DATABASE MANAGEMENT SYSTEMS

COMPLETE PRACTICAL APPROACH

DATABASE MANAGEMENT SYSTEMS

COMPLETE PRACTICAL APPROACH

By

SHARAD MAHESHWARI
M.Sc. (Comp. Sc.), Masters in IT

RUCHIN JAIN
M.C.A., M.Tech. (Comp. Sc.)

FIREWALL MEDIA

(An Imprint of Laxmi Publications Pvt. Ltd.)

An ISO 9001:2008 Company

BENGALURU • CHENNAI • COCHIN • GUWAHATI • HYDERABAD
JALANDHAR • KOLKATA • LUCKNOW • MUMBAI • RANCHI • NEW DELHI
BOSTON (USA) • ACCRA (GHANA) • NAIROBI (KENYA)

DATABASE MANAGEMENT SYSTEMS

Printed and bound in India
Typeset at : Goswami Associates, Delhi
First Edition : 2005, *Second Edition* : 2006, *New Edition* : 2016
ISBN : 978-81-7008-953-7

Branches

✆ **Bengaluru**	080-26 75 69 30
✆ **Chennai**	044-24 34 47 26
✆ **Cochin**	0484-237 70 04, 405 13 03
✆ **Guwahati**	0361-254 36 69, 251 38 81
✆ **Hyderabad**	040-27 55 53 83, 27 55 53 93
✆ **Jalandhar**	0181-222 12 72
✆ **Kolkata**	033-22 27 43 84
✆ **Lucknow**	0522-220 99 16
✆ **Mumbai**	022-24 91 54 15, 24 92 78 69
✆ **Ranchi**	0651-220 44 64

Published in India by

FIREWALL MEDIA

(An Imprint of Laxmi Publications Pvt. Ltd.)
An ISO 9001:2008 Company
113, GOLDEN HOUSE, DARYAGANJ, NEW DELHI-110002, INDIA
Telephone : 91-11-4353 2500, 4353 2501
Fax : 91-11-2325 2572, 4353 2528
www.laxmipublications.com info@laxmipublications.com

C—11116/015/12
Printed at : Ajit Printers, Delhi.

PREFACE

The Second Edition of this book provides a complete guide to the practical implementation of DBMS concepts including SQL, Oracle, Oracle Administration, PL/SQL development Forms and Reports using Oracle and developer 2000. This book assumes no prior knowledge by the reader on the subject. It is very useful for B.E., B.Tech, BCA, PGDCA, PGDIT, MCA, B.Sc (CSE/IT), M.Sc (CSE/IT), M.I.T., MBA, and M.Tech of all universities, computer institutes and also DOEACC students of O, A & B levels.

This book is also very useful for campus interviews, competitions where Oracle, SQL or DBMS practical knowledge is required. A large number of examples, practical questions, objectives, FAQ, descriptive questions are available in this book, which are very useful for universities and job-oriented examinations of various reputed companies.

This book covers the following topics in detail:

Foundation of Computers, Introduction to SQL, SQL Commands, SQL Functions, Relations, Various type of SQL queries, PL/SQL, Cursors, Triggers, Procedures, Packages, Customized Functions, DBA Commands, Forms & Reports.

For the successful publication of this book we express our hearty thanks to ALMIGHTY GOD, who had kindled the desire in our heart to write this book and supported us in every odd conditions and made our mind and determination strong enough to complete this book.

We are also very grateful to our families, friends, colleagues, students, institute administration, management and publisher.

We have tried our best to avoid error and mistakes, however their presence can not be ruled out. Your valuable suggestions and corrections are always welcome to improve the quality and standard of this book and will be deeply appreciated.

—**Authors**

ACKNOWLEDGMENTS

Many persons have contributed to make this book a reality, I would especially like to express my sincere gratitude to **Prof. P. S. Gill** for being by my side at each and every step of this wonderful experience. I would also like to thank my friend Ms. Ajanta Sharma, Debajeet Chanda, my father Shri. Narendra, mother Smt. Urmila and my wife Khushboo for their guidance throughout the preparation of the manuscript. Thanks are also due to all my family members, colleagues, friend and students.

Finally, I wish to express my appreciation to LAXMI PUBLICATIONS PVT. LTD. for letting me successfully complete this endeavor.

Sharad Maheshwari

I would especially like to express my gratitude to Mr. S.K. Goel for his unstinted support and encouragement. I would also like to thank my wife Neha and my sweet daughter Kriti for their guidance and moral support throughout the preparation of the manuscript. Thanks are also due to my father Shri D.K. Jain, my mother Smt. Rekha Jain, my all colleagues, friends and students for their great support and encouragement. We would like to thank Prof. B.N. Roy, (IT, BHU) for his well wishes and moral support.

Last but not the least, I would like to express my sincere thanks to LAXMI PUBLICATIONS PVT. LTD. for publishing this book.

Ruchin Jain

SYLLABUS

DBMS LAB

- Writing the queries for Data Definition and Data Manipulation Language.
- Write SQL queries using Logical Operators (=, <, >, etc.).
- Write SQL queries using SQL Operators (B/W./:/AND, IN(List), Like, ISNULL and also with negating expressions).
- Write SQL query using character, number, date and group function.
- Write SQL queries for Relational Algebra (UNION, INTERSECT, and MINUS etc.).
- Write SQL queries for extracting data from more than one table (Equi-Join, Non-Equi-Join , Outer Join).
- Write SQL queries for sub queries , nested queries.
- Write programs by the use of PL/SQL.
- Concepts for ROLL BACK, COMMIT and CHECK POINTS.
- Create VIEWS, CURSORS, and TRIGGERS and write ASSERTIONS.
- Create FORMS and REPORTS using Oracle 9i/Developer 2000.
- Objects and Basic Database administration.
- Competitive Examination Questions.

CONTENTS

DEDICATION

This book is dedicated to my loving parents my wife Khushboo and my all family members.

Sharad Maheshwari

This book is dedicated to my loving parents, wife Neha and my daughter Kriti.

Ruchin Jain

1 Introduction

Objectives :

- DBMS & RDBMS
- Codd's Rules for a Fully Relational DBMS
- Introduction of Various Types of Keys of DBMS
- Different Type of Relationship
- Introduction to DDL, DML & DCL

Exercise

DBMS & RDBMS

Database Management System. A Database Management is a collection of interrelated data and a set of programs to access this data. Collection of interrelated data is known as Database. *Example - Mark sheet & Student Records.* The main objective of a DBMS is to provide a convenient environment to retrieve and store database information. Database systems can support single user or multi-user environment. While, on one hand, **DBMS allows only one person to access the database at any given time like MS-Access & Fox Pro, on the other, RDBMS allows multiple users simultaneous access to the database like Oracle.**

Basically a Database System consists of two parts :

(*i*) Database Management System

(*ii*) Database Application

Database Management System is the program that organizes and maintains the information.

Database Application is the program that is used to view, retrieve and update information stored in the database.

DBMS offers the following services:

(*i*) **Data Definition.** It is a method of defining data and storage.

(*ii*) **Data Maintenance.** It checks whether each record has field containing all information for a particular record or not. For Example, in an employee table, all information about the employee like employee id, name, designation, salary, dept are recorded.

(*iii*) **Data manipulation.** It allows data in the database to be inserted, updated, deleted and sorted.

(*iv*) **Data Display.** It helps in viewing data.

(*v*) **Data Integrity.** It ensures the accuracy of the data.

Various Types of DBMS & RDBMS

Hierarchical Database Management Systems (HDBMS)

In the HDBMS data storage is arranged in the form of a parent-child relationship or in hierarchical manner. The origin place of data tree is known as root. Data located at various levels along a particular branch from the root is called the node. Last node in the series is referred as leaf.

Disadvantage: The links in hierarchical model are unidirectional, *i.e.*, we can travel from parent to the child only. The model does not support many- to-many relationship.

So in this model if you need any information from lower level then you have to follow complete hierarchy of the system.

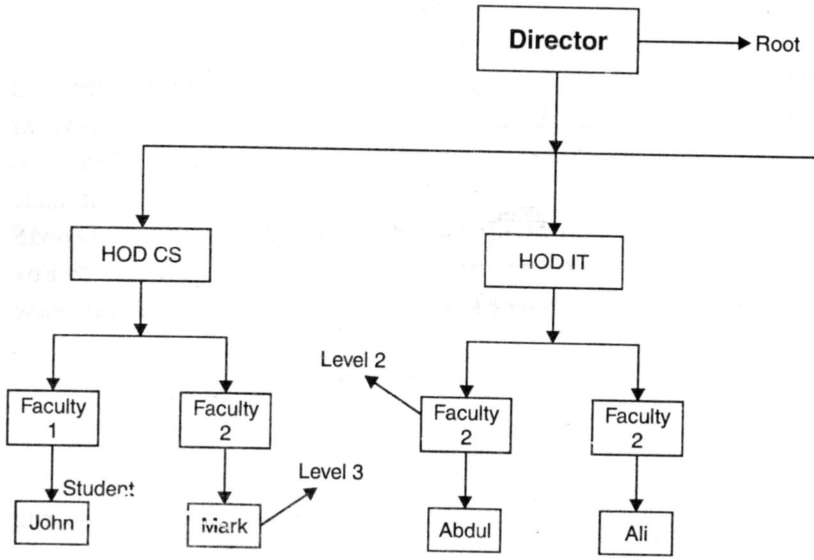

Figure 1.1. A Hierarchical Scheme for a College Database.

So in this system if Director need any information regarding a particular subject marks of any specific student then director will inquire to HOD, HOD will inquire to co-ordinator, co-ordinator will inquire to faculty of that class. So it will take much time.

Network Database Management System (NDBMS)

In networked database management system many users can access and share the one or more databases located on a network. The network model is the entity-relationship model with all relationship restricted to be either binary or many-one relationships.

The data is represented by collections of records, and relationships among data are represented as links, which can be diagrammatically be viewed as pointers. The pointers are used to locate a particular record.

Disadvantages: The use of pointers leads to a complex structure, which makes mapping of related data very difficult.

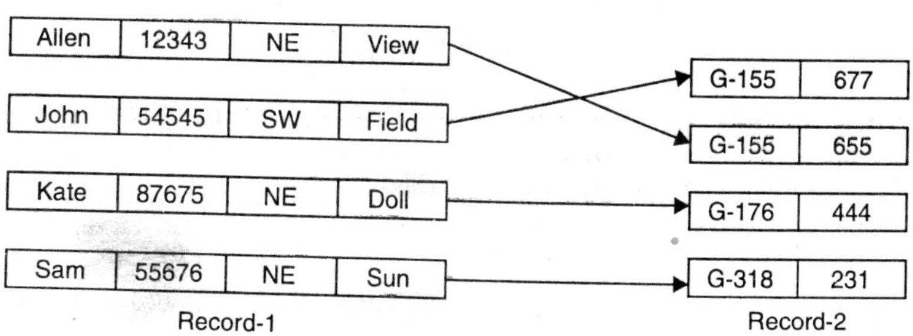

Figure 1.2. A Network Scheme for a Bank Database.

Relational Database Management System (RDBMS)

RDBMS stands for Relational Database Management System. An RDBMS is a computer program, which provides the user the facility to store and retrieve data in a manner consistent with a defined model, called the relational model.

RDBMS TERMINOLOGY

Formal Relational Term	Informal Equivalent (S)
Relation	Table
Tuple	Row, Record
Cardinality	Number of rows
Attribute	Column, Field
Degree	Number of columns
Primary key	Unique identifier
Domain	Set of legal values

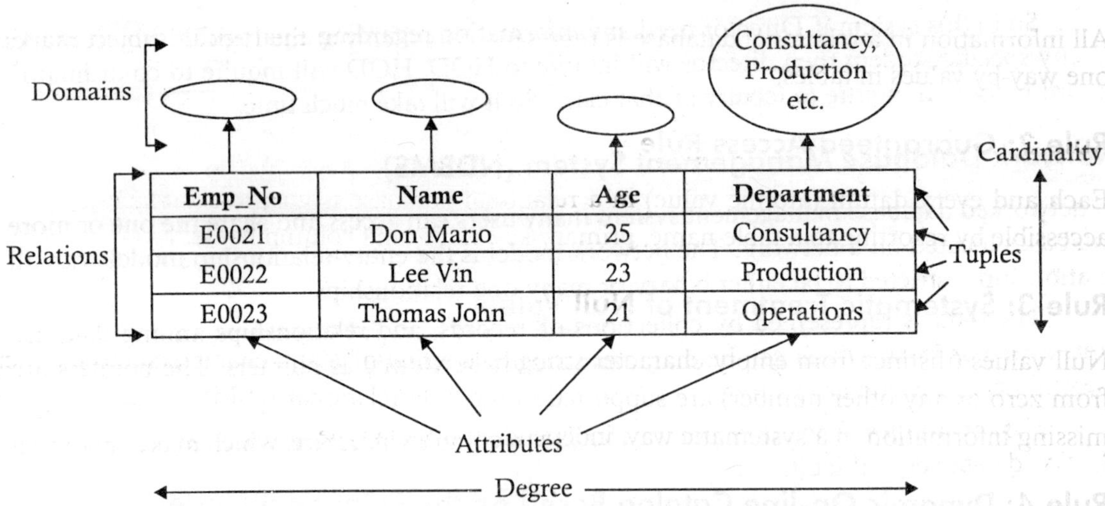

Figure 1.3

Object Relational Database Management System (ORDBMS)

When the relational database is extended to include object oriented concepts and structures such as abstract data types, nested tables and varying arrays, it is known as Object Relational Database Management System.

The first and most important concept that we describe is, of course, the concept of object. Object is an entity able to save a state (information) and which offers a number of operations (behavior) to either examine or affect this state. For example, 'Thomas' can be object and operations can be his college name, age, branch etc.

The benefits of ORDBMS include:

- The objects as such can be stored in the database.
- The language of the DBMS can be integrated with an object- oriented programming language. The language may even be exactly the same as that used in the application, which does not force the programmer to have two representations of his objects.

CODD'S RULES FOR A FULLY RELATIONAL DBMS

According to Elmasri and Navathe (1994), Dr. E. F. Codd, the originator of the relational data model, published a two-part article in ComputerWorld (Codd, 1985) that lists 12 rules for how to determine whether a DBMS is relational and to what extent it is relational. These rules provide a very useful yardstick for evaluating a relational system. Codd also mentions that, according to these rules, no fully relational system is available yet. In particular, rules 6, 9, 10, 11, and 12 are difficult to satisfy.

The 12 Rules

Rule 1: The Information Rule

All information in a relational database is represented explicitly at the logical level in exactly one way-by values in tables.

Rule 2: Guaranteed Access Rule

Each and every datum (atomic value) in a relational database is guaranteed to be logically accessible by resorting to a table name, primary key value, and column name.

Rule 3: Systematic Treatment of Null Values

Null values (distinct from empty character string or a string of blank characters and distinct from zero or any other number) are supported in the fully relational DBMS for representing missing information in a systematic way, independent of data type.

Rule 4: Dynamic On-line Catalog Based on the Relational Model

The database description is represented at the logical level in the same way as ordinary data, so authorized users can apply the same relational language to its interrogation as they apply to regular data.

Rule 5: Comprehensive Data Sublanguage Rule

A relational system may support several languages and various modes of terminal use (for example, the fill-in-blanks mode). However, there must be at least one language whose statements are expressible per some well-defined syntax, as character strings and whose ability to support all of the following is comprehensible: data definition, view definition, data manipulation (interactive and by program), integrity constraints, and transaction boundaries (begin, commit, and rollback).

Rule 6: View Updating Rule

All views that are theoretically updateable are also updateable by the system.

Rule 7: High-level Insert, Update, and Delete

The capability of handling a base relation or a derived relation as a single operand applies nor only to the retrieval of data but also to the insertion, update, and deletion of data.

Rule 8: Physical Data Independence

Application programs and terminal activities remain physical unimpaired whenever any changes are made in either storage representation or access methods.

Rule 9: Logical Data Independence

Application programs and terminal activities remain logically unimpaired when information preserving changes of any kind that theoretically permit unimpairment are made to the base tables.

Rule 10: Integrity Independence

Integrity constraints specific to a particular relational database must be definable in the relational data sublanguage and storable in the catalog, not in the application programs.

A minimum of the following two integrity constraints must be supported:

1. Entity integrity: No components of a primary key is allowed to have a null value.
2. Referential integrity: For each distinct non-null foreign key value in a relational database, there must exist a matching primary key value from the same domain.

Rule 11: Distribution Independence

A relational DBMS has distribution independence. Distribution independence implies that users should not have to be aware of whether a database is distributed.

Rule 12: Nonsubversion Rule

If a relational system has a low-level (single-record-at-a-time) language, that low-level language cannot be used to subvert or bypass the integrity rules or constraints expressed in the higher-level (multiple-records-at-a-time) relational language.

Note: There is a rider to these 12 rules known as **Rule Zero** "For any system that is claimed to be a relational database management system, that system must be able to manage data entirely through its relational capabilities."

On the basis of the above rules, there is no fully relational DBMS available today.

Entity

Person, place, event or concept about which the organization wishes to collect, track or maintain data. (Employee, student, patient, transaction, account, course, work center, machine, vehicle). It is fundamental construct of E-R model.

ER Model

A collection of entities and relationships among entities.

ER Diagram

Presents an ER model graphically.

Attribute

Properties or characteristics of an entity that is of interest to the organization (StudentID, CustomerName, VehicleNumber, EmployeeAddress).

Relationship

An association between one entity with another entity. Relationships are glue that holds together the various components of an E-R model.

Entity Type

A collection of entities that share common properties or characteristics (Customers, Vendors).

Entity Instance

A single occurrence of an entity type.

Identifier

An attribute that uniquely identifies an entity instance. This distinguishes one entity instance from other instances of the same type. Normally, a key is used to uniquely identify an entity instance. (For example, EmployeeID or SSN).

INTRODUCTION OF VARIOUS TYPES OF KEYS OF DBMS

Super Key

Any set of attributes which can uniquely identify an entity. For example, {name, s_no., salary}.

Candidate Key

Often abbreviate as just key

A minimal set of attributes whose values can uniquely identify an entity in the set.

For example, {s_no.}

Primary Key

A candidate key chosen to serve as the key for the entity set.

DIFFERENT TYPE OF RELATIONSHIP

One-To-Many Relationship/Many-To-One Relationship

One Manager can manage *zero, one or more* Department(s).

One Department can be managed by *at most one* Manager.

Given a Department, you can *uniquely* determine its Manager (if any).

Key of Departments à Key of Manager.

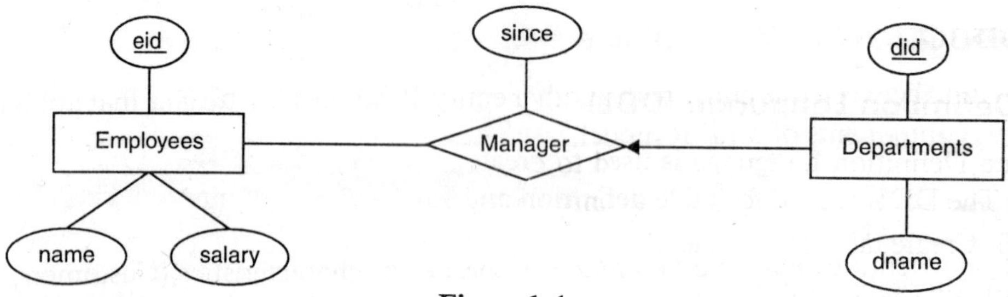

Figure 1.4

One-To-One Relationship

One Manager can manage *at most one* Department.

One Department can be managed by *at most one* Manager.

Given a Department, you can *uniquely* determine its Manager (if any).

Given an Employee, you can *uniquely* determine the Department s/he manages (if any).

Key of Departments *OR* Key of Employees à Key of Manager.

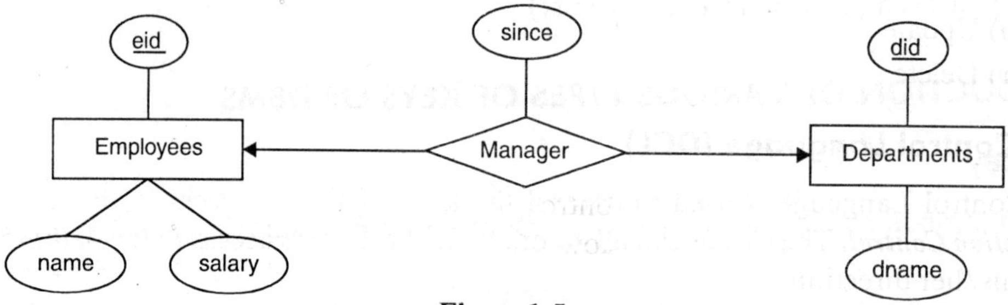

Figure 1.5

Many-To-Many Relationship

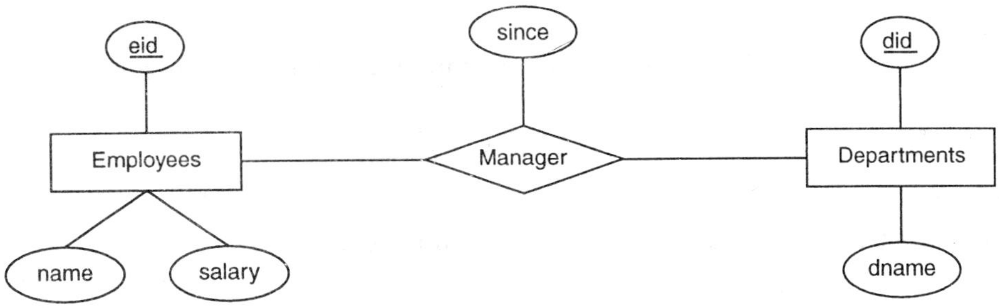

Figure 1.6

One Manager can manage *zero, one or more* Department(s).

One Department can be managed by *zero, one or more* Manager(s).

Union of Key of Employees and Key of Departments.

a Key of Managers.

Constraints should be determined by the application.

INTRODUCTION TO DDL, DML & DCL

Data Definition Language (DDL)

The Data Definition Language is used to create, remove and alter the structure of database objects. The DDL is used for table definition and can be classified into four categories -

(*i*) Create table command

(*ii*) Alter table command

(*iii*) Truncate table command

(*iv*) Drop table command

Data Manipulation Language (DML)

Data Manipulation Commands are used to query and manipulate existing database objects. Following are some DML commands:

(*i*) Insert

(*ii*) Select

(*iii*) Update

(*iv*) Delete

Data Control Language (DCL)

Data Control Language is used to control the kind of a data access to the database and ***Transaction Control.*** The owner can allow other database users access to the database objects as per his/her direction.

Example:

Grant, revoke are used for data access control.

Commit, Rollback and save point are transaction control commands.

(All commands are discussed in detail in later chapters.)

EXERCISE

1. What is a database? Explain the use of database.
2. What is the difference between DBMS and RDBMS ?
3. What are data models ? Differentiate between HDBMS and NDBMS?
4. Explain the following terms:
   (*i*) DDL (*ii*) DML (*iii*) DCL.
5. What is an ER Diagram?
6. What is a key? Differentiate between a primary key and a Super key?
7. What are the Codd's Rules? How many rules must be followed for a language to be a complete RDBMS?
8. Define these terms in brief :
   (*a*) Entity
   (*b*) Attribute
   (*c*) Identifier
   (*d*) Candidate Key.
9. Explain various types of relationships.

2 Getting Started

Objectives :

- Introduction to Oracle
- Oracle File Structure
- SQL vs SQL *PLUS
- Various Data Types of Oracle
- Creating a Table
- Reserved Words of SQL
- Constraints
- Inserting Rows to the Table
- Sequence
- To View the Rows in the Table
- Where Clause
- Rownum
- To Delete Rows from a Table
- Commit Statement
- The Rollback Statement
- The Savepoint Statement
- The Set Transaction Statement
- The Lock Table Statement
- To Update Rows in the Table
- Operators in SQL *Plus
- Not in
- Between
- Not Like
- Order by
- Column Aliases
- Column Format
- Some Important Commands

Lab Assignment-1
Lab Assignment-2
Lab Assignment-3
Lab Assignment-4

INTRODUCTION TO ORACLE

Oracle Corporation was founded in 1977 in Redwood, California. They introduced the first Relational Database Management System based on the **IBM System/R** model and the first database management system utilizing IBM's Structured Query Language (**SQL**) technology.

Today, the Oracle DBMS is supported on over 80 different operating environments, ranging from IBM mainframes, DEC VAX minicomputers, UNIX-based minicomputers, Windows NT and several proprietary hardware-operating system platforms, and is clearly the world's largest RDBMS vendor.

Lawrence Joseph (Larry) Ellison (Born: 1944, Chicago) is president and CEO of Oracle Corporation. Oracle Corporation, the company he founded with Robert N. (Bob) Miner and Edward A. (Ed) Oates back in 1977, has emerged as the world's largest vendor of software that helps large corporations and governments better manage their information.

Bruce **Scott** was one of the first employees at Oracle (then Software Development Laboratories). He co-founded Gupta Technology (now known as **Centura Software**) in 1984 with Umang Gupta, and later became CEO and founder of PointBase, Inc.

Bruce was co-author and co-architect of Oracle V1, V2 and V3. The SCOTT schema (EMP and DEPT tables), with password TIGER, was created by him. **Tiger** was the name of his cat.

The word **Oracle** means:

Prophecy or prediction; answer to a question believed to come from the gods; a statement believed to be infallible and authoritative; a shrine at which these answers are given

Oracle's main competitors in the **database** business are:

IBM with DB/2, Informix with the Informix DB, Microsoft with Access and SQL Server, CA with Ingres, Software AG with ADABAS, Sybase with Sybase System, PostgreSQL and MySQL etc.

Oracle's main competitors in the **applications** business are:

SAP (R/2 and R/3), Baan and Peoplesoft.

History of Oracle's

1977 Relational Software Inc. (RSI - currently Oracle Corporation) established.

1978 Oracle V1 ran on PDP-11 under RSX, 128 KB max memory. Written in assembly language. Implementation separated Oracle code and user code. Oracle V1 was never officially released.

1980 Oracle V2 released - the first commercially available relational database to use SQL. Oracle runs on DEC PDP-11 machines. Code is still written in PDP-11 assembly language, but now run under Vax/VMS.

1982 Oracle V3 released, Oracle became the first DBMS to run on mainframes, minicomputers, and PC's. First release to employ transactional processing. Oracle V3's server code was written in C.

1983 Relational Software Inc. changed its name to Oracle Corporation.

1984 Oracle V4 released, introduced read consistency, was ported to multiple platforms, first interoperability between PC and server.

1986 Oracle V5 released. Featured true client/server, VAX-cluster support, and distributed queries. (first DBMS with distributed capabilities).

1987 CASE and 4GL toolset.

1988 Oracle V6 released.

Oracle Financial Applications built on relational database.

1989 Released Oracle 6.2 with Symmetric cluster access using the Oracle Parallel Server.

1991 Reached power of 1,000 TPS on a parallel computing machine. First database to run on a massively parallel computer.

1992 Released Oracle7 for Unix.

1993 Rollout of Oracle's Cooperative Development Environment (CDE). Introduction of Oracle Industries and the Oracle Media Server.

1994 Headquarters moved to present location. Released Oracle7 for the PC.

1995 Reported gross revenues of almost $3 billion.

1997 Oracle8 released (supports more users, more data, higher availability, and object-relational features).

1998 Oracle announces support for the Intel Linux operating system.

1999 Oracle8i or Oracle 8.1.5 with Java integration (JVM in the database).

2000 Oracle8i Release 2.

Oracle now not only the number one in Databases but also in ERP Applications.

Oracle9i Application Server generally available: Oracle tools integrated in middle tier.

2001 Oracle9i Release 1 (with RAC and Advanced Analytic Service).

2002 Oracle9i Release 2.

2004 Oracle10g released.

Features of Oracle 9i

Oracle 9i improves the following technical aspects :

- database performance.
- ease of management.
- scalability.
- security.
- availability.
- Windows2000 integration and application areas.
- Internet content managemen.
- e-commerce integration.

- packaged applications.
- Business Intelligence.

1. Performance Improvements

Performance is always a big issue with databases, so what's new in Oracle9i in the way of performance enhancements ?Biggest improvements have been to Parallel Server which Oracle now calls Real Application Clusters and which allow applications to use clustered servers without modification. Other improvements include:

- native compilation of PL/SQL.
- reduction in latch contention (SGA locks) and I/O improvements.
- better Java performance (better compilation, improved garbage collection).
- distributed database performance enhancements.

2. Manageability Enhancements

Ease of management of the database has always been a bone of contention, especially configuration of rollback segments and such like, so Oracle have made great strides to improve manageability as the complexity of the database has increased. These improvements include:

- automatic rollback segment management.
- many operations management enhancements.
- Oracle Enterprise Manager enhancements.

3. Scalability Enhancements

As the demand for databases to be able to support more and more users continues, issues of scalability become more important. Improvements in this area consist of:

- Real Application Clusters–new servers can be added as required.
- reduced resource requirements per user.
- improved resource management features to give greater control at lower levels.

4. Security Enhancements

As the number of users increase and the locations and types of users become more diverse, better security (and privacy) features become essential. The security improvements for Oracle 9i are:

- enhanced 3-tier security (integration with LDAP ...).
- improved hosting security (through use of virtual private databases), fine-grained auditing and single sign-on.
- improved user security (more password management features, etc.).
- ability to encrypt stored data.
- row-level access control (Oracle Label Security).

5. Availability

For the last few releases Oracle have been putting a lot of effort into increasing database availability and this continues with Oracle 9i with new features including:

- Disaster recovery enhancements (standby database management, LogMiner).
- Reduction in off-line maintenance requirements (CREATE TABLE ... AS SELECT... etc.).
- Faster and more precise database repair (after corruption/instance failure).
- Enabling queries to go back in time with flashback queries.

6. Internet Content Management

Oracle 9i can be used for the storage and manipulation of many different types of data. The new features are:

- Internet File Store improvements.
- Searching/indexing of multimedia and XML data.
- Support for collaborative projects via the creation of shared workspaces, allowing multiple versions of content to exists simultaneously.
- Ability to create applications to make use of location information of clients and services (e.g. for use with mobile phones).

7. e-commerce Integration

The enhancements Oracle 9i provides in this area are:

- pre-built objects for creating store fronts, exchanges and portals to provide a faster time-to-market and enable easier integration with the back-end.
- support for standard messaging formats to enable faster integration of the store front with the back-end and external systems.

8. Packaged Applications

The improvements in this area comprise:

- Enhanced globalization features (enables multiple languages to be supported simultaneously on the same database through use of the UTF8 character set).
- Enhanced 3rd party development features (stored outlines and default column values).

9. Business Intelligence

The enhancements for business intelligence provided by Oracle can be grouped into 2 main categories:

- Enhancements to database performance, scalability and manageability (e.g., new list partitioning method).
- Enhanced analysis (OLAP), ETL (extraction, transformation and loading) and data mining features.

10. Windows Integration

Oracle 9i has been enhanced to take advantage of the new Windows features including:

- Integration of single sign-on and PKI with Active Directory and Microsoft Certificate Store.

- Better integration with IIS and Microsoft's Transaction Services and Message Queuing enhanced development features (Oracle Data Objects etc.).

INTRODUCTION TO ORACLE

Oracle 9i is an Object Relational Database Management System (ORDBMS). It offers capabilities of relational and object oriented database system. Oracle products are based on Client/Server technology. In this technology server performs all activities related to the database and the client performs activities that help the user to interact with the application.

Tools of Oracle

- SQL *Plus
- PL/SQL
- Forms
- Reports

SQL *Plus

SQL *Plus is a Structured Query Language supported by Oracle. Through SQL *Plus we can store, retrieve, edit and run SQL commands and PL/SQL blocks. Using SQL * Plus we can perform calculations, list column definitions for any table and can also format query results in the form of a report.

PL/SQL

PL/SQL is an extension of SQL. PL/SQL block can contain any number of SQL statements integrated with flow of control statements. PL/SQL is a procedural language for the oracle server and its client. In a PL/SQL program, SQL statements are used for data manipulation and transaction processing.

Forms

Form is a graphical tool used for generating and executing forms based applications. A form basically consists of block and fields. Multiple tables can be accessed over a single form base application with the help of transaction commands. Oracle form builder is the design component of oracle forms.

Reports

It is an application development tool of oracle for developing, executing, displaying and printing reports. We can create wide variety of reports, which have various modes. Oracle Reports are powerful and easy to use.

ORACLE FILE STRUCTURE

Oracle file has two representations: Logical file structure and the Physical file structure.

Logical Structure

This is the user's view of the data. The user sees the data to exist in the form of a two dimensional table or group of tables. The tables are created in tablespaces.

So, a database is made up of one or more tablespaces. When the database is created, the system tablespace is created. The system tablespace contains the Oracle Data Dictionary and System Rollback segments. It is best that other tables are created in other tablespaces. One tablespace can contain many data files. A new tablespace is created using CREATE TABLESPACE command.

Physical Structure

The physical files, which are stored in the disk.

1. **Data files:** Contains all the User's data and Oracle's data dictionary. A data file can be associated with only one database. Database files can have certain characteristics set to allow them to automatically extend when the database runs out of space.
2. **Log files:** Also referred to as the Redo log files or On-line log files. These files contain all the changes made to the data over a period of time. There will be at least two redo log files. These files are used to rebuild the database in case of a crash.
3. **Control files:** Control files contains a list of all the database files and the Redo log files and the current log sequence number.

Oracle Memory Structure and Processes

The basic memory structure associated with Oracle includes:

- Software Code Areas
- The System Global Area (SGA)
  (*a*) The Database Buffer Cache (*b*) The Redo log Buffer
  (*c*) The Shared Pool
- The Program Global Areas (PGA)
  (*a*) Stack Areas (*b*) Data Areas
  (*c*) Sort Areas

Oracle uses memory to store the following information:

1. Program code being executed.
2. Information about a connected session, even if it is not currently active.
3. Data needed during program execution (for example, the current state of a query from which rows are being fetched).
4. Information, which is shared and communicated among processes.
5. Cached information, which is also permanently stored on peripheral memory.

System Global Area (SGA)

The *System Global Area (SGA)* is a shared memory structure that contains data and control information for one Oracle database instance. An SGA and the Oracle background processes constitute an Oracle instance. If multiple users are concurrently connected to the same instance, the data in the instance's SGA is "shared" among the users. So. SGA is often referred to as either the "System Global Area" or the "Shared Global Area".

The information stored within an SGA is divided into several areas of memory:

- The database buffer cache
- The redo log buffer
- The shared pool
- Request and response queues (if multi-threaded server is used)
- The data dictionary cache

Other miscellaneous information.

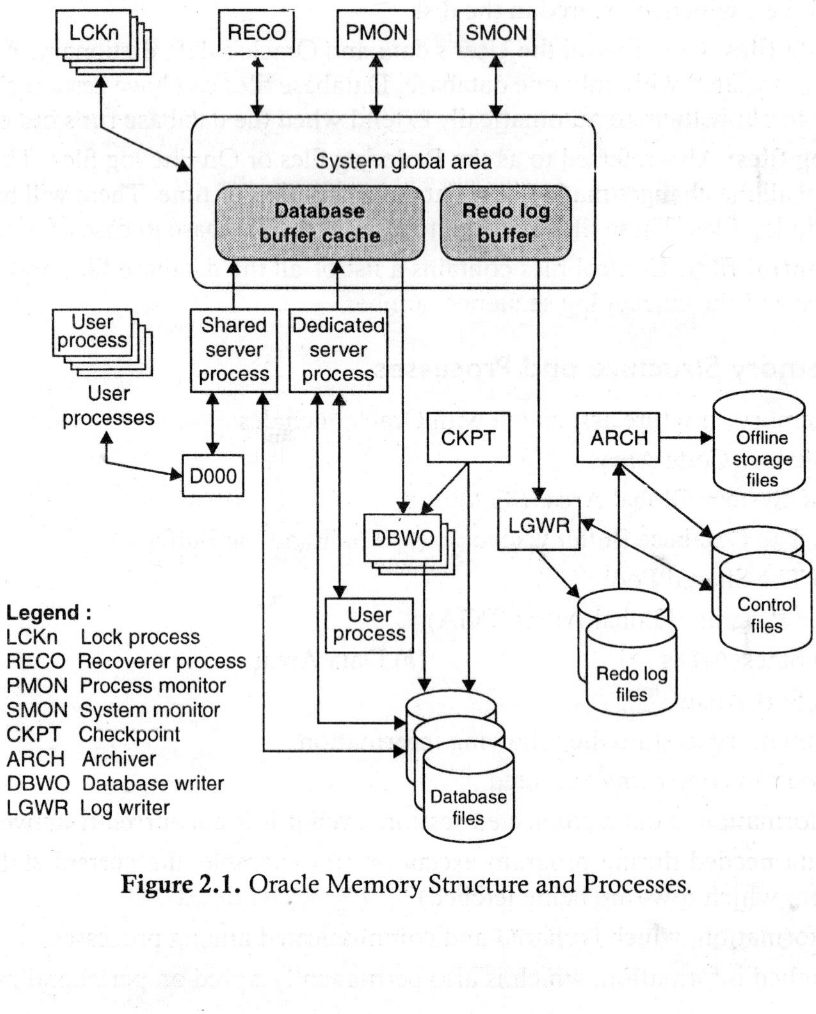

Figure 2.1. Oracle Memory Structure and Processes.

The Database Buffer Cache

A portion of SGA is a cache that holds database information. The buffers in the buffer cache hold copies of the data blocks read from the data files. The buffers are shared by all Oracle user processes concurrently connected to the instance.

The Redo Log Buffer

The Redo Log buffer is a circular buffer in the SGA that holds information about changes made to the database. The information is stored in redo entries. Redo entries describe the changes that are made to the database. They are written to on line Redo Log files so that they can be used in roll forward operations during database recoveries.

The Shared Pool

The shared pool is an area in the SGA that contains constructs such as shared SQL areas and the data dictionary cache. Oracle represents each SQL statement it executes with a shared part (a shared SQL area) and a private part (a private SQL area).

A shared SQL area is a memory area that contains the parse tree and execution plan for a single SQL statement. A private SQL area is a memory area that contains such items as binding information and runtime buffers.

The Program Global Area (PGA)

The *Program Global Area (PGA)* is a memory area that contains data and control information for a single process (server or background). A PGA is created by Oracle when a server process is started. The information in a PGA depends on the configuration of Oracle. PGA is also referred as the "Process Global Area".

Oracle Processes

- Database Writer (DBWR)
- Log Writer (LGWR)
- Checkpoint (CKPT)
- System Monitor (SMON)
- Process Monitor (PMON)
- Archiver (ARCH)
- Recover (RECHO)
- Lock (LCKn)
- Dispatcher (Dnnn)
- Server (Snnn)

Database Writer (DBWR)

All the writing of data files is performed by the Database Writer Process (DBWR). It is responsible for buffer cache management. When a buffer in the buffer cache is modified, it is marked "dirty"; the primary job of the DBWR process is to keep the buffer cache "clean" by writing "dirty" buffers to disk. DBWR manages the buffer cache so that user processes can always find free buffers to the disk.

Log Writer (LGWR)

The Redo Log buffer is written to a Redo Log buffer on disk by the Log Writer process. The LGWR is the only process that writes to the on-line Redo Log and the only one that directly reads the Redo Log buffers during normal operations.

LGWR Writes

- A commit record when a user process commits a transaction.
- Redo buffers every three seconds.
- Redo buffers when a Redo Log buffer is one third full.
- Redo buffers when the DBWR process writes modified buffers to the disk.

Checkpoint (CKPT)

Check points cause DBWR to write all of the blocks that have been modified since the last checkpoint to the data files and update the data files header and control files to record the checkpoint.

System Monitor (SMON)

The System Monitor Process (SMON) performs instance recovery at instance start up. SMON is also responsible for cleaning up temporary segments that are no longer in use, it also merges contiguous free extents to make longer blocks of free space available.

Process Monitor (PMON)

The Process Monitor performs process recovery when a user process fails. PMON is responsible for cleaning up the cache and freeing resources that the process was using. PMON also periodically checks the status of the dispatcher and server processes and restarts any that have died.

Recover (RECO)

The Recover process (RECO) is a process used with the distributed option that automatically resolves failure involving distributed transactions. If the RECO process of the database server attempts to establish communication with a remote server and the remote server is not available or the network connection has not been re-established, RECO will automatically try to connect again after a timed interval.

Archiver (ARCH)

The Archiver Process (ARCH) copies on line Redo Log files to a designated storage device once they become full. ARCH is present only when the Redo Log is used in ARCHIVELOG mode and automatic archiving is enabled.

LOCK (LCKn)

When the parallel server option is used, up to ten Lock processes (LCK0,……,LCK9) are used for inter instance locking.

Dispatcher (Dnnn)

The Dispatcher Process allows user processes to share a limited number of server processes. Without a dispatcher, each user process requires one dedicated server process. Multiple dispatcher processes can be created for a single database instance, at least one dispatcher must be created for each network protocol by which users will communicate with Oracle.

Server (Snnn)

Each *Shared Server Process* serves multiple client requests in the multithreaded server configuration.

SQL vs SQL*PLUS

SQL (pronounced "ess-que-el" or "sequel") stands for Structured Query Language. SQL is used to communicate with a database. According to ANSI (American National Standards Institute), it is the standard language for relational database management systems. This language is non procedural. SQL was introduced by IBM Corporation and standardized by ANSI and ISO (International Standard Organization) in 1986. Oracle was the first company to release a product that used SQL. SQL has structure just as English or any other language. It has rules of grammar and syntax and they are basically the normal rule of English speaking and easily understood. SQL statements are used to perform tasks such as update data on a database or retrieve data from a database. Some common relational database management systems that use SQL are: Oracle, Sybase, Microsoft SQL Server, Access, Ingres, etc. Although most database systems use SQL, most of them also have their own additional proprietary extensions that are usually only used on their system.

SQL *PLUS is an Oracle specific program, which accepts and executes SQL commands and PL/SQL blocks. SQL *PLUS allow us to manipulate SQL commands and PL/SQL blocks. It also performs many additional tasks as given below:

(*i*) enter, edit, retrieve, store and run SQL commands and PL/SQL blocks,

(*ii*) format, store, calculations and print query results in the form of reports,

(*iii*) list column definition for any table,

(*iv*) access and copy data between SQL databases,

(*v*) send and retrieve messages from end users.

VARIOUS DATA TYPES OF ORACLE

Table 2.1

SCALAR TYPES	COMPOSITE TYPES	REFERENCE TYPES	LOB TYPES
BINARY_INTEGER DEC DECIMAL DOUBLE PRECISION FLOAT INT INTEGER NATURAL NATURAL N NUMBER NUMERIC REAL SMALLINT CHAR CHARACTER LONG NCHAR VARCHAR2 RAW LONG RAW ROWID UROWID BOOLEAN (Other) DATE (Other)	RECORD TABLE VARRAY	REF CURSOR REF object_type	BFILE BLOB CLOB NCLOB

Binary_Integer

BINARY_INTEGER datatype is used to store signed integers. Its magnitude range is—2147483647.. 2147483647. BINARY_INTEGER values require less storage than NUMBER values.

Binary_Integer Subtypes

A base type is the datatype from which a subtype is derived. A subtype associates a base type with a constraint and so defines a subset of values.

BINARY_INTEGER subtypes:

NATURAL
NATURALN
POSITIVE
POSITIVEN
SIGNTYPE

The subtypes NATURAL and POSITIVE restrict us an integer variable to non-negative or positive values, respectively. NATURALN and POSITIVEN prevent the assigning of nulls to an integer variable. SIGNTYPE lets us restrict an integer variable to the values -1, 0, and 1, which is useful in programming tri-state logic.

Number

NUMBER datatype is used to store fixed-point or floating-point numbers of virtually any size. Its magnitude range is 1E-130 .. 10E125. If the value of an expression falls outside this range, we get a numeric overflow or underflow error. We can specify precision, which is the total number of digits and scale which is the number of digits to the right of the decimal point. The syntax follows:

NUMBER[(precision,scale)]

To declare fixed-point numbers, for which we must specify *scale*, use the following form:

NUMBER(precision,scale)

To declare floating-point numbers, for which we cannot specify *precision* or *scale* because the decimal point can "float" to any position, use the following form:

NUMBER

To declare integers, which have no decimal point, use this form:

NUMBER(precision) — same as NUMBER(precision,0)

We cannot use constants or variables to specify precision and scale, we must use integer literals. The maximum precision of a NUMBER value is 38 decimal digits. If you do not specify precision, it defaults to 38 or the maximum supported by your system whichever is less.

Scale, which can range from -84 to 127, determines where rounding occurs. For instance, a scale of 2 rounds to the nearest hundredth (3.457 becomes 3.46). A negative scale rounds to the left of the decimal point. For example, a scale of -3 rounds to the nearest thousand (3457 becomes 3000) and a scale of 0 rounds to the nearest whole number. If we do not specify scale, it defaults to 0.

Number Subtypes

NUMBER subtypes are used for compatibility with ANSI/ISO and IBM types or when we want a more descriptive name:

DEC
DECIMAL
DOUBLE PRECISION

FLOAT
INTEGER
INT
NUMERIC
REAL
SMALLINT

Use the subtypes DEC, DECIMAL, and NUMERIC to declare fixed-point numbers with a maximum precision of 38 decimal digits.

Use the subtypes DOUBLE PRECISION and FLOAT to declare floating-point numbers with a maximum precision of 126 binary digits, which is roughly equivalent to 38 decimal digits. Or, use the subtype REAL to declare floating-point numbers with a maximum precision of 63 binary digits, which is roughly equivalent to 18 decimal digits.

Use the subtypes INTEGER, INT, and SMALLINT to declare integers with a maximum precision of 38 decimal digits.

Character Types

Character types allow us to store alphanumeric data, represent words and text, and manipulate character strings.

CHAR

CHAR datatype is used to store fixed-length character data. Data represented internally depends on the database character set. The CHAR datatype takes an optional parameter that lets us specify a maximum length up to 32767 bytes. The syntax follows:

CHAR[(maximum_length)]

We cannot use a constant or variable to specify the maximum length, we must use an integer literal in the range 1 .. 32767.

If we do not specify a maximum length, it defaults to 1. Remember, we specify the maximum length in bytes not characters. So, if a CHAR(n) variable stores multi-byte characters, its maximum length is less than n characters. The maximum width of a CHAR database column is 2000 bytes. So, we cannot insert CHAR values longer than 2000 bytes into a CHAR column.

We can insert any CHAR(n) value into a LONG database column because the maximum width of a LONG column is 2147483647 bytes or 2 gigabytes. However, we cannot retrieve a value longer than 32767 bytes from a LONG column into a CHAR(n) variable.

CHAR Subtypes

The CHAR subtype CHARACTER has the same range of values as its base type. That is, CHARACTER is just another name for CHAR. We can use this subtype for compatibility with ANSI/ISO and IBM types or when we want an identifier more descriptive than CHAR.

VARCHAR2

VARCHAR2 datatype is used to store variable-length character data. Data represented internally depends on the database character set. The VARCHAR2 datatype takes a required parameter that specifies a maximum length up to 32767 bytes. The syntax follows:

VARCHAR2(maximum_length)

We cannot use a constant or variable to specify the maximum length, we must use an integer literal in the range 1 .. 32767.

The VARCHAR2 datatype involves a trade-off between memory use and efficiency. For a VARCHAR2 (>= 2000) variable, SQL dynamically allocates only enough memory to hold the actual value. However, for a VARCHAR2(< 2000) variable, SQL and PL/SQL preallocates enough memory to hold a maximum-size value. So, for example, if you assign the same 500 bytes value to a VARCHAR2(2000) variable and to a VARCHAR2(1999) variable, the latter uses 1499 bytes more memory.

Remember, we specify the maximum length of a VARCHAR2(n) variable in bytes, not characters. So, if a VARCHAR2(n) variable stores multi-byte characters, its maximum length is less than n characters. The maximum width of a VARCHAR2 database column is 4000 bytes. Therefore, we cannot insert VARCHAR2 values longer than 4000 bytes into a VARCHAR2 column.

We can insert any VARCHAR2(n) value into a LONG database column because the maximum width of a LONG column is 2147483647 bytes. However, we cannot retrieve a value longer than 32767 bytes from a LONG column into a VARCHAR2(n) variable.

VARCHAR2 Subtype

The VARCHAR2 subtype below have the same range of values as their base type. For example, VARCHAR is just another name for VARCHAR2.

VARCHAR

CHAR vs VARCHAR2

When we assign a character value to a CHAR variable, if the value is shorter than the declared length of the variable, Oracle blank-pads the value to the declared length. So, information about trailing blanks is lost. In the following example, the value assigned to last_name includes six trailing blanks, not just one:

last_name CHAR(10) : 'ANIL' — note trailing blank

If the character value is longer than the declared length of the CHAR variable, SQL and PL/SQL aborts the assignment and raises the predefined exception VALUE_ERROR. Oracle neither truncates the value nor tries to trim trailing blanks. For example, given the declaration

acronym CHAR(4);

the following assignment raises VALUE_ERROR:

acronym : 'ANIL'; — note trailing blank

When we assign a character value to a VARCHAR2 variable: the value is shorter than the declared length of the variable, SQL and PL/SQL neither blank-pads the value nor strips trailing blanks. Character values are assigned intact, so no information is lost. If the character value is longer than the declared length of the VARCHAR2 variable, SQL and PL/SQL aborts the assignment and raises VALUE_ERROR. SQL and PL/SQL neither truncates the value nor tries to trim trailing blanks.

LONG and LONG RAW

LONG datatype is used to store variable-length character strings. The LONG datatype is like the VARCHAR2 datatype, except that the maximum length of a LONG value is 32760 bytes.

We use the LONG RAW datatype to store binary data or byte strings. LONG RAW data is like LONG data, except that LONG RAW data is not interpreted by SQL and PL/SQL. The maximum length of a LONG RAW value is 32760 bytes.

We can insert any LONG value into a LONG database column because the maximum width of a LONG column is 2147483647 bytes. However, we cannot retrieve a value longer than 32760 bytes from a LONG column into a LONG variable.

We can insert any LONG RAW value into a LONG RAW database column because the maximum width of a LONG RAW column is 2147483647 bytes. However, we cannot retrieve a value longer than 32760 bytes from a LONG RAW column into a LONG RAW variable.

LONG columns can store text, arrays of characters, or even short documents. We can reference LONG columns in UPDATE, INSERT, and (most) SELECT statements, but *not* in expressions, SQL function calls, or certain SQL clauses such as WHERE, GROUP BY, and CONNECT BY.

RAW

RAW datatype is used to store binary data or byte strings. For example, a RAW variable might store a sequence of graphic characters or a digitized picture. Raw data is like VARCHAR2 data, except that SQL and PL/SQL does not interpret raw data. Likewise, Net8 does no character set conversions when we transmit raw data from one system to another.

The RAW datatype takes a required parameter that lets us specify a maximum length up to 32767 bytes. The syntax follows:

RAW(maximum_length)

We cannot use a constant or variable to specify the maximum length, we must use an integer literal in the range 1 .. 32767.

The maximum width of a RAW database column is 2000 bytes. So, we cannot insert RAW values longer than 2000 bytes into a RAW column. We can insert any RAW value into a LONG RAW database column because the maximum width of a LONG RAW column is 2147483647 bytes. However, we cannot retrieve a value longer than 32767 bytes from a LONG RAW column into a RAW variable.

ROWID and UROWID

Every database table has a ROWID pseudocolumn, which stores binary values called rowids. Each rowid represents the storage address of a row. A physical rowid identifies a row in an ordinary table. A logical rowid identifies a row in an index-organized table. The ROWID datatype can store only physical rowids. However, the UROWID (universal rowid) datatype can store physical, logical, or foreign (non-Oracle) rowids.

Use the ROWID datatype only for backward compatibility with old applications. For new applications, use the UROWID datatype.

When we select or fetch a ROWID into a UROWID variable, we can use the built-in function ROWIDTOCHAR, which converts the binary value into an 18-byte character string. Conversely, the function CHARTOROWID converts a UROWID character string into a rowid.

NCHAR

NCHAR datatype is used to store fixed-length (blank-padded if necessary) NLS character data. How the data is represented internally depends on the national character set, which might use a fixed-width encoding such as US7ASCII or a variable-width encoding such as JA16SJIS.

The NCHAR datatype takes an optional parameter that lets us specify a maximum length up to 32767 bytes. The syntax follows:

NCHAR[(maximum_length)]

We cannot use a constant or variable to specify the maximum length, we must use an integer literal in the range 1 .. 32767.

The maximum width of an NCHAR database column is 2000 bytes. So, we cannot insert NCHAR values longer than 2000 bytes into an NCHAR column. Remember, for fixed-width, multi-byte character sets, we cannot insert NCHAR values longer than the number of characters that fit in 2000 bytes.

If the NCHAR value is shorter than the defined width of the NCHAR column, Oracle blank-pads the value to the defined width. We cannot insert CHAR values into an NCHAR column. Likewise, we cannot insert NCHAR values into a CHAR column.

Other Types

The following types allow us to store and manipulate logical values and date/time values.

BOOLEAN

BOOLEAN datatype is used to store the logical values TRUE, FALSE, and NULL (which stand for a missing, unknown, or inapplicable value). Only logic operations are allowed on BOOLEAN variables.

The BOOLEAN datatype takes no parameters. Only the values TRUE, FALSE, and NULL can be assigned to a BOOLEAN variable. We cannot insert the values TRUE and FALSE into a database column. Also, we cannot select or fetch column values into a BOOLEAN variable.

DATE

DATE datatype is used to store fixed-length date/time values. DATE values include the time of day in seconds since midnight. The date portion defaults to the first day of the current month, the time portion defaults to midnight. The date function SYSDATE returns the current date and time.

Valid dates range from January 1, 4712 BC to December 31, 9999 AD. A Julian date is the number of days since January 1, 4712 BC. Julian dates allow continuous dating from a common reference.

LOB Types

The LOB (large object) datatypes BFILE, BLOB, CLOB, and NCLOB let us store blocks of unstructured data (such as text, graphic images, video clips, and sound waveforms) up to four gigabytes in size and, they allow efficient, random, piece-wise access to the data.

The LOB types differ from the LONG and LONG RAW types in several ways. For example, LOBs can be attributes of an object type, but LONGs cannot. The maximum size of a LOB is four gigabytes, but the maximum size of a LONG is two gigabytes. Also, LOBs support random access to data, but LONG supports only sequential access.

LOB types store values called lob locators that specify the location of large objects stored in an external file, in-line (inside the row) or out-of-line (outside the row). Database columns of type BLOB, CLOB, NCLOB, or BFILE store the locators. BLOB, CLOB, and NCLOB data is stored in the database, in or outside the row. BFILE data is stored in operating system files outside the database.

BFILE

BFILE datatype is used to store large binary objects in operating system files outside the database. Every BFILE variable stores a file locator, which points to a large binary file on the server. The locator includes a directory alias, which specifies a full path name (logical path names are not supported).

BFILEs are read-only. We cannot modify them. The size of a BFILE is system dependent but cannot exceed four gigabytes (2**32 - 1 bytes).

BLOB

BLOB datatype is used to store large binary objects in the database in-line or out-of-line. Every BLOB variable stores a locator, which points to a large binary object. The size of a BLOB cannot exceed four gigabytes.

CLOB

CLOB datatype is used to store large blocks of single-byte character data in the database, in-line or out-of-line. Both fixed-width and variable-width character sets are support. Every CLOB variable stores a locator, which points to a large block of character data. The size of a CLOB cannot exceed four gigabytes.

NCLOB

NCLOB datatype is used to store large blocks of multi-byte NCHAR data in the database, in-line or out-of-line. Both fixed-width and variable-width character sets are supported. Every NCLOB variable stores a locator, which points to a large block of NCHAR data. The size of an NCLOB cannot exceed four gigabytes.

How to Start Oracle SQL *PLUS

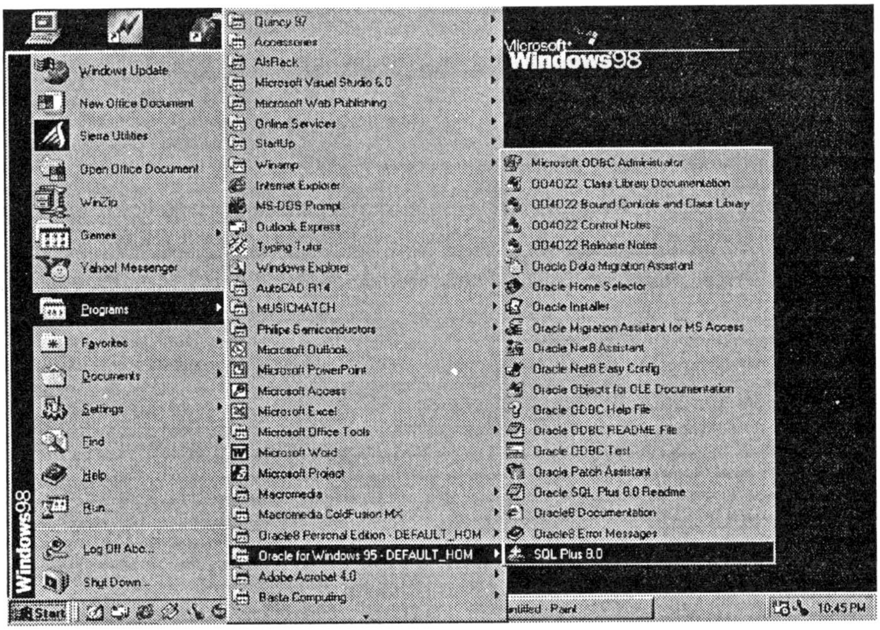

Figure 2.2

Click on SQL plus enter user name, Password & Host String and click OK button.

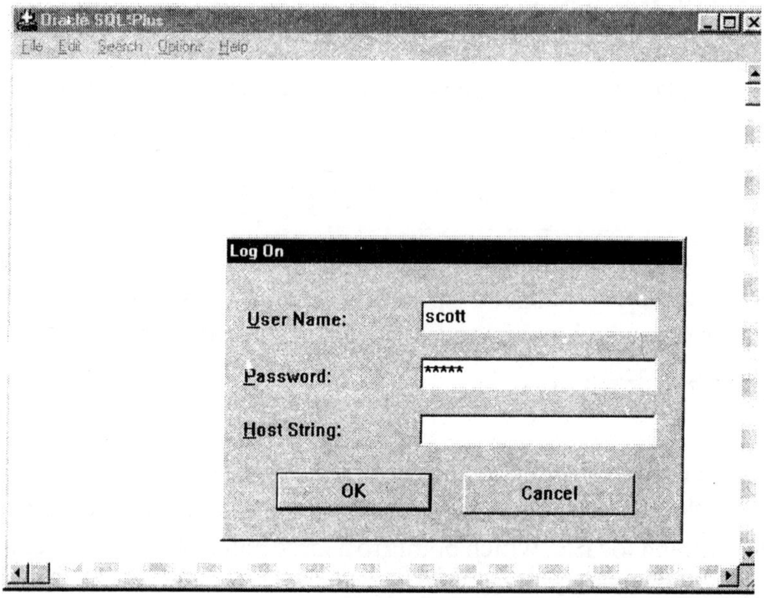

Figure 2.3

Then we will get the following SQL prompt and oracle is ready to execute the commands

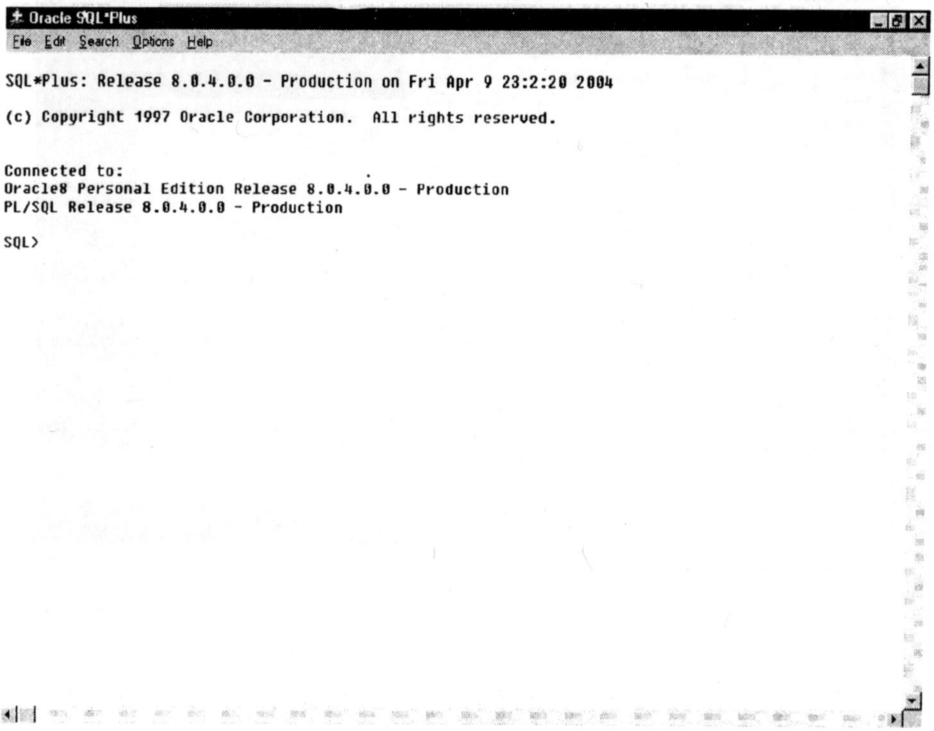

Figure 2.4

CREATING A TABLE

Rules for Table and Column Names

- Names can be upto 30 characters.
- Names must begin with an alphabet.
- Names cannot contain quotes.
- Names are not case sensitive.
- Names can contain characters a-z, 0-9, _, $ and #.
- Names cannot be reserved words.
- The above rules can be bypassed by using double quotes.

RESERVED WORDS OF SQL

The words listed are reserved by SQL. So, we should not use them to name schema objects such as columns, tables, or indexes.

ALL	DESC	LEVEL	PCTFREE	START
ALTER	DISTINCT	LIKE	PRIOR	SUCCESSFUL
AND	DROP	LOCK	PUBLIC	SYNONYM
ANY	ELSE	LONG	RAW	SYSDATE
AS	EXCLUSIVE	MAX	ROLLBACK	TABLE
ASC	EXISTS	MIN	ROW	THEN
BETWEEN	FLOAT	MINUS	ROWID	TO
BY	FOR	MLSLABEL	ROWNUM	TRIGGER
CHAR	FROM	MODE	SELECT	UID
CHECK	GROUP	NOT	SET	UNION
CLUSTER	HAVING	NOWAIT	SHARE	UNIQUE
COMMENT	IMMEDIATE	NULL	SMALLINT	UPDATE
COMPRESS	IN	NUMBER		USER
CONNECT	INDEX	OF		VALIDATE
CREATE	INSERT	ON		VALUES
CURRENT	INTEGER	OPTION		VARCHAR
DATE	INTERSECT	OR		VARCHAR2
DECIMAL	INTO	ORDER		VARIANCE
DEFAULT	IS			VIEW
DELETE				WHENEVER
				WHERE
				WITH

Spool

We can save our commands and results of queries in a notepad file using spool command permanently. This will create a file with extension .lst by default.

Example :

SQL > Spool Sharad

After that execute our queries in SQL then these queries result will be stored in Sharad file. At last for saving the file you have to type :

SQL > Spool Off

Create Table

The **create table** statement is used to create a new table. Here is the format of a simple **create table** statement:

Syntax

```
create table <tablename>
(column1 data-type(width),
 column2 data-type(width),
 column3 data-type(width)
);
```

This example below demonstrates how we can create a table named "Student", with five columns. The column names will be "Roll_no", "Name", "Class", "DOB", and "ADD1":

```
CREATE TABLE STUDENT
(
Roll_no    Number(6),
Name       Varchar2(15),
Class      Varchar2(5),
DOB        DATE,
ADD1       Varchar2(15)
);
```

After that we will get the message "Table created" on SQL prompt.

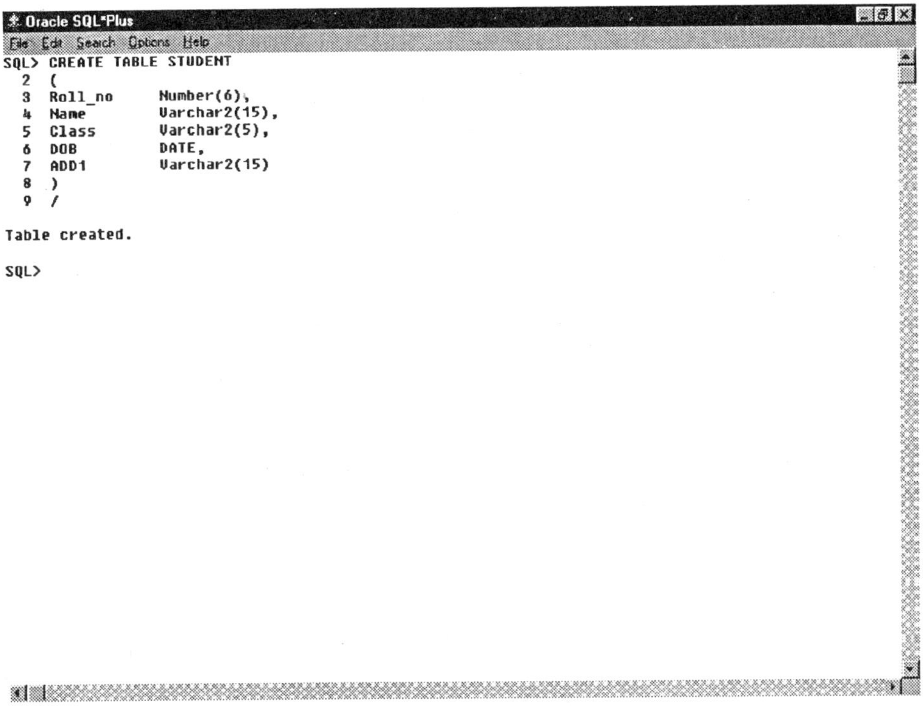

Figure 2.5

Example:

```
CREATE TABLE BOOK
(
  ISBN NUMBER(10),
  TITLE VARCHAR2(200),
  AUTHOR VARCHAR2(50),
  COST NUMBER(8,2),
  LENT_DATE DATE,
  RETURNED_DATE DATE,
  TIMES_LENT NUMBER(6),
  SECTION_ID NUMBER(3)
);
```

Example:

```
CREATE TABLE SECTION
(
  SECTION_ID NUMBER(3),
  SECTION_NAME CHAR(30),
  BOOK_COUNT NUMBER(6)
);
```

CONSTRAINTS

Constraints are rules that are used to control the invalid data entry in a column.

Some common constraints are:

(*i*) Primary Key
(*ii*) Foreign Key
(*iii*) Null
(*iv*) Not Null
(*v*) Unique
(*vi*) Check
(*vii*) Default.

Table 2.2

Constraint	Description
NULL / NOT NULL	NOT NULL specifies that a column must have some value. NULL (default) allows NULL values in the column.
DEFAULT	Specifies some default value if no value entered by user.
UNIQUE	Specifies that column(s) must have unique values
PRIMARY KEY	Specifies that column(s) are the table prime key and must have unique values. Index is automatically generated for column.
FOREIGN KEY	Specifies that column(s) are a table foreign key and will use referential uniqueness of parent table. Index is automatically generated for column. Foreign keys allow deletion cascades and table / business rule validation.
CHECK	Applies a condition to an input column value.

Primary Key

Primary key has two special attributes:

(*i*) It defines the column as a mandatory or we can say that column cannot be left blank or not null.

(*ii*) The data held across the column must be unique or values should not be repeated.

A single column primary key is known as Simple key and multicolumn primary key is defined as a Composite Primary Key. A table can have only one primary key. We cannot define two primary keys in a single table for that purpose you can use Composite Primary Key. Composite Primary Key is used when a record cannot be uniquely identified using the single column like E-mail ID and Password.

Example: **Simple Primary Key**

Create a Table to store the Customer Address Record.

```
Create Table Customer
(
Cust_No        Number(5)       Primary Key,
Name           Varchar2(20),
```

```
Address        Varchar2(20),
City           Varchar2(20),
State          Varchar2(10),
PIN            Number(6)
);
```

In the above example Cust_No is defined as Simple Primary Key.

Example: **Composite Primary Key**

```
Create Table Cust
(
order_no       Number(5),
prod_no        varchar2(10),
qty            number(8),
price          number(8,2),
Primary Key (order_no, prod_no)
);
```

In the above example order_no and prod_no both are defined as Composite Primary Key.

Foreign Key

Foreign key constraint is used to represent relationship between two or more tables.

(Foreign key constraint will be discussed in detail in Chapter - 05)

Null

If in a record any field that is created as nullable is not having value than Oracle will place a null value in that column. Null value is not equivalent to a blank or zero. Null value can be inserted into the columns of any data type. Null value will evaluate to null in all expressions. Example Null multiplied by 5 is null.

Not Null

The not null constraint ensures that the users always type the value for that column or column becomes a mandatory column. Not null constraint can be applied at column level only.

Unique

The unique key constraint ensures that information in the column(s) is unique or value entered in unique column must not be repeated across the column(s). A table may have more than one unique key. Unique key can be null at the time of data entry. So value is not mandatory in unique column.

Note : We can define a single column as Unique and Not null both than that constraint will work like primary key.

Example:

```
Create table cust1
(
cust_no    number(5)  unique not null,
name       varchar2(10) unique ,
age        number(3),
Address    varchar2(20)
);
```

In the above example **cust_no** column is defined as both unique and not null constraints, so it will act as a primary key and name column is defined as unique. So values in column **name** must not be repeated.

Check

Check constraint ensure that when data is entered, the data in the column is limited to specific values.

Like *a*, *b* or *c*.

Default

At the time of table creation a default value can be assigned to a column. When the user is entering the values and leaves this column empty, the oracle will automatically load this column with the default value. The data type of the default value should match the data type of that column.

Example:

```
Create table student12
(
Roll_no        number(5)       Primary Key,
Enroll_no      number(6)       Unique Not Null,
Name           varchar2(10),
Age            number(3)       Default 21,
Category       varchar2(5)     Check (category in ('SC','ST','OBC','GEN')),
Address        varchar2(10)
);
```

In the above example, Roll_no is primary key and Enroll_no is defined as unique and not null, so it will work like primary key. Check constraint is defined in Category column for checking the category in 'SC','ST','OBC', and 'GEN' at the time of data entry by the users.

To view the structure of the table

Syntax: DESCRIBE <table name>

Example:

SQL> DESCRIBE EMP;

OR

SQL> DESC EMP;

INSERTING ROWS TO THE TABLE

The INSERT INTO statement is used to insert new rows into a table.

Syntax

INSERT INTO table_name VALUES (value1, value2,....);

We can also specify the columns for which we want to insert data:

INSERT INTO table_name (column1, column2,...) VALUES (value1, value2,....);

Note. Character and date values are typed within single quotes and numeric values are typed as they are. Date format is 'DD-MON-YEAR' as '02-APR-04'.

Example:

Insert a New Row in "Persons" table where fields are given below:

LastName	FirstName	Address	City

Type this SQL statement:

INSERT INTO Persons VALUES ('Hetland', 'Camilla', 'Hagabakka 28', 'Sandnes');

Will give this result:

Last Name	FirstName	Address	City
Hetland	Camilla	Hagabakka 28	Sandnes

Insert Data in Specified Columns

This "Persons" table:

Last Name	FirstName	Address	City
Hetland	Camilla	Hagabakka 28	Sandnes

Type this SQL statement:

INSERT INTO Persons (LastName, City) VALUES ('Rasmussen', 'Storgt 68');

Will give this result:

Last Name	FirstName	Address	City
Hetland	Camilla	Hagabakka 28	Sandnes
Rasmussen			Storgt 68

To Add Fields Interactively

INSERT INTO Persons VALUES('&LastName','&FirstName','&Address','&City');

Note. That Names need not match the column names, the data types and order is important.

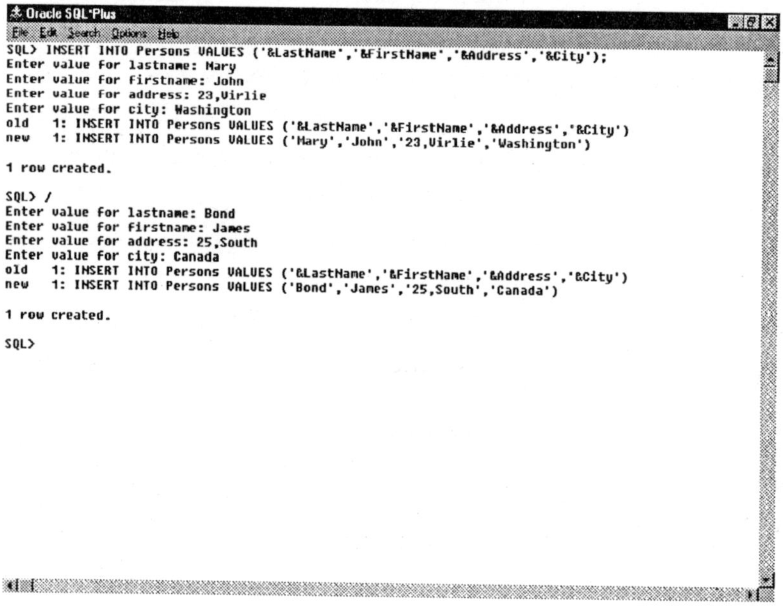

Figure 2.6

For executing the last command in SQL simply type (/) Forward slash. Than no need to type the whole command again and again. So we can enter the values frequently.

To Enter The Time Portion of a Date

To enter the time of date, the TO_DATE function must be used with a format mask indicating the time portion.

Syntax

To_date (char [, format])

Example: Insert into emp (empno,dob) values (7897,to_date('25-JUN-78 10:59 A.M.', 'DD-MON-YY HH:MI A.M.');

SEQUENCE

A sequence is a database object that generates unique, sequential integers values in Oracle. It can be used to automatically generate primary key or unique key column. A sequence can be either in an ascending or a descending order. When we create a sequence, we can specify its initial value and an increment or decrement .

Syntax

Create Sequence <seq_name> [increment by n] [start with n] [maxvalue n] [minvalue n] [cycle / nocycle] [cache/nocache];

INCREMENT BY	The interval value between sequence numbers.
START WITH	The starting value of the sequence.
MINVALUE/NOMINVALUE	The minimum sequence number.
MAXVALUE/NOMAXVALUE	The maximum sequence number.
CACHE/NOCACHE	How many values are kept in the cache - for performance reasons large databases using sequences very frequently will want a lot of values cached.
CYCLE/NOCYCLE	Specifies whether the sequence generator will cycle back to MINVALUE from MAXVALUE when MAXVALUE is met. For sequences providing key values it is probably not a good idea to cycle back.

[ ] are optional

Increment by n. 'n' is an integer that specifies the interval between sequence numbers. The default is 1. If n is positive, then the sequence ascends and if n is negative the sequence descends.

Start with n. Specifies the first sequence numbers to be generated.

Minvalue n. Specifies the minimum value of the sequence. By default, it is 1 for an ascending sequence and 10e26 - 1 for a descending sequence.

Maxvalue n. Specifies the maximum value that the sequence can generate. By default, it is -1 and 10e27 -1 for descending and ascending sequences respectively.

Cycle. Specifies that the sequence continues to generate values from the beginning after reaching either its max or min values.

No cycle. Specifies that the sequence cannot generate more values after reaching either its maxvalue or minvalue. The default value is 'no cycle'.

Cache. The cache option pre-allocates a set of sequence numbers and retains them in memory so that sequence numbers can be accessed faster. When the last of the sequence numbers in the cache has been used , Oracle reads another set of numbers into the cache.

Nocache. The default value 'nocache', does not preallocate sequence numbers for faster access.

Example:

Create Sequence ID increment by 1

start with 1

maxvalue 10

minvalue 1

cycle

cache 4;

After creating a sequence we can access its values with the help of currval and nextval.

CREATE SEQUENCE SECIDNUM INCREMENT BY 1 START WITH 1 MAXVALUE 100 NOCACHE;

CURRVAL returns the current value in a specified sequence which is the value returned by the last reference to nextval.

NEXTVAL returns the initial value of the sequence, when referred to, for the first time. Later reference to nextval will increment the sequence using the increment by clause and return the new value.

Insert into emp values (Id.nextval,'John','01-Jan-99',3500,'MGR');

To obtain the current or next value in a sequence, we must use dot notation, as follows:

sequence_name.CURRVAL

sequence_name.NEXTVAL

We can use CURRVAL and NEXTVAL in a SELECT , INSERT VALUES clause, and the Update clause.

Example: select id. currval from emp;

We may alter the INCREMENT BY, MINVALUE and MAXVALUE values of a sequence by using the ALTER command.

ALTER SEQUENCE SEQUENCENAME INCREMENT BY 2

ALTER SEQUENCE SEQUENCENAME MINVALUE 10

ALTER SEQUENCE SEQUENCENAME MAXVALUE 2500

We can remove a sequence by using the DROP command.

DROP SEQUENCE SEQUENCENAME

Drop Sequence Sequence_name:

Syntax

Drop sequence name;

Example: Drop sequence id;

TO VIEW THE ROWS IN THE TABLE

The SELECT Statement

The SELECT statement is used to view data from a table.

Syntax

SELECT column_name(s) FROM table_name ;

Select Some Columns

To select the columns named "LastName" and "FirstName", use a SELECT statement like this:

SELECT LastName, FirstName FROM Persons;

"Persons" table

Last Name	FirstName	Address	City
Hansen	Ola	Timoteivn 20	Sandnes
Svendson	Tove	Borgvn 25	Sandnes
Pettersen	Kari	Storgt 21	Stavanger

Result

Last Name	FirstName
Hansen	Ola
Svendson	Tove
Pettersen	Kari

Select All Columns

To select all columns from the "Persons" table, use a * (asterisk) symbol instead of column names, like this:

SELECT * FROM Persons;

Result

Last Name	FirstName	Address	City
Hansen	Ola	Timoteivn 20	Sandnes
Svendson	Tove	Borgvn 25	Sandnes
Pettersen	Kari	Storgt 21	Stavanger

WHERE CLAUSE

The optional WHERE condition has the general form:

WHERE *boolean_expr*

boolean_expr can consist of any expression which evaluates to a Boolean value. In many cases, this expression will be:

expr cond_op expr

or *log_op expr*

where *cond_op* can be one of: =, <, <=, >, >= or <>, a conditional operator like ALL, ANY, IN, LIKE, or a locally defined operator, and *log_op* can be one of: AND, OR, NOT. SELECT will ignore all rows for which the WHERE condition does not return TRUE.

The SELECT Statement with where clause

The SELECT statement is used to view data from a table for a particular condition also.

Syntax

SELECT column_name(s) FROM table_name where condition ;

```
Oracle SQL*Plus
File Edit Search Options Help
SQL> SELECT * FROM EMP;

    EMPNO ENAME      JOB             MGR HIREDATE        SAL      COMM    DEPTNO
--------- ---------- --------- --------- --------- --------- --------- ---------
     7782 CLARK      MANAGER        7839 09-JUN-81      2450       500        10
     7788 SCOTT      ANALYST        7566 19-APR-87      3000       500        20
     7839 KING       PRESIDENT           17=NOV=81      5000       500        10
     7844 TURNER     SALESMAN       7698 08-SEP-81      1500       500        30
     7876 ADAMS      CLERK          7788 23-MAY-87      1100       500        20

SQL> SELECT ENAME, JOB FROM EMP;

ENAME      JOB
---------- ---------
CLARK      MANAGER
SCOTT      ANALYST
KING       PRESIDENT
TURNER     SALESMAN
ADAMS      CLERK

SQL> SELECT * FROM EMP WHERE JOB = 'MANAGER';

    EMPNO ENAME      JOB             MGR HIREDATE        SAL      COMM    DEPTNO
--------- ---------- --------- --------- --------- --------- --------- ---------
     7782 CLARK      MANAGER        7839 09-JUN-81      2450       500        10

SQL> |
```

Figure 2.7

Multiple condition WHERE clauses

Multiple condition WHERE clauses are in the format—WHERE keyword, 1st comparison column, 1st operator, 1st condition, AND/OR operator, 2nd comparison column, 2nd operator, 2nd condition ad infinitum. The AND operator takes precedence unless we force priority to an OR operator with brackets. An example is given below :

SELECT * FROM BOOK WHERE SECTION_ID IN (9, 11) AND TIMES_LENT > 10;

The SELECT DISTINCT Statement

The DISTINCT keyword is used to return only distinct (different) values.

The SELECT statement returns information from table columns. But what if we only want to select distinct elements?

With SQL, all we need to do is to add a DISTINCT keyword to the SELECT statement:

Syntax

SELECT DISTINCT column_name(s) FROM table_name;

Using the DISTINCT keyword

To select ALL values from the column named "Company" we use a SELECT statement like this:

SELECT Company FROM Orders ;

"Orders" table

Company	Order Number
Sega	3412
LG	2312
Trio	4678
LG	6798

Result

Company
Sega
LG
Trio
LG

Note that "LG" is listed twice in the result-set.

To select only DIFFERENT values from the column named "Company" we use a SELECT DISTINCT statement like this:

SELECT DISTINCT Company FROM orders;

Result

Company
Sega
LG
Trio

ROWNUM

ROWNUM returns a number indicating the order in which a row was selected from a table. The first row selected has a ROWNUM of 1, the second row has a ROWNUM of 2, and so on. We can use ROWNUM in the WHERE clause of a SELECT statement to limit the number of rows retrieved, as follows:

```
Oracle SQL*Plus
File Edit Search Options Help
SQL> SELECT * FROM EMP WHERE ROWNUM = 1;

    EMPNO ENAME      JOB              MGR HIREDATE         SAL       COMM     DEPTNO
--------- ---------- --------- --------- --------- --------- --------- ---------
     7782 CLARK      MANAGER         7839 09-JUN-81       2450        500         10

SQL> SELECT * FROM EMP WHERE ROWNUM <= 3;

    EMPNO ENAME      JOB              MGR HIREDATE         SAL       COMM     DEPTNO
--------- ---------- --------- --------- --------- --------- --------- ---------
     7782 CLARK      MANAGER         7839 09-JUN-81       2450        500         10
     7788 SCOTT      ANALYST         7566 19-APR-87       3000        500         20
     7839 KING       PRESIDENT            17-NOV-81       5000        500         10

SQL>
```

Figure 2.8

TO DELETE ROWS FROM A TABLE

The Delete Statement

The DELETE command allows us to remove rows from a table, we can include a WHERE clause in the same fashion as the SELECT statement to indicate which row(s) we want deleted - in nearly all cases we should specify a WHERE clause, running a DELETE without a WHERE clause deletes. ALL rows from the table. Unlike the INSERT command the DELETE command can change multiple rows so we should take great care that we are deleting only the rows we want to remove.

Syntax

```
DELETE FROM table_name WHERE column_name = some_value;
```

Person:

Last Name	FirstName	Address	City
Nilsen	Bond	Kirkegt 56	Stavanger
Rasmussen	John	Stien 12	Stavanger

Delete a Row

"John" is going to be deleted:

DELETE FROM Person WHERE LastName = 'John';

Select * from person;

Result

Last Name	FirstName	Address	City
Nilsen	Bond	Kirkegt 56	Stavanger

Delete All Rows

It is possible to delete all rows in a table without deleting the table. This means that the table structure, attributes, and indexes will be intact:

DELETE FROM table_name;

or

DELETE * FROM table_name;

Drop Table and Truncate

Delete a Table or Database

To delete a table (the table structure, attributes, and indexes will also be deleted):

DROP TABLE table_name;

To delete a database:

DROP DATABASE database_name;

Truncate a Table

If we only want to get rid of the data inside a table, and not the table itself, we should use the TRUNCATE TABLE command (deletes only the data inside the table):

TRUNCATE TABLE table_name;

Transaction Management

The Oracle provides a robust transaction model, as we might expect for a relational database. We determine what constitutes a transaction, the logical unit of work that must be either saved together with a COMMIT statement or rolled back together with a ROLLBACK statement. A transaction begins implicitly with the first SQL statement issued since the last COMMIT or ROLLBACK (or with the start of a session).

SQL and PL/SQL provide the following statements for transaction management:

Commit

Saves all outstanding changes since the last COMMIT or ROLLBACK and releases all locks.

Rollback

Erases all outstanding changes since the last COMMIT or ROLLBACK and releases all locks.

Rollback to Savepoint

Erases all changes made since the specified savepoint was established.

Savepoint

Establishes a savepoint, which then allows us to perform partial ROLLBACKs.

Set Transaction

Allows us to begin a read-only or read-write session, establish an isolation level, or assign the current transaction to a specified rollback segment.

Lock Table

Allows us to lock an entire database table in the specified mode. This overrides the default row-level locking usually applied to a table.

COMMIT STATEMENT

When we COMMIT, we make any permanent changes made by our session to the database in the current transaction. Once we commit, our changes will be visible to other Oracle sessions or users. The syntax for the COMMIT statement is:

```
COMMIT [WORK] [COMMENT text];
```

The WORK keyword is optional and can be used to improve readability.

The COMMENT keyword specifies a comment, which is then associated with the current transaction. The text must be a quoted literal and can be not more than 50 characters in length. The COMMENT text is usually employed with distributed transactions.

Note that COMMIT releases any row and table locks issued in our session, such as with a SELECT FOR UPDATE statement. It also erases any savepoints issued since the last COMMIT or ROLLBACK. Once we COMMIT our changes, we cannot roll them back with a ROLLBACK statement.

The following statements are all valid uses of the COMMIT:

```
COMMIT;
COMMIT [WORK]
```

WORK is an optional keyword that does not change the semantics of COMMIT.

THE ROLLBACK STATEMENT

When we ROLLBACK, we undo some or all changes made by our session to the database in the current transaction. From an *ad hoc* SQL standpoint, the ROLLBACK gives us a way to erase mistakes we might have made, as in:

```
DELETE FROM orders;
```

The syntax for the ROLLBACK statement is:

```
ROLLBACK [WORK] [TO [SAVEPOINT] savepoint_name];
```

There are two basic ways to use ROLLBACK without parameters or with the TO clause to indicate a savepoint at which the ROLLBACK should stop.

The parameterless ROLLBACK undoes all outstanding changes in your transaction.

The ROLLBACK TO version allows us to undo all changes and release all acquired locks which were issued since the savepoint identified by savepoint_name was marked (see the next section on the SAVEPOINT statement for more information on how to mark a savepoint in our application).

The savepoint_name is an undeclared Oracle identifier. It cannot be a literal (enclosed in quotes) or variable name.

All of the following uses of ROLLBACK are valid:

```
ROLLBACK;
ROLLBACK WORK;
ROLLBACK TO begin_cleanup;
```

All of the following uses of ROLLBACK are invalid:

```
ROLLBACK SAVEPOINT;
— ORA-02181: invalid option to ROLLBACK WORK
— Must use TO keyword before SAVEPOINT.
ROLLBACK WORK TO;
— ORA-02182: save point name expected
— Must specify savepoint name.
ROLLBACK TO SAVEPOINT 'favorite_movies';
— ORA-03001: Unimplemented feature
— Savepoint cannot be in quotes.
```

Example:

Delete from emp where ename = 'Scott';

Commit;

If a commit is not issued, it is possible to undo the operation by issuing a Rollback.

Delete from emp where ename = 'Scott';

Rollback;

When we roll back to a specific savepoint, all savepoints issued after the specified savepoint_name are erased. The savepoint to which we roll back is not, however, erased. This means that we can restart our transaction from that point and, if necessary, roll back to that same savepoint if another error occurs.

Immediately before we execute an INSERT, UPDATE, or DELETE, SQL implicitly generates a savepoint. If our DML statement fails, a rollback is automatically performed to that implicit savepoint. In this way, only that last DML statement is undone.

THE SAVEPOINT STATEMENT

SAVEPOINT gives a name to and marks a point in the processing of our transaction. This marker allows us to ROLLBACK TO that point, erasing any changes and releasing any locks issued after that savepoint, but preserving any changes and locks which occurred before we marked the savepoint.

The syntax for the SAVEPOINT statement is:

SAVEPOINT savepoint_name;

where savepoint_name is an undeclared identifier. This means that it must conform to the rules for an Oracle identifier (up to 30 characters in length, starting with a letter, containing letters, numbers and #, $, or _), but that we do not need to (nor can we) declare that identifier.

Savepoints are not scoped to SQL blocks. If we reuse a savepoint name within the current transaction, that savepoint is "moved" from its original position to the current point in the transaction, regardless of the procedure, function, or anonymous block in which the SAVEPOINT statements are executed. As a corollary, if we issue a SAVEPOINT inside a recursive program, a new SAVEPOINT is executed at each level of recursion, but we can only roll back to the most recently marked savepoint.

Example:

Savepoint D1;

Delete from emp where ename = 'Scott';

Savepoint D2;

Delete from emp where ename ='King';

Rollback to D2;

Commit;

These will undo the second delete operation.

THE SET TRANSACTION STATEMENT

The SET TRANSACTION statement allows to begin a read-only or read-write session, establish an isolation level, or assign the current transaction to a specified rollback segment. This statement must be the first SQL statement processed in a transaction and it can appear only once. This statement comes in the following four types:

SET TRANSACTION READ ONLY

This version defines the current transaction as read-only. In a read-only transaction, all subsequent queries only see those changes, which were committed before the transaction began (providing a read-consistent view across tables and queries). This statement is useful when we are executing long-running, multiple query reports and you want to make sure that the data used in the report is consistent:

SET TRANSACTION READ WRITE

This version defines the current transaction as read-write:

SET TRANSACTION ISOLATION LEVEL
SERIALIZABLE | READ COMMITTED

If we specify READ COMMITTED, a DML which requires row-level locks held by another transaction will wait until those row locks are released:

SET TRANSACTION USE ROLLBACK SEGMENT rollback_segname

This version assigns the current transaction to the specified rollback segment and establishes the transaction as read-write. This statement cannot be used in conjunction with SET TRANSACTION READ ONLY.

THE LOCK TABLE STATEMENT

This statement allows us to lock an entire database table with the specified lock mode. By doing this, we can share or deny access to that table while we perform operations against it. The syntax for this statement is:

LOCK TABLE table_reference_list IN lock_mode MODE [NOWAIT]

where table_reference_list is a list of one or more table references (identifying either a local table/view or a remote entity through a database link), and lock_mode is the mode of the lock, which can be one of the following:

ROW SHARE
ROW EXCLUSIVE
SHARE UPDATE
SHARE
SHARE ROW EXCLUSIVE
EXCLUSIVE

If we specify the NOWAIT keyword, Oracle will not wait for the lock if the table has already been locked by another user. If we leave out the NOWAIT keyword, Oracle waits until the table is available (and there is no set limit on how long Oracle will wait). Locking a table never stops other users from querying or reading the table.

The following LOCK TABLE statements show valid variations:

```
LOCK TABLE emp IN ROW EXCLUSIVE MODE;
LOCK TABLE emp, dept IN SHARE MODE NOWAIT;
LOCK TABLE scott.emp@new_york IN SHARE UPDATE MODE;
```

TO UPDATE ROWS IN THE TABLE

The **update** statement is used to update or change records that match a specified criteria. This is accomplished by carefully constructing a where clause.

```
update tablename
set columnname =
  newvalue
 [,nextcolumn =
  newvalue2...]
where columnname
 OPERATOR value
 [and|or column
 OPERATOR value];
 [] = optional
```

Examples:

1. update phone_book
   set area_code = 623
   where prefix = 979;
2. update phone_book
   set last_name = 'Smith', prefix=555, suffix=9292
   where last_name = 'Jons';
3. update employee
   set age = age+1
   where first_name='Pattin' and last_name='William';

Remember if the where clause is not given, then all the rows in the table will be updated.

OPERATORS IN SQL *PLUS

OPERATERS in SQL *PLUS			
Arithmetic	**Relational or Comparison**	**Logical**	**Miscellaneous**
+ (Addition) – (Subtraction) * (Multiplication) / (Divison)	= (Equal) > (Greater than) < (Less than) >= (Greater than or equal to) <= (Less than or equal to) < > or != Not equal to LIKE	AND OR NOT	IN BETWEEN NOT IN NOT LIKE || (Concatenation)

EXAMPLE OF ARITHMETIC OPERATORS

```
Oracle SQL*Plus
File Edit Search Options Help
SQL> SELECT * FROM EMP;

    EMPNO ENAME      JOB             MGR HIREDATE        SAL      COMM    DEPTNO
--------- ---------- --------- --------- --------- --------- --------- ---------
     7782 CLARK      MANAGER        7839 09-JUN-81      2450       500        10
     7788 SCOTT      ANALYST        7566 19-APR-87      3000       500        20
     7839 KING       PRESIDENT           17-NOV-81      5000       500        10
     7844 TURNER     SALESMAN       7698 08-SEP-81      1500       500        30
     7876 ADAMS      CLERK          7788 23-MAY-87      1100       500        20

SQL> SELECT SAL+COMM FROM EMP;

 SAL+COMM
---------
     2950
     3500
     5500
     2000
     1600

SQL> SELECT SAL*COMM FROM EMP;

 SAL*COMM
---------
  1225000
  1500000
  2500000
   750000
   550000

SQL> SELECT SAL-COMM FROM EMP;

 SAL-COMM
---------
     1950
     2500
```

Figure 2.9

Example of Relational or Comparison Operators

```
SQL> SELECT * FROM EMP WHERE SAL < 3000;

    EMPNO ENAME      JOB              MGR HIREDATE         SAL      COMM    DEPTNO
--------- ---------- --------- --------- --------- --------- --------- ---------
     7782 CLARK      MANAGER         7839 09-JUN-81      2450       500        10
     7844 TURNER     SALESMAN        7698 08-SEP-81      1500       500        30
     7876 ADAMS      CLERK           7788 23-MAY-87      1100       500        20

SQL> SELECT * FROM EMP WHERE SAL > 3000;

    EMPNO ENAME      JOB              MGR HIREDATE         SAL      COMM    DEPTNO
--------- ---------- --------- --------- --------- --------- --------- ---------
     7839 KING       PRESIDENT            17-NOV-81      5000       500        10

SQL> SELECT * FROM EMP WHERE SAL >= 3000;

    EMPNO ENAME      JOB              MGR HIREDATE         SAL      COMM    DEPTNO
--------- ---------- --------- --------- --------- --------- --------- ---------
     7788 SCOTT      ANALYST         7566 19-APR-87      3000       500        20
     7839 KING       PRESIDENT            17-NOV-81      5000       500        10

SQL> SELECT * FROM EMP WHERE SAL <= 1500;

    EMPNO ENAME      JOB              MGR HIREDATE         SAL      COMM    DEPTNO
--------- ---------- --------- --------- --------- --------- --------- ---------
     7844 TURNER     SALESMAN        7698 08-SEP-81      1500       500        30
     7876 ADAMS      CLERK           7788 23-MAY-87      1100       500        20

SQL> SELECT * FROM EMP WHERE SAL <> 1500;

    EMPNO ENAME      JOB              MGR HIREDATE         SAL      COMM    DEPTNO
--------- ---------- --------- --------- --------- --------- --------- ---------
     7782 CLARK      MANAGER         7839 09-JUN-81      2450       500        10
     7788 SCOTT      ANALYST         7566 19-APR-87      3000       500        20
     7839 KING       PRESIDENT            17-NOV-81      5000       500        10
     7876 ADAMS      CLERK           7788 23-MAY-87      1100       500        20
```

Figure 2.10

Like Operator

The **LIKE** is a pattern matching operator and can also be used in the conditional selection of the where clause. Like is a very powerful operator that allows us to select only rows that are "like" what we specify. The percent sign "%" (percentage) and _ (underscore) can be used as a wild card to match any possible character that might appear before or after the characters specified. The % is used to denote **any number of unknown characters** and _ denotes **one unknown character**. To denote more than one unknown character using _, the number of _ (underscore) must be equal to the number of unknown characters.

For example:

```
select empno, job, hiredate
from emp
where ename LIKE 'C%';
```

This SQL statement will match any ename that start with 'C'.
Strings must be in single quotes.
Or we can specify,

select empno, job, hiredate
  from emp
where ename LIKE '%K';

This statement will match any ename that end in a 'K'.

select * from emp
where ename = 'SCOTT';

This will only select rows where the ename equals 'SCOTT' exactly.
To retrieve rows where the JOB contains the word 'NA' embedded in it.
Example: MANAGER, ANALYST.

SELECT * FROM EMP WHERE JOB LIKE '%NA%';

To retrieve rows where the ENAME starts with 'C' and end with 'K'.

SELECT * FROM EMP WHERE ENAME LIKE 'C%K';

To retrieve rows where the ENAME starts with 'C' and having four characters more after 'C'.

Example: CLERK, CLARK,CROWN,CAMIL

SELECT * FROM EMP WHERE ENAME LIKE 'C_ _ _ _';

Example of Logical Operators

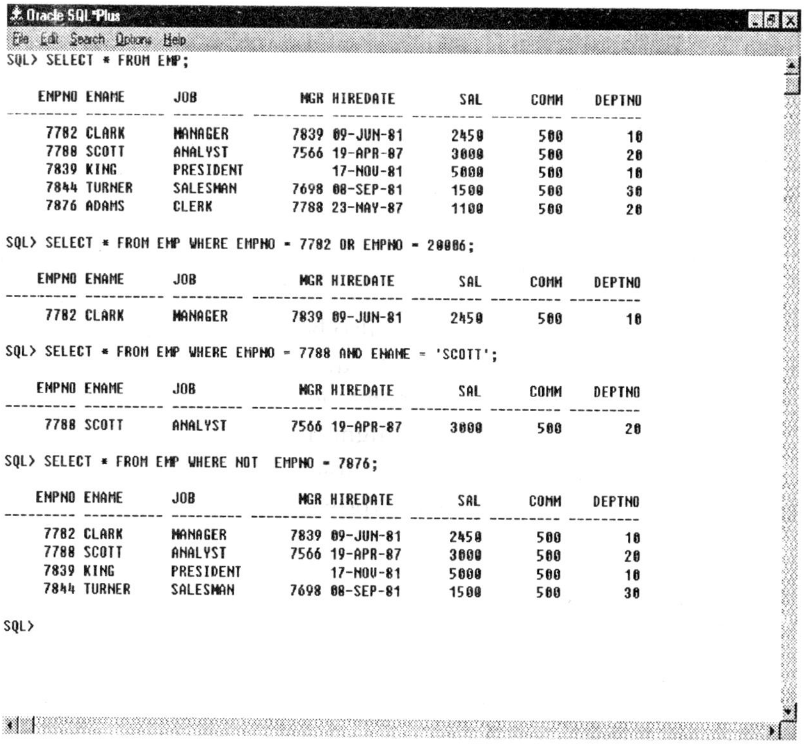

```
SQL> SELECT * FROM EMP;

    EMPNO ENAME      JOB              MGR HIREDATE        SAL       COMM     DEPTNO
--------- ---------- --------- --------- --------- --------- --------- ---------
     7782 CLARK      MANAGER         7839 09-JUN-81      2450       500        10
     7788 SCOTT      ANALYST         7566 19-APR-87      3000       500        20
     7839 KING       PRESIDENT            17-NOV-81      5000       500        10
     7844 TURNER     SALESMAN        7698 08-SEP-81      1500       500        30
     7876 ADAMS      CLERK           7788 23-MAY-87      1100       500        20

SQL> SELECT * FROM EMP WHERE EMPNO = 7782 OR EMPNO = 20006;

    EMPNO ENAME      JOB              MGR HIREDATE        SAL       COMM     DEPTNO
--------- ---------- --------- --------- --------- --------- --------- ---------
     7782 CLARK      MANAGER         7839 09-JUN-81      2450       500        10

SQL> SELECT * FROM EMP WHERE EMPNO = 7788 AND ENAME = 'SCOTT';

    EMPNO ENAME      JOB              MGR HIREDATE        SAL       COMM     DEPTNO
--------- ---------- --------- --------- --------- --------- --------- ---------
     7788 SCOTT      ANALYST         7566 19-APR-87      3000       500        20

SQL> SELECT * FROM EMP WHERE NOT  EMPNO = 7876;

    EMPNO ENAME      JOB              MGR HIREDATE        SAL       COMM     DEPTNO
--------- ---------- --------- --------- --------- --------- --------- ---------
     7782 CLARK      MANAGER         7839 09-JUN-81      2450       500        10
     7788 SCOTT      ANALYST         7566 19-APR-87      3000       500        20
     7839 KING       PRESIDENT            17-NOV-81      5000       500        10
     7844 TURNER     SALESMAN        7698 08-SEP-81      1500       500        30

SQL>
```

Figure 2.11

AND ensures that rows satisfying both the conditions are selected.

OR ensures that rows satisfying any one of the condition is retrieved.

NOT ensures that rows not satisfying the condition specified in the query.

IN - one of a set of values

Syntax

IN ({ Value [,...] } | SELECT-Command)

Description:

IN (Value [,...]) tells the DBMS , that one of the values must be in the specified value list.

Example:

SELECT *
FROM order
WHERE price IN (100,200,300,400,500);

Here are all records from the table order selected, where price have one of the values in the specified list.

select * from emp where empno IN (7782,7788,7876);

Here are all records from the table emp selected, where empno have one of the values in the specified list.

SELECT * FROM EMP WHERE JOB IN ('CLERK','MANAGER');

Here are all records from the table emp selected, where JOB have one of the values in the specified list.

NOT IN

NOT IN ({ Value [,...] } | SELECT-Command)

Description:

NOT IN (Value [,...]) tells the DBMS , that values must not be in the specified value list.

SELECT * FROM EMP WHERE JOB NOT IN ('CLERK','MANAGER');

Here are all records from the table emp selected, where JOB not have values in the specified list.

BETWEEN

BETWEEN - checks when an field is between two values

Syntax

BETWEEN Value1 AND Value2

Description:

BETWEEN W1 AND W2 tells the Oracle, that values must be between W1 and W2.

Example:

SELECT num, item, price

FROM order

WHERE price BETWEEN 100 AND 500

Here are the fields num, item and price from the table order selected, where the field price have a value between 100 and 500.

SELECT * FROM EMP WHERE SAL BETWEEN 1500 AND 2450;

Here are the fields from EMP table selected, where the SAL value between 1500 and 2450.

We can also use **NOT BETWEEN** to exclude the values between our range.

NOT LIKE

The **NOT LIKE** is a pattern matching operator and can also be used in the conditional selection of the where clause. NOT Like operator that allows us to select only rows that are "not like" what we specify. The percent sign "%" (percentage) and _ (underscore) can be used as a wild card to match any possible character that might appear before or after the characters specified.

For example:

Select empno, job, hiredate from emp where ename NOT LIKE 'C%';

Above query will select only those rows where ename not starts with 'C' character.

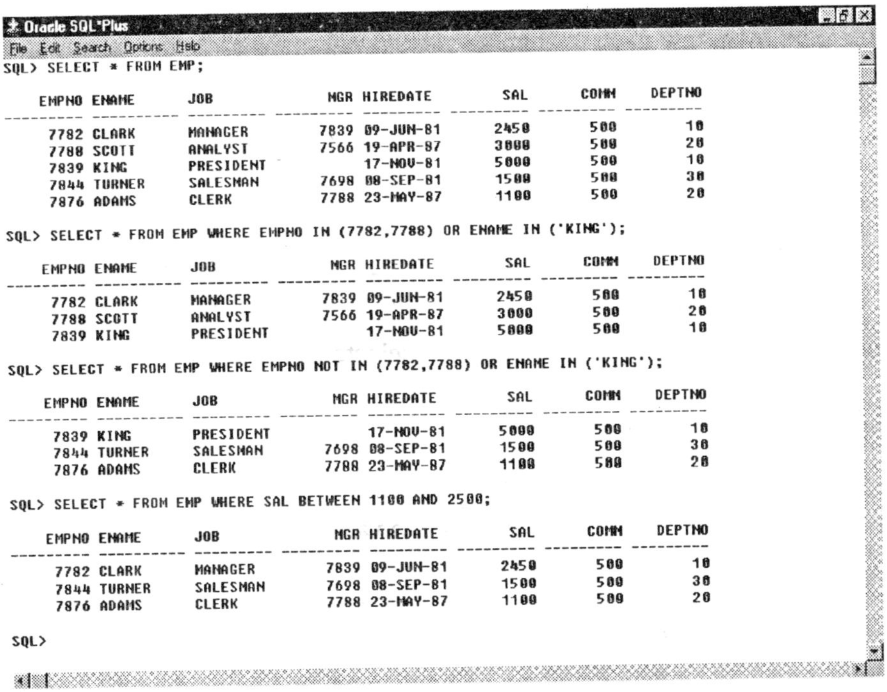

```
Oracle SQL*Plus
File Edit Search Options Help
SQL> SELECT * FROM EMP;

    EMPNO ENAME      JOB              MGR HIREDATE        SAL       COMM     DEPTNO
--------- ---------- --------- --------- --------- --------- --------- ---------
     7782 CLARK      MANAGER         7839 09-JUN-81      2450        500        10
     7788 SCOTT      ANALYST         7566 19-APR-87      3000        500        20
     7839 KING       PRESIDENT            17-NOV-81      5000        500        10
     7844 TURNER     SALESMAN        7698 08-SEP-81      1500        500        30
     7876 ADAMS      CLERK           7788 23-MAY-87      1100        500        20

SQL> SELECT * FROM EMP WHERE EMPNO IN (7782,7788) OR ENAME IN ('KING');

    EMPNO ENAME      JOB              MGR HIREDATE        SAL       COMM     DEPTNO
--------- ---------- --------- --------- --------- --------- --------- ---------
     7782 CLARK      MANAGER         7839 09-JUN-81      2450        500        10
     7788 SCOTT      ANALYST         7566 19-APR-87      3000        500        20
     7839 KING       PRESIDENT            17-NOV-81      5000        500        10

SQL> SELECT * FROM EMP WHERE EMPNO NOT IN (7782,7788) OR ENAME IN ('KING');

    EMPNO ENAME      JOB              MGR HIREDATE        SAL       COMM     DEPTNO
--------- ---------- --------- --------- --------- --------- --------- ---------
     7839 KING       PRESIDENT            17-NOV-81      5000        500        10
     7844 TURNER     SALESMAN        7698 08-SEP-81      1500        500        30
     7876 ADAMS      CLERK           7788 23-MAY-87      1100        500        20

SQL> SELECT * FROM EMP WHERE SAL BETWEEN 1100 AND 2500;

    EMPNO ENAME      JOB              MGR HIREDATE        SAL       COMM     DEPTNO
--------- ---------- --------- --------- --------- --------- --------- ---------
     7782 CLARK      MANAGER         7839 09-JUN-81      2450        500        10
     7844 TURNER     SALESMAN        7698 08-SEP-81      1500        500        30
     7876 ADAMS      CLERK           7788 23-MAY-87      1100        500        20

SQL>
```

Figure 2.12

ORDER BY

ORDER BY clause allows us to display the results of our query in a sorted order (either ascending order or descending order) based on the columns that we specify to order by.

ORDER BY clause syntax:

SELECT column1, SUM(column2)
FROM "list-of-tables"
ORDER BY
"column-list" ASC | DESC;

This statement will select the employee_id, dept, name, age, and salary from the employee table which results in ascending (default) order based on their Salary.

ASC = Ascending Order - default
DESC = Descending Order

For example:

SELECT employee_id, dept, name, age, salary
FROM employee
ORDER BY salary;

If we would like to order based on multiple columns, we must seperate the columns with commas.

For example:

Select fields from tablename ORDER BY field name desc;
SELECT employee_id, dept, name, age, salary
FROM employee
ORDER BY salary, age DESC;

In the above query Salary column will be arranged in ascending order and age column will be arranged in descending order.

To Rename a Table

Syntax: Rename oldtablename to newtablename;

Example:

Rename emp to newemp

Above query will change the table name emp to newemp.

Concatenation

There is just one string operator - || (split bar typed twice), for string concatenation. Both operands of || must be strings. The operator concatenates the second string to the end of the first.

For example:

'ab' || 'cd' => 'abcd'

Example:

SELECT ENAME ||'(' || JOB || ')' FROM EMP;

SELECT ENAME || ' WORKING AS ' || JOB || ' IN DEPARTMENT NO ' || DEPTNO || ' HAVING SALARY '|| SAL FROM EMP;

```
Oracle SQL*Plus
File Edit Search Options Help
SQL> SELECT * FROM EMP;

    EMPNO ENAME      JOB              MGR HIREDATE         SAL       COMM     DEPTNO
--------- ---------- --------- --------- --------- --------- ---------- ---------
     7782 CLARK      MANAGER         7839 09-JUN-81      2450        500         10
     7788 SCOTT      ANALYST         7566 19-APR-87      3000        500         20
     7839 KING       PRESIDENT            17-NOV-81      5000        500         10
     7844 TURNER     SALESMAN        7698 08-SEP-81      1500        500         30
     7876 ADAMS      CLERK           7788 23-MAY-87      1100        500         20

SQL> SELECT  ENAME  ||' ( ' || JOB || ' ) ' FROM EMP;

ENAME||'('||JOB||')'
-------------------------
CLARK ( MANAGER )
SCOTT ( ANALYST )
KING ( PRESIDENT )
TURNER ( SALESMAN )
ADAMS ( CLERK )

SQL> SELECT ENAME || ' WORKING AS  ' || JOB  || ' IN DEPARTMENT NO ' || DEPTNO ||
  2  ' HAVING  SALARY '|| SAL   FROM EMP
  3  /

ENAME||'WORKINGAS'||JOB||'INDEPARTMENTNO'||DEPTNO||'HAVINGSALARY'||SAL
--------------------------------------------------------------------------------
CLARK WORKING AS  MANAGER IN DEPARTMENT NO 10 HAVING  SALARY 2450
SCOTT WORKING AS  ANALYST IN DEPARTMENT NO 20 HAVING  SALARY 3000
KING WORKING AS  PRESIDENT IN DEPARTMENT NO 10 HAVING  SALARY 5000
TURNER WORKING AS  SALESMAN IN DEPARTMENT NO 30 HAVING  SALARY 1500
ADAMS WORKING AS  CLERK IN DEPARTMENT NO 20 HAVING  SALARY 1100

SQL> |
```

Figure 2.13

COLUMN ALIASES

The column of the table can be displayed with user defined heading or aliases instead of the column names appearing as the heading.

Syntax

Select column1, column2 "Alias" from tablename;

Example:

SELECT EMPNO "NUMBER", ENAME "NAME" FROM EMP;

```
Oracle SQL*Plus
File Edit Search Options Help
SQL> SELECT * FROM EMP;

    EMPNO ENAME      JOB              MGR HIREDATE        SAL      COMM    DEPTNO
--------- ---------- --------- --------- --------- --------- --------- ---------
     7782 CLARK      MANAGER         7839 09-JUN-81      2450       500        10
     7788 SCOTT      ANALYST         7566 19-APR-87      3000       500        20
     7839 KING       PRESIDENT            17-NOV-81      5000       500        10
     7844 TURNER     SALESMAN        7698 08-SEP-81      1500       500        30
     7876 ADAMS      CLERK           7788 23-MAY-87      1100       500        20

SQL> SELECT EMPNO "NUMBER", ENAME "NAME", SAL "SALARY" FROM EMP;

   NUMBER NAME           SALARY
--------- ---------- ---------
     7782 CLARK           2450
     7788 SCOTT           3000
     7839 KING            5000
     7844 TURNER          1500
     7876 ADAMS           1100

SQL> SELECT EMPNO, ENAME, SAL*12 "ANNUAL SAL" FROM EMP;

    EMPNO ENAME      ANNUAL SAL
--------- ---------- ----------
     7782 CLARK           29400
     7788 SCOTT           36000
     7839 KING            60000
     7844 TURNER          18000
     7876 ADAMS           13200

SQL>
```

Figure 2.14

COLUMN FORMAT

The column data can be formatted as per the requirement of the user.

Example:

COLUMN SAL FORMAT 9,99,999.99

SELECT * FROM EMP

The SAL column will now be displayed with commas wherever applicable and two decimal places.

COLUMN JOB FORMAT A5 TRUNC

SELECT * FROM EMP

The JOB column is formatted to display only five characters. If a job name is longer than five characters, it will be truncated in the display.

To release the formatting command is :
Clear column

```
Oracle SQL*Plus
File Edit Search Options Help
SQL> SELECT * FROM EMP;

    EMPNO ENAME      JOB             MGR HIREDATE        SAL      COMM    DEPTNO
--------- ---------- --------- --------- --------- --------- --------- ---------
     7782 CLARK      MANAGER        7839 09-JUN-81      2450       500        10
     7788 SCOTT      ANALYST        7566 19-APR-87      3000       500        20
     7839 KING       PRESIDENT           17-NOV-81      5000       500        10
     7844 TURNER     SALESMAN       7698 08-SEP-81      1500       500        30
     7876 ADAMS      CLERK          7788 23-MAY-87      1100       500        20

SQL> COLUMN SAL FORMAT 9,99,999.99;
SQL> SELECT * FROM EMP;

    EMPNO ENAME      JOB             MGR HIREDATE           SAL      COMM    DEPTNO
--------- ---------- --------- --------- --------- ------------ --------- ---------
     7782 CLARK      MANAGER        7839 09-JUN-81     2,450.00       500        10
     7788 SCOTT      ANALYST        7566 19-APR-87     3,000.00       500        20
     7839 KING       PRESIDENT           17-NOV-81     5,000.00       500        10
     7844 TURNER     SALESMAN       7698 08-SEP-81     1,500.00       500        30
     7876 ADAMS      CLERK          7788 23-MAY-87     1,100.00       500        20

SQL> COLUMN JOB FORMAT A5 TRUNC;
SQL> SELECT * FROM EMP;

    EMPNO ENAME      JOB         MGR HIREDATE           SAL      COMM    DEPTNO
--------- ---------- ----- --------- --------- ------------ --------- ---------
     7782 CLARK      MANAG      7839 09-JUN-81     2,450.00       500        10
     7788 SCOTT      ANALY      7566 19-APR-87     3,000.00       500        20
     7839 KING       PRESI           17-NOV-81     5,000.00       500        10
     7844 TURNER     SALES      7698 08-SEP-81     1,500.00       500        30
     7876 ADAMS      CLERK      7788 23-MAY-87     1,100.00       500        20

SQL> CLEAR COLUMN ;
columns cleared
SQL> |
```

Figure 2.15

SOME IMPORTANT COMMANDS

Command	Description
SPOOL filename	Write all console text from this point on to named text file.
SPOOL OFF	Close any open spool file, stop spooling.
DESCRIBE tablename	Describe the structure of the named table, abbreviate to DESC.
HELP	Call system help (if installed)
HOST command	Run command on local shell (UNIX or DOS)
CONNECT userid/password	Connect to another schema.
CONNECT userid/password@instname	Connect to another schema on another database instance.

ED	Start the local text editor and load the last SQL command. When we save the text file the SQL will be placed back into SQL *Plus.
SAVE commandfilename	Save the last SQL command to the named command file
LOAD commandfilename	Load a command file but don't run it.
START commandfilename	Load a command file and run it, also use @commandfilename.
PROMPT text	Output a line of text to any user of the command file with the PROMPT in it.
REMARK	Comment line in a command file.
PAUSE	In command file, forces command file to halt execution until any key is pressed.
SET	Used to set SQL *Plus environment variables.
/	Execute the last command stored in the buffer.
List or L	Display the commands stored in buffer
Input or I	Input some more line or text in the current command
Del	Delete the current line from the buffer
Change or C	To make Changes to the current line *Example:* Change/old-value/new-value or C/old-value/new-value.
Clear Screen	To Clear the Screen like CLS command in DOS

TO VIEW ALL THE TABLES

Select * from tab

These will display all the tables.

LAB ASSIGNMENT—1

1. Create the following tables:

(*i*) **EMPLOYEE**

Column Name	Data Type	Size
Empno	Varchar2	6 (Primary Key)
Ename	Varchar2	20 (Not Null)
Job	Char	10
Hiredate	Date	
Basic_Sal	Number	(9,2)
Comm	Number	(7,2)
Dept_no	Varchar2	(2)

Insert the following data into the above EMPLOYEE table:

Empno	Ename	Job	Hiredate	Basic_sal	Comm	Dept_no
E0001	Kim	Manager	15-Dec-02	5000	500	D001
E0002	Bruce	Analyst	24-Apr-99	4000	400	D002
E0003	Arnold	Clerk	10-Jan-01	2500	250	D004
E0004	Holyfield	Tester	10-Oct-01	3000	300	D002
E0005	Kelly	Admin	11-Apr-99	2000	200	D003

(*ii*) **DEPT Table**

Column Name	Data Type	Size
Deptno	Varchar2	8
Dname	Varchar2	20
Loc	Varchar2	20

Insert the following data into the above DEPT table:

Deptno	Dname	Loc
D001	Development	Noida
D002	R & D	Rocky Creek
D003	Admin	Seattle
D004	Accounts	Seattle
D005	Production	Noida

(*iii*) Client_Mast

Column Name	Data Type	Size
Client_no	Varchar2	6 (Primary Key)
Name	Varchar2	20 (Not Null)
Address	Varchar2	25
City	Varchar2	20
Pincode	Number	6
State	Varchar2	15
Bal_due	Number	(8,2)

Insert the following data into the above Client_Mast table :

Client_no	Name	Address	City	Pincode	State	Bal_due
B001	Procurez	12,sunbay street	Gainesville	1233	Florida	3500
B002	BMW	6, Rocky creek	Jacksonville	1234	Florida	3488
B003	Takenote	7, Hudson bay	Puria	6454	Illinois	4555
B004	Teoco	1243, princiton circle	Fairfax	3433	Virginia	4433
B005	ASAP	23,North city	Puria	4354	Illinois	3600

(*iv*) **Product_Mast**

Column Name	Data Type	Size
Product_no	Varchar2	6
Description	Varchar2	14
Profit_perc	Number	5,2
Units	Varchar2	10
Qty_Available	Number	6
Sell_Price	Number	7,2
Cost_price	Number	7,2

Insert the following data into the above Product_Mast table :

Product_no	Description	Profit_perc	Units	Qty_Available	Sell_Price	Cost_price
PR023	CD Player	5	Piece	100	210	200
PR045	Television	10	Piece	35	1320	1200
PR055	Refrigerator	15	Piece	60	920	800
PR065	Oven	12	Piece	40	504	450
PR075	Microwave	20	Piece	100	900	750

(*v*) **Salesman_Mast**

Column Name	Data Type	Size
Salesman_no	Varchar2	10
Name	Varchar2	20 (Not Null)
Address	Varchar2	20
City	Varchar2	18
Pincode	Number	6
State	Varchar2	15
Sal_amount	Number	(8,2)
Target	Number	5,2

Insert the following data into the above Salesman_Mast table :

Salesman_no	Name	Address	City	Pincode	State	Sal_amount	Target
SA001	Sammy	43, NW	Jacksonville	1234	Florida	2500	200
SA002	Aron	2, Avenue	Gainesville	1233	Florida	2500	200
SA003	Quincy	2,moon App	Janesville	1235	Florida	2500	200
SA004	Teddy	3, Silver-spoons	Harryville	1233	Tennessee	2300	200
SA005	Byron	4, St. Street	Puria	12	Illinois	3500	100

LAB ASSIGNMENT—2

1. Find out the names of all the clients from client_mast table.
2. Retrieve all the records from client_mast table.
3. Retrieve the list of names, address and city of all the clients from client_mast.
4. List all the clients who are staying in Florida from client_mast.
5. List the names of the employee who have a salary less than Rs 3000 from employee table.
6. List the employee name, job and department no, of everyone whose name fall in the alphabetical range 'C' to 'L' from employee table.
7. List all the employees whose name starts with the Letter 'K' from employee table.
8. List the department name which is Located in Noida and Rocky creek from Dept table.
9. List the employee name working in department D002 , D003 from employee table.
10. List all employee whose name start with 'A' and end with 'D' from employee table.
11. List all managers and salesman with salary over 2500 from employee table.
12. Display all the employee names in the ascending order of their date of joining from employee table.
13. Display all the employees in alphabetical order from employee table.
14. List all employee who where hired during 1999 from employee table.
15. List all the employees whose commission is more than Rs. 300 from employee table.

LAB ASSIGNMENT—3

1. Change the city of client_no 'B001' from 'Gainesville' to 'paul street' from client_mast table.
2. Change the bal_due of client_no B005 to Rs. 2000 from client_mast table.
3. Change the name to 'infospace' of client_no B004 in the table client_mast table.
4. Change the client_no 'B004' to 'B009' in the table client_mast.
5. Change the city of the salesman from 'Jacksonville' to 'Huston' from salesman_mast table.
6. Change the basic salary Rs 3000 where basic salary less than 2500 from employee table.
7. Change the basic_sal = 3000 where job in Clerk from employee table.
8. Change the basic salary of Employee Number E004 to Rs. 3500 from employee table.
9. Change the Department name to 'Sales' from the DEPT table where Deptno is 'D004'
10. Change the Description of Product Number 'PR065' to AC in the Product_mast table.
11. Change the Profit percent of Product Number 'PR065' to 25% in the Product_mast table.
12. Change the available quantity of Product Number 'PR065' to 120 in the Product_mast table.
13. Change the cost price and selling price of Product Number 'PR065' to 5000 and 6250 in the Product_mast table.
14. Change the units where Product Number 'PR065' to 'pack of 10' in the Product_mast table.
15. Create a sequence named counter which is incremented by 1 and starts with 1.
16. Create a sequence named counter which is incremented by 5 and starts with 25.

LAB ASSIGNMENT—4

1. Delete all salesman from the salesman_mast whose salaries are equal to Rs. 2000.
2. Write a query to undo the above delete query.
3. Delete all products from product_mast where the Qty_Available is equal to 100.
4. Write a query such that the above query cannot be undone.
5. Delete from client_mast where the state venue is 'Illinois'.
6. Delete all employees from employee where basic_sal is less than 2000.
7. Write a query to mark the above two queries such the the second delete operation is undone.
8. Delete employee from employee table where basic_sal equal to 3000 and job = 'Clerk'.
9. Delete employee from employee table where job = 'Clerk' or 'Manager'.
10. Delete all records from Dept table.
11. Delete all managers and salesman with salary over 1500 from employee table.
12. Delete all the employee name, job and department, no of everyone whose name fall in the alphabetical range 'C' to 'L' from employee table.
13. Write a Query so the following statement can be achieved 'Kim is working as Manager since 15-12-2002' where Employee number is E0001.
14. Rename the table name from Client_mast to T_client_mast.
15. Write a query in which the column name should be displayed as Employee Name from the Employee table.

3 Alter, Views and Index

Objectives :

- Alter Commands
- Synonym
- Views
- Index

Lab Assignment-5

ALTER COMMANDS

The ALTER command is used to modify the structure of a table and UPDATE command is used to modify the records or field of a table. So using alter command we can add new columns, modify existing columns, and add or drop integrity constraints.

ALTER can be used to make the following changes to any tables :

- Add new columns
- Add new integrity constraints
- Modify existing columns
    - — Expand length
    - — Change default
    - — Decrease length - all values in column must be null
    - — Change data type - all values in column must be null
- Drop integrity constraints

Note. We cannot drop or rename columns. The table must be rebuilt for this. But in Oracle 9i and higher versions you can drop a column.

We must have one of the following privileges to alter a table:

- Ownership of the table
- Alter privilege on the table
- Alter any table (Allows altering of tables outside your schema).

To add a new column

Syntax

Alter table tablename add(field datatype(width));

Example: Alter table emp add (Address varchar2 (20));

To change the width of existing field

Syntax

Alter table tablename modify(fieldname datatype(width));

Example: Alter table emp modify(Address varchar2 (25));

Many column can be added in a single alter statement

Syntax

Alter table tablename add (fieldname datatype(size), fieldname datatype(size), fieldname datatype(size) default 'ABC', fieldname datatype(size));

Example: Alter table emp add (Address varchar2 (20), City varchar2(8),D_O_B date);

To add a primary key

Syntax

Alter table tablename add primary key(field);

Example: Alter table emp add primary key(empno);

To remove primary key

Syntax

Alter table tablename drop primary key;

Example: Alter table emp drop primary key;

To drop primary key that has dependents tables

Syntax

Alter table tablename drop primary key cascade;

Example: Alter table emp drop primary key cascade;

To add a foreign key constraint to an existing column

Syntax

Alter table tablename add (foreign key (column) references master_table on delete cascade);

Example: Alter table emp add (foreign key (sup_code) references supplier_master on delete cascade);

(Foreign key concept is described in chapter - 05)

To drop a foreign key constraint

Syntax

Alter table tablename drop constraint column name;

Example: Alter table emp drop constraint Sup_code;

To add a not null constraint

Syntax

Alter table tablename modify column name NOT NULL;

Example: Alter table emp modify ename not null;

To drop a NOT NULL constraint

Syntax

Alter table tablename modify column name NULL;

Example: Alter table emp modify ename null;

To add a check constraints

Example: Alter table emp add constraint chkdeposit (check deposit between 2000 and 15000);

To drop the check constraints

Example: Alter table emp drop constraint chkdeposit;

To add a Foreign key constraint to an existing column

Example: Alter table emp add constraint supplier foreign key (su_code) references Supplier_Master on delete cascade;

To drop the foreign key constraint

Example: Alter table emp drop constraint supplier;

SYNONYM

A synonym is a database object, which is used as an alias (alternative names) for a table, view or sequence. They are used to

- Simplify SQL statements.
- Hide the name and owner of an object.
- Provide location transparency for remote objects of a distributed database.
- Provide public access to an object.

Synonym can either be private or public. The former is created by normal user, which is available only to that person whereas the latter is created by the DBA, which can be availed by any database user. Public synonyms are created by a Database Administrator to hide the identity of a base table and reduce the complexity of SQL statements.

The syntax for creating a synonym is given below.

Create [public] synonym <synonym_name> for <table_name>;

One such example of a public synonym is T AB, which we use for selecting the tables owned by the user. These public synonyms are owned by user group Public.

Example: SQL > Create table tab (no number (5));

We will get the message "table created."

Now select the values from tab, no rows will be selected.

Note: When we have public and local objects with the same name, the local objects takes precedence.

But we can use the public synonym as usual after dropping the local objects.

SQL > Drop table tab;

SQL> Select * from tab;

VIEWS

Views are logical tables of data extracted from existing tables. A view can be thought of as a 'stored query' or a "VIRTUAL TABLE". We can use views in most places where a table can be used. The tables upon which a view is based are called base tables. A query can be made just like a table, but does not require disk space.

A view is a method of organising table data to meet a specific need. Views are based on SELECT statements, which derive their data from real tables. A view allows us to reorganise the database data, we want to do this so that we can restrict data access, reduce selection complexity, provide improved data independence or allow desparate users to view the same data in different ways. Most of the Oracle data dictionary is readable via views which interpret internal Oracle tables.

Note: Views come in simple and complex forms. Simple views are based on a single table and data can be updated via DML commands (privilege issues aside), complex views are derived from multiple tables and DML commands cannot be used to update data.

Use of View

- It can be used to hide sensitive columns.
- It can be used to hide complex queries involving multiple tables. For example, a single view might be defined with a join, which is a collection of related columns or rows in multiple tables. However, the view hides the fact that this information actually originates from several tables.
- Views created with a check option, prevents the updating of other rows and columns.
- Views provide an additional level of table security by restricting to a predetermined set of rows and /or columns of a table.
- Views simplify commands for the user because they allow them to select information from multiple tables without actually knowing how to perform a join.
- Views isolate applications from changes in definitions of base tables. For example, if a view's defining query references three columns of a four-column table and a fifth column is added to the table, the view's definition is not affected and all applications using the view are not affected.
- Views provide data in a different perspective than that of a base table by renaming columns without affecting the base table.

To Create the View

Syntax

Create [or Replace][no][force] View <view-name> [column alias name..] as <query> [with [check option][read only][constraint]];

Example: Create view emp_view as select emp_no, emp_name from emp;

The Order by clause cannot be used in a create view statement.

To Display the View

Select * from emp_view;

To View the columns in a View

Desc emp_view;

To Delete a View

Syntax:

Drop view <view name>;

Example: Drop view emp_view;

VIEW cannot be updated if it contains

(*i*) Joins

(*ii*) Set operators (Union, Intersect, Minus)

(*iii*) Group functions

(*iv*) Group by clause

(*v*) Distinct.

Example: SQL> create view ven_view as select * from vendor_master;

The above command will create a view with name ven_view , which will have the same structure as the vendor_master table and all the rows of the base table are accessible through this view.

Example: The marketing division wants the accounts department to view only the pending orders and not the other orders. So a view is created with a 'where' condition which selects only the order_status with 'P'.

SQL> create view pending_view as select * from order_master where order_status ='P';

SQL>update pending_view set order_status = 'D' where order_status = 'P';

The above update command will work fine but this will produce rows which are not viewable through the view.

DML Statement and Join Views

Joining of table is also possible in a view. Any UPDATE, INSERT, or DELETE statement on a join view can modify only one underlying base table. The following example creates a view from two tables:

The orders are actually stored in two tables order_master and order_detail related by orderno. When a user wants to view the orders, he needs to perform a query separately or a join query on both the tables. Instead of doing this, a view can be created with the join query and the view in turn can be queried as a normal table.

SQL> create view orders as select o.orderno, odate, vencode, itemcode, qty_ord from order_master o, order_detail d where o.orderno = d.orderno

In the above example the view orders will contain information about vendor and also details about items he has purchased in that order. Since this information is spread across two tables, we use the concept of join to retrieve them.

Key-Preserved Tables

A table is key-preserved if every key of the table can also be a key of the result of the join. In our case ORDERNO of the ORDER_MASTER is the key to the view. So, ORDER_MASTER table is key-preserved table whose keys are preserved through a join.

Note. It is not necessary that the key or keys of a table has to be selected for it to be key-preserved. It is sufficient, if the key or keys were selected, then they would also be key(s) of the result of the join.

The following example shows an UPDATE statement that successfully modifies the ORDERS view.

Example: SQL> update orders set qty_ord = qty_ord * 2 where itemcode = 'b10';

The following update statement would be disallowed on the ORDERS view:

Example: SQL> update orders set odate = odate+1 where orderno = 'a10';

This statement fails and returns an ORA-01779 error ("cannot modify a column which maps to a non key-preserved tables"), because it attempts to modify the underlying ORDER_MASTER table, and the ORDER_MASTER table is not key-preserved in the ORDERS view.

The data dictionary view USER_UPDATABLE_COLUMNS will help in identifying the update table columns of a join view.

Functions in View

Single row functions comprising of number, character, date, group functioning and expressions can also be used in views. Consider the following example, which illustrates the usage of expressions in a view.

Example: SQL> create view itemsold as select itemcode, sum(qty_ord) sold_qty from order_detail group by itemcode;

Note. Functions are discussed in next chapter.

The above example calculates the discount offered for a product.

— View's query cannot select pseudo columns like currval and nextval.

— If a view's query contains joins, set operators, group functions and distinct clause then deletion, updation and insertion cannot be performed.

— The changes performed in a view will affect the base table and vice versa.

— Group functions and group by clause can also be included in views.

— While using functions the column should be given an alias name as shown in the above given example.

Partition View

With partition views, the data resides in separate tables. These tables are then brought together at run time using the relational operator Union all. The syntax for a partition view is given below:

```
Create view <viewname> as
select * from <tablename1>
Union all
select * from <tablename2>
```

```
Union all
select * from <tablename3>
```

Consider the following examples:

```
SQL> create view sales as
select * from sales_93
Union all
select * from sales_94
Union all
select * from sales_95
Union all
select * from sales_96;
```

Here sales is name assigned to the view created and sales_93, sales_94, sales_95, sales_96 are the table partitions which hold the respective for years 93, 94, 95, 96 etc.

If the records for the year 96 are required, then the partitions built on records for all the other years are skipped during the scanning of the data. Let us assume that the total number of records in the partition view 120,000,000 and that in the partition for the year 96 is 1,500,000. In such a case less than 15% of the records is only scanned. Thus the amount of records being scanned is drastically reduced. This process of skipping the scanning is called as partition elimination.

Dropping Views

The view can be dropped using the SQL command DROP VIEW. For Example, the following statement drops as view named venmast.

Syntax

```
Drop view <view_name>
```

Example:

```
SQL> Drop view venmast;
```

Querying user_views will provide details on views that the user has created.

INDEX

Indexes are optional structures associated with tables. We can create indexes explicitly to speed up SQL statement execution on a table. Similar to the indexes in books that helps us to locate information faster, an Oracle index provides a faster access path to table data.

The index points directly to the location of the rows containing the value. Indexes are the primary means reducing disk I/O when properly using appropriately. The absence or presence of an index does not require a change in the wording of any SQL statement. An Index is a fast access path to the data; it affects only the speed of execution.

We create an index on a column or combinations of columns using CREATE INDEX command as follows.

Assuming that the order_detail table has more than 10000 orders and the access on the table is time consuming. So the marketing division wants to speed up the access by creating index on the frequently queried column the itemcode.

Example: SQL> create index oditem on order_detail(itemcode);

When we create an index, Oracle fetches and sorts the column to be indexed, and stores the ROWID along with the index value for each row. Then Oracle loads the index from the bottom up. Oracle sorts the order_detail table on the itemcode column. It then loads the index with the itemcode and corresponding ROWID values in this sorted order. Using the index, Oracle does a quick search through the sorted itemcode values and then uses the associated ROWID values to locate the rows having the sought item code value.

Indexes are logically and physically independent of the data in associated table. We can create or drop an index at any time with affecting the base tables or order indexes. If we drop an index, all applications continue to work; however, access to previously indexed data might be slower. Indexes, as independent structures, requires storage space.

Oracle automatically maintains and uses indexes once they are created. Oracle automatically reflects changes to data, such as addition of new rows, updating rows, deleting rows, in all relevant indexes with additional action by users.

Retrieval performance of index data remains almost constant, even as new rows are inserted. However, the presence of more number of indexes on a table decreases the performance of updates, deletes, inserts because Oracle must also update the indexes associated with the table.

Unique Indexes

Indexes can be unique or non-unique. Unique indexes guarantee that no two rows of a table have duplicate values in the columns that define the index. Non-unique indexes do not impose this restriction on the column values. Oracle enforces unique integrity constraints by automatically defining a unique index on the unique key.

A Unique index is created by using create unique index command as follows.

Example: SQL> Create unique index ind2 on order_master(orderno);

Note. A unique index is automatically created when we create unique or primary key constraint. Alternatively a constraint is imposed on the column we created unique index. We cannot create index for a column which is already indexed.

Composite Index

A composite index (also called a concatenated index) is an index created on multiple columns of a table. Columns in a composite index can appear in any order and need not be adjacent columns of the table.

Composite indexes can enhance the retrieval speed of data for select statements in which the 'where' clause references all or the leading portion of the columns in the composite index. that is orderno. Therefore, we should pay due attention to the order of the columns used in that definition; generally, the most commonly accessed or most selective columns go first in the order of the column list.

Example: SQL> create index combind1 on order_detail(orderno, itemcode);

The index created with the above statement will be used to retrieve data, when the where clause has either both of these columns or orderno alone, but not while itemcode alone is used.

Reversed Key Indexes

Creating a reverse key index, when compared to a standard index, reverses each byte of the column being indexed while keeping the column order. Such an agreement can help avoid performance degradation in indexes where modifications to the index are concatenated on a small set of blocks. By reversing the key of the index, the insertion becomes distributed all over the index.

For example, the column value is stored in an index as shown below:

In Normal Index	In Reverse Index
A100001	100001A
A100002	200001A
A100003	300001A
A100004	400001A

Consider the above column values that are stored in a normal index. Then the rows will be stored together in one block as except the last number the value is almost same for all rows. When the same column is indexed in reverse mode then the column values will be stored in an index in different as the starting value differs. The difference between 100001 and 400001 will make the index data stored well apart. Even though the original difference is just 4 in actual data.

Using the reverse key arrangement eliminates the ability to run an index range-scanning query on the index. As lexically adjacent keys are not stored next to each other in a reverse-key index, only fetch-by-key or full-index(table) scans can be performed.

Under some circumstances using a reverse-key index can make application run faster.

Specify the keyword REVERSE along with the optional index specifications in create index statement.

Example: SQL> create index revind1 on order_master(orderno) reverse;

We can rebuild a reverse key index into normal index using the keyword NOREVERSE.

Example: SQL> Alter index revind1 rebuild noreverse;

Note. We cannot rebuild a normal index as a reverse key index.

Bitmap Indexes

The advantages of using bitmap indexes are greatest for low cardinality column; that is, column in which the number of distinct values is small compared to the number of rows in the table. If the values in a column are repeated more than a hundred times, the column is a candidate for bitmap index. For example, on a table with one million rows, a column with 10,000 distinct values is a candidate for bitmap index.

We can create a bitmap index using create bitmap index command.

Example: SQL> create bitmap index bitind1 on order_details(itemcode);

Itemcode is a low cardinality column in order_detail table because the itemcode are going to repeat for most of the orders and it is appropriate to create bitmap indexes on this columns, (*i.e.*, if there are 100 items available with us and there are more than 10000 orders a month). A bitmap index should not be created on orderno on order_master table because this is a high cardinality column. Instead a unique index on this column in order would provide the most efficient representation and retrieval.

Table

itemcode = 'A001'	**itemcode='B001'**	**itemcode='C001'**
1	0	0
0	1	0
0	0	1
0	0	1
0	1	0
0	1	0

Each entry (or "bit") in the bitmap corresponds to single row of the order_detail table. The value of each bit depends upon the values of the corresponding row in the table. For instance, the bitmap itemcode = 'A001' contains 1 as its first bit. This is because the itemcode is 'A001' in the first row of the order_detail table.

The bitmap itemcode = 'A001' has a zero for its other bits because none of the other rows of the table contains 'A001' as their value for itemcode.

In a bitmap index, a bitmap for each key value is used instead of a list or rowids. Each bit in the bitmap corresponds to possible rowid, and of the bit is set, it means that the row with the corrressponding rowid contains the key value.

A mapping fuction converts the bit position to an actual rowid, hence the bitmap index provide the same functionality as regular index even though it uses a different representation internally. If the number of different key values is small, bitmap index are very space efficient.

Bitmap indexing provides the following benefits:

— Reduce response time for large classes of ad hoc queries.

— A substantial reduction of space usage compared to other indexing techniques.

—- Dramatic performances gain even on very low end hardware.

Fully indexing a large table with a normal index can be prohabitatively expensive in terms of space since the index can be several times larger than the data in the table. Bitmap indexes are typically only a friction of the size of the index data in the table.

In ad hoc queries or similar situations, bitmap indexes can dramatically improve query performance. AND and OR conditions in the 'where' clause of a query can be quickly resolved by performing the corresponding boolean operations directly on the bitmaps before converting the resulting bitmap to row ids. If the resulting number of rows is small, the query can be answered very quickly without resorting to a full scan of the table.

Index-Organized Tables

An Index-Organized table differs from a regular table, in that the data for the table is held in its associated index. Changes to the table data, such as adding new rows, updating rows, or deleting rows, results only in updating the index.

The Index-Organized table is like a regular table with index on one or more of its columns. But instead of maintaining two separate storages for the table and the index, the database system only maintains a single index, which contains both the encoded key value and the associated column values for the corresponding row.

Instead of having the row ROWID as the second element of the index entry, the actual data of the row is stored in the index.

We can create an index organized table using create table command with ORGANIZATION INDEX clause.

Example: SQL> create table indiaorg (vencode number(4) primary key, venname varchar2(20)) organization index;

Note. Primary key is a must for creating index-organized table.

The data rows are built on primary key for the table, and each index entry contains <primary_key_value,non_primary_key_column_values >.

Index-organized tables are suitable for accessing data via primary key or via any other key which is a valid prefix of the primary key. There is no duplication of key values because only non-key column values are stored with the key.

Application manipulates the index-organized table just like a regular table, using SQL statements. However, the database system performs all operations by manipulating the corresponding index.

Comparison of index-organized tables with regular tables can be shown in the following ways:

Regular Table

— ROWID uniquely identifies a row; primary key can be optional specified.

— Implicit ROWID column; allows building physical secondary indexes.

— ROWID based access.

— Sequential scan returns all rows.

— UNIQUE constraint and triggers allowed

— A table can be stored in a cluster containing other tables.

— Distribution , Replication and Partitioning support

Index-Organized Table

— Primary Key uniquely identifies a row; primary key must be specified.

— No implicit rowid column cannot have physical secondary indexes.

— Primary key based access.

— Full-Index scan returns all rows in primary key order.

— UNIQUE constraint not allowed (ORACLE8 restriction) but triggers are allowed.

— An Index-organized table cannot be stored in a cluster.

— Distribution, Replication, Partitioning not supported (Oracle 8 Restriction).

Benefits of Index-Organized Tables

As rows are stored in the index, index-organized table provides a faster key-based access to table data for queries involving exact match and /or range search. The storage requirements are reduced as key columns are not duplicated in the table and the index. The data row stored with the key eliminated additional storage required for ROWIDS that link key values to corresponding rows in the case of an index for a regular table.

Partitioning in Index

Similar to partitioning tables, Oracle 8 allows us to partition indexes too. Like table partitions , index partitions could be in different table spaces.

The syntax for creating a partitioned index is :

Create index <index name>

on <tablename>(<col1>,<col2>) [global/local]

partition by range (<col2>)

partition values less than (<value1>) tablespace <tablespacename1>, partition values less than (<value2>) tablespace <tablespacename2>.

Where index name refers to the name which we would refer to the index in future, tablename refers to the name of the table for which we create the index, col1,col2 refers to the name of the table for which the index has to be created , col2 refers to that column based on which the partitioning has to be done, value1,value2 denote the criteria for the range and tablespacename1, tablespacename2 refers to the name of the table spaces which are associated with the partitions. The clauses tablespace <tablespacename> can be ignored, as partions are default user tablespace.

LAB ASSIGNMENT—5

1. Add a column "Telephone_No" of data type 'number' and size = '10' to the employee table.
2. Add a column "Country" of data type 'Char' and size = '15' to the client_mast table.
3. Increase the size of "description" field from 14 to 16 in product_mast table.
4. Modify the "product_no" key as a primary key from product_mast table.
5. Drop the primary key of Client_mast table.
6. Define the "Deptno" as not null constraint from Dept table.
7. Display Empno, Ename and Annual Salary of each employee from employee table with a column name "Annual Salary" on the basis of basic_sal.
8. Add two columns "HOD" and "Strength" of datatype varchar2 and size = 15 to the Dept table.
9. Add check constraint for deptno field to the Dept table check deptno from the 'D001','D002' and 'D003'.
10. Create a view as empview from employee table where basic_sal equal to 3000 and job = 'Clerk'.
11. Drop the above created empview.
12. Create an index for client_no on client_mast table.
13. Create a view as empview from employee table with basic_sal, empno and ename.
14. Create a view as clientview from client_mast with all columns of table.
15. Drop the above created empview view.

4 SQL *Plus Functions

Objectives :

- ➤ Date Functions
- ➤ Numeric Functions
- ➤ Character Functions
- ➤ Conversion Functions
- ➤ LOB and Miscellaneous Functions
- ➤ Aggregate Functions (Group Function)

  Lab Assignment-6

  Lab Assignment-7

SQL *Plus provides some special inbuilt functions to perform operations using the DML commands. A function takes one or more arguments and returns a value. There are mainly two types of functions.

1. Single row functions (Scalar Functions)
2. Group Functions (Aggregate Functions)

Single Row Functions

A single row or scalar function returns only one value for every row queried in the table. Single row functions can appear in a select commands and can also be included in a 'where' clause. The single row functions can be classified as:

- Date functions
- Numeric Functions
- Character Functions
- Conversion functions
- LOB and Miscellaneous functions

'DUAL' Table

Dual is a small Oracle worktable, which consists of only one row and one column, and contains the value x in that column. It supports date retrieval and its formatting and arithmetic calculations etc. We can use dual table with select statements, where clause and for retrieving the function results.

Example : SQL> Select 2*2 from dual;

SQL> Select sysdate from dual;

DATE FUNCTIONS

Table 4.1

Name	Description
ADD_MONTHS	Adds the specified number of months to a date.
LAST_DAY	Returns the last day in the month of the specified date..
MONTHS_ BETWEEN	Calculates the number of months between two dates.
NEW_TIME	Returns the date/time value, with the time shifted as requested by the specified time zones.
NEXT_DAY	Returns the date of the first weekday specified that is later than the date.
ROUND	Returns the date rounded by the specified format unit.
SYSDATE	Returns the current date and time in the Oracle Server.
TRUNC	Truncates the specified date of its time portion according to the format unit provided.

SYSDATE

The SYSDATE function returns the current system date and time as recorded in the database. The time component of SYSDATE provides the current time to the nearest second. It takes no arguments. The specification for SYSDATE is:

```
FUNCTION SYSDATE RETURN DATE

SQL > SELECT SYSDATE FROM dual;
```

ADD_MONTHS

The ADD_MONTHS function returns a new date with the specified number of months added to the input date. The specification for ADD_MONTHS is as follows:

```
FUNCTION ADD_MONTHS (date_in IN DATE, month_shift NUMBER)
RETURN DATE

FUNCTION ADD_MONTHS (month_shift NUMBER, date_in IN DATE)
RETURN DATE
```

ADD_MONTHS is an overloaded function. We can specify the date and the number of months by which we want to shift that date, or we can list the month_shift parameter first and then the date. Both arguments are required.

Date Arithmetic

SQL allows us to perform arithmetic operations directly on date variables. We may add numbers to a date or subtract numbers from a date. To move a date one day in the future, simply add 1 to the date as shown below:

```
join_date + 1
```

We can even add a fractional value to a date. For example, adding 1/24 to a date adds an hour to the time component of that value. Adding 1/(24*60) adds a single minute to the time component, and so on.

If the month_shift parameter is positive, ADD_MONTHS returns a date for that number of months into the future. If the number is negative, ADD_MONTHS returns a date for that number of months in the past. Here are some examples that use ADD_MONTHS:

Move ahead date by three months:

```
SQL > SELECT ADD_MONTHS ('12-JAN-1995', 3) FROM DUAL;
SQL > 12-APR-1995
```

Specify negative number of months in first position:

```
SQL > SELECT ADD_MONTHS (-12, '12-MAR-1990') FROM DUAL;
SQL > 12-MAR-1989
```

ADD_MONTHS always shifts the date by whole months. We can provide a fractional value for the month_shift parameter, but ADD_MONTHS will always round down to the whole number nearest zero, as shown in these examples:

SQL > SELECT ADD_MONTHS ('28-FEB-1989', 1.5) FROM DUAL;
same as
SQL > SELECT ADD_MONTHS ('28-FEB-1989', 1) FROM DUAL;
SQL > 31-MAR-1989

SQL > SELECT ADD_MONTHS ('28-FEB-1989', 1.9999)FROM DUAL;
same as
SQL > SELECT ADD_MONTHS ('28-FEB-1989', 1)FROM DUAL;
SQL > 31-MAR-1989

SQL > SELECT ADD_MONTHS ('28-FEB-1989', -1.9999)FROM DUAL;
same as
SQL > SELECT ADD_MONTHS ('28-FEB-1989', -1)FROM DUAL;
SQL > 31-JAN-1989

SQL > SELECT ADD_MONTHS ('28-FEB-1989', .5)FROM DUAL;
same as
SQL > SELECT ADD_MONTHS ('28-FEB-1989', 0)FROM DUAL;
SQL > 28-FEB-1989

If we want to shift a date by a fraction of a month, we should simply add to or subtract from the date the required number of days. SQL supports direct arithmetic operations between date values.

If the input date to ADD_MONTHS does not fall on the last day of the month, the date returned by ADD_MONTHS falls on the same day in the new month as in the original month. If the day number of the input date is greater than the last day of the month returned by ADD_MONTHS, the function sets the day number to the last day in the new month. For example, there is no 31st day in February, so ADD_MONTHS returns the last day in this month.

SQL >SELECT ADD_MONTHS ('31-JAN-1995', 1)FROM DUAL;
SQL > 28-FEB-1995

LAST_DAY

The LAST_DAY function returns the date of the last day of the month for a given date. The specification is:

FUNCTION LAST_DAY (date_in IN DATE) RETURN DATE

This function is useful because the number of days in a month varies throughout the year. With LAST_DAY, for example, you do not have to try to figure out if February of this or that year has 28 or 29 days. Just let LAST_DAY figure it out for you.

Here are some examples of LAST_DAY:

Go to the last day in the month:

```
SQL >SELECT LAST_DAY ('16-JAN-99') FROM DUAL;
SQL >31-JAN-1999
```

If already on the last day, just stay on that day:

```
SQL >SELECT LAST_DAY ('31-JAN-99')FROM DUAL;
SQL > 31-JAN-1999
```

Get the last day of the month three months after being hired:

```
SQL > SELECT LAST_DAY (ADD_MONTHS (hiredate, 3)) FROM EMP;
```

Tell the number of days until the end of the month:

```
SQL > SELECT LAST_DAY (SYSDATE)FROM DUAL;
SQL > (Last day of the current month)
```

MONTHS_BETWEEN

The MONTHS_BETWEEN function calculates the number of months between two dates and returns that difference as a number. The specification is:

```
FUNCTION MONTHS_BETWEEN (date1 IN DATE, date2 IN DATE)
RETURN NUMBER
```

The following rules apply to MONTHS_BETWEEN:

- If date1 comes after date2, then MONTHS_BETWEEN returns a positive number.
- If date1 comes before date2, then MONTHS_BETWEEN returns a negative number.
- If date1 and date2 are in the same month, then MONTHS_BETWEEN returns a fraction (a value between -1 and +1).
- If date1 and date2 both fall on the last day of their respective months, then MONTHS_BETWEEN returns a whole number (no fractional component).
- If date1 and date2 are in different months and at least one of the dates is not a last day in the month, MONTHS_BETWEEN returns a fractional number. The fractional component is calculated on a 31-day month basis and also takes into account any differences in the time component of date1 and date2.

Here are some examples of the uses of MONTHS_BETWEEN:

Calculate two ends of month, the first earlier than the second:

```
SQL > SELECT MONTHS_BETWEEN ('31-JAN-1994', '28-FEB-1994')
      FROM DUAL;
SQL > -1
```

Calculate two ends of month, the first later than the second:

```
SQL > SELECT MONTHS_BETWEEN ('31-MAR-1995', '28-FEB-1994')
      FROM DUAL;
SQL > 13
```

Calculate when both dates fall in the same month:

```
SQL > SELECT MONTHS_BETWEEN ('28-FEB-1994', '15-FEB-1994')
      FROM DUAL;
SQL >  0
```

Perform months_between calculations with a fractional component:

```
SQL >SELECT MONTHS_BETWEEN ('31-JAN-1994', '1-MAR-1994')
      FROM DUAL;
SQL >-1.0322581

SQL >SELECT MONTHS_BETWEEN ('31-JAN-1994', '2-MAR-1994')
      FROM DUAL;
SQL > -1.0645161

SQL >SELECT MONTHS_BETWEEN ('31-JAN-1994', '10-MAR-1994')
      FROM DUAL;
SQL > -1.3225806
```

If one detects a pattern here one is right. As we said, MONTHS_BETWEEN calculates the fractional component of the number of months by assuming that each month has 31 days. Therefore, each additional day over a complete month counts for 1/31 of a month, and

1 divided by 31 = .032258065 —more or less!

According to this rule, the number of months between January 31, 1994 and February 28, 1994 is one — a nice, clean integer. But to calculate the number of months between January 31, 1994 and March 1, 1994, we have to add an additional .032258065 to the difference (and make that additional number negative because in this case MONTHS_BETWEEN counts from the first date back to the second date.

NEW_TIME

This function converts dates (along with their time components) from one time zone to another. The specification for NEW_TIME is:

FUNCTION NEW_TIME (date_in DATE, zone1 VARCHAR2, zone2 VARCHAR2)

RETURN DATE

where date_in is the original date, zone1 is the starting point for the zone switch (usually, but not restricted to, our own local time zone), and zone2 is the time zone in which the date returned by NEW_TIME should be placed.

The valid time zones are shown in Table 4.2

Table 4.2: Time Zone Abbreviations and Descriptions

Time Zone Abbreviation	Description
AST	Atlantic Standard Time
ADT	Atlantic Daylight Time
BST	Bering Standard Time
BDT	Bering Daylight Time
CST	Central Standard Time
CDT	Central Daylight Time
EST	Eastern Standard Time
EDT	Eastern Daylight Time
GMT	Greenwich Mean Time
HST	Alaska-Hawaii Standard Time
HDT	Alaska-Hawaii Daylight Time
MST	Mountain Standard Time
MDT	Mountain Daylight Time
NST	Newfoundland Standard Time
PST	Pacific Standard Time
PDT	Pacific Daylight Time
YST	Yukon Standard Time
YDT	Yukon Daylight Time

The specification of time zones to NEW_TIME is not case-sensitive, as the following example shows:

SQL > SELECT TO_CHAR (NEW_TIME (TO_DATE ('09151994 12:30 AM', 'MMDDYYYY HH:MI AM'),'CST', 'hdt'),'Month DD, YYYY HH:MI AM')FROM DUAL;

SQL >'September 14, 1994 09:30 PM'

So, when it was 12:30 in the morning of September 15, 1994 in Chicago, it was 9:30 in the evening of September 14, 1994 in Anchorage.

Note. We used TO_DATE with a format mask to make sure that a time other than the default of midnight would be used in the calculation of the new date and time. We then used TO_CHAR with another date mask (this one intended to make the output more readable) to display the date and time, because by default SQL will not include the time component unless specifically requested to do so.

NEXT_DAY

The NEXT_DAY function returns the date of the first day after the specified date which falls on the specified day of the week. Here is the specification for NEXT_DAY:

FUNCTION NEXT_DAY (date_in IN DATE, day_name IN VARCHAR2) RETURN DATE

The day_name must be a day of the week in our session's date language (specified by the NLS_DATE_LANGUAGE database initialization parameter). The time component of the returned date is the same as that of the input date, date_in. If the day of the week of the input date matches the specified day_name, then NEXT_DAY will return the date seven days (one full week) after date_in. NEXT_DAY does not return the input date if the day names match.

Here are some examples of the use of NEXT_DAY.

Let's figure out the date of the first Monday and Wednesday in 1997 in all of these examples.

We can use both full and abbreviated day names:

SQL > SELECT NEXT_DAY ('01-JAN-1997', 'MONDAY') FROM DUAL;
SQL > 06-JAN-1997

SQL > SELECT NEXT_DAY ('01-JAN-1997', 'MON') FROM DUAL;
SQL > 06-JAN-1997

The case of the day name doesn't matter :

SQL >SELECT NEXT_DAY ('01-JAN-1997', 'monday') FROM DUAL;
SQL >06-JAN-1997

If the date language were Spanish:

SQL >SELECT NEXT_DAY ('01-JAN-1997', 'LUNES') FROM DUAL;
SQL >06-JAN-1997

NEXT_DAY of Wednesday moves the date up a full week:

SQL >SELECT NEXT_DAY ('01-JAN-1997', 'WEDNESDAY') FROM DUAL;
SQL >08-JAN-1997

ROUND

The ROUND function rounds a date value to the nearest date as specified by a format mask. It is just like the standard numeric ROUND function, which rounds a number to the nearest number of specified precision, except that it works with dates. The specification for ROUND is as follows:

FUNCTION ROUND (date_in IN DATE [, format_mask VARCHAR2]) RETURN DATE

The ROUND function always rounds the time component of a date to midnight (12:00 A.M.). The format mask is optional. If we do not include a format mask, ROUND rounds the date to the nearest day. In other words, it checks the time component of the date. If the time is past noon, then ROUND returns the next day with a time component of midnight

The set of format masks for ROUND is a bit different from those masks used by TO_CHAR and TO_DATE. The masks are listed in Table These same formats are used by the TRUNC function, described later in this chapter, to perform truncation on dates

Table 4.3: Format Masks for ROUND and TRUNC

Format Mask	**Rounds or Truncates to**
CC or SSC	Century
SYYY, YYYY, YEAR, SYEAR, YYY, YY, or Y	Year (rounds up to next year on July 1)
IYYY, IYY, IY, or I	Standard ISO year
Q	Quarter (rounds up on the sixteenth day of the second month of the quarter)
MONTH, MON, MM, or RM	Month (rounds up on the sixteenth day, which is not necessarily the same as the middle of the month)
WW	Same day of the week as the first day of the year
IW	Same day of the week as the first day of the ISO year
W	Same day of the week as the first day of the month
DDD, DD, or J	Day
DAY, DY, or D	Starting day of the week
HH, HH12, HH24	Hour
MI	Minute

Here are some examples of ROUND dates·

Round up to the next century:

SQL > SELECT TO_CHAR (ROUND (TO_DATE ('01-MAR-1994'), 'CC'), 'DD-MON-YYYY') FROM DUAL,
SQL > 01-JAN-2000

Round back to the beginning of the current century:

SQL >SELECT TO_CHAR (ROUND (TO_DATE ('01-MAR-1945') CC'), 'DD-MON-YYYY')FROM DUAL;
SQL >01-JAN-1900

Round down and up to the first of the vear.

SQL > SELECT ROUND (TO_DATE ('01-MAR-1994'), 'YYYY')FROM DUAL;
SQL > 01-JAN-1994

SQL > SELECT ROUND (TO_DATE ('01-SEP-1994'), 'YEAR')FROM DUAL;
SQL > 01-JAN-1995

Round up and down to the quarter (first date in the quarter):

SQL >SELECT ROUND (TO_DATE ('01-MAR-1994'), 'Q')FROM DUAL;
SQL >01-APR-1994

SQL >SELECT ROUND (TO_DATE ('15-APR-1994'), 'Q')FROM DUAL;
SQL >01-APR-1994

Round down and up to the first of the month:

SQL > SELECT ROUND (TO_DATE ('12-MAR-1994'), 'MONTH')FROM DUAL;
SQL > 01-MAR-1994

SQL > SELECT ROUND (TO_DATE ('17-MAR-1994'), 'MM') FROM DUAL;
SQL > 01-APR-1994

Day of first of year is Saturday:

SQL > SELECT TO_CHAR (TO_DATE ('01-JAN-1994'), 'DAY')FROM DUAL;
SQL > 'SATURDAY'

So round to date of nearest Saturday for '01-MAR-1994':

SQL > SELECT ROUND (TO_DATE ('01-MAR-1994'), 'WW')FROM DUAL;
SQL > 26-FEB-1994

First day in the month is a Friday:

```
SQL >SELECT TO_CHAR (TO_DATE ('01-APR-1994'), 'DAY')FROM DUAL;
SQL > FRIDAY
```

So round to date of nearest Friday from April 16, 1994:

```
SQL >SELECT TO_CHAR ('16-APR-1994'), 'DAY')FROM DUAL;
SQL >SATURDAY
```

```
SQL >SELECT ROUND (TO_DATE ('16-APR-1994'), 'W')FROM DUAL;
SQL > 15-APR-1994
```

```
SQL >SELECT TO_CHAR (ROUND (TO_DATE ('16-APR-1994'), 'W'),
'DAY')FROM DUAL;
SQL >FRIDAY
```

In the rest of the examples we use TO_DATE in order to pass a time component to the ROUND function, and TO_CHAR to display the new time.

Round back to nearest day (time always midnight):

```
SQL > SELECT TO_CHAR (ROUND (TO_DATE ('11-SEP-1994 10:00 AM',
'DD-MON-YY HH:MI AM'), 'DD'),'DD-MON-YY HH:MI AM')FROM DUAL;
SQL > 11-SEP-1994 12:00 AM
```

Round forward to the nearest day:

```
SQL >SELECT TO_CHAR (ROUND (TO_DATE ('11-SEP-1994 4:00 PM
'DD-MON-YY HH:MI AM'), 'DD'),'DD-MON-YY HH:MI AM')FROM DUAL;
SQL > 12-SEP-1994 12:00 AM
```

Round back to the nearest hour:

```
SQL >SELECT TO_CHAR (ROUND (TO_DATE ('11-SEP-1994 4:17 PM',
'DD-MON-YY HH:MI AM'), 'HH'),'DD-MON-YY HH:MI AM')FROM DUAL;
SQL > 11-SEP-1994 04:00 PM
```

TRUNC

The TRUNC function truncates date values according to the specified format mask. The specification for TRUNC is:

```
FUNCTION TRUNC (date_in IN DATE [, format_mask VARCHAR2]) RETURN
DATE
```

The TRUNC date function is similar to the numeric FLOOR function. Generally speaking, it rounds down to the beginning of the minute, hour, day, month, quarter, year, or century, as specified by the format mask.

TRUNC offers the easiest way to retrieve the first day of the month or first day of the year. It is also useful when you want to ignore the time component of dates. This is often the case when you perform comparisons with dates, such as the following:

```
IF request_date BETWEEN start_date AND end_date
THEN
...
```

The date component of date_entered and start_date might be the same, but if our application does not specify a time component for each of its dates, the comparison might fail. If, for example, the user enters a request_date and the screen does not include a time component, the time for request_date will be midnight or 12:00 A.M. of that day. If start_date was set from SYSDATE, however, its time component will reflect the time at which the assignment was made. Because 12:00 A.M. comes before any other time of the day, a comparison that looks to the naked eye like a match might well fail.

If you are not sure about the time components of date fields and variables and want to make sure that operations on dates disregard the time component, TRUNCate them:

```
IF TRUNC (request_date) BETWEEN TRUNC (start_date) AND TRUNC (end_date)
THEN
...
```

TRUNC levels the playing field with regard to the time component, all dates now have the same time of midnight (12:00 A.M.). The time will never be a reason for a comparison to fail.

Here are some examples of TRUNC for dates (all assuming a default date format mask of DD-MON-YYYY):

Without a format mask, TRUNC sets the time to 12:00 A.M. of the same day:

```
SQL > SELECT TO_CHAR (TRUNC (TO_DATE ('11-SEP-1994 9:36 AM', 'DD-MON-YYYY HH:MI AM'))FROM DUAL;
SQL > 11-SEP-1994 12:00 AM
```

Trunc to the beginning of the century in all cases:

```
SQL > SELECT TO_CHAR (TRUNC (TO_DATE ('01-MAR-1994'), 'CC'), 'DD-MON-YYYY')FROM DUAL;
SQL > 01-JAN-1900
```

SQL > SELECT TO_CHAR (TRUNC (TO_DATE ('01-MAR-1945'), 'CC'), 'DD-MON-YYYY')FROM DUAL;
SQL > 01-JAN-1900

Trunc to the first of the current year:

SQL >SELECT TRUNC (TO_DATE ('01-MAR-1994'), 'YYYY')FROM DUAL;
SQL > 01-JAN-1994

SQL >SELECT TRUNC (TO_DATE ('01-SEP-1994'), 'YEAR')FROM DUAL;
SQL >01-JAN-1994

Trunc to the first day of the quarter:

SQL >SELECT TRUNC (TO_DATE ('01-MAR-1994'), 'Q')FROM DUAL;
SQL > 01-JAN-1994

SQL >SELECT TRUNC (TO_DATE ('15-APR-1994'), 'Q')FROM DUAL;
SQL >01-APR-1994

Trunc to the first of the month:

SQL >SELECT TRUNC (TO_DATE ('12-MAR-1994'), 'MONTH')FROM DUAL;
SQL >01-MAR-1994

SQL >SELECT TRUNC (TO_DATE ('17-MAR-1994'), 'MM')FROM DUAL;
SQL >01-APR-1994

In the rest of the examples TO_DATE is used to pass a time component to the TRUNC function, and TO_CHAR to display the new time:

Trunc back to the beginning of the current day (time is always midnight):

SQL > SELECT TO_CHAR (TRUNC (TO_DATE ('11-SEP-1994 10:00 AM', 'DD-MON-YYYY HH:MI AM'), 'DD'),'DD-MON-YYYY HH:MI AM')FROM DUAL;
SQL > 11-SEP-1994 12:00 AM

SQL > SELECT TO_CHAR (TRUNC (TO_DATE ('11-SEP-1994 4:00 PM', 'DD-MON-YYYY HH:MI AM'), 'DD'),'DD-MON-YYYY HH:MI AM')FROM DUAL;
SQL > 11-SEP-1994 12:00 AM

Trunc to the beginning of the current hour:

SQL > SELECT TO_CHAR (TRUNC (TO_DATE ('11-SEP-1994 4:17 PM', 'DD-MON-YYYY HH:MI AM'), 'HH'),'DD-MON-YYYY HH:MI AM')FROM DUAL;
SQL > 11-SEP-1994 04:00 PM

NUMERIC FUNCTIONS

Table 4.4

Name	Description
ABS	Returns the absolute value of the number.
ACOS	Returns the inverse cosine.
ASIN	Returns the inverse sine.
ATAN	Returns the inverse tangent.
ATAN2	Returns the result of the tan2 inverse trigonometric function.
CEIL	Returns the smallest integer greater than or equal to the specified number.
COS	Returns the cosine.
COSH	Returns the hyperbolic cosine.
EXP (n)	Returns e raised to the nth power, where e = 2.71828183...
FLOOR	Returns the largest integer equal to or less than the specified number.
LN (a)	Returns the natural logarithm of a.
LOG (a, b)	Returns the logarithm, base a, of b.
MOD (a, b)	Returns the remainder of a divided by b.
POWER (a, b)	Returns a raised to the bth power.
ROUND (a, [b])	Returns a rounded to b decimal places.
SIGN (a)	Returns 1 if a is positive, if a is 0, and – 1 if a is less than 0.
SIN	Returns the sine.
SINH	Returns the hyperbolic sine.
SQRT	Returns the square root of the number.
TAN	Returns the tangent.
TANH	Returns the hyperbolic tangent.
TRUNC (a, [b])	Returns a truncated to b decimal places.
GREATEST	Returns the greatest of the specified list of values.
LEAST	Returns the least of the specified list of values.

ABS

The ABS function returns the absolute value of the input. The specification for the ABS function is:

FUNCTION ABS (n NUMBER) RETURN NUMBER's

```
SQL > select abs(-234.56) from dual;
SQL > 234.56
```

ACOS

The ACOS function returns the inverse cosine. The specification for the ACOS function is:

FUNCTION ACOS (n NUMBER) RETURN NUMBER;

where the number n must be between -1 and 1, and the value returned by ACOS is between 0 and pi.

ASIN

The ASIN function returns the inverse sine. The specification for the ASIN function is:

FUNCTION ASIN (n NUMBER) RETURN NUMBER;

where the number n must be between -1 and 1, and the value returned by ASIN is between -pi/ 2 and pi/2.

ATAN

The ATAN function returns the inverse tangent. The specification for the ATAN function is:

FUNCTION ATAN (n NUMBER) RETURN NUMBER;

where the number n must be between -infinity and infinity, and the value returned by ATAN is between -pi/2 and pi/2.

ATAN2

The ATAN2 function returns the result of the tan2 inverse trigonometric function. The specification for the ATAN2 function is:

FUNCTION ATAN (n NUMBER, m NUMBER) RETURN NUMBER

where the numbers n and m must be between -infinity and infinity, and the value returned by ATAN is between -pi and pi.

As a result, the following holds true:

- atan2(-0.00001, -1) is approximately -pi.
- atan2(0,-1) is pi.

CEIL

The CEIL ("ceiling") function returns the smallest integer greater than or equal to the specified number. The specification for the CEIL function is:

FUNCTION CEIL (n NUMBER) RETURN NUMBER;

Here are some examples of the effect of CEIL:

SQL > SELECT CEIL (6) FROM DUAL;
SQL > 6

SQL >SELECT CEIL (119.1)FROM DUAL;
SQL >120

SQL >SELECT CEIL (-17.2)FROM DUAL;
SQL > -17

COS

The COS trigonometric function returns the cosine of the specified angle. The specification for the COS function is:

FUNCTION COS (angle NUMBER) RETURN NUMBER;

where angle must be expressed in radians. A radian is equal to 180/pi or roughly 57.29578.

COSH

The COSH trigonometric function returns the hyperbolic cosine of the specified number. The specification for the COSH function is:

FUNCTION COSH (n NUMBER) RETURN NUMBER;

If n is a real number and i = v-1 (the imaginary square root of -1), then the relationship between COS and COSH can be expressed as follows:

COS (i * n) = COSH (h)

EXP

The EXP function returns the value e raised to the nth power, where n is the input argument. The specification for the EXP function is:

FUNCTION EXP (n NUMBER) RETURN NUMBER

The number e (approximately equal to 2.71828) is the base of the system of natural logarithms.

FLOOR

The FLOOR function, the opposite of the CEIL function, returns the largest integer that is less than or equal to the input number. The specification for the FLOOR function is:

FUNCTION FLOOR (n NUMBER) RETURN NUMBER;

Here are some examples of the values returned by FLOOR:

```
SQL > SELECT FLOOR (6.2)FROM DUAL;
SQL > 6

SQL > SELECT FLOOR (-89.4) FROM DUAL;
SQL > -90
```

LN

The LN function returns the natural logarithm of the input. The specification for the LN function is:

FUNCTION LN (n NUMBER) RETURN NUMBER;

The argument n must be greater than or equal to 0. If you pass LN a negative argument, you will receive the following error:

ORA-01428: argument '-1' is out of range

LOG

The LOG function returns the base-b logarithm of the input value. The specification for the LOG function is:

FUNCTION LOG (b NUMBER, n NUMBER) RETURN NUMBER;

The argument n must be greater than or equal to 0. The base b must be greater than 1. If you pass LOG an argument that violates either of these rules, you will receive the following error:

ORA-01428: argument '-1' is out of range

MOD

The MOD function returns the remainder of one number when divided by a second number. The specification for the MOD function is:

FUNCTION MOD (dividend NUMBER, divisor NUMBER) RETURN NUMBER;

If the divisor is zero, then the dividend is returned unchanged. Here are some examples of MOD:

```
SQL > SELECT MOD (10, 5) FROM DUAL;
SQL > 0
```

```
SQL > SELECT MOD (2, 1)FROM DUAL;
SQL > 0
```

```
SQL > SELECT MOD (3, 2)FROM DUAL;
SQL > 1
```

POWER

The POWER function raises the first argument to the power indicated by the second argument. The specification for the POWER function is:

FUNCTION POWER (base NUMBER, power NUMBER) RETURN NUMBER;

If base is negative, then power must be an integer. The following expression calculates the range of valid values for a BINARY_INTEGER variable (-231-1 through 231-1):

```
SQL > SELECT POWER (-2, 31) - 1 FROM DUAL;
SQL > -2147483637
```

```
SQL >SELECT POWER (2, 31) - 1 FROM DUAL;
SQL >2147483637
```

ROUND

The ROUND function returns the first argument rounded to the number of decimal places specified in the second argument. The specification for the ROUND function is:

FUNCTION ROUND (n NUMBER, [decimal_places NUMBER]) RETURN NUMBER;

The decimal_places argument is optional and defaults to 0, which means that n will be rounded to zero decimal places, a whole number. The value of decimal_places can be less than zero. A negative value for this argument directs ROUND to round digits to the left of the decimal point, rather than to the right. Here are some examples:

```
SQL > SELECT ROUND (153.46) FROM DUAL;
SQL > 153
```

```
SQL > SELECT ROUND (153.46, 1) FROM DUAL;
SQL > 153.5
```

```
SQL > SELECT ROUND (153, -1)FROM DUAL;
SQL > 150
```

The SIGN function

The SIGN function returns the sign of the input number. The specification for the SIGN function is:

FUNCTION SIGN (n NUMBER) RETURN NUMBER;

This function returns one of the three values shown below:

-1

n *is less than zero*

0

n *is equal to zero*

+1

n *is greater than zero*

SIN

The SIN trigonometric function returns the sine of the specified angle. The specification for the SIN function is:

FUNCTION SIN (angle NUMBER) RETURN NUMBER;

where angle must be expressed in radians. A radian is equal to 180/pi or roughly 57.29578.

SINH

The SINH trigonometric function returns the hyperbolic sine of the specified number. The specification for the SINH function is:

FUNCTION SINH (n NUMBER) RETURN NUMBER;

If n is a real number and i = v-1 (the imaginary square root of -1), then tne relationship between SIN and SINH can be expressed as follows:

SIN (i * n) = i * SINH (h)

SQRT

The SQRT function returns the square root of the input number. The specification for the SQRT function is:

FUNCTION SQRT (n NUMBER) RETURN NUMBER;

where n must be greater than or equal to 0. If n is negative, you will receive the following error:

ORA-01428: argument '-1' is out of range

TAN

The TAN trigonometric function returns the tangent of the specified angle. The specification for the TAN function is:

FUNCTION TAN (angle NUMBER) RETURN NUMBER;

where angle must be expressed in radians. A radian is equal to 180/pi or roughly 57.29578.

TANH

The TANH trigonometric function returns the hyperbolic tangent of the specified number. The specification for the TANH function is:

FUNCTION TANH (n NUMBER) RETURN NUMBER;

If n is a real number and i = v-1 (the imaginary square root of -1), then the relationship between TAN and TANH can be expressed as follows:

TAN (i * n) = i * TANH (h)

TRUNC

The TRUNC function truncates the first argument to the number of decimal places specified by the second argument. The specification for the TRUNC function is:

FUNCTION TRUNC (n NUMBER, [decimal_places NUMBER])
RETURN NUMBER;

The decimal_places argument is optional and defaults to 0, which means that n will be truncated to zero decimal places, a whole number. The value of decimal_places can be less than zero. A negative value for this argument directs TRUNC to truncate or zero-out digits to the left of the decimal point, rather than to the right. Here are some examples:

```
SQL > SELECT TRUNC (153.46) FROM DUAL;
SQL > 153

SQL > SELECT TRUNC (153.46, 1)FROM DUAL;
SQL > 153.4

SQL > SELECT TRUNC (-2003.16, -1)FROM DUAL;
SQL > -2000
```

GREATEST

The GREATEST function evaluates a list of values and returns the greatest value in that list. (The LEAST function, discussed below, returns the least value.) GREATEST accepts two or more arguments, and there is no upper limit on the number of values you can pass to GREATEST, which makes it especially useful. The specification for GREATEST is:

```
FUNCTION GREATEST (expr1, expr2 [, expr3 ...)
```

This example finds the greatest (most recent) of three dates:

```
SQL > SELECT GREATEST (SYSDATE, :emp.hire_date, '13-JAN-1994')
FROM DUAL;
```

First expression is a call to the SYSDATE function. Second expression is an Oracle Forms item of type DATE. Third expression is a literal string. This string is converted to a date by PL/SQL with an internal call to TO_DATE. The comparison of the values then proceeds.

LEAST

The LEAST function, the opposite of the GREATEST function, evaluates a list of values and returns the least value in that list. LEAST accepts two or more arguments; there is no upper limit on the number of values you can pass to LEAST, which makes it especially useful. The specification for LEAST is as follows:

```
FUNCTION LEAST (expr1, expr2 [, expr3 ...)
```

CHARACTER FUNCTIONS

Table 4.5: The Built-In Character Functions

Name	Description
ASCII	Returns the ASCII code of a character.
CHR	Returns the character associated with the specified collating code.
CONCAT	Concatenates two strings into one.
INITCAP	Sets the first letter of each word to uppercase. All other letters are set to lowercase.
INSTR	Returns the location in a string of the specified substring.
LENGTH	Returns the length of a string.
LOWER	Converts all letters to lowercase.
LPAD	Pads a string on the left with the specified characters.
LTRIM	Trims the left side of a string of all specified characters.
REPLACE	Replaces a character sequence in a string with a different set of characters.

RPAD	Pads a string on the right with the specified characters.
RTRIM	Trims the right side of a string of all specified characters.
SOUNDEX	Returns the "soundex" of a string.
SUBSTR	Returns the specified portion of a string.
TRANSLATE	Translates single characters in a string to different characters.
UPPER	Converts all letters in the string to uppercase.

ASCII

The ASCII function returns the NUMBER code that represents the specified character in the database character set. The specification of the ASCII function is:

FUNCTION ASCII (single_character IN VARCHAR2) RETURN NUMBER

where single_character is the character to be located in the collating sequence. Even though the function is named ASCII, it will return the code location in whatever the database character set is set to, such as EBCDIC Code or 7-bit ASCII. For example, in the 7-bit ASCII character set, ASCII ('a') returns 97. Remember that the collating code for uppercase letters is different from that for lowercase letters. ASCII ('A') returns 65 (in the 7-bit ASCII character set) because the uppercase letters come before the lowercase letters in the sequence.

If we pass more than one character in the parameter to ASCII, it returns the collating code for the first character and ignores the other characters. As a result, the following calls to ASCII all return the same value of 100:

```
SQL > ASCII ('defg')
SQL > 100
SQL > ASCII ('d')
SQL > 100

SQL > ASCII ('d_e_f_g')
SQL > 100
```

CHR

The CHR function is the inverse of ASCII. It returns a VARCHAR2 character (length 1) that corresponds to the location in the collating sequence provided as a parameter. The specification of the CHR function is:

FUNCTION CHR (code_location IN NUMBER) RETURN VARCHAR2

where code_location is the number specifying the location in the collating sequence.

The CHR function is especially valuable when we need to make reference to a nonprintable character in our code. For example, the location in the standard ASCII collating sequence for the newline character is ten. The CHR function therefore gives me a way to search for the linefeed control character in a string, and perform operations on a string based on the presence of that control character.

We can also insert a linefeed into a character string using the CHR function. Suppose, to build a report that displays the address of a company. A company can have up to four address strings (in addition to city, state, and zipcode). To put each address string on a new line, but we don't want any blank lines embedded in the address. The following SELECT will not do the trick:

```
SELECT name, address1, address2, address3, address4,
    city || ', ' || state || ' ' || zipcode location
    FROM company;
```

Assuming each column (report field) goes on a new line, we will end up using six lines per address, no matter how many of these address strings are NULL. For example:

```
HAROLD HENDERSON
22 BUNKER COURT
SUITE 100
WYANDANCH, MN 66557
```

We can use the CHR function to suppress these internal blank lines as follows:

```
SELECT name ||
    DECODE (address1, NULL, NULL, CHR (10) || address1) ||
    DECODE (address2, NULL, NULL, CHR (10) || address2) ||
    DECODE (address3, NULL, NULL, CHR (10) || address3) ||
    DECODE (address4, NULL, NULL, CHR (10) || address4) ||
    CHR (10) ||
    city || ', ' || state || ' ' || zipcode
 FROM company;
```

Now the query returns a single formatted column per company. The DECODE statement offers IF-THEN logic within SQL and executes as follows: "If the address string is NULL then concatenate NULL, otherwise insert a linefeed character. Then concatenate the address string."

In this way, blank address lines are ignored. If we now use wrap on the report field which holds this string, the address will be scrunched down to:

```
HAROLD HENDERSON
22 BUNKER COURT
SUITE 100
WYANDANCH, MN 66557
```

CONCAT

The CONCAT function concatenates by taking two VARCHAR2 strings and returning those strings appended together in the order specified. The specification of the CONCAT function is:

FUNCTION CONCAT (string1 IN VARCHAR2, string2 IN VARCHAR2)
RETURN VARCHAR2

CONCAT always appends string2 to the end of string1. If either string is NULL, CONCAT returns the non-NULL argument all by its lonesome. If both strings are NULL, CONCAT returns NULL. Here are some examples of uses of CONCAT:

SQL > CONCAT ('abc', 'defg');
SQL > 'abcdefg'

SQL > CONCAT (NULL, 'def');
SQL > 'def'

SQL > CONCAT ('ab', NULL);
SQL > 'ab'

SQL > CONCAT (NULL, NULL);
SQL > NULL

INITCAP

The INITCAP function reformats the case of the string argument, setting the first letter of each word to uppercase and the remainder of the letters in that word to lowercase. A word is a set of characters separated by a space or non alphanumeric characters (such as # or _). The specification of INITCAP is:

FUNCTION INITCAP (string_in IN VARCHAR2) RETURN VARCHAR2

Here are some examples of the INITCAP on your strings:

- Shift all lowercase to mixed case:

  SQL > INITCAP ('this is lower')
  SQL > 'This Is Lower'

- Shift all uppercase to mixed case:

  SQL > INITCAP ('BIG>AND^TALL')
  SQL > 'Big>And^Tall'

- Shift a confusing blend of cases to consistent initcap format:

    SQL >INITCAP ('wHatISthis_MESS?');

    SQL > 'Whatisthis_Mess?'

When and why would one use INITCAP? Many Oracle shops like to store all character string data in the database, such as names and addresses, in uppercase. This makes it easier to search for records that match certain criteria.

SQL > INITCAP ('HAMBURGERS BY THE BILLIONS AT MCDONALDS')

SQL > 'Hamburgers By The Billions At Mcdonalds'

Use INITCAP with caution when printing reports or displaying data, since the information it produces may not always be formatted correctly.

INSTR

The INSTR function searches a string to find a match for the substring and, if found, returns the position, in the source string, of the first character of that substring. If there is no match, then INSTR returns 0. In Oracle7, if nth_appearance is not positive (*i.e.*, if it is 0 or negative), then INSTR always returns 1. In Oracle8, a value of 0 or a negative number for nth_appearance causes INSTR to raise the VALUE_ERROR exception.

The specification of the INSTR function is:

```
FUNCTION INSTR
    (string1 IN VARCHAR2,
    string2 IN VARCHAR2
    [, start_position IN NUMBER := 1
    [, nth_appearance IN NUMBER := 1]])
RETURN NUMBER
```

where string1 is the string searched by INSTR for the position in which the nth_appearance of string2 is found. The start_position parameter is the position in the string where the search will start. It is optional and defaults to 1 (the beginning of string1). The nth_appearance parameter is also optional and also defaults to 1.

Both the start_position and nth_appearance parameters can be literals like 5 or 157, variables, or complex expressions, as follows:

INSTR (company_name, 'INC', (last_location + 5) * 10)

If start_position is negative, then INSTR counts back start_position number of characters from the end of the string and then searches from that point towards the beginning of the string for the nth match. Figure 4.1 illustrates the two directions in which INSTR searches, depending on the sign of the start_position parameter.

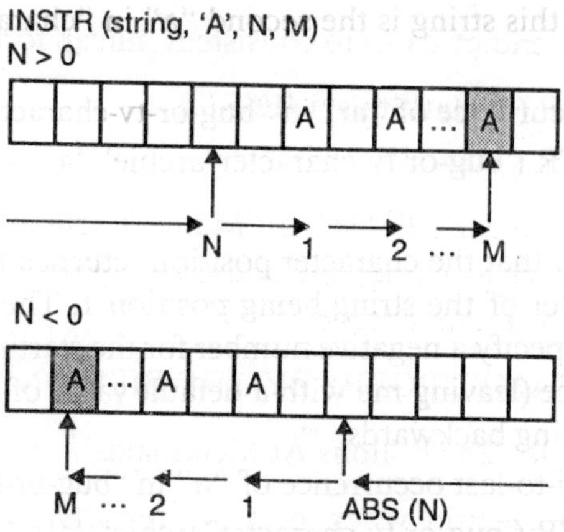

Figure 4.1. Forward and reverse searches with INSTR

We have found INSTR to be a very handy function — especially when used to the fullest extent possible. Most programmers make use of (and are even only aware of) only the first two parameters.

Let's look at some examples of INSTR. In these examples, we will see all four parameters used in all their permutations. As we write our own programs, keep in mind the different ways in which INSTR can be used to extract information from a string; it can greatly simplify the code we write to parse and analyze character data.

- Find the first occurrence of archie in "bug-or-tv-character?archie":

  SQL > INSTR ('bug-or-tv-character?archie', 'archie');

  SQL > 21

The starting position and the nth appearance both defaulted to 1.

- Find the first occurrence of archie in the following string starting from position 14:

  SQL > INSTR ('bug-or-tv-character?archie', 'ar', 14);

  SQL > 21

In this example We specified a starting position, which overrides the default of 1; the answer is still the same though. No matter where we start our search, the character position returned by INSTR is always calculated from the beginning of the string.

- Find the second occurrence of archie in the following string:

  SQL > INSTR ('bug-or-tv-character?archie', 'archie', 1, 2);

  SQL > 0

There is only one archie in the string, so INSTR returns 0. Even though the starting point is the default, I cannot leave it out if I also want to specify a nondefault nth appearance (2 in this case, for "second occurrence").

- Find the second occurrence of "a" in "bug-or-tv-character?archie":

  SQL > INSTR ('bug-or-tv-character?archie', 'a', 1, 2);

  SQL > 15

The second "a" in this string is the second "a" in "character," which is in the fifteenth position in the string.

- Find the last occurrence of "ar" in "bug-or-tv-character?archie".

SQL > INSTR ('bug-or-tv-character?archie', 'ar', -1)

SQL > 21

We must remember that the character position returned by INSTR is always calculated from the leftmost character of the string being position 1. The easiest way to find the last of anything in a string is to specify a negative number for the starting position. We did not have to specify the nth appearance (leaving me with a default value of 1), since the last occurrence is also the first when searching backwards.

- Find the second-to-last occurrence of "a" in "bug-or-tv-character?archie":

SQL > INSTR ('bug-or-tv-character?archie', 'a', -1, 2);

SQL > 15

No surprises here. Counting from the back of the string, INSTR passes over the "a" in archie, because that is the last occurrence, and searches for the next occurrence. Again, the character position is counted from the leftmost character, not the rightmost character, in the string.

- Find the position of the letter "t" closest to (but not past) the question mark in the following string: bug-or-tv-character?archie tophat:

SQL >INSTR ('bug-or-tv-character?archie tophat', 't', -14);

SQL > 17

To find the "t" just before the question mark. The phrase "just before" indicates that we should search backwards from the question mark for the first occurrence. We therefore counted through the characters and determined that the question mark appears at the 20th position. We specified -14 as the starting position so that INSTR would search backwards right from the question mark.

LENGTH

The LENGTH function returns the length of the specified string. The specification for LENGTH follows:

FUNCTION LENGTH (string1 VARCHAR2) RETURN NUMBER

If string1 is NULL, then LENGTH returns NULL — not zero (0)! Remember, a NULL string is a "nonvalue." Therefore, it cannot have a length, even a zero length.

The LENGTH function, in fact, will never return zero; it will always return either NULL or a positive number. Here are some examples:

SQL > LENGTH (NULL)

SQL > NULL

SQL > LENGTH ('')

SQL > NULL — Same as a NULL string.

```
SQL >LENGTH ('abcd')
SQL > 4
SQL >LENGTH ('abcd')
SQL > 5
```

If string1 is a fixed-length CHAR datatype, then LENGTH counts the trailing blanks in its calculation. So the LENGTH of a fixed-length string is always the declared length of the string. If you want to compute the length of the nonblank characters in string1, you will need to use the RTRIM function to remove the trailing blanks (RTRIM is discussed later in this chapter).

LOWER

The LOWER function converts all letters in the specified string to lowercase. The specifications for the LOWER function are:

```
FUNCTION LOWER (string1 IN CHAR) RETURN CHAR
FUNCTION LOWER (string1 IN VARCHAR2) RETURN VARCHAR2
```

As we have noted earlier, LOWER and UPPER will actually return a fixed-length string if the incoming string is fixed-length. LOWER will not change any characters in the string that are not letters, since case is irrelevant for numbers and special characters, such as the dollar sign ($).

Here are some examples of the effect of LOWER:

```
SQL > LOWER ('BIG FAT LETTERS');
SQL > 'big fat letters'
SQL > LOWER ('123ABC');
SQL > '123abc'
```

LOWER and its partner in case conversion, UPPER, are useful for guaranteeing a consistent case when comparing strings.

LPAD

By default, SQL strips all trailing blanks from a character string unless it is declared with a fixed-length CHAR datatype. There are occasions, however, when you really want some spaces (or even some other character) added to the front or back of your string. LPAD and its right-leaning cousin, RPAD give us this capability. The LPAD function returns a string padded to the left (hence the "L" in "LPAD") to a specified length, and with a specified pad string. The specification of the LPAD function is:

```
FUNCTION LPAD
  (string1 IN VARCHAR2,
   padded_length IN NUMBER
   [, pad_string IN VARCHAR2])
RETURN VARCHAR2
```

LPAD returns string1 padded on the left to length padded_length with the optional character string pad_string. If you do not specify pad_string, then string1 is padded on the left with spaces. We must specify the padded_length. If string1 already has a length equal to padded_length, then LPAD returns string1 without any additional characters. If padded_length is smaller than the length of string1, LPAD effectively truncates string1 — it returns only the first padded_length characters of the incoming string1.

As one can easily see, LPAD can do a lot more than just add spaces to the left of a string. Let's look at some examples of how useful LPAD can be.

- Display the number padded left with zeros to a length of 10:

  SQL > LPAD ('55', 10, '0');

  SQL > '0000000055'

- Display the number padded left with zeros to a length of 5:

  SQL > LPAD ('12345678', 5, '0');

  SQL > '12345'

LPAD interprets its padded_length as the maximum length of the string that it may return. As a result, it counts padded_length number of characters from the left (start of the string) and then simply returns that substring of the incoming value.

- Place the phrase "sell!" in front of the names of selected stocks, up to a string length of 45:

  SQL > LPAD ('HITOP TIES', 45, 'sell!');

  SQL > 'sell!sell!sell!sell!sell!sell!sell!HITOP TIES'

Because the length of "HITOP TIES" is 10 and the length of "sell!" is 5, there is room for seven repetitions of the pad string. LPAD does, in fact, generate a repetition of the pattern specified in the pad string.

- Place the phrase "sell!" in front of the names of selected stocks, up to a string length of 43.

  SQL > LPAD ('HITOP TIES', 43, 'sell!');

  SQL >'sell!sell!sell!sell!sell!sell!selHITOP TIES'

Because the length of "HITOP TIES" is 10 and the length of "sell!" is 5, there is no longer room for seven full repetitions of the pad string. As a result, the seventh repetition (counting from the left) of "sell!" lost its last two characters. So one can see that LPAD does not pad by adding to the left of the original string until it runs out of room. Instead, it figures out how many characters it must pad by to reach the total, then constructs that full padded fragment, and finally appends the original string to this fragment.

- Place three repetitions of the string "DRAFT-ONLY" in front of the article's title. Put two spaces between each repetition.

  SQL > LPAD ('Why I Love PL/SQL', 53, 'DRAFT-ONLY');

  SQL > 'DRAFT-ONLY DRAFT-ONLY DRAFT-ONLY Why I Love PL/SQL'

One can specify any number of characters to be padded in front of the incoming string value. The 53 that is hardcoded in that call to LPAD is the result of some hard calculations: the title is 17 characters and the prefix, including spaces, is 12 characters. As a result, make sure that padded length of at least 17 + 12*3 = 53.

LTRIM

The LTRIM function is the opposite of LPAD. Whereas LPAD adds characters to the left of a string, LTRIM removes, or trims, characters from the leading portion of the string. And just as with LPAD, LTRIM offers much more flexibility than simply removing leading blanks. The specification of the LTRIM function is:

```
FUNCTION LTRIM (string1 IN VARCHAR2 [, trim_string IN VARCHAR2])
RETURN VARCHAR2
```

LTRIM returns string1 with all leading characters removed up to the first character not found in the trim_string. The second parameter is optional and defaults to a single space.

There is one important difference between LTRIM and LPAD. LPAD pads to the left with the specified string, and repeats that string (or pattern of characters) until there is no more room. LTRIM, on the other hand removes all leading characters which appear in the trim string, not as a pattern, but as individual candidates for trimming.

Here are some examples:

- Trim all leading blanks from 'Way Out in Right Field':

```
SQL >LTRIM ('Way Out in Right Field');
SQL > 'Way Out in Right Field'
```

Because we did not specify a trim string, it defaults to a single space and so all leading spaces are removed.

- Trim '123' from the front of a string:

```
my_string := '123123123LotsaLuck123';
SQL >LTRIM (my_string, '123');
SQL > 'LotsaLuck123'
```

In this example, LTRIM stripped off all three leading repetitions of "123" from the specified string. Although it looks as though LTRIM trims by a specified pattern, this is not so, as the next example illustrates.

- Remove all numbers from the front of the string:

```
SQL > my_string := '70756234LotsaLuck';
SQL >LTRIM (my_string, '0987612345');
SQL > 'LotsaLuck'
```

By specifying every possible digit in our trim string, we ensured that any and all numbers would be trimmed, regardless of the order in which they occurred (and the order in which we place them in the trim string).

- Remove all a's, b's, and c's from the front of the string: 'abcabcccccI LOVE CHILI':

  SQL >LTRIM ('abcabcccccI LOVE CHILI', 'abc')

  SQL > 'I LOVE CHILI'

LTRIM removed the patterns of "abc", but also removed the individual instances of the letter "c". This worked out fine since the request was to remove any and all of those three letters. To remove only any instance of "abc" as a pattern from the front of the string? We couldn't use LTRIM since it trims off any matching individual characters. To remove a pattern from a string — or to replace one pattern with another pattern — you will want to make use of the REPLACE function, which is discussed next.

REPLACE

The REPLACE function returns a string in which all occurrences of a specified match string are replaced with a replacement string. REPLACE is useful for searching out patterns of characters and then changing all instances of that pattern in a single function call. The specification of the REPLACE function is:

```
FUNCTION REPLACE (string1 IN VARCHAR2, match_string IN VARCHAR2
        [, replace_string IN VARCHAR2])
RETURN VARCHAR2
```

If we do not specify the replacement string, then REPLACE simply removes all occurrences of the match_string in string1. If we specify neither a match string nor a replacement string, REPLACE returns NULL.

Here are several examples using REPLACE:

- Remove all instances of the letter "C" in the string "CAT CALL":

  SQL > REPLACE ('CAT CALL', 'C');

  SQL > 'AT ALL'

Because we did not specify a replacement string, REPLACE changed all occurrences of "C" to NULL.

- Replace all occurrences of "99" with "100" in the following string:

  SQL > REPLACE ('Zero defects in period 99 reached 99%!', '99', '100');

  SQL > 'Zero defects in period 100 reached 100%!'

- Replace all occurrences of "th" with the letter "z":

  SQL > REPLACE ('this that and the other', 'th', 'z');

  SQL > 'zis zat and ze ozer'

- Handle occurrences of a single quote (') within a query criteria string. The single quote is a string terminator symbol. It indicates the start and/or end of the literal string. We ran into this requirement while building query-by-example strings in Oracle Forms. If the user enters a string with a single quote in it, such as:

  Customer didn't have change

and then we concatenate that string into a larger string, the resulting SQL statement (created dynamically by Oracle Forms in Query Mode) fails, because there are unbalanced single quotes in the string.

We can resolve this problem in one of three ways:

1. Simply strip out the single quote before we execute the query. This is workable only if there aren't really any single quotes in the data in the database.
2. If we do allow single quotes, we can then either replace the single quote with a single character wildcard (_) or:
3. Embed that single quote inside other single quotes so that the SQL layer can properly parse the statement.

To replace the single quote with a wild card, one would code:

criteria_string := REPLACE (criteria_string, '''', '_');

Four single quotes in sequence are required for SQL to understand that one wants to search for one single quote in the criteria string. The first quote indicates the start of a literal. The fourth quote indicates the end of the string literal. The two inner single quotes parse into one single quote. That is, whenever one wants to embed a single quote inside a literal, one must place another single quote before it.

This principle comes in handy for the final resolution of the single quote in query criteria problem, change the single quote to two single quotes and then execute the query:

criteria_string := REPLACE (criteria_string, '''', '''''');

as in:

SQL > REPLACE ('Customer didn''t have change.', '''', '''''');

SQL > Customer didn''t have change.

Now, even if one places single quotes at the beginning and end of this string, the internal single quote will not signal termination of the literal.

- Remove all leading repetitions of "abc" from the string:

  "abcabcccccI LOVE CHILIabc"

This is the behavior we were looking at in the previous section on LTRIM. We want to remove all instances of the pattern "abc" from the beginning of the string, but we do not want to remove that pattern throughout the rest of the string. In addition, we want to remove "abc" only as a pattern, if we encounter three contiguous c's ("ccc"), on the other hand, they should not be removed from the string. This task is less straightforward than it might at first seem. If we simply apply REPLACE to the string, it will remove all occurrences of "abc" instead of just the leading instances. For example:

SQL > REPLACE ('abcabcccccI LOVE CHILIabc', 'abc');

SQL > 'cccI LOVE CHILI'

That is not what we want in this case. If we use LTRIM, on the other hand, we will be left with none of the leading c's, as demonstrated in a previous example:

SQL > LTRIM ('abcabcccccI LOVE CHILIabc', 'abc');

SQL > 'I LOVE CHILIabc'

If we want to be left with 'cccI LOVE CHILIabc' and it turns out that the way to get it is to use a combination of LTRIM and REPLACE. Suppose we create a local variable as follows:

```
my_string  := 'abcabccccI LOVE CHILIabc';
```

Then the following statement will achieve the desired effect by nesting calls to REPLACE and LTRIM within one another:

```
SQL >REPLACE
        (LTRIM
        (REPLACE (my_string, 'abc', '@'), '@'), '@', 'abc');
SQL >'cccI LOVE CHILIabc'
```

Here is how we describe in English what the above statement does:

"First replace all occurrences of 'abc' with the special character '@'. Then trim off all leading instances of '@'. Finally, replace all remaining occurrences of '@' with 'abc'."

RPAD

The RPAD function adds characters to the end of a character string. It returns a string padded to the right (hence the "R" in "RPAD") to a specified length, and with an optional pad string. The specification of the RPAD function is:

```
FUNCTION RPAD
  (string1 IN VARCHAR2,
  padded_length IN NUMBER
  [, pad_string IN VARCHAR2])
RETURN VARCHAR2
```

RPAD returns string1 padded on the right to length padded_length with the optional character string pad_string. If one does not specify pad_string, then string1 is padded on the right with spaces. One must specify the padded_length. If string1 already has a length equal to padded_length, then RPAD returns string1 without any additional characters. If padded_length is smaller than the length of string1, RPAD effectively truncates string1: it returns only the first padded_length characters of the incoming string1.

Let's look at some examples of RPAD:

- Display the number padded right with zeros to a length of 10:

```
SQL > RPAD ('55', 10, '0');
SQL > '5500000000'
```

One can also use TO_CHAR to convert from a number to a character

```
SQL >TO_CHAR (55 * 100000000);
SQL > '5500000000'
```

- Display the number padded right with zeros to a length of 5:

  SQL >RPAD ('12345678', 5);

  SQL > '12345'

RPAD interprets its padded_length as the maximum length of the string that it may return. As a result, it counts padded_length number of characters from the left (start of the string) and then simply returns that substring of the incoming value. This is the same behavior as that found with LPAD, described earlier in this chapter. Remember: RPAD does not return the rightmost five characters (in the above case "45678").

- Place the phrase "sell!" after the names of selected stocks, up to a string length of 45:

  SQL > RPAD ('HITOP TIES', 45, 'sell!');

  SQL >'HITOP TIESsell!sell!sell!sell!sell!sell!sell!'

Since the length of "HITOP TIES" is 10 and the length of "sell!" is 5, there is room for seven repetitions of the pad string. RPAD does, in fact, generate a repetition of the pattern specified in the pad string.

- Place the phrase "sell!" after the names of selected stocks, up to a string length of 43:

  SQL > RPAD ('HITOP TIES', 43, 'sell!');

  SQL > 'HITOP TIESsell!sell!sell!sell!sell!sell!sel'

Because the length of "HITOP TIES" is 10 and the length of "sell!" is 5, there is no longer room for seven full repetitions of the pad string. As a result, the seventh repetition of "sell!" lost its last two characters.

- Create a string of 60 dashes to use as a border in a report:

  SQL >RPAD ('-', 60, '-');

  SQL >'————————————————————'

One can use RPAD (and LPAD as well) to generate repetitive sequences of characters.

RTRIM

The RTRIM function is the opposite of RPAD, and the companion function to LTRIM. Where RPAD adds characters to the right of a string, RTRIM removes, or trims, characters from the end portion of the string. Just as with RPAD, RTRIM offers much more flexibility than simply removing trailing blanks. The specification of the RTRIM function is:

```
FUNCTION RTRIM (string1 IN VARCHAR2 [, trim_string IN VARCHAR2])
RETURN VARCHAR2
```

RTRIM returns string1 with all trailing characters removed up to the first character not found in the trim_string. The second parameter is optional and defaults to a single space.

Here are some examples of RTRIM:

- Trim all trailing blanks from a string:

SQL > RTRIM ('Way Out in Right Field');

SQL > 'Way Out in Right Field'

Since we did not specify a trim string, it defaults to a single space and so all trailing spaces are removed.

- Trim all the characters in "BAM! ARGH!" from the end of a string:
- my_string := 'Sound effects: BAM!ARGH!BAM!HAM';

SQL >RTRIM (my_string, 'BAM! ARGH!');

SQL > 'Sound effects:'

This use of RTRIM stripped off all the letters at the end of the string which are found in "BAM!ARGH!." This includes "BAM" and "HAM," so those words too are removed from the string even though "HAM" is not listed explicitly as a "word" in the trim string. Also, the inclusion of two exclamation marks in the trim string is unnecessary, because RTRIM is not looking for the word "ARGH!", but each of the letters in "ARGH!".

SOUNDEX

The SOUNDEX function allows us to perform string comparisons based on phonetics (the way a word sounds), as opposed to semantics (the way a word is spelt).[1] SOUNDEX returns a character string which is the "phonetic representation" of the argument. The specification of the SOUNDEX function is as follows:

[1] Oracle Corporation used the algorithm in The Art of Computer Programming, Volume 3, by Donald Knuth, to generate the phonetic representation.

FUNCTION SOUNDEX (string1 IN VARCHAR2) RETURN VARCHAR2

Here are some of the values SOUNDEX generated and how they vary according to the input string:

SQL >SOUNDEX ('smith');

SQL > 'S530'

SQL >SOUNDEX ('SMYTHE');

SQL > 'S530'

SQL >SOUNDEX ('smith smith');

SQL > 'S532'

SQL >SOUNDEX ('smith z');

SQl > 'S532'

SQL >SOUNDEX ('feuerstein');

SQL > 'F623'

SQL > SOUNDEX ('feuerst');
SQL 'F623'

Example:

SQL > Select City,temp from weather where
Soundex(City) = Soundex('Sidny');

Keep the following SOUNDEX rules in mind while using this function:

- The SOUNDEX value always begins with the first letter in the input string.
- SOUNDEX only uses the first five consonants in the string to generate the return value.
- Only consonants are used to compute the numeric portion of the SOUNDEX value. Except for a possible leading vowel, all vowels are ignored.
- SOUNDEX is not case-sensitive. Upper and lowercase letters return the same SOUNDEX value.

The SOUNDEX function is useful for *ad hoc* queries, and any other kinds of searches where the exact spelling of a database value is not known or easily determined.

SUBSTR

The SUBSTR function is one of the most useful and commonly used character functions. It allows us to extract a portion or subset of contiguous (connected) characters from a string. The substring is specified by starting position and a length.

The specification for the SUBSTR function is:

```
FUNCTION SUBSTR
   (string_in IN VARCHAR2,
   start_position_in IN NUMBER
   [, substr_length_in IN NUMBER])
RETURN VARCHAR2
```

where the arguments are used as follows:

string_in
: The source string

start_position_in
: The starting position of the substring in string_in

substr_length_in
: The length of the substring desired (the number of characters to be returned in the substring)

The last parameter, substr_length_in, is optional. If you do not specify a substring length, then SUBSTR returns all the characters to the end of string_in (from the starting position specified).

The start position cannot be zero. If the start position is less than zero, the substring is retrieved from the back of the string. SUBSTR counts backwards substr_length_in number of characters from the end of string_in. In this case, however, the characters which are extracted are still to the right of the starting position. See Figure 4.2 for an illustration of how the different arguments are used by SUBSTR.

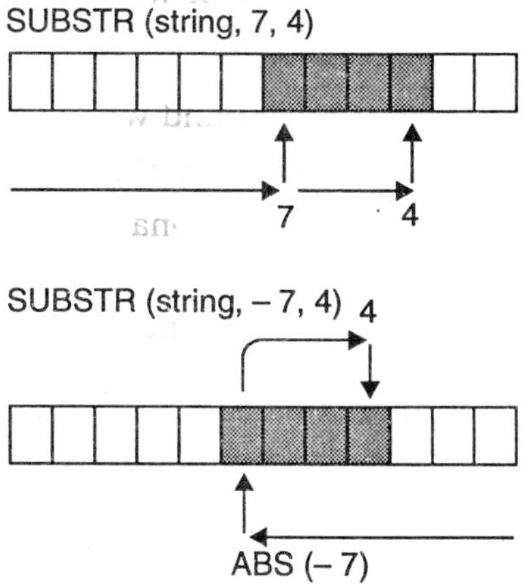

Figure 4.2. How arguments are used by SUBSTR

The substr_length_in argument must be greater than zero.

Here are some examples of SUBSTR:

- If the absolute value of the starting position exceeds the length of the input string, return to NULL:

```
        SQL > SUBSTR ('now_or_never', 200);
        SQL > NULL
    SQL > SUBSTR ('now_or_never', -200);
    SQL > NULL
```

- If starting position is 0, SUBSTR acts as though the starting position was actually 1:

```
        SQL >SUBSTR ('now_or_never', 0, 3);
        SQL > 'now'
    SQL > SUBSTR ('now_or_never', 0);
    SQL > 'now_or_never'
```

- If the substring length is less than or equal to zero, return NULL:

```
        SQL >SUBSTR ('now_or_never', 5, -2);
        SQL > NULL
    SQL >SUBSTR ('now_or_never', 1, 0);
    SQL >NULL
```

- Return the last character in a string:

```
SQL >SUBSTR ('Another sample string', -1)
SQL >'g'
```

This is the cleanest way to get the single last character. A more direct, but cumbersome, approach is this:

```
SQL >SUBSTR('Sample string', LENGTH ('Sample string'), 1);
SQL > 'g'
```

In other words, calculate the LENGTH of the string and the one character from the string that starts at that last position.

TRANSLATE

The TRANSLATE function is a variation on REPLACE. REPLACE replaces every instance of a set of characters with another set of characters, that is, REPLACE works with entire words or patterns. TRANSLATE replaces single characters at a time, translating the nth character in the match set with the nth character in the replacement set. The specification of the TRANSLATE is as follows:

```
FUNCTION TRANSLATE
  (string_in IN VARCHAR2,
  search_set IN VARCHAR2,
  replace_set VARCHAR2)
RETURN VARCHAR2
```

where string_in is the string in which characters are to be translated, search_set is the set of characters to be translated (if found), and replace_set is the set of characters which will be placed in the string. Unlike REPLACE, where the last argument could be left off, you must include all three arguments when you use TRANSLATE. Any of the three arguments may, however, be NULL, in which case TRANSLATE always returns NULL.

Here are some examples of the effect of TRANSLATE:

```
SQL > TRANSLATE ('abcd', 'ab', '12');
SQL > '12cd'

SQL > TRANSLATE ('12345', '15', 'xx');
SQL > 'x234x'

SQL > TRANSLATE ('grumpy old possum', 'uot', '%$*');
SQL > 'gr%mpy $ld p$ss%m'

SQL >TRANSLATE ('my language needs the letter e', 'egms', 'X');
SQL >'y lanuaX nXXd thX lXttXr X';

SQL >TRANSLATE ('please go away', 'a', NULL);
SQL > NULL
```

One can deduce a number of the usage rules for TRANSLATE from the above examples, namely:

- If the search set contains a character not found in the string, then no translation is performed for that character.
- If the string contains a character not found in the search set, then that character is not translated.
- If the search set contains more characters than the replace set, then all the "trailing" search characters that have no match in the replace set are removed from the string. In the following example, a, b, and c are changed to z, y, and x, respectively. But the letter "d" is removed from the return string entirely since it had no corresponding character in the replace set.

SQL > TRANSLATE ('abcdefg', 'abcd', 'zyx');
SQL > 'zyxefg'

In these cases, NULL is the matching "character" for all extra characters in the search set. When one replaces a character with NULL it is the same as removing that character from the string.

- If any of the three arguments is NULL, then the result of the translation is NULL. This is consistent with a basic tenet of NULLs: apply an operation to an unknown value and we always get an unknown value.

The UPPER function converts all letters in the specified string to uppercase. The specifications of the UPPER function are:

FUNCTION UPPER (string1 IN CHAR) RETURN CHAR
FUNCTION UPPER (string1 IN VARCHAR2) RETURN VARCHAR2

As we noted at the beginning of this chapter, UPPER and LOWER will actually return a fixed-length string if the incoming string is fixed length. UPPER will not change any characters in the string which are not letters, since case is irrelevant for numbers and special characters such as $.

Here are some examples of the effect of UPPER:

SQL > UPPER ('short little letters no more');
SQL > 'SHORT LITTLE LETTERS NO MORE'

SQL > UPPER ('123abc');
SQL > '123ABC'

SQL is not a case-sensitive language as concerns its own syntax and names of identifiers. It is sensitive to case, however, in character strings, whether found in named constants, literals, or variables. The string "ABC" is not the same as "abc", and this can cause problems in our programs if we are not careful and consistent in our handling of such values.

CONVERSION FUNCTIONS

Table 4.6

Name	Description
CHARTOROWID	Converts a string to a ROWID.
CONVERT	Converts a string from one character set to another.
HEXTORAW	Converts from hexadecimal to raw format.
RAWTOHEX	Converts from raw value to hexadecimal.
ROWIDTOCHAR	Converts a binary ROWID value to a character string.
TO_CHAR	Converts a number or date to a string.
TO_DATE	Converts a string to a date.
TO_NUMBER	Converts a string to a number.

CHARTOROWID

The CHARTOROWID function converts a string of either type CHAR or VARCHAR2 to a value of type ROWID. The specification of the CHARTOROWID function is:

FUNCTION CHARTOROWID (string_in IN CHAR) RETURN ROWID
FUNCTION CHARTOROWID (string_in IN VARCHAR2) RETURN ROWID

In order for CHARTOROWID to successfully convert the string, it must be of the format: BBBBBBBB.RRRR.FFFF

where BBBBBBBB is the number of the block in the database file, RRRR is the number of the row in the block, and FFFF is the number of the database file. All three numbers must be in hexadecimal format.

Example : SELECT ename FROM emp

If the input string does not conform to the above format, SQL raises the VALUE_ERROR exception.

CONVERT

The CONVERT function converts strings from one character set to another character set. The specification of the CONVERT function is:

```
FUNCTION CONVERT
   (string_in IN VARCHAR2,
   new_char_set VARCHAR2
   [, old_char_set VARCHAR2])
RETURN VARCHAR2
```

The old_char_set is an optional argument. If this third argument is not specified, then the default character set for the database instance is used.

The CONVERT function does not translate words or phrases from one language to another! CONVERT simply substitutes the letter or symbol in one character set with the corresponding letter or symbol in another character set. (A character set is not the same thing as a human language.)

Two commonly used character sets are US7ASCII (U.S. 7-bit ASCII character set) and F7DEC (DEC French 7-bit character set).

Example : SELECT CONVERT('Groß', 'US7ASCII', 'WE8HP')
"Conversion" FROM DUAL;

```
Conversion
__________
Gross
```

Common character sets include:

US7ASCI	US 7-bit ASCII character set
WE8DEC	DEC West European 8-bit character set
WE8HP	HP West European Laserjet 8-bit character set
F7DEC	DEC French 7-bit character set
WE8EBCD1C500	IBM West European EBCDIC Code Page 500
WE8PC850	IBM PC Code Page 850
WE8ISO8859P1	ISO 8859-1 West European 8-bit character set

HEXTORAW

The HEXTORAW function converts a hexadecimal string from type CHAR or VARCHAR2 to type RAW. The specification of the HEXTORAW function is:

```
FUNCTION HEXTORAW (string_in IN CHAR) RETURN RAW
FUNCTION HEXTORAW (string_in IN VARCHAR2) RETURN RAW
```

RAWTOHEX

The RAWTOHEX function converts a value from type RAW to a hexadecimal string of type VARCHAR2. The specification of the RAWTOHEX function is:

```
FUNCTION RAWTOHEX (binary_value_in IN RAW) RETURN VARCHAR2
```

RAWTOHEX always returns a variable-length string value, even if its mirror conversion function is overloaded to support both types of input.

ROWIDTOCHAR

The ROWIDTOCHAR function converts a binary value of type ROWID to a string of type VARCHAR2. The specification of the ROWIDTOCHAR function is:

```
FUNCTION ROWIDTOCHAR (row_in IN ROWID ) RETURN VARCHAR2
```

The string returned by this function has the format:

BBBBBBBB.RRRR.FFFF

where BBBBBBBB is the number of the block in the database file, RRRR is the number of the row in the block, and FFFF is the number of the database file. All three numbers are in hexadecimal format.

TO_CHAR (date conversion)

The TO_CHAR function can be used to convert both dates and numbers to a variable-length string. The following specification describes TO_CHAR for dates:

```
FUNCTION TO_CHAR
  (date_in IN DATE
  [, format_mask IN VARCHAR2
  [, nls_language IN VARCHAR2]])
RETURN VARCHAR2
```

where date_in is the date to be converted to character format, the format_mask is the mask made up of one or more of the date format elements, and nls_language is a string specifying a date language. Both the format mask and the NLS language parameters are optional.

If the format mask is not specified, then the default date format for the database instance is used. This format is DD-MON-YY, unless the initialization parameter NLS_DATE_FORMAT is included in the initialization file. The format of the specification of an alternative date mask is:

NLS_DATE_FORMAT = 'MM/DD/YYYY'

If the NLS language parameter is not specified, then the default date language for the instance is used. This is either the language for the instance specified by the NLS_LANGUAGE parameter, or the date language specified in the initialization file with the parameter NLS_DATE_LANGUAGE. Note that if one wants to specify a date language, one also must include a format mask. One cannot skip over the intervening parameters.

Here are some examples of TO_CHAR for date conversion:

- Notice that there are two blanks between month and day and a leading zero for the fifth day:

SQL > TO_CHAR (SYSDATE, 'Month DD, YYYY');
SQL > 'February 05, 1994'

- Use the FM fill mode element to suppress blanks and zeros:

SQL > TO_CHAR (SYSDATE, 'FMMonth DD, YYYY');
SQL > 'February 5, 1994'

- Note the case difference on the month abbreviations of the next two samples. One gets exactly what one asks for with Oracle date formats!

SQL > TO_CHAR (SYSDATE, 'MON DDth, YYYY');
SQL > 'FEB 05th, 1994'

SQL >TO_CHAR (SYSDATE, 'fmMon DDth, YYYY');
SQL > 'Feb 5th, 1994'

- Show the day of year, the month, and the week for the date:

SQL > TO_CHAR (SYSDATE, 'DDD DD D');
SQL > '036 05 7'

SQL >TO_CHAR (SYSDATE, 'fmDDD DD D')
SQL >'36 5 7'

- Some fancy formatting for reporting purposes:

SQL >TO_CHAR (SYSDATE, '"In month" RM "of year" YEAR');
SQL >'In month II   of year NINETEEN NINETY FOUR'

TO_CHAR (number conversion)

The TO_CHAR function converts numbers as well as dates. The specification of the TO_CHAR (number) function is:

```
FUNCTION TO_CHAR
   (number_in IN NUMBER
   [, format_mask IN VARCHAR2
   [, nls_language IN VARCHAR2]])
RETURN VARCHAR2;
```

where number_in is the number to be converted to character format, the format_mask is the mask made up of one or more of the number format elements, and nls_language is a string specifying one or more of the NLS parameters which affect the way numbers are displayed. Both the format mask and the NLS language parameters are optional.

If the format mask is not specified, then the default number format for the database instance is used.

Here are some examples of TO_CHAR for number conversion:

SQL > TO_CHAR (564.70, '$999.9');
SQL > $564.7

SQL >TO_CHAR (564.70, '$0000999.9');
SQL >$0000564.7

TO_DATE

The TO_DATE function converts a character string to a true DATE datatype. The specification of the TO_DATE function is overloaded for string and number input:

```
FUNCTION TO_DATE (string_in IN VARCHAR2
  [, format_mask IN VARCHAR2
  [, nls_language IN VARCHAR2 ]])
RETURN DATE;

FUNCTION TO_DATE
  (number_in IN NUMBER
  [, format_mask IN VARCHAR2   [, nls_language IN VARCHAR2 ]])
RETURN DATE;
```

The second version of TO_DATE can be used only with the format mask of J for Julian date. The Julian date is the number of days which have passed since January 1, 4712 B.C. Only in this use of TO_DATE can a number be passed as the first parameter of TO_DATE.

For all other cases, string_in is the string variable, literal, named constant, or expression to be converted, format_mask is the format mask TO_DATE will use to convert the string, and nls_language is a string which specifies the language which is to be used to interpret the names and abbreviations of both months and days in the string. The format of nls_language is as follows:

'NLS_DATE_LANGUAGE=<language>'

where <language> is a language recognized by the instance of the database. One can usually determine the acceptable languages by checking one's installation guide.

Here are some examples of the TO_DATE function:

- Convert the string '123188' to a date:

SQL >TO_DATE ('123188', 'MMDDYY');
SQL > 31-DEC-1988

- Convert a date using the Spanish language:

```
SQL >TO_DATE ('April 12 1991', 'Month DD YYYY',
'NLS_DATE_LANGUAGE=Spanish');
SQL >12-APR-1991
```

Any Oracle errors between ORA-01800 and ORA-01899 are related to the internal Oracle date function and can arise when one encounters date conversion errors. One can learn additional nuances of date conversion rules by perusing the different errors and reading about the documented causes of these errors. Some of these rules are:

- A date literal passed to TO_CHAR for conversion to a date cannot be longer than 220 characters.
- One cannot include both a Julian date element (J) and the day of year element (DDD) in a single format mask.
- One cannot include multiple elements for the same component of the date/time in the mask. For example, the format mask YYYY-YYY-DD-MM is illegal because it includes two year elements, YYYY and YYY.
- One cannot use the 24-hour time format (HH24) and a meridian element (For example, AM) in the same mask.

TO_NUMBER

The TO_NUMBER function converts both fixed and variable length strings to numbers using the associated format mask. The specification of the TO_NUMBER function is as follows:

```
FUNCTION TO_NUMBER
  (string_in IN CHAR
  [, format_mask VARCHAR2 [, nls_language VARCHAR2 ]])
RETURN NUMBER;

FUNCTION TO_NUMBER
  (string_in IN VARCHAR2
  [, format_mask VARCHAR2 [, nls_language VARCHAR2 ]])
RETURN NUMBER;
```

where string_in is the string containing a sequence of characters to be converted to a number, format_mask is the optional string directing TO_NUMBER how to convert the character bytes to a number, and nls_language is a string containing up to three specifications of National Language Support parameters, as follows:

NLS_NUMERIC_CHARACTERS

The characters used to specify the decimal point and the group separator in a number. The decimal point character for the American language is a dot (.) while the group separator is a comma (,).

NLS_CURRENCY

The character(s) used to specify the local currency symbol. The currency character for the American language is a dollar sign ($).

NLS_ISO_CURRENCY

The character(s) used to specify the international currency symbol in the string.

The format for nls_language in the call to TO_NUMBER is as follows:

'NLS_NUMERIC_CHARACTERS = "string"'

'NLS_CURRENCY = "string"'

'NLS_ISO_CURRENCY = "string"'

Two contiguous single quotes are needed before and after the values for each string value so that SQL will parse the entire parameter and leave behind a single quote around each value.

LOB AND MISCELLANEOUS FUNCTIONS

Table 4.7: The Built-in LOB Functions

Name	Description
BFILENAME	Initializes a BFILE column in an INSERT statement by associating it with a file in the server's filesystem.
EMPTY_BLOB	Returns an empty locator of type BLOB (binary large object).
EMPTY_CLOB	Returns an empty locator of type CLOB (character large object).

Table 4.8: The Built-in Miscellaneous Functions

Name	Description
DUMP	Returns a string containing a "dump" of the specified expression. This dump includes the datatype, length in bytes, and internal representation.
NVL	Returns a substitution value if the argument is NULL.
SQLCODE	Returns the number of the Oracle error for the most recent internal exception.
SQLERRM	Returns the error message associated with the error number returned by SQLCODE.
UID	Returns the User ID (a unique integer) of the current Oracle session.
USER	Returns the name of the current Oracle user.
USERENV	Returns a string containing information about the current session.
VSIZE	Returns the number of bytes in the internal representation of the specified value.

BFILENAME

The BFILENAME function initializes a BFILE column in a database table or a BFILE variable in SQL by returning a locator to a physical file in the server's filesystem. The header for BFILENAME is:

```
FUNCTION BFILENAME
   (directory_alias IN VARCHAR2, filename IN VARCHAR2
RETURN BFILE;
```

where directory_alias is a DIRECTORY database object which has already been defined with a CREATE DIRECTORY statement, and filename is the name of the file containing the large binary object.

This function will return NULL if we try to get a BFILE locator with a directory alias which does not yet exist.

We can use BFILENAME in SQL INSERT and UPDATE statements. We can also use it to initialize a BFILE locator in a PL/SQL program. Here are examples of both usages:

```
UPDATE school_report
   SET photo_op =
      BFILENAME ('projects', 'grasshoppers.atwork')
WHERE title = 'REPRODUCTIVE CYCLES OF BUGS';
```

There are several issues to keep in mind with directory aliases:

- An alias is a database object, an "internal" name for an external, filesystem-based directory location.
- One must create a directory alias before one can use it.
- To create a directory alias, one will need the CREATE DIRECTORY or CREATE ANY DIRECTORY privileges.
- To access a directory alias, one must be the owner or be granted the READ privilege on that alias.
- Directory aliases can be case-sensitive!

EMPTY_BLOB

The EMPTY_BLOB function returns an empty locator of type BLOB (binary large object). The specification for the EMPTY_BLOB function is:

```
FUNCTION EMPTY_BLOB RETURN BLOB;
```

We can call this function without any parentheses or with an empty pair. Here are some examples:

```
INSERT INTO family_member (name, photo)
      VALUES ('Steven Feuerstein', EMPTY_BLOB());
```

Use EMPTY_BLOB to initialize a BLOB to "empty." Before one can work with a BLOB, either to reference it in SQL DML statements such as INSERTs or to assign it a value in PL/SQL, it must contain a locator. It cannot be NULL. The locator might point to an empty BLOB value, but it will be a valid BLOB locator.

EMPTY_CLOB

The EMPTY_CLOB function returns an empty locator of type CLOB. The specification for the EMPTY_CLOB function is:

```
FUNCTION EMPTY_CLOB RETURN CLOB;
```

We can call this function without any parentheses or with an empty pair. Here are some examples:

```
INSERT INTO diary (entry, text) VALUES (SYSDATE, EMPTY_CLOB());
```

DUMP

The DUMP function "dumps," or returns, the internal representation of the input expression. DUMP is an overloaded function, as is shown by its specification:

```
FUNCTION DUMP (expr_in DATE
   [, return_format_in BINARY_INTEGER
   [, start_position_in BINARY_INTEGER
   [, length_in BINARY_INTEGER)
RETURN VARCHAR2

FUNCTION DUMP (expr_in NUMBER
   [, return_format_in BINARY_INTEGER
   [, start_position_in BINARY_INTEGER
   [, length_in BINARY_INTEGER)
RETURN VARCHAR2

FUNCTION DUMP (expr_in VARCHAR2
   [, return_format_in BINARY_INTEGER
   [, start_position_in BINARY_INTEGER
   [, length_in BINARY_INTEGER)
RETURN VARCHAR2
```

where expr_in is the expression to be dumped, return_format_in is a numeric code specifying the format of the returned string, start_position_in is the starting position of the portion of the internal representation to be returned, and length_in is the length of the portion to be returned. The starting position and length arguments perform the same way as in the SUBSTR function described in

Valid return format numbers are:

8 Returns result in octal notation

10 Returns result in decimal notation

16 Returns result in hexadecimal notation

17 Returns result as individual characters

The default for the return format is 10 (decimal), the default for the starting position is 1, and the default for length is the full length of the value. So, a fully default call to DUMP will return the full internal representation in decimal notation.

If expr_in IS NULL, then DUMP returns NULL.

NVL

The NVL function offers a concise way to return or substitute a non-NULL value if the specified value is NULL. One can think of NVL as an abbreviation for "if Null Value, then return X." The NVL function is massively overloaded because any type of data can also have a NULL value. Here is the specification:

```
FUNCTION NVL (string_in IN CHAR, replace_with_in IN CHAR)
  RETURN CHAR
FUNCTION NVL (string_in IN VARCHAR2, replace_with_in IN VARCHAR2)
  RETURN VARCHAR2
FUNCTION NVL (date_in IN DATE, replace_with_in IN DATE)
  RETURN DATE
FUNCTION NVL (date_in IN NUMBER, replace_with_in IN DATE)
  RETURN NUMBER
FUNCTION NVL (date_in IN CHAR, replace_with_in IN DATE)
  RETURN BOOLEAN
```

NVL simply provides a much cleaner and more concise way of coding this functionality. And since it is a function, we can call it inline to provide substitution of NULL values where such a state of data would disrupt your program. For example, if we calculate the total compensation of an employee as salary plus compensation, then the expression:

```
salary + commission
```

will be NULL when commission is NULL. With NVL, however, one can be sure that the calculated value will make sense:

```
salary + NVL (commission, 0)
```

SQLCODE

The SQLCODE function returns the number of the exception raised by SQL. The specification for this function is:

FUNCTION SQLCODE RETURN INTEGER

SQLCODE returns values as follows:

- If we reference SQLCODE outside of an exception section, it always returns 0, which means normal, successful completion.
- If we explicitly raise our own user-defined exception, then SQLCODE returns a value of +1.
- In all other cases, SQLCODE returns a negative value. In other words, if we try to convert a date to a string with TO_CHAR and use the wrong format mask, we might encounter the following error message:

ORA-01830: date format picture ends before converting entire input string

In this case, SQLCODE returns a value of -1830.

We will find SQLCODE and its sibling function, SQLERRM, most useful in the WHEN OTHERS exception handler. If an error is trapped by WHEN OTHERS, we do not know which exception was raised or which error was encountered. We can, however, use SQLCODE to find out, as shown in this example:

SQLERRM

The SQLERRM returns the error message associated with the specified code. The specification for this function is:

FUNCTION SQLERRM (code_in IN INTEGER := SQLCODE) RETURN VARCHAR2

If we do not provide an error code when we call SQLERRM, it uses the value returned by SQLCODE (see the preceding section). If SQLCODE returns 0, then SQLERRM returns the following message:

ORA-0000; normal, successful completion

If SQL and PL/SQL has raised an internal Oracle error or we pass a negative value to SQLERRM, then the function returns the error message provided by Oracle Corporation. If we pass (or allow SQLCODE to pass) a value of +100 to SQLERRM, it returns this message:

ORA-01403: no data found

Any other positive value passed to SQLERRM will result in this message:

User-Defined Exception

The maximum length of a message returned by SQLERRM is 512 bytes. This length includes the error code and all nested messages that may have been flagged by the compiler.

UID

The UID function returns an integer that uniquely identifies the current user. This integer is generated by the Oracle RDBMS when a user connects to the database. The specification for UID is as follows:

```
FUNCTION UID RETURN NUMBER
```

When called inline, the UID function looks like a variable since it has no arguments. Remember that when we call UID we will actually issue a SQL call to the RDBMS to extract the UID information for the user. Furthermore, in a distributed SQL statement, the UID always returns the value identifying the user on the local database. We cannot obtain the UID for connections to other, remote databases.

USER

The USER function returns the name of the current account. The specification for USER is as follows:

```
FUNCTION USER RETURN VARCHAR2
```

Like UID, when called inline, the USER function looks like a variable since it has no arguments. Remember that when we call USER we actually issue a SQL call to the RDBMS to extract the account name for the user. Furthermore, in a distributed SQL statement, the USER always returns the value identifying the user on the local database. We cannot obtain the USER for connections to other, remote databases.

The most common use for the USER function is to initialize an application session with configuration for a user.

Most of the applications we build have a system configuration table (with one row for each system or application) and a separate user configuration table (with one row for each user in each application). This user configuration table might have the following columns:

RDBMS account name

It is the name of Oracle account, which matches the value returned by USER.

User name

It is the actual name of the user, as in: STEVEN FEUERSTEIN.

Business data

It is the information about the user that relates to the business of the application, such as the user's department and default printer.

Preference data

It is the information about the preferences of the user, such as "Display Toolbar" or "Automatically pcp up a list of values boxes."

Assuming an Oracle Form-based set of screens, each screen the user is able to enter from a Windows icon will contain a When-New-Form-Instance trigger. This trigger calls a procedure to transfer the information from the user configuration table to GLOBAL variables that are then available to all screens for the duration of the session.

USERENV

The USERENV function returns information about the current user session or environment. The specification for USERENV is as follows:

```
FUNCTION USERENV (info_type_in IN VARCHAR2) RETURN VARCHAR2
```

where info_type_in can be one of these values (specified in a named constant or a literal string in single quotes). The following list gives options and descriptions of what they return:

ENTRYID

It is an auditing entry identifier.

LANGUAGE

The language, territory, and character set used by your session. The value is returned in this format: language_territory.characterset.

SESSIONID

It is an auditing session identifier.

TERMINAL

It is the operating system identifier for our current session's terminal. The format of this information will clearly be dependent on our underlying operating system.

VSIZE

The VSIZE function returns the number of bytes used by the internal representation of the input expression. The specification for VSIZE is:

```
FUNCTION VSIZE (expr_in IN DATE) RETURN NUMBER
FUNCTION VSIZE (expr_in IN VARCHAR2) RETURN NUMBER
FUNCTION VSIZE (expr_in IN NUMBER) RETURN NUMBER
FUNCTION VSIZE (expr_in IN CHAR) RETURN NUMBER
```

If the expression is NULL, then VSIZE returns to NULL.

SQL> SELECT VSIZE (hiredate) FROM emp WHERE ROWNUM=1;

```
VSIZE(HIREDATE)
---------------
              7
```

We included the WHERE clause for ROWNUM equal to 1 so that we would receive the answer (7 bytes) only once. Otherwise, we would have received the answer as the VSIZE of hiredate is 7 — for every record in the emp table.

The Decode Function

Unlike the translate function which performs a character by character replacement the DECODE function does a value by value replacement.

DECODE ***(s, search1, result1, search2, result2)*** - Compares *s* with *search1, search2,* etc. and returns the corresponding result when there is a match.

Or

DECODE(value,if1,then1,if2,then2,if3,then3,........,else)

SQL > Select vencode, decode (venname, 'frances','francis')name, tel_no from vendor_master where vencode = 'v001';

Venco	Name	Tel_no
v001	Francis	611892

Example : SQL > Select feature, section , decode(page,'1','Welcome','Go To || page) from newspaper;

In the above command page number is decoded. If the page number is 1 then the word 'Welcome' are substituted . If the page number is anything else then word 'Go To' are concated with page number.

AGGREGATE FUNCTIONS (GROUP FUNCTION)

Function	Usage
AVG(expression)	Computes the average value of a column by the expression
COUNT(expression)	Counts the rows defined by the expression
COUNT(*)	Counts all rows in the specified table or view
MIN(expression)	Finds the minimum value in a column by the expression
MAX(expression)	Finds the maximum value in a column by the expression
SUM(expression)	Computes the sum of column values by the expression
STDDEV(expression)	Standard devition of all values for group of rows
VARIANCE(expression)	Variance of all values for group of rows

The general syntax of an aggregate function is:

aggregate_function_name ([ALL | DISTINCT] expression)

The aggregate function name may be AVG, COUNT, MAX, MIN, or SUM. The ALL clause, which is the default behavior and does not actually need to be specified, evaluates all rows when aggregating the value of the function. The DISTINCT clause uses only distinct values when evaluating the function.

AVG

The AVG function returns the average value for the column when applied to a column containing numeric data. The following is the syntax for the AVG function.

AVG (column_name)

Example : SELECT AVG(commission_rate) FROM sales;

COUNT

The COUNT function has three variations.

COUNT(*) counts all the rows in the target table whether they include nulls or not.

COUNT(expression) computes the number of rows with non-NULL values in a specific column or expression.

COUNT(DISTINCT expression) computes the number of distinct non-NULL values in a column or expression.

Examples : This query counts all rows in a table:

SELECT COUNT(*) FROM publishers;

The following query finds the number of different countries where publishers are located:

SELECT COUNT(DISTINCT country) "Count of Countries"
FROM publishers

MIN

The MIN function returns the data item with the lowest value for a column when applied to a column containing numeric data. If we apply the MIN function to a CHARACTER value, it returns the first value in the sorted values for that column. The following syntax is for the MIN function.

MIN(column_name)

Example : SELECT MIN(commission_rate) FROM sales;

MAX

The MAX function returns the data item with the highest value for a column when applied to a column containing numeric data. If we apply the MAX function to a CHARACTER value, it returns the last value in the sorted values for that column. The following syntax is for the MAX function.

MAX(column_name)

Example : SELECT MAX(commission_rate) FROM sales;

SUM

The SUM function returns the sum of all values in the specified column. The result of the SUM function has the same precision as the column on which it is operating. The following syntax is for the SUM function.

SUM(column_name)

Example : SELECT SUM(ytd_sales) FROM sales;

STDDEV

The STDDEV function returns the standard deviation of values in the specified column. The result of the STDDEV function has the same precision as the column on which it is operating. The following syntax is for the STDDEV function.

STDDEV(column_name)

Example : SELECT STDDEV(Basic) FROM salary;

VARIANCE

The VARIANCE function returns the variance of values in the specified column. The result of the VARIANCE function has the same precision as the column on which it is operating. The following syntax is for the VARIANCE function.

VARIANCE(column_name)

Example : SELECT VARIANCE(Basic) FROM salary;

LAB ASSIGNMENT—6

1. Select the average salaries of each department where deptno is either D001 or D002 from employee table.
2. Select the name of the lowest paid employee from employee table.
3. Select the highest paid employee from employee table.
4. Display the total number of rows in the employee table.
5. Display only those jobs where max sal >=3000 in the employee table.
6. List the names and hiredate of the employees in deptno = D002, display date formatted as '12/03/03'.
7. List the name of employees whose hiredate is in the month of December using Substr function.
8. Count the number of people in department number D003.
9. Produce the following output using employee table:

   EMPLOYEE

   Kim (Manager)

   Bruce(Analyst)
10. Find out the difference between highest and lowest salaries.
11. How many months has the manager worked for the company (Round value).
12. Display the top three earners with name and salary in the company
13. Display the Sin and Sinh value of 45.
14. Display the ASCII value of "ORACLE".
15. Display all job types in smaller case from employee table.

LAB ASSIGNMENT—7

1. Select those clients whose bal_due is greater than value 2000 from client_mast table.
2. Count the total number of orders from product_mast table.
3. Calculate the average price of all the products from product_mast table.
4. Calculate the maximum and minimum product prices and rename the output as max_price and min_price respectively from product_mast table.
5. Count the number of products having price greater than or equal to 1200.
6. Display the employee number and day on which employee hired from employee table.
7. Display the Total number of working days of each employee from employee table.
8. Display the date, 20 days after today's date.
9. Count all distinct job types from employee table.
10. Using LPAD function pad the job types with 15 characters by '*' symbol.
11. Display the length of each employee name from employee table.
12. Display the value of 3 raised to 4 using power function.
13. Display the square root of 81.
14. Display the number of bytes used by ename from employee table.
15. Display the ename those are having sound like Kim from employee table.

5 Normalization

Objectives :

- ➤ First Normal Form
- ➤ Second Normal Form
- ➤ Third Normal Form
- ➤ Fourth Normal Form
- ➤ Fifth Normal Form

NORMALIZATION

Normalization theory was first described by E. F. Codd and is used in practice to aid in database design. The overall goals of the normalization process are to–

- Arrange data so that it can be represented in tabular form where each row-column position contains a single data element (no repeating groups).
- Ensure that data elements are associated with the correct keys, and thereby minimize data redundancy.

Normalization involves a series of steps that change the structure of the various records that make up a database by placing the data into a series of different forms called *first normal form, second normal form,* and so on.

FIRST NORMAL FORM

The first step of the normalization process is to place the data into first normal form. This involves the removal of repeating groups. We remove repeating groups by simply creating a separate record for each of the elements in the repeating group. Suppose we begin with the following employee data:

Employee

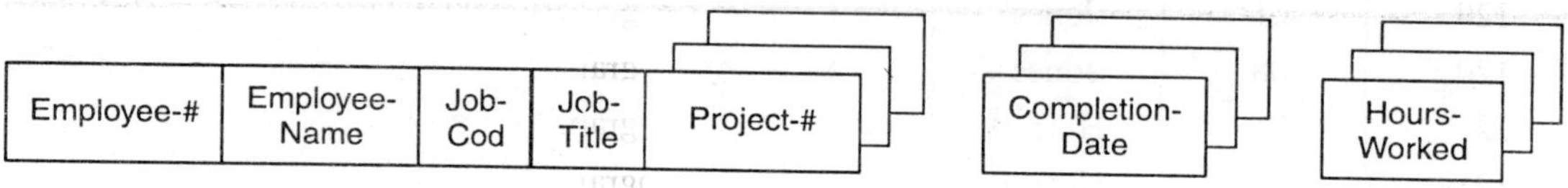

Here, a given record stores information about a number of different projects that a particular employee has worked on.

To represent this data in tabular form, we generate a separate record for each project by repeating the employee information in each record. Here is how the data would look in tabular form; each row represents a separate record occurrence:

Employee

Employee-#	Employee-Name	Job-Code	Job-Title	Project-#	Completion-Date	Hours-Worked
120	Jones	1	Programmer	01	7/17	37
120	Jones	1	Programmer	08	1/12	12
121	Harpo	1	Programmer	01	7/17	45
121	Harpo	1	Programmer	08	1/12	21
121	Harpo	1	Programmer	12	3/21	107
270	Garfunkel	2	Analyst	08	1/12	10
270	Garfunkel	2	Analyst	12	3/21	78

273	Selsi	3	Designer	01	7/17	22
274	Abrahms	2	Analyst	12	3/21	41
279	Higgins	1	Programmer	01	7/17	27
279	Higgins	1	Programmer	08	1/12	20
279	Higgins	1	Programmer	12	3/21	51
301	Flannel	1	Programmer	01	7/17	16
301	Flannel	1	Programmer	12	3/21	85
306	McGraw	3	Designer	12	3/21	67

It is generally useful to define a unique key that identifies each record occurrence. In some cases, it is possible to identify a single data element that uniquely identifies each record; in other cases, two or more data elements must be combined to from a *concatenated key*. In this case, we must use both the Employee-# and Project-# data elements as a concatenated key that uniquely identifies each record:

Employee

Employee-#	Project-#	Employee -Name	Job-Code	Job-Title	Completion-Date	Hours-Worked
120	01	Jones	1	Programmer	7/17	37
120	08	Jones	1	Programmer	1/12	12
121	01	Harpo	1	Programmer	7/17	45
121	08	Harpo	1	Programmer	1/12	21
121	12	Harpo	1	Programmer	3/21	107
270	08	Garfunkel	2	Analyst	1/12	10
270	12	Garfunkel	2	Analyst	3/21	78
273	01	Selsi	3	Designer	7/17	22
274	12	Abrahms	2	Analyst	3/21	41
279	01	Higgins	1	Programmer	7/17	27
279	08	Higgins	1	Programmer	1/12	20
279	12	Higgins	1	Programmer	3/21	51
301	01	Flannel	1	Programmer	7/17	16
301	12	Flannel	1	Programmer	3/21	85
306	12	McGraw	3	Designer	3/21	67

One of the goals of normalization is to reduce data redundancy. At this point, it appears that we have instead increased data redundancy by placing the data into first normal form; Job-Code and Job-Title data elements are repeated many times, and the same completion dates are stored multiple times as well. This increase in data redundancy is an important argument for why further normalization steps are required to produce a stable design. A record type that is in first normal form only and has not been further normalized may have many undesirable characteristics, of which data redundancy is only one. We will see how subsequent steps in the normalization process will reduce the redundancy that we have introduced and how additional normalization steps improve the data structure in other important ways as well.

SECOND NORMAL FORM

The second step in the normalization process places the data into *second normal form.* Second normal form involves the idea of *functional dependence.*

Functional Dependence

In general, a given data element, say, data element B, is functionally dependent on some other data element, say, data element A, if for any given value of data element A there is a single value of data element B associated with it. Saying that data element B is functionally dependent on data element A is equivalent to saying that data element A *identifies* data element B. Notice that there are three record occurrences that have an Employee-# value of 121, but in each of those records, the Employee-Name data element value is the same – Harpo.

Employee

Employee-#	Project-#	Employee -Name	Job-Code	Job-Title	Completion-Date	Hours-Worked
120	01	Jones	1	Programmer	7/17	37
120	08	Jones	1	Programmer	1/12	12
121	01	Harpo	1	Programmer	7/17	45
121	08	Harpo	1	Programmer	1/12	21
121	12	Harpo	1	Programmer	3/21	107
270	08	Garfunkel	2	Analyst	1/12	10
270	12	Garfunkel	2	Analyst	3/21	78
273	01	Selsi	3	Designer	7/17	22
274	12	Abrahms	2	Analyst	3/21	41
279	01	Higgins	1	Programmer	7/17	27
279	08	Higgins	1	Programmer	1/12	20
279	12	Higgins	1	Programmer	3/21	51
301	01	Flannel	1	Programmer	7/17	16
301	12	Flannel	1	Programmer	3/21	85
306	12	McGraw	3	Designer	3/21	67

A similar relationship exists between the Employee-# and Employee-Name data elements in the other record occurrences that have the same Employee-# value. Therefore, as long as we assume that no two employees can have the same employee number, Employee-Name is functionally dependent on Employee-#. We can use the same argument to show that Job-Code and Job-Title are also functionally dependent on Employee-#.

Full Functional Dependence

In some cases, a data element will not be functionally dependent on a single data element but will be functionally dependent on a group of data elements. For example, Hours-Worked is functionally dependent on the combination of Employee-# and Project-#. This leads to the idea of *full functional dependence*. A data element can be said to be fully functionally dependent on some collection of other data elements when it is functionally dependent on the entire set but not on any subset of that collection. Hours-Worked is fully functionally dependent on Employee-# and Project-#. However, Completion-Date is not fully functionally dependent on Employee-# and Project-#, since Completion-Date is functionally dependent on Project-# alone.

To place into second normal form a group of data elements that is in first normal form, we identify all the full functional dependencies that exist and create a separate record for each set of these. We begin by identifying a likely key – in this case Employee-# - and determining which other data elements are fully functionally dependent on that key. Employee-Name, Job-Code, and Job-Title are fully functionally dependent on Employee-#, so we move them to a separate Employee record type that has Employee-# as its primary key:

Employee

Employee-#	Employee-Name	Job-Code	Job-Title
120	Jones	1	Programmer
121	Harpo	1	Programmer
270	Garfunkel	2	Analyst
273	Selsi	3	Designer
274	Abrahms	2	Analyst
279	Higgins	1	Programmer
301	Flannel	1	Programmer
306	McGraw	3	Designer

Of the remaining data elements, Completion-Date is dependent on Project-#, so we move the Project-# and Completion-Date data elements to a separate Project record type that has Project-# as the primary key:

Project

Project-#	Completion-Date
01	7/17
08	1/17
12	3/21

This leaves the Hours-Worked data element. Hours-Worked is fully functionally dependent on the concatenated key that consists of Employee-# and Project-#. So we create a third record type called Hours that consists of Employee-#, Project-#, and Hours-Worked. The key of the Hours-Worked record type consists of Employee-# and Project-#:

Hours

Employee-#	Project-#	Hours-Worked
120	01	37
120	08	12
121	01	45
121	08	21
121	12	107
270	08	10
270	12	78
273	01	22
274	12	41
279	01	27
279	08	20
279	12	51
301	01	16
301	12	85
306	12	67

We can now say that our set of data elements is in second normal form because it is first normal form and every non-key data element is fully functionally dependent on the primary key of its record type.

Notice that we have repeated the Employee-# data element in two of the records (Employee, Hours) and that we have repeated the Project-# data element in two of the records (Project, Hours).

Duplicating data element types is perfectly valid and often occurs when converting records to second normal form. With a relational database, these duplicate data element types implement the relationships that exist between the record types. With a networked-structured database, these data element duplications can later be removed and the relationships between record types can be implemented using sets.

Notice that placing the data into second normal form has reduced much of the redundancy that existed in the original set of first normal form records. Job-Code and Job-Title data element values now appear only once per employee, and Completion-Date data element values appear only once per project.

Now that we have our data in the second normal form, we can point out another undesirable characteristic of a record type that is in first normal form only. When our data was in first normal form, we had a single record type whose primary key consisted of Employee-# and Project-#. With that structure, we needed to have valid values for both Employee-# and Project-# in order to create a new record occurrence. This means that we would be unable to store a record occurrence for an employee who is currently not assigned to a project unless we used a null Project-# value. Similarly, we would be unable to store a record occurrence for a project that currently has no employees assigned to it without using a null Employee-# value.

With our data elements in second normal form, we can add a new employee by adding only a employee record occurrence. After the new employee has been assigned to a project and has logged some time on that project, we can add an Hours record occurrence to describe the project assignment and the number of hours logged. In a similar manner, we can add only a Project record occurrence to describe a new project.

THIRD NORMAL FORM

The third step in the normalization process involves the idea of *transitive dependence*. Suppose we have a record type with data elements A, B, and C:

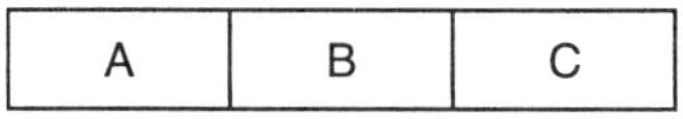

If data element C is functionally dependent on data element B, and data element B is functionally dependent on data element A, then data element C is functionally dependent on data element A:

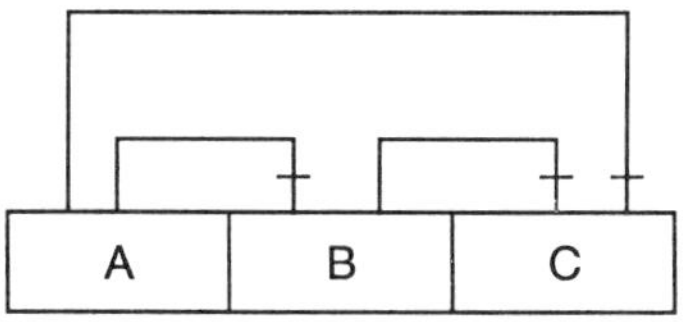

If similar dependencies are not true in the opposite direction (*i.e.*, data element A is not functionally dependent on data element B or data element B is not functionally dependent on data element C), then data element C is said to be transitively dependent on data element A:

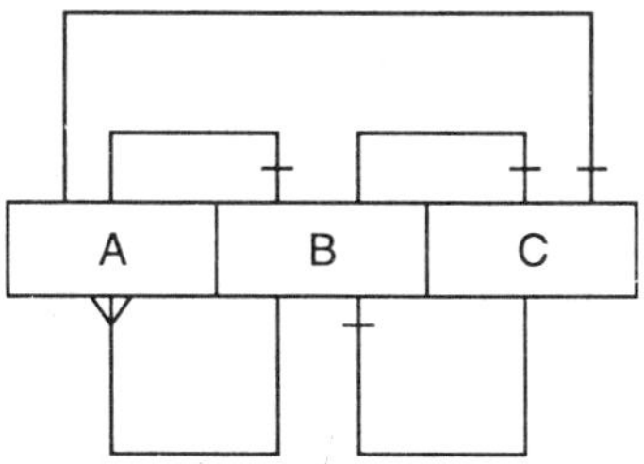

We said earlier that Job-Code and Job-Title were functionally dependent on Employee-#:

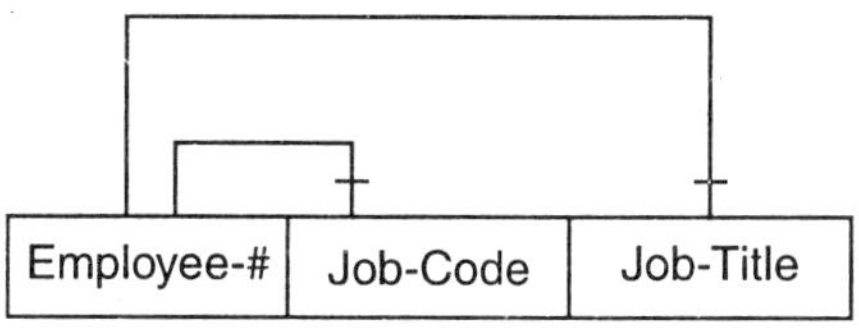

Assuming there is only one job title associated with a given job code, Job-Title is functionally dependent on Job-Code:

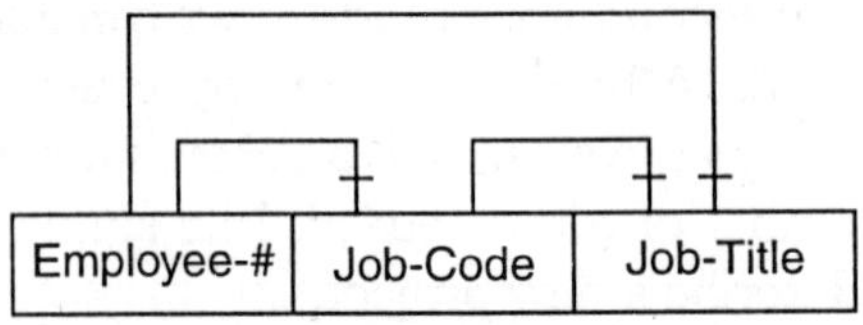

In the reverse direction Job-Code is functionally dependent on Job-Title as long as a given job title is associated with only one job code. However, many employees may have the same job code. So Employee-# is not functionally dependent on Job-Code. This means that Job-Title is transitively dependent on Employee-#:

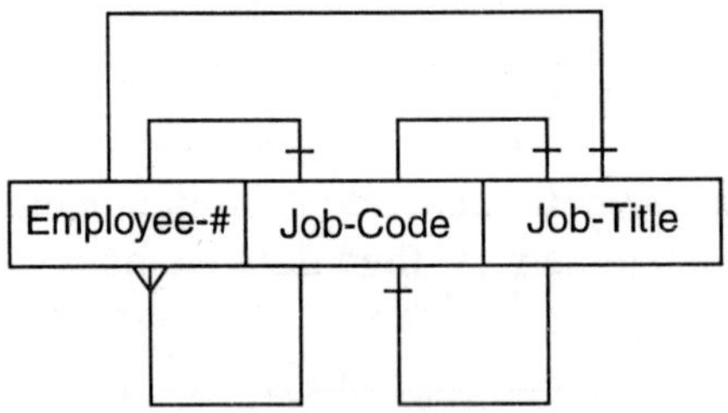

To place our data in third normal form, we must remove transitive dependencies. This is done by placing the Job-Title data element in a separate record type called Jobs with Job-Code as its primary key. The following shows the data after it has been placed into third normal form:

Employee

Employee-#	Employee-Name	Job-Code
120	Jones	1
121	Harpo	1
270	Garfunkel	2
273	Selsi	3
274	Abrahms	2
279	Higgins	1
301	Flannel	1
306	McGraw	3

Jobs

Job-Code	Job-Title
1	Programmer
2	Analysis
3	Designer

Project

Project-#	Completion-Date
01	7/17
08	1/12
12	3/21

Hours

Employee-#	Project-#	Hours-Worked
120	01	37
120	08	12
121	01	45
121	08	21
121	12	107
270	08	10
270	12	78
273	01	22
274	12	41
279	01	27
279	08	20
279	12	51
301	01	16
301	12	85
306	12	67

A record type is said to be in third normal form if it is second normal form and every non-key data element is non-transitively dependent on the primary key. We can give an informal definition of third normal form by saying that in third normal form, all the data elements of a record type are functionally dependent on the key, the whole key, and nothing but the key.

Placing data into third normal form eliminates additional potentially undesirable characteristics of data that is in only first or second normal form. The preceding set of records shows that a job title associated with a given job code now appears only in one place instead of appearing for each employee that has that job code. This makes it easier to change a job title, since the change has to be made in only one place. Also, we can now add a new job code with its associated job title even though no employee has yet been assigned that job code. And we will not lose the job title if we temporarily have no employees assigned a given job code.

FOURTH NORMAL FORM

In the great majority of cases, placing data into third normal form provides a sufficient level of normalization. Higher levels of normalization are possible, however, and it is occasionally beneficial to place into *fourth normal form*.

Suppose that an employee can be assigned to several projects concurrently. Also suppose that an employee can possess a series of skills. If we record this information in a single record type, we need to use all three data elements as the key, since no other data element grouping produces unique record identification.

Employee-Project-Skill

Employee-#	Project-#	Skill
120	01	Design
120	01	Program
120	01	Document
120	08	Design
120	08	Program
120	08	Document

Using a single record type, like the foregoing one, it is not desirable because values have to be repeated, which could cause consistency problems when updating. However, since there are no data elements in this record that are not part of the key, the record is in third normal form. We can represent the relationships in this record in a simpler manner if we split them into the following two separate all-key record types:

Employee-Project

Employee-#	Project-#
120	01
120	08

Employee-Skill

Employee-#	Skill
120	Design
120	Program
120	Document

These records are in fourth normal form. Fourth normal form involves the idea of multi-valued dependencies, in which a given value for a single data element identifies multiple values of another data element. A multi-valued dependency is defined in terms of the set of values of one data element type that is associated with a given pair of values from two other data element types. Look again at our original three data element record occurrences:

Employee-Project-Skill

Employee-#	Project-#	Skill
120	01	Design
120	01	Program
120	01	Document
120	08	Design
120	08	Program
120	08	Document

The relationship between Employee-# and Project-# is a multi-valued dependency because for each pair of (Employee-# / Skill) values, the associated set of Project-# values is determined only by Employee-# and is independent of Skill. Similarly, the relationship between Employee-# and Skill is a multi-valued dependency, since the set of Skill values for an (Employee-# / Project-#) pair is independent of Project-#. Conversion to fourth normal form involves decomposing the original record type into multiple record types so that the multi-valued dependencies are eliminated.

Notice that the two individual record types better represent the true relationships between the data elements because there is no real relationship between projects and skills. Also, there is less redundant data when we use two separate records, and the update behavior of the database is better as well. For example, if an employee acquires a new skill, we simply add a new Employee-Skill record occurrence. With the single record type, we would have to add multiple record occurrences, one for each of the projects the employee is assigned to.

Another way of looking at fourth normal form is that it gives us a good way of handling multiple repeating groups by placing each of them into separate record types. In actual practice, the earlier steps of normalization often identify such repeating groups and remove them, thus producing third normal form records that are already also in fourth normal form.

FIFTH NORMAL FORM

Fifth normal form is of interest mainly to users of relational database management systems that will be performing relational operations on the tables that make up the database. The relational operations that are concerned with fifth normal form are quite simple, so this discussion of fifth normal form can be understood even if the reader has no background in the relational database architecture.

In all the normalization steps that we have discussed so far, we have split record types into their constituent parts by performing what is essentially a relational *project operation*. A *project* operation produces a new set of record occurrences that contains all the original record occurrences but only a subset of the data elements from them. Any record occurrences that contain exactly the same values as some other record occurrence are then eliminated from the result. For example, let us begin with the following set of record occurrences that we looked at previously:

Employee-Project-Skill

Employee-#	Project-#	Skill
120	01	Design
120	01	Program
120	01	Document
120	08	Design
120	08	Program
120	08	Document

One projection of these set of records would produce a new set with only Employee-# and Project-# data elements:

Employee-Project

Employee-#	Project-#
120	01
120	01
120	01
120	08
120	08
120	08

Eliminating redundant occurrences, the final result would be:

Employee-Project

Employee-#	Project-#
120	01
120	08

In all the previous examples, we were able to split a set of record occurrences into a set of its projections that together contain all the original data elements while still retaining all the data contained in the original set of records. In other words, we were able to recombine the constituent sets of record occurrences to exactly recreate the original set of records.

There exist, however, some set of records whose record types are in fourth normal form and that contain three data element types but cannot be split into two projections and then recombined to form the original set of record occurrences. This phenomenon occurs because of the particular combination of data element values that exists in the records and is result of the inherent relationships in the data. Consider the following set of records:

Employee-Project-Skill

Employee-#	Project-#	Skill
120	01	Design
120	08	Program
120	01	Program
205	01	Program

In the preceding set of records, an employee is assigned to one or more projects and uses one or more skills on each project. However, in this case the particular combinations of data element values imply that there is a relationship not only between employees and skills (an employee has a particular skill) but also between projects and skills (certain skills are employed by each project). We can interpret these relationships to mean that an employee uses a skill that he or she possesses on a project only if that skill is *employed* by that project. This means that employees may *have* skills that are not *used* on projects to which they are assigned.

At first glance, the foregoing set of records seems to have the same characteristics as the records we looked at when examining fourth normal form. However, suppose we split the above set of records into two of its projections as we did earlier:

Employee-Project

Employee-#	Project-#
120	01
120	08
205	01

Employee-Skill

Employee-#	Skill
120	Design
120	Program
205	Program

Since we have two sets of records that together contain all the data elements from the original set of records, it appears as though these two new sets of records are equivalent to the original set of records. Let us now perform a relational join operation in an attempt to recreate the original records. A relational join operation combines two sets of records and results in a new set that combines all the data element types from both sets of records. The join operation is based on data element values that are common between the two sets of records. In this case, the resulting set of records is formed by matching up the Employee-# values from both sets of records. By performing the join we get the following result:

Employee-Project-Skill

Employee-#	Project-#	Skill
120	01	Design
120	08	Design
120	01	Program
120	08	Program
205	01	Program

Notice that there is now an extra record occurrence that the original set of records did not have (the second record occurrence). Project 08 now appears to use design skills when the original data shows no employee performing design tasks for that project. The reason this occurs is that the two new sets of records we created by performing *project* operations on the original set of records do not accurately represent all the associations inherent in the original records. In this case, the original combination of data element values implies that there *does* exist a relationship between projects and skills; each project only uses certain types of skills. This relationship is lost when we decompose the records into the two projections shown earlier.

It is interesting to note that the original set of records does *not* contain multi-valued dependencies and thus is already in fourth normal form. The set of Project-# values associated with each Employee-Skill pair is dependent on both Employee-# and Skill and not just on Employee-#. Similarly, sets of Skill values are dependent on both Employee-# and Project-#. Thus, it is not correct to separate the set of records into only *two* projections. Doing so loses one of the relationships.

This record can, however, be further normalized by placing the data into *fifth normal form*. This involves decomposing the set of records into *three* projections, thus retaining all three relationships that exist between the various data elements:

Employee-Project

Employee-#	Project-#
120	01
120	08
205	01

Employee-Skill

Employee-#	Skill
120	Design
120	Program
205	Program

Project-Skill

Project-#	Skill
01	Design
08	Program
01	Program

To rejoin the three sets of records, we first perform a relational join on the first two sets to form an intermediate result. We then join the intermediate set with the third set of records to form the final result of the three-way join operation. The result of the first join operation in this case corresponds to an intermediate result that shows all the skills that *might* be used on projects:

Employee-Project-Skill

Employee-#	Project-#	Skill
120	01	Design
120	08	Design
120	01	Program
120	08	Program
205	01	Program

The third set of records specifies the skills that each project *actually* uses. We then join the intermediate set with the third set:

Employee-Project-Skill

Employee-#	Project-#	Skill
120	01	Design
120	08	Design
120	01	Program
120	08	Program
205	01	Program

Project-Skill

Project-#	Skill
01	Design
08	Program
01	Program

In performing this join, we match up sets of both Project-# and Skill data element values. Because values for both Project 08 and Skill Design do not exist in both sets of records, the spurious record is eliminated, and we get a result that is identical to our original set of record occurrences:

Employee-Project-Skill

Employee-#	Project-#	Skill
120	01	Design
120	08	Program
120	01	Program
205	01	Program

The projections from the previous example, which can be rejoined to produce the original set of records, are in fifth normal form. This constraint on which projections can be validly rejoined is called *join dependency*.

A set of records that is in fourth normal form but not in fifth normal form has strange update behavior. Consider the following two record occurrences that show an employee using design skills on one project and programming skills on another project:

Employee-Project-Skill

Employee-#	Project-#	Skill
120	01	Design
120	08	Program

Suppose we added a new Employee record occurrence for an employee who uses programming skills on Project 01:

Employee-Project-Skill

Employee-#	Project-#	Skill
120	01	Design
120	08	Program
205	01	Program

The addition of that record occurrence on first glance seems to be valid. But let us now again decompose this new set of records into its three fifth normal form projections:

Employee-Project

Employee-#	Project-#
120	01
120	08
205	01

Employee-Skill

Employee-#	Skill
120	Design
120	Program
205	Program

Project-Skill

Project-#	Skill
01	Design
08	Program
01	Program

We now rejoin the three preceding sets of records, producing the following result:

Employee-Project-Skill

Employee-#	Project-#	Skill
120	01	Design
120	08	Program
120	01	Program
205	01	Program

Notice that we have an extra record occurrence that did not exist in the set of records that we began with. This result at first seems intuitively wrong. Does this mean that the three projections are not in fifth normal form? No, it means that it is not valid to add only that one record occurrence to the non-fifth normal form set of records. By adding the one new record to the non-fifth normal form set of records, we are actually stating three facts:

1. Employee 205 has been assigned to Project 01.
2. Employee 205 has programming skills.
3. Project 01 now uses programming skills.

By analyzing the contents of the original set of records, together with the foregoing facts, we can see that when we add the new record for Employee 205, Project 01, and the *programming* skill, then we must also add a new record for Employee 120, Project 01, and the *programming* skill. This is because Employee 120 already had the programming skill and was already assigned to Project 01; thus, Employee 120's programming skill is now available to Project 01, which, when we added the first record, we stated that Project 01 is now using.

The join dependencies that exist in the single set of records that is not in fifth normal form create constraints on the updating of the database. If the records are left in fourth normal form, then we must sometimes add two records at a time instead of only one. There can be similar problems with deletion. It is often quite difficult to determine when these updating anomalies can occur. Such arcane relationships are impossible for mere mortals to discern during normal update operations. But, by using the three individual record types (in fifth normal form) rather than the composite record type, we can be sure that all three facts stated above are reflected properly and completely in the database. When the data is in fifth normal form, we can add the Employee 205 data in a straightforward manner by simply adding a new record occurrence of each of the three record types. The two new records will then automatically appear in the result if we rejoin the three fifth normal form individual sets of records.

Placing the data into the fifth normal form also allows us to add data that couldn't be added when using the composite record type. For example, we can show an employee having a particular skill by adding an Employee-Skill record occurrence, even though no project currently uses that skill. This information cannot be added to the set of composite records without using a null Project-# value.

Research is continuing on normalization, and even higher forms of normalization have been identified. However, it can be shown that fifth normal form is the highest form of normalization that is possible with respect to the relational operations of projection and join, and fifth normal form is the highest form of normalization that is generally required in practice.

6 Relations, Join, Reports

Objectives :

- Foreign Key
- Join
- Set Operators
- Group by Clause
- Having Clause
- Subquery
- SQL*PLUS Report Commands

  Lab Assignment-8

  Lab Assignment-9

  Lab Assignment-10

FOREIGN KEY

Foreign key represents relationships between two or more tables. A foreign key is a column or a group of columns whose values are derived from the primary key or unique key of any other table.

The table in which the foreign key is defined is called a foreign table. The table that defines the primary or unique key and is referred by the foreign key is called master table.

The master table can be referred in the foreign key definition by using the **REFERENCES.** If the name of the table is not specified, by default, Oracle refers the primary key in the master table.

The syntax of the foreign key definition is given below:

[CONSTRAINT constraint-name]
FOREIGN KEY (column-comma-list) references-definition

Here the 'column-comma-list' is the name of the column or column that form the foreign key and the 'references-definition' take the following form:

REFERENCES base-table-name [(column-comma-list)]
[MATCH {FULL | PARTIAL}]
[ON DELETE {NO ACTION | CASCADE | SET DEFAULT | SET NULL}]
[ON UPDATE {NO ACTION | CASCADE | SET DEFAULT | SET NULL}]

The 'column-comma-list' in the FOREIGN KEY clause identifies the column or column combination that constitutes the foreign key. The 'base-table-name' in the reference-definition identifies the referenced column.

The optional 'MATCH' clause has no effect and can safely be ignored, if either the foreign key consists of a single column or if every component column of the foreign key has 'null not allowed specification'. But if any of these conditions are not true then MATCH will have significance. The 'MATCH FULL' option requires that foreign keys in a child table fully match a primary key in the parent table. The MATCH PARTIAL option allows null values in parts of the foreign key as long as the non-null values match the corresponding parts to some primary key in the parent table.

The optional 'ON DELETE' and 'ON UPDATE' clauses denote the referential actions. The idea behind the referential actions is that it might sometimes be possible to maintain referential integrity, not simply by rejecting an update that would violate it, but rather performing another compensating action in addition to the one that is requested.

The **ON DELETE** and **ON UPDATE** define the delete and update rules for the referenced candidate key.

1. Specifying the **'NO ACTION'** option is equivalent to omitting the ON DELETE / UPDATE clause entirely.
2. **ON DELETE CASCADE.** This option tells the RDBMS that when a parent row is deleted, all the child rows should also be automatically deleted from the child table.

For example, deleting a department from the DEPARTMENT table will result in the deletion of all the employees in that department from the EMPLOYEE table.

3. **ON UPDATE CASCADE.** This option tells the RDBMS that when a primary key value is changed in the parent row, the corresponding foreign key values in all its child rows should also automatically be changed in the child table, to match the new primary key value. Changing the department ID in the DEPARTMENT table will change the ID of that department for all the employees belonging to that department in the EMPLOYEE table.
4. **ON DELETE SET DEFAULT.** In this case, every component of the foreign key must have a defined value. So when the parent row is deleted, each component of the foreign key is set to the applicable default value for all child rows in the child table.
5. **ON UPDATE SET DEFAULT.** When a primary key value in a parent row is updated the components of the foreign key values in all of its child rows in the child table should automatically be set to the default values.
6. **ON DELETE SET NULL.** In this case, every component of the foreign key must have nulls allowed. So when the parent row is deleted, each component of the foreign key is set to NULL for the foreign key values of all the child rows in the child table.
7. **ON UPDATE SET NULL.** When the parent row is updated, the components of the foreign key that correspond to the updated components of the candidate key are set to NULL in all matching rows in the child table.

Consider the following example:

```
Create table LIST
(Book_id        char(3)          not null,
title           char(40),
Author_id       char(3),
Publisher_id    char(3)
Category_id     char(3)
Year            date
Price           numeric(12,2)
Primary key(Book_id),
Foreign Key(Author_id)      references author
            On delete cascade
            On update cascade,
Foreign Key(Publisher_id)   references publisher
            On delete cascade
            On update cascade,
Foreign Key(Category_id)    references category
            On delete cascade
            On update cascade);
```

Insert, Update and Delete Operation in Foreign Key

The existence of a foreign key implies that the table with the foreign key is related to the master table from which the foreign key is derived. A foreign key must have a corresponding primary key or unique key value in the master table.

If the user tries to delete a record in the master table when corresponding records exist in the foreign table oracle will display an error message.

Principles of Foreign Key/References Constraint

(*a*) Rejects an Insert or Update of a value, if a corresponding value does not currently exist in the master table.

(*b*) Rejects a Delete for the master table if corresponding records in the foreign table exist.

(*c*) Foreign key must reference a primary key or unique column in primary table.

(*d*) Foreign key requires that the foreign key column and the constraint column have same data types.

Example : For maintaining the record of students in a college we can create two tables as :

(*i*) Master Table Student_Address will contain only one record for every student like Roll_No, Name, Address, Place, Pin.

(*ii*) Marks Table will store more than one record for every student, *i.e.*, every time the student appears for an exam, a record will be added to the marks table like Roll_No, Subject, Exam_Date, Marks. So marks table will be considered as transaction file.

```
SQL > Create Table Student_Address
      (Roll_No        Number(4) Primary Key,
      Name            Varchar2(20),
      Address         Varchar2(20),
      Place           Varchar2(10),
      PIN             Number(6) );
SQL > Create Table Marks
      (Roll_No        Number(4) references Student_address on delete cascade,
      Subject         Varchar2(10),
      Exam_Date       Date,
      Marks           Number (3) );
```

Master Table

Student_Address

Roll_No	Name	Address	Place	Pin
1.	Don Mario	1, Alistonia	Tokio	21398
2.	Khaliona	2, Amaltash	Japan	23456
3.	Lee Vinn	5, King Estate	England	67864
4.	Uccharal	9, Queen Street	Singapore	89765
5.	Breet Lee	90, Alistonia	Kohima	98765

Foreign Table

Marks

Roll_No	Subject	Exam_Date	Marks
1.	Oracle	12-Jan-2004	90
2.	C++	12-Feb-2004	95
3.	OOPs	12-March-2004	85
4.	Windows-NT	12-March-2004	80

Can the marks file contain a row for roll number 10 from the above table ?

No it cannot and that is because roll number 10 does not exist in the student master table or there is no reference for that number in the Parent table. This is referential integrity which ensures that there are no rows in the transaction table if there is no reference for it in the master table.

Foreign Key Constraint at the Column Level

Syntax

```
columnname datatype(size) REFERENCES tablename [(columnname)]
[ON DELETE CASCADE]
```

Example: Create a table sales_order_detail table with its primary key as d_order_no and prod_no. The foreign key is d_order_no, referencing column order_no in the sale_order table.

```
SQL > Create table sale_order
    ( order_no  varchar2  (8) PRIMARY KEY,
      order_date    date,
      client_no     number  (6),
      order_status  varchar2(10) );
```

```
SQL > Create table sales_order_detail
      (d_order_no varchar2 (8) REFERENCES sale_order,
      prod_no     varchar2 (8),
      qty_ordered number (9),
      prod_price  number (6, 2),
       PRIMARY KEY (d_order_no,prod_no) );
```

In the above example the reference key word points to the table sale_order. The table sale_order has the column order_no as its primary key column. So when no column is specified in the foreign key definition, Oracle applies a default link to the primary key column like order_no of the table sale_order.

Foreign key definition will be specified as given below :

```
(d_order_no varchar2(8) REFERENCES sale_order (order_no) )
```

Foreign Key at the Table Level

Syntax

Foreign Key (column name) References tablename [(column name)]

Example :

```
SQL > Create table sales_order_detail
      (d_order_no varchar2 (8) REFERENCES sale_order,
       prod_no     varchar2 (8),
       qty_ordered number (9),
       prod_price  number (6, 2),
       PRIMARY KEY (d_order_no,prod_no),
       Foreign Key (d_order_no) REFERENCES sale_order );
```

JOIN

All of the queries up until this point have been useful with the exception of one major limitation—that is, we can select only one table at a time with SELECT statement. There is one of the most beneficial features of SQL & relational database systems - the "**Join**". "Join" makes relational database systems "relational".

Joins allow to link data from two or more tables together into a single query result from one single SELECT statement.

The FROM clause allows more than 1 table in its list, however simply listing more than one table will very rarely produce the expected results. The rows from one table must be correlated with the rows of the others. This correlation is known as joining.

pno	descr	color
P1	Wid	Blue
P2	Wid	Red
P3	Dongle	Green

P Table (Parts)

sno	name	city
S1	Pierre	Paris
S2	John	London
S3	Mario	Rome

S Table (Suppliers)

sno	pno	qty
S1	P1	NULL
S2	P1	200
S3	P1	1000
S3	P2	200

Sp Table

An example can best illustrate the relation behind joins. The following query:

SELECT * FROM sp, p

produces:

sno	pno	qty	pno	descry	color
S1	P1	NULL	P1	Wid	Blue
S1	P1	NULL	P2	Wid	Red
S1	P1	NULL	P3	Dongle	Green
S2	P1	200	P1	Wid	Blue
S2	P1	200	P2	Wid	Red
S2	P1	200	P3	Dongle	Green
S3	P1	1000	P1	Wid	Blue
S3	P1	1000	P2	Wid	Red
S3	P1	1000	P3	Dongle	Green
S3	P2	200	P1	Wid	Blue
S3	P2	200	P2	Wid	Red
S3	P2	200	P3	Dongle	Green

Each row in SP is arbitrarily combined with each row in P, giving 12 result rows (4 rows in SP × 3 rows in P.) This is known as a **cartesian product**.

Equi Join or Inner Join

A join, which is based on equalities, is called an equi join.The equi join combining rows that have equivalent values for the specified columns.

A more usable query would correlate the rows from SP with rows from P, for instance matching on the common column - pno:

```
SELECT *
FROM sp, p
WHERE sp.pno = p.pno
```

This produces:

sno	pno	qty	pno	descry	color
S1	P1	NULL	P1	Wid	Blue
S2	P1	200	P1	Wid	Blue
S3	P1	1000	P1	Wid	Blue
S3	P2	200	P2	Wid	Red

Rows for each part in P are combined with rows in SP for the same part by matching on part number (pno). In this query, the WHERE Clause provides the join predicate, matching pno from p with pno from sp.

The join in this example is known as an **inner equi-join**. equi meaning that the join predicate uses = (equals) to match the join columns. Other types of joins use different comparison operators. *For example,* a query might use a *greater-than* join.

The term *inner* means only rows that match are included. Rows in the first table that have no matching rows in the second table are excluded and vice versa (in the above join, the row in *p* with *pno* P3 is not included in the result.) An *outer* join includes unmatched rows in the result.

More than 2 tables can participate in a join. This is basically just an extension of a 2 table join. 3 tables—*a, b, c,* might be joined in various ways:

- *a* joins *b* which joins *c*
- *a* joins *b* and the join of *a* and *b* joins *c*
- *a* joins *b* and *a* joins *c*

Plus several other variations. With *inner* joins, this structure is not explicit. It is implicit in the nature of the join predicates. With *outer* joins, it is explicit.

This query performs a 3 table join:

```
SELECT name, qty, descr, color
FROM s, sp, p
WHERE s.sno = sp.sno
AND sp.pno = p.pno
```

It joins S to SP and SP to P, producing:

name	qty	descr	color
Pierre	NULL	Wid	Blue
John	200	Wid	Blue
Mario	1000	Wid	Blue
Mario	200	Wid	Red

Note that the *order* of tables listed in the FROM clause should have no significance, nor does the order of join predicates in the WHERE clause.

Another example:

```
SELECT employee_info.employeeid, employee_info.lastname,
employee_sales.comission
FROM employee_info, employee_sales
WHERE employee_info.employeeid = employee_sales.employeeid;
```

This statement will select the employeeid, lastname (from the employee_info table), and the comission value (from the employee_sales table) for all of the rows where the employeeid in the employee_info table matches the employeeid in the employee_sales table.

Non Equi-Join

A non equi join specifies the relationship between columns belonging to different tables by making use of the relational operators (>,<,<=,>=,<>) other than = (equal).

```
SQL > Select item, qty_order from item, order where (item.order < order.qty_order) ;
```

Outer Joins

An *inner* join excludes rows from either table that don't have a matching row in the other table. An *outer* join provides the ability to include unmatched rows in the query results. The outer join combines the unmatched row in one of the tables with an artificial row for the other table. This artificial row has all columns set to *null*.

The outer join is specified in the FROM clause and has the following general format:

table-1 { LEFT | RIGHT | FULL } OUTER JOIN table-2 ON predicate-1

predicate-1 is a join predicate for the outer join. It can only reference columns from the joined tables. The LEFT, RIGHT or FULL specifiers give the type of join:

- LEFT—only unmatched rows from the left side table (*table-1*) are retained
- RIGHT—only unmatched rows from the right side table (*table-2*) are retained
- FULL—unmatched rows from both tables (*table-1* and *table-2*) are retained

Outer join example:

```
SELECT pno, descr, color, sno, qty
FROM P LEFT OUTER JOIN Sp ON P.pno = Sp.pno
```

pno	descr	color	sno	qty
P1	Wid	Blue	S1	NULL
P1	Wid	Blue	S2	200
P1	Wid	Blue	S3	1000
P2	Wid	Red	S3	200
P3	Dongle	Green	NULL	NULL

We can use outer join using (+) plus symbol also:

Example :

Table : Player (ID_NO is the primary key)

ID_No	NAME
10	Sachin Tandulkar
20	Leander Paes
30	Mahesh Bhupathi
40	Saurav Ganguly

MATCH (MatchNO is the primary key, ID_NO is the foreign key)

MATCHNO	ID_NO	MATCH_DATE	OPPONENT
1	20	10-Aug-2003	Washington
2	30	12-Aug-2003	Vishwanathan
3	20	13-Aug-2003	Sampras
4	30	20-Mar-2004	London

SQL > Select player.id_no, name,match_date,opponent from player,match
Where player.id_no = match.id_no (+);

Above query will return following result :

ID_NO	NAME	MATCH_DATE	OPPONENT
10	Sachin Tandulkar	NULL	NULL
20	Leander Paes	10-Aug-2003	Washington
20	Leander Paes	13-Aug-2003	Sampras
30	Mahesh Bhupathi	12-Aug-2003	Vishwanathan
30	Mahesh Bhupathi	20-Mar-2004	London
40	Saurav Ganguly	NULL	NULL

If matching records are not present in the second file, certain names from the first file are not listed at all.To retrieve these records also we have to perform an outer join operation using the outer join operator(+). The data, which is not available in the second file, will be presented as null values.

Table Alias

The name of the table can be coded with an alias making the query easier to code. Table alias are used to make multiple table queries shorter and more readable. The alias can be used instead of the table name throughout the query.

Example :

SQL > Select PLAYER.RoLLNO, NAME, MATCH_DATE,OPPONENT FROM PLAYER, MATCH WHERE PLAYER.ROLLNO = MATCH.ROLLNO;

We can write the above query using alias as given below :

SQL > Select P.ROLLNO, NAME, MATCH_DATE, OPPONENT FROM PLAYER P, MATCH M WHERE P.ROLLNO = M.ROLLNO;

In the above example alias 'P' and 'M' is used for table names player and match. To retrieve all the columns from both the table we can write P.* and M.* also.

Self Joins

A query can join a table to itself. Self joins have a number of real world uses. For example, a self join can determine which parts have more than one supplier:

```
SELECT DISTINCT a.pno
FROM Sp a, Sp b
WHERE a.pno = b.pno
AND a.sno < > b.sno
```

pno
P1

As illustrated in the above example, self joins use *correlation* names to distinguish columns in the select list and where predicate. In this case, the references to the same table are renamed—*a* and *b*.

SET OPERATORS

The SQL UNION operator combines the results of two queries into a *composite* result. The following set operators are used by SQL in joining queries to retrieve rows :

- ➤ UNION
- ➤ UNION ALL
- ➤ INTERSECT
- ➤ MINUS

The columns in the select statement joined using the set operators should strictly follow the rules given below.

- The queries, which are related by a set operator should have the same number of columns and the corresponding columns, must be of the same data type.
- Such a query should not contain any column of type long.
- The label under which the rows are displayed are those from the first select statement.

UNION	Returns all rows returned by either query does not eliminates duplicates.
UNION ALL	Returns all rows returned by either query eliminates including duplicate rows.
INTERSECT	Returns all distinct rows or common rows returned by both queries.A row must exist in both query outputs to be returned in the final result.
MINUS	Produce rows returned by the first query but not the second.

Union

The union operator returns all distinct rows selected by both queries.

```
SQL > SELECT SECTION_ID FROM BOOK
      UNION
      SELECT SECTION_ID FROM SECTION ;
```

section_id
10
5
6
7
9
11

Note that the returned values have been grouped because only rows distinct in both tables are returned.

Union All

Union All returns all rows returned by either query eliminates including duplicate rows.

```
SQL >SELECT SECTION_ID FROM BOOK
     UNION ALL
     SELECT SECTION_ID FROM SECTION;
```

section_id
9
9
10
5
9
6
10
9
11
10
5
6
7
9
11

Now all the rows have been returned (including duplicates).

Intersect

Intersect returns all distinct rows or common rows returned by both queries. A row must exist in both query outputs to be returned in the final result.

If we want to see only the rows that match in both queries than we use INTERSECT.

```
SQL > SELECT SECTION_ID FROM BOOK
      INTERSECT
      SELECT SECTION_ID FROM SECTION;
```

section_id
10
5
6
9
11

Minus

Produce rows returned by the first query but not by the second query.

```
SQL > SELECT SECTION_ID FROM SECTION
      MINUS
      SELECT SECTION_ID FROM BOOK ;
```

section_id
10

Section_id 7 is returned as the only row that doesn't match in both result sets.

GROUP BY CLAUSE

The GROUP BY clause will gather all of the rows together that contain data in the specified column(s) and will allow aggregate functions to be performed on the one or more columns.

GROUP BY operates on the rows from the FROM clause as filtered by the WHERE clause. It collects the rows into groups based on common values in the grouping columns. Except nulls, rows with the same set of values for the grouping columns are placed in the same group. If any grouping column for a row contains a null, the row is given its own group.

GROUP BY was added to SQL because aggregate functions (like SUM) return the aggregate of all column values every time they are called, and without the GROUP BY function it was impossible to find the sum for each individual group of column values.

The syntax for the GROUP BY function is:

GROUP BY clause syntax:

```
SELECT column1,
SUM(column2),
FROM "list-of-tables"
GROUP BY "column-list";
```

Retrieve a list of the highest paid salaries in each dept:

```
SELECT max(salary), dept
FROM employee
GROUP BY dept;
```

This statement will select the maximum salary for the people in each unique department. Basically, the salary for the person who makes the most in each department will be displayed. Their salary and their department will be returned.

Example :

This "Sales" Table:

Company	Amount
NIIT	5500
IBM	4500
NIIT	7100

and this SQL:

SELECT Company, SUM(Amount) FROM Sales;

returns this result:

Company	SUM(Amount)
NIIT	17100
IBM	17100
NIIT	17100

The above code is invalid because the column returned is not part of an aggregate. A GROUP BY clause will solve this problem:

SELECT Company,SUM(Amount) FROM Sales GROUP BY Company;

returns this result:

Company	SUM(Amount)
NIIT	12600
IBM	4500

For example, take a look at the items_ordered table. Let's say we want to group everything of quantity 1 together, everything of quantity 2 together, everything of quantity 3 together, etc. If we like to determine what the largest cost item is for each grouped quantity (all quantity 1's, all quantity 2's, all quantity 3's, etc.), we would enter:

```
SQL > SELECT quantity, max(price) FROM items_ordered
      GROUP BY quantity;
```

Example Using the SUM Function

For example, we also use the SUM function to return the name of the department and the total sales (in the associated department).

```
SELECT department, SUM (sales) as "Total sales"
FROM order_details
GROUP BY department;
```

Because we have listed one column in our SELECT statement that is not encapsulated in the SUM function, we must use a GROUP BY clause. The department field must, therefore, be listed in the GROUP BY section.

Using the grouping the *sp* table on the *pno* column:

Sno	pno	qty	
S1	P1	NULL	'P1' Group
S2	P1	200	
S3	P1	1000	
S3	P2	200	'P2' Group

A Set Function can compute the total quantities for each group:

Sno	pno	qty		qty total
S1	P1	NULL	'P1' Group	1200
S2	P1	200		
S3	P1	1000		
S3	P2	200	'P2' Group	200

Null columns are ignored in computing the summary. The Set Function—SUM, computes the arithmetic sum of a numeric column in a set of grouped/aggregate rows. For example,

```
SELECT pno, SUM(qty)
FROM sp
GROUP BY pno;
```

Pno	
P1	1200
P2	200

Set Functions have the following general format:

set-function ([DISTINCT | ALL] column-1)

Example Using the COUNT Function

For example, we use the COUNT function to return the name of the department and the number of employees (in the associated department) that make over $25,000 / year.

```
SELECT department, COUNT (*) as "Number of employees"
FROM employees
WHERE salary > 25000
GROUP BY department;
```

Example Using the MIN Function

For example, we also use the MIN function to return the name of each department and the minimum salary in the department.

```
SELECT department, MIN (salary) as "Lowest salary"
FROM employees
GROUP BY department;
```

Example Using the MAX Function

For example, we also use the MAX function to return the name of each department and the maximum salary in the department.

```
SELECT department, MAX (salary) as "Highest salary"
FROM employees
GROUP BY department;
```

- COUNT—count of rows
- SUM—arithmetic sum of numeric column
- AVG—arithmetic average of numeric column; should be SUM()/COUNT().
- MIN—minimum value found in column
- MAX—maximum value found in column

The result of the COUNT function is always integer. The result of all other Set Functions is the same data type as the argument.

The Set Functions skip columns with *nulls*, summarizing *non-null* values. COUNT counts rows with non-null values, AVG averages non-null values, and so on. COUNT returns 0 when no non-null column values are found; the other functions return *null* when there are no values to summarize.

A Set Function argument can be a column or an scalar expression.

The DISTINCT and ALL specifiers are optional. ALL specifies that *all* non-null values are summarized; it is the default. DISTINCT specifies that *distinct* column values are summarized; duplicate values are skipped.

Note. DISTINCT has no effect on MIN and MAX results.

COUNT also has an alternate format:

COUNT(*)

Which counts the underlying rows regardless of column contents.

Set Function examples:

SQL > SELECT pno, MIN(sno), MAX(qty), AVG(qty), COUNT(DISTINCT sno)FROM sp GROUP BY pno;

pno				
P1	S1	1000	600	3
P2	S3	200	200	1

SQL > SELECT sno, COUNT(*) parts FROM sp GROUP BY sno;

sno	parts
S1	1
S2	1
S3	2

HAVING clause

The HAVING clause allows to specify conditions on the rows for each group - in other words, which rows should be selected will be based on the specified conditions. The HAVING clause should follow the GROUP BY clause.

HAVING was added to SQL because the WHERE keyword is used to specify conditions to retrieve rows of a table but where clause could not be used against aggregate functions (like SUM, AVG), and without HAVING it would be impossible to test for result conditions.

HAVING clause syntax:

SELECT column1, SUM(column2) FROM "list-of-tables"GROUP BY "column-list" HAVING "condition";

HAVING can best be described by example. Let's say we have an employee table containing the employee's name, department, salary, and age. If we like to select the average salary for each employee in each department, we enter:

```
SELECT dept, avg(salary)
FROM employee
GROUP BY dept;
```

But, let's say that we want ONLY to calculate & display the average if their salary is over 20000:

```
SELECT dept, avg(salary)
FROM employee
GROUP BY dept
HAVING avg(salary) > 20000;
    SQL > SELECT sno, COUNT(*) parts
    FROM sp
    GROUP BY sno
    HAVING COUNT(*) > 1
```

sno	parts
S3	2

SUBQUERY

A subquery is a query within a query. A select statement is used as part of another SQL statement. The outer statement is called the parent and the nested query passes a value to the outer query is called child.The nested query executes first.

Important Rules about Subquery

1. A subquery must produce a single column of data as its result. In other words, the subquery can have only a single select item in its SELECT clause. So you cannot use a 'SELECT *' in a subquery unless the table you are referring has only one column.
2. The ORDER BY clause cannot be specified in a subquery. Since the result of the subquery are used internally and are not displayed to the user, ordering does not make much sense. You can specify the ORDER BY clause in the main query to the order the results.
3. A subquery cannot be a UNION, only a single SELECT statement is allowed.

Example of Nested Subqueries or Predicate Subqueries

1. Get the details of the author whose book are being sold from the book shop

```
SELECT *
FROM AUTHOR
WHERE AUTHOR_NO IN (SELECT AUTHOR_NO
 FROM LIST
 WHERE BOOK_ID IN
 (SELECT DISTINCT BOOK_ID FROM ORDER_DETAILS));
```

2. **Get the ID, Name, Address, City, State and Pin of all the members who have placed an order for the book 'DBMS'.**

```
SELECT * FROM MEMBER WHERE MEMBER_ID IN
(SELECT MEMBER_ID FROM ORDER_SUMMARY WHERE
ORDER_NO IN (SELECT ORDER_NO FROM ORDER_DETAILS
WHERE BOOK_ID = (SELECT BOOK_ID FROM LIST WHERE
TITLE = "DBMS")));
```

3. **Get the title and price of all the books whose price is greater than the average price of the books in the 'COMPUTER' category.**

```
SELECT TITLE FROM LIST WHERE PRICE > (SELECT AVG(PRICE) FROM
LIST WHERE CATEGORY = (SELECT CATEGORY_ID FROM CATEGORY
WHERE DESCRIPTION = "COMPUTER"));
```

Parallel Subqueries

Parallel subqueries include more than one subquery into a query. In other words, a query, which has a compound WHERE clause – more than one component to which subqueries are attached–is a parallel subquery. In the case of parallel subqueries the subqueries will be executed first and the result will be put into the respective places of the outer query, which will then be executed. Consider the following examples:

1. **Get the details of the titles whose price is greater than the average price and whose year of publishing is greater than the average year of publishing.**

```
SELECT TITLE, YEAR, PRICE FROM LIST
WHERE PRICE > ( SELECT AVG (PRICE) FROM LIST)
AND YEAR > (SELECT AVG (YEAR) FROM LIST);
```

2. **Get the details of the authors who have 2 or more books in the list and the price of the books is greater than the average price of the books in the list and the year of publication of the book is after 1999.**

```
SELECT * FROM AUTHOR
WHERE AUTHOR_ID IN (SELECT AUTHOR_ID FROM LIST GROUP BY
AUTHOR_ID HAVING COUNT(*) > =2)
AND AUTHOR_ID IN (SELECT AUTHOR_ID FROM LIST
WHERE PRICE > (SELECT AVG(PRICE) FROM LIST))
AND AUTHOR_ID IN
(SELECT AUTHOR_ID FROM LIST WHERE YEAR > 1999);
```

There are 3 basic types of subqueries in SQL:

- **Predicate Subqueries**—extended logical constructs in the WHERE and HAVING clause.

- **Scalar Subqueries**—standalone queries that return a single value; they can be used anywhere a scalar value is used.
- **Table Subqueries**—queries nested in the FROM clause.

All subqueries must be enclosed in parentheses.

Predicate Subqueries

Predicate subqueries are used in the WHERE and HAVING clause. Each is a special logical construct. Except for EXISTS, predicate subqueries must retrieve one column (in their select list.)

- IN Subquery

The IN Subquery tests whether a scalar value matches the single query column value in any subquery result row. It has the following general format:

value-1 [NOT] IN (query-1)

Using NOT is equivalent to:

NOT value-1 IN (query-1)

For example, to list parts that have suppliers:

```
SELECT *
FROM p
WHERE pno IN (SELECT pno FROM sp);
```

pno	descr	color
P1	Wid	Blue
P2	Wid	Red

The self join example in the previous subsection can be expressed with an IN Subquery:

```
SELECT DISTINCT pno
FROM sp a
WHERE pno IN (SELECT pno FROM sp b WHERE a.sno <> b.sno);
```

pno
P1

Note that the subquery where clause references a column in the outer query (*a.sno*). This is known as an *outer reference*. Subqueries with outer references are sometimes known as *correlated subqueries*.

- **Quantified Subqueries**

A quantified subquery allows several types of tests and can use the full set of comparison operators. It has the following general format:

value-1 {=|>|<|>=|<=|<>} {ANY|ALL|SOME} (query-1)

The comparison operator specifies how to compare *value-1* to the single query column value from each subquery result row. The ANY, ALL, SOME specifiers give the type of match expected. ANY and SOME must match at least one row in the subquery. ALL must match all rows in the subquery.

For example, to list all parts that have suppliers:

```
SELECT *
FROM p
WHERE pno = ANY (SELECT pno FROM sp);
```

pno	descr	color
P1	Wid	Blue
P2	Wid	Red

A self join is used to list the supplier with the highest quantity of each part (ignoring *null* quantities):

```
SELECT *
FROM sp a
WHERE qty >ALL (SELECT qty FROM sp b
    WHERE a.pno = b.pno
    AND a.sno <> b.sno
    AND qty IS NOT NULL);
```

sno	pno	qty
S3	P1	1000
S3	P2	200

Example : Select all the fields of the table SALARY and the name from EMP for those employees who had BASIC less than the average salary.

```
SQL > SELECT SALARY.*,
      EMP_NAME from SALARY, EMP
      WHERE EMP.EMP_NO = SALARY.EMP_NO and
      BASIC < (SELECT AVG(BASIC) FROM SALARY);
```

- **EXISTS Subqueries**

The EXISTS Subquery tests whether a subquery retrieves at least one row, that is, whether a qualifying row *exists.* It has the following general format

EXISTS(query-1)

Any valid EXISTS subquery must contain an *outer reference*. It must be a *correlated subquery*.

Note. The select list in the EXISTS subquery is not actually used in evaluating the EXISTS, so it can contain any valid select list (though * is normally used).

To list parts that have suppliers:

```
SELECT *
FROM p
WHERE EXISTS(SELECT * FROM sp WHERE p.pno = sp.pno);
```

pno	descr	color
P1	Widget	Blue
P2	Widget	Red

Example: To display the names of che employees who belong to SLS department.

```
SELECT EMP_NAME FROM EMP
WHERE EXISTS (SELECT * FROM SALARY WHERE
EMP.EMP_NO = SALARY.EMP_NO AND DEPARTMENT = 'SLS');
```

Scalar Subqueries

The Scalar Subquery can be used anywhere a value can be used. The subquery must reference just one column in the select list. It must also retrieve no more than one row.

When the subquery returns a single row, the value of the single select list column becomes the value of the Scalar Subquery. When the subquery returns no rows, a database *null* is used as the result of the subquery. Should the subquery retrieve more than one row, it is a *run-time* error and aborts query execution.

A Scalar Subquery can appear as a scalar value in the select list and where predicate of an another query. The following query on the *sp* table uses a Scalar Subquery in the select list to retrieve the supplier city associated with the supplier number (*sno* column in *sp*):

```
SELECT pno, qty, (SELECT city FROM s WHERE s.sno = sp.sno)
    FROM sp;
```

pno	qty	city
P1	NULL	Paris
P1	200	London
P1	1000	Rome
P2	200	Rome

The next query on the *sp* table uses a Scalar Subquery in the where clause to match parts on the color associated with the part number (*pno* column in *sp*):

```
SELECT *
FROM sp
WHERE 'Blue' = (SELECT color FROM p WHERE p.pno = sp.pno);
```

sno	pno	qty
S1	P1	NULL
S2	P1	200
S3	P1	1000

Note that both example queries use outer references. This is normal in Scalar Subqueries. Often, Scalar Subqueries are Aggregate Queries.

Table Subqueries

Table Subqueries are queries used in the FROM clause, replacing a table name. Basically, the result set of the Table Subquery acts like a base table in the from list. Table Subqueries can have a correlation name in the from list. They can also be in outer joins.

The following two queries produce the same result:

```
SELECT p.*, qty
FROM p, sp
WHERE p.pno = sp.pno
AND sno = 'S3';
```

pno	descr	color	qty
P1	Wid	Blue	1000
P2	Wid	Red	200

```
SELECT p.*, qty
FROM p, (SELECT pno, qty FROM sp WHERE sno = 'S3')
WHERE p.pno = sp.pno;
```

pno	descr	color	qty
P1	Wid	Blue	1000
P2	Wid	Red	200

For example,

```
SELECT *
FROM p
WHERE (SELECT COUNT(*) FROM sp WHERE sp.pno = p.pno) > 0;
```

pno	descr	color
P1	Wid	Blue
P2	Wid	Red

Parts with multiple suppliers:

SELECT *

FROM p

WHERE (SELECT COUNT(DISTINCT sno) FROM sp WHERE sp.pno = p.pno) > 1;

pno	descr	color
P1	Wid	Blue

CREATE TABLE FROM A TABLE

Example:

SQL > Create table saldup as select * from salary;

A new table named saldup is created which will be a duplicate of the table named salary.

Example:

SQL > Create table empdup as select empno, ename, job from emp;

A new table empdup will be created with three columns of emp table like empno, ename, job.

Subquery to Copy Structure of a Table

SQL > Create table saldup as select * from salary where 1>2;

A new table named saldup is created which will have the structure of the table named, salary. The rows will not be copied because of the condition 1 > 2 that is always false. So you can copy the structure of any table using any false condition like 2 > 3 also.

Subquery to Insert Data

SQL > Insert into saldup (select * from salary where department = 'SLS');

Rows from the table salary where Department is SLS will be inserted into the table saldup.

SQL > Insert into saldup (emp_no, basic, department)(select emp_no, basic, department from salary where department = 'SLS');

Three columns from the table SALARY where Department is SLS will be inserted into the table SALDUP.

Subquery to DELETE Data

Syntax

Delete from <table> where <column_name> in (Select <column_name> from <table> where <query>);

Example:

SQL > Delete from emp where emp_no in (select emp_no from salary where deduction = 150);

Update Data using Subquery
SQL > Update saldup set
(Basic,Commission) = (select sum(basic),sum (commission)from salary
where emp_no = 1001) where department = 'SLS';

Reports Using SQL*PLUS

We can generate formatted reports by storing the SQL *PLUS commands in a file. The commands are typed in a file using any editor like notepad. For typing the commands in an editor type ed filename on SQL prompt.

Example:

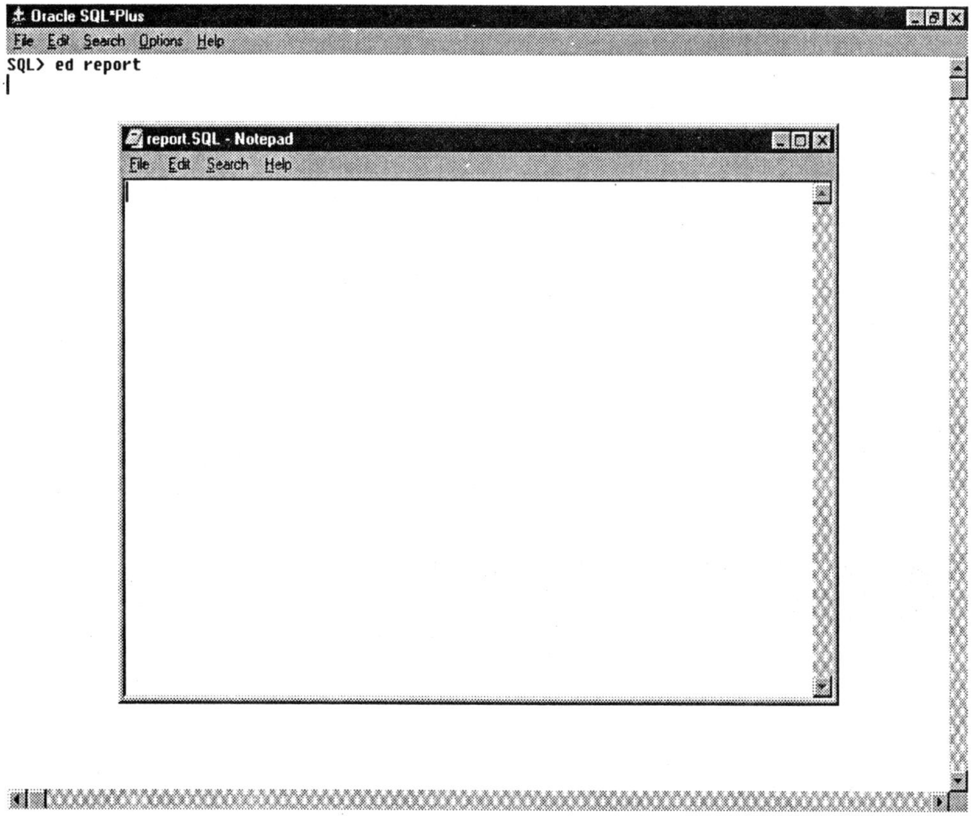

Now type the commands in notepad and after that save the file and close the editor then we will be at SQL prompt, now for execution of the file

SQL > start report or **SQL > @ report**

SQL * PLUS REPORT COMMANDS

COMMAND	DEFINITION
REMARK	Tells SQL *PLUS that the words to follow are to be treated as comments and not as instructions.
—	Marks the beginning and end of an inline comment within a SQL query. Treats everything from the marks to the end of the line as a comment This is also similar to remark.
TTITLE	Sets the top title for each page of a report
BTITLE	Sets the bottom title for each page of a report
COLUMN	Gives SQL *PLUS a variety of instructions in the heading format and treatment of a column
BREAK ON	Tells SQL * PLUS where to put spaces between sections of a report or where to break for subtotals and totals.
COMPUTE SUM	Makes SQL *PLUS calculate subtotals.
SET LINESIZE	Sets the maximum no. of characters allowed on any line of the report
SET PAGESIZE	Sets maximum no. of lines per page.
SET NEWPAGE	Sets the no. of blank spaces between pages
SET HEADSEP	Sets heading separator identifies the single character that tells SQL * PLUS to split a title onto two or more lines.
SPOOL	Moves a report into a file , which can be later printed
SAVE	Saves the SQL query we have created into the file of your choice.
HOST	Sends any command to the host operating system.
START	Tells SQL * PLUS to execute instructions saved in a file.
EDIT	Moves us out of SQL * PLUS and into an editor of our choice.
DEFINE_EDITOR	Tells SQL *PLUS the name of the editor of our choice.
SET PAGESIZE 60	Sets the pagesize 60 default size of page is 40.
SET LINESIZE 65	Sets the linesize 65 default size of line is 80.
SET NULL 'N/S'	Set 'N/S' in place of null default is Blank.
SET SPACE 10	Set the space is 10 default space is 1.
SET WRAP OFF	Set the word wrap off by default wrap is on.
SET PAUSE ON	Sets system to pause after each page.
SKIP 2	Skip two lines after specification.

Example: Type ed salrep at SQL prompt and type the following program :

```
— PROGRAM TO PRINT SALARY REPORT
SET PAGESIZE 25
SET LINESIZE 80
TTITLE CENTER 'SALARY REPORT'
BTITLE 'END OF REPORT'
COLUMN ENAME FORMAT A10 TRUNC
COLUMN "NET SALARY" FORMAT $9,999.00
SELECT EMPNO, ENAME, JOB, HIREDATE, SAL, COMM, SAL+ COMM "NET
SALARY" FROM EMP;
TTITLE OFF
BTITLE OFF
CLEAR COLUMN
—END OF PROGRAM
```

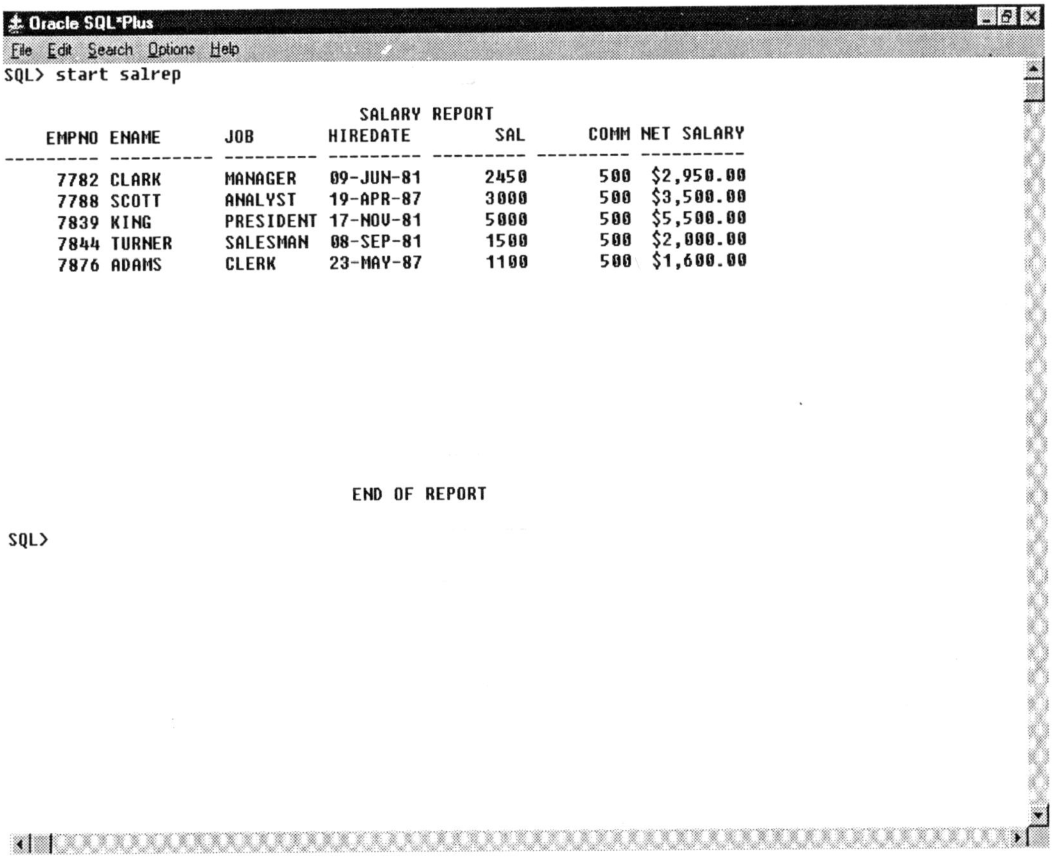

```
Oracle SQL*Plus
File Edit Search Options Help
SQL> start salrep

                                    SALARY REPORT
    EMPNO ENAME      JOB       HIREDATE        SAL      COMM NET SALARY
--------- ---------- --------- --------- --------- --------- ----------
     7782 CLARK      MANAGER   09-JUN-81      2450       500  $2,950.00
     7788 SCOTT      ANALYST   19-APR-87      3000       500  $3,500.00
     7839 KING       PRESIDENT 17-NOV-81      5000       500  $5,500.00
     7844 TURNER     SALESMAN  08-SEP-81      1500       500  $2,000.00
     7876 ADAMS      CLERK     23-MAY-87      1100       500  $1,600.00



                                   END OF REPORT

SQL>
```

Example: To generate a Departmentwise Salary report.

SQL > ed salaryrep then type the following program

```
Oracle SQL*Plus
File Edit Search Options Help
SQL> start salaryrep

                          SALARY REPORT - DEPARTMENTWISE
                                                               PAGE  1

EMPLOYEE
  NUMBER    DEPTNO EMP_NAME          SAL      COMM NET SALARY
--------- --------- ---------- ---------- --------- ----------
     7782        10 Clark         2450.00    500.00       2950
     7839           King          5000.00    500.00       5500
          *********                ---------- ---------
          sum                      7450.00   1000.00


     7788        20 Scott         3000.00    500.00       3500
     7876           Adams         1100.00    500.00       1600
          *********                ---------- ---------
          sum                      4100.00   1000.00


     7844        30 Turner        1500.00    500.00       2000
          *********                ---------- ---------
          sum                      1500.00    500.00


                                ---------- ---------
                          SALARY REPORT - DEPARTMENTWISE
                                                               PAGE  2

EMPLOYEE
  NUMBER    DEPTNO EMP_NAME          SAL      COMM NET SALARY
--------- --------- ---------- ---------- --------- ----------
sum                               13050.00   2500.00

SQL> |
```

```
—DEPARTMENTWISE SALARY
SET PAGESIZE 25
SET LINESIZE  85
COLUMN EMPNO FORMAT 9999
COLUMN SAL FORMAT 999999.99
COLUMN COMM FORMAT 99999.99
COLUMN ENAME FORMAT A10 TRUNC
COLUMN EMPNO HEADING "EMPLOYEE | NUMBER"
COLUMN ENAME HEADING "EMPLOYEE | NAME"
TTITLE CENTER 'SALARY REPORT - DEPARTMENTWISE' SKIP 1  RIGHT
'PAGE' FORMAT 99 SQL.PNO SKIP 2
BREAK ON REPORT ON DEPTNO SKIP 2
COMPUTE SUM OF COMM ON DEPTNO REPORT
COMPUTE SUM OF SAL ON DEPTNO REPORT
SPOOL SALARYREP
SELECT EMPNO, DEPTNO,INITCAP(ENAME) "EMP_NAME", SAL, COMM,
SAL+COMM "NET SALARY" FROM EMP ORDER BY DEPTNO;
```

```
SPOOL OFF
CLEAR COLUMN
TTITLE OFF
CLEAR BREAK
CLEAR COMPUTE
—END OF PROGRAM
```

Example: To Generate a Mailing List for the data in the emp table

```
SET HEADING OFF
COLUMN NAME FOLD_AFTER 1
COLUMN DEPTNO FOLD_AFTER 2
COLUMN EMPNO FOLD_AFTER 1
SELECT EMPNO,ENAME "NAME",DEPTNO "DEPARTMENT" FROM EMP;
SET HEADING ON
```

Run the above program and see the output.

SQL *PLUS INPUT & VARIABLES

SQL * PLUS allows interactive input using the Accept statement and the prompt statements.

The PROMPT statement is used to display message to the user.

PROMPT ENTER EMP NO.

The message displayed on the screen is,

Enter EMP NO.

ACCEPT is used to store the data in a variable.

The two commands Prompt and Accept can be combined.

ACCEPT

The ACCEPT command reads a line of input and stores it in a given user variable.

Syntax

```
ACCEPT variablename CHAR
ACCEPT variablename NUMBER or NUM
ACCEPT variablename CHAR HIDE (will hide the input as in passwords)
ACCEPT variablename PROMPT text
ACCEPT variablename NOPR[OMPT]
```

Variablename represents the name of the variable in which we wish to store a value. If variable does not exist, SQL * PLUS creates it.

NUMBER restricts the datatype of variable to the datatype Number. If the reply does not match the datatype , Accept gives an error message and terminates.

CHAR restricts the datatype of variable to the datatype CHAR. If the reply does not match the datatype, Accept gives an error message and terminates.

PROMPT text display text on screen before accepting the value of variable from the user.

NOPR[OMPT] skips a line and waits for input without displaying a prompt.

HIDE suppresses the display as we type the reply.

Example: To display the prompt, "SALARY :" and place the reply in a number variable named salary , enter :

SQL > Accept SALARY Number Prompt 'SALARY :'

To display the prompt , "Password :", to place the reply in a char variable named PWD, and to suppress the display enter :

SQL > Accept pwd CHAR PROMPT 'PASSWORD :' HIDE;

LAB ASSIGNMENT—8

1. Select the average salaries of each department where dept_no is either D001 or D002.
2. Find Average salary per job in each department_no.
3. Find avg,min,max salaries of employee for each dept_no.
4. Display the dept_no where more than two clerks are working.
5. Who was the first employee hired in each department_no ?
6. Display the average monthly salary bill for each job type within a department_no.
7. Find all departments which have more than 3 employees.
8. Display only those jobs where max sal >= 3000.
9. Find out the employees who earn the highest salary in each dept_no.
10. Display the employees who are doing the same job as 'KIM'.
11. List the cmp_name and minimum salary earned by employee in each dept_no.
12. Display empno, ename, job, basic_sal and total salary of each dept_no.
13. List names of employees who do not work in the marketing department.
14. Select all the fields of the table Dept and the name from EMPLOYEE for those employees who had Basic less than the average salary.
15. List all the employees in descending order of salaries where the first employee should be the last one to join the company.

LAB ASSIGNMENT—9

1. Create the tables described below :

(*a*) Table Name : Client_mast

Column Name	Data Type	Size	Attribute
Client_no	Varchar2	8	Primary Key / First letter must start with 'C'
Name	Varchar2	22	Not null
Address1	Varchar2	20	
Address2	Varchar2	20	
City	Varchar2	15	
Pincode	Number	6	
State	Varchar2	16	
Balance	Number	8, 2	

(*b*) Table Name : Product_mast

Column Name	Data Type	Size	Attribute
Prod_no	Varchar2	8	Primary Key/First letter must start with 'P'
Desc	Varchar2	15	Not null
Profit_perc	Varchar2	5, 2	Not null
Unit	Varchar2	10	Not null
Qty_available	Number	9	Not null
Reorder_level	Number	8	Not null
Sell_cost	Number	8, 2	Not Null, Cannot be 0.
Cost_price	Number	8, 2	Not Null, Cannot be 0.

(*c*) Table Name : salesman_mast

Column Name	Data Type	Size	Attribute
salesman_no	Varchar2	8	Primary Key / First letter must start with 'S'
Name	Varchar2	20	Not null
Address1	Varchar2	20	Not null

Address2	Varchar2	20	
City	Varchar2	15	
Pincode	Number	6	
State	Varchar2	20	
Sale_amt	Number	8,2	Not Null, Cannot be 0.
Target	Number	6,2	Not Null, Cannot be 0.
Units_sold	Number	6,2	Not null
Remarks	Varchar2	40	

(*d*) Table Name : sales_order

Column Name	Data Type	Size	Attribute
Order_no	Varchar2	8	Primary Key/First letter must start with 'O'
Ord_Date	Date		
Client_no	Varchar2	8	Foreign Key references client_no of client_mast table
Delivery_add	Varchar2	20	
Salesman_no	Varchar2	8	Foreign Key references salesman_no of salesman_mast table
Delivery_type	Char	1	Delivery : part (P)/Full (F) Default 'F'
Billed_yn	Char	1	
Del_date	Date		Cannot be less than ord_date
Order_status	Varchar2	10	Values ('Under Process', 'Completed', 'Back Order', 'Cancelled')

(*e*) Table Name : sales_order_detail

Column Name	Data Type	Size	Attribute
Order_no	Varchar2	8	Primary Key/Foreign Key references order_no of the sales_order table
Prod_no	Varchar2	8	Primary key/Foreign key references product_no of the product_mast table.
Qty_ordered	Number	8	
Qty_disp	Number	8	
Product_cost	Number	12, 2	

2. Insert the following data into their respective tables :

(*a*) Client_mast

Client_no	Name	City	Pincode	State	Balance
C001	Harry Potter	Washington	234576	Washington DC	15000
C002	Nav Norton	Honolulu	235436	United State	120
C003	Cao Min	Vietnam	876543	China	5000
C004	Abdul Rahman	Makka	765432	U.A.E	2000
C005	Lee Vin	Vietnam	76543	China	2000

(*b*) Product_mast

Prod_no	Desc	Profit_perc	Unit	Qty_available	Reorder_level	Sell_cost	Cost_price
P001	650 CD	5	Piece	100	20	525	500
P002	Mouse	6	Piece	10	3	120	100
P003	Keyboard	2	Piece	10	3	1250	1200
P004	RAM	2	Piece	10	3	1800	1750
P005	CD Drive	5	Piece	15	5	1250	1225

(*c*) Salesman_mast

Salesman _no	Name	Address1	City	Pincode	State	Sale _amt	Target	Units _sold	Remarks
S001	Shikhar	A-556	Noida	201301	UP	3000	100	50	Good
S002	Sanjeev	A-98	Delhi	110011	Delhi	4000	200	100	Good
S003	Sahil	B-098	Delhi	110987	Delhi	2500	200	100	Good
S004	Amit	C-145	Noida	201301	UP	3500	200	100	Good

(*d*) sale order

Order _no	Or _Date	Client _no	Salesman _no	Delivery _type	Billed _yn	Del _date	Order _status
O001	12-Feb-04	C001	S001	F	N	20-Jun-04	Under Process
O002	13-Feb-04	C002	S002	P	N	21-Jun-04	Cancelled
O003	14-Feb-04	C003	S003	F	Y	22-Jun-04	Completed
O004	15-Feb-04	C004	S004	P	Y	23-Jun-04	Completed
O005	16-Jun-04	C005	S005	P	Y	30-Jun-04	Under Process

(*e*) Sales_order_detail

Order_no	Prod_no	Qty_ordered	Qty_disp	Product_cost
O001	P001	4	4	525
O002	P002	6	5	120
O003	P003	8	7	1250
O004	P004	9	8	1800
O005	P005	9	8	1250

3. List names of employees who do not work in the D001 department from employee table.
4. Find the profit value of each product sold from product_mast table.
5. Find the products and their quantities that will have profit price greater than 10 from product_mast table.

LAB ASSIGNMENT—10

1. Display the desc and total qty sold for each product.
2. Calculate the average qty sold for each client that has a maximum order value of 3000.00.
3. Find out the sum total of all the billed orders for the month of February.
4. Find out the products which have been sold to 'Harry Potter'.
5. Find out the products and their quantities that will have to be delievered in the June month.
6. Find the names of clients who have purchased 'RAM'.
7. List the product_no and order_no of customers having qty_ordered less than 8 from the sales_order_detail table for the product RAM.
8. Find the products and their quantities for the orders placed by 'Harry Potter' and 'Lee Vin'.
9. Find the products and their quantities for the orders placed by client_no 'C001' and 'C003'.
10. Find the customer name, city and pincode for the client who has placed order no 'O001'.
11. Find the client names who have placed orders before the month of Jun '04.
12. Find the names of clients who have placed orders worth Rs. 3000 or more.
13. Create the Report of Product_mast table with Total Sell Price and Cost Price.
14. Create the Report of client_mast table with total of balance.
15. Create the report of salesman_mast table with total sale_amt and total units_sold.

7 Introduction to PL/SQL

Objectives :

- Introduction
- The Anonymous PL/SQL Block
- Lexical Units
- Reserved Words
- Variables and Data Types
- Records in PL/SQL
- Operator Precedence
- Control Structures
- Sequential Control
- Exception Handlers
- Advantages of PL/SQL

Lab Assignment-11

Lab Assignment-12

INTRODUCTION

PL/SQL stands for Procedural Language/SQL, superset of Structural Query Language (SQL). PL/SQL extends SQL by adding constructs found in procedural languages, resulting in a structural language that is more powerful than SQL. The basic unit in PL/SQL is a block. PL/SQL is a block-structured language. That is, the basic units (procedures, functions, and anonymous blocks) that make up a PL/SQL program are logical blocks, which can contain any number of nested sub-blocks. Each logical block corresponds to a problem or sub problem to be solved. PL/SQL supports the divide-and-conquer approach to problem solving called stepwise **refinement.**

If the block of PL/SQL code is not given a name, it is called anonymous block, each block performs a logical action in the program. A block is used to group logically related declarations and statements. We can place declarations close to where they are used. The declarations are local to the block and exist when the block completes.

As Figure 7.1 shows, a PL/SQL block has three parts: a declarative part, an executable part, and an exception-handling part. (In PL/SQL, error condition is called an exception.) Only the executable part is mandatory.

The order of the parts is logical. First comes the declarative part, in which items can be declared. Once declared, items can be manipulated in the executable part. Exceptions raised during execution can be dealt with in the exception-handling part.

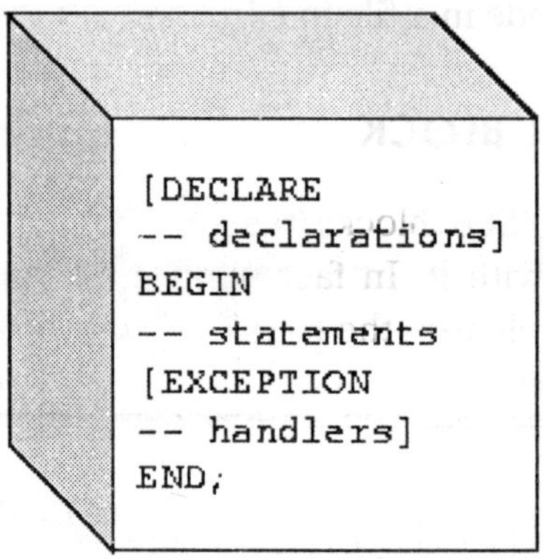

Figure 7.1. Block Structure

A block has the following structure:

DECLARE Declarative section: variables, types, and local subprograms.
BEGIN Executable section: procedural and SQL statements go here. This is the only section of the block that is required.

EXCEPTION Exception handling section: error-handling statements go here.
END;

The only SQL statements allowed in a PL/SQL program like SELECT, INSERT, UPDATE, DELETE and several other DML statements plus some transaction control. However, the SELECT statement has a special form in which a single record is placed in variables. DDL statements like CREATE, DROP, or ALTER are not allowed. The executable section also contains constructs such as assignments, branches, loops, procedure calls, and triggers, which are all described below. PL/SQL is not sensitive case. We can nest sub-blocks in the executable and exception-handling parts of a PL/SQL block or subprogram but not in the declarative part. Also, we can define local subprograms in the declarative part of any block. However, we can call local subprograms only from the block in which they are defined.

To execute a PL/SQL program, we must follow the program text itself by

- A line with a single dot ("."), and then
- A line with run;

As with Oracle SQL programs, we can invoke a PL/SQL program either by typing it in SQL *PLUS or by putting the code in a file in editor.

THE ANONYMOUS PL/SQL BLOCK

Unlike the other two types of PL/SQL blocks (the procedure and the function), the anonymous block has no name associated with it. In fact, the anonymous block is missing the header section altogether. Instead it simply uses the DECLARE reserved word to mark the beginning of its optional declaration section.

```
BEGIN                                      Execution Only
    DBMS_OUTPUT.PUT_LINE ('Hello world');
END;
```

Figure 7.2. An anonymous block without declaration and exception sections

Without a name, the anonymous block cannot be called by any other block — it doesn't have a handle for reference. Instead, anonymous blocks serve as scripts that execute PL/SQL statements, including calls to procedures and functions. Anonymous blocks can also serve as nested blocks inside procedures, functions, and other anonymous blocks.

Because an anonymous block can have its own declaration and exception sections, developers use anonymous blocks to provide a scope for identifiers and exception handling within a larger program.

The Structure of an Anonymous Block

The general format of an anonymous PL/SQL block is as follows:

```
[ DECLARE
  ... optional declaration statements ... ]
BEGIN
  ... executable statements ...
[ EXCEPTION
  ... optional exception handler statements ... ]
END;
```

The square brackets indicate an optional part of the syntax. As you can see, just about everything in an anonymous block is optional. You must have BEGIN and END statements and you must have at least one executable statement.

Examples of Anonymous Blocks

The following examples show the different combinations of block sections, all of which comprise valid PL/SQL blocks:

- A block with BEGIN-END terminators, but no declaration or exception sections:

```
BEGIN
  joindate : = SYSDATE;
END
```

- An anonymous block with a declaration section, but no exception section:

```
DECLARE
  rt_nw DATE := SYSDATE;
BEGIN
  joindate := rt_nw;
END
```

- An anonymous block containing declaration, execution, and exception sections:

```
DECLARE
  rt_nw DATE := SYSDATE;
  too_late EXCEPTION;
BEGIN
  IF :employee.joindate < ADD_MONTHS (rt_nw, 6)
  THEN
    RAISE too_late;
  ELSE
```

```
        :employee.joindate := rt_nw;
      END IF;
    EXCEPTION
      WHEN too_late
      THEN
        DBMS_OUTPUT.PUT_LINE
('You no longer qualify for free air.');
      WHEN OTHERS
      THEN
        DBMS_OUTPUT.PUT_LINE
       ('Error encountered: ' || SQLCODE);
END;
```

Note. Anonymous blocks execute a series of statements and then terminate, thus acting like procedures. In fact, all anonymous blocks are anonymous block procedures.

Nested Blocks

PL/SQL allows nesting or embedding anonymous blocks within another PL/SQL block. You can also nest anonymous blocks within anonymous blocks for more than one level, as shown in Figure 7.3.

```
DECLARE
     CURSOR emp_cur IS ...;
BEGIN
     DECLARE
         total_sales NUMBER;
     BEGIN
         DECLARE
             hiredate DATE;
         BEGIN
             ...
         END;
     END;
  END;
```

Figure 7.3. Anonymous blocks nested three levels deep

Character Set

We can write a PL/SQL program as lines of text using a specific set of characters. The PL/SQL character set includes

- the upper-case and lower-case letters A .. Z and a .. z
- the numerals 0 .. 9
- the symbols ( ) + - * / < > = ! ~ ^ ; : . ' @ % , " # $ & _ | { } ? [ ]
- tabs, spaces, and carriage returns

Note. PL/SQL is not case sensitive, so lower-case letters are equivalent to corresponding upper-case letters except within string and character literals.

LEXICAL UNITS

A line of PL/SQL text contains groups of characters known as lexical units, which can be classified as follows:

- **delimiters (simple and compound symbols)**
- **identifiers, which include reserved words**
- **literals**
- **comments**

For example, the line

bonus := salary * 0.90; — compute bonus

Contains the following lexical units:

- identifiers bonus and salary
- compound symbol :=
- simple symbols * and ;
- numeric literal 0.90
- comment - - compute bonus

To improve readability, we can separate lexical units by spaces. In fact, we separate adjacent identifiers by a space or punctuation. The following line is illegal because the reserved words END and IF are joined:

IF x > y THEN high := x; ENDIF; — illegal

However, we cannot include spaces in lexical units except for string literals and comments. For example, the following line is illegal because the compound symbol for assignment (:=) is split:

count : = count + 1; — illegal

Delimiters

A delimiter is a simple or compound symbol that has a special meaning to PL/SQL. For example, we use delimiters to represent arithmetic operations such as addition and subtraction. Simple symbols consist of one character. A list follows:

Symbol	Meaning
+	addition operator
%	attribute indicator
‘	character string delimiter
.	component selector
/	division operator
(	expression or list delimiter
)	expression or list delimiter
:	host variable indicator
,	item separator
*	multiplication operator
“	quoted identifier delimiter
=	relational operator
<	relational operator
>	relational operator
@	remote access indicator
;	statement terminator
-	subtraction/ negation operator

Compound symbols consist of two characters. A list follows:

<table>
<tr><th>Symbol</th><th>Meaning</th></tr>
<tr><td>: =</td><td>assignment operator</td></tr>
<tr><td>=></td><td>association operator</td></tr>
<tr><td>||</td><td>concatenation operator</td></tr>
<tr><td>**</td><td>exponentiation operator</td></tr>
<tr><td><<</td><td>label delimiter (begin)</td></tr>
<tr><td>>></td><td>label delimiter (end)</td></tr>
<tr><td>/*</td><td>multi-line comment delimiter (begin)</td></tr>
<tr><td>*/</td><td>multi-line comment delimiter (end)</td></tr>
<tr><td>..</td><td>range operator</td></tr>
<tr><td><></td><td>relational operator</td></tr>
<tr><td>!=</td><td>relational operator</td></tr>
<tr><td>~=</td><td>relational operator</td></tr>
<tr><td>^=</td><td>relational operator</td></tr>
<tr><td><=</td><td>relational operator</td></tr>
<tr><td>>=</td><td>relational operator</td></tr>
<tr><td>- -</td><td>single-line comment indicator</td></tr>
</table>

Identifiers

We will use identifiers to name PL/SQL program items and units, which include constants, variables, exceptions, cursors, cursor variables, subprograms, and packages. Some examples of identifiers follow:

X
t2
PIN#
credit_limit
LastName

An identifier consists of a letter optionally followed by more letters, numerals, dollar signs, underscores, and number signs. Other characters such as hyphens(-), slashes(/), and spaces are illegal, as the following examples show:

mine&yours — illegal ampersand
debit-amount — illegal hyphen
on /off —illegal slash
user id — illegal space

The next examples show that adjoining and trailing dollar signs, underscores, and number signs are allowed:

money$$$tree
SNO##
try_again_

We can use upper, lower, or mixed case to write identifiers. PL/SQL is not case sensitive except within string and character literals. So, if the only difference between identifiers is the case of corresponding letters, PL/SQL considers the identifiers to be the same, as the following example shows:

lastname
LastName — same as lastname

The length of an identifier cannot exceed 30 characters. But, every character, including dollar signs, underscores, and number signs, is significant. For example, PL/SQL considers the following identifiers to be different:

lastname
last_name

Identifiers should be descriptive. So, avoid confusing names such as cpm. Instead, use meaningful names such as cost_per_Minute.

RESERVED WORDS

The words listed here are reserved by PL/SQL. That is, they have a special syntactic meaning to PL/SQL. So, we should not use them to name program objects such as constants, variables, or cursors, functions. Some of these words (marked by an asterisk) are also reserved by SQL. So, we should not use them to name schema objects such as columns, tables, or indexes.

ALL*
ALTER*
AND*
ANY*
ARRAY
AS*
ASC*
AUTHID
AVG
BEGIN
BETWEEN*
BINARY_INTEGER
BODY
BOOLEAN
BULK
BY*
CHAR*
CHAR_BASE
CHECK*
CLOSE
CLUSTER*
COLLECT
COMMENT*
COMMIT
COMPRESS*
CONNECT*
CONSTANT
CREATE*
CURRENT*
CURRVAL
CURSOR
DATE*
DAY
DECLARE
DECIMAL*
DEFAULT*
DELETE*
DESC*
DISTINCT*
DO
DROP*
ELSE*
ELSIF
END
EXCEPTION
EXCLUSIVE*
EXECUTE
EXISTS*
EXIT
EXTENDS
FALSE
FETCH
FLOAT*
FOR*
FORALL
FROM*
FUNCTION
GOTO
GROUP*
HAVING*
HEAP
HOUR
IF
IMMEDIATE*
IN*
INDEX*
INDICATOR
INSERT*
INTEGER*
INTERFACE
INTERSECT*
INTERVAL
INTO*
IS*
ISOLATION
JAVA
LEVEL*
LIKE*
LIMITED
LOCK*
LONG*
LOOP
MAX
MIN
MINUS*
MINUTE
MLSLABEL*
MOD
MODE*
MONTH
NATURAL
NATURALN
NEW
NEXTVAL
NOCOPY
NOT*
NOWATT*
NULL*
NUMBER*
NUMBER_BASE
OCIROWID
OF*
ON*
OPAQUE
OPEN
OPERATOR
OPTION*
OR*
ORDER*
ORGANIZATION
OTHERS
OUT
PACKAGE
PARTITION
PCTFREE*
PLS_INTEGER
POSITIVE
POSITIVEN
PRAGMA
PRIOR*
PRIVATE
PROCEDURE
PUBLIC*
RAISE
RANGE
RAW*
REAL
RECORD
REF
RELEASE
RETURN
REVERSE
ROLLBACK
ROW*
ROWID*
ROWLEBEL
ROWNUM*
ROWTYPE
SAVEPOINT
SECOND
SELECT*
SEPARATE
SET*
SHARE*
SMALLINT*
SPACE
SQL
SQLCODE
SQLERRM
START*
STDDEV
SUBTYPE
SUCCESSFUL*
SUM
SYNONYM*
SYSDATE*
TABLE*
THEN*
TIME
TIMESTAMP
TO*
TRIGGER*
TRUE
TYPE
UID*
UNION*
UNIQUE*
UPDATE*
USE
USER*
VALIDATE*
VALUES*
VARCHAR*
VARCHAR2*
VARIANCE
VIEW*
WHEN
WHENEVER*
WHERE*
WHILE
WITH*
WORK
WRITE
YEAR
ZONE

Predefined Identifiers

Identifiers globally declared in package STANDARD, such as the exception INVALID_NUMBER, can be redeclared. Redeclaring predefined identifiers is error prone because our local declaration overrides the global declaration.

Quoted Identifiers

PL/SQL provides enclosed identifiers within double quotes. They can contain any sequence of printable characters including spaces but excluding double quotes. Thus, the following identifiers are valid:

```
'X+Y"
"last name"
"on/off switch"
"employee(s)"
"*** header info ***"
```

Note. The maximum length of a quoted identifier is 30 characters not counting the double quotes. Though allowed, using PL/SQL reserved words, as quoted identifiers is a poor programming practice.

Some PL/SQL reserved words are not reserved by SQL. For example, we can use the PL/SQL reserved word TYPE in a CREATE TABLE statement to name a database column. But, if a SQL statement in your program refers to that column, we get a compilation error, as the following example shows:

```
SELECT acct, type, amt INTO ... — causes compilation error
```

To prevent the error, enclose the uppercase column name in double quotes, as follows:

```
SELECT acct, "TYPE", amt INTO ...
```

The column name cannot appear in lower or mixed case (unless it was defined that way in the CREATE TABLE statement). For example, the following statement is invalid:

```
SELECT acct, "type", bal INTO ... — causes compilation error
```

Alternatively, we can create a view that renames the troublesome column, then use the view instead of the base table in SQL statements.

Literals

A literal is an explicit numeric, character, string, or Boolean value not represented by an identifier. The numeric literal 149 and the Boolean literal TRUE are examples.

Numeric Literals

Two kinds of numeric literals can be used in arithmetic expressions: integers and reals. An integer literal is an optionally signed whole number without a decimal point. Some examples follow:

```
020  7  -16  0  +32767
```

A real literal is an optionally signed whole or fractional number with a decimal point. Several examples follow:

6.6687, 0.0, -12.0, 3.14158, +8300.00, .5, 25

PL/SQL considers numbers such as 12.0 and 25 to be reals even though they have integral values.

Numeric literals cannot contain dollar signs or commas, but can be written using scientific notation. Simply suffix the number with an E (or e) followed by an optionally signed integer. A few examples follow:

2E5, 1.0E-7, 3.14159e0, -1E38, -9.5e-3

E stands for "times ten to the power of." As the next example shows, the number after E is the power of ten by which the number before E must be multiplied (the double asterisk (**) is the exponentiation operator):

5E3 = 5, 10**3 = 5, 1000 = 5000

The number after E also corresponds to the number of places the decimal point shifts. In the last example, the implicit decimal point shifted three places to the right. In this example, it shifts three places to the left:

5E-3 = 5, 10**-3 = 5, 0.001 = 0.005

As the following example shows, if the value of a numeric literal falls outside the range 1E-130 .. 10E125, you get a compilation error:

```
DECLARE
  n NUMBER;
BEGIN
  n := 10E127;  — causes a 'numeric overflow or underflow' error
```

Character Literals

A character literal is an individual character enclosed by single quotes (apostrophes). Character literals include all the printable characters in the PL/SQL character set: letters, numerals, spaces, and special symbols. Some examples follow:

'A' '%' '8' ' ' 'z' '('

PL/SQL is case sensitive within character literals. For example, PL/SQL considers the literals 'Z' and 'z' to be different. Also, the character literals '0'..'9' are not equivalent to integer literals but can be used in arithmetic expressions because they are implicitly convertible to integers.

String Literals

A character value can be represented by an identifier or explicitly written as a string literal, which is a sequence of zero or more characters enclosed by single quotes. Several examples follow:

'Hello, Everybody!'

'ABC Limited'

'11-NOV-04'

'$2,00,00'

All string literals except the null string ('') have datatype CHAR.

Given that apostrophes (single quotes) delimit string literals, as the next example shows how do we represent an apostrophe within a string? Note that we write two single quotes, which is not the same as writing a double quote:

'Don''t leave without doing your work.'

Note. PL/SQL is case sensitive within string literals. For example, PL/SQL considers the following literals to be different:

'baker'

'Baker'

Boolean Literals

Boolean literals are the predefined values TRUE, FALSE, and NULL (which stands for a missing, unknown, or inapplicable value). Remember, Boolean literals are values, not strings. For example, TRUE is no less a value than the number 25.

Comments

The PL/SQL compiler ignores comments, but we should not. Adding comments to our program promotes readability and understanding. Generally, we use comments to describe the purpose and use of each code segment. PL/SQL supports two type of comment styles: single-line and multi-line.

Single-Line

Single-line comments begin with a double hyphen (—) anywhere on a line and extend to the end of the line.

Examples:

```
— begin processing
SELECT sal INTO salary FROM emp — get current salary
  WHERE empno = emp_id;
bonus := salary * 0.15; — compute bonus amount
```

Notice that comments can appear within a statement at the end of a line.

While testing or debugging a program, you might want to disable a line of code. The following example shows how you can "comment-out" the line:

```
— DELETE FROM emp WHERE comm IS NULL;
```

Multi-line

Multi-line comments begin with a slash-asterisk (/*), end with an asterisk-slash (*/), and can span multiple lines.

Examples :

```
BEGIN
  ...
  /* Compute a 25% bonus for top-rated employees. */
  IF rating > 80 THEN
    bonus := salary * 0.25 /* bonus is based on salary */
  ELSE
    bonus := 0;
  END If;
  ...
  /* The following line computes the area of a
    circle using pi, which is the ratio between
    the circumference and diameter. */
  area := pi * radius**2;
END;
```

VARIABLES AND DATA TYPES

Information is transmitted between a PL/SQL program and the database through variables. Every variable has a specific type associated with it. That type can be

- One of the types used by SQL for database columns
- A generic type used in PL/SQL such as NUMBER
- Declared to be the same as the type of some database column

PL/SQL offers a comprehensive set of predefined scalar and composite datatypes. A scalar datatype is an atomic; it is not made up of other variable components. A composite datatype has internal structure or components. The two composite types currently supported by PL/SQL are the record and table. The scalar datatypes fall into one of four categories : number, character, Boolean, and date-time

Table 7.1: Datatype Categories

Category	Datatype
Number	BINARY_INTEGER
	DEC
	DECIMAL
	DOUBLE PRECISION

	FLOAT
	INT
	INTEGER
	NATURAL
	NUMBER
	NUMERIC
	PLS_INTEGER
	POSITIVE
	REAL
	SMALLINT
Character	CHAR
	CHARACTER
	LONG
	LONG RAW
	NCHAR
	NVARCHAR2
	RAW
	ROWID
	STRING
	VARCHAR
	VARCHAR2
Boolean	BOOLEAN
Date-time	DATE
Large object (LOB)	BFILE
	BLOB
	CLOB
	NCLOB

These datatypes are already discussed in Chapter 3.

The most commonly used generic type is NUMBER. Variables of type NUMBER can hold either an integer or a real number. The most commonly used character string type is VARCHAR(n), where n is the maximum length of the string in bytes. This length is required, and there is no default. For example, we might declare:

```
DECLARE
   price NUMBER;
   myvariable VARCHAR(20);
```

Note that PL/SQL allows BOOLEAN variables, even though Oracle does not support BOOLEAN as a type for database columns.

Bind Variable

Bind variables are variables which can be used to communicate from a PL/SQL block to SQL *PLUS.

Bind variables are created by syntax,

Variable <name> <type>

The <type> can be : Char (Do not specify width)
Number (Do not specify width)
Varchar2(Width can be specified)

Example:

```
SQL > Variable salary number
SQL > Begin
      :SAL := 2000;
      END;
      /
PL/SQL procedure successfully completed.
SQL > Print Salary
SALARY
--------------------
2000
```

RECORDS IN PL/SQL

Records in PL/SQL programs are very similar in concept and structure to the rows of a table. A record is a composite data structure, which means that it is composed of more than one element or component, each with its own value. The record as a whole does not have value of its own; instead, each individual field has a value. The record gives us a way to store and access these values as a group.

Different Types of Records

PL/SQL supports three different kinds of records: **table-based, cursor-based, and programmer-defined.** These different types of records are used in different ways and for different purposes, but all three share the same internal structure: every record is composed of one or more fields.

However, the way these fields are defined in the record depend on the record type. Table 7.2 shows this information about each record type.

Table 7.2 : PL/SQL Record Types

Record Type	Description	Fields in Record
Table-based	A record based on a table's column structure.	Each field corresponds to—(and has the same name as)—a column in a table.
Cursor-based	A record based on the cursor's SELECT statement.	Each field corresponds to a column or expression in the cursor SELECT statement.
Programmer-defined	A record whose structure you, the programmer, get to define with a declaration statement.	Each field is defined explicitly (its name and datatype) in the TYPE statement for that record; a field in a programmer-defined record can even be another record.

Accessing Record-Based Data

We can access the fields within a record using dot notation, just as we would identify a column from a database table, in the following format:

```
<record name>.<field name>
```

We would reference the first_name column from the employee table as follows:

```
employee.first_name
```

We would reference the emp_full_name field in the employee PL/SQL record as:

```
employee_rec.emp_full_name
```

The record structure of relational database tables has proven to be a very powerful way to represent data in a database, and records in our programs offer similar advantages.

Benefits of Using Records

The record data structure provides a high-level way of addressing and manipulating program-based data. This approach offers the following benefits:

(1) Data abstraction

(2) Aggregate operations

(3) Leaner, cleaner code

Referencing a Record and its Fields

The rules must follow for refering a record in its entity set or a particular field in the record are the same for all types of records: table, cursor, and programmer-defined.

A record's structure is similar to that of a database table. Where a table has columns, a record has fields. We refer a table's column by its name in a SQL statement, as in:

```
SELECT com_id FROM company;
```

The fully qualified name of a column is:

```
<table_name>.<column_name>
```

This full name is often required in a SQL statement to avoid ambiguity, as is true in the following statement:

```
SELECT employee.com_id, COUNT(*) total_employee
FROM company, employee
WHERE company.com_id = employee.comp_id;
```

If we do not preface the name of com_id with the appropriate table name, the SQL compiler will not know to which table that column belongs. The same is true for a record's fields. We refer a record by its name, and we refer a record's field by its full name using dot notation, as in:

```
<record_name>.<field_name>
```

So if we create a record named company_rec, which contains a company_id field, then we would refer this field as follows:

```
company_rec.comp_id
```

We must always use the fully qualified name of a field when refering that field. If we don't, PL/SQL will never be able to determine the "default" record for a field, as it does in a SQL statement.

```
DECLARE
   TYPE cust_sales_rectype IS RECORD (...);
   cust_rec cust_sales_rectype;
BEGIN
   display_sales_data (cust_rec);
END;
```

We didn't make a single dotted reference to any particular field in the customer record. Instead we declared the record type, used it to create the record, used the record type again to define the type for the parameter in the procedure specification, and finally called the procedure, passing it the specific record we declared.

Comparing Two Records

If we want to compare records, for example, we must always do so through comparison of the records' individual fields.

Suppose we want to know if the old company information is the same as the new company information, both being stored in records of the same structure. The following test for equality will not compile:

```
IF old_comp_rec = new_comp_rec          */ Illegal syntax!
    THEN
     ...
    END IF;
```

even though the structures of the two records are absolutely identical and based on the same record type (in this case, a table record type).

PL/SQL will not automatically compare each individual field in the old company record to the corresponding field in the new company record. Instead, we will have to perform that detailed check ourself, as in:

```
IF old_comp_rec.name = new_comp_rec.name AND
old_comp_rec.incorp_date = new_comp_rec.incorp_date AND
old_comp_rec.address1 = new_comp_rec.address1
AND
    THEN
      ... the two records are identical ...
    END IF;
```

Types in PL/SQL can be tricky. In many cases, a PL/SQL variable will be used to manipulate data stored in an existing relation. In this case, it is essential that the variable have the same type as the relation column. If there is any type mismatch, variable assignments and comparisons may not work the way we expect. To be safe, instead of hard coding the type of a variable, we should use the %TYPE operator.

Example:

```
DECLARE
  myvar variables.name%TYPE;
```

gives PL/SQL variable myvar whatever type was declared for the name column in relation variables.

A variable may also have a type that is a record with several fields. The simplest way to declare such a variable is to use %ROWTYPE on a relation name. The result is a record type in which the fields have the same names and types as the attributes of the relation. For instance:

```
DECLARE
   Emp Tuple emp%ROWTYPE;
```

makes variable Emp Tuple be a record with fields name and manufacture, assuming that the relation has the schema emp(empno, name, sal, dept).

The initial value of any variable, regardless of its type, is NULL. We can assign values to variables, using the ":=" operator. The assignment can occur either immediately after the type of the variable is declared, or anywhere in the executable portion of the program.

For example:

```
DECLARE
   a NUMBER := 9;
BEGIN
   a := a + 1;
END;
run;
```

This program has no effect when run, because there are no changes to the database.

Our program stores values in variables and constants. As the program executes, the values of variables can change, but the values of constants cannot.

We can declare variables and constants in the declarative part of any PL/SQL block. Declarations allocate storage space for a value, specify its datatype, and name the storage location so that we can refer to it.

Examples:

```
dob DATE;
emp_count SMALLINT := 0;
```

The first declaration names a variable of type DATE. The second declaration names a variable of type SMALLINT and uses the assignment operator to assign an initial value of zero to the variable.

The next examples show that the expression following the assignment operator can be arbitrarily complex and can refer to previously initialized variables:

```
pi       REAL := 3.14159;
radius   REAL := 1;
area     REAL := pi * radius**2;
```

By default, variables are initialized to NULL. So, these declarations are equivalent:

```
dob DATE;
dob DATE := NULL;
```

In the declaration of a constant, the keyword CONSTANT must precede the type specifier, as the following example shows:

```
crdt_limit CONSTANT REAL := 6000.00;
```

This declaration names a constant of type REAL and assigns an initial (also final) value of 6000 to the constant. A constant must be initialized in its declaration. Otherwise, we get a compilation error when the declaration is elaborated.

Using DEFAULT

We can use the keyword DEFAULT instead of the assignment operator to initialize variables. For example, the declaration

```
blood_type CHAR := 'A';
```

can be rewritten as follows:

```
blood_type CHAR DEFAULT 'A';
```

Use DEFAULT for variables that have a typical value. Use the assignment operator for variables (such as counters and accumulators) that have no typical value.

```
hours_worked   INTEGER DEFAULT 40;
employee_count INTEGER := 0;
```

We can also use DEFAULT to initialize subprogram parameters, cursor parameters, and fields in a user-defined record.

Using NOT NULL

Besides assigning an initial value, declarations can impose the NOT NULL constraint, as the following example shows:

```
acc_id INTEGER(5) NOT NULL := 99999;
```

We cannot assign nulls to a variable defined as NOT NULL. If we try, PL/SQL raises the predefined exception VALUE_ERROR. The NOT NULL constraint must be followed by an initialization clause. For example, the following declaration is illegal:

```
acc_id INTEGER(5) NOT NULL;  – illegal; not initialized
```

Recall that the subtypes NATURALN and POSITIVEN are predefined as NOT NULL. For instance, the following declarations are equivalent:

```
emp_count NATURAL NOT NULL := 0;
emp_count NATURALN := 0;
```

In NATURALN and POSITIVEN declarations, the type specifier must be followed by an initialization clause. Otherwise, you get a compilation error. For example, the following declaration is illegal:

```
line_item POSITIVEN;  – illegal; not initialized
```

Using %TYPE

The %TYPE attribute provides the datatype of a variable or database column. In the following example, %TYPE provides the datatype of a variable:

```
credit REAL(8,2);
debit credit%TYPE;
```

Variables declared using %TYPE are treated like those declared using a datatype specifier. For example, given the previous declarations, PL/SQL treats debit like a REAL(8,2) variable.

```
balance        NUMBER(6,2);
minimum_balance balance%TYPE := 5000.00;
```

The %TYPE attribute is particularly useful when declaring variables that refer to database columns. We can refer to a table and column, or we can refer to an owner, table, and column, as in

```
my_dname scott.dept.dname%TYPE;
```

Using %TYPE to declare my_dname has two advantages. First, we need not know the exact datatype of dname. Second, if the database definition of dname changes, the datatype of my_dname changes accordingly at run time.

However, %TYPE variables do not inherit the NOT NULL column constraint. In the next example, even though the database column empno is defined as NOT NULL, we can assign a null to the variable my_empno:

```
DECLARE
  my_empno emp.empno%TYPE;
  ...
BEGIN
  my_empno := NULL; — this works
```

Using %ROWTYPE

The %ROWTYPE attribute provides a record type that represents a row in a table (or view). The record can store an entire row of data selected from the table or fetched from a cursor or strongly typed cursor variable. In the example below, we declare two records. The first record stores a row selected from the emp table. The second record stores a row fetched from cursor c1.

```
DECLARE
  emp_rec emp%ROWTYPE;
  CURSOR c1 IS SELECT deptno, dname, loc FROM dept;
  dept_rec c1%ROWTYPE;
```

Columns in a row and corresponding fields in a record have the same names and datatypes. However, fields in a %ROWTYPE record do not inherit the NOT NULL column constraint.

In the following example, we select column values into record emp_rec:

```
BEGIN
  SELECT * INTO emp_rec FROM emp WHERE ...
```

The column values returned by the SELECT statement are stored in fields. To reference a field, we use dot notation. For example, we might reference the deptno field as follows:

```
IF emp_rec.deptno = 50 THEN ...
```

We can also assign the value of an expression to a specific field, as the following examples show:

```
emp_rec.ename := 'WILLIAM';
emp_rec.sal := emp_rec.sal * 1.20;
```

In the final example, we use %ROWTYPE to define a packaged cursor:

```
CREATE PACKAGE emp_actions AS
  CURSOR c1 RETURN emp%ROWTYPE;  — declare cursor specification
  ...
END emp_actions;
CREATE PACKAGE BODY emp_actions AS
  CURSOR c1 RETURN emp%ROWTYPE IS  — define cursor body
    SELECT * FROM emp WHERE sal > 4000;
  ...
END emp_actions;
DECLARE
  dept_rec1 dept%ROWTYPE;
  dept_rec2 dept%ROWTYPE;
  CURSOR c1 IS SELECT deptno, dname, loc FROM dept;
  dept_rec3 c1%ROWTYPE;
BEGIN
  ...
  dept_rec1 := dept_rec2;
```

However, because dept_rec2 is based on a table and dept_rec3 is based on a cursor, the following assignment is illegal:

```
dept_rec2 := dept_rec3;  — illegal
```

Second, we can assign a list of column values to a record by using the SELECT or FETCH statement, as the example below shows. The column names must appear in the order in which they were defined by the CREATE TABLE or CREATE VIEW statement.

```
DECLARE
  dep_rec dept%ROWTYPE;
  ...
BEGIN
  SELECT deptno, dname, loc INTO dept_rec FROM dept
    WHERE deptno = 40;
```

However, we cannot assign a list of column values to a record by using an assignment statement. So, the following syntax is illegal:

```
record_name := (value1, value2, value3, ...); — illegal
```

Although we can retrieve entire records, we cannot insert or update them. For example, the following statement is illegal:

```
INSERT INTO dept VALUES (dep_rec); — illegal
```

Restrictions

PL/SQL does not allow forward references. We must declare a variable or constant before referencing it in other statements, including other declarative statements. For example, the following declaration of maxi is illegal:

```
maxi INTEGER := 5 * mini; — illegal
mini INTEGER := 17;
```

However, PL/SQL does allow the forward declaration of subprograms.

Some languages allow us to declare a list of variables that have the same datatype. PL/SQL does not allow this. For example, the following declaration is illegal:

```
i, j, k SMALLINT; — illegal
```

The legal version follows:

```
i SMALLINT;
j SMALLINT;
k SMALLINT;
```

Datatype Conversion

Sometimes it is necessary to convert a value from one datatype to another. For example, if we want to examine a rowid, we must convert it to a character string. PL/SQL supports both explicit and implicit (automatic) datatype conversion.

Explicit Conversion

To convert values from one datatype to another, we use built-in functions. For example, to convert a CHAR value to a DATE or NUMBER value, we use the function TO_DATE or TO_NUMBER, respectively. Conversely, to convert a DATE or NUMBER value to a CHAR value, we use the function TO_CHAR. For more information about these functions refer chapter - 04.

Implicit Conversion

PL/SQL can convert the datatype of a value implicitly. This allows you to use literals, variables, and parameters of one type where another type is expected. In the example below, the CHAR variables start_time and finish_time hold string values representing the number of seconds past midnight. The difference between those values must be assigned to the NUMBER variable elapsed_time. So, PL/SQL converts the CHAR values to NUMBER values automatically.

```
DECLARE
   st_time  CHAR(5);
   fi_time  CHAR(5);
   elapsed_time NUMBER(5);
BEGIN
   /* Get system time as seconds past midnight. */
   SELECT TO_CHAR(SYSDATE,'SSSSS') INTO st_time FROM sys.dual;
   -- do something
   /* Get system time again. */
   SELECT TO_CHAR(SYSDATE,'SSSSS') INTO fi_time FROM sys.dual;
   /* Compute elapsed time in seconds. */
   elapsed_time := fi_time - st_time;
   INSERT INTO results VALUES (elapsed_time, ...);
END;
```

Before assigning a selected column value to a variable, PL/SQL will, if necessary, convert the value from the datatype of the source column to the datatype of the variable. This happens, for example, when we select a DATE column value into a VARCHAR2 variable.

Likewise, before assigning the value of a variable to a database column, PL/SQL will, if necessary, convert the value from the datatype of the variable to the datatype of the target column. If PL/SQL cannot determine which implicit conversion is needed, we get a compilation error. In such cases, we must use a datatype conversion function.

Naming Conventions

The same naming conventions apply to all PL/SQL program items and units including constants, variables, cursors, cursor variables, exceptions, procedures, functions, and packages. Names can be simple, qualified, remote, or both qualified and remote. For example, we might use the procedure name raise_salary in any of the following ways:

```
raise_salary(...);                          — simple
emp_actions.raise_salary(...);              — qualified
raise_salary@newyork(...);                  — remote
emp_actions.raise_salary@newyork(...);      — qualified and remote
```

In the first case, simply use the procedure name. In the second case, we must qualify the name using dot notation because the procedure is stored in a package called emp_actions. In the third case, using the remote access indicator (@), we reference the database link newyork because the procedure is stored in a remote database. In the fourth case, qualify the procedure name and reference a database link.

Synonyms

We can create synonyms to provide location transparency for remote schema objects such as tables, sequences, views, stand-alone subprograms, and packages. However, we cannot create synonyms for items declared within subprograms or packages that include constants, variables, cursors, cursor variables, exceptions, and packaged subprograms.

Name Resolution

In potentially ambiguous SQL statements, the names of database columns take precedence over the names of local variables and formal parameters. For example, the following DELETE statement removes all employees from the emp table, not just 'KING', because Oracle assumes that both enames in the WHERE clause refer to the database column:

```
DECLARE
  ename VARCHAR2(10) := 'KING';
BEGIN
  DELETE FROM emp WHERE ename = ename;
```

In such cases, to avoid ambiguity, we prefix the names of local variables and formal parameters with my_, as follows:

```
DECLARE
  my_ename VARCHAR2(10);
```

Or, use a block label to qualify references, as in

```
<<main>>
DECLARE
  ename VARCHAR2(10) := 'KING';
BEGIN
  DELETE FROM emp WHERE ename = main.ename;
```

The next example shows that we can use a subprogram name to qualify references to local variables and formal parameters:

```
FUNCTION bonus (deptno IN NUMBER, ...) RETURN REAL IS
  job CHAR(10);
BEGIN
SELECT ... WHERE deptno = bonus.deptno AND job = bonus.job;
```

Scope and Visibility

The scope of an identifier is that region of a program unit (block, subprogram, or package) from which we can reference the identifier. An identifier is visible only in the regions from which we can reference the identifier using an unqualified name. Figure 7.4 shows the scope and visibility of a variable named x, which is declared in an enclosing block, then redeclared in a sub-block.

Identifiers declared in a PL/SQL block are considered local to that block and global to all its sub-blocks. If a global identifier is redeclared in a sub-block, both identifiers remain in scope. Within the sub-block, however, only the local identifier is visible because we must use a qualified name to reference the global identifier.

Although we cannot declare an identifier twice in the same block, we can declare the same identifier in two different blocks. The two items represented by the identifier are distinct, and any change in one does not affect the other. However, a block cannot reference identifiers declared in other blocks at the same level because those identifiers are neither local nor global to the block.

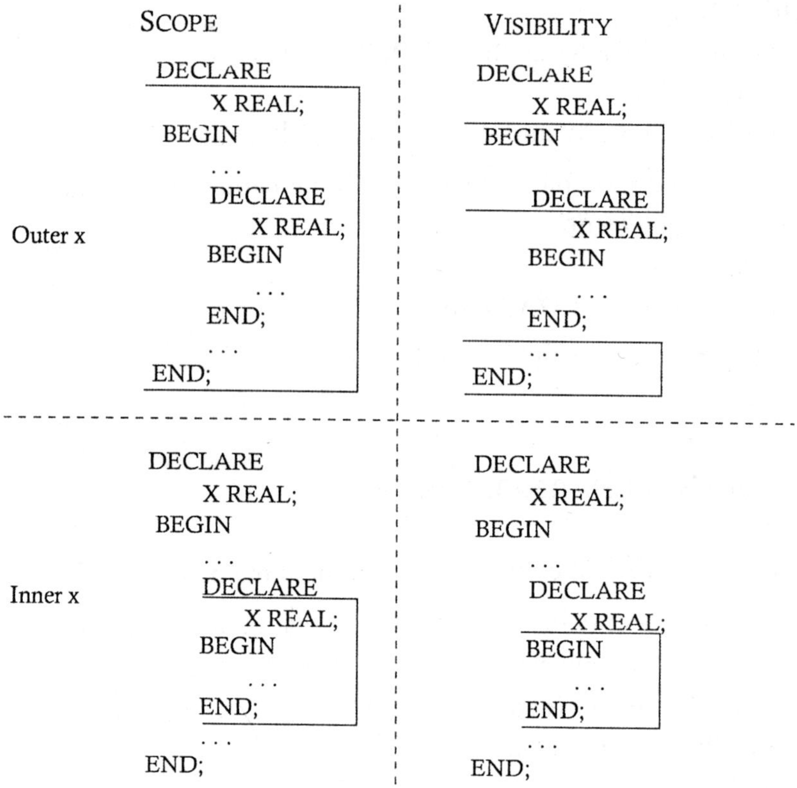

Figure 7.4. Scope and Visibility

The example below illustrates the scope rules.

Note. The identifiers declared in one sub-block cannot be referenced in the other sub-block. That is because a block cannot reference identifiers declared in other blocks nested at the same level.

```
DECLARE
  a CHAR;
  b REAL;
```

```
BEGIN
  -- identifiers available here: a (CHAR), b

DECLARE
  a INTEGER;
  c REAL;
BEGIN
  -- identifiers available here: a (INTEGER), b, c
END;
DECLARE
  d REAL;
BEGIN
  -- identifiers available here: a (CHAR), b, d
END;
  -- identifiers available here: a (CHAR), b
END;
```

Recall that global identifiers can be redeclared in a sub-block, in which case the local declaration prevails and the sub-block cannot reference the global identifier unless we use a qualified name. The qualifier can be the label of an enclosing block, as the following example shows:

```
<<outer>>
DECLARE
  birthdate DATE;
BEGIN
  DECLARE
    birthdate DATE;
  BEGIN
    ...
    IF birthdate = outer.birthdate THEN ...
```

As the next example shows, the qualifier can also be the name of an enclosing subprogram:

```
PROCEDURE check_credit (...) IS
  rating NUMBER;
  FUNCTION valid (...) RETURN BOOLEAN IS
    rating NUMBER;
  BEGIN
    ...
    IF check_credit.rating < 3 THEN ...
```

However, within the same scope, a label and a subprogram cannot have the same name.

Boolean Values

Only the values TRUE, FALSE, and NULL can be assigned to a Boolean variable. For example, given the declaration

```
DECLARE
  done BOOLEAN;
```

the following statements are legal:

```
BEGIN
  done := FALSE;
  WHILE NOT done LOOP
    ...
  END LOOP;
```

When applied to an expression, the relational operators return a Boolean value. So, the following assignment is legal:

```
done := (count > 500);
```

Database Values

We can use the SELECT statement to have Oracle assign values to a variable. For each item in the select list, there must be a corresponding, type-compatible variable in the INTO list. An example follows:

```
DECLARE
  my_empno emp.empno%TYPE;
  my_ename emp.ename%TYPE;
  wages NUMBER(7,2);
BEGIN
  ...
  SELECT ename, sal + comm
    INTO last_name, wages FROM emp
    WHERE empno = emp_id;
```

Note. We cannot select column values into a Boolean variable.

Expressions and Comparisons

Expressions are constructed using operands and operators. An operand is a variable, constant, literal, or function call that contributes a value to an expression. An example of a simple arithmetic expression follows:

```
-X / 2 + 3
```

Ternary operators such as the negation operator (-) operate on one operand; binary operators such as the division operator (/) operate on two operands. PL/SQL has no ternary operators.

The simplest expressions consist of a single variable, which yields a value directly. PL/SQL evaluates an expression by combining the values of the operands in ways specified by the operators. This always yields a single value and datatype. PL/SQL determines the datatype by examining the expression and the context in which it appears.

OPERATOR PRECEDENCE

The operations within an expression are done in a particular order depending on their precedence (priority). Table 7.3 shows the default order of operations from first to last (top to bottom).

Table 7.3: Operator Precedence

<table>
<tr><th>Operator</th><th>Operation</th></tr>
<tr><td>**, NOT</td><td>exponentiation, logical negation</td></tr>
<tr><td>+, –</td><td>identity, negation</td></tr>
<tr><td>*, /</td><td>multiplication, division</td></tr>
<tr><td>+, –, ||</td><td>addition, subtraction, concatenation</td></tr>
<tr><td>=, <, >, <=, >=, <>, !=, ~=, ^=,
IS NULL, LIKE, BETWEEN, IN</td><td>comparison</td></tr>
<tr><td>AND</td><td>conjunction</td></tr>
<tr><td>OR</td><td>inclusion</td></tr>
</table>

Operators with higher precedence are applied first. In the example below, both expressions yield 8 because division has a higher precedence than addition. Operators with the same precedence are applied in no particular order.

```
5 + 12 / 4
12 / 4 + 5
```

In the next example, the subtraction is done before the division because the most deeply nested sub expression is always evaluated first:

```
100 + (20 / 5 + (8 - 3))
```

The following example shows that we can always use parentheses to improve readability, even when they are not needed:

```
(salary * 0.05) + (commission * 0.35)
```

Logical Operators

The logical operators AND, OR, and NOT follow the tri-state logic shown in Table 7.4. AND and OR are binary operators; NOT is a unary operator.

Table 7.4: Logic Truth Table

x	y	x AND y	x OR y	NOT x
TRUE	TRUE	TRUE	TRUE	FALSE
TRUE	FALSE	FALSE	TRUE	TRUE
TRUE	NULL	NULL	TRUE	NULL
FALSE	TRUE	FALSE	TRUE	
FALSE	FALSE	FALSE	FALSE	
FALSE	NULL	FALSE	NULL	
NULL	TRUE	NULL	TRUE	
NULL	FALSE	FALSE	NULL	
NULL	NULL	NULL	NULL	

As the truth table shows, AND returns TRUE only if both its operands are true. On the other hand, OR returns TRUE if either of its operands is true. NOT returns the opposite value (logical negation) of its operand. For example, NOT TRUE returns FALSE.

NOT NULL returns NULL because nulls are indeterminate. It follows that if we apply the NOT operator to a null, the result is also indeterminate.

Order of Evaluation

When we do not use parentheses to specify the order of evaluation, operator precedence determines the order. Compare the following expressions:

NOT (valid AND done) | NOT valid AND done

If the Boolean variables valid and done have the value FALSE, the first expression yields TRUE. However, the second expression yields FALSE because NOT has a higher precedence than AND. Therefore, the second expression is equivalent to:

(NOT valid) AND done

In the following example, notice that when valid has the value FALSE, the whole expression yields FALSE regardless of the value of done:

valid AND done

Likewise, in the next example, when valid has the value TRUE, the whole expression yields TRUE regardless of the value of done:

```
valid OR done
```

Short-Circuit Evaluation

When evaluating a logical expression, PL/SQL uses short-circuit evaluation. That is, PL/SQL stops evaluating the expression as soon as the result can be determined. This allows us to write expressions that might otherwise cause an error. Consider the following OR expression:

```
DECLARE
   ...
   on_hand  INTEGER;
   on_order INTEGER;
BEGIN
   ...
   IF (on_hand = 0) OR ((on_order / on_hand) < 5) THEN
      ...
   END IF;
END,
```

When the value of on_hand is zero, the left operand yields TRUE, so PL/SQL need not evaluate the right operand. If PL/SQL were to evaluate both operands before applying the OR operator, the right operand would cause a division by zero error. In any case, it is a poor programming practice to rely on short-circuit evaluation.

Comparison Operators

Comparison operators compare one expression to another. The result is always true, false, or null. Typically, we use comparison operators in conditional control statements and in the WHERE clause of SQL data manipulation statements. Here are a couple of examples:

```
IF quantity_on_hand > 0 THEN
   UPDATE inventory SET quantity = quantity - 1
      WHERE part_number = item_number;
ELSE
   ...
END IF;
```

Relational Operators

The relational operators allow us to compare arbitrarily complex expressions. The following list gives the meaning of each operator:

Operator	Meaning
=	equal to
<>, !=, ~=, ^=	not equal to
<	less than
>	greater than
<=	less than or equal to
>=	greater than or equal to

IS NULL Operator

The IS NULL operator returns the Boolean value TRUE if its operand is null or FALSE if it is not null. Comparisons involving nulls always yield NULL. Therefore, to test for nullity (the state of being null), do not use the statement

IF variable = NULL THEN ...

Instead, use the following statement:

IF variable IS NULL THEN ...

LIKE Operator

LIKE operator is used to compare a character value to a pattern. Case is significant. LIKE returns the Boolean value TRUE if the character patterns match or FALSE if they do not match.

The patterns matched by LIKE can include two special-purpose characters called wildcards like DOS. An underscore (_) matches exactly one character; a percent sign (%) matches zero or more characters. For example, if the value of ename is 'JOHNSON', the following expression is true:

ename LIKE 'J%SON'

BETWEEN Operator

The BETWEEN operator tests whether a value lies in a specified range. It means "greater than or equal to low value and less than or equal to high value." For example, the following expression is false:

45 BETWEEN 38 AND 44

IN Operator

The IN operator tests set membership. It means "equal to any member of." The set can contain nulls, but they are ignored. For example, the following statement does not delete rows in which the ename column is null:

DELETE FROM emp WHERE ename IN (NULL, 'KING', 'FORD');

Furthermore, expressions of the form value NOT IN set yield FALSE if the set contains a null. For example, instead of deleting rows in which the ename column is not null and not 'KING', the following statement deletes no rows:

DELETE FROM emp WHERE ename NOT IN (NULL, 'KING');

Concatenation Operator

Double vertical bars (||) serve as the concatenation operator, which appends one string to another. For example, the expression

'Techn' || 'ology'

returns the following value:

'Technology'

If both operands have datatype CHAR, the concatenation operator returns a CHAR value. Otherwise, it returns a VARCHAR2 value.

Boolean Expressions

PL/SQL lets you compare variables and constants in both SQL and procedural statements. These comparisons, called Boolean expressions, consist of simple or complex expressions separated by relational operators. Often, Boolean expressions are connected by the logical operators AND, OR, and NOT. A Boolean expression always yields TRUE, FALSE, or NULL.

In a SQL statement, Boolean expressions let us specify the rows in a table that are affected by the statement. In a procedural statement, Boolean expressions are the basis for conditional control. There are three kinds of Boolean expressions: arithmetic, character, and date.

Arithmetic Expressions

We can use the relational operators to compare numbers for equality or inequality. Comparisons are quantitative; that is, one number is greater than another if it represents a larger quantity. For example, for the given assignments

number1 := 85;
number2 := 80;

the following expression is true:

number1 > number2

Character Expressions

We can also compare character values for equality or inequality. Comparisons are based on the collating sequence used for the database character set. A collating sequence is an internal ordering of the character set in which a range of numeric codes represents the individual characters. One character value is greater than another if its internal numeric value is larger. For example, for the given assignments

```
string1 := 'Katy';
string2 := 'Katleen';
```

the following expression is true:

```
string1 > string2
```

However, there are semantic differences between the CHAR and VARCHAR2 base types that come into play when we compare character values.

Date Expressions

We can also compare dates. Comparisons are chronological, that is, one date is greater than the other if it is more recent. For example, for the given assignments

```
date1 := '04-JAN-91';
date2 := '30-DEC-90';
```

the following expression is true:

```
date1 > date2
```

Guidelines

In general, do not compare real numbers for exact equality or inequality. Real numbers are stored as approximate values. So, for example, the following IF condition might not yield TRUE:

```
count := 1;
IF count = 1.0 THEN ...
```

It is a good idea to use parentheses when doing comparisons. For example, the following expression is illegal because 100 < tax yields a Boolean value, which cannot be compared with the number 500:

```
100 < tax < 500 — illegal
```

The debugged version follows:

```
(100 < tax) AND (tax < 500)
```

A Boolean variable is itself either true or false. So, comparisons with the Boolean values TRUE and FALSE are redundant. For example, assuming the variable done is of type BOOLEAN, the WHILE statement

```
WHILE NOT (done = TRUE) LOOP
...
END LOOP;
```

can be simplified as follows:

```
WHILE NOT done LOOP
   ...
END LOOP;
```

Handling Nulls

When working with nulls, we can avoid some common mistakes by keeping in mind the following rules:

- Comparisons involving nulls always yield NULL
- Applying the logical operator NOT to a null yields NULL
- In conditional control statements, if the condition yields NULL, its associated sequence of statements is not executed

In the example below, we might expect the sequence of statements to execute because x and y seem unequal. But, nulls are indeterminate. Whether or not x is equal to y is unknown. Therefore, the IF condition yields NULL and the sequence of statements is bypassed.

```
x := 5;
y := NULL;
...
IF x != y THEN  — yields NULL, not TRUE
   sequence_of_statements;  — not executed
END IF;
```

In the next example, we might expect the sequence of statements to execute because a and b seem equal. But, again, that is unknown, so the IF condition yields NULL and the sequence of statements is bypassed.

```
a := NULL;
b := NULL;
   ...
IF a = b THEN  — yields NULL, not TRUE
   sequence_of_statements;  — not executed
END IF;
```

NOT Operator

Recall that applying the logical operator NOT to a null yields NULL. Thus, the following two statements are not always equivalent:

IF x > y THEN
   high := x;
ELSE
   high := y;
END IF;
	IF NOT x > y THEN
	   high := y;
	ELSE
	   high := x;
	END IF;

The sequence of statements in the ELSE clause is executed when the IF condition yields FALSE or NULL. If neither x nor y is null, both IF statements assign the same value to high. However, if either x or y is null, the first IF statement assigns the value of y to high, but the second IF statement assigns the value of x to high.

Zero-Length Strings

PL/SQL treats any zero-length string like a null. This includes values returned by character functions and Boolean expressions. For example, the following statements assign nulls to the target variables:

```
null_string := TO_VARCHAR2('');
zip_code := SUBSTR(address, 25, 0);
valid := (name != '');
```

So, use the IS NULL operator to test for null strings, as follows:

```
IF my_string IS NULL THEN ...
```

Concatenation Operator

The concatenation operator ignores null operands. For example, the expression

```
'apple' || NULL || NULL || 'sauce'
```

returns the following value:

```
'applesauce'
```

Functions

If a null argument is passed to a built-in function, a null is returned except in the following cases.

The function DECODE compares its first argument to one or more search expressions, which are paired with result expressions. Any search or result expression can be null. If a search is successful, the corresponding result is returned. In the following example, if the column rating is null, DECODE returns the value 1000:

```
SELECT DECODE(rating, NULL, 1000, 'C', 2000, 'B', 4000, 'A', 5000)
  INTO credit_limit FROM accts WHERE acctno = my_acctno;
```

The function NVL returns the value of its second argument if its first argument is null. In the example below, if hire_date is null, NVL returns the value of SYSDATE. Otherwise, NVL returns the value of hire_date:

```
start_date := NVL(hire_date, SYSDATE);
```

The function REPLACE returns the value of its first argument if its second argument is null, whether the optional third argument is present or not. For instance, after the assignment

```
new_string := REPLACE(old_string, NULL, my_string);
```

the values of old_string and new_string are the same.

If its third argument is null, REPLACE returns its first argument with every occurrence of its second argument removed. For example, after the assignments

```
syllabified_name := 'Gold-i-locks';
name := REPLACE(syllabified_name, '-', NULL);
```

the value of name is 'goldilocks'

If its second and third arguments are null, REPLACE simply returns its first argument.

CONTROL STRUCTURES

Now we will learn how statements are connected by simple but powerful control structures that have a single entry and exit point. Collectively, these structures can handle any situation. Their proper use leads naturally to a well-structured program.

1. Conditional Control : IF Statements
2. Iterative Control : LOOPS and EXIT Statements
3. Sequential Control : GOTO and NULL Statements

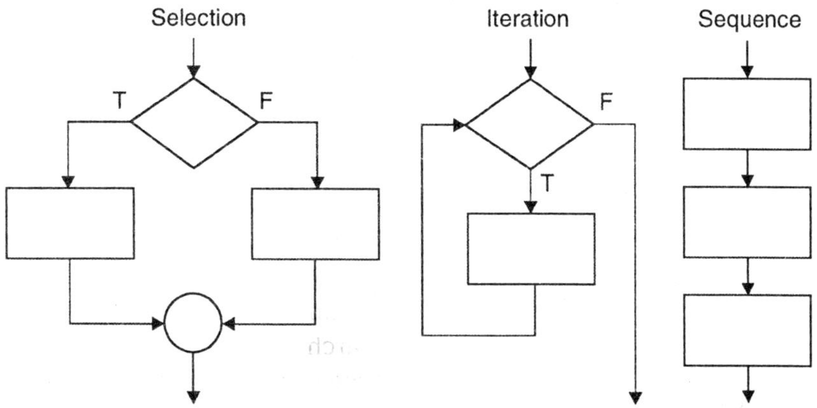

Figure 7.5. Control Structures

The selection structure tests a condition, then executes one sequence of statements instead of another, depending on whether the condition is true or false. A condition is any variable or expression that returns a Boolean value (TRUE or FALSE). The iteration structure executes a sequence of statements repeatedly as long as a condition holds true. The sequence structure simply executes a sequence of statements in the order in which they occur.

Conditional Control: IF Statements

We need to be able to implement requirements such as:

If the salary is between ten and twenty thousand, then apply a bonus of $1500.

If the salary is between twenty and forty thousand, apply a bonus of $1000.

If the salary is over forty thousand, give the employee a bonus of $500.

or:

If the user preference includes the toolbar, display the toolbar when the window first opens.

The IF statement allows to design conditional logic in your programs. The IF statement comes in three types:

IF **THEN** **END IF;**	This is the simplest form of the IF statement. The condition between the IF and THEN determines whether the set of statements between the THEN and END IF should be executed. If the condition evaluates to false, then the code is not executed.
IF **ELSE** **END IF;**	This combination implements an either/or logic: based on the condition between the IF and THEN keywords, either execute the code between the THEN and ELSE or between the ELSE and END IF. One of these two sections of executable statements is performed.
IF **ELSIF** **ELSE** **END IF;**	This last and most complex form of the IF statement selects an action from a series of mutually exclusive conditions and then executes the set of statements associated with that condition.

The IF-THEN Combination

The general format of the IF-THEN syntax is as follows:

```
IF <condition>
THEN
  ... sequence of executable statements ...
END IF;
```

The <condition> is a Boolean variable, constant, or expression that evaluates to TRUE, FALSE, or NULL. If <condition> evaluates to TRUE, then the executable statements found after the THEN keyword and before the matching END IF statement are executed. If the <condition> evaluates to FALSE or NULL, then those statements are not executed.

Here are some examples of the simple IF-THEN structure:

The following IF condition compares two different numeric values. Remember that if one of these two variables is NULL, then the entire Boolean expression returns NULL and the discount is not applied:

```
IF :company.total_sales > system_average_sales
THEN
apply_discount (:company.company_id);
END IF;
```

Here is an example of an IF statement with a single Boolean variable (or function — one really can't tell the difference just by looking at this line of code):

```
IF report_requested
THEN
print_report (report_id);
     END IF;
```

In the previous example, we used a single Boolean variable in my condition. If the variable report_requested evaluates to TRUE, then the report prints. Otherwise, the print step is skipped. The same IF statement is as follows:

```
IF report_requested = TRUE
THEN
print_report (report_id);
END IF;
```

While the code in the third example is logically equivalent to the IF report_requested formulation, it is superfluous and works against the nature of a Boolean variable. A Boolean variable itself evaluates to TRUE, FALSE, or NULL; we don't have to test the variable against those values. If we name our Boolean variables properly, we will be able to easily read the logic and intent of our IF-THEN logic by leaving out the unnecessary parts of the statement.

The IF-THEN-ELSE Combination

We use the IF-THEN-ELSE format when we want to choose between two mutually exclusive actions. The format of this either/or version of the IF statement is as follows:

```
IF <condition>
THEN
  ... TRUE sequence of executable statements ...
ELSE
  ... FALSE/NULL sequence of executable statements ...
END IF;
```

The <condition> is a Boolean variable, constant, or expression. If <condition> evaluates to TRUE, then the executable statements found after the THEN keyword and before the ELSE keyword are executed (the "TRUE sequence of executable statements"). If the <condition> evaluates to FALSE or NULL, then the executable statements that come after the ELSE keywords and before the matching END IF keywords are executed (the "FALSE/NULL sequence of executable statements").

The important thing to remember is that one of these sequences of statements will always execute, because it is an either/or construct. Once the appropriate set of statements has been executed, control passes to the statement immediately following the END IF statement.

Note. The ELSE clause does not have a THEN associated with it.

Here are some examples of the IF-THEN-ELSE construct:

In this example, if there is a VIP caller, we generate an express response, otherwise, we use normal delivery:

```
IF caller_type = 'VIP'
THEN
generate_response ('EXCLUSIVE');
ELSE
generate_response ('GENERAL');
END IF;
```

We can put an entire IF-THEN-ELSE on a single line as shown below:

```
IF new_caller THEN get_next_id; ELSE use_current_id; END IF;
```

This example sets the order_exceeds_balance Boolean variable based on the order total:

```
IF :customer.order_total > max_allowable_order
THEN
    order_exceeds_balance := TRUE;
ELSE
    order_exceeds_balance := FALSE;
END IF;
```

In the last example, the IF statement is not only unnecessary, but confusing. Remember: we can assign a TRUE/FALSE value directly to a Boolean variable. We do not need the IF-THEN-ELSE construct to decide how to set order_exceeds_balance. Instead, we can assign the value directly, as follows:

```
order_exceeds_balance :=  :customer.order_total >
max_allowable_order;
```

This assignment sets the order_exceeds_balance variable to TRUE if the customer's order total is greater than the maximum allowed, and sets it to FALSE otherwise. In other words, it achieves exactly the same result as the IF-THEN-ELSE and does it more clearly and with less code.

The IF-ELSIF Combination

This last form of the IF statement comes in handy when we have to implement logic which has many alternatives; it is not an either/or situation. The IF-ELSIF formulation provides the most straightforward and natural way to handle multiple, mutually exclusive alternatives. The general format for this variation of the IF statement is:

```
IF <condition-1>
THEN
    <statements-1>
...
ELSIF <condition-N>
THEN
    <statements-N>
[ELSE
    <else_statements>]
END IF;
```

Logically speaking, the IF-ELSIF implements the CASE statement in PL/SQL. The sequence of evaluation and execution for this statement is:

If <condition1> is true then execute <statements1>.

Otherwise ... if <condition n> is true then execute <statements n>.

Otherwise execute the <else_statements>.

Each ELSIF clause must have a THEN after its condition. Only the ELSE keyword does not need the THEN keyword. The ELSE clause in the IF-ELSIF is the "otherwise" of the statement. If none of the conditions evaluate to TRUE, then the statements in the ELSE clause are executed. But the ELSE clause is also optional. We can code an IF-ELSIF that has only IF and ELSIF clauses. In this case, if none of the conditions are TRUE, then no statements inside the IF block are executed.

The conditions in the IF-ELSIF are always evaluated in the order of first condition to last condition. Once a condition evaluates to TRUE, the remaining conditions are not evaluated at all.

IF-ELSIF examples

Here are some examples of the possible variations in the format of the IF-ELSIF structure:

- We have three different caller types to check. If the caller type is not one of VIP, BILL_COLLECTOR, or INTERNATIONAL, then send the response with normal delivery:

```
IF caller_type = 'VIP'
THEN
   generate_response ('EXPRESS');
ELSIF caller_type = 'BILL_COLLECTOR'
THEN
   generate_response ('THROUGH_CHICAGO');
ELSIF caller_type = 'INTERNATIONAL'
THEN
```

```
   generate_response ('AIR');
ELSE
   generate_response ('NORMAL');
  END IF;
```

- Here's an IF-ELSIF with just a single ELSIF — and no ELSE. In this case, however, we could just as well have used an IF-THEN-ELSE structure because the two conditions are mutually exclusive. The ELSIF statements execute only if the IF condition is FALSE. The advantage of including the ELSIF is that it documents more clearly the condition under which its executable statements will be run.

```
IF start_date > SYSDATE AND order_total >= min_order_total
THEN
  fill_order (order_id);
ELSIF start_date <= SYSDATE OR order_total < min_order_total
THEN
  queue_order_for_addtl_parts (order_id);
  END IF;
```

Mutually Exclusive IF-ELSIF Conditions

Make sure that our IF-ELSIF conditions are mutually exclusive. The conditions in the IF-ELSIF are always evaluated in the order of first to last. Once a condition evaluates to TRUE, the remaining conditions are not evaluated at all. If we have an overlap in the conditions so that more than one condition could be TRUE, we probably have an error in our logic. Either the conditions in the IF statement should be changed to make them exclusive, or we'll sometimes run the risk of not executing the right set of code in our IF statement. The following example illustrates these points. Translate the following rules:

If the salary is between ten and twenty thousand, then apply a bonus of $1600.
If the salary is between twenty and forty thousand, apply a bonus of $1100.
If the salary is over forty thousand, give the employee a bonus of $600.
into this code:

```
IF salary BETWEEN 10000 AND 20000
THEN
    bonus := 1600;
ELSIF salary BETWEEN 20000 AND 40000
THEN
    bonus := 1100;
ELSIF salary > 40000
THEN
```

```
      bonus := 600;
   END IF;
```

What will be the bonus if the salary is $20,000 ? Will the person receive a bonus of $1100 or $1600? The way the IF-ELSIF is currently written, a person making $20,000 will always receive a bonus of $1600. Actually, the problem here is that the original phrasing of the specification is ambiguous — and even incomplete. It assumes that no one ever has a salary of less than $10,000 (or, if we did not want to give the author of this specification the benefit of the doubt, we would say, "Anyone with a salary under $10,000 gets no bonus").

We can close up the holes in this logic by moving away from the BETWEEN operator and instead relying on < and >. This clarifies those break-points in the salary:

```
IF salary < 10000
THEN
  bonus := 2100;
ELSIF salary < 20000
THEN
  bonus := 1600;
ELSIF salary < 40000
THEN
  bonus := 1100;
ELSE — same as ELSIF salary >= 40000
  bonus := 600;
END IF;
```

Now the conditions are mutually exclusive and the people who get the lowest salary get the largest bonus.

Here is an example of an IF-ELSIF with a condition that will never evaluate to TRUE; the code associated with it, therefore, will never be executed. See if we can figure out which condition that is:

```
IF order_date > SYSDATE AND order_total >= min_order_total
THEN
  fill_order (order_id, 'HIGH PRIORITY');
ELSIF order_date < SYSDATE OR order_date = SYSDATE
THEN
  fill_order (order_id, 'LOW PRIORITY');
ELSIF order_date <= SYSDATE AND order_total < min_order_total
THEN
  queue_order_for_addtl_parts (order_id);
```

```
ELSIF order_total = 0
THEN
  MESSAGE (' No items have been placed in this order!');
END IF;
```

The only executable statement that we can say with complete confidence will never be executed is:

```
queue_order_for_addtl_parts (order_id);
```

An order is put in the queue to wait for additional parts (to boost up the order total) only if the third condition evalutes to TRUE:

The order was placed today or earlier and the total for the order is under the minimum.

The reason that queue_order_for_addtl_parts will never be executed lies in the second condition:

An order is filled with LOW PRIORITY whenever the order date was no later than the system date.

The second condition is a logical subset of the third condition. Whenever the second condition is FALSE, the third condition will also be FALSE. Whenever the third condition evaluates to TRUE, the second condition will also evaluate to TRUE. Because it comes before the third condition in the evaluation sequence, the second condition will catch any scenarios that would otherwise satisfy the third condition.

When we write an IF-ELSIF, especially one with more than three alternatives, we review our logic closely and make sure there is no overlap in the conditions. For any particular set of values or circumstances, at most one — and perhaps none — of the conditions should evaluate to be TRUE.

Nested IF Statements

We can nest any IF statement within any other IF statement. The following IF statement shows several layers of nesting:

```
IF <condition1>
THEN
    IF <condition2>
    THEN
       <statements2>
    ELSE
       IF <condition3>
       THEN
         <statements3>
       ELSIF <condition4>
       THEN
         <statements4>
```

```
            END IF;
        END IF;
    END IF;
```

Nested IF statements are often necessary to implement complex logic rules, but we should use them carefully. Nested IF statements, like nested loops, can be very difficult to understand and debug. If we find that we need to nest more than three levels deep in our conditional logic, we should review that logic and see if there is a simpler way to code the same requirement. If not, then consider creating one or more local modules to hide the innermost IF statements.

A key advantage to the nested IF structure is that it defers evaluation of inner conditions. The conditions of an inner IF statement are evaluated only if the condition for the outer IF statement that encloses them evaluates to TRUE.

If the evaluation of a condition is very expensive (in CPU or memory terms), one may want to defer that processing to an inner IF statement so that it is executed only when absolutely necessary. This is especially true of code that will be performed frequently or in areas of the application where quick response time is critical.

The following IF statement illustrates this concept:

```
IF condition1 AND condition2
THEN
  ...
END IF;
```

The PL/SQL run-time engine evaluates both conditions in order to determine if the Boolean expression A AND B evaluates to TRUE. Suppose that condition2 is an expression which PL/SQL can process simply and efficiently, such as:

```
total_sales > 100000
```

but that condition1 is a much more complex and CPU-intensive expression, perhaps calling a stored function which executes a query against the database. If condition2 is evaluated in a tenth of a second to TRUE and condition1 is evaluated in three seconds to FALSE, then it would take more than three seconds to determine that the code inside the IF statement should not be executed.

Now consider this next version of the same IF statement:

```
IF condition2
THEN
    IF condition1
    THEN
        ...
    END IF;
END IF;
```

Now condition1 will be evaluated only if condition2 evaluates to be TRUE. In those situations where total_sales <= 100000, the user will never have to wait the extra three seconds to continue.

Special Notes about IF

Keep these points in mind about IF statement syntax:

- Always match up an IF with an END IF. In all three variations of the IF statement, we must close off the executable statements associated with the conditional structure with an END IF statement.
- We must have a space between the keywords END and IF. If we type ENDIF instead of END IF, the compiler will get very confused and give us the following hard-to-understand error messages:
  ORA-06550: line 14, column 4:
  PLS-00103: Encountered the symbol ";" when expecting one of the following:
  if
- The ELSIF keyword does not have an embedded "E". If we use type ELSEIF in place of ELSIF, the compiler will get very confused and not recognize the ELSEIF as part of the IF statement. It will interpret it as a variable name or program name.
- Place a semicolon (;) only after the END IF keywords. The keywords THEN, ELSE, and ELSIF should not have a semicolon after them. They are not standalone executable statements and, unlike END IF, do not complete a statement. If we include a semicolon after these keywords, the compiler will issue messages indicating that it is looking for a statement of some kind before the semicolon.

Iterative Control: LOOP and EXIT Statements

LOOP statements let us execute a sequence of statements multiple times. There are three forms of LOOP statements:

(1) LOOP

(2) WHILE-LOOP

(3) FOR-LOOP

LOOP

The structure of the simple loop is the most basic of all the loop constructs. It consists of the LOOP keyword, the body of executable code, and the END LOOP keywords, as shown here:

```
LOOP
   <executable statement(s)>
END LOOP;
```

The loop boundary consists solely of the LOOP and END LOOP reserved words. The body must consist of at least one executable statement. The following table summarizes the properties of the single loop:

Property	Description
How the loop is terminated	The simple loop is terminated when an EXIT statement is executed in the body of the loop. If this statement is not executed, the simple loop becomes a true infinite loop.
When the test for termination takes place	The test takes place inside the body of the loop—and then only if an EXIT or EXIT WHEN statement is executed. Therefore, the body—or part of the body—of the simple loop will always execute at least once.
Reason to use this loop	Use the simple loop when: • We are not sure how many times you will want the loop to execute, and • We want the loop to run at least once.

This loop is useful when we want to guarantee that the body (or at least part of the body) executes at least one time. As there is no condition associated with the loop boundary that determines whether or not it should execute, the body of the loop will always execute the first time.

The simple loop will terminate only when an EXIT statement is executed in its body (see "Terminating a Single Loop: EXIT and EXIT WHEN" below). As this doesn't have to be the case, a simple loop can also become an infinite loop. This could cause difficulties in your program and is something to be avoided.

The following example shows a simple loop which is truly infinite; it keeps checking for messages from a particular pipe so that it can respond immediately and display the information in the pipe.

```
DECLARE
  pipe_status INTEGER;
  message_text VARCHAR2
BEGIN
  LOOP
    pipe_status := DBMS_PIPE.RECEIVE_MESSAGE
('execution_trace');
    IF pipe_status = 0
    THEN
      DBMS_PIPE.UNPACK_MESSAGE (message_text);
      DBMS_OUTPUT.PUT_LINE (message_text);
```

```
    END IF;
  END LOOP;
END;
```

Terminating a Simple Loop

EXIT and EXIT WHEN

Be very careful when you use simple loops. Make sure they always have a way to stop. To force a simple loop to stop processing, execute an EXIT or EXIT WHEN statement within the body of the loop. The syntax for these statements is as follows:

```
EXIT:
EXIT WHEN condition;
```

where condition is a Boolean expression.

The following example demonstrates how the EXIT forces the loop to immediately halt execution and pass control to the next statement after the END LOOP statement. The account_balance procedure returns the amount of money remaining in the account specified by the account ID. If there is less than $1000 left, the EXIT statement is executed and the loop is terminated. Otherwise, the program applies the balance to the outstanding orders for that account.

```
    LOOP
      balance_remaining := account_balance (account_id);
      IF balance_remaining < 1000
      THEN
         EXIT;
    ELSE
         apply_balance (account_id, balance_remaining);
    END IF;
END LOOP;
```

One can use an EXIT statement only within a LOOP.

PL/SQL also offers the EXIT WHEN statement, which supports the concept of "conditional termination" of the loop. Essentially, the EXIT WHEN combines an IF-THEN statement with the EXIT statement. Using the same example we showed above, the EXIT WHEN changes the loop to:

```
LOOP
  /* Calculate the balance */
  balance_remaining := account_balance (account_id);
  /* Embed the IF logic into the EXIT statement */
  EXIT WHEN balance_remaining < 1000;
```

```
    /* Apply balance if still executing the loop */
    apply_balance (account_id, balance_remaining);
END LOOP;
```

Notice that the loop no longer requires an IF statement to determine when it should exit. Instead, that conditional logic is embedded inside the EXIT WHEN statement.

EXIT WHEN is a very concise and readable way to terminate a simple loop; we recommend its use over the unconditional EXIT statement. After all, you should always have an EXIT statement nested within an IF-THEN. If you don't, then you either have an infinite loop or you have a loop that executes just once. In the latter case, it is better to execute the body of the loop without using a loop. If the EXIT is always included within the IF-THEN, you'd be better off using a language construct built specifically for the purpose. The EXIT WHEN construct also reduces the amount of code you need to write.

Emulating a REPEAT UNTIL Loop

PL/SQL does not provide a REPEAT UNTIL loop in which the condition is tested after the body of the loop is executed and thus guarantees that the loop always executes at least once. You can, however, emulate a REPEAT UNTIL with a simple loop, as follows:

```
LOOP
    ... body of loop ...
  EXIT WHEN boolean_condition;
END LOOP;
```

where boolean_condition is a Boolean variable or an expression that evaluates to a Boolean value of TRUE or FALSE.

The WHILE Loop

The WHILE loop is a conditional loop that continues to execute as long as the Boolean condition defined in the loop boundary evaluates to TRUE. Because the WHILE loop execution depends on a condition and is not fixed, use a WHILE loop if you don't know ahead of time the number of times a loop must execute.

Here is the general syntax for the WHILE loop:

```
WHILE <condition>
LOOP
  <executable statement(s)>
END LOOP;
```

where <condition> is a Boolean variable or an expression that evaluates to a Boolean value of TRUE, FALSE, or NULL. Each time an iteration of the loop's body is to be executed, the condition is checked. If it evaluates to TRUE, then the body is executed. If it evaluates to FALSE or to NULL, then the loop terminates and control passes to the next executable statement following the END LOOP statement.

The following table summarizes the properties of the WHILE loop

Table 7.5

Property	Description
How the loop is terminated	The WHILE loop terminates when the Boolean expression in its boundary evaluates to FALSE or NULL.
When the test for termination takes place	The test for termination of a WHILE loop takes place in the loop boundary. This evaluation occurs prior to the first and each subsequent execution of the body. The WHILE loop, therefore, cannot be guaranteed to always execute its loop even a single time.
Reason to use this loop	Use the WHILE loop when: You are not sure how many times you must execute the loop body, and • You will want to conditionally terminate the loop, and • You don't have to execute the body at least one time.

The WHILE loop's condition is tested at the beginning of the loop's iteration, before the body of the loop is executed. There are two consequences to this pre-execution test:

- All the information needed to evaluate the condition must be set before the loop is executed for the first time.
- It is possible that the WHILE loop will not execute even a single time.

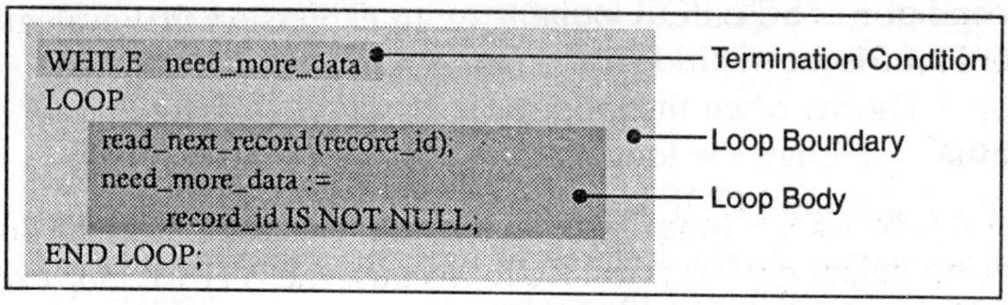

The Infinite WHILE Loop

One of the dangers of the simple loop is that it could be an infinite loop if the body of the loop never executes an EXIT statement. While this is less of a problem with the WHILE loop, we should be aware that it is certainly possible to construct a WHILE loop that is syntactically equivalent to the infinite LOOP. The most obvious version of an infinite WHILE loop is the following:

```
WHILE TRUE
LOOP
   <executable statement(s)>
END LOOP;
```

Sometimes, however, an infinite WHILE loop can be disguised by poor programming techniques. The following WHILE loop will terminate only when end_of_analysis is set to TRUE:

```
WHILE NOT end_of_analysis
LOOP
  perform_analysis;
  get_next_record;
  IF analysis_cursor%NOTFOUND AND
     next_analysis_step IS NULL
  THEN
     end_of_analysis := TRUE;
  END IF;
END LOOP;
```

In this WHILE loop, the end_of_analysis Boolean variable is set to TRUE only if the analysis_cursor fetches no data and we are at the last step of the analysis.

Unfortunately, both the cursor and the next_analysis_step variable are completely invisible in the loop itself. How is next_analysis_step set? Where is the cursor declared? How is a record fetched? This is a very dangerous way to structure code because if we do fall into an infinite loop, the information we need to resolve the problem is not readily available.

FOR Loop

There are two kinds of PL/SQL FOR loops: the numeric FOR loop and the cursor FOR loop. The numeric FOR loop is the traditional and familiar "counted" loop. The number of iterations of the FOR loop is known when the loop starts; it is specified in the loop boundary's range scheme. The number of times the loop executes is actually determined by the range scheme found between the FOR and LOOP keywords in the boundary.

The range scheme implicitly declares the loop index (if it has not already been declared), specifies the start and end points of the range, and optionally dictates the order in which the loop index proceeds (from lowest to highest or highest to lowest).

Here is the general syntax of the numeric FOR loop:

```
FOR <loop index> IN [REVERSE] <lowest number> ..
<highest number>
LOOP
     <executable statement(s)>
END LOOP;
```

We must have at least one executable statement between the LOOP and END LOOP key words.

The following table summarizes the properties of the numeric FOR loop:

Table 7.6

Property	Description
How the loop is terminated	The numeric FOR loop terminates unconditionally when the number of times specified in its range scheme has been satisfied. You can also terminate the loop with an EXIT statement, but this is not recommended.
When the test for termination takes place	After each execution of the loop body, PL/SQL checks the value of the loop index. When it exceeds the difference between the upper and lower bounds of the range scheme, the loop terminates. If the lower bound is greater than the upper bound of the range scheme, the loop never executes its body.
Reason to use this loop	Use the numeric FOR loop when you want to execute a body of code a fixed number of times, and you do not want to halt that looping prematurely.

Rules for Numeric FOR Loops

- Do not declare the loop index. PL/SQL automatically and implicitly declares it as a local variable with datatype INTEGER. The scope of this index is the loop itself; you cannot refer to the loop index outside the loop.
- Expressions used in the range scheme (both for lowest and highest bounds) are evaluated once, when the loop starts. The range is not re-evaluated during the execution of the loop. If you make changes within the loop to the variables which you used to determine the FOR loop range, those changes will have no effect.
- Never change the values of either the loop index or the range boundary from within the loop. This is an extremely bad programming practice. In most cases, PL/SQL will not let you compile such code.
- Do not use an EXIT statement inside a FOR loop in order to cause early execution of the loop. If you are going to use a numeric FOR loop, then you should let the loop execute as it is designed: from start value to end value. If you need more control over how frequently a loop is to execute and, particularly, when it is to terminate, do not use the FOR loop. Instead, use the WHILE loop or simple loop with EXIT WHEN constructs.
- Use the REVERSE keyword to force the loop to decrement from the upper bound to the lower bound. You must still make sure that the first value in the range specification (the N in N .. M) is less than the second value. Do not reverse the order in which you specify these values when you use the REVERSE keyword.

Examples of Numeric FOR Loops

The following examples demonstrate some variations of the numeric FOR loop syntax:

- The loop executes ten times; loop_counter starts at 1 and ends at 10:

```
FOR loop_counter IN 1 .. 10
LOOP
  ... executable statements ...
END LOOP;
```

- The loop executes ten times loop_counter starts at 10 and ends at 1:

```
FOR loop_counter IN REVERSE 1 .. 10
LOOP
  ... executable statements ...
END LOOP;
```

- Here is a loop that doesn't execute even once. We specified REVERSE so the loop index, loop_counter, will start at the highest value and end with the lowest.

```
FOR loop_counter IN REVERSE 10 .. 1
LOOP
  /* This loop body will never execute even once! */
END LOOP;
```

Even when we specify a REVERSE direction, we must still list the lowest bound before the highest bound. If the first number is greater than the second number, the body of the loop will not execute at all. If the lowest and highest bounds have the same value, then the loop will execute just once.

- Loop executes for a range determined by the values in the variable and expression:

```
FOR calc_index IN start_period_number ..
 LEAST (end_period_number, current_period)
LOOP
  ... executable statements ...
END LOOP;
```

Note that in this example we do not know the values for the lowest and highest bounds at the time of the writing of the code. The actual or dynamic range is determined at runtime and is fully supported by PL/SQL. In other words, the numeric FOR loop needs to know when it starts and how many times it will execute, but you do not have to know this when you write the program.

Handling Nontrivial Increments

PL/SQL does not provide a "step" syntax, whereby you can specify that the loop index increment. In all variations of the PL/SQL numeric FOR loop, the loop index is always incremented or decremented by one.

If you have a loop body which you want to be executed for a nontrivial (different from one) increment, you will have to write some cute code. For example, what will happen if you want your loop to execute only for all even numbers between 1 and 100? You can make use of the numeric MOD function, as follows:

```
FOR loop_index IN 1 .. 100
LOOP
  IF MOD (loop_index, 2) = 0
  THEN
    /* We have an even number, so perform calculation */
    calc_values (loop_index);
  END IF;
END LOOP;
```

Or you can use simple multiplication inside a loop with half the iterations:

```
FOR even_number IN 1 .. 50
LOOP
  calc_values (even_number*2);
END LOOP;
```

In both cases, the calc_values procedure executes only for even numbers. In the first example, the FOR loop executes 100 times. In the second example, the FOR loop executes only 50 times.

Note. Comments would be very helpful for the maintenance programmer who has to understand why you would code something like that.

SEQUENTIAL CONTROL

GOTO and NULL Statements

To execute a section of code more than once. PL/SQL offers two other statements to handle out of the ordinary requirements for sequential processing: GOTO and NULL. The GOTO statement allows you to perform unconditional branching to another executable statement in the same execution section of a PL/SQL block. The NULL statement gives you a way to tell the compiler to do absolutely nothing.

The GOTO Statement

The GOTO statement performs unconditional branching to a named label. The general format for a GOTO statement is:

```
GOTO label_name;
```

where label_name is the name of a label.

This GOTO label is defined in the program as follows:

```
<<label_name>>
```

You must surround the label name with double enclosing angle brackets (<< >>). In this case, the label names a loop. This label can then be appended to the END LOOP statement, making the termination of the loop more visible. You can also issue an EXIT statement for a particular labeled loop from within another (enclosed) loop. Finally, you can GOTO that loop label, even though it was "designed" for a loop.

When PL/SQL encounters a GOTO statement, it immediately shifts control to the first executable statement following the label.

Contrary to popular opinion (including mine), the GOTO statement can come in handy. There are cases where a GOTO statement can simplify the logic in your program. On the other hand, PL/SQL provides so many different control constructs and modularization techniques that you can almost always find a better way to do something than with a GOTO.

There are several restrictions regarding the GOTO statement, described in the sections below:

At least one executable statement must follow a label

A label itself is not an executable statement (notice that it does not have a semicolon (;) after the label brackets), so it cannot take the place of one. All of the uses of the loop label in the following blocks are illegal because the labels are not followed by an executable statement:

```
IF status_inout = 'COMPLETED'
THEN
  <<all_done>> /* Illegal! */
ELSE
  schedule_activity;
END IF;
```

Target labels and scope of GOTO

The target label must be in the same scope as the GOTO statement. In the context of the GOTO statement, each of the following constructs maintains its own scope: functions, procedures, anonymous blocks, IF statements, LOOP statements, and exception handlers. All of the code examples below generate the same PL/SQL error:

```
PLS-00375: illegal GOTO statement; this GOTO cannot branch to
label
```

- *IF conditions.* The only way to enter an IF statement is through an evaluation to TRUE of an IF condition. Therefore, this code produces an error:

```
GOTO label_inside_IF;
IF status = 'NEW'
THEN
```

```
    <<label_inside_IF>> /* Out of scope! */
    show_new_one;
  END IF;
```

- *BEGIN statements.* The only way to enter a block-within-a-block is through the sub-block's BEGIN statement. PL/SQL insists on orderly entrances and exits. This code produces an error because it doesn't comply with this structure:

```
GOTO label_inside_subblock;
BEGIN
  <<label_inside_subblock>> /* Crosses block boundary! */
  NULL;
  END;
```

- *Scope of IF statements.* Each IF clause of the IF statement is its own scope. A GOTO may not transfer from one clause to another. This code produces an error:

```
IF status = 'NEW'
THEN
  <<new_status>>
  GOTO old_status; /* Crosses IF clause boundary! */
ELSIF status = 'OLD'
THEN
  <<old_status>>
  GOTO new_status; /* Crosses IF clause boundary! */
END IF;
```

- *Don't jump into the middle of a loop.* One cannot jump into the middle of a loop with a GOTO. This code produces an error:

```
FOR month_num IN 1 .. 12
LOOP
  <<do_a_month>>
  schedule_activity (month_num);
END LOOP;
 GOTO do_a_month; /* Can't go back into loop. */
```

- *Don't GOTO a local module.* One also cannot issue a GOTO inside of a module to a label in the main body. This code produces an error:

```
DECLARE
  FUNCTION local_null IS
  BEGIN
    <<descrip_case_statement>>
```

```
      NULL;
    END;
  BEGIN
    GOTO descrip_case_statement; /* Label not visible here.
  */
    END;
```

Target labels and PL/SQL blocks

The target label must be in the same part of the PL/SQL block as the GOTO statement. A GOTO in the executable section may not go to a label in the exception section. Similarly, a GOTO in the exception section may not go to a label in the executable section. A GOTO in an exception handler may refer to a label in the same handler. The code example below generates the same PL/SQL error shown in the previous section (PLS-00375):

```
BEGIN
  /*
  || The label and GOTO must be in the same section!
  */
  GOTO out_of_here;
EXCEPTION
  WHEN OTHERS
  THEN
    <<out_of_here>> /* Out of scope! */
    NULL;
END;
```

The NULL Statement

Usually when we write a statement in a program, we want it to do something. There are cases, however, when we want to tell PL/SQL to do absolutely nothing, and that is where the NULL statement comes in handy. The NULL statement has the following format:

```
NULL;
```

Well, you wouldn't want a do-nothing statement to be complicated, would you? The NULL statement is simply the reserved word followed by a semicolon (;) to indicate that this is a statement and not the NULL value reserved word. The NULL statement does nothing except pass control to the next executable statement.

Why would you want to use the NULL statement? There are several reasons, described in the following sections.

Improving the Readability of Your Program

There are many situations in our program where we logically do not want to take any action. In most of these cases, PL/SQL will let us write nothing and the program will execute as we wish. The only drawback is the ambiguity surrounding this solution:

Consider the IF statement. When we write an IF statement we do not have to include an ELSE clause. To produce a report based on a selection, we can code:

```
IF :report.selection = 'DETAIL'
THEN
  exec_detail_report;
END IF;
```

What should the program have been doing if the report selection is not 'DETAIL'? One would assume that the program was supposed to do nothing. But because this is not explicitly stated in the code, one is left to wonder if perhaps there was an oversight. If, on the other hand, we include an explicit ELSE clause that does nothing.

```
IF :report.selection = 'DETAIL'
THEN
  exec_detail_report;
ELSE
  NULL;
END IF;
```

Using NULL with GOTO to Avoid Additional Statement Execution

In some cases, we can pair NULL with GOTO to avoid having to execute additional statements. Most of us will never have to use the GOTO statement; there are very few occasions where it is truly needed. If you ever do use GOTO, however, you should remember that when you GOTO a label, at least one executable statement must follow that label. In the following example, we use a GOTO statement to quickly move to the end of our program if the state of our data indicates that no further processing is required:

```
PROCEDURE process_data (data_in IN orders%ROWTYPE,
                        data_action IN VARCHAR2) IS
BEGIN
  – First in series of validations.
  IF data_in.ship_date IS NOT NULL
  THEN
    status := validate_shipdate (data_in.ship_date);
    IF status != 0 THEN GOTO end_of_procedure;
```

```
    END IF;
    – Second in series of validations.
    IF data_in.order_date IS NOT NULL
    THEN
      status := validate_orderdate (data_in.order_date);
      IF status != 0 THEN GOTO end_of_procedure;
    END IF;
    ... more validations ...
    << end_of_procedure >>
    NULL;
END;
```

With this approach, if we encounter an error in any single section, we can use the GOTO to bypass all remaining validation checks. Because we do not have to do anything at the termination of the procedure, we place a NULL statement after the label because at least one statement is required there.

EXCEPTION HANDLERS

In the PL/SQL language, errors of any kind are treated as exceptions — situations that should not occur — in our program. An exception can be one of the following:

- An error generated by the system (such as "out of memory" or "duplicate value in index")
- An error caused by a user action
- A warning issued by the application to the user

PL/SQL traps and responds to errors using an architecture of exception handlers. The exception-handler mechanism allows us to cleanly separate our error processing code from our executable statements. It also provides an event-driven model, as opposed to a linear code model, for processing errors. In other words, no matter how a particular exception is raised, it is handled by the same exception handler in the exception section.

When an error occurs in PL/SQL, whether a system error or an application error, an exception is raised. The processing in the current PL/SQL block's execution section halts and control is transferred to the separate exception section of your program, if one exists, to handle the exception. We cannot return to that block after we finish handling the exception. Instead, control is passed to the enclosing block, if any.

Figure 7.6 illustrates how control is transferred to the exception section when an exception is raised.

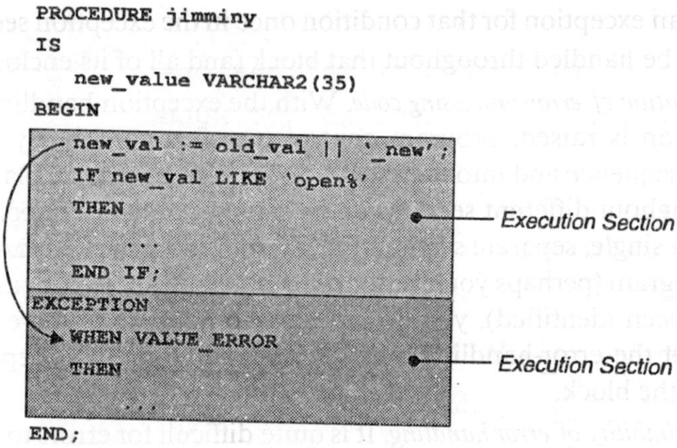

Figure 7.6. Exception handling architecture

Why Exception Handling?

It is a sad fact of life that most programmers never take the time to properly error-proof their programs. Instead, wishful thinking often reigns. Most of us find it hard enough to simply write the code that implements the positive aspects of an application: maintaining customers, generating invoices, etc. It is difficult from both a psychological standpoint and a resource perspective to focus on the negative side: what happens when the user presses the wrong key? If the database is unavailable, what should we do?

As a result, we write applications that often assume the best of all possible worlds, hoping that our programs are bug-free, that users will enter only the correct data in only the correct fashion, and that all systems (hardware and software) will always be a "go."

Of course, harsh reality is that, there will always be one more bug in our application. And our users will always find just the right sequence of keystrokes it takes to make a screen implode. The situation is clear: either we spend the time up front to properly debug and bulletproof our programs, or we fight an unending series of battles, taking frantic calls from our users and putting out the fires.

Fortunately, PL/SQL offers a powerful and flexible way to trap and handle errors in our programs. It is entirely feasible within the PL/SQL language to build an application which fully protects the user and the database from errors.

The exception handler model offers the following advantages:

- *Event-driven handling of errors.* As we've mentioned, PL/SQL exception handling follows an event-driven rather than a linear code model. No matter how a particular exception is raised, it is handled by the same exception handler in the exception section. You do not have to check repeatedly for a condition in your code, but instead can insert an exception for that condition once in the exception section and be certain that it will be handled throughout that block (and all of its enclosing blocks).

- *Clean separation of error-processing code.* With the exception-handling model, whenever an exception is raised, program control transfers completely out of the normal execution sequence and into the exception section. Instead of placing error-handling logic throughout different sections of your program, you can consolidate all of this logic into a single, separate section. Furthermore, if you need to add new exceptions in your program (perhaps you overlooked a possible problem, or a new kind of system error has been identified), you do not have to figure out where in your executable code to put the error-handling logic. Simply add another exception handler at the bottom of the block.
- *Improved reliability of error handling.* It is quite difficult for errors to go undetected with the PL/SQL error-handling model. If there is a handler, then that exception will be dealt with in the current block or in an enclosing block. Even if there is no explicit handler for that error, normal code execution will still stop. Your program cannot simply "work through" an error — unless you explicitly organize your code to allow this.

There is no avoiding the fact that if we want to trap errors in our PL/SQL programs we will have to write some additional code. The exception handler architecture, however, minimizes the amount of code we need to write, and offers the possibility of guarding against all problems that might arise in our application.

A PL/SQL block (of which procedures, functions, and anonymous blocks are all instances) consists of up to four parts: the header, declaration section, execution section, and exception section, as shown in the following anonymous block:

```
DECLARE
  ... declarations ...
BEGIN
  ... executable statements ...
[ EXCEPTION
  ... exception handlers ... ]
END;
```

When an exception is raised within the execution section of a PL/SQL block, control passes to the exception section. PL/SQL then scans through the exception handlers to see if that exception is handled.

The syntax for an exception section follows:

```
EXCEPTION
  WHEN exception_name [ OR exception_name ... ]
  THEN
     <executable statements>
END;
```

We can have multiple exception handlers in a single exception section. The exception handlers are structured much like a conditional CASE statement, as shown below:

The Exception Section	An English-like Translation

`EXCEPTION`
`WHEN NO_DATA_FOUND`
`THEN`
`executable_statements1;`
	If the NO_DATA_FOUND exception was raised, then execute the first set of statements.

`WHEN payment_overdue`
`THEN`
`executable_statements2;`
	If the payment is overdue, then execute the second set of statements.

`WHEN OTHERS`
`THEN`
`executable_statements3;`
`END;`
	If any other exception is encountered, then execute the third set of statements.

An exception is handled if an exception that is named in a WHEN clause matches the exception that was raised.

Note. The WHEN clause traps errors only by exception name, not by error codes. If a match is found, then the executable statements associated with that exception are run. If the exception that has been raised is not handled or does not match any of the named exceptions, the executable statements associated with the WHEN OTHERS clause — if present — will be run.

The WHEN OTHERS clause is optional; if it is not present, then any unhandled exception is immediately raised in the enclosing block, if any.

If the exception is not handled by any PL/SQL block, then the error number and message are presented directly to the user of the application. The exception remains, in other words, unhandled and it disrupts the execution of the application.

We define, raise, and handle exceptions in PL/SQL.

Types of Exceptions

There are four kinds of exceptions in PL/SQL:

- **Named system exceptions.** Exceptions that have been given names by PL/SQL and raised as a result of an error in PL/SQL or RDBMS processing.
- **Named programmer-defined exceptions.** Exceptions that are raised as a result of errors in our application code. We give these exceptions names by declaring them in the declaration section. We then raise the exceptions explicitly in the program.

- **Unnamed system exceptions.** Exceptions that are raised as a result of an error in PL/SQL or RDBMS processing but have not been given names by PL/SQL. Only the most common errors are so named; the rest have numbers and can be assigned names with the special PRAGMA EXCEPTION_INIT syntax.
- **Unnamed programmer-defined exceptions.** Exceptions that are defined and raised in the server by the programmer. In this case, the programmer provides both an error number (between -20000 and -20999) and an error message, and raises that exception with a call to RAISE_APPLICATION_ERROR. That error, along with its message, is propagated back to the client-side application.

The system exceptions (both named and unnamed) are raised by PL/SQL whenever a program violates a rule in the RDBMS (such as "duplicate value in index") or causes a resource limit to be exceeded (such as "maximum open cursors exceeded"). Each of these RDBMS errors has a number associated with it. In addition, PL/SQL predefines names for some of the most commonly encountered errors.

Named System Exceptions

The exceptions which are already given names by PL/SQL are declared in the STANDARD package in PL/SQL. You do not have to declare them in your own programs. SQLCODE is a PL/SQL built-in function that returns the status code of the last-executed statement. SQLCODE returns zero if the last statement executed without errors. In most, but not all, cases, the SQLCODE value is the same as the Oracle error code.

If you do so, in fact, you will have declared your own local exception. It will not be raised when the internal error with that name occurs. Avoid declaring an exception with the same name as a predefined exception.

Here is an example of how you can use the exceptions table. Suppose that your program generates an unhandled exception for error ORA-6511. Looking up this error, you find that it is associated with the CURSOR_ALREADY_OPEN exception. Locate the PL/SQL block in which the error occurs and add an exception handler for CURSOR_ALREADY_OPEN, as shown below:

```
EXCEPTION
  WHEN CURSOR_ALREADY_OPEN
  THEN
    CLOSE my_cursor;
END;
```

Of course, you would be even better off analyzing your code to determine proactively which of the predefined exceptions might occur. Then you could decide which of those exceptions you want to handle specifically, which should be covered by the WHEN OTHERS clause, and which would best be left unhandled.

Table 7.7: Predefined Exceptions in PL/SQL

Oracle Error/SQLCODE	Description
CURSOR_ALREADY_OPEN ORA-6511 SQLCODE= – 6511	You tried to OPEN a cursor that was already OPEN. You must CLOSE a cursor before you try to OPEN or re-OPEN it.
DUP_VAL_ON_INDEX ORA-00001 SQLCODE= – 1	Your INSERT or UPDATE statement attempted to store duplicate values in a column or columns in a row which is restricted by a unique index.
INVALID_CURSOR ORA-01001 SQLCODE= – 1001	You made reference to a cursor that did not exist. This usually happens when you try to FETCH from a cursor or CLOSE a cursor before that cursor is OPENed.
INVALID_NUMBER ORA-01722 SQLCODE = – 1722	PL/SQL executes a SQL statement that cannot convert a character string successfully to a number. This exception is different from the VALUE_ERROR exception, as it is raised only from within a SQL statement.
LOGIN_DENIED ORA-01017 SQLCODE= – 1017	Your program tried to log onto the Oracle RDBMS with an invalid username-password combination. This exception is usually encountered when you embed PL/SQL in a 3GL language.
NO_DATA_FOUND ORA-01403 SQLCODE= + 100	This exception is raised in three different scenarios: (1) You executed a SELECT INTO statement (implicit cursor) that returned no rows. (2) You referred to an uninitialized row in a local PL/SQL table. (3) You read past end of file with UTL_FILE package.
NOT_LOGGED_ON ORA-01012 SQLCODE= – 1012	Your program tried to execute a call to the database (usually with a DML statement) before it had logged into the Oracle RDBMS.
PROGRAM_ERROR ORA-06501 SQLCODE= – 6501	PL/SQL encounters an internal problem. The message text usually also tells you to "Contact Oracle Support."
STORAGE_ERROR ORA-06500 SQLCODE= – 6500	Your program run out of memory or memory was in some way corrupted.
TIMEOUT_ON_RESOURCE ORA-00051 SQLCODE= – 51	A timeout occurred in the RDBMS while waiting for a resource.

TOO_MANY_ROWS ORA-01422 SQLCODE= – 1422	A SELECT INTO statement returned more than one row. A SELECT INTO can return only one row; if your SQL statement returns more than one row you should place the SELECT statement in an explicit CURSOR declaration and FETCH from that cursor one row at a time.
TRANSACTION_BACKED_OUT ORA-00061 SQLCODE= – 61	The remote part of a transaction is rolled back, either with an explicit ROLLBACK command or as the result of some other action.
VALUE_ERROR ORA-06502 SQLCODE= – 6502	PL/SQL raises the VALUE_ERROR whenever it encounters an error having to do with the conversion, truncation, or invalid constraining of numeric and character data. This is a very general and common exception. If this same type of error is encountered in a SQL DML statement within a PL/SQL block, then the INVALID_NUMBER exception is raised.
ZERO_DIVIDE ORA-01476 SQLCODE= –1476	Your program tried to divide by zero.

Named Programmer-Defined Exceptions

The exceptions that PL/SQL has declared in the STANDARD package cover internal or system-generated errors. Many of the problems a user will encounter (or cause) in an application, however, are specific to that application. Your program might need to trap and handle errors such as "negative balance in account" or "call date cannot be in the past." While different in nature from "division by zero," these errors are still exceptions to normal processing and should be handled gracefully by your program.

One of the most useful aspects of the PL/SQL exception handling model is that it does not make any structural distinction between internal errors and application-specific errors. Once an exception is raised, it can and should be handled in the exception section, regardless of the type or source of error.

Of course, to handle an exception, you must have a name for that exception. Because PL/SQL cannot name these exceptions for you (they are specific to your application), you must do so yourself by declaring an exception in the declaration section of your PL/SQL block. You declare an exception by listing the name of the exception you want to raise in your program, followed by the keyword EXCEPTION, as follows:

```
exception_name EXCEPTION;
```

The following declaration section of the calc_annual_sales contains three programmer-defined exception declarations:

```
PROCEDURE calc_annual_sales
  (company_id_in IN company.company_id%TYPE)
IS
```

```
    invalid_company_id    EXCEPTION;
    no_sales_for_company EXCEPTION;
    negative_balance      EXCEPTION;

    duplicate_company     BOOLEAN;
  BEGIN
    ... body of executable statements ...
  EXCEPTION
    WHEN invalid_company_id
    THEN
      ...
    WHEN no_sales_for_company
    THEN
      ...
    WHEN negative_balance
    THEN
      ...
  END;
```

The names for exceptions are similar in format to (and "read" just like) Boolean variable names, but can be referred in only two ways:

- In a RAISE statement in the execution section of the program (to raise the exception), as in:

```
RAISE no_sales_for_company;
```

- In the WHEN clauses of the exception section (to handle the raised exception), as in:

```
WHEN no_sales_for_company THEN
```

Unnamed System Exceptions

What do you do when you want to trap an internal error raised by PL/SQL or the SQL engine, but it is not one of the lucky errors that have been given a predefined name? Although this error is identified only by its internal error number, exception handlers need a name by which they can check for a match. Sure, you can always use the WHEN OTHERS clause to simply catch any exceptions not previously handled. In many cases, however, you will want to trap specific errors in a way that clearly documents and highlights them in your code. To do this, you assign your own name to the Oracle or PL/SQL error that might be raised in your program, and then write a specific exception handler for that custom-named exception.

The EXCEPTION_INIT pragma

You can use a compiler construct called a pragma to associate a name with an internal error code. A pragma is a special instruction to the compiler that is processed at compile time instead of at runtime. A pragma called EXCEPTION_INIT instructs the compiler to associate or initialize a programmer-defined exception with a specific Oracle error number. With a name for that error, you can then raise this exception and write a handler which will trap that error. While in most cases you will leave it to Oracle to raise these system exceptions, you could also raise them yourself.

The pragma EXCEPTION_INIT must appear in the declaration section of a block, after the declaration of the exception name used in the pragma, as shown below:

```
DECLARE
   exception_name EXCEPTION;
   PRAGMA EXCEPTION_INIT (exception_name, error_code_literal);
BEGIN
```

where exception_name is the name of an exception and error_code_literal is the number of the Oracle error (including the minus sign, if the error code is negative, as is almost always the case).

In the following program code, we declare and associate an exception for this error:

```
ORA-2292 violated integrity constraining (OWNER.CONSTRAINT) -
         child record found.
```

This error occurs if we try to delete a parent record while there are child records still in that table. A child record is a record with a foreign key reference to the parent table:

```
PROCEDURE delete_company (company_id_in IN NUMBER)
IS
  /* Declare the exception. */
  still_have_employees EXCEPTION;

  /* Associate the exception name with an error number. */
  PRAGMA EXCEPTION_INIT (still_have_employees, -2292);
BEGIN
  /* Try to delete the company. */
  DELETE FROM company
    WHERE company_id = company_id_in;
EXCEPTION
  /* If child records were found, this exception is raised!
  */
    WHEN still_have_employees
    THEN
      DBMS_OUTPUT.PUT_LINE
        (' Please delete employees for company first.');
END;
```

When you use EXCEPTION_INIT, you must supply a literal number for the second argument of the pragma call. By explicitly naming this system exception, the purpose of the exception handler is self-evident.

The EXCEPTION_INIT pragma improves the readability of your programs by assigning names to otherwise obscure error numbers. You can employ the EXCEPTION_INIT pragma more than once in your program. You can even assign more than one exception name to the same error number.

Unnamed Programmer-Defined Exceptions

The final type of exception is the unnamed, yet programmer-defined exception. This kind of exception occurs when you need to raise an application-specific error from within the server and communicate this error back to the client application process. This scenario is more common than you might at first imagine. For example, even when you run all your Oracle software in a single hardware environment (such as a character-based SQL*Forms applications running on UNIX against an Oracle server on the same UNIX platform), you still have a separation between your client (SQL*Forms screen) and your server (the RDBMS).

You will trap some, perhaps most, application-specific errors on the client side. On the other hand, the Oracle7 architecture allows you to embed many of your business rules directly into your database structure, using database triggers, constraints, and stored procedures. In many cases, you will want to let the RDBMS trap and reject invalid database actions. To do this, you need a way to identify application-specific errors and return information about those error back to the client. This kind of error communication is illustrated in Figure 7.7.

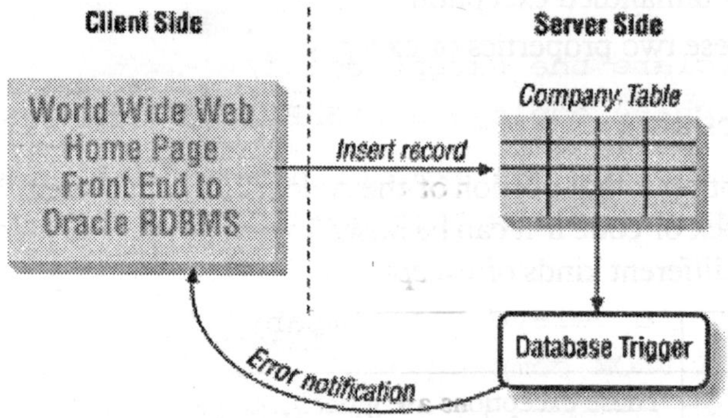

Figure 7.7. Error communication from server to client

We have called this type of exception "unnamed" and "programmer-defined." The programmer-defined aspect should be clear: because the error is application-specific, you cannot expect PL/SQL to have already defined it for you. The reason this type of exception is also unnamed is that you cannot name or declare an exception within a server-based program or database trigger and have the client-side tool handle that named exception. This identifier simply doesn't cross the great division between client and server.

To get around this problem, Oracle provides a special procedure to allow communication of an unnamed, yet programmer-defined, server-side exception: RAISE_APPLICATION_ERROR. The specification for this procedure is as follows:

```
PROCEDURE RAISE_APPLICATION_ERROR
   (error_number_in IN NUMBER, error_msg_in IN VARCHAR2);
```

where error_number_in is the error number you have assigned to this error. The error_msg_in argument is the message that will be sent back with the error code to the client program.

Determining Exception-Handling Behavior

A PL/SQL program is an anonymous block, a procedure, or a function. This program, or "highest-level" block, can call other procedures or functions, or nest an anonymous block within that block. So at any given point in execution, there might be several layers of PL/SQL blocks nested within other blocks. Each PL/SQL block can have its own exception section, or it can be totally void of exception handlers.

To determine the appropriate exception-handling behavior, PL/SQL follows rules regarding:

Scope

The PL/SQL block or blocks in which an exception can be raised and handled.

Propagation

The way in which an exception is passed back through enclosing blocks until it is handled or is resolved to be an unhandled exception

Let's look at these two properties of exceptions.

Scope of an Exception

The scope of an exception is that portion of the code which is "covered" by that exception. An exception covers a block of code if it can be raised in that block. The following table shows the scope for each of the different kinds of exceptions:

Exception Type	Description of Scope
Named system exceptions	These exceptions are globally available because they are not declared in or confined to any particular block of code. You can raise and handle a named system exception in any block.
Named programmer-defined exceptions	These exceptions can only be raised and handled in the execution and exception sections of the block in which they are declared (and all nested blocks).
Unnamed system exceptions	These exceptions can be handled in any PL/SQL exception section via the WHEN OTHERS section. If they are assigned a name, then the scope of that name is the same as that of the named programmer-defined exception.

Exception Type	Description of Scope
Unnamed programmer-defined exceptions	This exception is only defined in the call to RAISE_APPLICATION_ERROR and then is passed back to the calling program.

Scope of Programmer-defined Exception

Consider the following example of the exception overdue_balance declared in procedure check_account. The scope of that exception is the check_account procedure, and nothing else:

```
PROCEDURE check_account (company_id_in IN NUMBER)
IS
  overdue_balance EXCEPTION;
BEGIN
  ... executable statements ...
  LOOP
    ...
    IF ... THEN
      RAISE overdue_balance;
    END IF;
  END LOOP;
EXCEPTION
  WHEN overdue_balance THEN ...
END;
```

We can RAISE the overdue_balance inside the check_account procedure, but we cannot raise that exception from a program that calls check_account. The following anonymous block will generate the associated compile error:

```
DECLARE
  company_id NUMBER := 100;
BEGIN
  check_account (100);
EXCEPTION
  WHEN overdue_balance /* PL/SQL cannot resolve this
     reference. */
  THEN ...
END;

PLS-00201: identifier "OVERDUE_BALANCE" must be declared
```

The check_account procedure is a "black box" as far as the anonymous block is concerned. Any identifiers — including exceptions — which are declared inside check_account are invisible outside of that program.

Raising Exceptions in Nested Blocks

When you declare an exception in a block, it is local to that block, but global to all the blocks which are enclosed by that block (nested blocks). In the version of check_account shown in the following example, the procedure contains an anonymous subblock which also raises the overdue_balance. Because the subblock is enclosed by the procedure block, PL/SQL can resolve the reference to that exception:

```
PROCEDURE check_account (company_id_in IN NUMBER)
IS
  overdue_balance EXCEPTION;
BEGIN
  ... executable statements ...
  – Start of sub-block inside check_account
  BEGIN
    ... statements within sub-block ...
   RAISE overdue_balance;  – Exception raised in sub-block.
  END;
  – End of sub-block inside check_account
   LOOP
    ...
    IF ... THEN
       RAISE overdue_balance; – Exception raised in main
         block.
    END IF;
  END LOOP;
EXCEPTION
  WHEN overdue_balance THEN ... – Exception handled in
    main block.
END;
```

When the overdue_balance exception is raised in either the subblock or the main block, control is transferred immediately to the main block — the only exception section in the entire procedure. Because overdue_balance was declared for the whole procedure, the name is known throughout all subblocks.

Overlapping Exception Names

You never have to declare a named system exception because they have all been declared in the STANDARD package, which is instantiated as soon as you run any PL/SQL code. You can, on the other hand, declare your own exceptions with the same name as a previously defined system exception, as shown on next page.

```
DECLARE
  no_data_found EXCEPTION;
BEGIN
```

This locally declared exception will take precedence over the system exception. As a result, the following exception handler will not trap an error caused by an implicit query that returns no rows:

```
EXCEPTION
  WHEN no_data_found – This is MY exception, not PL/SQL's.
  THEN
  ...
END;
```

Qualifying Exception Names

If we really want to name a local exception the same as a predefined exception and handle the latter in that same PL/SQL block, we need to use the dot notation on the predefined exception. This notation distinguishes between the two and allows PL/SQL to find the handler for the predefined exception. we can then handle those two different exceptions separately, or we can combine them in a single expression:

```
EXCEPTION
  WHEN no_data_found
  THEN
    DBMS_OUTPUT.PUT_LINE ('My own local exception');
  WHEN STANDARD.NO_DATA_FOUND
  THEN
    DBMS_OUTPUT.PUT_LINE ('The predefined exception');
END;
```

or:

```
EXCEPTION
  WHEN no_data_found OR STANDARD.NO_DATA_FOUND
  THEN
    DBMS_OUTPUT.PUT_LINE ('Could not find the data');
END;
```

Of course, the best solution is to never declare exceptions with the same name as a named system exception.

Referencing Duplicate Exceptions in Nested Blocks

We cannot declare the same exception more than once in a single block, but we can declare an exception in a nested block with the same name as that of an enclosing block. When we do this, the declaration of local to that nested block takes precedence over the global exception. When we raise that exception, we are raising the local exception, which is a completely different exception from the outer exception, even though they share the same name.

In the following version of check_account, our nested block contains its own declaration of the overdue_balance exception:

```
PROCEDURE check_account (company_id_in IN NUMBER)
IS
   /* Main block exception declaration */
   overdue_balance EXCEPTION;
BEGIN
   ... executable statements ...

   /* Start of sub-block inside check_account */
   DECLARE
      /* Sub-block exception declaration */
      overdue_balance EXCEPTION;
   BEGIN
      ... statements within sub-block ...

      /* Exception raised in sub-block. */
      RAISE overdue_balance;
   END;
   /* End of sub-block inside check_account */

   LOOP

      IF ... THEN
         /* Exception raised in main block. */
         RAISE overdue_balance;
      END IF;
   END LOOP;

EXCEPTION
   /* Exception handled in main block. */
   WHEN overdue_balance
   THEN
      DBMS_OUTPUT.PUT_LINE ('Balance is overdue. Pay up!')
END;
```

This program will compile. Even though the overdue_balance exception is declared twice, each declaration takes place in a different PL/SQL block, hence in a different scope. The procedure-level overdue_balance is declared on line 4. The exception of the same name for the nested block is declared on line 11. Following these declarations, there are two RAISE statements — one within the nested block on line 16 and one in the main body of the procedure on line 24. Finally, there is just a single exception section and one handler for overdue_balance on line 30.

Well, the overdue_balance exception is certainly declared in every block in which it is raised. Yet the exception-handling behavior of check_account may not be as you would expect. What happens, for example, when the RAISE statement on line 16 executes? Do you see this:

```
'Balance is overdue. Pay up!'
```

or this:

```
ORA-06501: PL/SQL: unhandled user-defined exception
ORA-6512: at "USER.CHECK_ACCOUNT", line N
```

You will, in fact, have raised an unhandled exception when you RAISE overdue_balance in the nested block. How can this be?

Remember that the nested block does not have its own exception section — yet it does have its own, locally declared exception. So when the exception is raised on line 16, the nested block cannot handle the exception. Instead, that exception (declared only in that nested block) is passed on to the enclosing block and PL/SQL tries to handle it there.

As soon as control passes to the enclosing block, however, the nested block terminates and all local identifiers are erased. This includes the exception which was just raised. It is no longer defined and therefore cannot be handled in the outer block, even though it seems to have an handler precisely for that exception.

But there is still a glitch. The enclosing block doesn't know anything about the local overdue_balance, only its own rendition. And even though they appear to have the same name, these exceptions are different exceptions as far as the compiler is concerned. As a result, the nested block overdue_balance exception goes unhandled.

How can you get around this problem? First of all, you should avoid such duplication of exception names. This only makes the code very hard to understand and follow. But if you insist on these overlapping names, you can take any of the following steps:

1. Raise the procedure-level overdue_balance exception within the subblock if the enclosing block has a name (if it is a procedure or a function). You can use dot notation to distinguish the local exception from its global counterpart as follows:

   ```
   RAISE check_account.overdue_balance;
   ```

2. Make sure that the locally raised overdue_balance is handled by the main check_account exception section by including a WHEN OTHERS clause to trap any exceptions not otherwise handled.
3. Remove the local declaration of overdue_balance so this exception is declared only once in the program unit.

Propagation of an Exception

The scope rules for exceptions determine the block in which an exception can be raised. The rules for exception propagation address the way in which an exception is handled, once it has been raised.

When an exception is raised, PL/SQL looks for an exception handler in the current block (anonymous block, procedure, or function) for this exception. If it does not find a match, then PL/SQL propagates the exception to the enclosing block of that current block. PL/SQL then attempts to handle the exception by raising that exception once more in the enclosing block. It continues to do this in each successive enclosing block until there are no more blocks in which to raise the exception. When all blocks are exhausted, PL/SQL returns an unhandled exception to the application environment that executed the outermost PL/SQL block. An unhandled exception halts the execution of the host program.

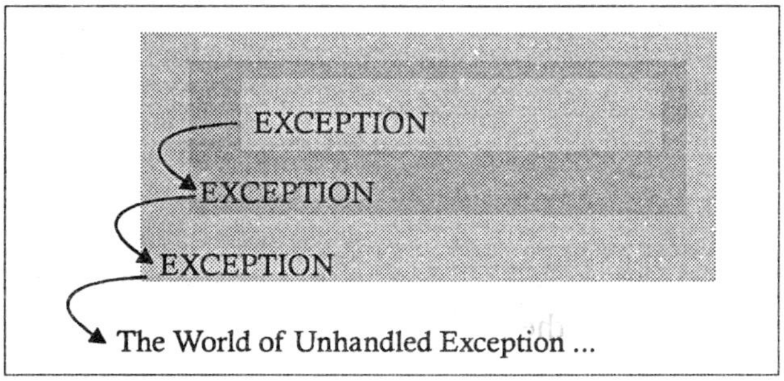

Figure 7.8. Propagation of exception through nested blocks

One very direct consequence of this propagation method is that if PL/SQL cannot locate an exception handler in the current block for a local, programmer-defined exception, the exception will not be handled at all. The exception is not recognized outside the current block, so propagating to enclosing blocks will never cause the exception to be handled (unless you use the blanket WHEN OTHERS handler).

Let's look at a few examples of the way exceptions propagate through enclosing blocks.

Figure 7.9 shows the exception raised in the inner block too_many_faults is handled by the next enclosing block.

The innermost block has an exception section, so PL/SQL first checks to see if the too_many_faults is handled in this section. Because it was not handled, PL/SQL closes that block and raises the too_many_faults exception in the enclosing block, Nested Block 1. Control immediately passes to the exception section of Nested Block 1. (The executable statements after Nested Block 2 are not executed.) PL/SQL scans the exception handlers and finds that too_many_faults have been handled in this block, so the code for that handler is executed, after which control passes back to the main list_my_faults procedure.

```
PROCEDURE list_my_faults IS
BEGIN
  ...
DECLARE                                                  Nested Block 1
  too_my_faults EXCEPTION;
BEGIN
  ... executable statements before new block ...
  BEGIN                                                  Nested Block 2
    SELECT SUM (faults) INTO num_faults FROM profile ... ;
    IF num_faults > 100
    THEN
      RAISE too_many_faults;
    END IF;
  EXCEPTION
    WHEN NO_DATA_FOUND THEN ... ;
  END;
  ... executable statements after Nested Block 2 ...
EXCEPTION
  WHEN too_many_faults THEN ... ;
END;
END list_my_faults;
```

Figure 7.9. Propagation of exception handling to first nested block

Notice that if the NO_DATA_FOUND exception had been raised in the innermost block (Nested Block 2), then the exception section for Nested Block 2 would have handled the exception. Then control would pass back to Nested Block 1 and the executable statements which come after Nested Block 2 would be executed.

In Figure 7.10, the exception raised in the inner block is handled by the outermost block.

The outermost block is the only one with an exception section, so when Nested Block 2 raises the too_many_faults exception, PL/SQL terminates execution of that block and raises that exception in the enclosing block, Nested Block 1. Again, this block has no exception section so PL/SQL immediately terminates Nested Block 1 and passes control to the outermost block (the list_my_faults procedure). This procedure does have an exception section, so PL/SQL scans the exception handlers, finds a match for too_many_faults, executes the code for that handler, and then returns control to whatever program called list_my_faults.

```
PROCEDURE list_my_faults
IS
   too_my_faults EXCEPTION;
BEGIN
 ...
 BEGIN
     BEGIN
         SELCT SUM (faults) INTO num_faults FROM profile ... ;
         IF num_faults > 100
         THEN
             RAISE too_many_faults;
         END IF;
     END;
 END;
EXCEPTION
   WHEN too_many_faults THEN ... ;
END list_my_faults;
```

Figure 7.10. Exception raised in nested block handled by outermost block

Raising an Exception

There are four ways that you or the PL/SQL runtime engine can raise an exception:

- *The PL/SQL runtime engine raised a named system exception.* These exceptions are raised automatically by the program. You cannot control when PL/SQL will raise a system exception. You can, however, write code to handle those exceptions when they are raised.
- *The programmer raises a named exception.* The programmer can use an explicit call to the RAISE statement to raise a programmer-defined or system-named exception.
- *The programmer raises an unnamed, programmer-defined exception.* These are raised with an explicit call to the RAISE_APPLICATION_ERROR procedure in the DBMS_STANDARD package.
- *The programmer re-raises the "current" exception.* From within an exception handler, you can re-raise the same exception for propagation to the enclosing block.

Who Raises the Exception?

The next sections show how you can let PL/SQL raise a system error or you can check for the error yourself and then raise that same system error.

PL/SQL raises ZERO_DIVIDE exception

In the following example, we raise our own exception, sales_domination, when the percentage of a customer's sales is over 50% of total sales. If, on the other hand, the total_sales is zero (as will be the case in the senseless code below), PL/SQL will automatically raise the ZERO_DIVIDE exception. Because we include a handler for that specific problem, the application does not abort when this code is executed. Instead, a message is displayed informing the user of a serious problem:

```
DECLARE
   total_sales NUMBER := 0;
   cust_sales NUMBER;
   sales_domination EXCEPTION;
BEGIN
   SELECT SUM (sales) INTO cust_sales
     FROM invoice WHERE customer_id = 1001;
   IF cust_sales / total_sales > .5
   THEN
      RAISE sales_domination;
   END IF;
EXCEPTION
   WHEN ZERO_DIVIDE
   THEN
      DBMS_OUTPUT.PUT_LINE
         (' We haven''t sold anything. We are bankrupt!');
   WHEN sales_domination
   THEN
      DBMS_OUTPUT.PUT_LINE
         (' Customer 1001 accounts for more than half of all
sales!');
END;
```

Notice that there is no RAISE statement for the ZERO_DIVIDE exception in the body of the program. Instead, we leave it to PL/SQL to raise such internally generated exceptions.

Programmer Raises ZERO_DIVIDE Exception

You could recode the previous anonymous block as follows:

```
DECLARE
  total_sales NUMBER := 0;
```

```
    cust_sales NUMBER;
    sales_domination EXCEPTION;
BEGIN
    SELECT SUM (sales) INTO cust_sales
      FROM invoice WHERE customer_id = 1001;

    /* Check for zero divisor and raise exception if necessary */
    IF total_sales = .0
    THEN
       RAISE ZERO_DIVIDE;
    ELSIF cust_sales / total_sales > .5
    THEN
       RAISE sales_domination;
    END IF;
EXCEPTION
    ... unchanged ...
END;
```

We know that a total_sales of zero will result in a division by zero. With either approach, the result is the same. Regardless of how the ZERO_DIVIDE exception is raised, the same exception handler will trap the error.

Impact of Unhandled Exceptions

If an exception is raised in a PL/SQL block and goes unhandled, there are several consequences to consider. First, if the program contains OUT or IN OUT parameters, then the PL/SQL runtime engine does not assign values to those parameters. Any changes to those parameters made during the program execution are, in essence, rolled back. Second, the runtime engine does not roll back any database work performed by that PL/SQL block. Instead, you must issue an explicit ROLLBACK statement to achieve this effect.

Re-Raising an Exception

When you are inside an exception handler in an exception section, you can re-raise the exception that "got you there" by issuing an unqualified RAISE statement as follows:

```
RAISE;
```

Since you do not specify an exception, the PL/SQL runtime engine re-raises the current exception (whose error number would be returned by a call to the SQLCODE function).

Here is an example of using raise in this way:

```
EXCEPTION
  WHEN OTHERS
  THEN
    send_error_to_pipe (SQLCODE);
    RAISE;
END;
```

This re-raise functionality comes in very handy when you need to raise exceptions which have not been assigned a name through use of the EXCEPTION_INIT pragma.

Exceptions Raised in a Declaration

When an exception is raised in the declaration section of a block, control is passed immediately to the enclosing block, if there is one, not to the exception section of the current block, as shown in Figure 7.11.

The assignment of the default value to little_string is too big for the variable. This causes PL/SQL to raise the VALUE_ERROR exception. This exception will not, however, be handled by the VALUE_ERROR handler in the anonymous block's exception section. Instead, PL/SQL will terminate the anonymous block and try to handle the exception in early_failure's exception section.

```
PROCEDURE list_my_faults
IS
BEGIN
   DECLARATION
      little_string VARCHAR2(2) := 'BIG STRING';
   BEGIN

      /* body of anonymous block */

   EXCEPTION
      WHEN VALUE_ERROR
      THEN
   END;
EXCEPTION

   WHEN VALUE_ERROR
   THEN

END;
```

Figure 7.11. VALUE_ERROR raised in nested block declaration section

The reason for this behavior is simple, as we describe in the next section.

Exceptions Raised in an Exception Handler

You can raise another exception from within an exception handler, but that exception can be handled only in the exception section of an enclosing block — never in the current block. The exception section of the current PL/SQL block will only handle exceptions raised in the execution section of that block.

When an exception is raised, the execution in the current block is immediately terminated, and control is passed in to the exception section, as shown in Figure 7.12. Once a match for the exception has been found, the rest of the exception section is inaccessible. At this point it is impossible to re-enter this same exception section because the corresponding execution section has been exited.

```
PROCEDURE hoptoit IS
BEGIN
   ...
   BEGIN
   EXCEPTION

      WHEN VALUE_ERROR
      THEN
         RAISE NO_DATA_FOUND;

      WHEN NO_DATA_FOUND
      THEN
         ...
   END;
   ...
EXCEPTION
   WHEN NO_DATA_FOUND
   THEN
      ...
END;
```

Figure 7.12. Exception raised in exception handler immediately exits the exception section

Why would you want to raise an exception inside an exception handler? You will find it useful to raise new exceptions from the current exception section when you do not want the enclosing block to continue normal processing after an exception in the subblock. You may instead want execution to branch off in a different direction, or to skip the rest of the enclosing block and move immediately to the enclosing block of that enclosing block.

In the following example, we have a triple nesting of anonymous blocks. When the innermost block raises an exception, we want to terminate both the second and third blocks, but continue normal processing in the outermost block. Raising an exception from within an exception block produces this behavior for us:

```
DECLARE – Outermost block
BEGIN
  DECLARE – First sub-block.
  – An exception whose scope is the two sub-blocks.
      skip_sub_block EXCEPTION;
  BEGIN
     ... executable statements for first sub-block ...
    BEGIN – Second sub-block.
       ... executable statements for innermost block ...
   EXCEPTION
        WHEN NO_DATA_FOUND – A table fetch returned no values.
   THEN
     RAISE skip_sub_block; – Raise exception in enclosing block.
   END;
  EXCEPTION
    WHEN skip_sub_block
    THEN
    NULL; – Terminate this sub-block, return to main block.
   END;
   – Now continue with main block processing.
   ... executable statements ...
END;
```

Handling Exceptions

Once an exception is raised, the current PL/SQL block stops its regular execution and transfer control to the exception section. The exception is then either handled by an exception handler in the current PL/SQL block or passed to the enclosing block.

Note. Once an exception is raised, the execution section is terminated. We cannot return to that body of code.

To handle or trap an exception once it is raised, you must write an exception handler for that exception. In your code, your exception handlers must appear after all the executable statements in your program but before the END statement of the block. The EXCEPTION keyword indicates the start of the exception section and the individual exception handlers.

The structure of the exception section is very similar to a CASE statement (which is not available in PL/SQL):

```
EXCEPTION
    WHEN exception_name1
```

```
    THEN
        <executable statements>
    WHEN exception_nameN
    THEN
        <executable statements>
    WHEN OTHERS
    THEN
        <executable statements>
END;
```

where exception_name1 is the name of the first exception handled in the section, exception_nameN is the name of the last named exception handled in the section, and the WHEN OTHERS clause provides the "otherwise" portion of the CASE statement. Of course, the code for each exception handler need not be on the same line, as shown in the preceding example. Every executable statement after a THEN and before the next WHEN or the final END statement belongs to the exception named by the previous WHEN statement, and is executed when that exception is raised.

The WHEN OTHERS clause must be the last exception handler in the exception section. If you place any other WHEN clauses after WHEN OTHER, you will receive the following compilation error:

```
PLS-00370: OTHERS handler must be last among the exception
handlers
           of a block
```

Unhandled Exceptions

If an exception is raised in your program and that exception is not handled by an exception section in either the current or enclosing PL/SQL blocks, that exception is "unhandled." PL/SQL returns the error which raised an unhandled exception all the way back to the application environment from which PL/SQL was run. That application environment (a tool like SQL*Plus, Oracle Forms, or a Powerbuilder program) then takes an action appropriate to the situation.

A well-designed application will not allow unhandled exceptions to occur. The best way to avoid unhandled exceptions is to make sure that the outermost PL/SQL block (whether it is an anonymous block in SQL*Plus or a stored procedure in the database) contains a WHEN OTHERS clause in its exception section.

Using SQLCODE and SQLERRM in WHEN OTHERS Clause

You can use the WHEN OTHERS clause in the exception section to trap all otherwise unhandled exceptions, including internal errors which are not predefined by PL/SQL. Once inside the exception handler, however, you will often want to know which error occurred. You can use the SQLCODE function to obtain this information.

Consider the following situation. The application maintains companies and orders entered for those companies. Foreign key constraint on company_id in the orders table guarantees that we cannot delete a company if there are still child records (orders) in the database for that company. The following procedure deletes companies and handles any exceptions which might arise:

```
PROCEDURE delete_company (company_id_in IN NUMBER)
IS
BEGIN
   DELETE FROM company WHERE company_id = company_id_in;
EXCEPTION
   WHEN OTHERS
   THEN
      DBMS_OUTPUT.PUT_LINE (' Error deleting company.');
END;
```

Notice the generic nature of the error message. Did the delete fail because there were orders still present? Then perhaps we would want to delete them and then delete the company. Fortunately, Oracle provides two functions, SQLCODE and SQLERRM, which return, respectively, the error code and the error message resulting from the most recently raised exception

Combined with WHEN OTHERS, SQLCODE provides a way for you to handle different, specific exceptions without having to use the EXCEPTION_INIT pragma. In the next example, we trap both of the parent-child exceptions, -2292 and -2291, and then take an action appropriate to each situation:

```
    PROCEDURE delete_company (company_id_in IN NUMBER)
IS
BEGIN
   DELETE FROM company
    WHERE company_id = company_id_in;
EXCEPTION
   WHEN OTHERS
   THEN
      /*
      || Anonymous block inside the exception handler lets me declare
       || local variables to hold the error code information.
```

```
*/
DECLARE
   error_code NUMBER := SQLCODE;
   error_msg  VARCHAR2 (300) := SQLERRM;
BEGIN
   IF error_code = -2292
   THEN
/* Child records found. Delete those too! */
      DELETE FROM employee
       WHERE company_id = company_id_in;

      /* Now delete parent again. */
      DELETE FROM company
       WHERE company_id = company_id_in;

   ELSIF error_code = -2291
   THEN
      /* Parent key not found. */
      DBMS_OUTPUT.PUTLINE
 Invalid company ID: '||TO_CHAR (company_id_in);
   ELSE
/* This is like a WHEN OTHERS inside a WHEN OTHERS! */

DBMS_OUTPUT.PUT_LINE
(' Error deleting company, error: '||error_msg);
 END IF;
      END; – End of anonymous block.

END delete_company;
```

Note. The PL/SQL block can be created using any editor, like Notepad.

Save the file with .sql extension.

Close the editor.

At the sql prompt, execute the program by typing start or @ followed by file name.

SQL > Start filename or @filename.

The program will be executed if there are no errors in the program. If any error message appears, switch to notepad, correct the errors and save the file. After saving switch back to the SQL *and execute the program.

DBMS_OUTPUT.PUT_LINE: To output data from a PL/SQL block we make use of a procedure named, Put_Line is part of a system package called, DBMS_OUTPUT.To use this procedure, we must also use another option, SET SERVEROUTPUT ON.(Discussed in detail later)

Examples:

PL/SQL block to find out the square of a numbe

```
SET SERVEROUTPUT ON
Declare
x number: &x;
Y number;
Begin
Y:=x*x;
Dbms_output.put_line ('The square is = '||y);
End;
/
```

To print 1..10 numbers

```
SET SERVEROUTPUT ON
BEGIN
DBMS_OUTPUT.PUT_LINE('This is a demo of for loop');
For Ctr in 1...10 Loop
DBMS_OUTPUT.PUT_LINE('Loop Number'|| CTR);
END LOOP;
/
```

Reverse for Loop

```
SET SERVEROUTPUT ON
BEGIN
DBMS_OUTPUT.PUT_LINE('The For loop begins :');
FOR CTR IN REVERSE 1..10 LOOP
DBMS_OUTPUT.PUT_LINE('LOOP NUMBER:'||CTR);
END LOOP;
END;
/
SET SERVEROUTPUT OFF
```

Note. Variable CTR need not be declared.

Loop

```
Set Serveroutput ON
```

```
Declare
Ctr number (2): = 0;
Begin
Dbms_output.put_line ('The LOOP loop begins:');
LOOP
CTR: = CTR+1;
Exit When CTR >10;
DBMS_OUTPUT.PUT_LINE ('LOOP NUMBER:' || CTR);
END LOOP;
END;
/
SET SERVEROUTPUT OFF
```

To Print 1 to 10 using while loop

```
Set Serveroutput on
Declare
Ctr Number(2):=1;
Begin
Dbms_output.put_line('The while loop begins:');
While ctr <=10 Loop
DBMS_OUTPUT.PUT_LINE('Loop Number :' || CTR);
Ctr:= ctr+1;
End loop;
End;
/
```

Program to Retrieve Name, Basic, Designation of employee from emp table queried by the user.

```
Set serveroutput on
Prompt Enter Employee Number
Accept N
Declare
DNAME emp.emp_name%type;
Dbasic    emp.join_basic%type;
Ddesig emp.design%Type;
```

```
Begin
Select emp_name, join_basic,desig into dname,dbasic,ddesig from emp where
emp_no=&N;
DBMS_OUTPUT.PUT_LINE('Name:'|| DNAME);
DBMS_OUTPUT.PUT_LINE('SALARY:'|| DBASIC);
DBMS_OUTPUT.PUT_LINE('DESIGNATION:'||DDESIG);
END;
/
SET SERVEROUTPUT OFF
```

ADVANTAGES OF PL/SQL

PL/SQL is a completely portable, high-performance transaction processing language that offers the following advantages:

- support for SQL
- support for object-oriented programming
- better performance
- higher productivity
- full portability
- tight integration with Oracle
- security

LAB ASSIGNMENT—11

1. Write a PL/SQL Block to find out the square of a number.
2. Write a PL/SQL block to compute the area of the circle and square
3. Write a PL/SQL Block to conversion of Celsius to Fahrenheit and vice versa.
4. Write a PL/SQL Block to find the Largest from the three numbers.
5. Write a PL/SQL Block to find the Factorial value of any number.
6. Write a PL/SQL Block to accept the marks for three subjects from a student, calculate its average. If average < 50 then print Fail, Average is between 50 to 60 then Second division, Average is between 60 to 75 then First division and average is in between 75 and above then print Distinction.
7. Write a PL/SQL Block to accept the emp number from employee table and calculate the tax on salary based on following-

Join Basic	**Tax**
Less than 1500	5% of salary
1500 to 2500	7% of salary
2501 to 3500	9% of salary
3501 and above	10% of salary.

8. Write a PL/SQL Block to find out whether the entered year is the leap year or not a leap year.
9. Write a PL/SQL Block to display the first 10 odd numbers.
10. Write a PL/SQL Block to display the first ten numbers that are divisible by both 3 and 5.

LAB ASSIGNMENT—12

1. Write a PL/SQL Block to print the Fibonacci series.
2. Write a PL/SQL Block to calculate Gross salary on the basis of basic salary if DA is 40% of basic, HRA is 20% of basic and PF deduction is 12% of basic salary.
3. Write a PL/SQL Block to calculate the sum of digits of a number entered through keyboard.
4. Write a PL/SQL Block to calculate the electricity bill on the basis of following details.

Consumption Units	Rate of Charge
0-200	Rs. 0.50 per Unit
201-400	Rs.100 plus Rs. 0.65 per unit excess of 200.
401-600	Rs.230 plus Rs.0.80 per unit excess of 400.
601 and above	Rs. 390 plus Rs. 1.00 per unit excess of 600.

5. Write a PL/SQL Block to print the table of number entered by user.
6. Write a PL/SQL block. Take the salary of an employee into a variable and check if his or her salary is less than 3000 then update the salary with 4000.

8 Cursors

Objectives :

- Cursors in PL/SQL
- Types of Cursors
- Cursor Operations
- Declaring Cursors
- Opening Cursors
- Fetching from Cursors
- Closing Cursors
- Cursor Attributes
- Cursor Variables
- The Cursor FOR Loop

Lab Assignment-13
Lab Assignment-14

CURSORS IN PL/SQL

When we execute a SQL statement from PL/SQL, the Oracle RDBMS assigns a private work area for that statement. This work area contains information about the SQL statement and the set of data returned or affected by that statement. The PL/SQL cursor is a mechanism by which we can name that work area and manipulate the information within it.

In its simplest form, we can think of a cursor as a pointer into a table in the database. For example, the following cursor declaration associates the entire employee table with the cursor named employee_cur:

```
CURSOR employee_cur IS SELECT * FROM employee;
```

Once we have declared the cursor, we can open it:

```
OPEN employee_cur;
```

And then we can fetch rows from it:

```
FETCH employee_cur INTO employee_rec;
```

and, finally, we can close the cursor:

```
CLOSE employee_cur;
```

In this case, each record fetched from this cursor represents an entire record in the employee table. We can, however, associate any valid SELECT statement with a cursor. In the next example we can see a join of three tables in cursor declaration:

```
DECLARE
    CURSOR jo_feed
    IS
        SELECT J.name, R.laugh_volume, C.name
            FROM joke S, response R, comedian C
        WHERE S.joke_id = R.joke_id
            AND S.joker_id = C.joker_id;
BEGIN
  ...
END;
```

Here, the cursor does not act as a pointer into any actual table in the database. Instead, the cursor is a pointer into the virtual table represented by the SELECT statement (SELECT is called a virtual table because the data it produces has the same structure as a table — rows and columns—but it exists only for the duration of the execution of the SQL statement). If the triple-join returns 20 rows, each row containing the three columns in the preceding example, then the cursor functions as a pointer into those 20 rows.

TYPES OF CURSORS

We have lots of options in PL/SQL for executing SQL, and all of them occur as some type of cursor. Generally, there are two types of SQL that we can execute in PL/SQL: static and dynamic. SQL is static if the content of the SQL statement is determined at compile time. A SQL statement is dynamic if it is constructed at runtime and then executed.

Dynamic SQL is made possible in PL/SQL only through the use of the DBMS_SQL built-in package. All other forms of SQL executed inside a PL/SQL program represent static SQL; these forms of cursors are the focus of the remainder of this chapter.

Even within the category of static SQL, we have further differentiation. With the advent of PL/SQL , we can choose between two distinct types of cursor objects:

Static cursor objects

These are the really static cursors of PL/SQL. The SQL is determined at compile time, and the cursor always refers to one SQL statement, which is known at compile time.

Cursor variables

We can declare a variable, which references a cursor object in the database. Our variable may refer to different SQL statements at different times (but that SQL is defined at compile time, not run time).

The cursor variable is one of the newest enhancements to PL/SQL. Cursor variables act as references to cursor objects. A cursor variable can change its value as our program executes. The variable can refer to different cursor objects (queries) at different times. We can also pass a cursor variable as a parameter to a procedure or function.

The static cursor itself comes in two types : implicit and explicit.

PL/SQL declares and manages an implicit cursor every time we execute a SQL DML statement, such as an INSERT or a SELECT that returns a single row.

We can define our own explicit cursors in our code. We must use an explicit cursor when we need to retrieve more than one row of data at a time through a SELECT statement. We can then use the cursor to fetch these rows one at a time. The set of rows returned by the query associated with an explicit cursor is called the active set or result set of the cursor. The row to which the explicit cursor points is called the current *row* of the result set.

CURSOR OPERATIONS

Parse

The first step in processing an SQL statement is to parse it to make sure it is valid and to determine the execution plan (using either the rule-based or cost-based optimizer).

Bind

When we bind, we associate values from program (host variables) with placeholders inside SQL statement. For static SQL, the SQL engine itself performs these binds. When we use dynamic SQL, we explicitly request a binding of variable values.

Open

When we open a cursor, the bind variables are used to determine the result set for the SQL statement. The pointer to the active or current row is set to the first row. Sometimes we will not explicitly open a cursor; instead the PL/SQL engine will perform this operation for us (as with implicit cursors).

Execute

In the execute phase, the statement is run within the SQL engine.

Fetch

If you are performing a query, the FETCH command retrieves the next row from the cursor's result set. Each time you fetch, PL/SQL moves the pointer forward in the result set. When working with explicit cursors, remember that if there are no more rows to retrieve, then FETCH does nothing (it does not raise an error).

Close

The CLOSE statement closes the cursor and releases all memory used by the cursor. Once closed, the cursor no longer has a result set. Sometimes you will not explicitly close a cursor; instead the PL/SQL engine will perform this operation for you (as with implicit cursors).

Figure 8.1 shows how some of these different operations are used to fetch information from the database into your PL/SQL program.

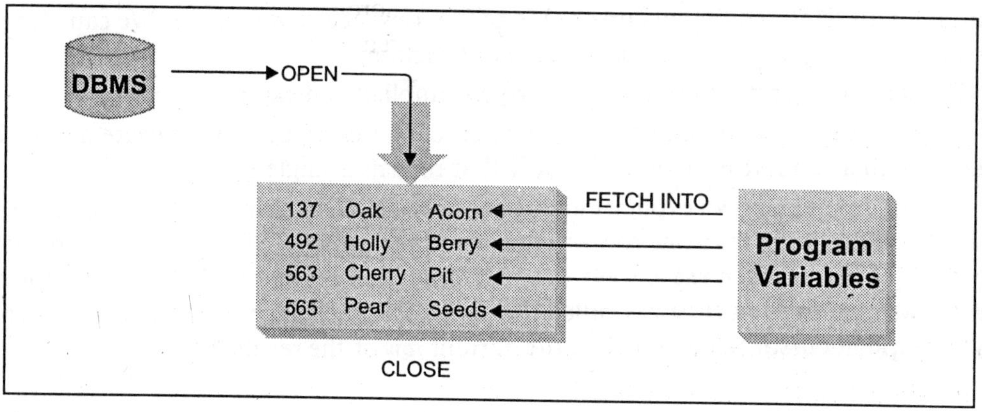

Figure 8.1. Using cursor operations to fetch database information into your program

Implicit and Explicit Cursors

Let's take a closer look at implicit and explicit cursors and the ways you can put them in your programs.

Implicit Cursors

PL/SQL issues an implicit cursor whenever you execute a SQL statement directly in your code, as long as that code does not employ an explicit cursor. It is called an "implicit" cursor because you, do not explicitly declare a cursor for the SQL statement.

If you use an implicit cursor, Oracle performs the open, fetches, and close for you automatically; these actions are outside of your programmatic control. You can, however, obtain information about the most recently executed SQL statement by examining the values in the implicit SQL cursor attributes.

PL/SQL employs an implicit cursor for each UPDATE, DELETE, or INSERT statement you execute in a program. You cannot execute these statements within an explicit cursor, even if you want to. You have a choice between using an implicit or explicit cursor only when you execute a single-row SELECT statement (a SELECT that returns only one row).

In the following UPDATE statement, which gives everyone in the company a 10% raise, PL/SQL creates an implicit cursor to identify the set of rows in the table which would be affected by the update:

```
UPDATE employee
 SET salary = salary * 1.1;
```

The following single-row query calculates and returns the total salary for a department. Once again, PL/SQL creates an implicit cursor for this statement:

```
SELECT SUM (salary) INTO department_total
 FROM employee
 WHERE department_number = 10;
```

If you have a SELECT statement that returns more than one row, you must use an explicit cursor for that query and then process the rows returned one at a time. PL/SQL does not yet support any kind of array interface between a database table and a composite PL/SQL datatype such as a PL/SQL table.

Drawbacks of Implicit Cursors

The implicit cursor has the following drawbacks:

- It is less efficient than an explicit cursor
- It is more vulnerable to data errors
- It gives you less programmatic control

The following sections explore each of these limitations to the implicit cursor.

Explicit Cursors

An explicit cursor is a SELECT statement that is explicitly defined in the declaration section of your code and, in the process, assigned a name. There is no such thing as an explicit cursor for UPDATE, DELETE, and INSERT statements.

With explicit cursors, you have complete control over how to access information in the database. You decide when to OPEN the cursor, when to FETCH records from the cursor (and therefore from the table or tables in the SELECT statement of the cursor) how many records to fetch, and when to CLOSE the cursor. Information about the current state of your cursor is available through examination of the cursor attributes. This granularity of control makes the explicit cursor an invaluable tool for your development effort.

Let's look at an example. The following anonymous block looks up the employee type description for an employee type code:

```
1. DECLARE
2. /* Explicit declaration of a cursor */
```

```
3. CURSOR emp_cur IS
4. SELECT emp.type_desc
5. FROM employees emp, employee_type emptyp
6. WHERE emp.type_code = emptyp.type_code;
7. BEGIN
8. /* Check to see if cursor is already open. If not, open it. */
9. IF NOT emp_cur%ISOPEN
10. THEN
11. OPEN emp_cur;
12. END IF;
13.
14. /* Fetch row from cursor directly into an Oracle Forms item */
15. FETCH emp_cur INTO :emp.type_desc;
16.
17. /* Close the cursor */
18. CLOSE emp_cur;
19. END;
```

This PL/SQL block performs the following cursor actions:

Action	Line(s)
Declare the cursor	3
Open the cursor (if not already open)	9, 11
Fetch one or more rows from the cursor	15
Close the cursor	18

The next few sections examine each of these steps in more detail. For the remainder of this chapter, unless noted otherwise, the word "cursor" refers to the explicit cursor.

DECLARING CURSORS

To use an explicit cursor, you must first declare it in the declaration section of your PL/SQL block or in a package, as shown here:

```
CURSOR cursor_name [ ( [ parameter [, parameter ...] ) ]
  [ RETURN return_specification ]
  IS SELECT_statement;
```

where cursor_name is the name of the cursor, return_specification is an optional RETURN clause for the cursor, and SELECT_statement is any valid SQL SELECT statement.

Once you have declared a cursor you can then OPEN it and FETCH from it.

Here are some examples of explicit cursor declarations:

- *A cursor without parameters.* The result set of this cursor is the set of company ID numbers for each record in the table:

```
CURSOR company_cur IS
SELECT company_id FROM company;
```

- *A cursor with parameters.* The result set of this cursor is the name of the company which matches the company ID passed to the cursor via the parameter:

```
CURSOR name_cur (company_id_in IN NUMBER)
IS
  SELECT name FROM company
   WHERE company_id = company_id_in;
```

- *A cursor with a* RETURN *clause.* The result set of this cursor is all columns (same structure as the underlying table) from all employee records in department 10:

```
CURSOR emp_cur RETURN employee%ROWTYPE
IS
  SELECT * FROM employee
   WHERE department_id = 10;
```

The Cursor Name

The name of an explicit cursor is not a PL/SQL variable. Instead, it is an undeclared identifier used to point to or refer to the query. We cannot assign values to a cursor, nor can we use it in an expression.

As a result, both of the executable statements after the BEGIN line below are invalid:

```
DECLARE
  CURSOR company_cur IS
    SELECT company_id FROM company;
BEGIN
  company_cur := 15009; /* Invalid syntax */

  IF company_cur IS NOT NULL THEN ... ;  /* Invalid syntax */
```

The name of a cursor can be up to 30 characters in length and follows the rules for any other identifier in PL/SQL.

PL/SQL Variables in a Cursor

Because a cursor must be associated with a SELECT statement, every cursor must refer at least one table from the database and determine from that (and from the WHERE clause) which rows will be returned in the active set. The list of expressions that appears after the SELECT keyword and before the FROM keyword is called the select list.

In native SQL, this select list may contain both columns and expressions (SQL functions on those columns, constants, etc.). In PL/SQL, the select list of a SELECT may contain PL/SQL variables, expressions, and even functions.

In the following cursor, the SELECT statement retrieves rows based on the employee table, but the information returned in the select list contains a combination of table columns, a PL/SQL variable, and a bind variable from the host environment (such as an Oracle Forms item):

```
DECLARE
  /* A local PL/SQL variable */
  projected_bonus NUMBER := 1000;
  /*
  || Cursor adds $1000 to the salary of each employee
  || hired more than three years ago.
  */
  CURSOR employee_cur
  IS
    SELECT employee_id,
         salary + projected_bonus new_salary, /* Column alias */
         :review.evaluation                  /* Bind variable */
     FROM employee
    WHERE hiredate < ADD_MONTHS (SYSDATE, -36);

BEGIN
  ...
END;
```

We can refer local PL/SQL program data (PL/SQL variables and constants), as well as host language bind variables in the WHERE, GROUP, and HAVING clauses of the cursor's SELECT statement.

Identifier Precedence in a Cursor

Be careful about naming identifiers when you mix PL/SQL variables in with database columns. It is a common practice to give a variable the same name as the column whose data it is supposed to represent. This makes perfect sense until we want to refer those local variables in a SQL statement along with the column.

In the following example, we want to fetch each employee who was hired more than three years ago and, using a local variable, add $1000 to their salary. The employee table has a column named "salary." Unfortunately, this procedure relies on a local variable of the same name to achieve its ends. Although this code will compile without error, it will not produce the desired result:

```
PROCEDURE improve_QOL
IS
  /* Local variable with same name as column: */
  salary NUMBER := 1000;

  CURSOR double_sal_cur
  IS
    SELECT salary + salary
     FROM employee
    WHERE hiredate < ADD_MONTHS (SYSDATE, -36);
BEGIN
```

Instead of adding $1000 to each person's salary, this code will instead double his or her salary. Inside the SQL statement, any unqualified reference to "salary" is resolved by using the column named "salary."

We could achieve the desired effect by qualifying the PL/SQL variable with the name of the procedure, as follows:

```
CURSOR double_sal_cur
IS
  SELECT salary + improve_QOL.salary
   FROM employee
  WHERE hiredate < ADD_MONTHS (SYSDATE, -36);
```

In this situation, we inform the compiler that the second reference to salary is that variable "owned" by the improve_QOL procedure. It will then add the current value of that variable to the salary column value.

If local variable names conflict with database column or table names, *change the name of variable.* Avoid this kind of duplication by using a standard naming convention for local variables which represent database information.

The Cursor RETURN Clause

One of the most significant new features in PL/SQL is the full support for packages and the resulting modularization of code that is now possible with that construct. Packages introduce an enhancement to the way you can declare a cursor: the RETURN clause.

When you group programs together into a package, you can make only the specification, or header information, of those programs available to developers. Although a developer can tell from the specification what the module is called and how to call it, he or she does not need to see any of the underlying code. As a result, you can create true black boxes behind which you can hide complex implementational details.

With PL/SQL you can accomplish the same objective with cursors by using the cursor RETURN clause. The RETURN clause allows you to create a specification for a cursor which is separate from its body (the SELECT statement). You may then place cursors in packages and hide the implementation details from developers.

Consider the following cursor declaration with RETURN clause:

```
CURSOR caller_cur (id_in IN NUMBER) RETURN caller%ROWTYPE
IS
   SELECT * FROM caller WHERE caller_id = id_in;
```

The specification of the caller_cur cursor is:

```
CURSOR caller_cur (id_in IN NUMBER) RETURN caller%ROWTYPE
```

while the *body* of the caller_cur cursor is:

```
SELECT * FROM caller WHERE caller_id = id_in:
```

Everything up to but not including the IS keyword is the specification, while everything following the IS keyword is the body.

Note. You can include a RETURN clause for any cursor you write in PL/SQL Version 2, but it is required only for cursors which are contained in a package specification.

The RETURN clause may be made up of any of the following datatype structures:

- A record defined from a database table, using the %ROWTYPE attribute
- A record defined from a programmer-defined record

Here is an example of a cursor defined in a package. First, the package specification provides the name of the cursor and the RETURN datatype (an entire row from the company table):

```
PACKAGE company
IS
  CURSOR company_cur (id_in NUMBER) RETURN company%ROWTYPE;
END company;
```

Then the following package body repeats the cursor specification and adds the SQL statement:

```
PACKAGE BODY company
IS
  CURSOR company_cur (id_in NUMBER) RETURN company%ROWTYPE
  IS
    SELECT * FROM company
     WHERE company_id = id_in;

END company;
```

The number of expressions in the cursor's select list must match the number of columns in the record identified by table_name%ROWTYPE or PLSQL_record%ROWTYPE. The datatypes of the elements must also be compatible. If the second element in the select list is type NUMBER, then the second column in the RETURN record cannot be type VARCHAR2 or BOOLEAN.

OPENING CURSORS

The first step in using a cursor is to define it in the declaration section. The next step you must perform before you try to extract or fetch records from a cursor is to open that cursor.

The syntax for the OPEN statement is simplicity itself:

```
OPEN <cursor_name> [ ( argument [, argument ...] ) ];
```

where <cursor_name> is the name of the cursor you declared and the arguments are the values to be passed if the cursor was declared with a parameter list.

When you open a cursor, PL/SQL executes the query for that cursor. It also identifies the active set of data — that is, the rows from all involved tables that meet the criteria in the WHERE clause and join conditions. The OPEN does not itself actually retrieve any of these rows — that action is performed by the FETCH statement.

Note. From the moment you open your cursor until the moment that cursor is closed, all data fetched through the cursor will ignore any inserts, updates, and deletes performed after the cursor was opened.

Furthermore, if the SELECT statement in your cursor uses a FOR UPDATE clause, then, when the cursor is opened, all the rows identified by the query are locked.

You should open a cursor only if it has been closed or was never opened. If you try to open a cursor that is already open you will get the following error:

```
ORA-06511: PL/SQL: cursor already open
```

You can be sure of a cursor's status by checking the %ISOPEN cursor attribute before you try to open the cursor:

```
IF NOT company_cur%ISOPEN
THEN
  OPEN company_cur;
END IF;
```

FETCHING FROM CURSORS

A SELECT statement creates a virtual table in SQL: its return set is a series of rows determined by the WHERE clause and with columns determined by the column list of the SELECT. So a cursor represents that virtual table within your PL/SQL program. In almost every situation, the point of declaring and opening a cursor is to return, or fetch, the rows of data from the cursor and then manipulate the information retrieved. PL/SQL provides a FETCH statement for this action.

The general syntax for a FETCH is shown below:

```
FETCH <cursor_name> INTO <record_or_variable_list>;
```

where <cursor_name> is the name of the cursor from which the record is fetched and <record_or_variable_list> is the PL/SQL data structure into which the next row of the active set of records is copied. You can fetch into a record structure (declared with the %ROWTYPE attribute or TYPE declaration statement) or you can fetch into a list of one or more variables (PL/SQL variables or application-specific bind variables such as Oracle Forms items).

The following examples illustrate the variety of possible fetches:

- Fetch into a PL/SQL record:

```
FETCH company_cur INTO company_rec;
```

- Fetch into a variable:

```
FETCH new_balance_cur INTO new_balance_dollars;
```

- Fetch into the row of a PL/SQL table row, a variable, and an Oracle Forms bind variable:

```
FETCH emp_name_cur INTO emp_name (1), hiredate, :dept.min_salary;
```

Matching Column List with INTO Clause

When you fetch into a list of variables, the number of variables must match the number of expressions in the SELECT list of the cursor. When you fetch into a record, the number of columns in the record must match the number of expressions in the SELECT list of the cursor.

If you do not match up the column list in the cursor's query with the INTO elements in the FETCH, you will receive the following compile error:

```
PLS-00394: wrong number of values in the INTO list of a FETCH statement
```

Let's look at variations of FETCH to see what will and will not work. Suppose we have declared the following cursor, records, and variables:

- Cursor that selects just three columns from dr_love table and a record based on that cursor:

```
CURSOR green_eggs_cur (character_in IN VARCHAR2)
IS
  SELECT ham_quantity, times_refused, excuse
   FROM dr_love
  WHERE book_title = 'GREEN EGGS AND HAM'
   AND character_name = character_in;
   green_eggs_rec green_eggs_cur%ROWTYPE;
```

- Cursor for all columns in dr_love table and a record based on the dr_love table:

```
CURSOR dr_love_cur
IS
  SELECT * FROM dr_love;
   dr_love_rec dr_love_cur%ROWTYPE;
```

- Programmer-defined record type which contains all three of the green_eggs_cur columns, followed by declaration of record:

```
TYPE green_eggs_rectype IS RECORD
  (ham# dr_love.ham_quantity%TYPE;
   saidno# dr_love.times_refused%TYPE,
```

```
    reason dr_love.excuse%TYPE);
full_green_eggs_rec green_eggs_rectype;
```

- Programmer-defined record type which contains only two of the three cursor columns, following by declaration of record:

```
TYPE partial_green_eggs_rectype IS RECORD
  (ham# dr_seuss.ham_quantity%TYPE;
   saidno# dr_seuss.times_refused%TYPE);
partial_rec partial_green_eggs_rectype;
```

- A set of local PL/SQL variables:

```
ham_amount NUMBER;
refused_count INTEGER;
lousy_excuse VARCHAR2(60);
```

Now that everything is declared, then we OPEN the cursor for the "Sharad I Am" character (passed as an argument) as follows:

```
OPEN green_eggs_cur ('Sharad I Am');
```

All of the following fetches will compile without error because the number and type of items in the INTO clause match those of the cursor:

```
FETCH green_eggs_cur INTO green_eggs_rec;
FETCH green_eggs_cur INTO ham_amount, refused_count, lousy_excuse;
FETCH green_eggs_cur INTO full_green_eggs_rec;
FETCH dr_love_cur INTO dr_love_rec;
```

Notice that you can FETCH a cursor's row into either a table-based or a programmer-defined record. You do not have to worry about record type compatibility in this situation. PL/SQL just needs to be able to match up a cursor column/expression with a variable/field in the INTO clause.

As you can see from the above FETCHes, you are not restricted to using any single record or variable list for a particular FETCH — even in the same program. You can declare multiple records for the same cursor and use all those different records for different fetches. You can also fetch once INTO a record and then later INTO a variable list, as shown below:

```
OPEN green_eggs_cur ('Sharad I Am');
FETCH green_eggs_cur INTO green_eggs_rec;
FETCH green_eggs_cur INTO amount_of_ham, num_rejections, reason;
CLOSE green_eggs_cur;
```

PL/SQL is very flexible in how it matches up the cursor columns with the INTO clause.

Fetching Past the Last Row

Once you open a cursor, you can FETCH from it until there are no more records left in the active set. At this point the %NOTFOUND cursor attribute for the cursor is set to TRUE.

Actually, you can even FETCH past the last record! In this case, PL/SQL will not raise any exceptions. Because there is nothing left to fetch, it will not modify the values in the INTO list of the FETCH and the fetch will not set those values to NULL.

Column Aliases in Cursors

The SELECT statement of the cursor includes the list of columns that are returned by that cursor. Just as with any SELECT statement, this column list may contain either actual column names or column expressions, which are also referred to as calculated or virtual columns.

A column alias is an alternative name you provide to a column or column expression in a query. You may have used column aliases in SQL*Plus in order to improve the readability of ad hoc report output. In that situation, such aliases are completely optional. In an explicit cursor, on the other hand, column aliases are required for calculated columns when:

- You FETCH into a record declared with a %ROWTYPE declaration against that cursor.
- You refer the calculated column in your program.

Consider the following query. For all companies with sales activity during 2004, the SELECT statement retrieves the company name and the total amount invoiced to that company (assume that the default date format mask for this instance is 'DD-MON-YYYY'):

```
SELECT company_name, SUM (inv_amt)
 FROM company C, invoice I
WHERE C.company_id = I.company_id
  AND I.invoice_date BETWEEN '01-JAN-2004' AND '31-DEC-2004';
```

If you run this SQL statement in SQL*Plus, the output will look something like this:

COMPANY_NAME	SUM (INV_AMT)
ACME TURBO CO.	1000
WASHINGTON GLASS CO.	25.20

SUM (INV_AMT) does not make a particularly attractive column header for a report, but it works well enough for a quick dip into the data as an ad hoc query. Let's now use this same query in an explicit cursor and add a column alias:

```
DECLARE
  CURSOR comp_cur IS
    SELECT company_name, SUM (inv_amt) total_sales
     FROM company C, invoice I
    WHERE C.company_id = I.company_id
      AND I.invoice_date BETWEEN '01-JAN-1994' AND '31-DEC-1994';
  comp_rec comp_cur%ROWTYPE;
BEGIN
  OPEN comp_cur;
```

```
        FETCH comp_cur INTO comp_rec;
        ...
      END;
```

With the alias in place, we can get at that information just as we would any other column in the query:

```
IF comp_rec.total_sales > 5000
THEN
  DBMS_OUTPUT.PUT_LINE
    (' You have exceeded your credit limit of $5000 by ' ||
     TO_CHAR (5000-company_rec.total_sales, '$9999'));
END IF;
```

If we fetch a row into a record declared with %ROWTYPE, the only way to access the column or column expression value is to do so by the column name.

CLOSING CURSORS

When you are done with a cursor, close it.

Here is the syntax for a CLOSE cursor statement:

```
CLOSE <cursor_name>
```

where <cursor_name> is the name of the cursor you are closing.

An open cursor uses a certain amount of memory; the exact amount depends on the active set for the cursor. It can, therefore, use up quite a lot of the Shared Global Area of the RDBMS. The cursor can also cause the database to issue row-level locks when the FOR UPDATE clause is used in the SELECT statement.

Maximum Number of Cursors

When database instance is started, an initialization parameter called OPEN_CURSORS specifies the maximum number of open cursors that a single-user process can have at once. This parameter does not control a system-wide feature, but rather the maximum address/memory space used by each process. If you are sloppy and do not close your cursors, all the other users might encounter the dreaded error message:

```
ORA-01000:  maximum open cursors exceeded
```

Go through your code and check for opened cursors which have not been closed.

You should close a cursor only if it is currently open. Be sure of a cursor's status by checking the %ISOPEN cursor attribute before you try to close the cursor:

```
IF company_cur%ISOPEN
THEN
  CLOSE company_cur;
END IF;
```

Closing Local Cursors

If you declare a cursor in a PL/SQL block (an anonymous block, procedure, or function), the cursor is only defined within (is "local to") that block. When execution of the block terminates, PL/SQL will automatically close any local cursors which were left open without raising an exception.

In addition, if your cursor is defined in a package, then its scope is not limited to any particular PL/SQL block. If you open such a cursor, it will stay open until you CLOSE it explicitly or you disconnect your Oracle session.

CURSOR ATTRIBUTES

You can manipulate cursors using the OPEN, FETCH, and CLOSE statements. When you need to get information about the current status of your cursor, or the result of the last fetch from a cursor, you will access cursor attributes.

Both explicit and implicit cursors have four attributes, as shown in Table 8.1.

Table 8.1: Cursor Attributes

Name	Description
%FOUND	Returns TRUE if record was fetched successfully, FALSE otherwise.
%NOTFOUND	Returns TRUE if record was not fetched successfully, FALSE otherwise.
%ROWCOUNT	Returns number of records fetched from cursor at that point in time.
%ISOPEN	Returns TRUE if cursor is open, FALSE otherwise.

To obtain information about the execution of the cursor, you append the cursor attribute name to the name of your cursor. For example, if you declare a cursor as follows:

```
CURSOR call_cur IS
  SELECT call_id, company_id FROM call;
```

then the four attributes associated with the cursor are:

```
call_cur%FOUND
call_cur%NOTFOUND
call_cur%ROWCOUNT
call_cur%ISOPEN
```

Some of the ways you can access the attributes of an explicit cursor are shown below in bold:

```
DECLARE
  CURSOR call_cur IS
    SELECT call_id, company_id FROM call;
  call_rec call_cur%ROWTYPE;
BEGIN
  /* Only open the cursor if it is not yet open */
  IF NOT call_cur%ISOPEN
  THEN
    OPEN call_cur
  END IF;
  FETCH call_cur INTO call_rec;

  /* Keep fetching until no more records are FOUND */
  WHILE call_cur%FOUND
  LOOP
    DBMS_OUTPUT.PUT_LINE
      ('Just fetched record number ' ||
       TO_CHAR (call_cur%ROWCOUNT));
    FETCH call_cur INTO call_rec;
  END LOOP;
  CLOSE call_cur;
END;
```

PL/SQL does provide the same attributes for an implicit cursor. As an implicit cursor has no name, PL/SQL assigns the generic name SQL to it. Using this name, you can access the attributes of an implicit cursor.

You can reference cursor attributes in your PL/SQL code, as shown in the preceding example, but cannot use those attributes inside a SQL statement. If you try to use the %ROWCOUNT attribute in the WHERE clause of a SELECT, for example:

```
SELECT call_id, company_id
  FROM call
 WHERE company_id = company_cur%ROWCOUNT;
```

then you will get a compile error:

```
PLS-00229: Attribute expression within SQL expression
```

The four explicit cursor attributes are examined in detail in the following sections:

The %FOUND Attribute

The %FOUND attribute reports on the status of your most recent FETCH against the cursor. The attribute evaluates to TRUE if the most recent FETCH against the explicit cursor returned a row, or FALSE if no row was returned.

If the cursor has not yet been opened, a reference to the %FOUND attribute raises the INVALID_CURSOR exception. You can evaluate the %FOUND attribute of any open cursor, because you refer the cursor by name.

In the following example, loop through all the call in the call_cur cursor, assign all calls entered before today to that particular caller, and then fetch the next record. If you have reached the last record, then the %NOTFOUND attribute is set to TRUE and exit the simple loop.

```
OPEN call_cur;
LOOP
  FETCH call_cur INTO call_rec;
  EXIT WHEN NOT call_cur%FOUND;

  UPDATE call
    SET call_id = call_rec.call_id
   WHERE call_timestamp < SYSDATE;
END LOOP;
CLOSE call_cur;
```

In the next example, keep a count of the total number of orders entered for a particular company. If we have fetched last order (%FOUND is FALSE), then we display a message in Oracle Forms informing the user of the total number of orders:

```
OPEN order_cur;
LOOP
  FETCH order_cur INTO order_number, company_id;
  EXIT WHEN order_cur%NOTFOUND;
  do_other_stuff_then_keep_count;
  :order.count_orders := :order.count_orders + 1;
END LOOP;
CLOSE order_cur;

IF :order.count_orders > 1
THEN
  DBMS_OUTPUT.PUT_LINE
    ('A total of ' || TO_CHAR (:order.count_orders) ||
     ' orders have been found.');
```

```
ELSE
   DBMS_OUTPUT.PUT_LINE('Just one order was found.');
END IF;
```

The %NOTFOUND Attribute

The %NOTFOUND attribute is the opposite of %FOUND. It returns TRUE if the explicit cursor is unable to fetch another row because the last row was fetched. If the cursor is unable to return a row because of an error, the appropriate exception is raised. If the cursor has not yet been opened, a reference to the %NOTFOUND attribute raises the INVALID_CURSOR exception. You can evaluate the %NOTFOUND attribute of any open cursor, because you refer the cursor by name.

The two attributes are directly, logically opposed, so whatever you can do with one you can also do with a NOT of the other. In other words, once a fetch has been performed against the open cursor <cursor_name>, the following expressions are equivalent:

```
<cursor_name>%FOUND          = NOT <cursor_name>%NOTFOUND
<cursor_name>%NOTFOUND       = NOT <cursor_name>%FOUND
```

Use whichever formulation fits most naturally in your code. In a previous example, we issued the following statement:

```
EXIT WHEN NOT call_cur%FOUND;
```

to terminate the loop. A simpler and more direct statement would use the %NOTFOUND instead of %FOUND, as follows:

```
EXIT WHEN call_rec%NOTFOUND;
```

The %ROWCOUNT Attribute

The %ROWCOUNT attribute returns the number of records fetched from a cursor at the time that the attribute is queried. When you first open a cursor, its %ROWCOUNT is set to zero. If you refer the %ROWCOUNT attribute of a cursor that is not open, you will raise the INVALID_CURSOR exception. After each record is fetched, %ROWCOUNT is increased by one. This attribute can be referred in a PL/SQL statement, but not in a SQL statement.

You can use %ROWCOUNT to limit the number of records fetched from a cursor. The following example retrieves only the first ten records from the cursor, providing the top ten companies placing orders in 2003:

```
DECLARE
  CURSOR company_cur IS
    SELECT company_name, company_id, total_order
     FROM company_revenue_view
     WHERE TO_NUMBER (TO_CHAR (order_date)) = 2003
     ORDER BY total_order DESC;
  company_rec company_cur%ROWTYPE;
```

```
BEGIN
OPEN company_cur;
LOOP
  FETCH company_cur INTO company_rec;
  EXIT WHEN company_cur%ROWCOUNT > 10 OR
      company_cur%NOTFOUND;

  DBMS_OUTPUT.PUT_LINE
  ('Company ' || company_rec.company_name ||
   'ranked number ' || TO_CHAR (company_cur%ROWCOUNT) || '.');
END LOOP;
CLOSE company_cur;
```

The %ISOPEN Attribute

The %ISOPEN attribute returns TRUE if the cursor is open; otherwise, it returns FALSE. In most cases when you use a cursor, you open it, fetch from it, and close it, all within one routine. Most of the time it is easy to know whether your cursor is open or closed. In some cases, however, you will spread your cursor actions out over a wider area of code, perhaps across different routines (possible if the cursor is declared in a package). If so, it will make sense to use the %ISOPEN attribute to make sure that a cursor is open before you perform a fetch:

```
IF NOT call_cur%ISOPEN
THEN
  OPEN call_cur;
END IF;
FETCH call_cur INTO call_rec;
...
```

Note. *Remember that if you try to open a cursor that has already been opened, you will receive a runtime error:*

ORA-06511: PL/SQL: cursor already open

Implicit SQL Cursor Attributes

When the RDBMS opens an implicit cursor to process your request (whether it is a query or an INSERT or an UPDATE), it makes cursor attributes available to you with the SQL cursor. This is not a cursor in the way of an explicit cursor. You cannot open, fetch from, or close the SQL cursor, but you can access information about the most recently executed SQL statement through SQL cursor attributes. The SQL cursor has the same four attributes as an explicit cursor:

```
SQL%FOUND
SQL%NOTFOUND
SQL%ROWCOUNT
SQL%ISOPEN
```

Differences Between Implicit and Explicit Cursor Attributes

The values returned by implicit cursor attributes differ from those of explicit cursor attributes in the following ways:

- If the RDBMS has not opened an implicit SQL cursor in the session, then the SQL%ROWCOUNT attribute returns NULL instead of raising the INVALID_CURSOR error. References to the other attributes (ISOPEN, FOUND, NOTFOUND) all return FALSE. You will never raise the INVALID_CURSOR error with an implicit cursor attribute reference.
- The %ISOPEN attribute will always return FALSE — before and after the SQL statement. After the statement is executed (whether it is SELECT, UPDATE, DELETE, or INSERT), the implicit cursor will already have been opened and closed implicitly. An implicit cursor can never be open outside of the statement itself.
- SQL cursor attributes are always set according to the results of the most recently executed SQL statement. That SQL statement might have been executed in a stored procedure which your program called; you might not even be aware of that SQL statement execution. If you plan to make use of a SQL cursor attribute, make sure that you reference that attribute immediately after you execute the SQL statement.
- The %FOUND attribute returns TRUE if an UPDATE, DELETE, or INSERT affected at least one record. It will return FALSE if those statements failed to affect any records. It returns TRUE if an implicit SELECT returns one row.
- The behavior of the %NOTFOUND attribute for UPDATE, DELETE, or INSERT statements is the opposite of %FOUND. The situation for an implicit SELECT is a bit different: when you use an implicit SELECT statement, never rely on the %NOTFOUND and %FOUND attributes.
- When an implicit SELECT statement does not return any rows, PL/SQL immediately raises the NO_DATA_FOUND exception. When an implicit SELECT statement returns more than one row, PL/SQL immediately raises the TOO_MANY_ROWS exception. In either case, once the exception is raised, control shifts to the exception section of the PL/SQL block.

Select for Update in Cursors

When you issue a SELECT statement against the database to query some records, no locks are placed on the selected rows. In general, this is a wonderful feature because the number of records locked at any given time is (by default) kept to the absolute minimum: only those records which have been changed but not yet committed are locked. Even then, others will be able to read those records as they appeared before the change.

There are times, however, when you will want to lock a set of records even before you change them in your program. Oracle offers the FOR UPDATE clause of the SELECT statement to perform this locking.

When you issue a SELECT...FOR UPDATE statement, the RDBMS automatically obtains exclusive row-level locks on all the rows identified by the SELECT statement, holding the records "for your changes only" as you move through the rows retrieved by the cursor. No one else will be able to change any of these records until you perform a ROLLBACK or a COMMIT.

Here are two examples of the FOR UPDATE clause used in a cursor:

```
CURSOR toys_cur IS
   SELECT name, manufacturer, preference_level, sell_at_yardsale_flag
    FROM my_sons_collection
   WHERE hours_used = 0
    FOR UPDATE;

CURSOR fall_job_cur IS
   SELECT task, expected_hours, tools_required, do_it_yourself_flag
    FROM winterize
   WHERE year = TO_CHAR (SYSDATE, 'YYYY')
    FOR UPDATE OF task;
```

The first cursor uses the unqualified FOR UPDATE clause, while the second cursor qualifies the FOR UPDATE with a column name from the query.

You can use the FOR UPDATE clause in a SELECT against multiple tables. In this case, rows in a table are locked only if the FOR UPDATE clause references a column in that table. In the following example the FOR UPDATE clause does not result in any locked rows in the winterize table:

```
CURSOR fall_job_cur IS
   SELECT w.task, w.expected_hours,
         w.tools_required, w.do_it_yourself_flag
    FROM winterize w, husband_config hc
   WHERE year = TO_CHAR (SYSDATE, 'YYYY')
    FOR UPDATE OF husband_config.max_procrastination_allowed;
```

The FOR UPDATE OF clause only mentions the max_procrastination_allowed column; no columns in the winterize table are listed.

The OF list of the FOR UPDATE clause does not restrict you to changing only those columns listed. Locks are still placed on all rows, the OF list just gives you a way to document more clearly what you intend to change.

Note. If you simply state FOR UPDATE in the query and do not include one or more columns after the OF keyword, then the database will then lock all identified rows across all tables listed in the FROM clause.

Furthermore, you do not have to actually UPDATE or DELETE any records just because you issued a SELECT...FOR UPDATE — which simply states your intention to be able to do so.

Finally, you can append the optional keyword NOWAIT to the FOR UPDATE clause to tell Oracle not to wait if the table has been locked by another user. In this case, control will be returned immediately to your program so that you can perform other work or simply wait for a period of time before trying again. Without the NOWAIT clause, your process will block until the table is available. There is no limit to the wait time unless the table is remote. For remote objects, the Oracle initialization parameter, DISTRIBUTED_LOCK_TIMEOUT, is used to set the limit.

Releasing Locks with COMMIT

As soon as a cursor with a FOR UPDATE clause is OPENed, all rows identified in the result set of the cursor are locked and remain locked until your session issues either a COMMIT statement to save any changes or a ROLLBACK statement to cancel those changes. When either of these actions occurs, the locks on the rows are released. As a result, you cannot execute another FETCH against a FOR UPDATE cursor after you COMMIT or ROLLBACK. You will have lost your position in the cursor.

If you ever need to execute a COMMIT or ROLLBACK as you FETCH records from a SELECT FOR UPDATE cursor, you should include code (such as a loop EXIT or other conditional logic) to halt any further fetches from the cursor.

The WHERE CURRENT OF Clause

PL/SQL provides the WHERE CURRENT OF clause for both UPDATE and DELETE statements inside a cursor in order to allow you to easily make changes to the most recently fetched row of data.

The general format for the WHERE CURRENT OF clause is as follows:

```
UPDATE table_name
   SET set_clause
 WHERE CURRENT OF cursor_name;

DELETE
  FROM table_name
 WHERE CURRENT OF cursor_name;
```

Notice that the WHERE CURRENT OF clause references the cursor and not the record into which the next fetched row is deposited.

The most important advantage to using WHERE CURRENT OF where you need to change the row fetched last is that you do not have to code in two (or more) places the criteria used to uniquely identify a row in a table. Without WHERE CURRENT OF, you would need to repeat the WHERE clause of your cursor in the WHERE clause of the associated UPDATEs and DELETEs. As a result, if the table structure changes in a way that affects the construction of the primary key, you have to make sure that each SQL statement is upgraded to support this change. If you use WHERE CURRENT OF, on the other hand, you only have to modify the WHERE clause of the SELECT statement.

This might seem like a relatively minor issue, but it is one of many areas in your code where you can leverage sub features in PL/SQL to minimize code redundancies. Utilization of

WHERE CURRENT OF, %TYPE, and %ROWTYPE declaration attributes, cursor FOR loops, local modularization, and other PL/SQL language constructs can have a big impact on reducing the pain you may experience when you maintain your Oracle-based applications.

Delete the record you just fetched.

or

Update these columns in that row you just fetched.

A perfect fit for WHERE CURRENT OF! The next version of our winterization program below uses this clause. We have also switched to a simple loop from FOR loop because We want to exit conditionally from the loop:

```
DECLARE
  CURSOR fall_jobs_cur IS SELECT ... same as before ... ;
  job_rec fall_jobs_cur%ROWTYPE;
BEGIN
  OPEN fall_jobs_cur;
  LOOP
    FETCH fall_jobs_cur INTO job_rec;

    IF fall_jobs_cur%NOTFOUND
    THEN
      EXIT;

    ELSIF job_rec.do_it_yourself_flag = 'YOUCANDOIT'
    THEN
      UPDATE winterize SET responsible = 'STEVEN'
       WHERE CURRENT OF fall_jobs_cur;
      COMMIT;
      EXIT;
    END IF;
  END LOOP;
  CLOSE fall_jobs_cur;
END;
```

CURSOR VARIABLES

In PL/SQL you can create and use cursor variables. Unlike an explicit cursor, which names the PL/SQL work area for the result set, a cursor variable is instead a reference to that work area. Explicit and implicit cursors are both static in that they are tied to specific queries. The cursor variable can be opened for any query, even different queries within a single program execution.

The most important benefit of the cursor variable is that it provides a mechanism for passing results of queries (the rows returned by fetches against a cursor) between different PL/SQL programs—even between client and server PL/SQL programs. Prior to PL/SQL, you would have had to fetch all data from the cursor, store it in PL/SQL variables (perhaps a PL/SQL table), and then pass those variables as arguments. With cursor variables, you simply pass the reference to that cursor. This improves performance and streamlines your code.

It also means that the cursor is, in effect, shared among the programs which have access to the cursor variable. In a client-server environment, for example, a program on the client side could open and start fetching from the cursor variable, then pass that variable as an argument to a stored procedure on the server. This stored program could then continue fetching and pass control back to the client program to close the cursor. You can also perform the same steps between different stored programs, on the same or different database instances.

This process, shown in Figure 8.2, offers new dramatic possibilities for data sharing and cursor management in PL/SQL programs.

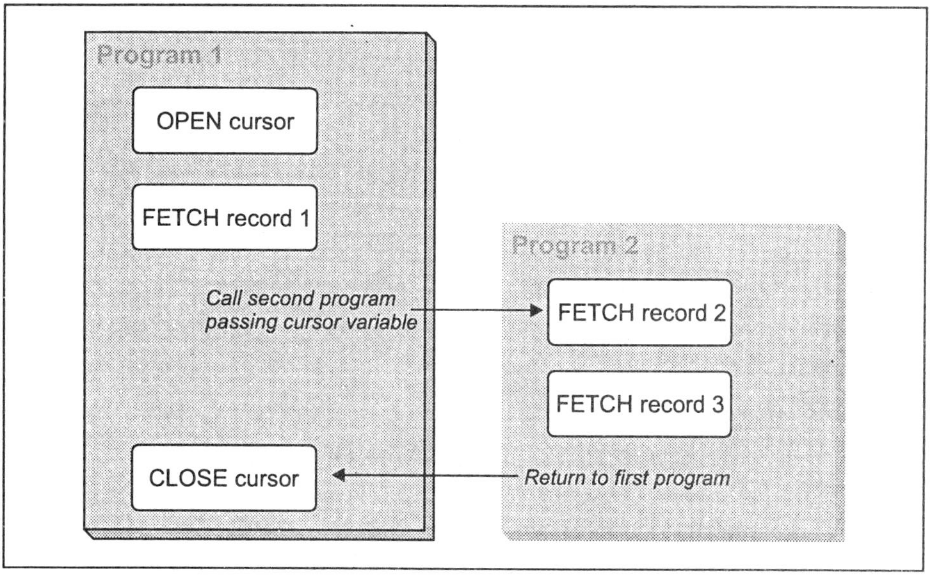

Figure 8.2. Referencing a cursor variable across two programs

The code you write to take advantage of cursor variables is very similar to that for explicit cursors. The following example declares a cursor type (called a REF CURSOR type) for the company table, then opens, fetches from and closes the cursor:

```
DECLARE
  /* Create the cursor type. */
  TYPE company_curtype IS REF CURSOR RETURN company%ROWTYPE;

  /* Declare a cursor variable of that type. */
  company_curvar company_curtype;
```

```
    /* Declare a record with same structure as cursor variable. */
    company_rec company%ROWTYPE;
  BEGIN
    /* Open the cursor variable, associating with it a SQL statement. */
    OPEN company_curvar FOR SELECT * FROM company;

    /* Fetch from the cursor variable. */
    FETCH company_curvar INTO company_rec;

    /* Close the cursor object associated with variable. */
    CLOSE company_curvar;
  END;
```

That looks an awful lot like explicit cursor operations, except for the following:

- The REF CURSOR type declaration
- The OPEN FOR syntax which specified the query at the time of the open

While the syntax is very similar, the fact that the cursor variable is a variable opens up many new opportunities in our programs. These are explored in the remainder of this section.

Features of Cursor Variables

Cursor variables let us:

- Associate a cursor variable with different queries at different times in our program execution. In other words, a single cursor variable can be used to fetch from different result sets.
- Pass a cursor variable as an argument to a procedure or function. We can share the results of a cursor by passing the reference to that result set.
- Employ the full functionality of static PL/SQL cursors for cursor variables. We can OPEN, CLOSE, and FETCH with cursor variables within your PL/SQL programs. We can reference the standard cursor attributes—%ISOPEN, %FOUND, %NOTFOUND, and %ROWCOUNT—for cursor variables.
- Assign the contents of one cursor (and its result set) to another cursor variable. Because the cursor variable is a variable, it can be used in assignment operations. There are, however, restrictions on referencing this kind of variable, addressed later in this chapter.

Declaring REF CURSOR Types and Cursor Variables

Just as with a PL/SQL table or a programmer-defined record, you must perform two distinct declaration steps in order to create a cursor variable:

1. Create a referenced cursor TYPE.
2. Declare the actual cursor variable based on that type.

The syntax for creating a referenced cursor type is as follows:

```
TYPE cursor_type_name IS REF CURSOR [ RETURN return_type ];
```

where cursor_type_name is the name of the type of cursor and return_type is the RETURN data specification for the cursor type. The return_type can be any of the data structures valid for a normal cursor RETURN clause, defined using the %ROWTYPE attribute or by referencing a previously-defined record TYPE.

Notice that the RETURN clause is optional with the REF CURSOR type statement. Both of the following declarations are valid:

```
TYPE company_curtype IS REF CURSOR RETURN company%ROWTYPE;
TYPE generic_curtype IS REF CURSOR;
```

The first form of the REF CURSOR statement is called a *strong type* because it attaches a record type (or row type) to the cursor variable type at the moment of declaration. Any cursor variable declared using that type can only be used with SQL statement and FETCH INTO data structures which match the specified record type. The advantage of a strong REF TYPE is that the compiler can determine whether or not the developer has properly matched up the cursor variable's FETCH statements with its cursor object's query list.

The second form of the REF CURSOR statement, in which the RETURN clause is missing, is called a *weak type.* This cursor variable type is not associated with any record data structure. Cursor variables declared without the RETURN clause can be used in much more flexible ways than the strong type. They can be used with any query, with any rowtype structure—varying even within the course of a single program.

Declaring Cursor Variables

The syntax for declaring a cursor variable is:

```
cursor_name cursor_type_name;
```

where cursor_name is the name of the cursor and cursor_type_name is the name of the type of cursor previously defined with a TYPE statement.

Here is an example of the creation of a cursor variable:

```
DECLARE
  /* Create a cursor type for sports cars. */
  TYPE sports_car_cur_type IS REF CURSOR RETURN car%ROWTYPE;

  /* Create a cursor variable for sports cars. */
  sports_car_cur sports_car_cur_type;
BEGIN
  ...
END;
```

It is very important to distinguish between declaring a cursor variable and creating an actual cursor object—the result set identified by the cursor SQL statement. The cursor variable is nothing more than a reference or pointer. A constant is nothing more than a value, whereas a variable points to its value. Similarly, a static cursor acts as a constant, whereas a cursor variable points to a cursor object. These distinctions are shown in Figure 8.3. Notice that two different cursor variables in different programs both refer to the same cursor object.

Declaration of a cursor variable does not create a cursor object. To do that, you must instead use the OPEN FOR syntax to create a new cursor object and assign it to the variable.

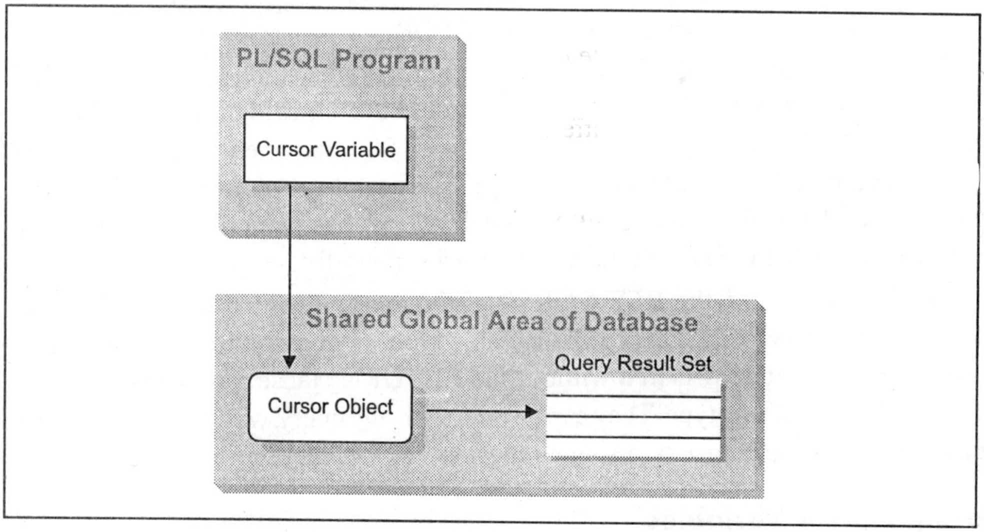

Figure 8.3. The referencing character of cursor variables

Opening Cursor Variables

You assign a value (the cursor object) to a cursor when you OPEN the cursor. So the syntax for the OPEN statement is now modified in PL/SQL Release 2.3 to accept a SELECT statement after the FOR clause, as shown below:

```
OPEN cursor_name FOR select_statement;
```

where cursor_name is the name of a cursor or cursor variable and select_statement is a SQL SELECT statement.

For strong REF CURSOR type cursor variables, the structure of the SELECT statement (the number and datatypes of the columns) must match or be compatible with the structure specified in the RETURN clause of the type statement. Figure 8.4 offers an example of the kind of compatibility required. Figure 8.4 contains the full set of compatibility rules.

```
DECLARE
   TYPE emp_curtype IS
      REF CURSOR RETURN emp%ROWTYPE;
   emp_curvar emp_curtype;
BEGIN
   OPEN emp_curvar FOR
                    SELECT * FROM emp;
END;
```

Figure 8.4. Compatible REF CURSOR rowtype and SELECT list

If cursor_name is a cursor variable defined with a weak REF CURSOR type, you can OPEN it for any query, with any structure. In the following example, We open (assign a value to) the cursor variable twice, with two different queries:

```
DECLARE
  TYPE emp_curtype IS REF CURSOR;
  emp_curvar emp_curtype;
BEGIN
  OPEN emp_curvar FOR SELECT * FROM emp;
  OPEN emp_curvar FOR SELECT employee_id FROM emp;
  OPEN emp_curvar FOR SELECT company_id, name FROM company;
END;
```

That last open didn't even have anything to do with the employee table!

If the cursor variable has not yet been assigned to any cursor object, the OPEN FOR statement implicitly creates an object for the variable.

If at the time of the OPEN the cursor variable is already pointing to a cursor object, then OPEN FOR does not create a new object. Instead, it reuses the existing object and attaches a new query to that object. The cursor object is maintained separately from the cursor or query itself.

Fetching from Cursor Variables

As mentioned earlier, the syntax for a FETCH statement using a cursor variable is the same as that for static cursors:

```
FETCH <cursor variable name> INTO <record name>;
FETCH <cursor variable name> INTO <variable name>, <variable name> ...;
```

When the cursor variable was declared with a strong REF CURSOR type, the PL/SQL compiler makes sure that the data structure(s) listed after the INTO keyword are compatible with the structure of the query associated with cursor variable.

Strong and Weak REF CURSOR Types

If the cursor variable is of the weak REF CURSOR type, the PL/SQL compiler cannot perform the same kind of check. Such a cursor variable can FETCH into any data structures, because the REF CURSOR type it is not identified with a rowtype at the time of declaration. At compile time, there is no way to know which cursor object (and associated SQL statement) will be assigned to that variable.

Consequently, the check for compatibility must happen at run time, when the FETCH is about to be executed. At this point, if the query and the INTO clause do not structurally match (and PL/SQL will use implicit conversions if necessary and possible), then the PL/SQL runtime engine will raise the predefined ROWTYPE_MISMATCH exception.

Rules for Cursor Variables

This section examines in more detail the rules and issues regarding the use of cursor variables in your programs. This includes rowtype matching rules, cursor variable aliases and scoping issues.

Remember that the cursor variable is a reference to a cursor object or query in the database. It is not the object itself. A cursor variable is said to "refer to a given query" if either of the following is true:

- An OPEN statement FOR that query was executed with the cursor variable.
- A cursor variable was assigned a value from another cursor variable that refers to that query.

You can perform assignment operations with cursor variables and also pass these variables as arguments to procedures and functions. In order to perform such actions between cursor variables (and to bind a cursor variable to a parameter), the different cursor variables must follow a set of compile-time and runtime rowtype matching rules.

Compile-time rowtype matching rules

These are the rules that PL/SQL follows at compile-time:

- Two cursor variables (including procedure parameters) are compatible for assignments and argument passing if any of the following are true:
  - Both variables (or parameters) are of a strong REF CURSOR type with the same <rowtype_name>.
  - Both variables (or parameters) are of some weak REF CURSOR type, regardless of the <rowtype_name>.
  - One variable (parameter) is of any strong REF CURSOR type, and the other is of any weak REF CURSOR type.
- A cursor variable (parameter) of a strong REF CURSOR type may be OPEN FOR a query that returns a rowtype which is structurally equal to the <rowtype_name> in the original type declaration.

- A cursor variable (parameter) of a weak REF CURSOR type may be OPEN FOR any query. The FETCH from such a variable is allowed INTO any list of variables or record structure.

In other words, if either of the cursor variables are of the weak REF CURSOR type, then the PL/SQL compiler cannot really validate whether the two different cursor variables will be compatible. That will happen at runtime, the rules are covered in the next section.

Run-time rowtype matching rules

These are the rules that PL/SQL follows at run time:

- A cursor variable (parameter) of a weak REF CURSOR type may be made to refer to a query of any rowtype regardless of the query or cursor object to which it may have referred earlier.
- A cursor variable (parameter) of a strong REF CURSOR type may be made to refer only to a query which matches structurally the <rowtype_name> of the RETURN clause of the REF CURSOR type declaration.
- Two records (or lists of variables) are considered structurally matching with implicit conversions if both of the following are true:
  - The number of fields is the same in both records (lists).
  - For each field in one record (or variable on one list), a corresponding field in the second list (or variable in second list) has the same PL/SQL datatype, or one which can be converted implicitly by PL/SQL to match the fi
- For a cursor variable (parameter) used in a FETCH statement, the query associated with the cursor variable must structurally match with implicit conversions the record or list of variables of the INTO clause of the FETCH statement. This is, by the way, the same rule used for static cursors.

Passing Cursor Variables as Arguments

You can pass a cursor variable as an argument in a call to a procedure or function. When you use a cursor variable in the parameter list of a program, you need to specify the mode of the parameter and the datatype (the REF CURSOR type).

Identifying the REF CURSOR type

In your program header, you must identify the REF CURSOR type of your cursor variable parameter. To do this, that cursor type must be defined earlier.

If you are creating a local module within another program , then you can also define the cursor type in the same program. It will then be available for the parameter. This approach is shown below:

```
DECLARE
  /* Define the REF CURSOR type. */
  TYPE curvar_type IS REF CURSOR RETURN company%ROWTYPE;
```

```
    /* Reference it in the parameter list. */
    PROCEDURE open_query (curvar_out OUT curvar_type)
    IS
      local_cur curvar_type;
    BEGIN
      OPEN local_cur FOR SELECT * FROM company;
      curvar_out := local_cur;
    END;
  BEGIN
    ...
  END;
```

If you are creating a standalone procedure or function, then the only to refer a pre-existing REF CURSOR type is by placing that type statement in a package. All variables declared in the specification of a package act as globals within your session, so you can then reference this cursor type using the dot notation as shown below:

1. Create the package with a REF CURSOR type declaration:

```
2.    PACKAGE company
3.    IS
4.      /* Define the REF CURSOR type. */
5.      TYPE curvar_type IS REF CURSOR RETURN company%ROWTYPE;
      END package;
```

6. In a standalone procedure, reference the REF CURSOR type by prefacing the name of the cursor type with the name of the package:

```
7.    PROCEDURE open_company (curvar_out OUT company.curvar_type) IS
8.    BEGIN
9.      ...
      END;
```

Setting the parameter mode

Just like other parameters, a cursor variable argument can have one of the following three modes:

IN	Can only be read by program
OUT	Can only be written to by program
IN OUT	Read/write in program

Remember that the value of a cursor variable is the reference to the cursor object and not the state of the cursor object. In other words, the value of a cursor variable does not change after you fetch from or close a cursor.

Only two operations, in fact, may change the value of a cursor variable change, that is, the cursor object to which the variable points:

- An assignment to the cursor variable
- An OPEN FOR statement

If the cursor variable already pointed to a cursor object, then the OPEN FOR wouldn't actually change the reference. It would simply change the query associated with the object.

The FETCH and CLOSE operations affect the state of the cursor object, but not the reference to the cursor object itself, which is the value of the cursor variable.

Here is an example of a program which has cursor variables as parameters:

```
PROCEDURE assign_curvar
  (old_curvar_in IN company.curvar_type,
   new_curvar_out OUT company.curvar_type)
IS
BEGIN
  new_curvar_out := old_curvar_in;
END;
```

This procedure copies the old company cursor variable to the new variable. The first parameter is an IN parameter because it appears only on the right-hand side of the assignment. The second parameter must be an OUT (or IN OUT) parameter, because its value is changed inside the procedure. Notice that the curvar_type is defined within the company package.

Cursor Variable Restrictions

Cursor variables are subject to the following restrictions; Oracle may remove some of these in future releases.

- Cursor variables cannot be declared in a package since they do not have a persistent state.
- RPCs (Remote Procedure Calls) to pass cursor variables from one server to another cannot be used.
- If a cursor variable is passed as a bind or host variable to PL/SQL, you will not be able to fetch from it from within the server unless you also open it in that same server call.
- The query associated with a cursor variable in an OPEN-FOR statement cannot use the FOR UPDATE clause.
- A cursor variable equality, inequality, or nullity using comparison operators cannot be tested.
- NULLs to a cursor variable cannot be assigned.
- Database columns cannot store cursor variable values. You will not be able to use REF CURSOR types to specify column types in statements to CREATE TABLEs or CREATE VIEWs.

- The elements in a nested table, index-by table, or variable array (VARRAY) cannot store the values of cursor variables. You will not be able to use REF CURSOR types to specify the element type of a collection.
- Cursor variables cannot be used with dynamic SQL (through use of the DBMS_SQL package).

THE CURSOR FOR LOOP

A cursor FOR loop is a loop that is associated with (actually defined by) an explicit cursor or a SELECT statement incorporated directly within the loop boundary. Use the cursor FOR loop whenever (and only if) you need to fetch and process each and every record from a cursor, which is a high percentage of the time with cursors.

The cursor FOR loop is one of the best PL/SQL features. It leverages fully the tight and effective integration of the procedural constructs with the power of the SQL database language. It reduces the volume of code you need to write to fetch data from a cursor. It greatly lessens the chance of introducing loop errors in your programming — and loops are one of the more error-prone parts of a program.

Here is the basic syntax of a cursor FOR loop:

```
FOR record_index IN cursor_name
LOOP
  <executable statement(s)>
END LOOP;
```

where record_index is a record declared implicitly by PL/SQL with the %ROWTYPE attribute against the cursor specified by cursor_name.

The following table summarizes the properties of the cursor FOR loop where record_index is a record declared implicitly by PL/SQL with the %ROWTYPE attribute against the cursor specified by cursor_name:

Property	Description
How the loop is terminated	The cursor FOR loop terminates unconditionally when all of the records in the associated cursor have been fetched. You can also terminate the loop with an EXIT statement, but this is not recommended.
When the test for termination takes place	After each execution of the loop body, PL/SQL performs another fetch. If the %NOTFOUND attribute of the cursor evalutes to TRUE, then the loop terminates. If the cursor returns no rows, then the loop never executes its body.
Reason to use this loop	Use the cursor FOR loop when you want to fetch and process every record in a cursor.

Let's take a look at how to use the cursor FOR loop to streamline the code and reduce opportunities for error.

Example of Cursor for Loops

Suppose we need to update the bills for all pets staying in pet hotel. The example below contains an anonymous block that uses a cursor, occupancy_cur, to select the room number and pet ID number for all occupants at the Hotel. The procedure update_bill adds any new changes to that pet's room charges:

```
1. DECLARE
2.   CURSOR occupancy_cur IS
3.     SELECT pet_id, room_number
4.     FROM occupancy WHERE occupied_dt = SYSDATE;
5.   occupancy_rec occupancy_cur%ROWTYPE;
6. BEGIN
7.   OPEN occupancy_cur;
8.   LOOP
9.     FETCH occupancy_cur INTO occupancy_rec;
10.    EXIT WHEN occupancy_cur%NOTFOUND;
11.    update_bill
12.      (occupancy_rec.pet_id, occupancy_rec.room_number);
13.  END LOOP;
14.  CLOSE occupancy_cur;
15. END;
```

This code leaves nothing to the imagination. In addition to defining the cursor (line 2), you must explicitly declare the record for the cursor (line 5), open the cursor (line 7), start up an infinite loop, fetch a row from the cursor set into the record (line 9), check for an end-of-data condition with the cursor attribute (line 10), and finally perform the update. Remember to close the cursor (line 14).

If we convert this PL/SQL block to use a cursor FOR loop, then we have:

```
DECLARE
  CURSOR occupancy_cur IS
    SELECT pet_id, room_number
     FROM occupancy WHERE occupied_dt = SYSDATE;
BEGIN
  FOR occupancy_rec IN occupancy_cur
  LOOP
    update_bill (occupancy_rec.pet_id, occupancy_rec.room_number);
  END LOOP;
END;
```

As with all other cursors, you can pass parameters to the cursor in a cursor FOR loop. If any of the columns in the select list of the cursor is an expression, remember to specify an alias for that expression in the select list. Within the loop, the only way to access a particular value in the cursor record is with the dot notation (cursor_name.column_name, as in occupancy_rec.room_number), so a column name associated with the expression.

The Cursor for Loop Record

The record which functions as the index for the cursor FOR loop is, like the loop index of a numeric FOR loop, defined only within the loop itself. You cannot reference that record outside the loop. Furthermore, PL/SQL declares that record itself. Programmer, should never declare a record for use as the index in a cursor FOR loop. If you do include such a declaration, the effect will not be as you intended.

Consider the code shown below. This code contains explicit declarations for both the cursor (line 2) and a record for that cursor (line 5). The block then uses a cursor FOR loop with that cursor and specifies as its index a record with the same name as the declared record:

```
1. DECLARE
2. CURSOR occupancy_cur IS
3.    SELECT pet_id, room_number
4.      FROM occupancy WHERE occupied_dt = SYSDATE;
5.  occupancy_rec occupancy_cur%ROWTYPE;
6.
7. BEGIN
8.  FOR occupancy_rec IN occupancy_cur
9.  LOOP
10.   update_bill
11.      (occupancy_rec.pet_id, occupancy_rec.room_number);
12.  END LOOP;
13.
14.  DBMS_OUTPUT.PUT_LINE
15.  ('Last pet ID updated: ' || TO_CHAR (occupancy_rec.pet_id));
16. END;
```

When to Use the Cursor for Loop

As you have seen, the cursor FOR loop offers many advantages to loop through all of the records returned by a cursor. This type of loop is not appropriate, however, when you need to apply conditions to each fetched record to determine if you should halt execution of the loop. Suppose you need to scan through each of the records from a cursor and stop when a total accumulation of a column like the maximum number of pets exceeds a maximum, as shown in the code below. Although you can do this with a cursor FOR loop by issuing an EXIT statement inside the loop, that is an inappropriate use of this construct:

```
DECLARE
  CURSOR occupancy_cur IS
    SELECT pet_id, room_number
     FROM occupancy WHERE occupied_dt = SYSDATE;
  pet_count INTEGER := 0;
BEGIN
  FOR occupancy_rec IN occupancy_cur
  LOOP
    update_bill
       (occupancy_rec.pet_id, occupancy_rec.room_number);
     pet_count := pet_count + 1;
     EXIT WHEN pet_count > :GLOBAL.max_pets;
  END LOOP;
END;
```

The FOR loop explicitly states: "We are going to execute the body of this loop n times" (where n is a number in a numeric FOR loop, or each record in a cursor FOR loop). An EXIT inside the FOR loop short-circuits this logic. The result is code which is difficult to follow and debug.

To terminate a loop based on information fetched by the cursor FOR loop, use a WHILE loop or infinite loop in its place. Then the structure of the code will more clearly state your intentions.

Example

For displaying the salary from emp

```
declare
var number;
cursor c1 is
select sal from emp;
begin
dbms_output.put_line('SALARIES');
open c1;
loop
fetch c1 into var;
dbms_output.put_line(var);
```

```
exit when c1% notfound;
end loop;
close c1;
end;
/
```

Example

Top 3 Earners from emp table.

```
declare
eno emp.empno%type;
enam emp.ename%type;
sal1  emp.sal%type;

cursor cur_sal is
select distinct empno, ename, sal from emp order by sal desc;

Begin
open cur_sal;
loop
fetch cur_sal into eno,enam,sal1;
exit when cur_sal%notfound;
Exit when (cur_sal%rowcount>3);
dbms_output.put_line(eno ||' '||enam||' '||sal1);
end loop;
close cur_sal;
end;
/
```

Example

Cursor for delete records of emp where sal <1000.

```
declare
rec_sal emp%rowtype;
cursor cur_sal is
select * from emp where sal < 1000 for update;
begin
open cur_sal;
loop
fetch cur_sal into rec_sal;
```

```
exit when cur_sal%notfound;
delete from emp where current of cur_sal;
end loop;
close cur_sal;
end;
/
```

Same as previous with user defined exception

```
declare
rec_sal emp%rowtype;
cursor cur_sal is
select * from emp where sal < 1000 for update;
NPF EXCEPTION;
begin
open cur_sal;
loop
fetch cur_sal into rec_sal;
delete from emp where current of cur_sal;
end loop;
if cur_sal%rowcount = 0 then
close cur_sal;
raise NPF;
EXCEPTION
when NPF then
DBMS_OUTPUT.PUT_LINE('NO EmPLOYEES HAVING SAL < 1000 have been
deleted');
end;
/
```

Update all sal < avg sal to sal = 3000.

```
Set serveroutput on
Set verify off
Declare
Ctr        number(2):=0;
Dno        number(4);
Dname      varchar2(30);
Ddate            date;
```

```
Cursor cur_mgr is
Select emp_no,emp_name,join_date from emp where upper(design) = 'MGR';
NO_MANAGER_FOUND EXCEPTION;
Begin
Open cur_mgr;
Loop
      FETCH cur_mgr into Dno,Dname,Ddate;
      Exit When Cur_Mgr%Notfound;
      Ctr:=Ctr+1;
      Dbms_output.put_line(CTR||' Record Inserted into Newemp');
      Dbms_output.put_line(Dno||' '||Dname||' '||Ddate);
      Insert into newemp values(dno,dname,ddate);
End loop;
      If cur_mgr%rowcount = 0 then
      Close cur_mgr;
      Raise no_manager_found;
      End if;
      Dbms_output.put_line('Total number of records'||ctr);
      Close cur_mgr;
      Exception
      When no_manager_found then
      Dbms_output.put_line('No records found');
      End;
/
```

LAB ASSIGNMENT—13

1. Display all clerks from emp table using cursor
2. Insert the record of all managers from emp table to newemp and display on the screen the No, Name, Join_date using user defined exception.
3. Update all sal < 1000 to sal = 2000 using cursor.
4. Write a PL/SQL block to delete all employees belonging to department 50 and check if atleast one row has been processed.Use the SQL%FOUND attribute.Insert the value into a table del_history and see the result.
5. Write a PL/SQL block to delete all employees whose job = 'CLERK' and update the EMP file with job ='CAPTAIN' and sal =8000.And check if any rows have been processed.Use the SQL%NOTFOUND attribute.If it is true the ROLLBACK if it is FALSE then commit.

LAB ASSIGNMENT—14

1. Declare a cursor that select all employees in a given department and raise the salary by .05% and updates the table and also updates another table which keeps track of raised amount.
2. Write a block which uses a Cursor FOR loop to select the five highest earners from the EMP table and write their details to the MESSAGES table. Results should look something like this:

Numcol1	Numcol2	charcol1
7839	5000	KING
7902	3000	FORD
7788	3000	SCOTT
7566	2975	JONES
7698	2850	BLAKE

3. Write a PL/SQL cursor to Update all salary of emp table by 5000 where salary is less then by minimum salary.
4. Write a PL/SQL Cursor for delete records of emp table where salary >2000.
5. Write a PL/SQL cursor to display the five lowest paid employees.

9 Trigger

Objectives :

- Assertions
- Introduction
- Basic Trigger Syntax
- Trigger Events
- Type of Triggers
- Trigger Example
- Viewing Defined Trigger
- Advantages of Triggers

Lab Assignment-15

Lab Assignment-16

ASSERTIONS

An assertion is a predicate expressing a condition that we wish the database always to satisfy. Domain constraints and referential-integrity constraints are special forms of assertions. They are easily tested and apply to a wide range of database applications.

An assertion in SQL takes the form

Syntax :

Create assertion < assertion-name > check <predicate>

Some examples of such constraints are

1. **The sum of all loan amounts for each branch must be less than the sum of all account balances at the branch.**

```
Create assertion sum-constraint check
(not exists (select sum(amount)from loan where
loan.branch-name = branch.branch-name) >=
(select sum(balance) from account where
account.branch_name = branch.branch_name)))
```

2. **Every loan has at least one customer who maintains an account with a minimum balance of Rs. 10000.**

```
Create assertion balance_constraint check
(not exists (select * from loan
where not exists (select * from borrower, depositor, account
where loan.loan_number = borrower.loan_number
and borrower.customer_name = depositor.customer_name
and depositor.account_number = account.account_number
and account.balance >= 10,000)));
```

When an assertion is created, the system tests it for validity. If the assertion is valid then any future modification to the database is allowed only if it does not cause that assertion to be violated. This testing may introduce a significant amount of overhead if complex assertions have been made. Hence, assertion should be used with great care.

INTRODUCTION

A trigger consists of PL/SQL code, which defines some action that the database should take when some database related event occurs.

Triggers are programs that execute in response to change in table data or certain database events. There is a predefined set of events that can be "hooked" with a trigger, enabling to integrate our own processing with that of the database.

Oracle allows us to define procedures that are implicitly executed when an insert, update or delete statement is issued against the associated table. These types of procedures are called database triggers. A trigger can include SQL and PL/SQL statements to execute as a unit and can invoke other stored procedures. However, procedures and triggers differ in the way that they are invoked. While a procedure is explicitly executed by a user or an application, a trigger is implicitly fired (executed) by ORACLE when a triggering INSERT, UPDATE or DELETE statement is issued, no matter what user is connected or what application is being used.

In Oracle there is no limitation to the number of triggers that can be associated with a given table.

BASIC TRIGGER SYNTAX

Below is the syntax for creating a trigger in Oracle (which differs slightly from standard SQL syntax):

```
CREATE [OR REPLACE] TRIGGER <trigger_name>
    {BEFORE|AFTER} {INSERT|DELETE|UPDATE} ON <table_name>
    [REFERENCING [NEW AS <new_row_name>] [OLD AS <old_row_name>]
    [FOR EACH ROW [WHEN (<trigger_condition>)]]
    <trigger_body>
```

Some important points to note:

- We can create only BEFORE and AFTER triggers for tables. (INSTEAD OF triggers are only available for views; typically they are used to implement view updates.)
- We may specify up to three triggering events using the keyword OR. Furthermore, UPDATE can be optionally followed by the keyword OF and a list of attribute(s) in <table_name>. If present, the OF clause defines the event to be only an update of the attribute(s) listed after OF. Here are some examples:

  ... INSERT ON R ...

  ... INSERT OR DELETE OR UPDATE ON R ...

  ... UPDATE OF A, B OR INSERT ON R ...
- If FOR EACH ROW option is specified, the trigger is row-level; otherwise, the trigger is statement-level.
- Only for row-level triggers:
  - ➤ The special variables NEW and OLD are available to refer to new and old tuples respectively.

    Note. In the trigger body, NEW and OLD must be preceded by a colon (":"), but in the WHEN clause, they do not have a preceding colon!
  - ➤ The REFERENCING clause can be used to assign aliases to the variables NEW and OLD.
  - ➤ A trigger restriction can be specified in the WHEN clause, enclosed by parentheses. The trigger restriction is a SQL condition that must be satisfied in order for Oracle

to fire the trigger. This condition cannot contain subqueries. Without the WHEN clause, the trigger is fired for each row.

- <trigger_body> is a PL/SQL block, rather than sequence of SQL statements. Oracle has placed certain restrictions on what we can do in <trigger_body>, in order to avoid situations where one trigger performs an action that triggers a second trigger, which then triggers a third, and so on, which could potentially create an infinite loop. The restrictions on <trigger_body> include:
  - We cannot modify the same relation whose modification is the event triggering the trigger.
  - We cannot modify a relation connected to the triggering relation by another constraint such as a foreign-key constraint.

TRIGGER EVENTS

Trigger events are defined in the following table:

Trigger Event	Description
INSERT	Fires whenever a row is added to the table_reference.
UPDATE	Fires whenever an UPDATE changes the table_reference. UPDATE triggers can additionally specify an OF clause to restrict firing to updates OF certain columns. See the following examples.
DELETE	Fires whenever a row is deleted from the table_reference. It does not fire on TRUNCATE of the table.
CREATE (Oracle8i)	Fires whenever a CREATE statement adds a new object to the database. In this context, objects are things like tables or packages (found in ALL_OBJECTS). It can apply to a single schema or the entire database.
ALTER (Oracle8i)	Fires whenever an ALTER statement changes a database object. In this context, objects are things like tables or packages (found in ALL_OBJECTS). It can apply to single schema or the entire database.
DROP (Oracle8i)	Fires whenever a DROP statement removes an object from the database. In this context, objects are things like tables or packages (found in ALL_OBJECTS). It can apply to a single schema or the entire database.
SERVERERROR (Oracle8i)	Fires whenever a server error message is logged. Only AFTER triggers are allowed in this context.
LOGON (Oracle8i)	Fires whenever a session is created (a user connects to the database). Only AFTER triggers are allowed in this context.
LOGOFF (Oracle8i)	Fires whenever a session is terminated (a user disconnects from the database). Only BEFORE triggers are allowed in this context.
STARTUP (Oracle8i)	Fires when the database is opened. Only AFTER triggers are allowed in this context.
SHUTDOWN (Oracle8i)	Fires when the database is closed. Only BEFORE triggers are allowed in this context.

TYPE OF TRIGGERS

Row Triggers: A row trigger is fired each time a row in the table is affected by the triggering statement. For example, if a delete statement deletes multiple rows of a table, a row trigger is fired once for each row affected by the delete statement. If the triggering statement affects no rows, the trigger is not executed. Row triggers must be used when some processing is required whenever a triggering statement affects a single row in a table.

Statement Triggers: A statement trigger is fired once on behalf of the triggering statement, independent of the number of rows the triggering statement affects. Statement triggers should be used when a triggering statement affects rows in a table but the processing required is completely independent of the number of row affected.

Before & After Triggers: There are 14 types of combination of before & after triggers. A trigger type is defined by the type of triggering transaction and by the level at which the trigger is executed. Here is the list of the triggering actions with their explanations and relative restrictions.

Name	Explanation	With For each Row option
BEFORE option	Oracle fires the trigger only once, before executing the triggering statement	Oracle fires the trigger before modifying each row affected by the triggering statement
AFTER option	Oracle fires the trigger only once after executing the triggering statement	Oracle fires [illegible] trigger for each row, to do s[illegible]hing else instead of perform[illegible] the action that executed the [illegible]
INSTEAD OF option	Oracle fires the trigger only once, to do so something else instead of performing the action that executed the trigger.	Oracle fires the trigger for each row, to do something else instead of performing the action that executed the trigger.

Referencing

It specifies correlation names. The user could use the correlation names in the PL/SQL block WHEN clause of a row trigger to refer specifically to old and new values of the current row associated with a table named OLD or NEW, this clause can be used to specify different names to avoid confusion between the table name and the correlation name.

When

It specifies the trigger restriction. This condition has to be satisfied to fire the trigger. This condition can be specified for the ROW TRIGGER.

— Statement-Level Triggers

Statement level triggers execute once for each transaction. For example, if a single transaction inserted with 100 rows into the EMP table, then a statement-level trigger on that level table would only be executed once. Statement level triggers therefore are not often used for data-related activities, they are normally used to enforce additional security measures on the types of transaction that may be performed on a table. Statement-level triggers are the default type of triggers created via the create trigger command.

While combining different types of triggering actions, there are 14 possible valid trigger types available to us.

The possible configurations are:

— BEFORE INSERT row

— BEFORE INSERT statement

— AFTER INSERT row

— AFTER INSERT statement

— BEFORE UPDATE row

— BEFORE UPDATE statement

— AFTER UPDATE row

— AFTER UPDATE statement

— BEFORE DELETE row

— BEFORE DELETE statement

— AFTER DELETE row

— AFTER DELETE statement

— INSTEAD OF row

— INSTEAD OF statement

- ➤ There can be many triggers for one table.
- ➤ There can be only one trigger of a particular type (*i.e.*, Update, Insert or Delete).
- ➤ Only one table can be specified in the triggering statement.
- ➤ Triggers cannot include Commit, Rollback and Savepoint.
- ➤ Inside the triggers, the correlation names: new and old can be made of use to refer to data on the command line and data in the table respectively.

NEW TRIGGER FEATURES IN ORACLE 9I

Oracle9*i* expands significantly the use of triggers to administer a database and publish information about events taking place within the database. By employing database triggers on the system events defined in Oracle9*i*, and using Oracle Advanced Queuing within those triggers, you can take advantage of the publish/subscribe capabilities of Oracle9*i*.

The database event publication feature allows applications to subscribe to database events just as they subscribe to messages from other applications. Trigger syntax is extended to support system and other data events on the database level or on a particular schema level. Trigger syntax also supports a CALL to a procedure as the trigger body.

You can now define a programmatic trigger on the following actions:

- DML statements (DELETE, INSERT, and UPDATE)
- DDL events (e.g., CREATE, DROP, and ALTER)
- Database events (SERVERERROR, LOGON, LOGOFF, STARTUP, and SHUTDOWN)

Here are the new trigger features available in Oracle9*i*:

Triggers on nested table columns

Use of the CAST...MULTISET operation allows you to trigger activity when only an attribute in a nested table column is modified.

Database-level (also known as system-level) event triggers

You can now define triggers to respond to such database-level events as LOGON, DATABASE SHUTDOWN, and even SERVERERROR.

Schema-level (also known as user-level) event triggers

You can now define triggers to respond to such schema-level events as CREATE, DROP, and ALTER.

Triggers on Nested Table View Columns

Oracle 9*i* allowed developers to create INSTEAD OF triggers, which could then be applied to any view but were especially handy with object views and any inherently unmodifiable view. Oracle9*i* expands further the usefulness of triggers by allowing you to define a trigger to fire when one or more attributes of a nested table view column are modified. This feature allows you to change an element of a collection synthesized using the CAST...MULTISET operation.

Figure 9.1 illustrates the ability of the nested table trigger to zoom inside the outer table structure and respond to changes made to the nested table.

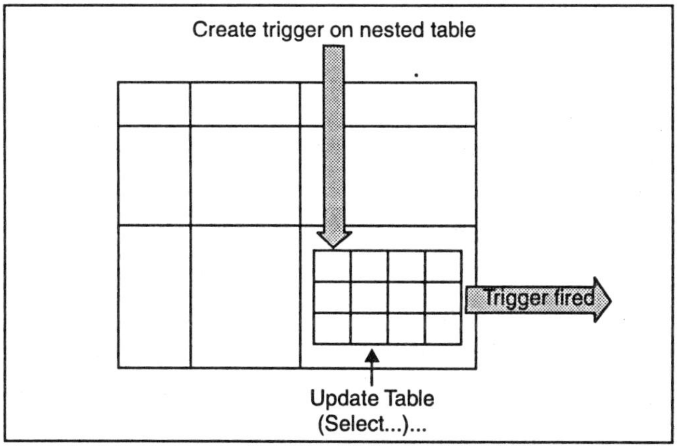

Figure 9.1. Nested table trigger fired by change to nested table

```
/* nesttrig.sql */
CREATE TABLE nra_members (
   person_id INTEGER,
   last_name VARCHAR2(100),
   first_name VARCHAR2(20), );
   age NUMBER);

CREATE TABLE non_killers (
   person_id INTEGER,
   gun_name VARCHAR2(75)
```

We want to build an object view over these two tables that implements the non_killers table as a nested table column. First we must create two object types:

```
CREATE OR REPLACE TYPE gun_name_ot AS OBJECT (
   gun_name VARCHAR2(75)


CREATE OR REPLACE TYPE non_killer_t
   AS TABLE OF gun_name ot;

CREATE OR REPLACE TYPE nra_member_t
AS OBJECT (
   person_id INTEGER,
   last_name VARCHAR2(100),
   first_name VARCHAR2(12),
   age INTEGER.
   gun_names non_killer_t
);
/
```

Now we can create our object view, using CAST...MULTISET to convert my normalized relational table into a nested table column:

```
CREATE OR REPLACE VIEW nra_members_ov
   OF nra_member_t
   WITH OBJECT OID (person_id)
AS
   SELECT luvguns.person_id,
      luvguns.last_name,
      luvguns.first_name,
      luvguns.age,
```

```
        CAST (MULTISET (
          SELECT gun_name
          FROM non_killers bestfriend
          WHERE bestfriend.person_id =
            bestfriend.person_id)
          AS non_killer_t)
    FROM nra_members luvguns;
```

Once we have this view in place, we also need to provide INSTEAD OF triggers to allow a user to update, insert, or delete through the view, making the illusion of my use of objects complete. We will, instead, focus on the new nested table trigger capability.

Here is the trigger definition; notice that the only difference is the line in bold, indicating that the trigger applies only to the specified nested table:

```
/* Filename: nesttrig.sql */
CREATE OR REPLACE TRIGGER nra_members_gun_rename
INSTEAD OF INSERT OR UPDATE

ON NESTED TABLE gun_names OF nra_members_ov
BEGIN
   IF INSERTING
   THEN
      INSERT INTO non_killers (person_id, gun_name)
      VALUES (:PARENT.person_id, :NEW.gun_name);
   END IF;

   IF UPDATING
   THEN
      UPDATE non_killers
         SET gun_name = :NEW.gun_name
      WHERE gun_name = :OLD.gun_name
         AND person_id = :PARENT.person_id;
   END IF;
END;
/
```

Let's try it out. we insert Charlton Heston and hypothetical information about his guns into the two tables:

```
INSERT INTO nra_members (
   person_id, last_name, first_name, age)
VALUES (100, 'HESTON', 'CHARLTON', 70);
```

```
INSERT INTO non_killers (
    person_id, gun_name)
    VALUES (100, 'COLT-45');
INSERT INTO non_killers (
    person_id, gun_name)
    VALUES (100, 'M-16');
INSERT INTO non_killers (
    person_id, gun_name)
    VALUES (100, 'DOUBLE-BARRELED JUSTICE');
```

Suppose then that Charlton Heston undergoes a sea change in philosophy. To demonstrate his new principles, he renames each of his guns, stored in that nested table. Here is the update in a single statement:

```
UPDATE TABLE (SELECT gun_names
            FROM nra_members_ov
            WHERE person_id = 100)
    SET gun_name =
      DECODE (gun_name,
        'COLT-45', 'Pretty Pony',
        'M-16', 'I Love Mom',
        'DOUBLE-BARRELED JUSTICE', 'Peace on Earth',
        gun_name);
```

We use the TABLE...SELECT combination to extract just the nested table column from the object view. The SET clause then applies to the attributes of that nested table.

Database-Level Event Triggers

Oracle9*i* allows you to define triggers to respond to database-level events (also known as system-level events), including the following:

- Logon to and logoff from a schema
- Startup and shutdown of the database
- Response to a server error

Here is the syntax for these triggers:

```
CREATE [ OR REPLACE ] TRIGGER trigger_name
    { BEFORE | AFTER }
    { SERVERERROR |
      LOGON | LOGOFF |
      STARTUP | SHUTDOWN }
    ON DATABASE
BEGIN
pl/sql_statements
END;
```

To create a trigger at the database level, you must have the ADMINISTER DATABASE TRIGGER system privilege. You will also need privileges to access any of the external references in the trigger's PL/SQL code.

Table 9.2 lists the different database-level events on which you may define a trigger.

Table 9.2. Database-Level Events for Trigger Definitions

Event	Description
SERVERERROR	Oracle fires the trigger whenever a server error message is logged.
LOGON	Oracle fires the trigger after a client application logs on to the database successfully.
LOGOFF	Oracle fires the trigger before a client application logs off the database.
STARTUP	Oracle fires the trigger immediately after the database is opened.
SHUTDOWN	Oracle fires the trigger just before the server starts a shutdown of an instance of the database. Note that a SHUTDOWN trigger will only fire if the database is shut down cleanly using SHUTDOWN or SHUTDOWN IMMEDIATE. If an instance shuts down abnormally (SHUTDOWN ABORT), this event will not be fired.

Each database-level event has an associated with it a set of attributes. These attributes are actually functions owned by SYS that return the values of characteristics relevant to the event. Table 9.3 lists the current set of attributes.

Table 9.3. Attributes for Database-Level Events

Name	Datatype	Description
SYSEVENT	VARCHAR2(30)	The database-level event firing the trigger; this value matches the name used in the syntax of the trigger.
LOGIN_USER	VARCHAR2(30)	The login username.
INSTANCE_NUM	NUMBER	The instance number.
DATABASE_NAME	VARCHAR2(50)	The name of the database.
SERVER_ERROR	NUMBER	This function returns the error at the n th position in the stack. You must specify a position (1 equals "top") when you call this function. For example: SERVER_ERROR(1)
IS_SERVERERROR	BOOLEAN	Returns TRUE if the specified error is on the current error stack; FALSE otherwise.

Table 9.4 lists the restrictions and attributes for each database-level event.

Table 9.4. Restrictions and Attributes for Database-Level Events

Event	Conditions/Restrictions	Attributes
SERVERERROR	You can specify a condition that will restrict the trigger to firing only when the specified exception is raised. Otherwise, it will fire for all errors.	SYSEVENT LOGIN_USER INSTANCE_NUM DATABASE_NAME SERVER_ERROR IS_SERVERERROR
LOGON	You can specify a condition using either USERID( ) or USERNAME( ).	SYSEVENT LOGIN_USER INSTANCE_NUM DATABASE_NAME
LOGOFF	You can specify a condition using either USERID( ) or USERNAME( ).	SYSEVENT LOGIN_USER INSTANCE_NUM DATABASE_NAME
STARTUP	No database operations (DML and queries) are allowed. Instead, you might start up listener programs, pin code in memory, etc.	SYSEVENT LOGIN_USER INSTANCE_NUM DATABASE_NAME
SHUTDOWN	No database operations (DML and queries) are allowed. Instead, you might shut down listener programs, run performance collection utilities that write logs to files, etc.	SYSEVENT LOGIN_USER INSTANCE_NUM DATABASE_NAME

Keep in mind the following rules when working with these triggers:

- Whenever a database-level event trigger fires, Oracle opens an autonomous transaction, fires the trigger, and commits any DML in the trigger logic independently of the existing user transaction.
- When defining LOGON, STARTUP, and SERVERERROR triggers, you can only specify the AFTER context. If you specify BEFORE, you will get this error:

  ORA-30500: database open triggers and server error
          triggers cannot have BEFORE type
- When defining LOGOFF and SHUTDOWN triggers, you can only specify the BEFORE context. If you specify AFTER, you will get this error:

  ORA-30509: client logoff triggers cannot have AFTER type
- You cannot define AFTER STARTUP and BEFORE SHUTDOWN triggers for a schema; these apply only to DATABASE.
- Calls to DBMS_OUTPUT.PUT_LINE do not generate any visible output in the current session. If you want to obtain a record of actions that occurred, you will need

to write information to a database table, database pipe, or operating system file. You could also use DBMS_AQ.ENQUEUE to place a message in a queue.

- A SERVERERROR trigger will not fire for any of the following errors:
  ORA-01403: no data found
  ORA-01422: exact fetch returns more than requested number of rows
  ORA-04030: out of process memory when trying to allocate *nnn* bytes
  ORA-01034: ORACLE not available
  ORA-01007: variable not in select list

Examples of Database-Level Event Triggers

There are many different ways you can use database-level event triggers to manage your database. The following examples offer some simple models from which you can build your own, more complex variations.

Pinning packages on database startup

A common requirement for a high-performance database is to pin one or more packages into shared memory. By pinning your code, it is exempted from the least recently used algorithm and will *never* be aged out of the shared pool area.

Before the existence of STARTUP triggers, the DBA would have to set up a script to run after the database was started. Now, we can create a STARTUP trigger like the following:

```
/* Filename: startup.trg */
CREATE OR REPLACE TRIGGER pin_code_on_startup
   AFTER STARTUP ON DATABASE
BEGIN
   /* Pin the default packages of PL/SQL to
      improve runtime performance. */
   DBMS_SHARED_POOL.KEEP (
      'SYS.STANDARD', 'P');
   DBMS_SHARED_POOL.KEEP (
      'SYS.DBMS_STANDARD', 'P');
END;
/
```

With this trigger in place, we guarantee that all of our large code elements (including cursors, types, and triggers) and even sequences are cached in the shared pool until the instance goes down.

If you are going to be pinning objects, you should consider building an infrastructure table to store the names of elements you want pinned. Then instead of hard-coding your pin commands in a trigger (as just shown), you could run a procedure that reads through the table and pins each element found.

Tracking logins to the database

Suppose that we want to keep track of logins to my database instance. To make this information available in a structured fashion, We are going to send our login information to a queue using the Oracle Advanced Queuing (AQ) facility.

These steps are illustrated in Figure 9.6. You will find all of the AQ-related steps in the *aq.sql* script on the companion disk; We will concentrate on the trigger-related components here.

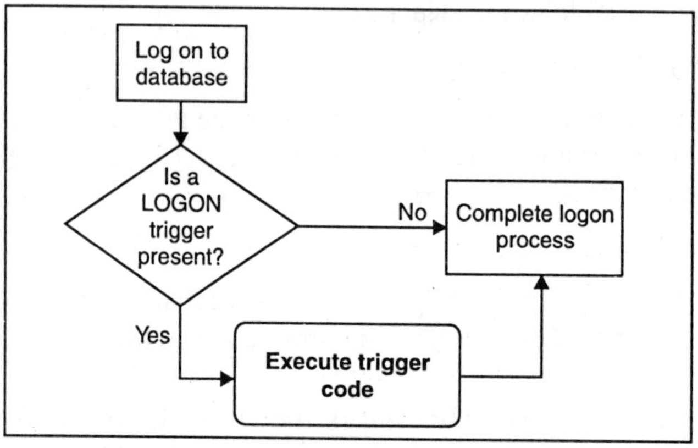

Figure 9.6. Logical flow of LOGON trigger

Let's start in reverse. Here is the LOGON trigger:

```
/* Filename: aq.sql */
CREATE OR REPLACE TRIGGER publish_logon
AFTER LOGON ON DATABASE
BEGIN
    oraevent.put ('This is a logon');
END;
/
```

As you can see, there isn't much to it: every time someone logs in to the database, we'll put a message in the queue with a call to oraevent.put. So let's take a look at that procedure:

```
PROCEDURE oraevent.put (details_in IN VARCHAR2)
IS
    q_opts DBMS_AQ.ENQUEUE_OPTIONS_T;
    msg_props DBMS_AQ.MESSAGE_PROPERTIES_T;
    msg_handle RAW(16);
    event_l Event_t;
BEGIN
    /* Setting visibility to IMMEDIATE will
    || force the queue to "commit" before the
```

```
    || client transaction commits.
    */
    q_opts.visibility := DBMS_AQ.IMMEDIATE;
    event_l := Event_t.make(details_in);

 DBMS_AQ.ENQUEUE(queue_name => 'aqadmin.loginQ'
    enqueue_options => q_opts,
    message_properties => msg_props,
    payload => event_l,
    msgid => msg_handle);
END;
```

This procedure calls DMBS_AQ.ENQUEUE to place a message, or *payload*, in the loginQ queue. Each message is an object of type Event_t, defined as follows:

```
CREATE TYPE Event_t AS OBJECT (
    eventname VARCHAR2(64),
    details VARCHAR2(512),
    username VARCHAR2(30),
    timestamp DATE,
    STATIC FUNCTION make (
       details_in IN VARCHAR2) RETURN Event_t
);
/
CREATE OR REPLACE TYPE BODY Event_t
AS
    STATIC FUNCTION make (
       details_in IN VARCHAR2) RETURN Event_t
    IS
    BEGIN
       RETURN Event_t(
          SYSEVENT,
          details_in,
          LOGIN_USER,
          SYSDATE);
    END;
END;
/
```

The RETURN statement relies on two of the event-related functions, SYSEVENT and LOGIN_USER, to record characteristics at the time of login.

Run the *aq.sql* script to create all elements and then test the code by spawning a second SQL*Plus session to watch or dequeue the login messages.

Trapping system errors

The SERVERERROR event will prove to be a very handy mechanism. You can define it at the database level, which means that any error raised in any schema will be interceptable through the trigger. You can also define a trigger for this event at the schema level, limiting the scope of firing of the trigger.

Suppose that you simply want to keep track of errors raised in a particular application running on your instance. When an error occurs, you write a message to a database pipe. Another session (running asynchronously to the application users) can then wake up and dump the contents of the pipe and examine the errors.

To facilitate that process, We have created and included on the disk a package called watch. Stored in *watch.pkg* on the companion disk, this package allows you to watch actions and then direct a message constructed for that action to either the screen via DBMS_OUTPUT or to a pipe via DBMS_PIPE.

Using the watch package, We first create a utility procedure that We will call in my SERVERERROR triggers:

```
/* Filename: serverr.trg */
CREATE OR REPLACE PROCEDURE pipe_error (
   context IN VARCHAR2, msg IN VARCHAR2)
IS
BEGIN
   /* Send the information to a pipe. */
   watch.topipe;

   /* Retrieve all system event attributes. */
   watch.action (context || ' trap_error', msg);
END;
/
```

We can then define a trigger at the database level that displays all of the attributes available from within this trigger:

```
CREATE OR REPLACE TRIGGER trap_error
 AFTER SERVERERROR ON DATABASE
BEGIN
   pipe_error ('DATABASE',
      sysevent || '-' ||
      instance_num || '-' ||
      database_name || '-' ||
```

```
        SQLCODE || '-' ||
        server_error (1) || '-' ||
        login_user
        );
END;
/
```

We will also define a SERVERERROR trigger for the SCOTT schema, so we can explore the way multiple triggers of the same type fire:

```
CREATE OR REPLACE TRIGGER scott_trap_error
   AFTER SERVERERROR ON SCOTT.SCHEMA
BEGIN
   pipe_error (login_user,
      sysevent || '-' ||
      instance_num || '-' ||
      database_name || '-' ||
      SQLCODE || '-' ||
      server_error (1) || '-' ||
      login_user
      );
END;
/
```

To test these triggers, We created the following script:

```
/* Filename: serverr.tst */
DECLARE
   exc EXCEPTION;
   PRAGMA EXCEPTION_INIT (exc, -&1);
BEGIN
   RAISE exc;
END;
/
```

Now We will connect as SCOTT and run the script emulating a date-related error:

```
SQL> @serverr.tst 1855
*
ERROR at line 1:
ORA-01855: AM/A.M. or PM/P.M. required
```

If the triggers fired, the watch pipe should contain some information. We can dump the contents of the pipe with a call to watch.show:

```
SQL> exec watch.show

Contents of WATCH Trace:
***WATCHing at: June 1, 1999 12:54:14
   Context: SCOTT trap_error
   Message: SERVERERROR-1-ORACLE-0-1855-SCOTT
***WATCHing at: June 1, 1999 12:54:14
   Context: DATABASE trap_error
   Message: SERVERERROR-1-ORACLE-0-1855-SCOTT
```

We learn a few things from this execution:

- The schema-level trigger fires before the database-level trigger.
- By the time the SERVERERROR trigger fires, the SQLCODE function does not return the error that was raised. Instead, it returns 0. You must rely on the SERVER_ERROR function to retrieve the error at the top of the error stack.

Now we will connect to the DEMO account in our Oracle instance and run this script for a different error:

```
SQL> connect demo/demo.
SQL> @serverr.tst 1652
*

ERROR at line 1:
ORA-01652: unable to extend temp segment by nnn in tablespace
```

When we take a look at our pipe contents, We have only one entry:

```
SQL> exec watch.show
Contents of WATCH Trace:
***WATCHing at: June 1, 1999 13:01:38
Context: DATABASE trap_error
Message: SERVERERROR-1-ORACLE-0-1652-DEMO
```

And that is because We did not create a SERVERERROR trigger in the DEMO schema; only the database-level trigger is fired.

Checking for specific errors

One other useful technique in this type of trigger is to check for a specific error and then take special action in that instance. There are two ways to do this:

- Use the trigger WHEN clause to restrict the execution of the trigger logic for a specific error.

- Use the IS_SERVERERROR function to determine if a specific error has been raised anywhere within the error call stack and then take action.

Let's see how each approach would work. First, suppose that I want to qualify my SERVERERROR trigger at the database level to fire only when the ORA-02292 error occurs ("integrity constraint (*constant name*) violated - child record found").

We can create my trigger as follows:

```
/* Filename: serverr2.trg */
CREATE OR REPLACE TRIGGER scott_trap_parent_key
   AFTER SERVERERROR ON DATABASE
WHEN (SYS.SERVER_ERROR(1) = 2292)
BEGIN
   pipe_error (
      'DATABASE trap parent key',
      'Invalid attempt to delete primary key by' ||
   LOGIN_USER);
END;
/
```

Our call to SYS.SERVER_ERROR(1) retrieves the error at the top of the error stack. There are two things to note in this procedure:

- If we do not qualify the call to SERVER_ERROR with its owner, SYS, we get the following error:

```
AFTER SERVERERROR ON DATABASE
                 *
ERROR at line 2:
ORA-00942: table or view does not exist
```

- We must specify the error number as a positive, not negative, integer value. Otherwise, no match will be detected.

Once the trigger is defined, we test it by trying to delete a row from the dept table whose parent key is referenced by an employee:

```
SQL> DELETE FROM dept WHERE deptno=10;
*
ERROR at line 1:
ORA-02292: integrity constraint (SCOTT.FK_DEPTNO) violated -
           child record found
```

we can now see what information was sent to my pipe within the trigger as follows:

```
SQL> exec watch.show
```

```
Contents of WATCH Trace:
***WATCHing at: June 2, 1999 16:27:09
   Context: DATABASE trap parent key trap_error
   Message: Invalid attempt to delete primary key by SCOTT
```

Here we will demonstrate the IS_SERVERERROR approach with a modified version of the database-level trigger:

```
/* Filename: serverr.trg */
CREATE OR REPLACE TRIGGER trap_error
   AFTER SERVERERROR ON DATABASE
BEGIN
   /* Same tracking as before. */
   pipe_error ('DATABASE', ...);

   IF IS_SERVERERROR (1652) — POSITIVE NUMBER REQUIRED!
   THEN
      /* Add a file to the tablespace... just a dummy
         entry for the book. */
      pipe_error ('DATABASE', 'Add to tablespace');
   END IF;
END;
/
```

And now if the ORA-01652 error is raised *anywhere* in the error stack from the SCOTT schema, we see three entries in the error pipe:

```
SQL> DECLARE
     exc EXCEPTION;
     PRAGMA EXCEPTION_INIT (exc, -1652);
           BEGIN
     RAISE exc;
           EXCEPTION
     WHEN OTHERS THEN
        RAISE VALUE_ERROR;
           END;
/

ERROR at line 1:
ORA-06502: PL/SQL: numeric or value error
ORA-01652: unable to extend temp segment by nnn in tablespace
```

```
SQL> exec watch.show
Contents of WATCH Trace:

***WATCHing at: June 3, 1999 09:47:05
 Context: SCOTT trap_error
 Message: SERVERERROR-1-ORACLE-0-6502-SCOTT

***WATCHing at: June 3, 1999 09:47:05
 Context: DATABASE trap_error
 Message: SERVERERROR-1-ORACLE-0-6502-SCOTT

***WATCHing at: June 3, 1999 09:47:05
 Context: DATABASE trap_error
 Message: Add to tablespace
```

TRIGGER EXAMPLE

To create a trigger for the EMP table, which makes the entry in ENAME column in uppercase.

```
CREATE OR REPLACE TRIGGER upper_trigger
BEFORE INSERT OR UPDATE OF ename ON emp
FOR EACH ROW

BEGIN
:new.ename := UPPER (:new.ename);
END;
```

The above example also illustrates the use of the new keyword which refers to the new value of the column and the old keyword, which refers to the old value of the column. While referencing the new and old keywords in the PL/SQL block they are preceeded by colon(:).

Note. *Use of new/old keyords is allowed with row level triggers only.*

Example: Write a trigger total_salary to maintain a derived column to instal that stores total salary of all members in a department

```
CREATE OR REPLACE TRIGGER total_salary
AFTER DELETE OR INSERT OR UPDATE OF DEPTNO, SAL ON emp
FOR EACH ROW
BEGIN
IF DELETING [OR (UPDATING AND :old.deptno = :new.deptno)] THEN
UPDATE dept
SET totsal = totsal - :old.sal
WHERE deptno = : old.deptno;
```

```
END IF;
IF inserting [OR (UPDATING AND :old.deptno = :new.deptno)] THEN
UPDATE dept
SET totsal = totsal + :new.sal
WHERE deptno = : new.deptno;
END IF;
IF UPDATING [AND :old.deptno = :new.deptno AND old.sal != : new.sal ]THEN
UPDATE dept
SET totsal = totsal - :old.sal + :new.sal
WHERE deptno = : new.deptno;
END IF;
END,
```

— raise_application_error

— The raise_application_error is a built-in Oracle procedure, which lets the user issue user defined error messages.

Example:

```
..........
..........

/* IF SALARY IS OUT OF RANGE */
IF (:NEW.SAL < MINSAL OR :NEW.SAL > MAXSAL) THEN
RAISE_APPLICATION_ERROR (-20230, ' SALARY OUT OF RANGE');
END IF;
.............
.............
```

The user can give any message. The integer value with the message can vary from -20000 to -20999.

Note. *Except INSTEAD OF TRIGGERS, all triggers can be used only on tables. INSTEAD OF triggers can be used only on views.*

In oracle 8i, INSTEAD OF triggers tells Oracle what to do instead of performing the actions that executed the trigger.

Example:

```
SQL > Create view v1 as
Select EMPNO, ENAME, EMP.DEPTNO, JOB, SAL, DNAME, LOC FROM EMP, DEPT WHERE EMP.DEPTNO = DEPT.DEPTNO;
```

View Created

```
SQL > Create Trigger T1
        Instead of delete on V1
        For each row
        Begin
              Delete from emp
              Where deptno = : OLD.DEPTNO;
              Delete from dept
              Where Deptno  = : OLD.DEPTNO;
        End;
```

Trigger Created

Now if a delete statement is fired on view V1, for an employee name, then the corresponding employee's record gets deleted from the emp table.

We illustrate Oracle's syntax for creating a trigger through an example based on the following two tables:

```
CREATE TABLE T4 (a INTEGER, b CHAR(10));
CREATE TABLE T5 (c CHAR(10), d INTEGER);
```

We create a trigger that may insert a tuple into T5 when a tuple is inserted into T4. Specifically, the trigger checks whether the new tuple has a first component 10 or less, and if so inserts the reverse tuple into T5:

```
CREATE TRIGGER trig1
  AFTER INSERT ON T4
  REFERENCING NEW AS newRow
  FOR EACH ROW
  WHEN (newRow.a <= 10)
  BEGIN
     INSERT INTO T5 VALUES(:newRow.b, :newRow.a);
  END trig1;

run;
```

Notice that we end the CREATE TRIGGER statement with a dot and run, as for all PL/SQL statements in general. Running the CREATE TRIGGER statement only creates the trigger; it does not execute the trigger. Only a triggering event, such as an insertion into T4 in this example, causes the trigger to execute.

Example:

```
create or replace trigger updsal
before update or delete
```

```
on emp
for each row
begin
Insert into emp1 values (:old.empno,:old.ename,:old.job,:old.mgr,:old.hiredate,
:old.sal,:old.comm,:old.deptno);
end;
/
```

Displaying Trigger Definition Errors

As for PL/SQL procedures, if you get a message

Warning: Trigger created with compilation errors.

we can see the error messages by typing

show errors trigger <trigger_name>;

Alternatively, we can type, SHO ERR (short for SHOW ERRORS) to see the most recent compilation error. Note that the reported line numbers where the errors occur are not accurate.

VIEWING DEFINED TRIGGER

To view a list of all defined triggers, use:

```
select trigger_name from user_triggers;
```

For more details on a particular trigger:

```
select trigger_type, triggering_event, table_name, referencing_names, trigger_body
from user_triggers
where trigger_name = '<trigger_name>';
```

Dropping Triggers

To drop a trigger:

```
drop trigger <trigger_name>;
```

Disabling Triggers

To disable or enable a trigger:

```
alter trigger <trigger_name> {disable|enable};
```

Aborting Triggers with Error

Triggers can often be used to enforce constraints. The WHEN clause or body of the trigger can check for the violation of certain conditions and signal an error accordingly using the Oracle built-in function RAISE_APPLICATION_ERROR. The action that activated the trigger (insert, update, or delete) would be aborted. For example, the following trigger enforces the constraint Person.age >= 0:

```
create table Person (age int);
CREATE TRIGGER PersonCheckAge
AFTER INSERT OR UPDATE OF age ON Person
FOR EACH ROW
BEGIN
   IF (:new.age < 0) THEN
  RAISE_APPLICATION_ERROR(-20000, 'no negative age allowed');
   END IF;
END;
RUN;
```

If we attempt to execute the insertion:

```
insert into Person values (-3);
```

we would get the error message:

```
ERROR at line 1:
ORA-20000: no negative age allowed
ORA-06512: at "MYNAME.PERSONCHECKAGE", line 3
ORA-04088: error during execution of trigger 'MYNAME.PERSONCHECKAGE'
```

and nothing would be inserted. In general, the effects of both the trigger and the triggering statement are rolled back.

ADVANTAGES OF TRIGGERS

1. To enforce rules that cannot be coded through referential integrity.
2. To enforce certain business rules (validation) in an application.
3. To maintain an audit of changes made to data.
4. Derive column values.
5. To customize complex security authorizations.
6. To generate data automatically.
7. To maintain replicate tables.

LAB ASSIGNMENT—15

1. Create a table dupemp with the records those are inserted, updated or deleted from emp table using trigger.
2. Create a trigger for emp table for basic salary should be greater than 1000 at the time of records insertion else show error message.
3. Create a trigger for does not permit deletion of any row from emp table on Sunday.
4. Create a trigger for total_salary to maintain a derived column totsal that stores total salary of all members in a company.
5. Replace the commission by 500 if user insert the comm less than 500 using trigger.
6. Create a trigger, which prevents duplicate entry of deptno in dept table.
7. Create an Instead of trigger on view V1 which contains columns DNAME, ENAME and salary from tables dept and emp joined on the basis of deptno. If salary on an employee is updated in the view, it should be updated in the EMP table.

LAB ASSIGNMENT—16

1. What is a trigger?
2. For which of the following events can you create a trigger?
   (*a*) An INSERT, UPDATE, or DELETE statement on a specific object
   (*b*) An execution of a specific procedure
   (*c*) A user logon (or logoff)
   (*d*) A DDL statement, such as DROP or ALTER, on a specific object.
3. What is one of the main differences between the execution of a trigger and the execution of a stored procedure?
4. What are the two modes a trigger can have?
5. Which of the following terms describes the situation in which the execution of one trigger results in the execution of another, or possibly more, different triggers?
   (*a*) Trigger torrent
   (*b*) Cascading triggers
   (*c*) Chain reaction
   (*d*) Interlock
   (*e*) Recursive nesting
6. What is the difference between a statement-level trigger and a row-level trigger?
7. What clause makes a trigger fire only when a specific condition is true?
8. Which of the following triggers populates the employee_id column of the employee table with the next employee_seq sequence value?

   (*a*)

```
CREATE OR REPLACE TRIGGER employee_t1
  BEFORE INSERT
  ON employee
  FOR EACH ROW
BEGIN
  INSERT INTO employee (employee_id)
     VALUES (employee_seq.nextval);
END;
```

   (*b*)

```
CREATE OR REPLACE TRIGGER employee_t1
  BEFORE INSERT
  ON employee
  FOR EACH ROW
BEGIN
  SELECT employee_seq.nextval
```

```
    INTO :new.employee_id
    FROM dual;
  END;
```

9. Which of these special "pseudo" records are allowed inside a trigger?
   (*a*) :NEW
   (*b*) :CURRENT
   (*c*) :OLDEST
   (*d*) :PARENT
   (*e*) :OLD
   (*f*) :NEWEST
   (*g*) :RECORD
10. What system privileges are required to create a trigger?
11. What is the difference between the ALTER ANY TRIGGER privilege and the CREATE ANY TRIGGER privilege?
12. Why does the following trigger generate a "ORA-00920: invalid relational operator" error?

```
CREATE OR REPLACE TRIGGER emp_beforeins_t
  BEFORE INSERT
  ON employee
  FOR EACH ROW
  WHEN (:NEW.mgr is null)
BEGIN
  IF (:NEW.sal > 800)
  THEN
    :NEW.sal := 850;
  END IF;
END;
```

13. How can you view a trigger's compilation errors?
14. How many different ways can you recompile a trigger?
15. Why might you want to omit the OR REPLACE clause when you first create a trigger?
16. Which of the following statements are correct, and which are incorrect?
   (*a*) A user can create a trigger in any database schema if she has the CREATE ANY TRIGGER privilege.
   (*b*) A user can create a trigger in any database schema (with the exception of SYS) if she has the CREATE ANY TRIGGER privilege.
   (*c*) Triggers can trap only DML events such as INSERT, DELETE, and UPDATE.

17. True or false? You can define a trigger for:

(*a*) Any schema-level object
(*b*) A table
(*c*) A view
(*d*) Any nested table
(*e*) The entire database or a user schema

18. Examine the following trigger:

```
CREATE OR REPLACE TRIGGER upd_employee_commision
FOR EACH ROW
BEGIN
  <<Trigger logic>>
END;
```

Which of the following statements must you add to the trigger definition to make sure this trigger executes only after updating the comm column of the emp table?

(*a*) AFTER UPDATE(comm) ON emp
(*b*) AFTER UPDATE ON emp
(*c*) AFTER UPDATE OF comm ON emp
(*d*) AFTER comm UPDATE ON emp

19. Examine the following trigger:

```
CREATE OR REPLACE TRIGGER insert_employee
  AFTER INSERT ON emp
BEGIN
  <<Trigger logic>>
END;
```

Which of the following statements must you add to the trigger definition to make sure it executes only once for each INSERT operation on the emp table?

(*a*) FOR EVERY ROW
(*b*) WHEN (new.sal IS NULL)
(*c*) FOR EACH ROW
(*d*) No modifications are necessary

20. Why does the following trigger fail when it's executed?

```
CREATE OR REPLACE TRIGGER in_emp_summary
  AFTER INSERT
  ON emp
BEGIN
  INSERT INTO emp_summary (empno, period, ytd_salary)
    VALUES (:new.empno, SYSDATE, :new.sal);
END;
```

21. Provide a template for a trigger that raises an error when a client application violates a business rule (For example, a trigger that raises an error if a user attempts to delete a row from the employee table).
22. You want to issue DML statements or execute PL/SQL stored programs inside a trigger. Which of the following describes how you must grant the necessary privileges on the underlying object?
    (*a*) Privileges on the underlying object must be granted through the database roles.
    (*b*) Privileges on the underlying object must be granted directly from the user who owns the object.
    (*c*) Privileges can be granted either through database roles or directly from the user who owns the object.
23. DDL and transaction control statements such as ROLLBACK, COMMIT, and SAVEPOINT are not allowed in the body of a trigger. Can you circumvent this restriction by calling a stored procedure, which does contain the statement, in the trigger's body?
24. Sometimes, depending on the context of the application being constructed, you need to implement logic that requires explicit (or implicit) transaction control. For example, suppose you want to create a sequence when a user inserts a row into a table. How would you perform this function in Oracle8i? In previous versions of Oracle?
25. True or false?
    (*a*) The trigger body cannot contain more than 32 lines of PL/SQL code.
    (*b*) The size of a trigger cannot be more than 32K.
    (*c*) Oracle allows up to 32 triggers to cascade at any one time.
    (*d*) LONG or LONG RAW column can be referenced in a SQL statement within a trigger only if they can be converted into a constrained datatype. The maximum length for these datatypes can be up to 32K.
26. Sometimes you need to enable or disable triggers when you perform certain tasks, such as loading data or reorganizing a table. Write a script that enables or disables all triggers for the user who runs it.
27. If you create several triggers of the same type for the same table, in what order do the triggers fire?
28. Optimize the performance of the following trigger and explain how this technique can minimize the number of times the trigger fires:

```
CREATE OR REPLACE TRIGGER emp_ins_t1
  AFTER UPDATE OR DELETE OR INSERT
  ON employee
  FOR EACH ROW
BEGIN
  IF (UPDATING) THEN
```

```
    IF :old.sal <> :new.sal THEN
      Employee_pkg.update_emp (:new.employee_id, :new.sal);
    END IF;
  END IF;
END;
```

29. An HR system has an employee table that holds a row for each employee within the company. Each record in the table has a manager field, (mgr), that holds the id for the employee's manager. Write a trigger so that when a manager record is deleted, the mgr field of that manager's employees is set to NULL. In other words, implement the following SQL statement:

```
WHEN AN EMPLOYEE IS DELETED,
  UPDATE employee SET
    mgr = null
  WHERE
    mgr = employee id of the deleted employee
```

30. What are the possible implications of using the pseudo-column names :OLD and :NEW in the following trigger, which uses autonomous transactions?

```
CREATE OR REPLACE TRIGGER ins_emp
  AFTER INSERT
  ON emp
 FOR EACH ROW
DECLARE
  PRAGMA AUTONOMOUS_TRANSACTION;
  vsal  NUMBER;
BEGIN
  SELECT SUM (sal)
   INTO vsal
   FROM emp e
  WHERE e.deptno = :new.deptno;

  BEGIN
    INSERT INTO dept_history
       VALUES (:new.deptno, vsal);
  EXCEPTION
    WHEN DUP_VAL_ON_INDEX
    THEN
      UPDATE dept_history
        SET sal = vsal
```

```
        WHERE deptno = :new.deptno;
    END;

    COMMIT;
  END;
```

31. Suppose that the procedures called by the following triggers are recompiled. What happens at the next execution of each trigger?

```
CREATE OR REPLACE TRIGGER loc_trigger
  BEFORE UPDATE
  ON bonus
  FOR EACH ROW
BEGIN
  update_bonus;
END;
/

CREATE OR REPLACE TRIGGER rem_trigger
  BEFORE UPDATE
  ON bonus
  FOR EACH ROW
BEGIN
  update_bonus@rdb;
END;
    /
```

10 Subprograms: Procedure and Functions

Objectives :

- Subprograms
- Advantages of Subprograms
- Modular Code
- Functions
- Actual and Formal Parameters
- Matching Actual and Formal Parameters in PL/SQL
- Recursion

Lab Assignment-17

SUBPROGRAMS

Subprograms are named PL/SQL blocks that can take parameters and be invoked. PL/SQL has two types of subprograms called procedures and functions. Generally, we use a procedure to perform an action and a function to compute a value.

Like unnamed or anonymous PL/SQL blocks, subprograms have a declarative part, an executable part, and an optional exception-handling part. The declarative part contains declarations of types, cursors, constants, variables, exceptions, and nested subprograms. These items are local and cease to exist when you exit the subprogram. The executable part contains statements that assign values, control execution, and manipulate Oracle data. The exception-handling part contains exception handlers, which deal with exceptions raised during execution.

Consider the following procedure named debit_account, which debits a bank account:

```
PROCEDURE debit_account (acct_id INTEGER, amount REAL) IS
  old_balance REAL;
  new_balance REAL;
  overdrawn   EXCEPTION;
BEGIN
  SELECT bal INTO old_balance FROM accts
    WHERE acct_no = acct_id;
  new_balance := old_balance - amount;
  IF new_balance < 0 THEN
    RAISE overdrawn;
  ELSE
    UPDATE accts SET bal = new_balance
      WHERE acct_no = acct_id;
  END IF;
EXCEPTION
  WHEN overdrawn THEN
    ...
END debit_account;
```

When invoked or called, this procedure accepts an account number and a debit amount. It uses the account number to select the account balance from the accts database table. Then, it uses the debit amount to compute a new balance. If the new balance is less than zero, an exception is raised, otherwise, the bank account is updated.

ADVANTAGES OF SUBPROGRAMS

Subprograms provide extensibility, that is, they let you tailor the PL/SQL language to suit your needs. For example, if you need a procedure that creates new departments, you can easily write one, as follows:

```
PROCEDURE create_dept (new_dname VARCHAR2, new_loc VARCHAR2) IS
```

```
BEGIN
  INSERT INTO dept
    VALUES (deptno_seq.NEXTVAL, new_dname, new_loc);
END create_dept;
```

Subprograms also provide **modularity**, that is, they let us break a program down into manageable, well-defined logic modules. This supports top-down design and the stepwise refinement approach to problem solving.

In addition, subprograms promote **reusability** and **maintainability**. Once validated, a subprogram can be used with confidence in any number of applications. If its definition changes, only the subprogram is affected. This simplifies maintenance and enhancement.

Finally, subprograms aid **abstraction**, the mental separation from particulars. To use subprograms, you must know what they do, not how they work. Therefore, you can design applications from the top down without worrying about implementation details.

MODULAR CODE

Modularization is the process by which we can break up large blocks of code into smaller pieces — modules — which can be called by other modules. Modularization of code is analogous to normalization of data, with many of the same benefits (and a few additional advantages which accrue specifically to code). With modularization, code becomes:

- **More reusable.** By breaking up a large program or entire application into individual components which "plug-and-play" together, you will usually find that many modules will be used by more than one other program in your current application. Designed properly, these utility programs could even be of use in other applications.
- **More manageable.** Which would you rather debug: a 10,000-line program or five individual 2,000 line programs that call each other as needed? Our minds work better when we can focus on smaller tasks. You can also test and debug on a smaller scale (unit test) before individual modules are combined for a more complicated system test.
- **More readable.** Modules have names and names describe behavior. The more you move or hide your code behind a programmatic interface, the easier it is to read and understand what that program is doing. Modularization helps you focus on the big picture rather than the individual executable statements.
- **More reliable.** The code you produce will have fewer errors. The errors you do find will be easier to fix because they will be isolated within a module. In addition, your code will be easier to maintain since there is less of it and it is more readable.

PL/SQL offers the following structures which modularize your code in different ways:

(*a*) Procedure (*b*) Function

Procedure

A named PL/SQL block that performs one or more actions and is called as an executable PL/SQL statement. You can pass information into and out of a procedure through its parameter list.

Function

A named PL/SQL block that returns a single value and is used just like a PL/SQL expression. You can pass information into a function through its parameter list.

Procedure

A procedure is a module performing one or more actions. Because a procedure is a standalone executable statement in PL/SQL, a PL/SQL block could consist of nothing more than a single call to a procedure. Procedures are key building blocks of modular code, allowing you to both consolidate and reuse your program logic.

The general format of a PL/SQL procedure is as follows:

```
PROCEDURE name [ ( parameter [, parameter ... ] ) ]
IS
  [declaration statements]

BEGIN
  executable-statements

[ EXCEPTION
   exception handler statements]

END [ name ];
```

where each component is used in the following ways:

name

The name of the procedure comes directly after the keyword PROCEDURE.

parameters

An optional list of parameters that you define to both pass information into the procedure and send information out of the procedure, back to the calling program.

declaration statements

The declarations of local identifiers for that procedure. If you do not have any declarations, then there will not be any statements between the IS and BEGIN statements.

executable statements

The statements that the procedure executes when it is called. You must have at least one executable statement after the BEGIN and before the END or EXCEPTION keywords.

exception handler statements

The optional exception handlers for the procedure. If you do not explicitly handle any exceptions, then you can leave out the EXCEPTION keyword and simply terminate the execution section with the END keyword.

Figure 10.1 shows the apply_discount procedure, which contains all four sections of the named PL/SQL block, as well as a parameter list.

```
PROCEDURE apply_discount                                        Header
  (company_id_in IN company, company_id&TYPE, discount_in IN NUMBER)
IS
  min_discount CONSTANT NUMBER:=.05;
  max_discount CONSTANT NUMBER:=.25;                            Declaration
  invalid_discount EXCEPTION;
BEGIN
  IF discount_in BETWEEN min_discount AND max_discount
    THEN
      UPDATE item
        SET item_amount:=item_amount*(1-discount_in):
      WHERE EXISTS (SELECT 'x' FROM order
        WHERE order.order_id=item.order_id                      Execution
          AND order.company_id=company_id_in);
  IF SQL%ROWCOUNT = 0 THEN RAISE NO_DATA_FOUND; END IF;
ELSE
  RAISE invalid_discount;
 END IF;
EXCEPTION
  WHEN invalid_discount
  THEN
   DBMS_OUTPUT.PUT_LINE('The specified discount is invalid.');
                                                                Exception
  WHEN NO_DATA_FOUND
  THEN
   DBMS_OUTPUT.PUT_LINE('No orders in the system for company:' ||
        TO_CHAR(company_id_in));
END apply_discount;
```

Figure 10.1. The apply_discount procedure

Calling a Procedure

A procedure is called as an executable PL/SQL statement. In other words, a call to a procedure must end with a semicolon (;) and be executed before and after other SQL or PL/SQL statements.

The following executable statement runs the apply_discount procedure:

apply_discount(new_company_id, 0.15); — 15% discount

If the procedure does not have any parameters, then you must call the procedure without any parentheses:

display_store_summary;

Procedure Header

The portion of the procedure definition that comes before the IS keyword is called the procedure header. The header provides all the information a programmer needs to call that procedure, namely:

- The procedure name
- The parameter list, if any

A programmer does not need to know about the inside of the procedure in order to be ble to call it properly from another program.

The header for the apply_discount procedure discussed above is:

```
PROCEDURE apply_discount
  (company_id_in IN company.company_id%TYPE,
  discount_in IN NUMBER)
```

It consists of the module type, the name, and a list of two parameters.

Procedure Body

The body of the procedure is the code required to implement the procedure. It consists of the declaration, execution, and exception sections of the function. Everything after the IS keyword in the procedure makes up that procedure's body.

Once again, the declaration and exception sections are optional. If you have no exception handlers, you will leave off the EXCEPTION keyword and simply enter the END statement to terminate the procedure.

If you do not have any declarations, the BEGIN statement simply follows immediately after the IS keyword (see the do_nothing procedure below for an example of this structure.).

You must supply at least one executable statement in a procedure.

```
PROCEDURE do_nothing IS
BEGIN
  NULL;
END;
```

Note. A procedure that doesn't do anything can, in fact, be very useful when you are creating stubs for modules in a top-down design effort. You can also use this kind of procedure when building templates. do_nothing procedure acts initially as a placeholder in code, but then also provides a mechanism for customization of the templates.

The END Label

You can append the name of the procedure directly after the END keyword when you complete your procedure, as shown below:

```
PROCEDURE display_stores (region_in IN VARCHAR2) IS
BEGIN
  ...
END display_stores;
```

This name serves as a label that explicitly links up the end of the program with its beginning. You should as a matter of habit use an END label. It is especially important to do so when you have a procedure that spans more than a single page, or is one in a series of procedures and functions in a package body.

FUNCTIONS

A function is a module that returns a value. A function returns a value, it can be said to have a datatype. A function can be used in place of an expression in a PL/SQL statement having the same datatype as the function.

We have already done built-in functions in function chapter. You can also write your own functions — numeric functions, VARCHAR2 functions, and even functions that return a PL/SQL table or record. The programmer-defined function, a powerful addition to your tool chest, will aid greatly in making your code more flexible and easier to understand.

Structure of a Function

The structure of a function is the same as that of a procedure, except that the function also has a RETURN clause. The general format of a function follows:

```
FUNCTION name [ ( parameter [, parameter ... ] ) ]
  RETURN return_datatype
IS
  [ declaration statements ]

BEGIN
  executable statements

[ EXCEPTION
  exception handler statements ]

END [ name ];
```

where each component is used in the following ways:

name

The name of the procedure comes directly after the keyword FUNCTION.

parameters

An optional list of parameters that you define to both pass information into the procedure and send information out of the procedure, back to the calling program.

return_datatype

The datatype of the value returned by the function. This is required in the function header and is explained in more detail in the next section.

declaration statements

The declarations of local identifiers for that function. If you do not have any declarations, then there will not be any statements between the IS and BEGIN statements.

executable statements

The statements or the function executes when it is called. You must have at least one executable statement after the BEGIN and before the END or EXCEPTION keywords.

exception handler statements

The optional exception handlers for the function. If you do not explicitly handle any exceptions, then you can leave out the EXCEPTION keyword and simply terminate the execution section with the END keyword.

Rules for Functions

- When called from a SELECT statement or a parallelized INSERT, UPDATE, or DELETE statement, the function cannot modify any database tables.
- When called from an INSERT, UPDATE, or DELETE statement, the function cannot query or modify any database tables modified by that statement.
- When called from a SELECT, INSERT, UPDATE, or DELETE statement, the function cannot execute SQL transaction control statements (such as COMMIT), session control statements (such as SET ROLE), or system control statements (such as ALTER SYSTEM). Also, it cannot execute DDL statements (such as CREATE) because they are followed by an automatic commit.

If any SQL statement inside the function body violates a rule, you get an error at run time (when the statement is parsed).

Figure 10.2 illustrates the PL/SQL function and its different sections. Notice that the tot_sales function does not have an exception section.

```
FUNCTION tot_sales
  (company_id_in IN company.company_id%TYPE,
   status_in IN order.status_code%TYPE:=NULL)
RETURN NUMBER
IS
  /*Internal upper-cased version of status code */
  status_int order.status_code%TYPE:=UPPER(status_in);

  /*Parameterized cursor returns total discounted sales. */
  CURSOR sales_cur {status_in IN status_code%TYPE) IS
    SELECT SUN (amount*discount)
     FROM item
    WHERE EXISTS (SELECT 'X' FROM order
          WHERE order.order_id=item.order_id
          AND company_id=company_id_in
          AND status_code LIKE status_in);

  /*Return value for function*/
  return value NUMBER;
BEGIN
  OPEN sales_cur (status_int);
  FETCH sales_cur INTO return_value;
  IF sales_cur%NOTFOUND
  THEN
       CLOSE sales_cur;
       RETURN NULL;
  ELSE
       CLOSE sales_cur;
       RETURN return_value;
  END IF;
END tot_sales;
```

Header

Declaration

Execution

Figure 10.2. The tot_sales function

The RETURN Datatype

The return_datatype is the datatype of the value returned by the function. This datatype can be any datatype (and many complex structures) supported by PL/SQL, including scalars like these:

- VARCHAR2
- NUMBER
- BINARY_INTEGER
- BOOLEAN

Functions can also return complex and composite datatypes, such as:

- PL/SQL table
- Nested table or variable array (VARRAY)
- PL/SQL record
- Object type
- Large objects (LOBs) such as BFILEs and CLOBs

The datatype of a function cannot be either of the following:

Named exception

Once we declare an exception, we can refer that exception only in a RAISE statement and in the exception handler itself.

Cursor name

We cannot return a cursor from a function. (Note that PL/SQL Release 2.2 and beyond provides a REF CURSOR TYPE declaration that will allow us to return a cursor and even declare a parameter as a cursor.)

The END Label

We can append the name of the function directly after the END keyword when you complete our function, as shown below:

```
FUNCTION tot_sales (company_in IN INTEGER) RETURN NUMBER
IS
BEGIN
  ...
END tot_sales;
```

This name serves as a label that explicitly links up the end of the program with its beginning. We should as a matter of habit use an END label. It is especially important to do so when you have a function that spans more than a single page or is one in a series of functions and procedures in a package body.

Calling a Function

A function is called as part of an executable PL/SQL statement wherever an expression can be used. The following examples illustrate the different ways that the tot_sales function.

Example:

Call tot_sales to assign a value to a local PL/SQL variable:

```
sales_for_1995 := tot_sales (1504, 'C');
```

Example:

Use a call to tot_sales to set a default value for a variable:

```
DECLARE
  sales_for_1995 NUMBER DEFAULT tot_sales (1504, 'C');
BEGIN
```

Example:

Use tot_sales directly in an expression:

```
IF tot_sales (275, 'O') > 10000
THEN
...
```

Functions without parameters

If a function has no parameters, the function call must be written without parentheses, as the line below illustrates:

```
IF tot_sales THEN ...
```

Notice that we cannot tell just by looking at the above line of code whether tot_sales is a function or a variable. We would, in fact, have to check the declaration section of our PL/SQL block if we really needed to know. And that's the whole point. A function returns a value, as does a variable. The function just happens to execute some code to come up with that value whereas a variable has that value as its very attribute available for immediate return.

Function Header

The portion of the function definition that comes before the IS keyword is called the function header. The header provides all the information a programmer needs to call that function, namely:

- The function name
- The parameter list, if any
- The RETURN datatype

A programmer does not need to know about the inside of the function in order to be able to call it properly from another program.

The header for the tot_sales function discussed above is:

```
FUNCTION tot_sales
  (company_id_in IN company.company_id%TYPE,
   status_in IN order.status_code%TYPE := NULL)
RETURN NUMBER
```

It consists of the module type, the name, a list of two parameters, and a RETURN datatype of NUMBER. This means that the PL/SQL statement containing a call to tot_sales must be able to use a numeric value.

Function Body

The body of the function is the code required to implement the function. It consists of the declaration, execution, and exception sections of the function. Everything after the IS keyword in the function makes up that function's body.

Once again, the declaration and exception sections are optional. If we have no exception handlers, we will simply leave off the EXCEPTION keyword and enter the END statement to terminate the function.

If we do not have any declarations, the BEGIN statement simply follows immediately after the IS keyword (see the does_nothing function below for an example of this structure).

A Small Function

We must supply at least one executable statement in a function. Here is Boolean function with the smallest possible body in PL/SQL:

```
FUNCTION does_nothing RETURN BOOLEAN IS
BEGIN
  RETURN TRUE;
END;
```

We would call does_nothing as follows:

```
IF does_nothing
THEN
  NULL;
END IF;
```

The RETURN Statement

A function must have at least one RETURN statement in its execution section of statements. It can have more than one RETURN, but only one of those statements is executed each time the function is called. The RETURN statement that is executed by the function determines the value that is returned by that function. When a RETURN statement is processed, the function terminates immediately and returns control to the calling PL/SQL block.

The RETURN clause in the header of the function is different from the RETURN statement in the execution section of the body of the function. While the RETURN clause indicates the datatype of the return or result value of the function, the RETURN statement specifies the actual value that is returned. We have to specify the RETURN datatype in the header, but then also include at least one RETURN statement in the function.

Multiple RETURNs

In the tot_sales function we used two different RETURN statements to handle different situations in the function, as follows:

```
IF sales_cur%NOTFOUND
THEN
  CLOSE sales_cur;
  RETURN NULL;
ELSE
  CLOSE sales_cur;
  RETURN return_value;
END IF;
```

In other words, if we could not obtain sales information from the cursor, we will return NULL (which is different from zero). If we do get a value from the cursor,we return it to the calling program.

Note. In both of these cases the RETURN statement passes back a value; in one case the NULL value, and in the other the return_value variable.

RETURN Any Valid Expression

The RETURN statement can accept any expression for evaluation and return. This expression can be composed of calls to other functions, complex calculations, and even data conversions. All the following usages of RETURN are valid:

```
RETURN 'buy me lunch';
RETURN POWER (max_salary, 5);
RETURN (100 - pct_of_total_salary (employee_id));
RETURN TO_DATE ('01' || earliest_month || initial_year, 'DDMMYY');
```

An expression in the RETURN statement is evaluated when the RETURN is executed. When control is passed back to the calling form, the result of the evaluated expression is passed along, too.

No RETURN is Executed

What happens when you include one or any number of RETURN statements in your functions but none of them is executed? PL/SQL raises an error.

The following function:

```
FUNCTION company_type (type_code_in IN VARCHAR2)
  RETURN VARCHAR2 IS
BEGIN
  IF type_code_in = 'S'
  THEN
    RETURN 'SUBSIDIARY';
```

```
    ELSIF type_code_in = 'P'
    THEN
      RETURN 'PARTNER';
    END IF;
  END;
```

is then called in this executable statement:

```
  type_description := company_type ('R');
```

Because the RETURN statements are executed only when the type code is 'S' or 'P', the function never hits a RETURN. It does, however, execute to the end of the function and then raise an error, as follows:

ORA-6503: PL/SQL: Function returned without value

We can avoid this kind of problem (which we may never encounter in testing since we always pass a sensible value to the function) by restructuring our use of the RETURN statement.

Parameters

Procedures and functions can both use parameters to pass information back and forth between the module and the calling PL/SQL block.

The parameters of a module are at least as important as the code that implements the module (the module's body). Sure, you have to make certain that your module fulfills its promise. But the whole point of creating a module is that it can be called, you hope by more than one other module. If the parameter list is confusing or badly designed, it will be very difficult for programmers to make use of the module. The result will be that few people will use that module. And it doesn't much matter how well you implemented a program that no one uses.

Many developers do not give enough attention to a module's set of parameters. Considerations regarding parameters include:

- **The number of parameters.** Too few parameters can limit the reusability of your program. Too many parameters, and no one will want to reuse your program.
- **The types of parameters.** Should you use read-only, write-only, or read-write parameters?
- **The names of parameters.** How should you name your parameters so that their purpose in a module is properly and easily understood?
- **Default values for parameters.** How do you set defaults? When should a parameter be given defaults and when should the programmer be forced to enter a value?

Defining the Parameters

Formal parameters are defined in the parameter list of the program. A parameter definition parallels closely the syntax for declaring variables in the declaration section of a PL/SQL block. There is one important distinction: a parameter declaration must be unconstrained.

A *constrained declaration* is one that constrains or limits the kind of value that can be assigned to a variable declared with that datatype. An *unconstrained declaration* is one that does not limit values in this way. The following declaration of the variable company_name constrains the variable to 60 characters:

```
DECLARE
  company_name VARCHAR2(60);
BEGIN
```

When you declare a parameter, however, you must leave out the constraining part of the declaration:

```
PROCEDURE display_company (company_name IN VARCHAR2) IS ...
```

%TYPE and %ROWTYPE

You can use the %TYPE and %ROWTYPE anchoring attributes in the parameter list, even if the %TYPE refer a constrained declaration somewhere back along the line, as in a CREATE TABLE statement. The following parameter list will compile just fine:

```
PROCEDURE fun_and_games (ride_id_in IN rides.ride_id%TYPE)
```

If you are using PL/SQL Version 2, you can also declare parameters as PL/SQL tables through use of the TABLE type statement, as shown in this example:

```
PACKAGE pet_hotel
IS
  /* Define a table type and declare a table */
  TYPE breeds_type IS
    TABLE OF breed.breed_name%TYPE INDEX BY BINARY_INTEGER;
  TYPE avail_rooms_type IS
    TABLE OF room.room_number%TYPE INDEX BY BINARY_INTEGER;

  /* Specification of function which takes a table argument */
  FUNCTION room_by_breeds (breed_table_in IN breeds_type)
    RETURN avail_rooms_type;
END;
```

The %TYPE and %ROWTYPE attributes are allowed for parameters because both result in unconstrained declarations. The actual sizes of the parameters depend on the structures of the tables and columns to which the attributes point. This size is resolved only at compilation time.

Parameter Modes

When we define the parameter we also specify the way in which the parameter can be used. There are three different modes of parameters:

The mode determines how the program can use and manipulate the value assigned to the formal parameter. We specify the mode of the parameter immediately after the parameter name and before the parameter's datatype and optional default value. The following procedure header uses all three modes of parameters:

```
PROCEDURE predict_activity
  (last_date_in IN DATE,
```

```
task_desc_inout IN OUT VARCHAR2,
next_date_out OUT DATE)
```

The predict_activity procedure takes in two pieces of information: the date of the last activity and a description of the activity. It then returns or sends out two pieces of information: a possibly modified task description and the date of the next activity. Because the task_desc_inout parameter is IN OUT, the program can both read the value of the argument and change the value of that argument.

Let's look at each of these parameter modes in detail.

IN mode

The IN parameter allows us to pass values into the module, but will not pass anything out of the module and back to the calling PL/SQL block. In other words, for the purpose of the program, its IN parameters function like constants. Just like constants, the value of the formal IN parameter cannot be changed within the program. We cannot assign values to the IN parameter or in any other way modify its value.

IN is the default mode for parameters. If we do not specify a parameter mode, then the parameter is automatically considered an IN parameter. We recommend, however, that you always specify a parameter mode with your parameters. Your intended use of the parameter is then documented explicitly in the code itself.

IN parameters can be given default values in the program header.

The actual parameter for an IN parameter can be a variable, a named constant, a literal, or an expression. All of the following calls to display_title are valid:

```
DECLARE
  happy_title CONSTANT VARCHAR2(30)  := 'HAPPY BIRTHDAY';
  changing_title VARCHAR2(30) := 'Happy Anniversary';
  spc VARCHAR2(1) := ' ';
BEGIN
  display_title ('Happy Birthday');          — a literal
  display_title (happy_title);             — a constant

  changing_title := happy_title;

  display_title (changing_title);           — a variable
  display_title ('Happy' || spc || 'Birthday'); — an expression
  display_title (INITCAP (happy_title));      — another expression
END;
```

OUT mode

An OUT parameter is the opposite of the IN parameter. Use the OUT parameter to pass a value back from the program to the calling PL/SQL block. An OUT parameter is like the return value for a function, but it appears in the parameter list and you can, of course, have as many OUT parameters as you like.

Inside the program, an OUT parameter acts like a variable that has not been initialized. In fact, the OUT parameter has no value at all until the program terminates successfully (without raising an exception, that is, during the execution of the program, any assignments to an OUT parameter are actually made to an internal copy of the OUT parameter. When the program terminates successfully and returns control to the calling block, the value in that local copy is then transferred to the actual OUT parameter. That value is then available in the calling PL/SQL block.

There are several consequences of these rules concerning OUT parameters:

- You cannot assign an OUT parameter's value to another variable or even use it in a re-assignment to itself. An OUT parameter can be found only on the left side of an assignment operation.
- You also cannot provide a default value to an OUT parameter. You can only assign a value to an OUT parameter inside the body of the module.
- Any assignments made to OUT parameters are rolled back when an exception is raised in the program. Because the value for an OUT parameter is not actually assigned until a program completes successfully, any intermediate assignments to OUT parameters are therefore ignored. Unless an exception handler traps the exception and then assigns a value to the OUT parameter, no assignment is made to that parameter. The variable will retain the same value it had before the program was called.
- An OUT actual parameter has to be a variable. It cannot be a constant, literal, or expression, since these formats do not provide a receptacle in which PL/SQL can place the OUTgoing value.

OUT parameters are very restrictive in how they can and should be used. These restrictions place more of a burden on the programmer to understand the parameter modes and their impact. On the other hand, the OUT parameter provides a level of security and a narrowing of functionality which, when appropriate, is invaluable.

The IN OUT mode

With an IN OUT parameter, you can pass values into the program and return a value back to the calling program (either the original, unchanged value or a new value set within the program). The IN OUT parameter shares two restrictions with the OUT parameter:

1. An IN OUT parameter cannot have a default value.
2. An IN OUT actual parameter or argument must be a variable. It cannot be a constant, literal, or expression, since these formats do not provide a receptacle in which PL/SQL can place the outgoing value.

Beyond these restrictions, none of the other restrictions apply.

You can use the IN OUT parameter in both sides of an assignment, because it functions like an initialized, rather than uninitialized, variable. PL/SQL does not lose the value of an IN OUT parameter when it begins execution of the program. Instead, it uses that value as necessary within the program.

The combine_and_format_names procedure shown here combines the first and last names into a full name in the format specified ("LAST, FIRST" or "FIRST LAST"). It uses all three different modes of parameters: IN, IN OUT, and OUT.

```
PROCEDURE combine_and_format_names
  (first_name_inout IN OUT VARCHAR2,
   last_name_inout IN OUT VARCHAR2,
   full_name_out OUT VARCHAR2,
   name_format_in IN VARCHAR2 := 'LAST, FIRST')
IS
BEGIN
  /* Upper-case the first and last names. */
  first_name_inout := UPPER (first_name_inout);
  last_name_inout := UPPER (last_name_inout);

  /* Combine the names as directed by the name format string. */
  IF name_format_in = 'LAST, FIRST'
  THEN
    full_name_out := last_name_inout || ', ' || first_name_inout;

  ELSIF name_format_in = 'FIRST LAST'
  THEN
    full_name_out := first_name_inout || ' ' || last_name_inout;
  END IF;
END;
```

The first name and last name parameters must be IN OUT. We need the incoming names for the combined action, and we will uppercase the first and last names for future use in the program (thereby enforcing the application standard of all uppercase for names of people and things).

The full_name_out is just an OUT parameter because we create the full name from its parts. If the actual parameter used to receive the full name has a value going into the procedure, we certainly don't want to use it! Finally, the name_format_in parameter is a mere IN parameter since it is used to determine how to format the full name, but is not changed or changeable in any way.

Each parameter mode has its own characteristics and purpose. You should choose carefully which mode to apply to each of your parameters so that the parameter is used properly within the module.

ACTUAL AND FORMAL PARAMETERS

When we talk about parameters, we need to distinguish between two different kinds of parameters: actual and formal parameters. The formal parameters are the names that are declared in the parameter list of the header of a module. The actual parameters are the values or expressions placed in the parameter list of the actual call to the module.

Let's examine the differences between actual and formal parameters using the example of tot_sales. Here, again, is tot_sales' header:

```
FUNCTION tot_sales
  (company_id_in IN company.company_id%TYPE,
   status_in IN order.status_code%TYPE := NULL)
RETURN std_types.dollar_amount;
```

The formal parameters of tot_sales are:

company_id_in

The primary key of the company

status_in

The status of the orders to be included in the sales calculation.

They do not exist outside of the function. You can think of them as place holders for real or actual parameter values that are passed into the function when it is used in a program.

When you use tot_sales in your code, the formal parameters disappear. In their place you list the actual parameters or variables, whose values will be passed to tot_sales. In the following example, the company_id variable contains the primary key pointing to a company record. In the first three calls to tot_sales a different, hardcoded status is passed to the function. The last call to tot_sales does not specify a status; in this case the function assigns the default value (provided in the function header) to the status_in parameter:

```
new_sales      : = tot_sales (company_id, 'N');
paid_sales     : = tot_sales (company_id, 'P');
shipped_sales  : = tot_sales (company_id, 'S');
all_sales      : = tot_sales (company_id);
```

When tot_sales is called, all the actual parameters are evaluated. The results of the evaluations are then assigned to the formal parameters inside the function to which they correspond.

The actual parameters must be evaluated because they can be expressions, as well as pointers, to non-PL/SQL objects such as bind variables in the development tool.

The formal parameter and the actual parameter that corresponds to the formal parameter (when called) must be of the same or compatible datatypes. PL/SQL will perform datatype conversions for you in many situations. Generally, however, you are better off avoiding all implicit datatype conversions so you are sure of what is happening in your code. Use a formal conversion function like TO_CHAR or TO_DATE, so you know exactly what kind of data you are passing into your modules.

MATCHING ACTUAL AND FORMAL PARAMETERS IN PL/SQL

How does PL/SQL know which actual parameter goes with which formal parameter when a program is executed? PL/SQL actually offers you two different ways to make the association:

Positional notation

Associate the actual parameter implicitly (by position) with the formal parameter.

Named notation

Associate an actual parameter explicitly (by name) with the formal parameter.

Positional notation

In every example you've seen so far, we have employed positional notation in order to guide PL/SQL through the parameters. With positional notation, PL/SQL relies on the relative positions of the parameters to make the correspondence. PL/SQL associates the nth actual parameter in the call to a program with the nth formal parameter in the program's header.

With the tot_sales example shown below, PL/SQL associates the first actual parameter, :order.company_id, with the first formal parameter, company_id_in. It then associates the second actual parameter, N, with the second format parameter, status_in:

```
new_sales := tot_sales (:order.company_id, 'N');

FUNCTION tot_sales
  (company_id_in IN company.company_id%TYPE,
   status_in IN order.status_code%TYPE := NULL)
RETURN std_types.dollar_amount;
```

Now you know the name for the way compilers pass values through parameters to modules. Positional notation, shown graphically in Figure 10.3, is certainly the most obvious method.

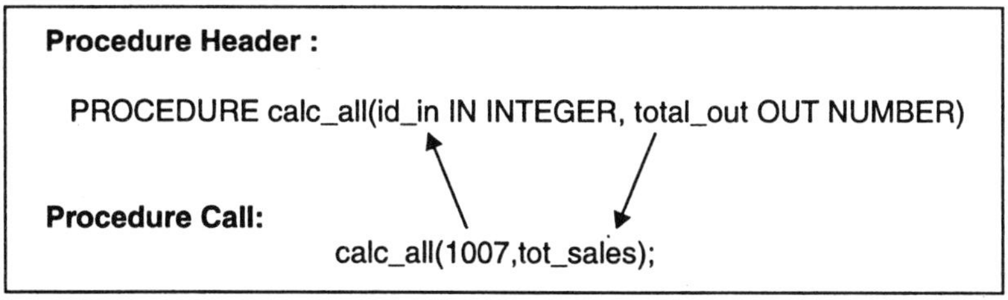

Figure 10.3. Matching actual with formal parameters (positional notation)

Named notation

With named notation, you explicitly associate the formal parameter (the name of the parameter) with the actual parameter (the value of the parameter), right in the call to the program, using the combination symbol =>.

The general syntax for named notation is:

formal_parameter_name => argument_value

Because you provide explicitly the name of the formal parameter, PL/SQL no longer needs to rely on the order of the parameters to make the association from actual to formal. So, if you use named notation, you do not need to list the parameters in your call to the program in the same order as the formal parameters are listed in the header. tot_sales for new orders in either of these two ways:

```
new_sales :=
  tot_sales (company_id_in => :order.company_id, status_in =>'N');

new_sales :=
  tot_sales (status_in =>'N', company_id_in => :order.company_id);
```

You can also mix named and positional notation in the same program call:

```
:order.new_sales := tot_sales (:order.company_id, status_in =>'N');
```

Benefits of named notation

Now you are aware of different ways to notate the order and association of parameters. One obvious question that you might ask is why you would ever use named notation. Here are some possibilities:

- *Named notation is self-documenting.* When you use named notation, the call to the program clearly describes the formal parameter to which the actual parameter is assigned. The names of formal parameters can and should be designed so that their use/purpose is self-explanatory. In a way, the descriptive aspect of named notation is another form of program documentation. If you are not familiar with all the modules called by an application, the listing of the formal parameters helps reinforce your understanding of a particular program call. In some development environments, the standard for parameter notation is named notation for just this reason.
- *Named notation gives you complete flexibility over parameter specification.* You can list the parameters in any order you want. You can also include only the parameters you want or need in the parameter list. Complex applications may at times require procedures with literally dozens of parameters. Any parameter with a default value can be left out of the call to the procedure. By using named notation, the developer can use the procedure, passing only the values needed for that usage.

Remember that whether you use named or positional notation, the actual module (both header and body) remains unchanged. The only difference is in the way the module is called.

Default Values

As you have seen from previous examples, you can provide a default value for IN parameters. If an IN parameter has a default value, you do not need to include that parameter in the call to the program. You must, of course, include an actual parameter for any IN OUT parameters, even if they have default values. A parameter's default value is used by the program only if the call to that program does not include that parameter in the list.

The parameter default value works the same way as a specification of a default value for a declared variable. There are two ways to specify a default value: either with the keyword DEFAULT or with the assignment operator (:=), as the following example illustrates:

```
PROCEDURE astrology_reading
  (sign_in IN VARCHAR2 := 'LIBRA',
   birth_time_in IN NUMBER DEFAULT 800) IS
```

By using default values, you can call programs using different numbers of actual parameters. The program uses the default value of any unspecified parameters. It also overrides the default values of any parameters in the list that have default values. Here are all the different ways you can ask for your astrology reading using positional notation:

```
astrology_reading ('SCORPIO', 1756);
astrology_reading ('SCORPIO');
astrology_reading;
```

The first line specifies both parameters explicitly. In the second call to astrology_reading, only the first actual parameter is included, so birth_time_in is set to 8:00 A.M. In the third line, no parameters are specified, so we cannot include the parentheses. Both the default values are used in the body of the procedure.

What if you want to specify a birth time, but not a sign? The following call to astrology_reading compiles properly since PL/SQL will convert NUMBER to VARCHAR2 automatically, but it results in assigning the string "1757" to the sign, and 8:00 A.M. to the birth time:

```
astrology_reading (1757);
```

Not exactly what you might have had in mind! You also cannot use a comma (,) to indicate a placeholder, as in, "There should be a parameter here so use the default value!" This next call does not even compile:

```
astrology_reading (,1757); — Invalid skipped argument
```

If you wish to leave out leading and defaulted parameters from your program call, you need to switch to named notation. By including the name of the formal parameter, you can list only those parameters to which you need to pass (or retrieve) values. In this (thankfully) last request for a star-based reading of my fate, I have successfully passed in a default of Libra as my sign and an overridden birth time of 5:56 P.M.

```
astrology_reading (birth_time_in => 1757);
```

RECURSION

Recursion is a powerful technique for simplifying the design of algorithms. Basically, *recursion* means self-reference. In a recursive mathematical sequence, each term is derived by applying a formula to preceding terms. The Fibonacci sequence (1, 1, 2, 3, 5, 8, 13, 21, ...), which was first used to model the growth of a rabbit colony, is an example. Each term in the sequence (after the second) is the sum of the two terms that immediately precede it.

In a recursive definition, something is defined in terms of simpler versions of itself. Consider the definition of *n* factorial (*n*!), the product of all integers from 1 to *n*:

$$n! = n * (n - 1)!$$

Recursive Subprograms

A recursive subprogram is one that calls itself. Think of a recursive call as a call to some other subprogram that does the same task as your subprogram. Each recursive call creates a new instance of any items declared in the subprogram, including parameters, variables, cursors, and exceptions. Likewise, new instances of SQL statements are created at each level in the recursive descent.

Be careful where you place a recursive call. If you place it inside a cursor FOR loop or between OPEN and CLOSE statements, another cursor is opened at each call. As a result, your program might exceed the limit set by the Oracle initialization parameter OPEN_CURSORS.

There must be at least two paths through a recursive subprogram: one that leads to the recursive call and one that does not. At least one path must lead to a *terminating condition*. Otherwise, the recursion would (theoretically) go on forever. In practice, if a recursive subprogram strays into infinite regress, PL/SQL eventually runs out of memory and raises the predefined exception STORAGE_ERROR.

Example 1: **To solve some programming problems, you must repeat a sequence of statements until a condition is met. You can use iteration or recursion to solve such problems. Use recursion when the problem can be broken down into simpler versions of itself. For example, you can evaluate 3! as follows:**

```
0! = 1 —by definition
1! = 1 * 0! = 1
2! = 2 * 1! = 2
3! = 3 * 2! = 6
```

To implement this algorithm, you might write the following recursive function, which returns the factorial of a positive integer:

```
FUNCTION fac (n POSITIVE) RETURN INTEGER IS —returns n!
BEGIN
  IF n = 1 THEN —terminating condition
    RETURN 1;
  ELSE
    RETURN n * fac(n - 1); —recursive call
  END IF;
END fac;
```

At each recursive call, n is decremented. Eventually, n becomes 1 and the recursion stops.

Example 2: **Consider the procedure below, which finds the staff of a given manager. The procedure declares two formal parameters, mgr_no and tier, which represent the manager's employee number and a tier in his or her departmental organization. Staff members reporting directly to the manager occupy the first tier.**

```
PROCEDURE find_staff (mgr_no NUMBER, tier NUMBER := 1) IS
  boss_name  CHAR(10);
  CURSOR c1 (boss_no NUMBER) IS
    SELECT empno, ename FROM emp WHERE mgr = boss_no;
BEGIN
  /* Get manager's name. */
  SELECT ename INTO boss_name FROM emp WHERE empno = mgr_no;
  IF tier = 1 THEN
    INSERT INTO staff  — single-column output table
      VALUES (boss_name || ' manages the staff');
  END IF;
  /* Find staff members who report directly to manager. */
  FOR ee IN c1 (mgr_no) LOOP
    INSERT INTO staff
      VALUES (boss_name || 'manages' || ee.ename
        || ' on tier ' || TO_CHAR(tier));
    /* Drop to next tier in organization. */
    find_staff(ee.empno, tier + 1);  — recursive call
  END LOOP;
  COMMIT;
END;
```

When called, the procedure accepts a value for mgr_no but uses the default value of tier. For example, you might call the procedure as follows:

```
find_staff(7839);
```

The procedure passes mgr_no to a cursor in a cursor FOR loop, which finds staff members at successively lower tiers in the organization. At each recursive call, a new instance of the FOR loop is created and another cursor is opened, but prior cursors stay positioned on the next row in their result sets.

When a fetch fails to return a row, the cursor is closed automatically and the FOR loop is exited. Since the recursive call is inside the FOR loop, the recursion stops. Unlike the initial call, each recursive call passes a second actual parameter (the next tier) to the procedure.

The last example illustrates recursion, not the efficient use of set-oriented SQL statements. You might want to compare the performance of the recursive procedure to that of the following SQL statement, which does the same task:

```
INSERT INTO staff
  SELECT PRIOR ename || ' manages ' || ename
    || ' on tier ' || TO_CHAR(LEVEL - 1)
  FROM emp
  START WITH empno = 7839
  CONNECT BY PRIOR empno = mgr;
```

The SQL statement is appreciably faster. However, the procedure is more flexible. For example, a multi-table query cannot contain the CONNECT BY clause. So, unlike the procedure, the SQL statement cannot be modified to do joins. (A *join* combines rows from two or more database tables.) In addition, a procedure can process data in ways that a single SQL statement cannot.

Example:

```
FUNCTION balance (acct_id INTEGER) RETURN REAL IS
  acct_bal REAL;
BEGIN
  SELECT bal INTO acct_bal FROM accts
    WHERE acct_no = acct_id;
  RETURN acct_bal;
END balance;
```

Example:

```
FUNCTION compound (
  years  NUMBER,
  amount NUMBER,
  rate   NUMBER) RETURN NUMBER IS
BEGIN
  RETURN amount * POWER((rate / 100) + 1, years);
END compound;
```

Example:

Function to return the square of a given number.

```
Create or Replace Function Sqno (NO Number)
Return Number
IS
Begin
Return NO*NO;
End;
```

Test the function

```
SQL > Select Sqno (10) from dual;
```

Function to return the netsalary of given employee number.

```
Create or replace function netsalary
(id in emp.empno%type)
return number
is
netsal emp.sal%type;
begin
select sum (sal) + sum (comm) into netsal from emp where empno = id;
return (netsal);
end;
/
```

LAB ASSIGNMENT—17

1. Create a procedure for credit a bank account.
2. Create a procedure for hike the salary by 10% of all employees.
3. Create a function for cube of any number.
4. Create a function for simple interest.
5. Create a function for calculation the total profit amount.
6. Create a recursive function for Fibonnaci series.

11 Packages

Objectives :

- Introduction
- Advantages of Packages
- Public and Private Package Elements
- How to Reference Package Elements
- Quick Tour of a Package
- Packages without Bodies
- Overloading
- Product-Specific Packages

Lab Assignment-18

INTRODUCTION

A package is a collection of PL/SQL objects that are packaged or grouped together within a special BEGIN-END syntax, a kind of "meta-block." Here is a partial list of the kinds of objects we can place in a package:

- Cursors
- Variables (scalars, records, tables, etc.)
- Constants
- Exception names
- PL/SQL table and record TYPE statements
- Procedures
- Functions

Packages are among the least understood and most underutilized features of PL/SQL. Packages provide a structure in which we can organize our modules and other PL/SQL elements. They encourage proper structured programming techniques in an environment that often befuddles the implementation of structured programming.

Oracle Corporation itself uses the package construct to extend the PL/SQL language. In fact, the most basic operators of the PL/SQL language, such as the + and LIKE operators and the INSTR function, are all defined in a special package called STANDARD.

Packages are, by nature, highly modular. When we place a program unit into a package we automatically create a context for that program. By collecting related PL/SQL elements in a package, we express that relationship in the very structure of the code itself. Packages are often called "the poor man's objects" because they support some, but not all, object-oriented rules. For example, packages allow us to encapsulate and abstract our data and functions.

ADVANTAGES OF PACKAGES

- Enforced Information Hiding
- Object-Oriented Design
- Top-Down Design
- Object Persistence
- Performance Improvement

Overview of Package Structure

A package provides an extra layer of code and structure over that of an individual module. Many of the concepts needed to understand a package's structure are familiar to us. In fact, a package is very similar in structure to a PL/SQL module that has local modules defined within it.

Whereas a module has a header and a body, a package has a specification and a body. Just as the module's header explains to a developer how to call that module, the package specification describes the different elements of the package that can be called. Beyond that, however, there are key differences between the constructs in the module and in the package.

A module's specification and body are connected by the IS keyword; both are required and one cannot be written without the other. The specification determines how we call the module. The body, after the IS keyword, contains the code that is executed when the function is used. These two components of a module are coded together and are completely inseparable.

A package also has a specification and a body, but the package's two parts are structured differently, and have a different significance, from those for a single module. With a package, the specification and body are completely distinct objects. You can write and compile the specification independently of the body. When we create and replace stored packages in the database, we perform this action separately for each of the specification and body.

This separation of specification and body allows us to employ top-down design techniques in a powerful way.

The Specification

The package specification contains the definition or specification of all elements in the package that may be referred outside the package. These are called the public elements of the package specification containing two module definitions.

```
PACKAGE sp_timer
IS
    PROCEDURE capture (context_in IN VARCHAR2);
    PROCEDURE show_elapsed;
END sp_timer;
```

Figure 11.1. The specification of sp_timer package

Like the module, the package specification contains all the code that is needed for a developer to understand how to call the objects in the package. A developer should never have to examine the code behind the specification (which is the body) in order to understand how to use and benefit from the package.

The Body

The body of the package contains all the code behind the package specification: the implementation of the modules, cursors, and other objects. Figure 11.2 illustrates the body required to implement the specification of the sp_timer package shown in Figure 11.1.

```
PACKAGE BODY sp_timer
IS
    last_timing NUMBER := NULL;

    PROCEDURE capture
            (context_in IN VARCHAR2) IS
    BEGIN
            last_timing := DBMS_UTILITY.GET_TIME;
    END;

    PROCEDURE show_elapsed IS
    BEGIN
            DBMS_OUTPUT.PUT.LINE
                    (DBMS_UTILITY.GET_TIME - last timing);
    END;
END sp_timer;
```

Figure 11.2. The body of sp_timer package

The body may also contain elements that do not appear in the specification. These are called the private elements of the package. A private element cannot be referred outside the package, since it does not appear in the specification.

The body of the package resembles a standalone module's declaration section. It contains both declarations of variables and the definitions of all package modules. The package body may also contain an execution section, which is called the *initialization section* because it is only run once, to initialize the package.

Package Syntax

The general syntax for the two parts of a package follows:

- The package specification:

```
PACKAGE package_name
IS
[ declarations of variables and types ]
[ specifications of cursors ]
[ specifications of modules ]
  END [ package_name ];
```

We can declare variables and include specifications of both cursors and modules (and only the specifications). We must have at least one declaration or specification statement in the package specification.

Notice that the package specification has its own BEGIN-END block syntax. This enables its independent existence and compilation from the package body.

- The package body:

```
PACKAGE BODY package_name
IS
[ declarations of variables and types ]
[ specification and SELECT statement of cursors ]
[ specification and body of modules ]
[ BEGIN
  executable statements ]
[ EXCEPTION
  exception handlers ]
  END [ package_name ];
```

In the body we can declare other variables, but we do not repeat the declarations in the specification. The body contains the full implementation of cursors and modules. In the case of a cursor, the package body contains both specification and SQL statement for the cursor. In the case of a module the package body contains both the specification and body of the module.

The BEGIN keyword indicates the presence of an execution or initialization section for the package. This section can also optionally include an exception section.

As with a procedure or function, you can add the name of the package, as a label, after the END keyword in both the specification and package.

PUBLIC AND PRIVATE PACKAGE ELEMENTS

A central concept of packages is the privacy level of its elements. One of the most valuable aspects of a package is its ability to actually enforce information hiding. With a package you can not only modularize your secrets behind a procedural interface, you can keep these parts of your application completely private.

An element of a package, whether it is a variable or a module, can either be private or public, as defined below:

Public

Defined in the specification. A public element can be referenced from other programs and PL/SQL blocks.

Private

Defined only in the body of the package, but does not appear in the specification. A private element cannot be referenced outside of the package. Any other element of the package may, however, reference and use a private element. Private elements in a package must be defined before they can be referenced by other elements of the package. If, in other words, a public procedure calls a private function, that function must be defined above the public procedure in the package body. We can, alternatively, use a forward declaration if we wish to keep our private programs at the bottom of the package body.

If we find that a formerly private object such as a module or cursor should instead be made public, we simply add that object to the package specification and recompile. It will then be visible outside the package.

The distinct difference between public and private elements gives PL/SQL developers unprecedented control over their data structures and programs. Figure 11.3 shows a Booch diagram for the package that displays private and public package elements.

This diagram is named after Grady Booch, who pioneered many of the ideas of the package, particularly in the context of object-oriented design.

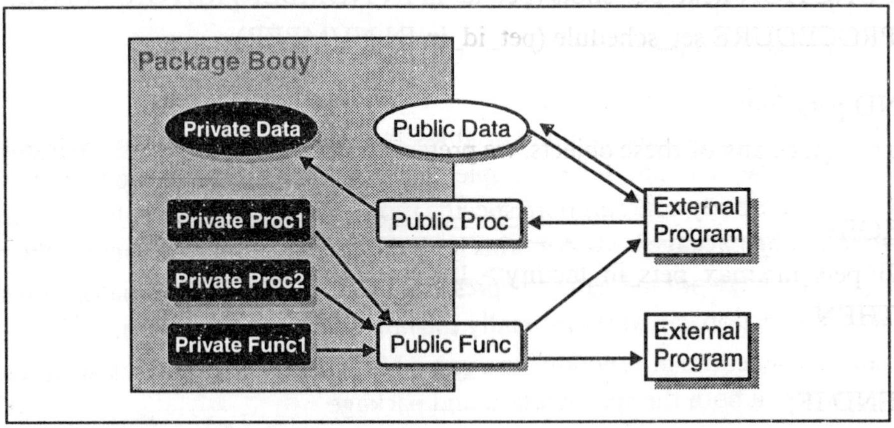

Figure 11.3. Booch diagram showing public and private package elements

The diagram offers a clear representation of the public/private character of PL/SQL packages. The large rectangle establishes the graphical boundary of the package. A program external to the package may only call a package element if a part of the element extends past the boundary of the package. Thus, all public elements defined in the specification straddle the package boundary. Part of the element is inside the boundary, and part lies outside, accessible to other programs.

All the objects (data and modules) that are completely surrounded by the boundary of the package are private objects. These are defined only in the package body and do not appear in the specification. Because they are wholly contained, no external program can reference those elements.

As the border of the public elements exists both outside and inside the package boundary, so all elements in the package (private and public) can use those elements.

The next section offers a quick tour of a simple package which illustrates these concepts.

HOW TO REFERENCE PACKAGE ELEMENTS

A package owns its objects, just as a table owns its columns. We use the same dot notation to provide a fully qualified specification for a package's object as we would for a table's column.

The following package specification declares a constant, an exception, a cursor, and several modules:

```
PACKAGE pets_inc
IS
  max_pets_in_facility CONSTANT INTEGER := 120;
  pet_is_sick EXCEPTION;

  CURSOR pet_cur RETURN pet%ROWTYPE;

  FUNCTION next_pet_shots (pet_id_in IN NUMBER) RETURN DATE;
  PROCEDURE set_schedule (pet_id_in IN NUMBER);

END pets_inc;
```

To reference any of these objects, we preface the object name with the package name, as follows:

```
BEGIN
  IF pets_inc.max_pets_in_facility > 100
  THEN
    ...
  END IF;
EXCEPTION
  WHEN pets_inc.pet_is_sick
  THEN
    ...
END;

OPEN pets_inc.pet_cur;

:pet_master.next_appointment
    := pets_inc.next_pet_shots (:pet_master.pet_id);
```

If we do not preface the call to next_pet_shots with the package name, pets_inc, PL/SQL is not able to resolve the reference and the compile fails.

So, the rule for referencing package elements is simple and clear: *To reference a stored package element, use dot notation.* The one exception is that inside a package, we do not need to qualify references to other elements of that package. PL/SQL will automatically resolve our reference within the scope of the package.

Suppose, for example, that the set_schedule procedure of pets_inc references the max_pets_in_facility constant. Such a reference would be unqualified as shown here:

```
PROCEDURE set_schedule (pet_id_in IN NUMBER)
IS
  ...
BEGIN
  ...
  IF total_pets < max_pets_in_facility
  THEN
    ...
  END IF;
END;
```

Of course, if we want to reference the element of a second package inside the current package, we will need to include the name of that package.

QUICK TOUR OF A PACKAGE

The pet maintenance package defined below is used by veterinarians to keep track of their patients and to determine when a pet needs another visit. Its specification identifies the public elements of the package. The body implements those elements and also creates two private elements.

The pets_inc package specification

The specification for the pets_inc package establishes the five public elements:

Name	Type	Description
petid_type	Subtype definition	Creates a programmer-defined subtype for the pet table primary key.
petid_nu	Variable declaration	Represents the primary key in pet table.
pet_cur	Cursor specification	Retrieves information about specified pet.
next_pet_shots	Function specification	Returns the date for next shots.
set_schedule	Procedure specification	Sets the schedule for the specified pet.

Here is the pets_inc package specification:

```
PACKAGE pets_inc
IS
  SUBTYPE petid_type IS pet.pet_id%TYPE;
  petid_nu petid_type;
```

```
   CURSOR pet_cur (pet_name_in IN VARCHAR2) RETURN pet%ROWTYPE;
   FUNCTION next_pet_shots (pet_id_in IN petid_type) RETURN DATE;
   PROCEDURE set_schedule (pet_id_in IN petid_type)
END pets_inc;
```

The header for the package specification simply states PACKAGE. We do not explicitly indicate that it is the specification, as in PACKAGE SPECIFICATION. Instead, when we create the body of a package, we indicate explicitly in the first line of the definition that we are defining the body of the pets_inc package.

Since all of these elements are in the package, we can reference them in other programs, such as the following procedure:

```
PROCEDURE show_next_visit (pet_in IN VARCHAR2)
IS
  next_visit DATE;

  /* Declare record to receive row fetched from package cursor. */
  pet_rec pets_inc.pet_cur%ROWTYPE;
BEGIN
  /* Open the package-based cursor. */
  OPEN pets_inc.pet_cur (pet_in);

  /* Fetch from cursor into local record. */
  FETCH pets_inc.pet_cur INTO pet_rec;

  IF pets_inc.pet_cur%FOUND
  THEN
    /* Call packaged function to get next visit date. */
    next_visit := pets_inc.next_pet_shots (pet_rec.pet_id);

    /* Display the information. */
    DBMS_OUTPUT.PUT_LINE
      ('Schedule next visit for ' || pet_in || ' on ' ||
       TO_CHAR (next_visit));
  END IF;

  CLOSE pets_inc.pet_cur;
END;
```

The pets_inc package body

The package body for pets_inc contains elements shown in the following table:

Name	Type	Description
max_date	Constant declaration	Private variable. Maximum date allowed.
pet_cur	Cursor declaration	The cursor specification and SQL statement that retrieves information about specified pet.
pet_status	Function definition	Private module. The specification and body for the function that returns the status of the pet.
next_pet_shots	Function definition	The specification and body for the function that returns date for next shots.
set_schedule	Procedure definition	The specification and body for the procedure that sets the schedule for the specified pet.

Here is the pets_inc package body:

```
PACKAGE BODY pets_inc
IS
  max_date CONSTANT DATE := SYSDATE + 10;

  CURSOR pet_cur (pet_name_in IN VARCHAR2) RETURN pet%ROWTYPE IS
    SELECT * FROM pet;

  FUNCTION pet_status  (pet_id_in IN petid_type) RETURN VARCHAR2
  IS
  BEGIN
    ... code behind the module ...
  END;
  FUNCTION next_pet_shots (pet_id_in IN petid_type) RETURN DATE
  IS
  BEGIN
    ... the code behind the module ...
  END;

  PROCEDURE set_schedule (pet_id_in IN petid_type)
  IS
  BEGIN
    ... the code behind the module ...
  END;

END pets_inc;
```

The body for the pet maintenance package contains the SELECT statement for the pet_cur cursor as well as the code required to implement all the modules.

This package body contains two private elements: max_date and pet_status. The max_date constant is used inside the package modules to validate dates that are manipulated in the package. The pet_status function is used by other modules to retrieve the status of the pet.

Since these elements are private, they can only be referenced by other elements of the package.

Observations about pets_inc

There are several interesting facts to point out about the previous two package components:

- The package specification does not contain any executable statements or exception handlers. A specification only specifies, or declares, those objects in the package that are public—that is, visible outside the package and callable by other programs.
- The declaration of the petid_nu variable and the petid_type subtype are not repeated inside the body. The declaration in the specification is enough for the whole package. Any module in the body can reference variables declared in the specification.
- Both the body and the specification of pets_inc are actually extended declaration sections. The package body can, however, also contain execution and exception sections. These two parts of the package body make up the initialization section of the package, which is explored later in this chapter.

The Package Specification

The specification of a package lists all the objects in that package that are available for use in applications, and provides all the information a developer needs in order to use objects in the package. A package specification may contain any of the following object specification statements:

- Variable declaration. Any kind of variable declaration statement, from a Boolean variable to a character string to a number. This variable is then available outside of the package (as well as within the body of the package).
- TYPE declaration. Any kind of valid TYPE statement, such as those to create a programmer-defined record type or a PL/SQL table. These complex data structures are then available outside of the package (as well as within the body of the package).
- Exception declaration. Declare exceptions in a package that can then be raised and handled outside of the package.
- Cursor specification. Specify a cursor's name and its RETURN clause. This cursor can then be opened, fetched, and closed outside of the package (as well as within the body of the package). This is available only in PL/SQL Version 2 because Version 1 does not support the required RETURN clause for a cursor.
- Module specification. Place the full specification for a module in the package specification. A module specification is the module type (PROCEDURE or FUNCTION), module name, parameter list, and RETURN clause (for a function). This module can then be called both from within and outside of the package.

Of these object specification statements, only the cursor and the module need to be defined in the body of the package. The cursor and module, in other words, are not completely determined by the specification alone. The cursor needs its SELECT statement. The module needs its executable section.

The variable TYPE and exception declarations, on the other hand, do not need any additional code for completion—they need only their declaration statements. We can, therefore, write a package that consists solely of a specification and has nobody at all, as you will see in the next section.

The pets_inc package specification shown earlier contains a variable, cursor and two modules. We do not need to know how the package function next_pet_shots determines the date when a pet will next need its shots. We need to know just the name of the function, its parameters, and the function's return data type. Similarly, the package makes available a predefined cursor that gets everything we need to know about a pet based on its primary key, pet_id. The cursor might use a SELECT statement against a base table or against a three-way join with a sub-SELECT.

PACKAGES WITHOUT BODIES

A package only requires a body if one of the following is true:

- You want to define private package elements
- You have included a cursor or module in your specification

A package may consist solely of declarations of public package elements. In this case, there is no need for a package body. This section offers two examples of scenarios where a bodyless package may be just the ticket.

A package of exceptions

The exception handler package in the next example declares a set of programmer-defined exception numbers and exceptions to go with them. It also declares a PL/SQL table to hold the associated error messages.

```
PACKAGE exchdlr
IS
   en_general_error NUMBER := -20000;
   exc_general_error EXCEPTION;
   PRAGMA EXCEPTION_INIT (exc_general_error, -20000);

   en_must_be_eighteen  NUMBER := -20001;
   exc_must_be_eighteen EXCEPTION;
   PRAGMA EXCEPTION_INIT (exc_must_be_eighteen, -20001);

   max_error_number_used NUMBER := -20001;

   TYPE error_msg_tabtype IS TABLE OF VARCHAR2 (240)
```

```
    INDEX BY BINARY_INTEGER;
  error_msg_table error_msg_tabtype;

END exchdlr;
```

Because this package does not specify any cursors or modules, we do not need to create a body for the exception handler package.

Top-down design with bodyless packages

There is another motivation for writing a package without a body: we don't yet know what the body is going to look like. If we follow a top-down design methodology, we start with a general description of an application and gradually decompose into separate functional areas, programs, or individual statements. With the package structure we can immediately translate high-level refinements into code, while at the same time postponing a resolution of the actual implementation of that code. We can even compile references to unimplemented package modules as long as that module specification is available in a package specification.

Suppose we need to build an application to track calls about product quality. The functional areas of this application include call entry/maintenance, data validation, call analysis, and call assignment, and are represented in the packages shown below:

- Package to maintain support calls:

```
PACKAGE support
IS
  PROCEDURE add_call (call_id IN INTEGER);
  PROCEDURE remove_call (call_id IN INTEGER);
END support;
```

- Package to perform analysis on call workload:

```
PACKAGE workload
IS
  FUNCTION average (dept_id IN INTEGER)
    RETURN NUMBER;
  FUNCTION operator (operator_id IN INTEGER)
    RETURN NUMBER;
END workload;
```

Notice that we have only created package specifications. There is nobody yet for these modules. Still, we can now implement the assigncall procedure below, referencing our "stubs." This procedure will compile successfully.

```
PROCEDURE assigncall
  (call_id IN INTEGER,
   operator_id IN INTEGER,
   dept_id IN INTEGER)
IS
```

```
BEGIN
  IF workload.operator (operator_id) < workload.average (dept_id)
  THEN
    support.add_call (call_id);
  END IF;
END;
```

It all goes back to the public/private boundary of packages. The package provides all the information we need to call package modules: name, parameters, RETURN type. We need not know how a module is implemented. Conversely, the implementation of a module can change, and it should not affect our code—unless the module's header was affected (a parameter was removed, for example). When we write our own programs, the only thing PL/SQL needs to know at compile time is whether our call to a package module conforms to its specification. Of course, when we want to actually execute our application, we should throw some code into the package body.

The separation of specification and body in packages offers us tremendous flexibility in performing high-level design and implementation of our complex applications.

EXAMPLES

Consider the package below named emp_actions. The package specification declares the following types, items, and subprograms:

- types EmpRecTyp and DeptRecTyp
- cursor desc_salary
- exception salary_missing
- functions hire_employee, nth_highest_salary, and rank
- procedures fire_employee and raise_salary

After writing the package, we can develop applications that reference its types, call its subprograms, use its cursor, and raise its exception. When we create the package, it is stored in an Oracle database for general use.

```
CREATE PACKAGE emp_actions AS
  /* Declare externally visible types, cursor, exception. */
  TYPE EmpRecTyp IS RECORD (emp_id INTEGER, salary REAL);
  TYPE DeptRecTyp IS RECORD (dept_id INTEGER, location VARCHAR2);
  CURSOR desc_salary RETURN EmpRecTyp;
  salary_missing EXCEPTION;

  /* Declare externally callable subprograms. */
  FUNCTION hire_employee (
    ename  VARCHAR2,
    job    VARCHAR2,
```

```
    mgr   NUMBER,
    sal   NUMBER,
    comm   NUMBER,
    deptno NUMBER) RETURN INTEGER;
  PROCEDURE fire_employee (emp_id INTEGER);
  PROCEDURE raise_salary (emp_id INTEGER, amount NUMBER);
  FUNCTION nth_highest_salary (n INTEGER) RETURN EmpRecTyp;
END emp_actions;

CREATE PACKAGE BODY emp_actions AS
  number_hired  INTEGER;  — visible only in this package

  /* Fully define cursor specified in package. */
  CURSOR desc_salary RETURN EmpRecTyp IS
    SELECT empno, sal FROM emp ORDER BY sal DESC;

  /* Fully define subprograms specified in package. */
  FUNCTION hire_employee (
    ename  VARCHAR2,
    job   VARCHAR2,
    mgr   NUMBER,
    sal   NUMBER,
    comm   NUMBER,
    deptno NUMBER) RETURN INTEGER IS
    new_empno  INTEGER;
  BEGIN
    SELECT empno_seq.NEXTVAL INTO new_empno FROM dual;
    INSERT INTO emp VALUES (new_empno, ename, job,
      mgr, SYSDATE, sal, comm, deptno);
    number_hired := number_hired + 1;
    RETURN new_empno;
  END hire_employee;

  PROCEDURE fire_employee (emp_id INTEGER) IS
  BEGIN
    DELETE FROM emp WHERE empno = emp_id;
  END fire_employee;

  PROCEDURE raise_salary (emp_id INTEGER, amount NUMBER) IS
```

```
    current_salary NUMBER;
  BEGIN
    SELECT sal INTO current_salary FROM emp
      WHERE empno = emp_id;
    IF current_salary IS NULL THEN
      RAISE salary_missing;
    ELSE
      UPDATE emp SET sal = sal + amount WHERE empno = emp_id;
    END IF;
  END raise_salary;

  FUNCTION nth_highest_salary (n INTEGER) RETURN EmpRecTyp IS
    emp_rec  EmpRecTyp;
  BEGIN
    OPEN desc_salary;
    FOR i IN 1..n LOOP
      FETCH desc_salary INTO emp_rec;
    END LOOP;
    CLOSE desc_salary;
    RETURN emp_rec;
  END nth_highest_salary;

  /* Define local function, available only in package. */
  FUNCTION rank (emp_id INTEGER, job_title VARCHAR2)
    RETURN INTEGER IS
  /* Return rank (highest = 1) of employee in a given
    job classification based on performance rating. */
    head_count INTEGER;
    score      NUMBER;
  BEGIN
    SELECT COUNT(*) INTO head_count FROM emp
      WHERE job = job_title;
    SELECT rating INTO score FROM reviews
      WHERE empno = emp_id;
    score := score / 100;  — maximum score is 100
    RETURN (head_count + 1) - ROUND(head_count * score);
  END rank;
```

```
BEGIN — initialization part starts here
  INSERT INTO emp_audit VALUES (SYSDATE, USER, 'EMP_ACTIONS');
  number_hired := 0;
END emp_actions;
```

Remember: The initialization part of a package is run just once, the first time we refer the package. So, in the last example, only one row is inserted into the database table emp_audit. Likewise, the variable number_hired is initialized only once.

Every time the procedure hire_employee is called, the variable number_hired is updated. However, the count kept by number_hired is session specific. That is, the count reflects the number of new employees processed by one user, *not* the number processed by all users.

In the next example, we package some typical bank transactions. We assume that debit and credit transactions are entered after business hours via automatic teller machines, then applied to accounts the next morning.

```
CREATE PACKAGE bank_transactions AS
  /* Declare externally visible constant. */
  minimum_balance  CONSTANT NUMBER := 100.00;
  /* Declare externally callable procedures. */
  PROCEDURE apply_transactions;
  PROCEDURE enter_transaction (
    acct   NUMBER,
    kind   CHAR,
    amount NUMBER);
END bank_transactions;

CREATE PACKAGE BODY bank_transactions AS
  /* Declare global variable to hold transaction status. */
  new_status  VARCHAR2(70) := 'Unknown';

  /* Use forward declarations because apply_transactions
    calls credit_account and debit_account, which are not
    yet declared when the calls are made. */
  PROCEDURE credit_account (acct NUMBER, credit REAL);
  PROCEDURE debit_account (acct NUMBER, debit REAL);

  /* Fully define procedures specified in package. */
  PROCEDURE apply_transactions IS
  /* Apply pending transactions in transactions table
    to accounts table. Use cursor to fetch rows. */
    CURSOR trans_cursor IS
```

```
    SELECT acct_id, kind, amount FROM transactions
      WHERE status = 'Pending'
      ORDER BY time_tag
      FOR UPDATE OF status; — to lock rows
BEGIN
  FOR trans IN trans_cursor LOOP
    IF trans.kind = 'D' THEN
      debit_account(trans.acct_id, trans.amount);
    ELSIF trans.kind = 'C' THEN
      credit_account(trans.acct_id, trans.amount);
    ELSE
      new_status := 'Rejected';
    END IF;
    UPDATE transactions SET status = new_status
      WHERE CURRENT OF trans_cursor;
  END LOOP;
END apply_transactions;

PROCEDURE enter_transaction (
/* Add a transaction to transactions table. */
  acct   NUMBER,
  kind   CHAR,
  amount NUMBER) IS
BEGIN
  INSERT INTO transactions
    VALUES (acct, kind, amount, 'Pending', SYSDATE);
END enter_transaction;

/* Define local procedures, available only in package. */
PROCEDURE do_journal_entry (
/* Record transaction in journal. */
  acct    NUMBER,
  kind    CHAR,
  new_bal NUMBER) IS
BEGIN
  INSERT INTO journal
    VALUES (acct, kind, new_bal, sysdate);
```

```
  IF kind = 'D' THEN
    new_status := 'Debit applied';
  ELSE
    new_status := 'Credit applied';
  END IF;
END do_journal_entry;

PROCEDURE credit_account (acct NUMBER, credit REAL) IS
/* Credit account unless account number is bad. */
  old_balance NUMBER;
  new_balance NUMBER;
BEGIN
  SELECT balance INTO old_balance FROM accounts
    WHERE acct_id = acct
    FOR UPDATE OF balance; — to lock the row
  new_balance := old_balance + credit;
  UPDATE accounts SET balance = new_balance
    WHERE acct_id = acct;
  do_journal_entry(acct, 'C', new_balance);
EXCEPTION
  WHEN NO_DATA_FOUND THEN
    new_status := 'Bad account number';
  WHEN OTHERS THEN
    new_status := SUBSTR(SQLERRM,1,70);
END credit_account;

PROCEDURE debit_account (acct NUMBER, debit REAL) IS
/* Debit account unless account number is bad or
  account has insufficient funds. */
  old_balance NUMBER;
  new_balance NUMBER;
  insufficient_funds EXCEPTION;
BEGIN
  SELECT balance INTO old_balance FROM accounts
    WHERE acct_id = acct
    FOR UPDATE OF balance; — to lock the row
  new_balance := old_balance - debit;
  IF new_balance >= minimum_balance THEN
```

```
    UPDATE accounts SET balance = new_balance
      WHERE acct_id = acct;
    do_journal_entry(acct, 'D', new_balance);
  ELSE
    RAISE insufficient_funds;
  END IF;
EXCEPTION
  WHEN NO_DATA_FOUND THEN
    new_status := 'Bad account number';
  WHEN insufficient_funds THEN
    new_status := 'Insufficient funds';
  WHEN OTHERS THEN
    new_status := SUBSTR(SQLERRM,1,70);
 END debit_account;
END bank_transactions;
```

Note. In this package, the initialization part is not used.

OVERLOADING

PL/SQL allows two or more packaged subprograms to have the same name. This option is useful when we want a subprogram to accept parameters that have different datatypes. For example, the following package defines two procedures named journalize:

```
CREATE PACKAGE journal_entries AS
  ...
  PROCEDURE journalize (amount NUMBER, trans_date VARCHAR2);
  PROCEDURE journalize (amount NUMBER, trans_date NUMBER );
END journal_entries;

CREATE PACKAGE BODY journal_entries AS
  ...
  PROCEDURE journalize (amount NUMBER, trans_date VARCHAR2) IS
  BEGIN
    INSERT INTO journal
      VALUES (amount, TO_DATE(trans_date, 'DD-MON-YYYY'));
  END journalize;

  PROCEDURE journalize (amount NUMBER, trans_date NUMBER) IS
  BEGIN
```

```
    INSERT INTO journal
      VALUES (amount, TO_DATE(trans_date, 'J'));
  END journalize;
END journal_entries;
```

The first procedure accepts trans_date as a character string, while the second procedure accepts it as a number (the Julian day). Yet, each procedure handles the data appropriately.

Package STANDARD

A package named STANDARD defines the PL/SQL environment. The package specification globally declares types, exceptions, and subprograms, which are available automatically to every PL/SQL program. For example, package STANDARD declares the following built-in function named ABS, which returns the absolute value of its argument:

```
FUNCTION ABS (n NUMBER) RETURN NUMBER;
```

The contents of package STANDARD are directly visible to applications. So, we can call ABS from database triggers, stored subprograms, 3GL applications, and various Oracle tools.

If you redeclare ABS in a PL/SQL program, your local declaration overrides the global declaration. However, we can still call the built-in function by using dot notation, as follows:

```
... STANDARD.ABS(x) ...
```

Most built-in functions are overloaded. For example, package STANDARD contains the following declarations:

```
FUNCTION TO_CHAR (right DATE) RETURN VARCHAR2;
FUNCTION TO_CHAR (left NUMBER) RETURN VARCHAR2;
FUNCTION TO_CHAR (left DATE, right VARCHAR2) RETURN VARCHAR2;
FUNCTION TO_CHAR (left NUMBER, right VARCHAR2) RETURN VARCHAR2;
```

PL/SQL resolves a call to TO_CHAR by matching the number and datatypes of the formal and actual parameters.

PRODUCT-SPECIFIC PACKAGES

Package Name	Description
DBMS_ALERT	Provides support for notification of database events on an asynchronous basis. Registers a process with an alert and then waits for a signal from that alert.
DBMS_AQ	Offers an interface to Oracle/AQ, the Advanced Queueing Facility of Oracle8 (PL/SQL8 only).
DBMS_AQADM	Is used to perform administrative tasks for Oracle/AQ (PL/SQL8 only).

DBMS_DDL	Provides programmatic access to some of the SQL DDL statements.
DBMS_JOB	Submits and manages regularly scheduled jobs for execution inside the database.
DBMS_LOB	Provides a set of programs to manipulate LOBs (large objects) (PL/SQL8 only).
DBMS_LOCK	Lets you create your own user locks in the database.
DBMS_MAIL	Interfaces to Oracle Office (formerly known as Oracle*Mail).
DBMS_OUTPUT	Displays output from PL/SQL programs to the terminal.
DBMS_PIPE	Communicates between different Oracle sessions through a pipe in the RDBMS shared memory.
DBMS_ROWID	Encapsulates information about the structure of the ROWID datatype and allows for conversion between restricted and extended ROWIDs (PL/SQL8 only).
DBMS_SESSION	Provides a programmatic interface to several SQL ALTER SESSION commands and other session-level commands.
DBMS_SNAPSHOT	Provides a programmatic interface through which you can manage snapshots and purge snapshot logs. You might use modules in this package to build scripts to automate maintenance of snapshots.
DBMS_SQL	Provides full support for dynamic SQL within PL/SQL. Dynamic SQL refers to statements that are not prewritten into your programs. They are, instead, constructed at run time as character strings and then passed to the SQL engine for execution.
DBMS_TRANSACTION	Provides a programmatic interface to a number of the SQL transaction statements, such as SET TRANSACTION.
DBMS_UTILITY	Provides the miscellaneous package. It contains various useful utilities, such as FORMAT_CALL_STACK, which returns the current stack of called modules.
UTL_FILE	Allows PL/SQL programs to read from and write to operating system files.

LAB ASSIGNMENT—18

1. Create a package for checking the even or odd numbers.
2. Create a package for displaying the salary in descending order.
3. Create a package for displaying the emp_name in ascending order of their hire date, highest salary and rank.
4. Create a package for bank transactions for account debit and credit.
5. What are the major advantages of package?

12 Oracle Utilities

Objectives :

- ➤ Oracle Enterprise Manager
- ➤ Database Administration Tools
- ➤ Oracle Net 9
- ➤ Partitioning
- ➤ Backup
- ➤ Export
- ➤ Import
- ➤ SQL * Loader Basics

ORACLE ENTERPRISE MANAGER

Oracle Enterprise Manager combines a graphical console, agents, common services, and tools to provide an integrated, comprehensive systems management platform for managing Oracle products. From Enterprise Manager's Console, you can:

- Administer, diagnose, and tune multiple databases.
- Distribute software to multiple servers and clients.
- Schedule jobs on multiple nodes at varying time intervals.
- Monitor objects and events throughout the network.
- Customize your display using multiple graphic maps and groups of network objects, such as nodes and databases.
- Integrate participating Oracle and third-party tools.

Enterprise Manager's Components

Enterprise Manager consists of multiple components that integrate into a powerful and easy-to-use graphical user interface.

- Console
- Intelligent Agents
- Administrator Toolbar
- Database Administration (DBA) Tools and Utilities
- Server Manager Line Mode
- Online Help
- Value-Added Products

Console

The Oracle Enterprise Manager Console is a graphical user interface that provides menus, toolbars, launch palettes, and the framework to access Oracle tools and utilities available through other vendors. The format of the Console and the tools available are determined by the products purchased and user preferences.

Console menus, toolbars, and tool palettes provide access to the Console components and database administration (DBA) applications. The components of the Console include:

- Navigator
- Map
- Job Scheduling
- Event Management
- Repository
- Communication Daemon
- Discovery Cache

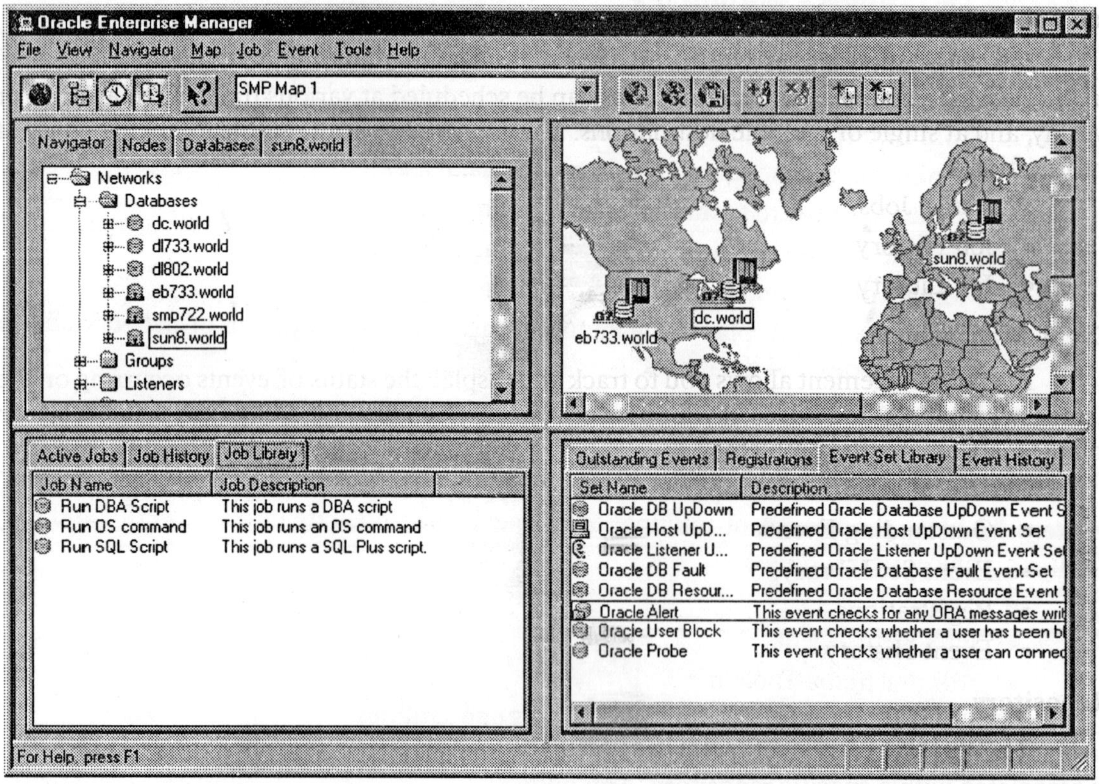

Figure 12.1. Enterprise Manager Console

Navigator

The Navigator discovers and displays a tree list of all the services and objects in a network, providing a direct view of objects such as databases, groups, listeners, and nodes, plus the objects that they contain. While specific types of objects can be viewed in the tree lists of the DBA tools, the Navigator shows all the network objects with their relationships to other objects.

The Navigator tree is populated by the Navigator Service Discovery feature or by reading an Oracle Parallel Server (OPS) topology file (topo_ops.ora) for OPS databases that cannot be added with Service Discovery.

Through the Navigator, you can also launch administration tasks with various objects, such as users and tablespaces. You can also perform some administration tasks in the Navigator, such as creating, editing, or dropping a user.

Map

The Map system allows you to monitor network objects with a graphical display. With the Map system, you can create, save, modify, and recall views of the network. You simply drag and drop objects from the Navigator into the Map view to create groups that you want to monitor.

Job Scheduling

Job Scheduling allows you to manage job scheduling among the databases, listeners, and nodes that you are administering. Jobs can be scheduled at various times, such as daily or weekly, and at single or multiple destinations. The Job window contains the following pages of information:

- Active Jobs
- Job History
- Job Library

Event Management

Event Management allows you to track and display the status of events occurring on the databases, listeners, and nodes in your network system. You can also create jobs that can be run to automatically fix the problems.

The Event window contains the following pages of information:

- Outstanding Events
- Event Set Library
- Registrations
- Event History

Repository

The repository is a set of tables in a user account of an Oracle database. Each administrator is associated with a specific repository. Any information related to the tasks performed by the administrator is stored in that repository. For example, the repository contains information about the jobs submitted and the events monitored by an administrator. The repository also stores information about maps and groups that are created by the administrator.

The repository can be stored in any database accessible to the Console and is automatically created or upgraded when you start the Console. An administrator can log on to the repository database from any machine. The repositories for the administrators do not have to be in the same database.

Note. Only one repository should be set up for each username. Creating identical users with repositories in different databases can cause problems with agent notifications. The intelligent agents use the unique username when tracking jobs and events. The username is appended to the Console location when creating a return address for notifications. When you log in to the Console, you must enter the connect information for the database that contains your repository. The Console looks up the repository associated with your username.

You should not log on to the Console repository multiple times with the same username. A warning displays if you attempt this. You should only ignore the warning if the previous Console session was aborted or a machine was disconnected. When a username is logged in multiple times, agent notifications are sent to most recent login. The information in the repository can be updated by third-party applications that integrate into the Enterprise Manager Console.

Communication Daemon

Enterprise Manager uses a Communication Daemon, which runs on the Console machine, to manage Console communication activities, such as communicating with the intelligent agents running on remote nodes in the system.

The Communication Daemon is also one of the components responsible for discovering services in the network environment that populate the Navigator tree.

Discovery Cache

The discovery cache is an efficient in-memory list of information about services and nodes. While you are logged into the Console, the discovery cache stores the current view of the network, including the user-defined groups and the states of nodes and services. When you log out of the Console, the contents of the discovery cache are stored in the repository.

The next time you start the Console, the discovery cache is loaded with information from the repository and updated with any new information that has been discovered. The new information can include a new service or object discovered by the daemon, or a state that changed since the last login.

The information in the discovery cache can be accessed by third-party applications that integrate into the Enterprise Manager Console.

Intelligent Agents

The agents are intelligent processes running on remote nodes in the network. Oracle Enterprise Manager uses Intelligent Agents to run jobs and monitor events on remote sites. The Intelligent Agent can also be used to discover services on the node where it resides. The Console Communication Daemon communicates with the Intelligent Agents on the remote nodes in the system.

Administrator Toolbar

The Administrator Toolbar provides a quick and easy method for launching database administration tools without the Console. The toolbar is installed with several database administration tools loaded in the toolbar. You can customize the toolbar with the tools that you want to display and the databases that you want to administer.

DATABASE ADMINISTRATION TOOLS

Enterprise Manager provides DBA tools for administrative tasks such as:

- Instance Manager for managing instances and sessions
- Schema Manager for managing schema objects
- Security Manager for setting up users and controlling security
- Storage Manager for managing storage and rollback segments
- SQL*Worksheet for entering and executing DBA commands, SQL statements, and PL/SQL commands

- Backup Manager for backing up an Oracle database
- Data Manager for exporting, importing, and loading data in and out of an Oracle database
- Software Manager for distributing, installing, and de-installing software packages on servers and clients throughout the network

The DBA tools provide both tree and multi-column views of objects. Some of the functions of these tools can also be performed from the Navigator; however, the full set of functions is accessed through each application. For example, to run tasks on a specific group of objects, such as users, you would launch the Security application, which provides complete task-oriented administration of the user objects.

Server Manager Line Mode

For the times when a command line interface is necessary or desirable, Oracle Server Manager provides a conversational line mode. In line mode, you can explicitly execute database administration (DBA) commands on a command line.

You may want to use Server Manager in line mode when a graphical device is unavailable, such as when dialing-in from a non-GUI terminal, or when performing unattended operations, such as running nightly batch jobs or batch scripts that do not require user intervention.

To start Server Manager, enter the operating-specific command name, such as svrmgrl (Unix) or svrmgr30 (Windows NT), at a system prompt.

Online Help

Enterprise Manager uses the Microsoft Windows online help system to provide information for windows and dialog boxes in the Console and database tools. The Help system is context sensitive, but you can also search through the online help contents or index to find a particular topic.

There are several ways of accessing the online Help system. In a main window, such as the Console window, you can access the Help system by pressing F1 or choosing Contents from the Help menu. In a dialog box, select the Help button or press F1 to access the online Help system.

Value Added Products

Oracle produces additional administration utilities that can be integrated into the Enterprise Manager Console. These include:

Oracle Performance Pack

Oracle Performance Pack provides easy-to-use tools for monitoring and diagnosing databases. These utilities include Oracle Performance Manager, Expert, Trace, Tablespace Manager, TopSessions, and Lock Manager. These utilities gather and inspect specific performance statistics that are useful for tuning your database.

Oracle Replication Manager

Oracle Replication Manager enables you to perform many system management tasks for a replicated environment.

Oracle Rdb for NT

Oracle Rdb for NT provides graphical tools to administer an Oracle Rdb database.

Oracle Fail Safe Manager

Oracle Fail Safe Manager is the graphical, high-availability option for Oracle solutions on Windows NT clusters.

Oracle Security Server Manager

Security Server Manager is a security product based on public-key cryptography that supports authentication and authorization in an Oracle network environment.

Oracle Biometrics Manager

Oracle Biometrics Manager administers the biometric credentials (fingerprints) of Oracle database users that use the Oracle Advanced Networking Option.

ORACLE NET 9

Net9 replaces SQL*Net as the networking services and connectivity component for Oracle9i. Net9 has evolved considerably from SQL*Net, supporting application programming interfaces, Java-enabled Internet browsers and network services such as naming and security-hence the name change.

Net9 is the foundation of Oracle's family of networking products, allowing databases and their applications to reside on different computers and communicate as peer applications. Net9 allows clients to communicate with Oracle9 and Oracle8 servers through *service names*, which are easy to remember aliases for database addresses. Setting up Net9 primarily involves creating service names for clients so a simple connect string, such as CONNECT SCOTT/ TIGER@*SERVICE_NAME*, can be used to make a connection from a client to a server.

Depending on your needs, service names can be stored in a variety of places, including the Domain Name System (DNS), configuration files on each client, a centrally located Oracle Names Server, or a non-Oracle naming service. Wherever you choose to store your service names, Net9 offers tools to easily configure service names.

Oracle Connectivity Overview

The main function of Net9 is to establish sessions and transfer data between a client and a server or between two servers. Once a session is established, Net9 acts as a data courier for the client and the server. The connection operation is initiated during any standard database login between the client application and the server, with information such as the client machine name and user name passed to the remote machine.

Sessions are established with the help of a network listener, located on the server. The network listener brokers the client request, handing off the request to the server. Every time a client (or server acting as a client) requests a session with a server, a network listener receives the actual request. The network listener determines the location of the server and enables the client to connect to the server. The network listener is a separate process whose responsibility is to listen for incoming client connection requests and manage the traffic to the server.

Client Request

The user requests a database connection from the server by supplying input (SQL command) through a client-side application such as SQL*Plus. The application sends the request to Net9 to be transported across the network to the server. After the connection request is accepted by the network listener on the server, the client application requests database information from the server.

Server Response to Client Request

The server runs the Oracle9 database software and a Net9 network listener program. The Net9 network listener, through an Oracle Protocol Adapter, accepts connections from client applications on the network.

Net9 on the server delivers the client data transfer request to the Oracle9i database. The database performs the function requested by the user on the client machine. Finally, Net9 transfers the results of the database functions to the client machine.

Architectural Overview

Net9, the networking layer formerly known as SQL*Net, uses the Transparent Network Substrate (TNS) and standard industry network protocols to connect a client to a server and establish an Oracle session. The following figure shows the basic connectivity architecture and process, with a connection request originating from a client side application. The database returns the queried information in the reverse direction.

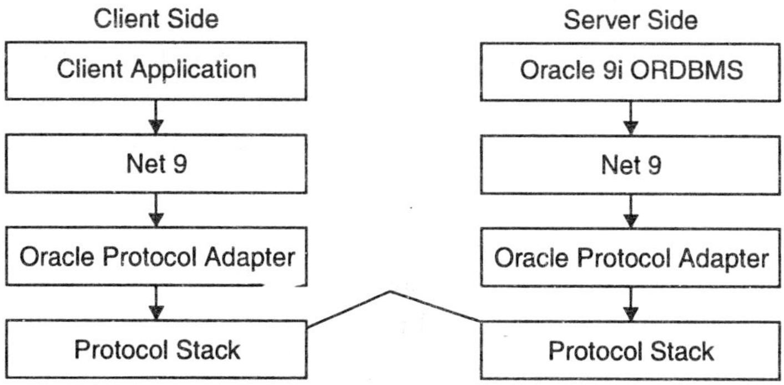

Physical Network

The following is an overview of Oracle network connectivity components:

- Net9
- Oracle Protocol Adapters
- Network-Specific Protocol Stack (third-party component)

Net 9

Net9 is a software layer that is required to communicate between Oracle clients and servers. The role of Net9 is to establish and maintain a connection between the client application and the server and exchange messages between them. It provides both client to server and server to server communications across any network. It enables client tools to access, modify, share, and store data on Oracle9i Servers over a network. The communication between client applications and servers takes place across one or more networks and is referred to as client/server communication.

Transparent Network Substrate (TNS)

The TNS is an underlying layer of Net9 that receives requests and settles all generic connectivity functions such as opening and closing a session or sending and receiving requests or responses. TNS then passes control to an Oracle Protocol Adapter to make the protocol-specific call.

Oracle Protocol Adapters

The Oracle Protocol Adapters are responsible for mapping TNS functionality to industry-standard protocols used in the client/server connection. Each adapter is responsible for mapping the equivalent functions between TNS and a specific protocol.

An Oracle Protocol Adapter translates (or adapts):

- function calls of specific network protocols (such as TCP/IP) into equivalent function calls of the Oracle Transparent Network Substrate (TNS).
- TNS generic function calls into specific function calls for the underlying network protocol.

PARTITIONING

Partitioning addresses the key problem of supporting very large tables and indexes by allowing you to decompose them into smaller and more manageable pieces called *partitions.*

Once partitions are defined, SQL statements can access and manipulate the partitions rather than entire tables or indexes. Partitions are especially useful in data warehouse applications, which commonly store and analyze large amounts of historical data.

All partitions of a table or index have the same logical attributes, although their physical attributes can be different. For example, all partitions in a table share the same column and constraint definitions; and all partitions in an index share the same index columns. However, storage specifications and other physical attributes such as PCTFREE, PCTUSED, INITRANS, and MAXTRANS can vary for different partitions of the same table or index.

Each partition is stored in a separate segment. Optionally, you can store each partition in a separate tablespace, which has the given advantages:

- You can contain the impact of damaged data.
- You can back up and recover each partition independently.
- You can balance I/O load by mapping partitions to disk drives.

In Figure 12.2, the **sales** table contains historical data divided by week number into 13 four-week partitions. This SQL statement creates the partitioned table:

```
CREATE TABLE sales ( acct_no          NUMBER(5),
                     acct_name        CHAR(30),
                     amount_of_sale   NUMBER(6),
                     week_no          INTEGER )
     PARTITION BY RANGE ( week_no ) ...
        (PARTITION sales1 VALUES LESS THAN ( 4 ) TABLESPACE ts0,
         PARTITION sales2 VALUES LESS THAN ( 8 ) TABLESPACE ts1,
         ...
         PARTITION sales13 VALUES LESS THAN ( 52 ) TABLESPACE ts12 );
```

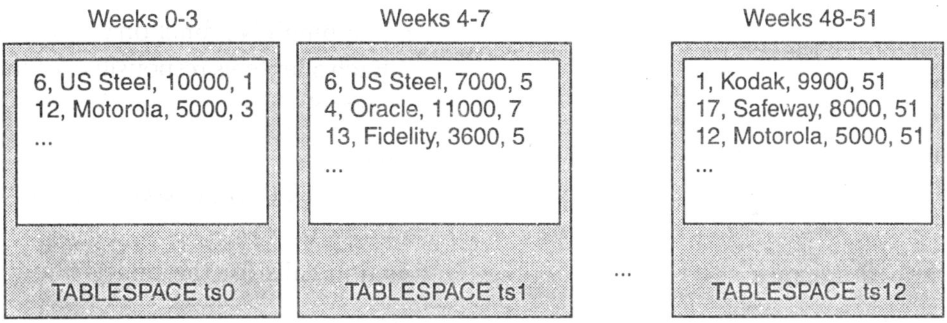

Figure 12.2. SALES Table Partitioned by Week

Partition Pruning

The Oracle server incorporates the intelligence to explicitly recognize partitions. This knowledge is exploited in optimizing SQL statements to mark the partitions that need to be accessed, eliminating ("pruning") unnecessary partitions from access by those SQL statements.

For each SQL statement, depending on the selection criteria specified, unneeded partitions can be eliminated. For example, if a query only involves Q1 sales data, there is no need to retrieve data for the remaining three quarters. Such intelligent pruning can dramatically reduce the data volume, resulting in substantial improvements in query performance.

If the optimizer determines that the selection criteria used for pruning are satisfied by all the rows in the accessed partition, it removes those criteria from the predicate list (WHERE clause) during evaluation in order to improve performance.

Partition pruning can eliminate index partitions even when the underlying table's partitions cannot be eliminated, if the index and table are partitioned on different columns.

You can often improve the performance of operations on large tables by creating partitioned indexes, which reduce the amount of data that your SQL statements need to access or modify.

The ability to prune unneeded partitions from SQL statements increases performance and availability for many purposes, including partition-level load, purge, backup, restore, reorganization, and index building.

BACKUP

Simply speaking, a database backup is a representative copy of data. When the original data is lost, you can use the backup to reconstruct lost information (the physical files that constitute your Oracle database). This copy includes important parts of your database, such as the control file, archive logs and datafiles-structures described later in this chapter and throughout this book. In the event of a media failure, your database backup is the key to successfully recovering your data.

Why Are Backups Important?

Imagine the magnitude of lost revenue (not to mention the degree of customer dissatisfaction!) if the production database of a catalog company, express delivery service, bank or airline suddenly became unavailable, even for just 5 or 10 minutes; or, if you lose datafiles due to media failure and cannot restore or recover them because you do not have a backup. From your enterprise's perspective, the results may be quite grim. You must restore and recover your data quickly to resume operations. The key to your success in this situation is a well-defined backup and recovery strategy.

When to Take Backups

You should tailor your backup strategy to the needs of your business. For example, if it is acceptable to lose data in the event of a disk failure, you may not need to perform frequent backups. What if your database must be available twenty-four hours a day, seven days a week? In this case, your database would have to be frequently backed up. The frequency of your backups and types of backups performed is determined in large part by the needs of your business.

Types of Failures

An unfortunate aspect of every database system is the possibility of a system or hardware failure. The most common types of failure are described below.

Failure type	Description
statement and process failure	Statement failure occurs when there is a logical failure in the handling of a statement in an Oracle program (for example, the statement is not a valid SQL construction). When statement failure occurs, the effects (if any) of the statement are automatically undone by Oracle and control is returned to the user. A *process failure* is a failure in a user process accessing Oracle, such as an abnormal disconnection or process termination. The failed user process cannot continue work, although Oracle and other user processes can.

instance failure	*Instance failure* occurs when a problem arises that prevents an instance (system global area and background processes) from continuing work. Instance failure may result from a hardware problem such as a power outage, or a software problem such as an operating system crash. When an instance failure occurs, the data in the buffers of the system global area is not written to the datafiles. Oracle automatically recovers from instance failure when the database opens.
user or application error	User errors can require a database to be recovered to a point in time before the error occurred. For example, a user might accidentally delete data from a table that is still required (for example, payroll taxes). To allow recovery from user errors and accommodate other unique recovery requirements, Oracle provides for exact point-in-time recovery. For example, if a user accidentally deletes data, the database can be recovered to the instant in time before the data was deleted.
media (disk) failure	An error can arise when trying to write or read a file that is required to operate the database. This is called disk failure because there is a physical problem reading or writing physical files on disk. A common example is a disk head crash, which causes the loss of all files on a disk drive. Different files may be affected by this type of disk failure, including the datafiles, the redo log files, and the control files. Also, because the database instance cannot continue to function properly, the data in the database buffers of the system global area cannot be permanently written to the datafiles.

EXPORT / IMPORT

Export writes data from an Oracle database into a transportable operating system file. Import reads data from this file back into an Oracle database. You can use Export and Import to accomplish the following tasks:

- move data between Oracle databases, even if the databases are on different systems or platforms
- move data from one tablespace or schema to another
- repartition data in tables
- store definitions of database objects (such as tables, clusters, and indexes) with or without the data
- archive inactive data or store temporary data
- store Oracle data in operating system files outside a database
- upgrade to new releases of Oracle
- back up entire Oracle databases or back up only tables whose data changed since the last export, using an incremental export or a cumulative export
- selectively back up parts of a database in a way that requires less storage space than a system backup
- restore a database by importing from incremental or cumulative exports
- restore tables that were dropped, if they had been exported previously

- move data between older and newer versions or releases of Oracle
- save space or reduce fragmentation on the platform used by the Oracle database

Export

Export provides a simple way for you to transfer data objects between Oracle database. Export extracts the object definitions and table data from an Oracle database and stores them in an Oracle binary-format Export dump file located typically on disk or tape.

Such files can then be FTPed or physically transported (in the case of tape) to a different site and used, with the Import utility, to transfer data between databases that are on machines not connected via a network or as backups in addition to normal backup procedures.

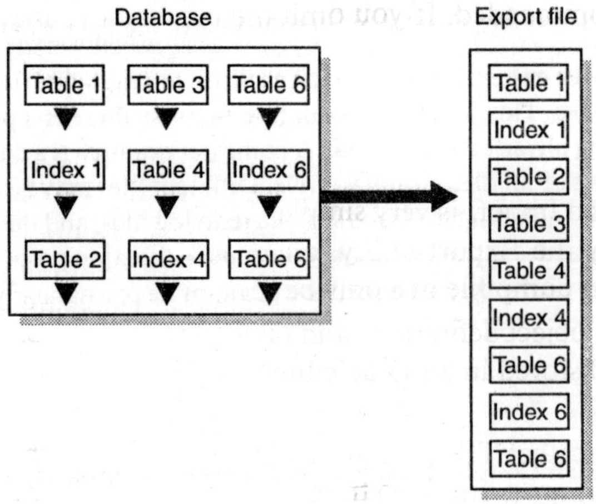

Figure 12.3. Exporting a Database

Invoking Export

You can invoke Export in one of the following ways:

- Enter the following command:
- exp *username/password* PARFILE=*filename*

  PARFILE is a file containing the export parameters you typically use. If you use different parameters for different databases, you can have multiple parameter files. This is the recommended method.
- Enter the command
- exp username/password

  followed by the parameters you need.

Note. The number of parameters cannot exceed the maximum length of a command line on the system.

Enter only the command exp username/password to begin an interactive session and let Export prompt you for the information it needs. The interactive method provides less functionality than the parameter-driven method. It exists for backward compatibility.

You can use a combination of the first and second options. That is, you can list parameters both in the parameters file and on the command line. In fact, you can specify the same parameter in both places. The position of the PARFILE parameter and other parameters on the command line determines what parameters override others. For example, assume the parameters file params.dat contains the parameter INDEXES=Y and

Export is invoked with the following line:

```
exp system/manager PARFILE=params.dat INDEXES=N
```

In this case, because INDEXES=N occurs *after* PARFILE=params.dat, INDEXES=N overrides the value of the INDEXES parameter in the PARFILE.

You can specify the username and password in the parameter file, although, for security reasons, this is not recommended. If you omit the username/password combination, Export prompts you for it.

IMPORT

The basic concept behind Import is very simple. Import inserts the data objects extracted from one Oracle database by the Export utility (and stored in an Export dump file) into another Oracle database. Export dump file can only be read by Import.

Import reads the object definitions and table data that the Export utility extracted from an Oracle database and stored in an Oracle binary-format Export dump file located typically on disk or tape.

Such files are typically FTPed or physically transported (in the case of tape) to a different site and used, with the Import utility, to transfer data between databases that are on machines not connected via a network or as backups in addition to normal backup procedures.

Order of Import

Table objects are imported as they are read from the export file. The export file contains objects in the following order:

1. table definitions
2. table data
3. table indexes
4. integrity constraints, triggers, and bitmap indexes

First, new tables are created. Then, data is imported and indexes are built. Then triggers are imported, integrity constraints are enabled on the new tables, and any bitmap indexes are built. This sequence prevents data from being rejected due to the order in which tables are imported. This sequence also prevents redundant triggers from firing twice on the same data (once when it was originally inserted and again during the import).

For example, if the EMP table has a referential integrity constraint on the DEPT table and the EMP table is imported first, all EMP rows that reference departments that have not yet been imported into DEPT would be rejected if the constraints were enabled.

When data is imported into existing tables however, the order of import can still produce referential integrity failures. In the situation just given, if the EMP table already existed and referential integrity constraints were in force, many rows could be rejected.

A similar situation occurs when a referential integrity constraint on a table references itself. For example, if SCOTT's manager in the EMP table is DRAKE, and DRAKE's row has not yet been loaded, SCOTT's row will fail, even though it would be valid at the end of the import.

Suggestion: For the reasons mentioned previously, it is a good idea to disable referential constraints when importing into an existing table. You can then re-enable the constraints after the import is completed.

Invoking Import

You can invoke Import in three ways:

- Enter the following command:
- imp *username/password* PARFILE=*filename*

  PARFILE is a file containing the Import parameters you typically use. If you use different parameters for different databases, you can have multiple parameter files.
- Enter the command

  imp username/password <parameters>

  replacing <parameters> with various parameters you intend to use. Note that the number of parameters cannot exceed the maximum length of a command line on your operating system.
- Enter the command

  imp username/password

to begin an interactive session, and let Import prompt you for the information it needs. Note that the interactive method does not provide as much functionality as the parameter-driven method. It exists for backward compatibility.

You can use a combination of the first and second options. That is, you can list parameters both in the parameters file and on the command line. In fact, you can specify the same parameter in both places. The position of the PARFILE parameter and other parameters on the command line determines what parameters override others. For example, assume the parameters file params.dat contains the parameter INDEXES=Y and Import is invoked with the following line:

```
imp system/manager PARFILE=params.dat INDEXES=N
```

In this case, because INDEXES=N occurs *after* PARFILE=params.dat, INDEXES=N overrides the value of the INDEXES parameter in the PARFILE.

You can specify the username and password in the parameter file, although, for security reasons, this is not recommended. If you omit the username and password, Import prompts you for it.

SQL*LOADER BASICS

SQL*Loader loads data from external files into tables in an Oracle database. SQL*Loader has many features of the DB2 Load Utility from IBM, as well as several other features that give it additional power and flexibility. SQL*Loader accepts input data in a variety of formats, can perform filtering (selectively loading records based upon their data values), and can load data into multiple Oracle database tables during the same load session.

Figure 12.4 shows the basic components of a SQL*Loader session in operation.

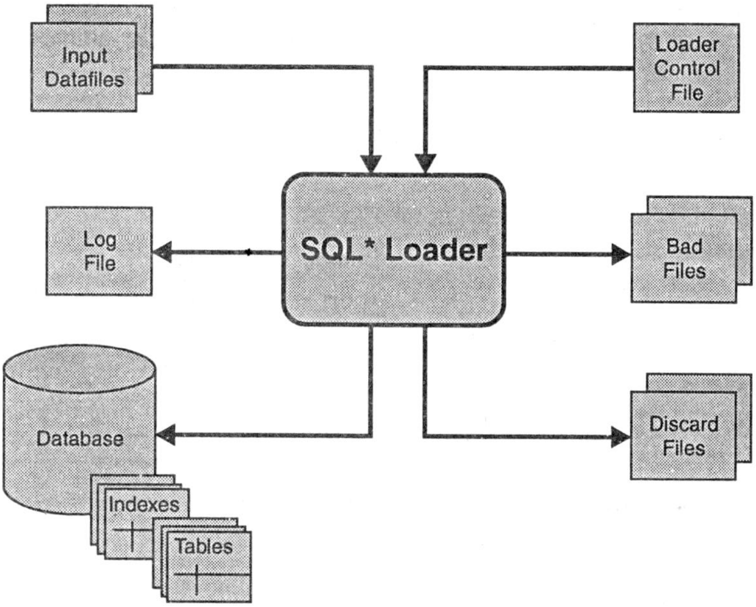

Figure 12.4. SQL*Loader Overview

SQL*Loader takes a *control file* as its input, which describes the load to SQL*Loader. The control file also specifies the *input datafile*(s).

As it executes, SQL*Loader produces a *log file* where it writes information about the load. If records are rejected (typically because of incorrect data), it produces a *bad file* containing the rejected records. It also may produce a *discard file* containing records that did not meet the specified selection criteria.

SQL*Loader can:

- Load data from multiple input datafiles of different file types
- Handle fixed-format, delimited-format, and variable-length records
- Manipulate data fields with SQL functions before inserting the data into database columns
- Support a wide range of datatypes, including DATE, BINARY, PACKED DECIMAL, and ZONED DECIMAL
- Load multiple tables during the same run, loading selected rows into each table

- Combine multiple physical records into a single logical record
- Handle a single physical record as multiple logical records
- Generate unique, sequential key values in specified columns
- Use the operating system's file or record management system to access datafiles
- Load data from disk, tape, or named pipes
- Thoroughly report errors so you can easily adjust and load all records
- Use high-performance "direct" loads to load data directly into database files without Oracle processing

SQL*Loader Control File

The control file, written in SQL*Loader data definition language (DDL), specifies how to interpret the data, what tables and columns to insert the data into, and may also include input datafile management information.

The data for SQL*Loader to load into an Oracle database must be in files accessible to SQL*Loader (typically a file in a file system, on tape, or a named pipe, depending on the platform). SQL*Loader requires information about the data to be loaded which provides instructions for mapping the input data to columns of a table. These instructions are written in SQL*Loader DDL, typically by the DBA using the system text editor. Following are some of the items that are specified in the SQL*Loader control file:

- Specifications for loading logical records into tables
- Field condition specifications
- Column and field specifications
- Data-field position specifications
- Datatype specifications
- Bind array size specifications
- Specifications for setting columns to null or zero
- Specifications for loading all-blank fields
- Specifications for trimming blanks and tabs
- Specifications to preserve white space
- Specifications for applying SQL operators to fields

SQL*Loader DDL is upwardly compatible with the DB2 Load Utility from IBM. Normally you can use a control file for the DB2 Load Utility as a control file for SQL*Loader.

13 Oracle Forms

Objectives :

- ➤ Introduction
- ➤ Prerequisites
- ➤ Developer Tools
- ➤ The Oracle Forms Designer Main Screen
- ➤ Forms Design
- ➤ Creating and Running a Form with a Single Block
- ➤ Creating and Master—Detail Form
- ➤ List of Values (LOV) and Non-Base Table Fields
- ➤ Oracle Forms Program Units and Stored Program Units
- ➤ Adding Alerts

  Lab Assignment-19

INTRODUCTION

Developer/2000 is an Oracle tool that helps to create forms and reports based on the tables that you have created using Designer/2000. We can use Developer/2000 to:

- Design and customize forms and reports.
- Add various functionality, like radio buttons, combo boxes, and list of values to make your forms and reports more user friendly.
- Write triggers on your objects to add functionality to them and capture errors.

PREREQUISITES

Use the Oracle SQL*Plus tool to create three tables named EMPLOYEE, DEPARTMENT and DEPENDENT with the following attributes.

Table 13.1. EMPLOYEE Table

Attribute	Data Type
FNAME	VARCHAR(8)
MINIT	VARCHAR(2)
LNAME	VARCHAR(8)
SSN	NUMBER(12)
BDATE	DATE
ADDRESS	VARCHAR(30)
SEX	VARCHAR(1)
SALARY	NUMBER(7)
SUPERSSN	NUMBER(12)
DNO	NUMBER(2)

Table 13.2. DEPARTMENT Table

Attribute	Data Type
DNAME	VARCHAR(15)
DNUMBER	NUMBER(2)
MGRSSN	NUMBER(12)
MGRSTARTDATE	DATE

Table 13.3. DEPENDENT Table

Attribute	Data Type
ESSN	NUMBER(12)
DEPENDENT_NAME	VARCHAR(10)
SEX	VARCHAR(1)
BDATE	DATE
RELATIONSHIP	VARCHAR(10)

The following CREATE TABLE and INSERT statements can be used to create the above tables and insert some baseline data using the Oracle SQL*Plus tool. Note that different versions of Oracle accept either 2 digit or 4 digit year designations in the DATE datatype. The INSERT statements below should be formatted accordingly.

```
CREATE TABLE employee
(FNAME          VARCHAR2(15),
MINIT           VARCHAR2(2),
LNAME           VARCHAR2(15),
SSN             NUMBER(12) NOT NULL,
BDATE           DATE,
```

```
ADDRESS              ARCHAR2(35),
SEX                  VARCHAR2(1),
SALARY               NUMBER(7) NOT NULL,
SUPERSSN             NUMBER(12),
DNO                  NUMBER(2) NOT NULL) ;
ALTER TABLE employee ADD CONSTRAINT pk_employee
PRIMARY KEY (ssn);
CREATE TABLE DEPARTMENT
(DNAME               VARCHAR2(15),
DNUMBER              NUMBER(2) NOT NULL.
MGRSSN               NUMBER(12),
MGRSTARTDATE DATE) ;

ALTER TABLE department ADD CONSTRAINT pk_department
PRIMARY KEY (dnumber);
CREATE TABLE DEPENDENT
(ESSN                NUMBER(12),
DEPENDENT_NAME       VARCHAR2(15),
SEX                  VARCHAR2(1),
BDATE                DATE,
RELATIONSHIP         VARCHAR2(12)) ;
ALTER TABLE dependent ADD CONSTRAINT pk_dependent
PRIMARY KEY (essn, dependent_name);
ALTER TABLE dependent ADD CONSTRAINT fk_employee
FOREIGN KEY (essn) REFERENCES employee (ssn);
ALTER TABLE employee ADD CONSTRAINT fk_department
FOREIGN KEY (dno) REFERENCES department (dnumber);
INSERT INTO DEPARTMENT VALUES ('RESEARCH', 5, 333445555, '22-MAY-1978') ;
INSERT INTO DEPARTMENT VALUES ('ADMINISTRATION', 4, 987654321,
'01-JAN-1985') ;
INSERT INTO DEPARTMENT VALUES ('HEADQUARTERS', 1, 888665555,
'19-JUN-1971') ;
INSERT INTO EMPLOYEE VALUES
('JOHN','B','SMITH',123456789,'09-JAN-1955','731 FONDREN, HOUSTON, TX',
'M',30000,333445555,5) ;
INSERT INTO EMPLOYEE VALUES
('FRANKLIN','T','WONG',333445555,'08-DEC-1945','638 VOSS,HOUSTON TX',
'M',40000,888665555,5) ;
INSERT INTO EMPLOYEE VALUES
('ALICIA','J','ZELAYA',999887777,'19-JUL-1958','3321 CASTLE, SPRING, TX',
'F',25000,987654321,4) ;
```

DEVELOPER TOOLS

Oracle Developer contains 3 main components:

1. Oracle Forms - For designing data entry forms.
2. Oracle Reports - For designing reports.
3. Oracle Graphics - For designing graphics such as charts that can be added to forms or reports.

Additional components include:

1. Procedure Builder - An integrated development environment to write and debug stored procedures (program units) for use in the Oracle database or in any of the Developer tools.
2. Query Builder - A GUI based query builder tool. Queries can be stored in the data dictionary or in a file system for later use and sharing.
3. Schema Builder - A GUI tool for creating and modifying tables, views and constraints.
4. Translation Builder - A tool for creating foreign language versions of applications written in Developer.
5. Project Builder - A software development project management system that manages source code for all Developer components.
6. PECS - The Oracle Performance Evaluation/Collection System - For profiling the execution and performance of applications developed with Oracle tools.
7. Discoverer - A data browsing tool that can be customized for end-users.

In the following section, the procedures to run Oracle Forms under MS Windows 95/98/NT/2000 will be given.

Starting Developer tools under Windows 95/98/NT/2000

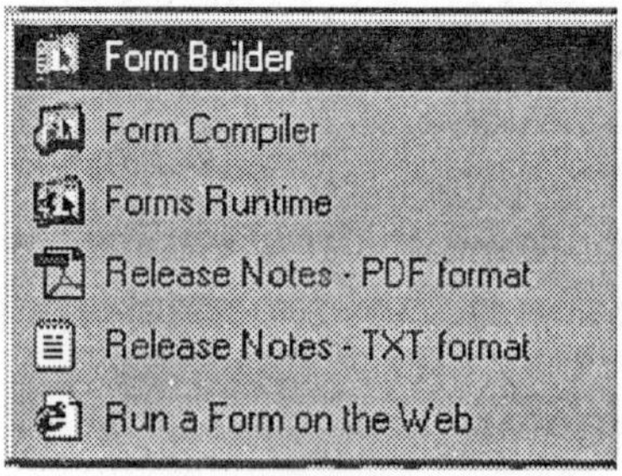

A typical installation of Developer creates several folders under the Start Programs menu. The main folders for the Developer programs for Oracle Forms 6i are found under the menu item: Oracle Forms 6i and include these items on next page.

To run Oracle Forms 6i under Windows 95/98/NT/2000, click on the Start -> Programs -> Oracle Forms 6i -> Form Builder menu item.

To run Oracle Reports under Windows 95/98/NT/2000, click on the Start -> Programs -> Oracle Reports 6i -> Report Builder menu item.

To run Oracle Graphics under Windows 95/98/NT/2000, click on the Start -> Programs -> Oracle Forms & Reports 6i -> Graphics Builder menu item.

For older versions of Oracle Developer the start menu would might have items such as: Developer 2000 R2.1 or Developer 2000 R2.0 and so on.

THE ORACLE FORMS DESIGNER MAIN SCREEN

Once the appropriate menu item has been clicked on (for Windows 95/98/NT/2000), the Oracle Forms Builder Welcome Screen will appear:

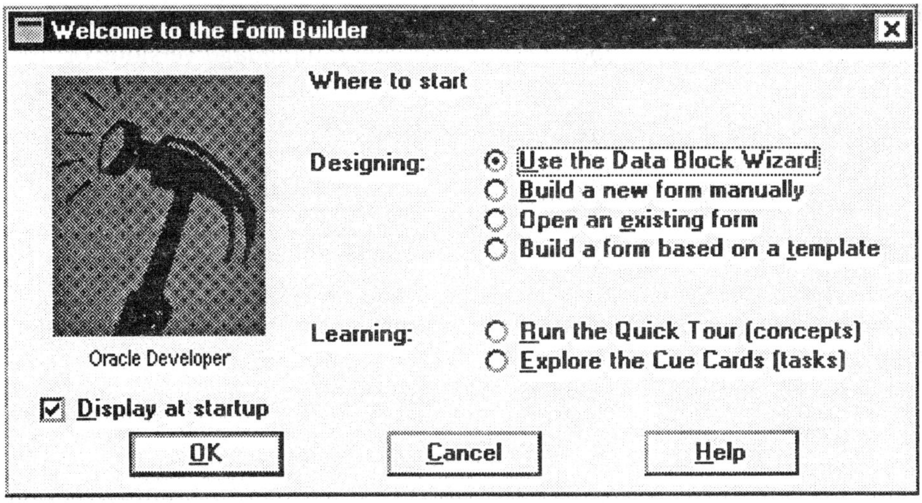

Forms 6.0 displays this welcome screen as a quick way to start working and designing forms.

To continue to the Object Navigator from the Welcome screen, click on the Cancel button or select the "Build a form Manually" option and click OK. In either case, the Object Navigator will appear.

Oracle Forms Object Navigator

After starting up Oracle Forms, the main screen will be presented.

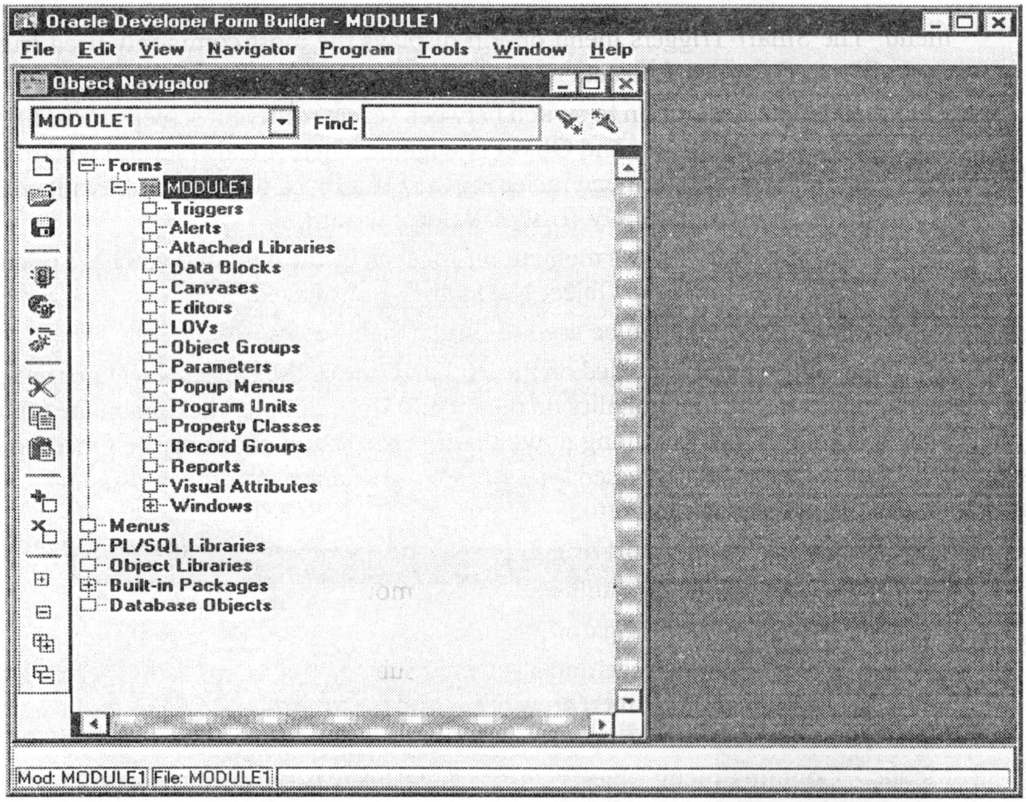

This screen is called the *Object Navigator* and displays all of the form elements, data blocks, menu items, user defined code libraries, built-in procedures and functions, and database objects (tables, views). The display is in the form of a collapsible tree. In general, clicking on a + will expand the current item to show its details. Clicking on a - will collapse the current list details.

The menu bar across the top provides access to almost all of the features of Oracle Forms.

- The File menu has options to create, open, save and print forms. This menu also includes an option to connect to the database and the Administration option that is used to compile forms and menu code. The last option on the File menu is the Exit option that will exit Oracle Forms Builder.
- The Edit menu has options to cut, copy and paste objects, to invoke an editor and to undo an operation.
- The View menu toggles the object navigator display between visual elements and ownership elements.
- The Navigator menu has items that control the display of the object navigator including expanding and collapsing tree branches. The Navigator menu can also be used to create and delete objects using the Create and Delete menu options respectively.
- The Program menu has items that control form compilation, generation and execution (Run). Triggers, Procedures and other PL/SQL code can also be created from this

menu. The Smart Triggers menu option displays the most commonly used triggers according to the type of object currently selected in the object navigator.

- The Tools menu has option to switch between several different screens including the Layout editor, Menu editor and Object Navigator. There are also several wizards that can be launched from this menu including the Data Block wizard, the Layout wizard, the Chart wizard and the LOV (List of Values) wizard.

  The Windows menu displays menu items for each of the windows you have open. By default, only one item - the Object Navigator - is displayed.
- Finally, the Help menu can be used to display help topics.

By default, a button bar is provided on the left hand side of the Object Navigator window. Each button duplicates some functionality on the menus. For example, clicking on the top icon (an opened folder) is the same as pulling down the File menu and choosing the Open option. To see what a button might do if pressed, place the mouse cursor over the button and a short message will appear describing the button's function.

In Developer 6.0, a form, report or graphic is generally referred to as a *Module*.

When first starting the Forms Builder, a default module is created called: MODULE1

The content of the Object Navigator is broken down into 6 major sections:

1. Forms - Contains form objects and all of their sub-objects such as data blocks, triggers, alerts, canvases, program units (procedures and functions), parameters and windows. More than one form can be open at a time.
2. Menus - Contains menu objects and all of their sub-objects such as menu items, parameters and program units. More than one menu can be open at a time.
3. PL/SQL Libraries - These are libraries of PL/SQL code (stored either in the database or in .plb files). Libraries can be shared among different forms and among different developers
4. Object Libraries - These are libraries containing a collection of objects (anything that can appear on a form).
5. Built-in Packages - Lists all of the packages (PL/SQL procedures) available by default to all forms, reports, etc.
6. Database Objects - Lists all of the database objects (Tables, Views, PL/SQL Libraries, and Stored Program Units) in the user's Oracle database schema.

As objects are created, they are displayed under the appropriate section. Context sensitive menus can be displayed for each object by clicking on an object with the right mouse button.

Connecting to the Database

The first step in working with any of the Developer tools is to establish a connection to an Oracle database. This is accomplished by pulling down the File menu and selecting the Connect menu item. Fill in your Oracle Username and Oracle Password (press the tab key to move between the fields).

For the Database field, type in the service name for your Oracle database. For example, if you are using Personal Oracle Lite, the Database: would be ODBC:POLITE. If you have a local database running on the same machine, you may be able to connect directly to it by leaving this field blank. If you are working in a client/server environment where the Oralce server resides on another machine, you will have to configure the Oracle Net9 middleware to establish a connection with that server. You would then supply the Net9 service name in the Database field. Alternatively, contact your system administrator to learn the service name for your Oracle database and provide that information in the Database: field.

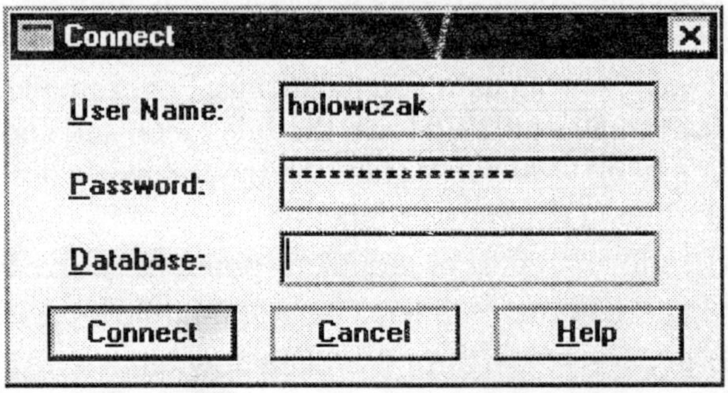

Click on the Connect button to complete the connection (Under some versions of UNIX, the button is labeled OK). If the user name or password is mistyped or incorrect, the dialog box will be re-displayed. Be sure to provide your Oracle username and password (not your UNIX host or Local Area Network password).

Each time any of the Developer Builder tools are executed, the first step will be to connect to an Oracle database in this fashion.

FORMS DESIGN

A typical database schema contains dozens of tables, each with several columns of various data types. We develop applications (forms, reports, menus, etc.) to make the job of manipulating data in those tables easier for users. In Oracle Forms, a form (or data entry form) acts like a window into the database schema. An individual focuses the attention of the user to one or a few of the tables at a time. In addition, a form can give prompts so the user knows what kind of input is expected and how data is to be entered and manipulated.

By default, every form in Oracle Forms has the capability to query existing data in a table, modify existing data and add new data (records) to the table. A form is built up using one or more *data blocks* that correspond to tables in the database. Fields within the data block correspond to columns in the database table. A data block is similar to a DataWindow object in PowerBuilder. In the next figure, a typical form is shown.

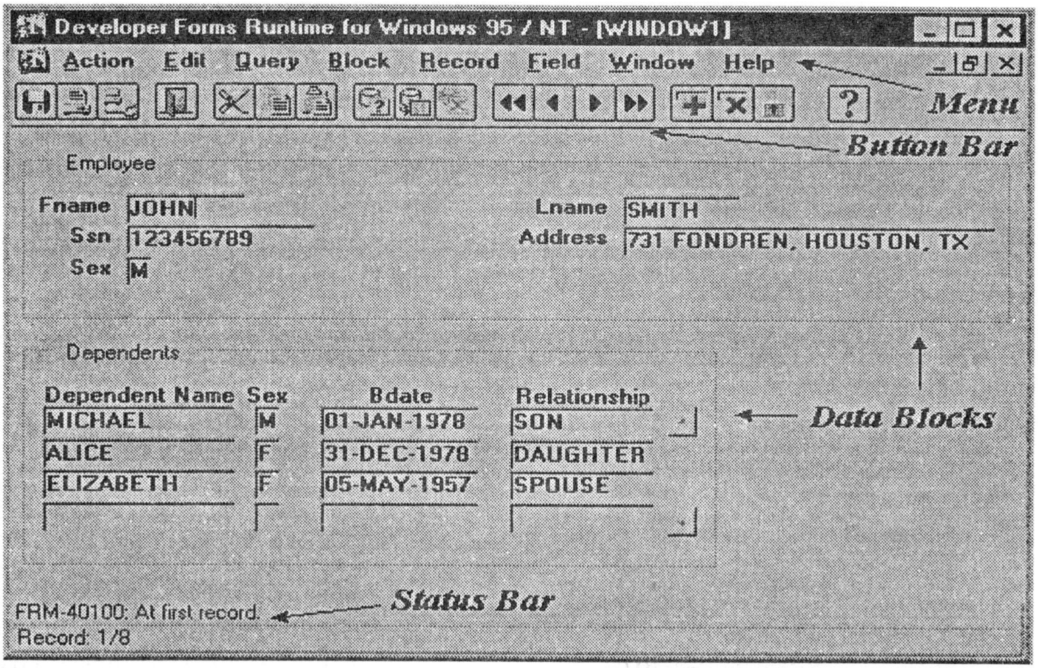

This form has two data blocks, one for the EMPLOYEE table, and one for the DEPENDENT table. These data blocks are arranged in a *Master/Detail* setup where a single Employee record (the master) is associated with one or more Dependents records (the details).

By default, forms also gives a button bar and a menu. These can be used to scroll through the records in a block, navigate between blocks, set up and perform queries against the tables, insert, update and delete records, clear the form and exit the form. Finally, at the bottom of each form is a status bar that displays any relevant prompts or error messages and an indication of the records in the current data block.

CREATING AND RUNNING A FORM WITH A SINGLE BLOCK

In this section, the basic steps for creating a basic data entry and query form for a single database table will be covered.

In general, a *Data Block* on a form corresponds to a table in the database. This is called the *Base Table* for the data block. For each table displayed on the form, a new data block will be created. For this example, only one data block will be created for the EMPLOYEE table.

A block appears on a *Canvas* which is contained in a *Window*. There are many options to control multiple canvas views and multiple windows per form. In these examples, we concentrate on a simple arrangement using a single canvas and a single window.

There are a number of ways to create a data block. One way is to manually define the base table and columns, and their positions on the form. While this is possible, it can be very tedious.

Oracle Forms 6.0 provides two wizards (programs that guide the developer in performing common tasks) to create data blocks:

1. The *Data Block wizard* guides the developer through the steps of choosing a base table and columns.
2. The *Layout wizard* guides the developer through arranging the base table and columns on the form.

Creating a New Block

To create a new block, pull down the Tools menu and select the Data Block wizard menu item. The following dialog box will appear:

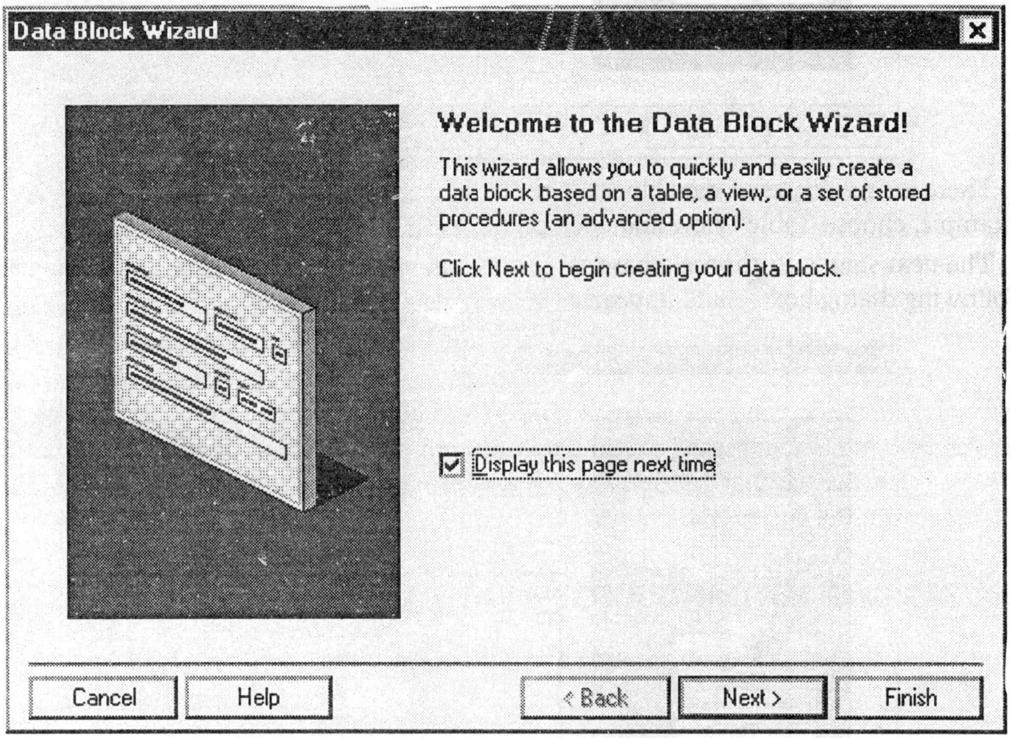

Click on the Next button. The following dialog box will appear:

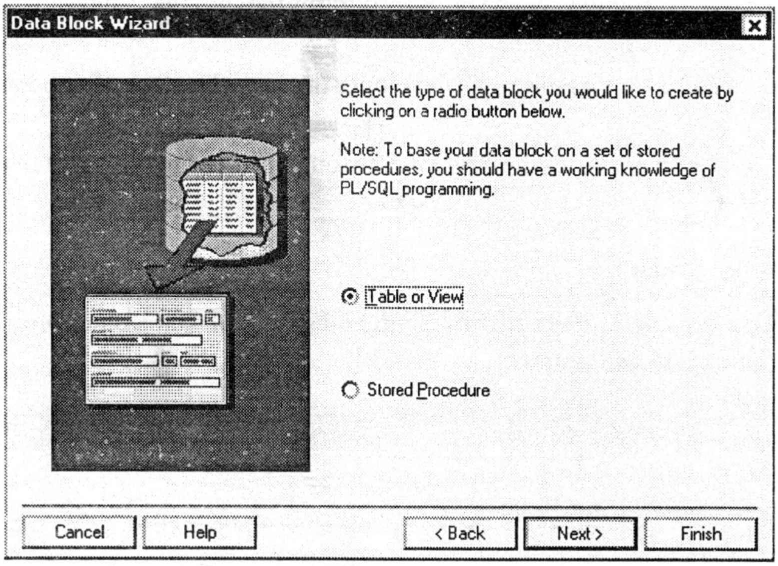

There are two types of data blocks that can be created. Table/View and Procedures. For this example, choose Table/View and click on the Next button.

The next step is to choose a base table and columns that will belong to the data block. The following dialog box should appear:

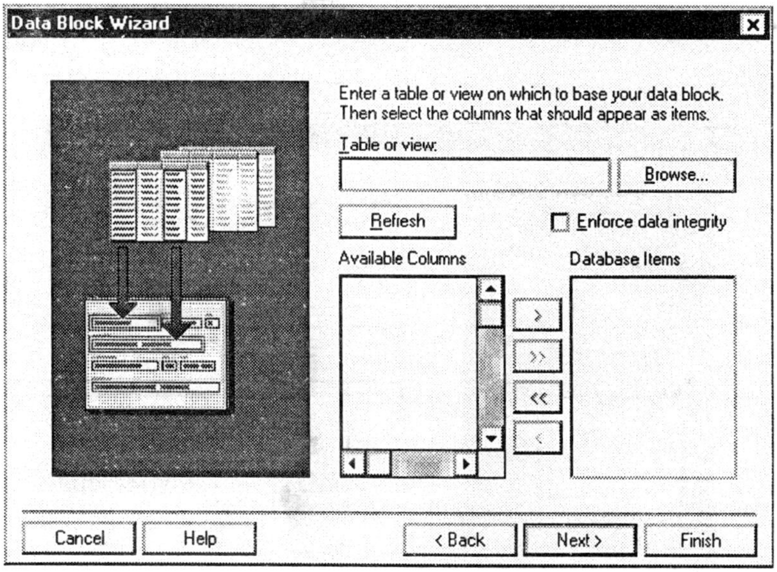

To associate a database table with the block, click on the Browse... button to the right of the Table or View field. The following dialog box will pop up:

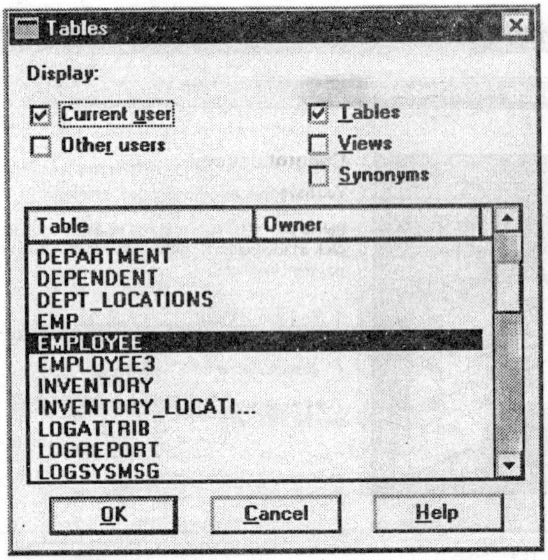

Make sure the Current User and Tables buttons are selected A list of your tables will appear. Highlight the name of the database table (EMPLOYEE in this example) and click on the OK button.

The wizard should reappear with the name of the table and a list of available columns displayed. To include a column in the data block, highlight the column name and click on the right arrow. The name of the column should move over to the right hand side.

For this example, select the FNAME, LNAME, SSN, BDATE, SALARY and DNO as in the following figure:

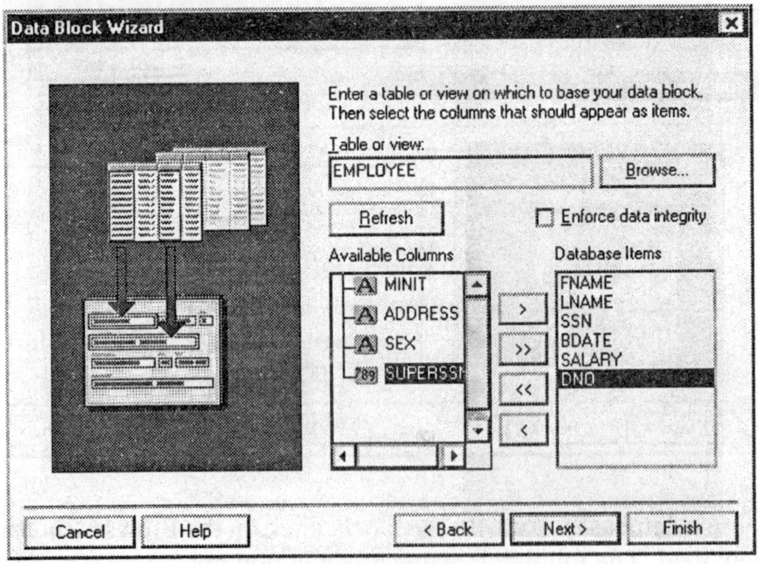

Click on the Next button, and the final dialog box for the Data Block wizard will appear:

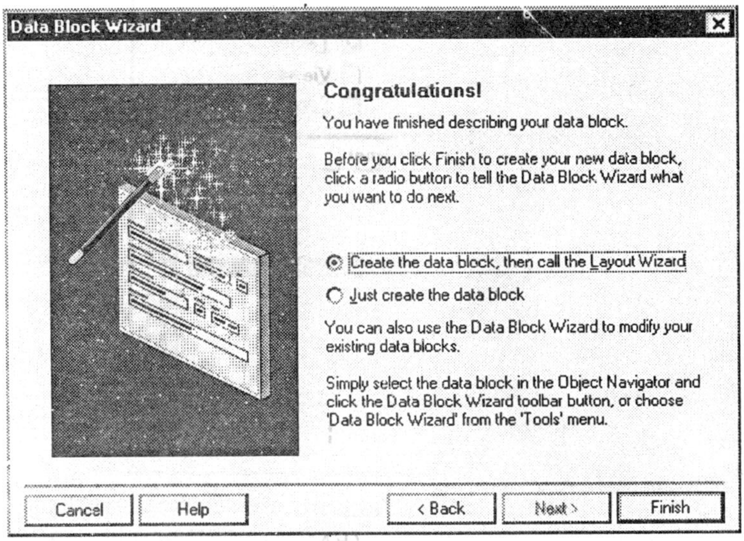

In this example, we want to continue on to the Layout wizard in order to specify how the new form will appear. Make sure the Create the block, then call the Layout wizard option is selected and click on the Finish button.

The data block will be created (as can be seen in the Object Navigator in the background). The objects created include the EMPLOYEE data block containing items for each of the columns that were selected in the third step of the wizard.

Once the new data block and items are created, the first dialog box in the Layout wizard will appear:

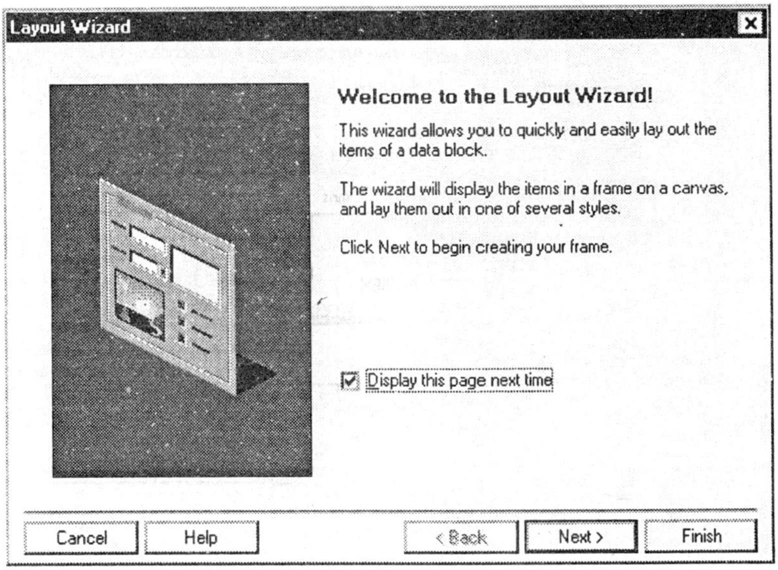

Click on the Next button and the following dialog box will appear:

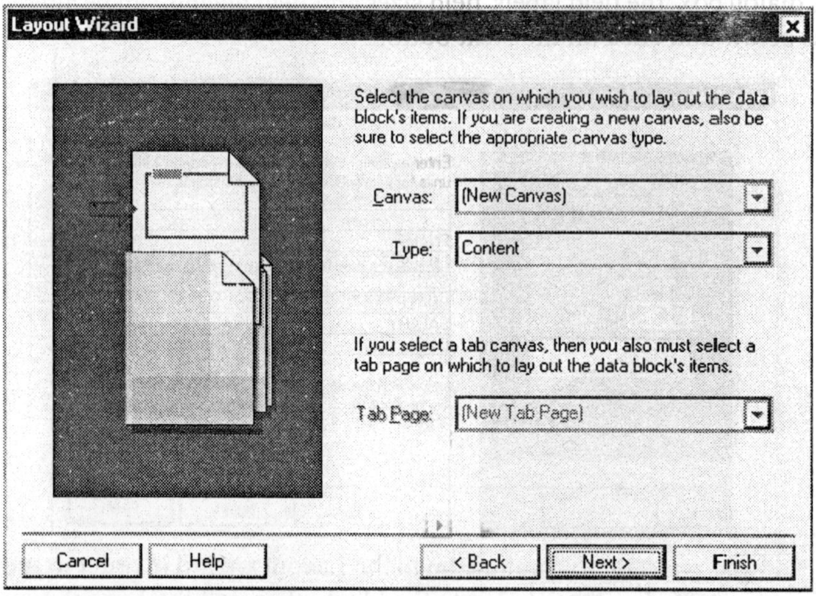

The layout for a data block may be placed on any existing canvas. In this case, there are no canvases so the only option available is to create a new canvas.

Click on the Next button to display the following dialog box:

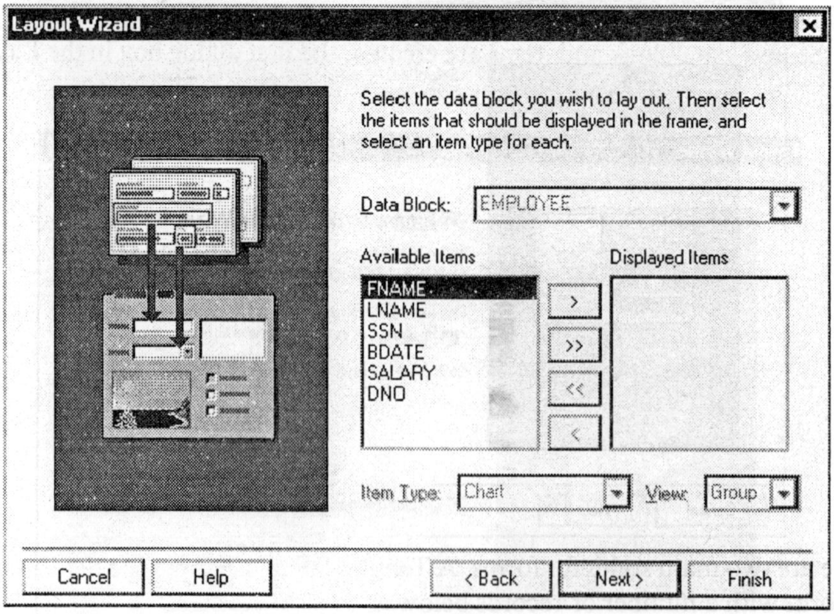

In this dialog box, the columns from a given base table on a data block can be added to the layout. Since we are laying out the EMPLOYEE data block, it is highlighted automatically.

Move all of the Available Columns over to the Displayed Items side by clicking on the double right arrow and click on the Next button.

In this dialog box, the field labels, field sizes and field heights can be altered. Change the field labels as below and click on the Next button:

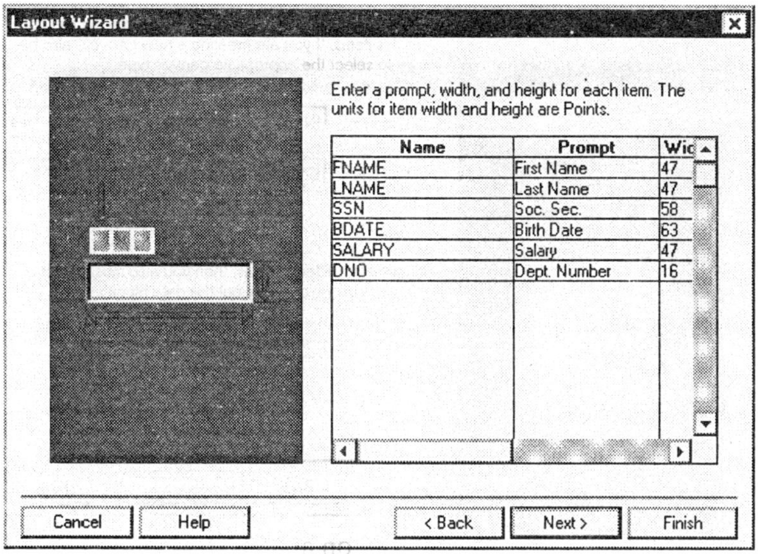

The following dialog box will appear:

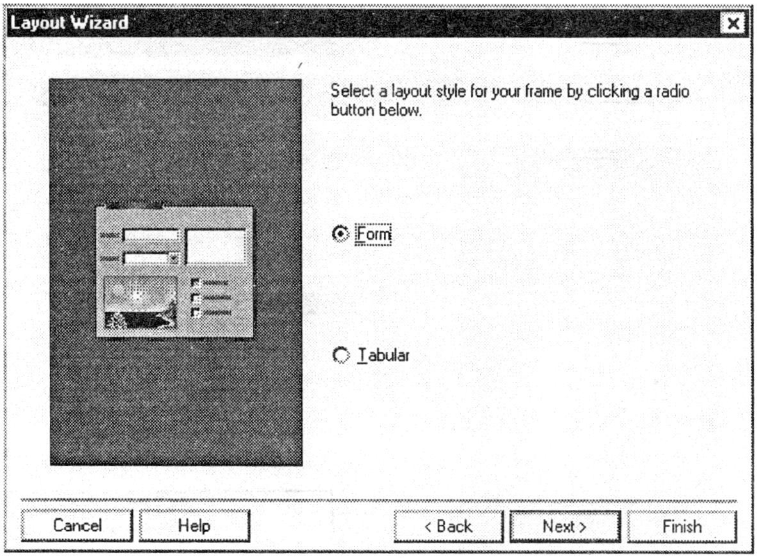

There are two main styles for forms. A Tabular layout arranges the field labels across the top of the form with a number of records below as in a spreadsheet.

A Form layout places the field labels to the left of the fields. Generally only one record is displayed at a time.

For this example, choose a Form layout and click on the Next button.

In the following dialog box, type a title for the frame (around the data block) and check the option to include a scroll bar.

The number of records displayed for a *Form* layout should be 1. The number of records displayed in a *Tabular* layout can be more than 1.

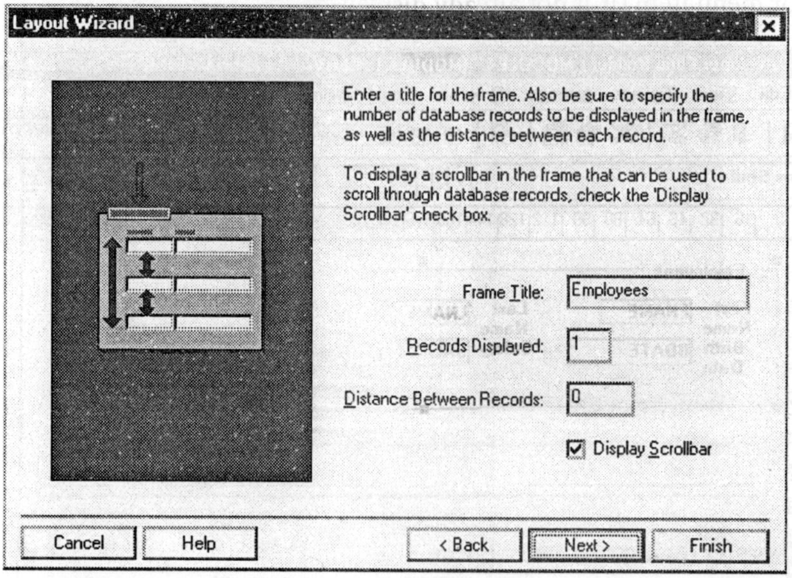

Click on the Next button and the final dialog box for the Layout wizard will appear.

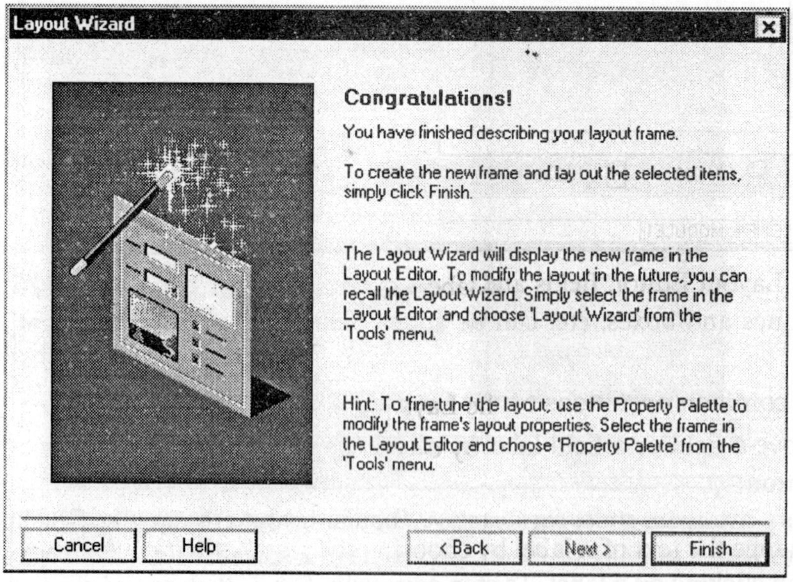

Click on the Finish button to create the layout. A new Canvas will be created.

At this point the Layout Editor should appear and the new form with the data block will appear.

The Layout Editor

To view the actual form and its blocks and fields, pull down the Tools menu and select the Layout Editor menu item (if it not already displayed).

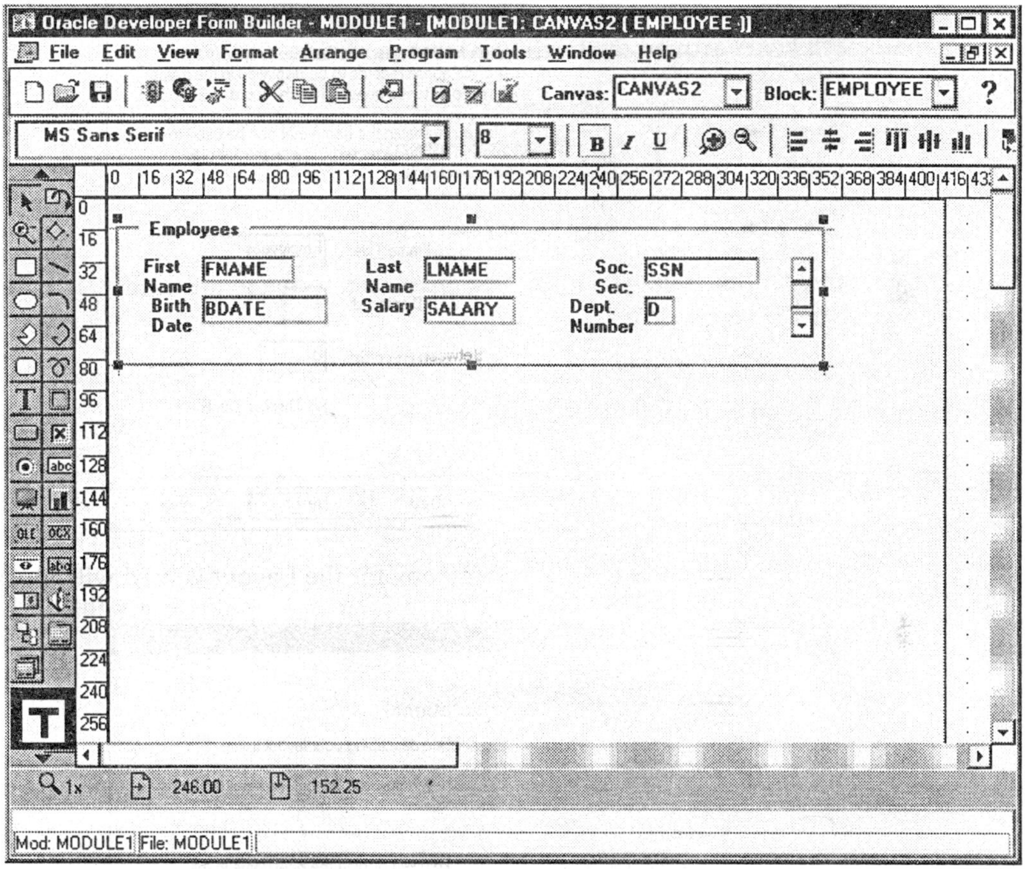

In the Layout Editor, fields and labels can be moved around by clicking and dragging. Other text, lines and boxes, etc. can be added using the tool palette on the left side of the window.

Some common operations on the Layout Editor include:

- Move a field or a field label by clicking and dragging the item with the left mouse button.

- Change the text of a label by choosing the text tool button  from the tool bar and then clicking on a label. To stop editing the label, click anywhere outside of the label text.

- Add text to the block by choosing the text tool button from the tool bar and then clicking on a open area. Type the new text. To change the font, highlight the text, pull down the Format menu and click on the Font menu item.

  To change the text color of a label, use the pointer tool to highlight a label and then click on the Text Color palette button to choose the color.
- Change the width of a field by clicking on the field. Then drag one of the handles (small black boxes around the field) to re-size the field.

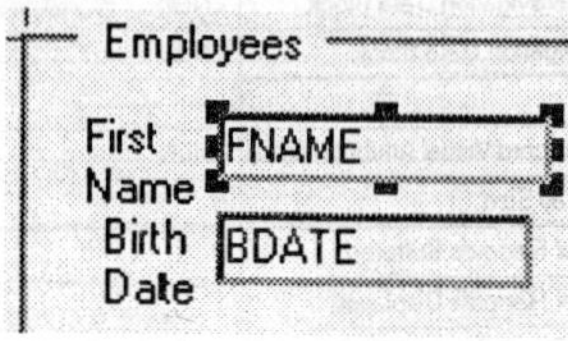

  For exampe, on the employee form, you may wish to make the SEX field wider to accomodate the capital letter 'M'.

- Use the Zoom In tool to zoom in to the form (e.g., make everything appear larger). Or use the Zoom Out tool to zoom out of the form.

Displaying Properties

While in the Layout Editor, double clicking on an object will bring up that object's *properties*. Optionally, clicking on an object with the right mouse button will bring up a small menu which has the Properties menu item on it. The following figure shows the properties for the FNAME item.

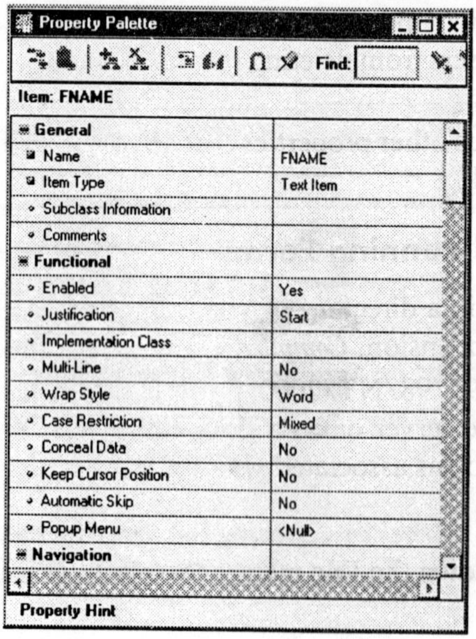

Each type of object has a slightly different set of properties. For example, double clicking on the EMPLOYEE data block in the Object Navigator will display that data block's properties.

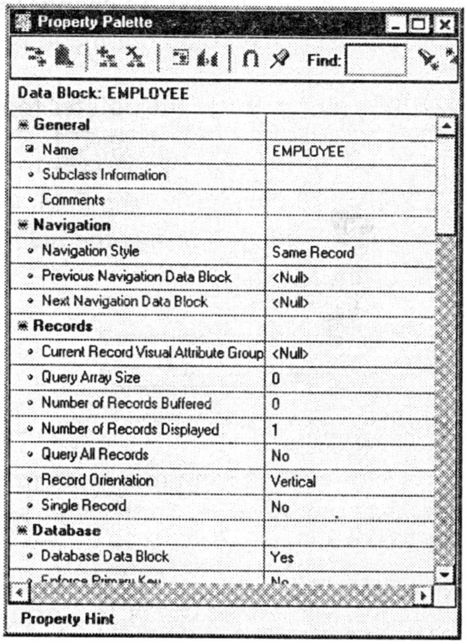

Some properties of interest for a data block include:

- WHERE Clause - specify a WHERE clause to filter the selection of rows from the base table.
- ORDER BY Clause - specify an ORDER BY clause to alter the displayed order of the records.
- Delete Allowed, Insert Allowed, Query Allowed and Update Allowed - toggle these properties to allow or prevent the action. For example, setting Delete Allowed to FALSE prevents users from deleting records from the corresponding base table using this form.
- There are numerous other properties that affect the fonts, colors, size and position of objects in the block.

Saving, Compiling and Running Forms

Forms can be saved in files in a directory of your choosing. The "source code" for a form is stored in a file with a .fmb extension. *Compiled* forms have a .fmx extension.

Under MS Windows 95/98/NT/2000, forms can be saved in a folder (subdirectory) on the local hard disk, on a file server or on a floppy disk. It is desirable to maintain separate subdirectories (folders) for forms associated with different projects.

Saving a Form

To save a form, pull down the File menu and select the Save menu item.

Under MS Windows 95/98/NT/2000, this dialog box looks like:

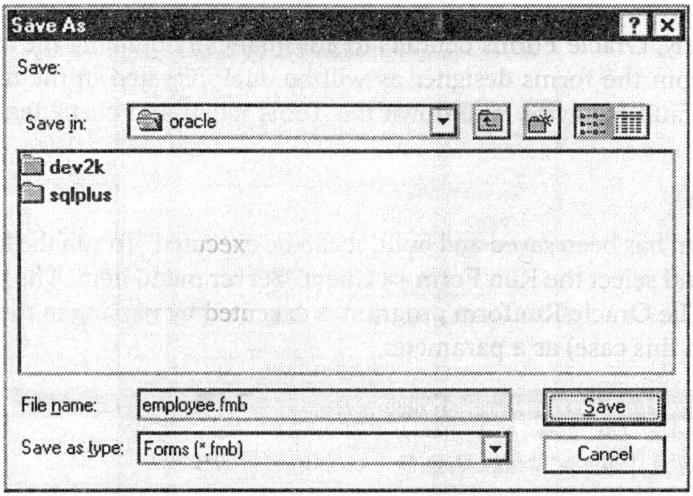

Note that in your company or organization, forms and other files may have to be saved on floppy disk or in a special directory. The above figure is simply an example.

Fill in a file name in the File Name: field. Be sure it ends with .fmb

Click on the Save button to save the file. For this example, use the file name employee.fmb

To save this form on a floppy disk in the A: drive, use the file name: A:\employee.fmb

To enhance portability of forms across different operating systems, use file names that begin with a letter, contain no spaces or punctuation (except for the underscore character), have all lower case letters and are relatively short.

If you are working on a form and wish to save it under a *different* file name, follow the same steps as above, only select the Save As menu item in place of the Save menu item. For example, if you have finished working on the Employee form and wish to save off a copy before adding some code or programming some program units, the Save As menu item can be used to save off a copy before proceeding.

Compiling/Building a Form

Before a form can be executed (run), it must be *Compiled* and *Built*. Compiling runs a PL/SQL compiler on all of the procedures and triggers in the form. Building (or compiling the file) creates the .fmx file that is then used to run the form.

To compile a form, first make sure the form is saved. Pull down the Program menu and select the Compile menu item. Then choose All in the flyout menu.

If a form has errors (e.g., in the PL/SQL code, or if the database schema changes) they will be displayed in a window as they are encountered. A record of the compilation process, including error messages, is kept in a file with a .err extension. For example, if the form is named employee then the record of the compilation will be stored in employee.err.

To *Build* the .fmx file for a form, pull down the File menu, click on the Administration menu item and then choose Compile File from the fly-out menu. If the forms generation is successful, the phrase *Module built successfully* will appear on the status bar at the bottom of the screen.

Alternatively, Oracle Forms defaults to automatically building the form each time it is executed (run) from the forms designer as will be demonstrated in the next step. For more details on the default behavior, pull down the Tools menu and check the Preferences menu item.

Running a Form

After a form has been saved and built, it can be executed. To run the form, pull down the Program menu and select the Run Form -> Client/Server menu item. The form will display in a new window. The Oracle Runform program is executed by passing in the name of the form (employee.fmx in this case) as a parameter.

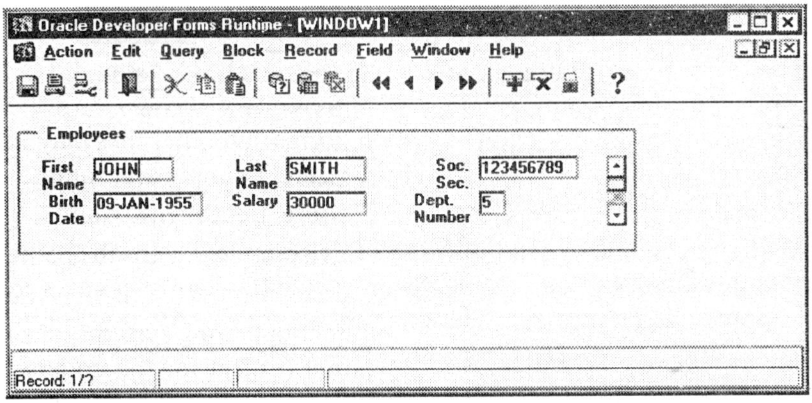

Use the various menus and items to query the form, enter new data and save new and changed data. Please read the section below on Query By Example to see how to query data from the underlying tables and populate the fields in the form.

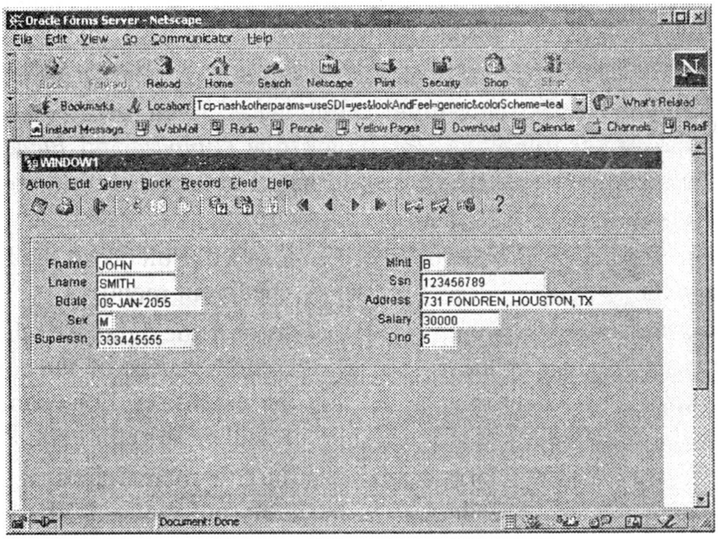

Forms 6i provides a simple test web page located under the Oracle Forms 6i program group called "Run a Form on the Web". One can make use of that to test if the Forms server, load balancer, and web server on the middle tier are running correctly.

Please note that getting Oracle Forms and Reports to run in this fashion is not a trivial undertaking. It requires extensive knowledge of web servers, Windows NT/2000 services and the way in which the forms applications are processed across the three tier architecture.

Query By Example

When a Developer Form is first executed, no records will appear. That is, the blank form will appear with no data in the fields. This is similar to running a word processor where the opening screen is blank. From this blank or empty form, the user can immediately begin to enter new data records by simply typing them in.

However, in may cases, the user would first like to see if there are any records in the database. To do this, the user must *query* the database using the query capabilities that are built into every Oracle form. This will bring a copy of the records from the database into the form.

When a tool such as SQL*Plus is used, the user must form the SQL query by typing it directly in. In the case of embedded SQL, the SQL statements are programmed into the host language (such as "C" or Java) and automatically executed for the user. In the case of Oracle Forms, complex queries can be formulated and submitted to the database using a technique called Query By Example or QBE. In QBE, the name of the table or tables is fixed as are the names of the columns that will be returned from the tables. The user can supply their own criteria by supplying values for the fields. These values become part of the query that is submitted to the database on behalf of the user.

Querying a form in Oracle Forms is a two step process. Clicking on the Query button or choosing Enter Query from the Query menu places the form in *Enter Query* mode. In enter query mode, the form is cleared and the user can navigate in the various fields. Example values can be supplied as criteria for the query. For example, a user looking for all employees in the RESEARCH department might type a "5" in the DNO field while in enter query mode.

Clicking on the Query button a second time executes the current query using any supplied data as criteria in a WHERE clause. If no criteria are supplied, then all records in the table will be displayed. Continuing the above example, supplying a "5" for the DNO field while in enter query mode would cause the following SQL query to be submitted to the database:

```
SELECT fname, lname, ssn, bdate, salary, dno
FROM employee
WHERE dno = 5;
```

Most of the commands on the menus and on the button bar can also be activated using special key combinations or function keys. For example, under MS Windows 95/98/NT/2000, pressing the F7 function key places the form in Enter Query mode. Pressing the F8 function key executes a query. To see a list of keys and their functions, pull down the Help menu and choose the Keys option.

Once data has been queried, it is retrieved from the database and stored in a buffer in the associated data block on the form. This means that a local copy of the data now exists in the client's memory. Appropriate locks are placed on the data so that the client maintains a consistent view of the data in the associated tables.

The user can navigate through the data in a block by pressing the up and down arrow keys to scroll between records. To change data in a form, the user can TAB to the field of interest, and type over the existing data.

To enter new data into the form, the user can scroll to the last record and then down once more to move to a blank record. Data can then be typed into the fields and the TAB key can be pressed to move between fields on the form.

To save both changed and new records on a form, pull down the Action menu and choose the Save menu item. Any records that have been changed are collected and submitted to the database as SQL UPDATE statements. Any new records are collected and submitted to the database as INSERT statements. These statements are submitted as a single logical unit of work. Thus if a failure occurs during any of the statements, the entire transaction will be rolled back.

If the user attempts to clear the block or exit the form and there are some changes that have not yet been applied to the database, they will be prompted to commit the changes before exiting or clearing the form. The block is cleared when the Enter Query mode is invoked. A block can also be cleared using the Clear Block and Clear Form menu items.

To exit from a running form, pull down the Action menu and select the Exit menu item.

As a review, here are a few basic functions that can be performed by default in any Form:

Forms function	Notes
Querying a form	To see all records in the table, simply "Execute Query" (via Query menu or by pressing F8 in Windows). To filter the record, "enter query" mode, specify the query parameters in the fields and then "Execute Query".
Inserting new records	Scroll to the last record and then scroll once more to get a blank record. Type in data for each field and then commit these changes by pulling down the Action menu and choose the Save menu item. For master/detail forms (discussed below) first either query a master record or insert and save a master record (in the master data block), then navigate to the detail block and insert new records there.
Updating existing records	Query the database and scroll to the record of interest. Change the values in the fields and then save the changes. For master/detail forms, changes to the key in the master block may be prevented if detail records exist (thus insuring relational integrity).
Deleting records	Query the database and scroll to the record of interest. Pull down the Records menu and choose Delete record. Then save the changes. For master/detail forms, attempting to delete a master record when detail records exist typically results in an error. In such cases, all of the detail records should be deleted first and then the master record should be able to be deleted.

Exercise: Creating a Single Block Form

Create a simple data entry form for the DEPARTMENT table with the following characteristics:

- Select and display all of the columns in the DEPARTMENT table.
- In the layout wizard, use the Tabular layout and display 5 Records in the form. Add a scrollbar.
- In the Layout Editor, make the DNAME field a bit wider to accommodate longer department names.
- Change the Properties of the DEPARTMENT block so that that data is ORDER BY DNUMBER.
- Save the form under the file name: depart.fmb

The resulting form should look like the following:

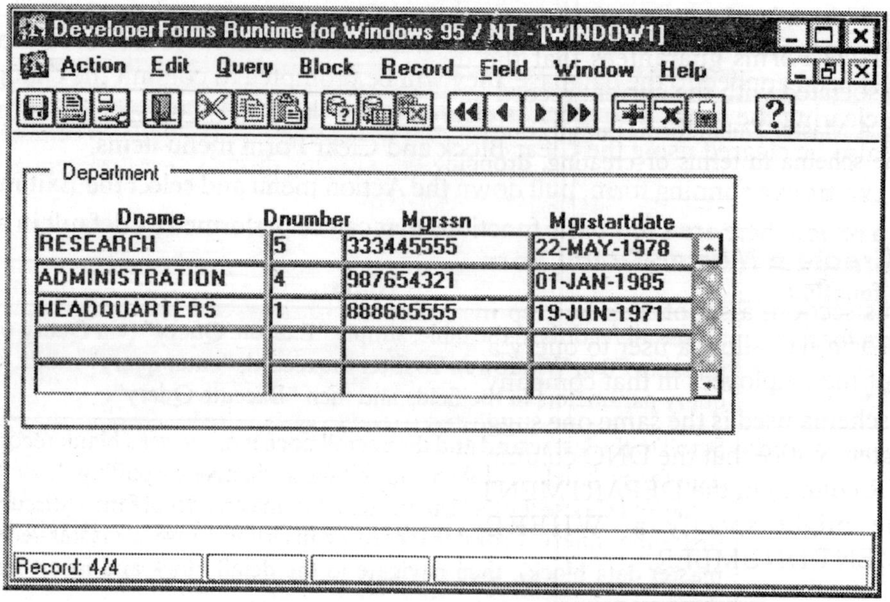

Use the enter query mode and execute query functions to query the department table for a specific department name and/or number.

CREATING A MASTER-DETAIL FORM

In this section, the basic steps for creating a Master/Detail form are introduced. A Master/Detail form is a form that has two blocks arranged in a master-detail relationship.

The Master-Detail Relationship

The Master-Detail relationship is a common relationship between entities in a business. In an Entity-Relationship diagram, these are shown as "One to Many" relationships. In a physical database design, a single *Master* record references one or more *detail* records in another table. A record in the detail table will relate to exactly one master record in the master table. Another name for this relationship is called parent-child. Examples of this relationship include:

- A Customer Order with many OrderItems.
- A Department with many Employees.
- An Employee with many Dependents.
- A Company with many Branch Offices.
- A Recipe with many Recipe Steps.
- An Inventory location with many Inventory Items.

Oracle Forms implements the master-detail relationship using two data blocks. The first block corresponds to the master table and the second block corresponds to the detail table. There are two major functions in a Master-Detail form:

- Oracle Forms coordinates values between the two blocks through a series of form and block level *triggers*.
- Oracle Forms guarantees that the detail block will display only records that are associated with the current record in the master block.

Note. A Master-Detail form is simply one way of viewing the data in two related tables. Forms do not affect the schema in terms of creating, dropping or enforcing database level referential integrity constraints.

Steps to Create a Master-Detail Form

In this section, a set of step by step instructions for creating a Master-detail form are given. The form will allow a user to query a given department in the company and then will display all of the employees in that company.

The schema used is the same one suggested in the Prerequisites section at the beginning of this chapter. Notice that the DNO column in the EMPLOYEE table gets its values from the DNUMBER column in the DEPARTMENT table. In other words, to join the two tables in a query, one might specify a WHERE clause such that: EMPLOYEE.DNO = DEPARTMENT.DNUMBER.

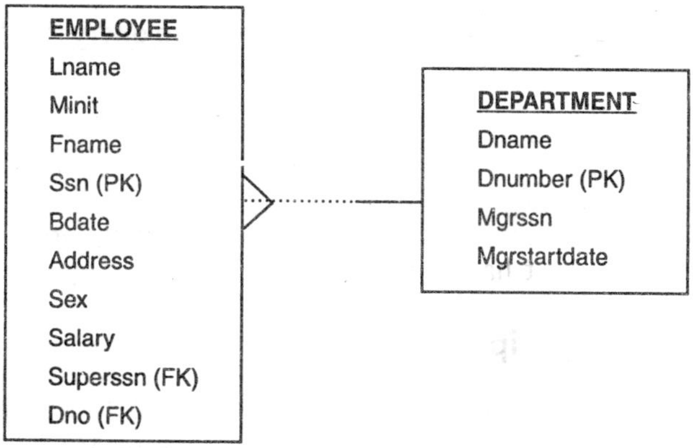

Create the Master Block

In the Object Navigator, click on the Forms branch at the very top. Create a new form by pulling down the File menu and choosing the New menu item. Then choose Form from the flyout menu.

Using the same steps given in the prior section on Creating a Form with a Single Block, create a new block named DEPARTMENT that contains all of the columns in the DEPARTMENT table. Briefly:

1. Pull down the Tools menu and choose the Data Block wizard.
2. Create a data block for a table/view.
3. Specify the DEPARTMENT table and select all of the columns (DNAME, DNUMBER, MGRSSN and MGRSTARTDATE).
4. Create the data block and then go on to the Layout wizard.
5. Apply the Department data block to a new canvas.
6. Add all of the columns as Displayed Items.
7. Change the labels to:
   Dept. Name
   Dept. Number
   Mgr. Ssn
   Mgr. Start Date
8. Choose a *Form* layout.
9. Specify a frame title of "Departments" and select only 1 record to be displayed.
10. Save the form as deptemp.fmb and then compile and run it to make sure it is working properly.
11. Use the QBE features to retrieve only those departments with DNUMBER greater than 2. Then, do another QBE query to retrieve only those departments with the letter H in their name (try %H%).

After this first step, the deptemp form should look like the following:

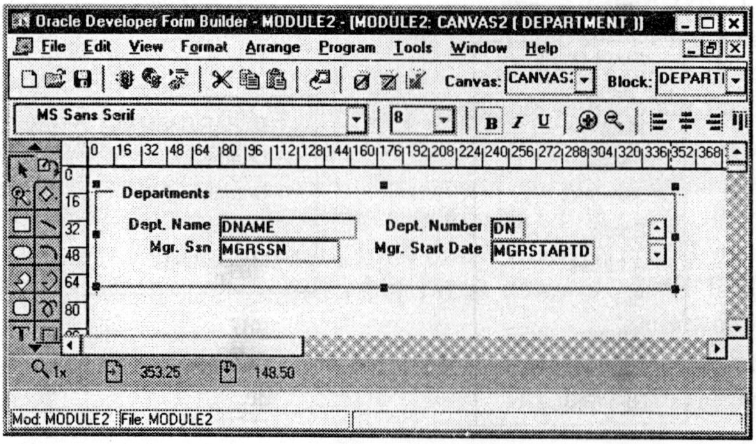

Create the Detail Block

Now that we have the master block DEPARTMENT created, we can now create the detail block EMPLOYEE and associate it with the master block. Perform the following steps:

1. Return to the Object Navigator (pull down the Tools menu and choose Object Navigator).
2. In the Object Navigator, click on the Data Blocks branch of the DEPTEMP form (do not click on the department data block, however).
3. Pull down the Tools menu and choose the Data Block wizard. *Note:* If the DEPARTMENT data block (or any of its items) is still selected, activating the Data Block wizard will cause the existing block to be edited instead of creating a new block.
4. Select the EMPLOYEE table and include the FNAME, LNAME, SSN, BDATE, SALARY and DNO columns.

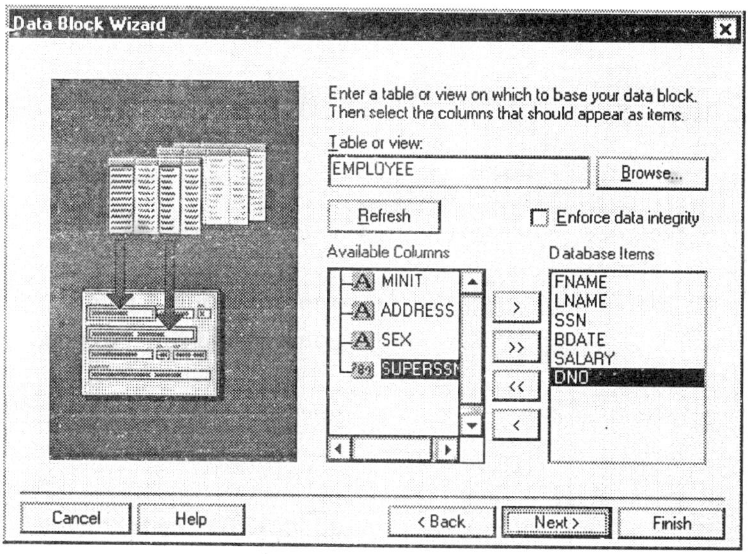

5. Because at least one data block already exists in the form, the next step in the wizard will be to create a relationship between the existing data block (DEPARTMENT in this case) and the new block being created.

   The wizard can construct the relationship based on table level constraints it learns from the database schema. For example, in the CREATE TABLE and ALTER TABLE statements given at the start of this tutorial, foreign key constraints were specified between DEPARTMENT and EMPLOYEE, and between EMPLOYEE and DEPENDENT. However, such relationships are not always implemented in table level constraints.

   The developer can also specify the relationship manually. In this case, the relationship will be specified manually.

De-select the Auto-join data blocks option.

Click on the Create Relationship button to list the available data blocks.

In the next dialog box Relation Type, choose Based on a join condition and click the OK button.

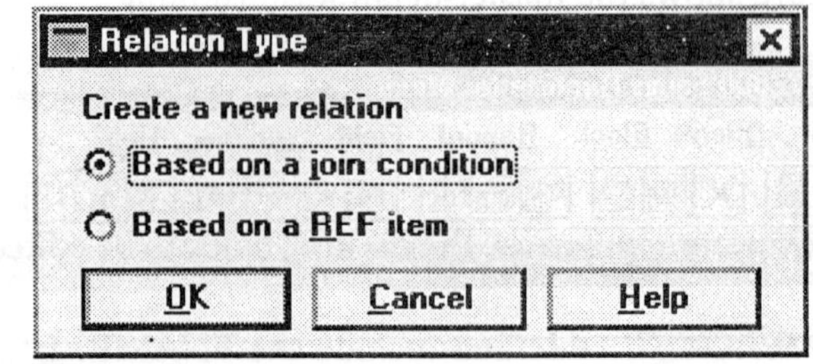

When the list of blocks appears, choose the DEPARTMENT data block. Arrange the Detail Item (DNO) and Master Item (DNUMBER) such as that the join condition becomes: EMPLOYEE.DNO = DEPARTMENT.DNUMBER

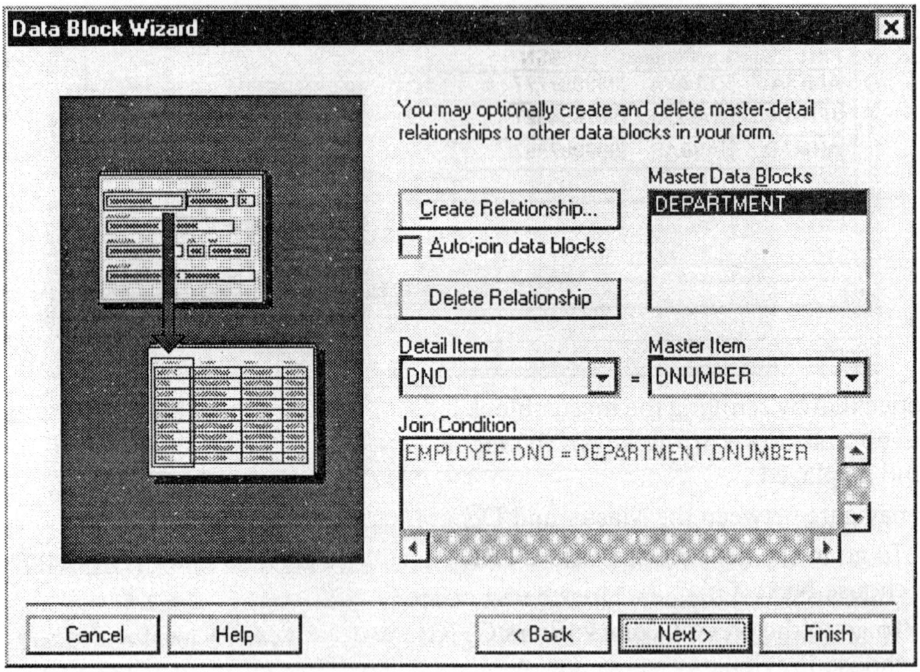

6. Create the data block and then call the Layout wizard.
7. Be sure to choose the existing canvas (CANVAS2 in this example) and include all of the items *except the DNO* as displayed.

   The DNO column (item) will still be a part of the EMPLOYEE data block, however, it will not be displayed to the user.
8. Touch up the labels for the fields and choose the *Tabular* layout.

9. Give the Frame Title as "Employees" and select 5 Records displayed with 0 distance between records.
10. Save the form (it should already have the name deptemp.fmb) and then compile and run it. Note that after compilation, any errors encountered will be displayed.

The following figure shows the master-detail form running:

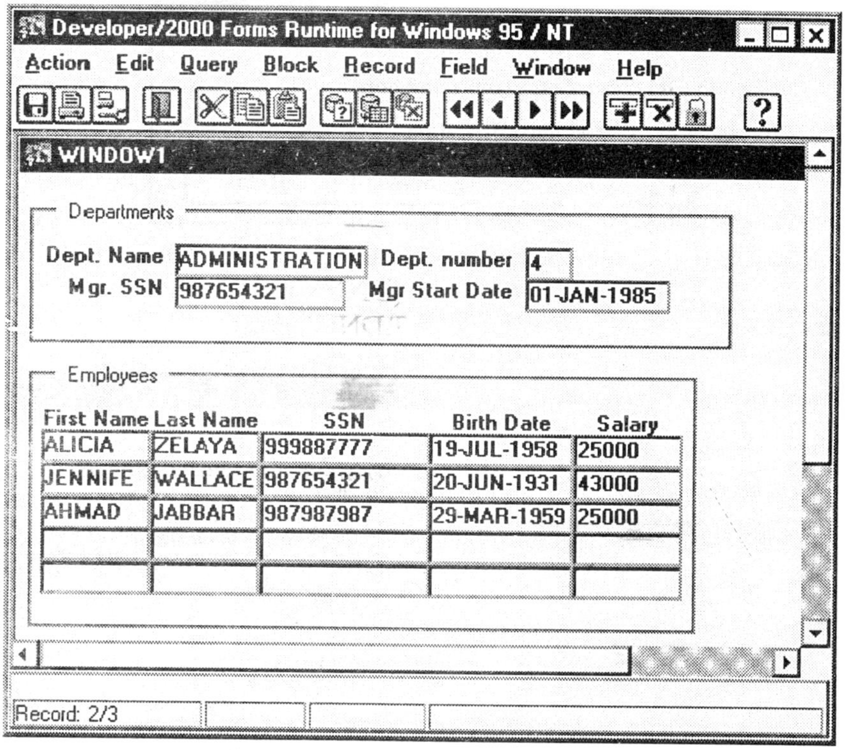

Notice that by scrolling the master block DEPARTMENT to a new department number (using the up and down arrow keys), the employees for that department are automatically queried and displayed.

To navigate between the Master and Detail blocks, use:

- To go to the next block: Press CTRL-PageDown or pull down the Block menu and choose Next
- To go to the previous block: Press CTRL-PageUp or pull down the Block menu and choose Previous

Relation Properties of a Master-Detail Form

There are a number of properties in a master-detail form that can be changed to suit particular behavior of the form. In the figure on next page, the Object Navigator has several new objects on it including *Relations*.

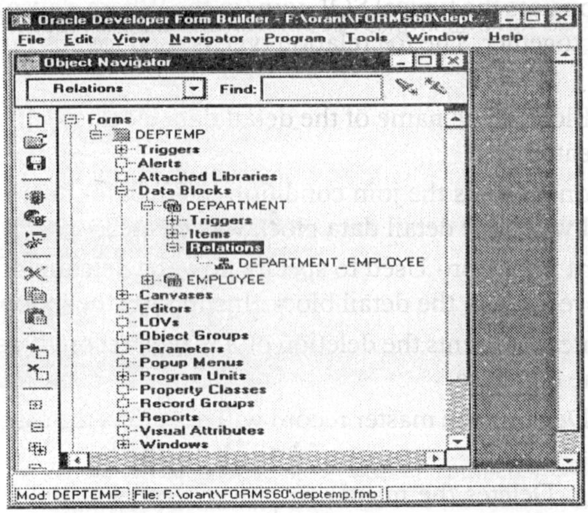

To view the properties for the DEPARTMENT_EMPLOYEE relation, open up the DEPARTMENT block and then open the Relations block by clicking on the + symbols. Then click on the DEPARTMENT_EMPLOYEE relation with the right mouse button and select Properties.

There are several interesting properties in the relations property sheet:

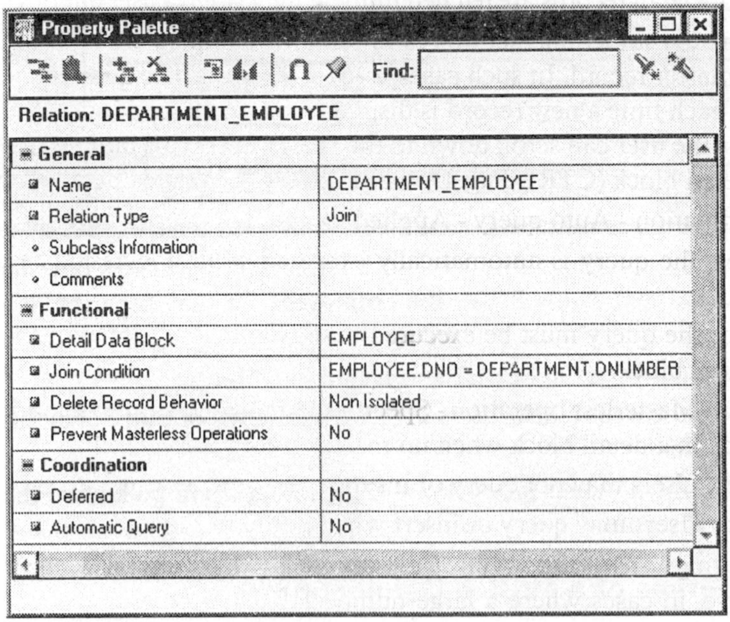

- Name - The name of the Relation. This is typically made up of the names of the blocks.
- Relation Type - The type of the relation: Join or Ref.

A Join relation uses the typical SQL join (in the Where clause) to bring the two tables (data blocks) together. The *Ref* relation type is used for abstract data types and object references.

- Detail Data Block - The name of the detail data block specified when the detail data block was created.
- Join Condition - This is the join condition in effect for queries to the database. This was specified when the detail data block was created.
- Delete Record Behavior - Used to specify how the deletion of a record in the master block affects records in the detail block. It supports the following settings:
  - Non-isolated: Prevents the deletion of a master record if associated detail records exist in the database.
  - Isolated: Deleting the master record will not affect the associated detail records in the database.
  - Cascading: Deletes the master record and automatically deletes any associated detail records.
- Coordination - Deferred - Indicates when detail records should be queried when a master record is queried.
  - Yes: Form does not query the detail records until the user navigates to the detail block.
  - No: Detail records are fetched immediately when a user queries the master record.

  Deferred is sometimes set to Yes in cases where there are a lot of detail records for each master record. In such cases, a lot of data must be queried and delivered to the client each time a new record is displayed in the master block. When Deferred is set to Yes, the user can scroll down to the master record of interest and then navigate to the detail block (CTRL-PageDown) to query the related detail records.
- Coordination - Auto-query - Applied to deferred queries only
  - Yes: the query is automatically executed when the user navigates to the detail block.
  - No: the query must be executed manually by the user after they navigate to the detail block.
- Prevent Masterless operation - Specifies whether users are allowed to query or insert records in a detail block when no master record is in place.
  - Yes: Users may not query or insert when no master record is in place.
  - No: Users may query or insert when no master record is in place.

These settings are used to "tune" the overall performance of a master-detail form. As mentioned above, in cases where a large number of detail records are associated with each master record, it is a good idea to set coordination-Deferred to Yes to avoid unnecessary transfers of data between the server and client. This will also speed up the display of master records as the user can freely scroll through them without a pause to query and deliver the detail records.

Program Units in a Master-Detail Form

When a Master-detail form is created, three basic *Program Units* (PL/SQL Procedures) are created by default. These procedures are used to coordinate the query and navigation of the detail records when the master record is changed (e.g., when the user scrolls to a different master record), updated or deleted. The procedures can be seen listed in the Object Navigator:

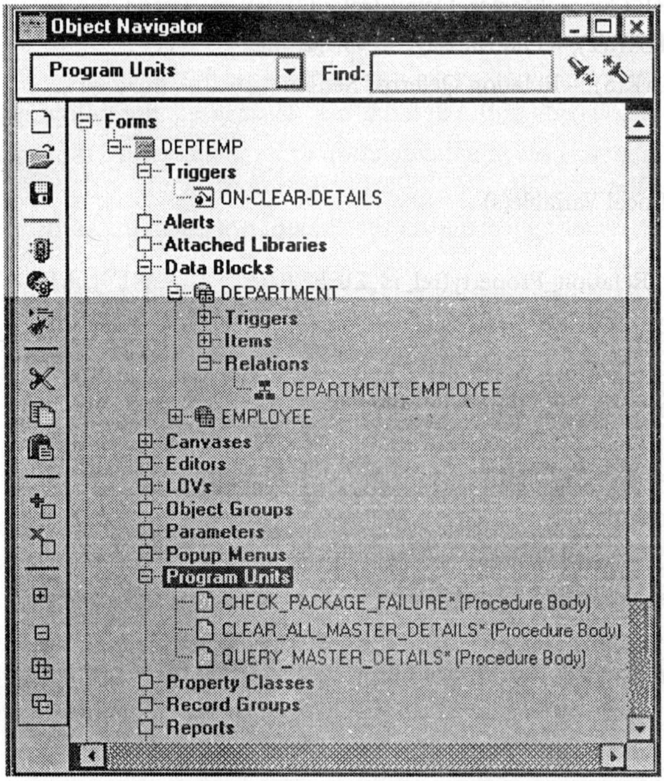

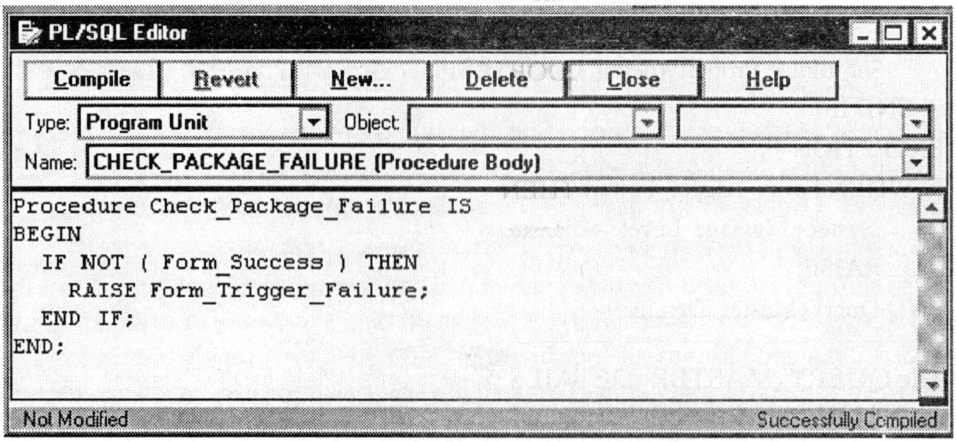

The CHECK_PACKAGE_FAILURE procedure checks to see if a prior form command or SQL statement was successful or if it failed.

Below is the PL/SQL code for the QUERY_MASTER_DETAILS procedure. The text after the -- (two minus signs) are comments.

```
PROCEDURE Query_Master_Details(rel_id Relation, detail CHAR) IS
   oldmsg CHAR(2); -- Old Message Level Setting
   reldef CHAR(5); -- Relation Deferred Setting
BEGIN
--
-- Initialize Local Variable(s)
--
reldef := Get_Relation_Property(rel_id, DEFERRED_COORDINATION);
oldmsg := :System.Message_Level;
   --
   -- If NOT Deferred, Goto detail and execute the query.
   --
   IF reldef = 'FALSE' THEN
      Go_Block(detail);
      Check_Package_Failure;
      :System.Message_Level := '10';
      Execute_Query;
      :System.Message_Level := oldmsg;
      ELSE
      --
      -- Relation is deferred, mark the detail block as un-coordinated
      --
      Set_Block_Property(detail, COORDINATION_STATUS, NON_COORDINATED);
   END IF;
EXCEPTION
   WHEN Form_Trigger_Failure THEN
      :System.Message_Level := oldmsg;
      RAISE;
END Query_Master_Details;
```

The QUERY_MASTER_DETAILS procedure is executed whenever the user navigates to the detail block in a master detail form. If the Deferred Coordination property is set to false, then the detail block is automatically queried.

Finally, the CLEAR_MASTER_DETAILS procedure is called each time a new master record is retrieved (e.g., when the user scrolls to a different master record) or deleted. In this case, if any of the detail records have been inserted, updated or deleted, the changes must be saved into the database before the detail block can be cleared. If there are any outstanding changes to be saved, the user will be prompted to save those changes before the detail bock is cleared.

Extending Master-Detail Forms

Master-Detail forms can be extended to include additional levels of details. For example, consider a Customer listing with detail on Orders a customer has placed. For each Order, there are then many Items. An extension to the above example would be to include the DEPENDENTS of the employees as a details of the EMPLOYEES block. The steps outlined above can be repeated allowing several levels of detail to be added. Each additional level of detail will add a new block that is related to the level above it.

Exercise: Creating a Master/Detail Form

For this exercise, create a Master/Detail form using the EMPLOYEE and DEPENDENT tables. Employee will be the Master block and Dependents will be the Detail block. The join condition between the two tables is where the SSN column of EMPLOYEE is equal to the ESSN column of DEPENDENT.

The following is an outline of the steps:

1. Create the Employee data block and include the FNAME, LNAME, SSN, ADDRESS and SEX fields on the form. Use the Form layout and only display one record at a time.
2. Go back to the Object Navigator and select the "Data Blocks" tree. Make sure the EMPLOYEE block is not selected and run the Data Block Wizard again.
3. Create the Dependents data block and include all of the columns. For the master/Detail relationship, de-select the "auto" option, use a Join relationship, choose the EMPLOYEE data block as the Master and set DEPENDENT.ESSN = EMPLOYEE.SSN for the join relationship.
4. In the Layout Wizard for the Dependents data block, display all of the fields *except the ESSN field*. The ESSN field will remain part of the data block but it will not be visible on the form. Choose a Tabular style and display 4 up to records at once with 0 space between each record.
5. Save the form using the name: empdepn.fmb

The completed form should look like the following:

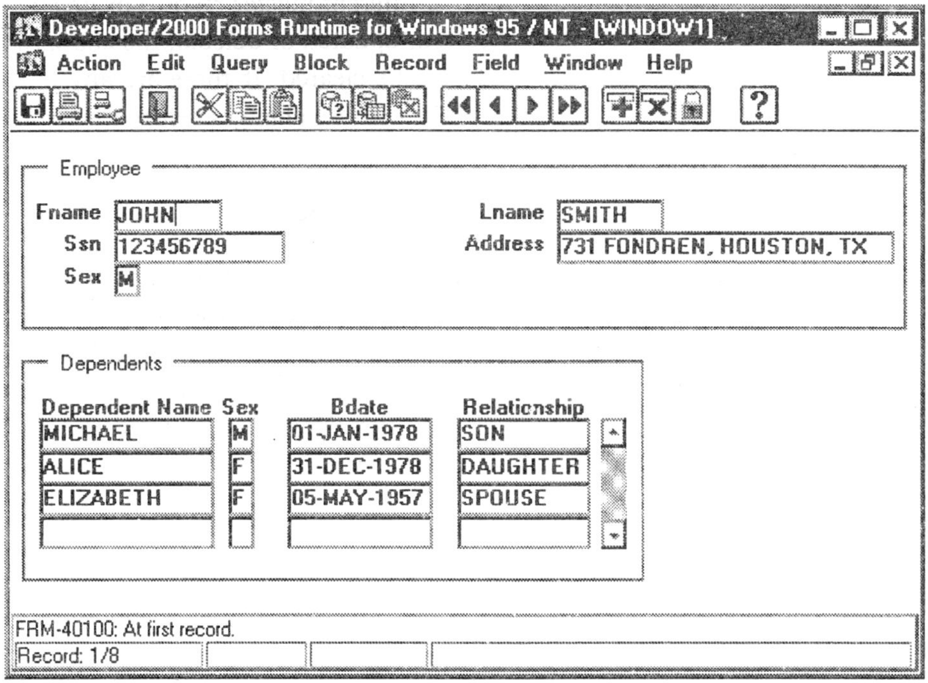

Query the master block and practice navigating between the two blocks using the CTRL-PageDown and CTRL-PageUp keys.

While in the Employee block, scroll to the Employee named JENNIFER WALLACE, navigate to the Dependents block and add a new record for a SON named ANDREW born on 20-OCT-1962. Navigate back to the Employee block and attempt to scroll to another employee record. A prompt should be displayed to save the new Dependent record.

While in the Master block for Employees, scroll to an employee who has some dependents. Try to delete the Employee record and see if an error message appears.

Finally, alter the EMPLOYEE_DEPENDENT relation properties and set the Coordination-Deferred to Yes and then run the form. Notice now that the detail records will not be displayed automatically. Navigate to the Dependents block and hit the Execute query button (or pull down the Query menu and choose Execute). Notice that only those Dependent records matching the Employee are displayed.

LIST OF VALUES (LOV) AND NON-BASE TABLE FIELDS

It is cumbersome for a user to have to remember various codes and numbers while entering data into a data entry form. For example, in the Employee form, it might be difficult to have all of the department numbers memorized when inserting new employee data.

One solution to this problem is to make a list of appropriate values available when the user navigates to Department Number field (DNO). In Oracle Forms, these are called List of Values (LOVs). The next section will illustrate creating LOVs for fields. These examples are based on the single block Employee form created at the beginning of this tutorial.

To prepare for this part of the tutorial, close any forms you currently have open by pulling down the File menu and selecting the Close menu item.

Once all of the forms are closed, pull down the File menu and choose the Open menu item to open up the employee.fmb form that was created previously.

A List of Values is based on a *Record Group*. In Oracle Forms, a record group is a query that returns some collection of records. Record groups can be used to populate blocks or LOVs and they can be used in procedures. When the user navigates to an item with an LOV attached to it, the LOV key (F9 in MS Windows) can be pressed to call up the LOV. At that time, the query associated with the record group is executed and the results are displayed in a pop up window. Once the user makes a selection from the list, the value or values are returned to the form and placed in the appropriate fields.

In the example below, a record group and LOV for the DNO (department number) field in the Employee table will be created.

Creating a List of Values

Creating a List of Values requires 4 basic steps.

Create a new LOV Object

To create an LOV, click on the LOVs node in the Object Navigator. Then pull down the Navigator menu and choose the Create menu item. A dialog box will appear asking if you would like to create the LOV manually or if you would like to use the LOV Wizard.

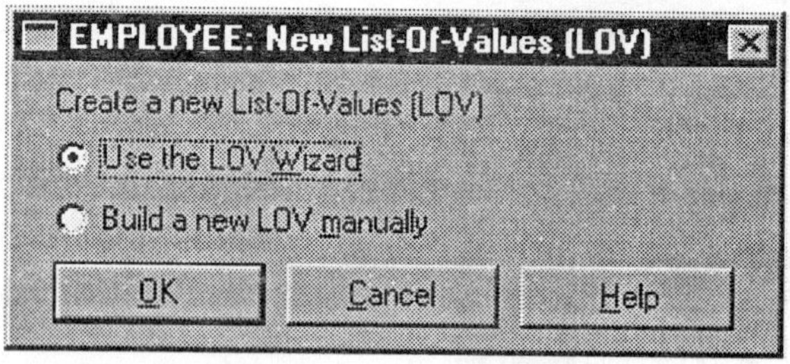

Choose "Use the LOV Wizard" and click the OK button. The first step of the LOV Wizard will appear as on next page:

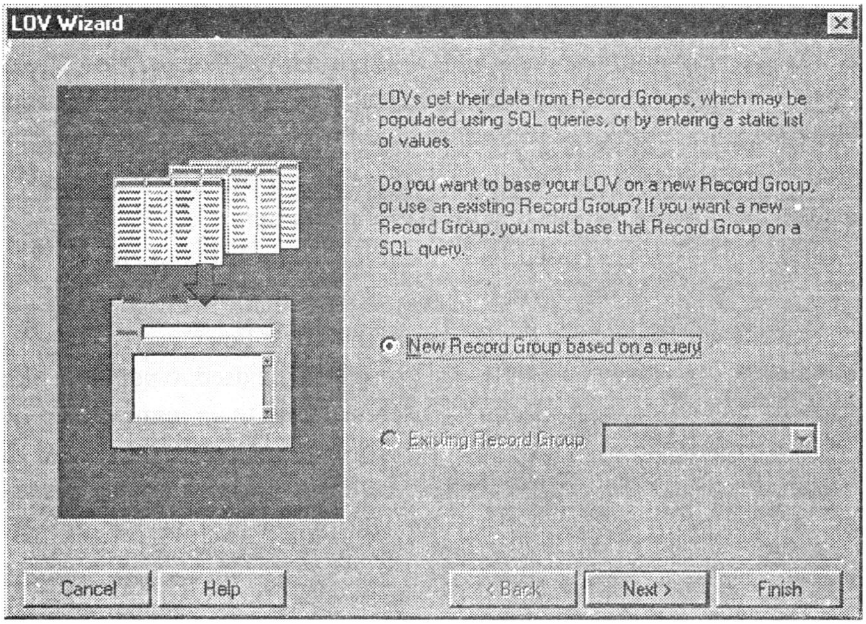

The default is set to create a new Record Group. Make sure this selection is highlighted and then click the Next button.

In most cases, you will not have a record group created previously. However, one can be created on the fly at this point by specifying a query. In this example, enter the LOV query as follows: SELECT DNUMBER FROM DEPARTMENT

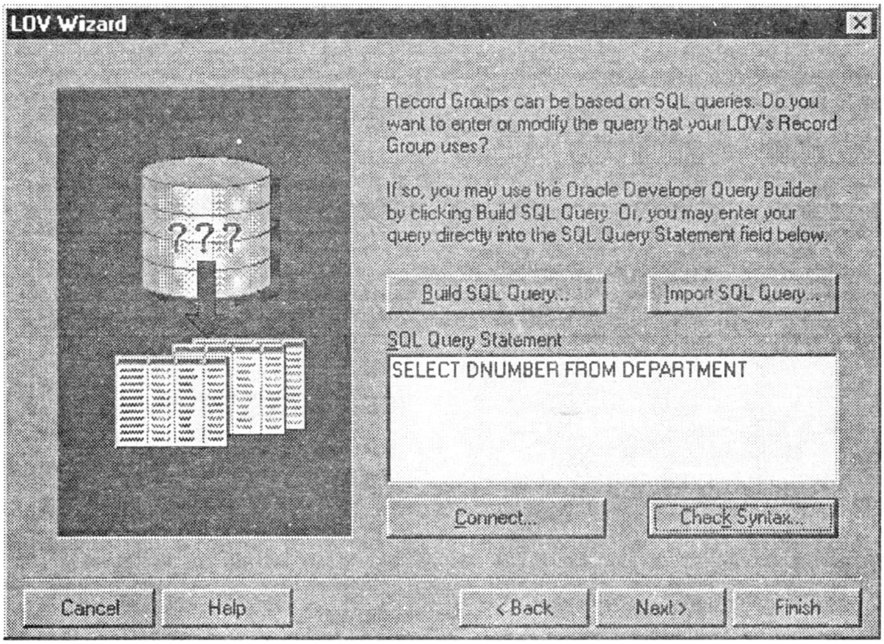

Then click on the Next button.

The next step is to specify which columns in the record group will be returned to for use by the LOV. In this example, we only return DNUMBER so select that column as shown below and click Next.

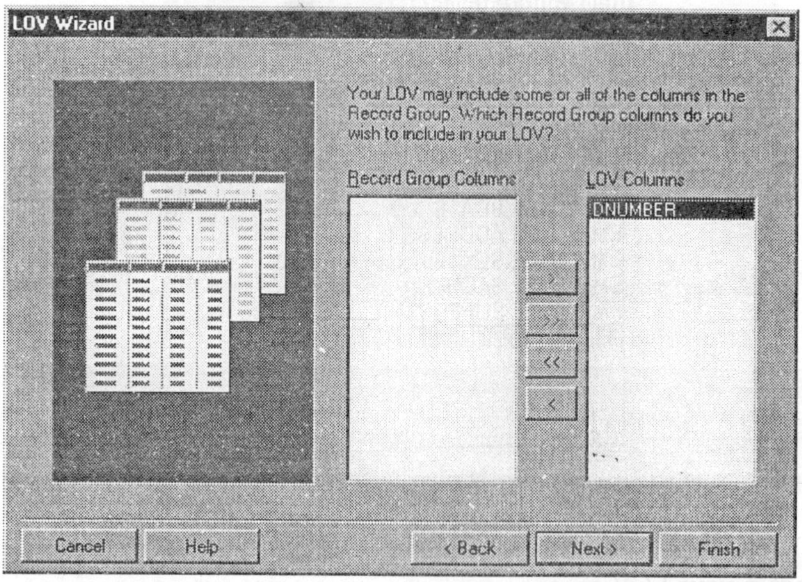

The next step is to specify the display properties of the LOV columns and also to map the LOV item to the field on the form.

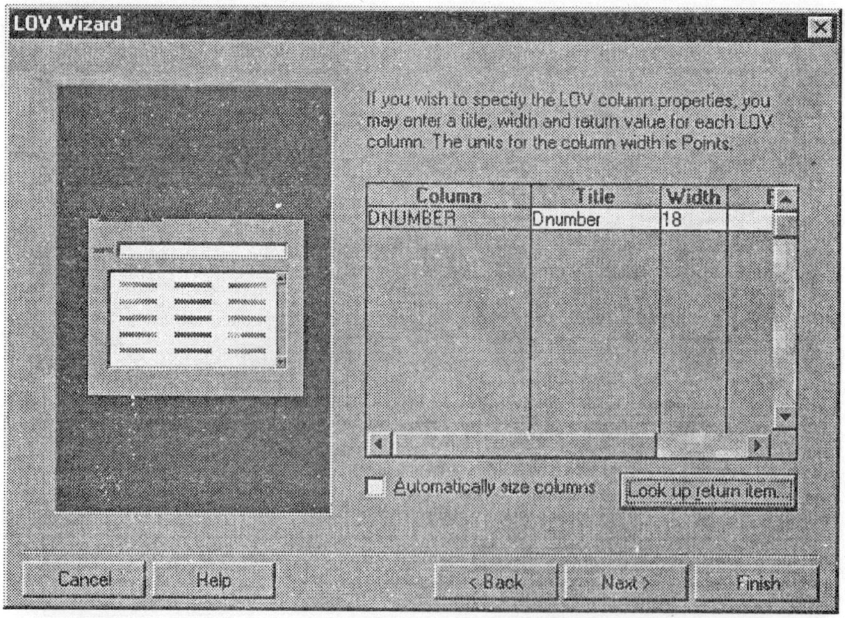

To map the LOV column to a field, click on the DNUMBER entry and then click on the "Look up return Item" button. Highlight the EMPLOYEE.DNO field and click on the OK button.

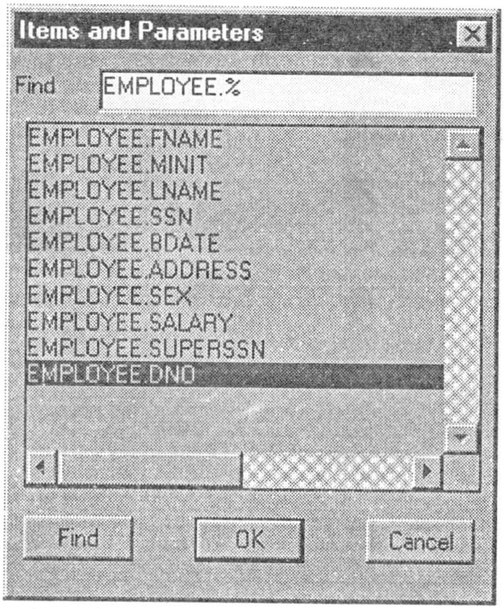

Note that if your LOV contains more than one item, at this time you would also map them as well (this is not the case with this example, but in the next example we will need to map two LOV columns). Click on the Next button.

Specify a title for LOV window. At this point you may also specify the size and positioning of the LOV. For this example, leave them as the defaults and click the Next button.

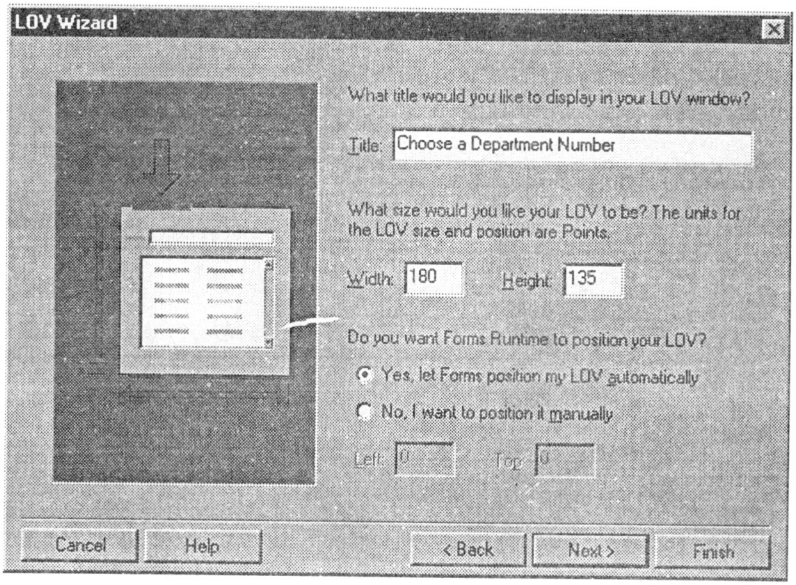

The advanced properties relate to how the records should be fetched for the LOV. If there are many hundreds or thousands of possible records returned by the LOV, you may consider changing these options. Otherwise, for this example, simply click Next.

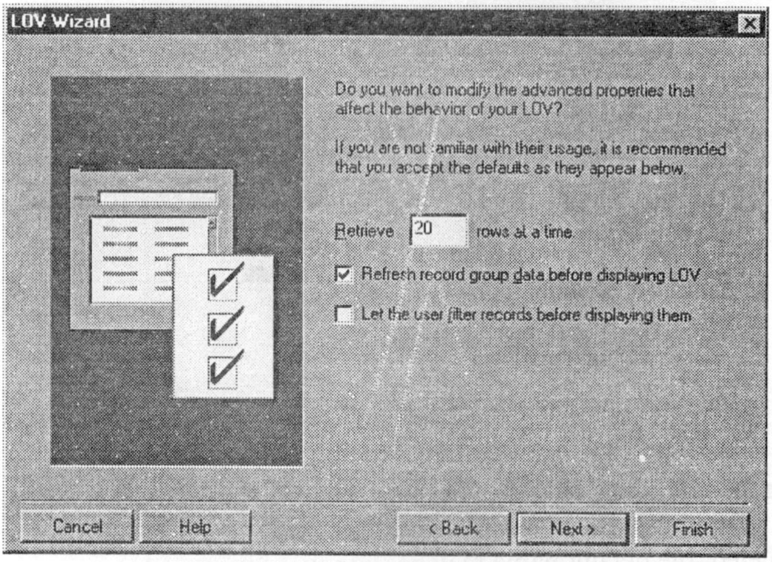

In this final step, the LOV is returning some columns and they were assigned to fields on the form in a previous step. At this point, we need to associate the LOV with a particular item on the form. For example, by assigning the LOV to the EMPLOYEE.DNO field, the user will be able to call up the LOV only when the cursor is positioned in the EMPLOYEE.DNO field. Choose EMPLOYEE.DNO and click the Next button.

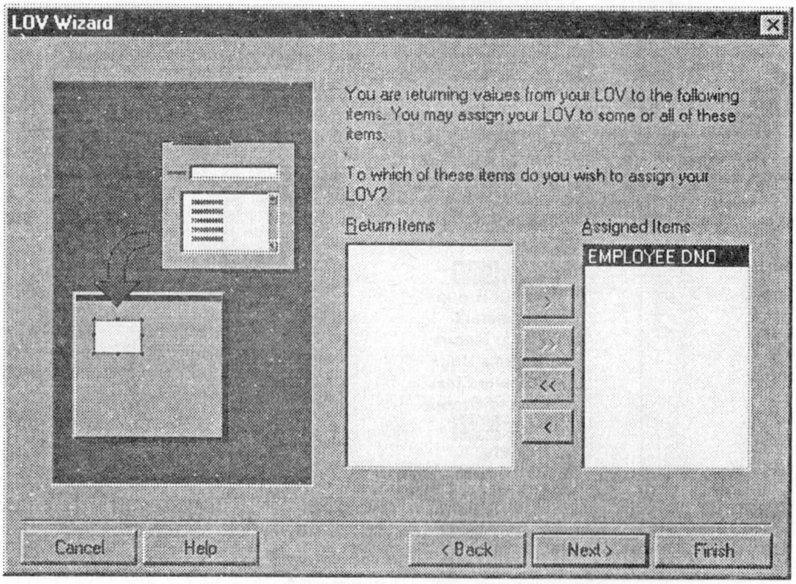

Finally, click Finish to create the Record Group and the LOV.

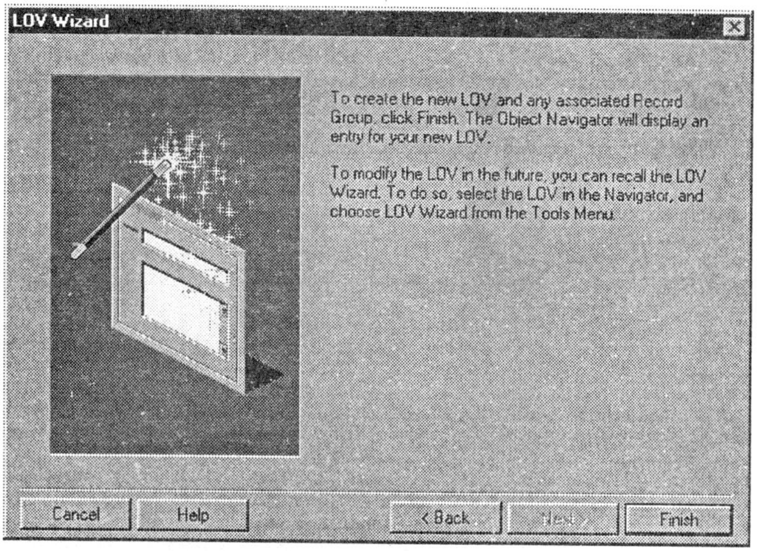

In the figure below, the LOV has been created. A default name of LOV4 was given to both the LOV and to its associated record group. Depending on what other parts of this chapter you have completed, the default name may be slightly different.

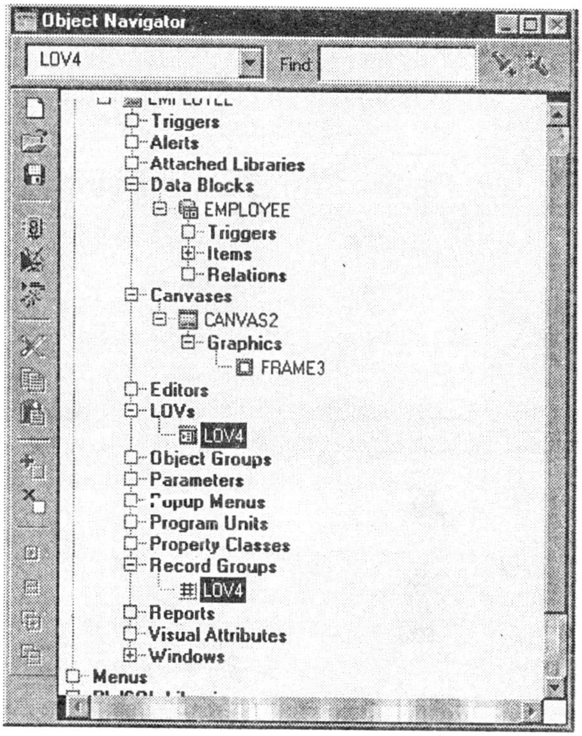

Save, Compile and Run the form. When entering new data, navigate to the DNO (Department number) field. Notice at the bottom of the form, a message appears: List of Values indicating a list of values is available for this field.

Under UNIX, the key to display the list of values is Control-l.

Under MS Windows 95/98/NT/2000 the key to display the list of values is F9.

To see the appropriate keys to press, pull down the Help menu and choose the Keys item.

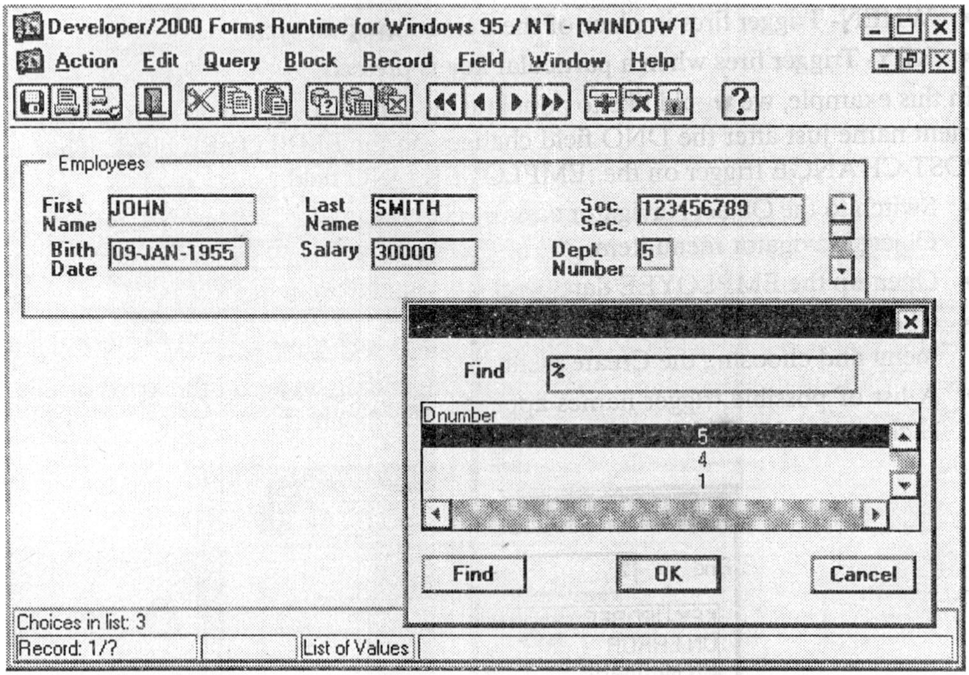

Non-Base Table fields

In the previous example of adding a List of Values, the supplied list of appropriate values can be useful in cases where the values themselves are self-explanatory. However, in the prior example, the department numbers may not have meaning to the user.

It would be more helpful to include the name of the department both in the pop-up list of values and on the form. However, the department name is not part of the EMPLOYEE table or data block. Thus we need a way to display this information on the EMPLOYEE data block in a *non base table field*.

Adding this item and making it functional will take several steps:

1. First the new item will have to be added to the EMPLOYEE data block. We'll call this new item DEPTNAME.
2. Next, the DEPTNAME field should be populated with the department name each time the value of the DNO field changes. A trigger will be created to handle this functionality.

3. Finally, the list of values will be changed to include the Department name in the LOV.

Creating a Trigger

Next, we will create a trigger to populate the DEPTNAME field whenever the value of DNO changes. Triggers in Oracle Forms have four general forms:

- PRE- Trigger fires before an event is executed.
- POST- Trigger fires after an event is executed.
- WHEN- Trigger fires in place of the execution of an event.
- KEY- Trigger fires when a particular key is pressed.

In this example, we would like to populate the DEPTNAME field with the appropriate department name just after the DNO field changes on the EMPLOYEE block. Thus we will use a POST-CHANGE trigger on the :EMPLOYEE.DNO field.

- Switch to the Object Navigator view by clicking on the Tools menu and choosing the Object Navigator menu item.
- Open up the EMPLOYEE data block and the DNO item.
- Click on the Triggers property and create a new trigger by pulling down the Navigator menu and choosing the Create menu item.
- A list of possible trigger names appears. Choose the POST-CHANGE trigger and click on the OK button.

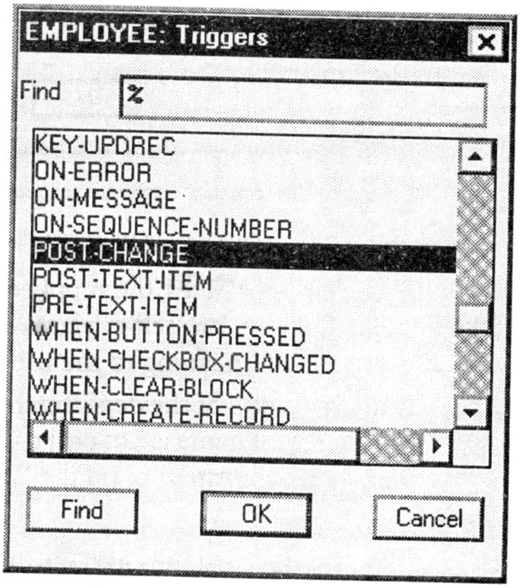

When the PL/SQL editor appears, type the following PL/SQL code:

-- Populate the non-base table field :EMPLOYEE.DEPTNAME

-- using a value from the DEPARTMENT table.

```
BEGIN
   SELECT DNAME
   INTO :EMPLOYEE.DEPTNAME
   FROM DEPARTMENT
   WHERE DEPARTMENT.DNUMBER = :EMPLOYEE.DNO;
      END;
```

Items on a block are preceded by a full colon to differentiate them from columns in a table.

Compile the trigger by clicking on the Compile button.

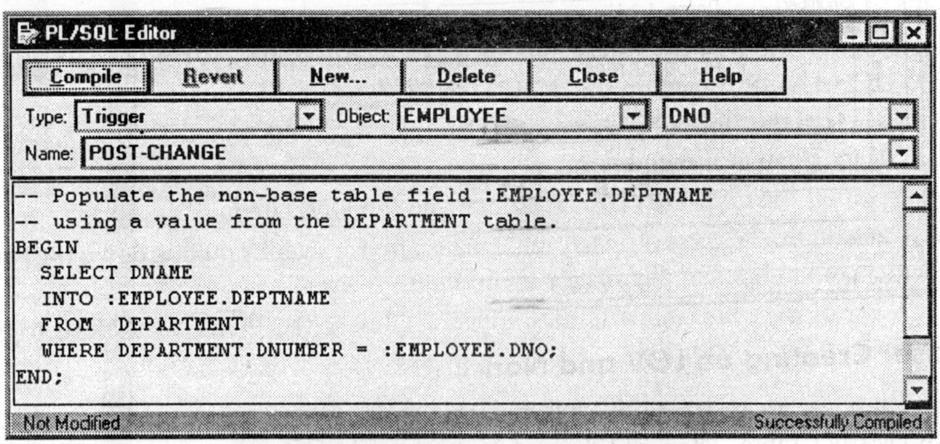

Close the PL/SQL editor by clicking on the Close button. Then save, compile/build and run the form to test the functionality. Notice that when the EMPLOYEE block is queried, the associated department name now appears in the new DEPTNAME field.

Create a new List of Values

Finally, a new list of values should be created to display both the department number and name when the user calls up the LOV.

- From the Object Navigator, click on the LOVs for the EMPLOYEE form. Pull down the Navigator menu and choose the Create menu item. Choose the LOV Wizard.
- Type the following SQL statement into the Query Text field:
- SELECT DEPARTMENT.DNUMBER, DEPARTMENT.DNAME FROM DEPARTMENT

  Then click on the Next button.

  Include both the DNUMBER and DNAME columns from the Record Group in the LOV.

  Map the DNUMBER LOV column to the :EMPLOYEE.DNO text item and map the DNAME LOV column to the :EMPLOYEE.DEPTNAME text item (created in the previous section).

- Give a title for your list of values and return both DNUMBER and DNAME from the LOV.
- Finally, Save, Compile and Run the form. Note that displaying the LOV for the DNO item now causes both the department number and the name to appear.

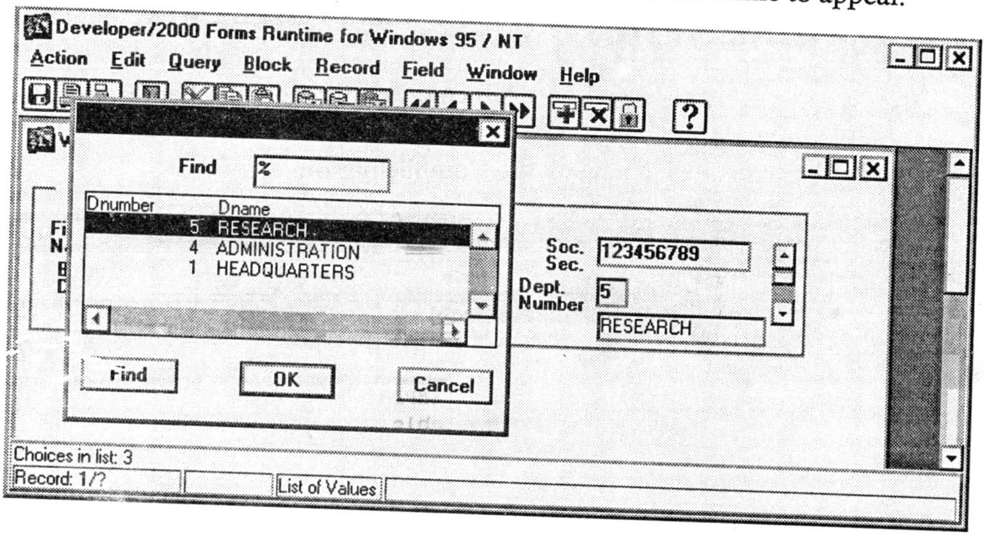

Exercise: Creating an LOV and Non-Base table field

For this exercise, create a new, single data block form based on all of the columns in the DEPARTMENT table. Then add a non-base table field for the last name of the department manager and create an LOV to populate it:

- Create a new form called departmg.fmb that includes all of the columns in the DEPARTMENT table. In the layout wizard, use the Tabular layout and display 5 Records in the form. Add a scrollbar.
- In the Layout Editor, create a new text item called MGR_LAST_NAME in the DEPARTMENT data block. Be sure the DEPARTMENT block is selected when the new item is created. Change the properties of MGR_LAST_NAME so it is not a Database item.
- Create a list of values called LOV_MGR based upon the query:
- SELECT ssn, lname FROM employee
  Assign LOV_MGR to the MGRSSN item.
- Create a POST-CHANGE trigger on the MGRSSN item so that when it changes, the following code will execute:
- SELECT lname
- INTO :DEPARTMENT.MGR_LAST_NAME
- FROM employee
- WHERE employee.ssn = :DEPARTMENT.MGRSSN;

This will automatically populate the non base table field MGR_LAST_NAME on the form when the form is queried. The form should look like the following:

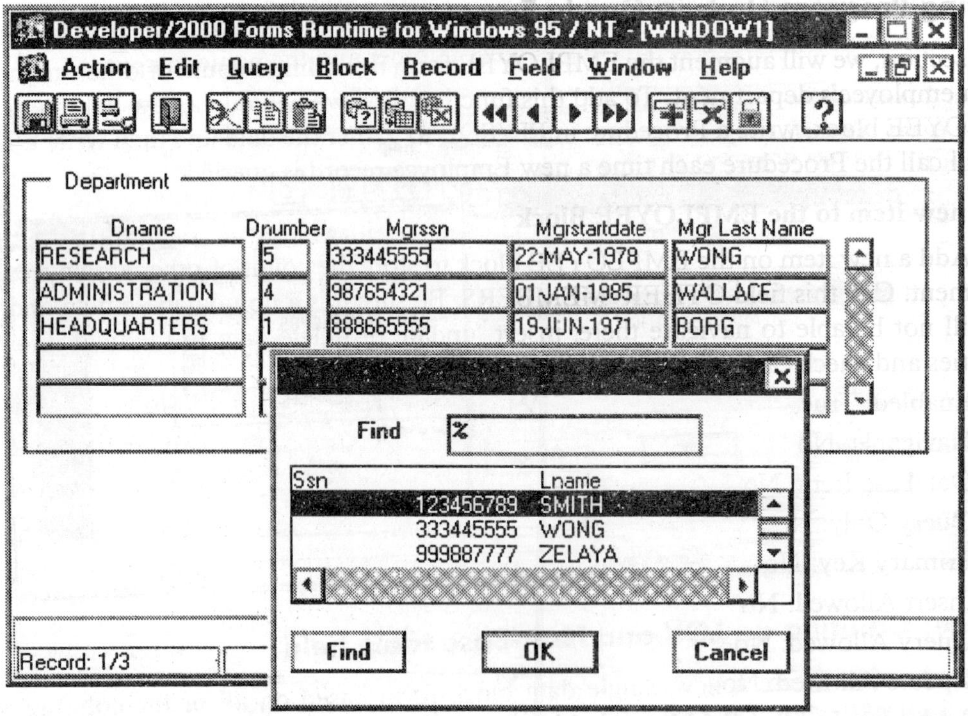

ORACLE FORMS PROGRAM UNITS AND STORED PROGRAM UNITS

Oracle Forms provides a mechanism to store procedures (called Program Units) written in the PL/SQL language within a form. Program Units can be used to add functionality that is not possible through Structured Query Language (SQL) or through the Oracle Forms interface.. By storing a Program Unit within a form, many blocks in the form can take advantage of the same procedure which reduces code duplication and improves the maintainability of the code.

Procedures written in PL/SQL may also be stored within the Oracle Database itself as an object in the schema. Such Stored Program Units (also called Stored Procedures) are ideal for situations where highly standardized business rules or applications logic must be implemented across many forms or applications. In addition, procedures that require several queries be made to the database may be best implemented in the database as this reduces the network traffic and can significantly improve performance. A user may create stored procedures with the Oracle SQL*Plus command line tool.

Oracle Forms can make calls to both internal Program Units as well as to Stored Program Units. This flexibility allows application designers extensive control over the execution of applications and facilitates performance tuning.

In the following sections, examples of Oracle Forms Program Units and Stored Program Units will be given.

Creating Program Units in Oracle Forms

In this section, we will augment the EMPLOYEE form by adding a count of other members of a given employee's department. To add this functionality, we will add a new field item to the EMPLOYEE block, write a Procedure in PL/SQL to gather the data and then write a Trigger that will call the Procedure each time a new Employee record is queried.

Add a new item to the EMPLOYEE Block

Add a new item on the EMPLOYEE block to store the count of other employees in the department. Call this field OTHER_MEMBERS. Be sure it is a non-database field and that a user will not be able to navigate there, insert, update or delete data in the field. Go to the Properties and check each of them:

Enabled: True

Navigable: No

Database Item: No

Query Only: No

Primary Key: No

Insert Allowed: No

Query Allowed: No

Update Allowed: No

Add a label to this field by switching to the Layout Editor, choosing the text tool and clicking next to the OTHER_MEMBERS field.

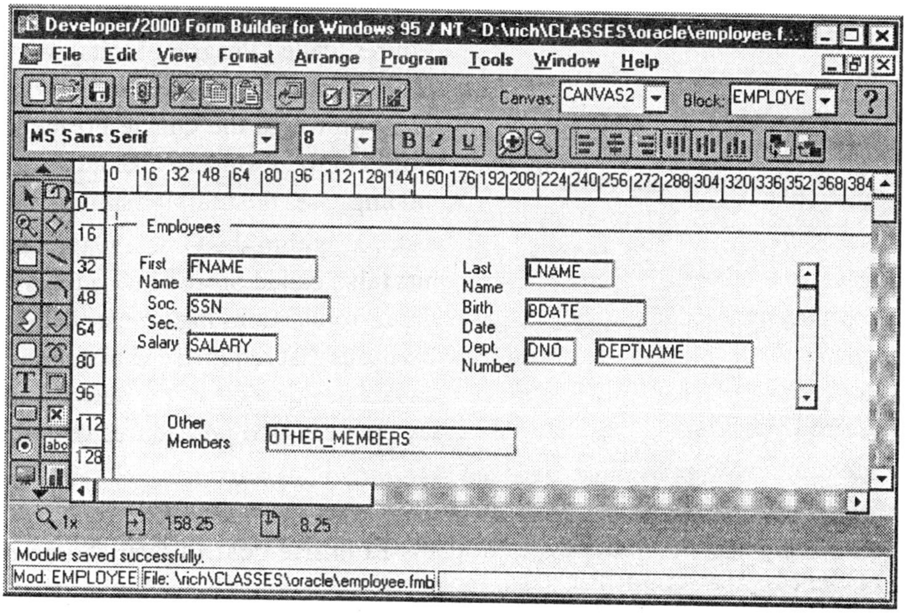

Create a Procedure to Count Other Department Members

In this step, create a Program Unit (procedure) in Oracle Forms to count the number of other members in the same department. For this procedure, we will pass in a parameter called IN_EMPLOYEE_SSN that will contain an employee's social security number. The procedure will return a value in the parameter OUT_COUNT_OTHER_MEMBERS that will contain the number of other employees who are in the same department.

To create this procedure, switch to the Object Navigator and scroll down to the Program Units branch. Pull down the Navigator menu and choose the Create menu item. A dialog box will appear asking you to name the new procedure. Type in the name

OTHER_DEPARTMENT_MEMBERS and click on the OK button.

At this point, the PL/SQL editor will appear. Type in the following procedure body. An explanation of each part of the procedure is given afterwards:

```
-- Given an Employee's SSN, return the number of other employees
-- in the same department.
PROCEDURE OTHER_DEPARTMENT_MEMBERS (IN_EMPLOYEE_SSN IN NUMBER,
        OUT_COUNT_OTHER_MEMBERS OUT NUMBER) IS
  TEMP_COUNT NUMBER; -- Placeholder for count
BEGIN
  TEMP_COUNT := 0; -- Initialize to 0
  -- Try and fill TEMP_COUNT with the count of other
  -- Employees in the department
  SELECT COUNT(*)
  INTO TEMP_COUNT
  FROM EMPLOYEE
  WHERE EMPLOYEE.DNO =
  (SELECT EMPLOYEE.DNO
  FROM EMPLOYEE
  WHERE EMPLOYEE.SSN = IN_EMPLOYEE_SSN);
  -- See if we got a meaningful result
  IF (NVL(TEMP_COUNT, 0) <> 0) THEN
    OUT_COUNT_OTHER_MEMBERS := (TEMP_COUNT - 1 );
  ELSE
    OUT_COUNT_OTHER_MEMBERS := 0;
  END IF;
END;
```

The procedure is written in three main sections. Any lines starting with -- are comments and are ignored by Oracle forms.

The heading for the procedure definition indicates that one parameter, IN_EMPLOYEE_SSN, is a NUMBER data type and the procedure should expect a value to be passed in. The other parameter, OUT_COUNT_OTHER_MEMBERS, is also a NUMBER data type and a value will be passed back to the calling program through it.

To finish off the procedure header, the TEMP_COUNT variable is declared for use within this procedure only.

The BEGIN statement starts the body of the procedure. TEMP_COUNT is initialized to 0 and then a query is performed on the database to find the total number of employees in the same department as the employee whose SSN was supplied to the procedure.

The result in TEMP_COUNT is checked to see if it is a NULL value. If TEMP_COUNT is not NULL and it is not 0, then OUT_COUNT_OTHER_MEMBERS is set to equal TEMP_COUNT-1. Otherwise OUT_COUNT_OTHER_MEMBERS is set to 0.

The last END statement ends the body of the procedure.

Be sure to check to see that the procedure compiles by clicking on the Compile button. Any errors in the procedure will be highlighted. Some common problems include forgetting to use := in an assignment statement (like the Pascal language) and leaving off the END IF to finish up IF ... THEN statements.

When done, click on the Close button to close the PL/SQL editor.

Create a Trigger to Call the Procedure

Create a trigger to call the OTHER_DEPARTMENT_MEMBERS procedure. In the Object Navigator, open up the EMPLOYEE block and the SSN item. Highlight the Trigger branch for the SSN item, pull down the Navigator menu and choose the Create menu item.

A pop up list of trigger names will appear. Choose POST-CHANGE and click on the OK button to open the PL/SQL editor for this new trigger. Type in the following code for the POST-CHANGE trigger on the SSN item:

```
DECLARE
return_count NUMBER;
BEGIN
-- Call the Forms Procedure to get the
-- count of others in the department.
OTHER_DEPARTMENT_MEMBERS(:EMPLOYEE.SSN, return_count);
-- Assign the return count to the field on
-- the EMPLOYEE block.
:EMPLOYEE.OTHER_MEMBERS := return_count;
END;
```

Again, click on the Compile button to be sure the trigger compiles correctly and then click on the Close button to return to the Object Navigator.

Save, Compile/Build and Run the Form

To this point, we have added a new non-base table field to the EMPLOYEE block, written a procedure (Program Unit) to count other employees in the same department and added a trigger to call the procedure each time a new employee record is queried.

To save the work, use the Save As menu item on the File menu and save this form under the name: emp_memb.fmb

Save, Compile/Build, and Run the form to check its functionality. Note that when scrolling to a new employee's record, the OTHER_MEMBERS field is automatically populated with values indicating the number of other employees in the same department.

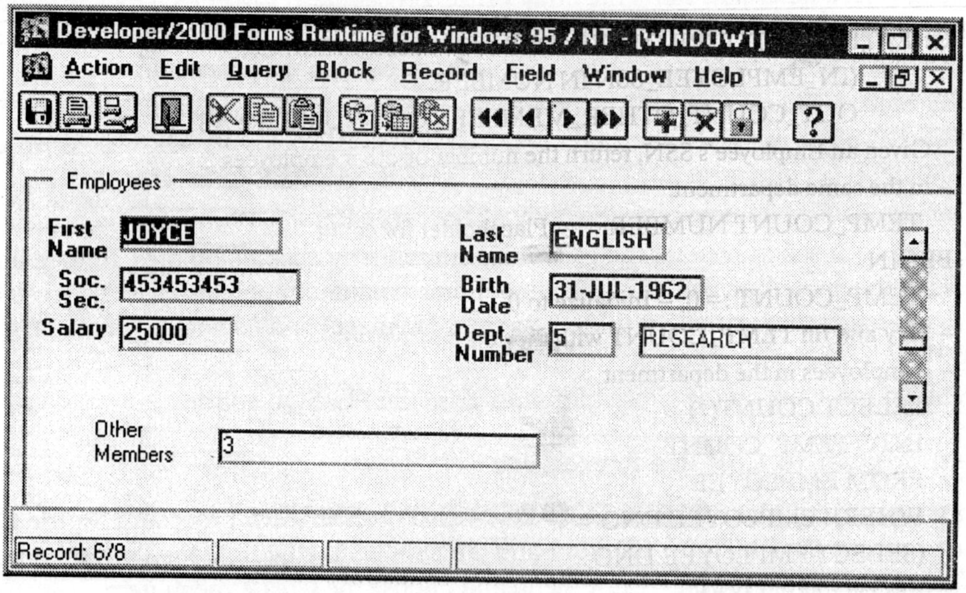

Creating Stored Procedures in SQL*Plus

In the previous example, we added a procedure (Program Unit) in Oracle Forms to perform a query on the database. The procedure is stored as part of the form's source code and is compiled when the form is built. Upon examination, each call of this procedure produces:

1. A local call from the POST-CHANGE trigger to the procedure passing an employee's SSN.
2. A remote access from the procedure to the database passing a SQL query.
3. A remote return from the database containing a count.
4. A small amount of processing in the procedure (IF ... THEN).
5. A local return from the procedure to the trigger.

In this exchange, the highest costs are incurred by the network traffic required to go back and forth between client and server (steps 2 and 3). The lowest costs are incurred by the local calls between trigger and procedure and the local processing (steps 1, 4 and 5).

In this example, the SQL Query in steps 2 and 3 does not return a significant amount of data. However, there are situations where, if a large amount of data were to be returned for each query, such queries would severely impact performance.

One solution to this problem is to move the queries and as much processing as possible "closer" to the data in the database. Thus our example for this section will be to implement the

OTHER_DEPARTMENT_MEMBERS procedure in the Oracle database. To achieve this, we will need to use Oracle SQL*Plus (a command-line tool) to create a stored procedure.

Log in to SQL*Plus and enter the following CREATE PROCEDURE statement. Alternatively, save this statement in a text file and execute it using the START command in SQL*Plus.

```
CREATE PROCEDURE OTHER_DEPARTMENT_MEMBERS
        (IN_EMPLOYEE_SSN IN NUMBER,
        OUT_COUNT_OTHER_MEMBERS OUT NUMBER) AS
-- Given an Employee's SSN, return the number of other employees
-- in the same department.
   TEMP_COUNT NUMBER;    -- Placeholder for count
BEGIN
   TEMP_COUNT := 0; -- Initialize to 0
-- Try and fill TEMP_COUNT with the count of other
-- Employees in the department
   SELECT COUNT(*)
   INTO TEMP_COUNT
   FROM EMPLOYEE
   WHERE EMPLOYEE.DNO =
   (SELECT EMPLOYEE.DNO
   FROM EMPLOYEE
   WHERE EMPLOYEE.SSN = IN_EMPLOYEE_SSN);
   -- See if we got a meaningful result
   IF (NVL(TEMP_COUNT, 0) <> 0) THEN
      OUT_COUNT_OTHER_MEMBERS := (TEMP_COUNT - 1 );
   ELSE
      OUT_COUNT_OTHER_MEMBERS := 0;
   END IF;
END;
```

After typing in this statement, be sure to RUN the command in the SQL*Plus buffer by typing RUN or by typing the forward slash /

Note. While creating a stored procedure, you may receive an error similar to the following:

ORA-01031: insufficient privileges

This indicates the DBA has not granted you the authorization to create stored procedures. Please contact your DBA to obtain this authorization.

To see if the procedure compiled correctly, look in view USER_ERRORS as follows:

```
SQL> SELECT * FROM user_errors;
no rows selected
```

If the message no rows selected appears, then no errors were found in the trigger.

Another alternative is to use the SQL*Plus command called show errors. After submitting a trigger or a stored procedure, any errors found during compilation can be displayed using the show errors command.

In some versions of SQL*Plus, the show errors command will not work due to a lack of buffer memory on the client computer. An error message may appear as in the following example:

```
SQL> CREATE PROCEDURE test AS
2 BEGIN
3 SELECT SYSDATE INTO :temp FROM dual;
4 END;
5 /
Warning: Procedure created with compilation errors.
SQL> show errors
buffer overflow. Use SET command to reduce ARRAYSIZE or increase MAXDATA.
No errors.
```

If the buffer overflow message appears, set the ARRAYSIZE variable to a lower number such as 2 with the following command:

```
SQL> SET ARRAYSIZE 2
```

Then use the show errors command as described:

```
SQL> show errors
Errors for PROCEDURE TEST:
LINE/COL ERROR
-------- ------------------------------------------------------
3/23     PLS-00049: bad bind variable 'TEMP'
```

To see what stored procedures you have created, query the USER_SOURCE view in the data dictionary.

The only major difference between the stored procedure created in the database schema through SQL*Plus and the procedure created in Oracle Forms is the way the header is formatted. Creating a stored procedure uses the following syntax:

```
CREATE PROCEDURE OTHER_DEPARTMENT_MEMBERS
    (IN_EMPLOYEE_SSN IN NUMBER,
    OUT_COUNT_OTHER_MEMBERS OUT NUMBER) AS
```

Contrast this with the procedure done in Oracle Forms:

```
PROCEDURE OTHER_DEPARTMENT_MEMBERS
    (IN_EMPLOYEE_SSN IN NUMBER,
    OUT_COUNT_OTHER_MEMBERS OUT NUMBER) IS
```

Once the OTHER_DEPARTMENT_MEMBERS procedure (Program Unit) has been created in SQL*Plus, it is stored as an object in your schema and will remain there until a

DROP PROCEDURE OTHER_DEPARTMENT_MEMBERS statement is issued. Any Oracle Form, Report or other procedure can make calls to OTHER_DEPARTMENT_MEMBERS as if it were a local procedure.

To see the stored procedure in action, open the emp_memb.fmb form and remove (delete) the Program Unit (procedure) OTHER_DEPARTMENT_MEMBERS from it. Save the form, compile, generate and run it.

The POST-CHANGE trigger on :EMPLOYEE.SSN will automatically make a call to the stored procedure version of OTHER_DEPARTMENT_MEMBERS located in the schema.

To view the available Stored Program Units from within Oracle Forms, switch to the Object Navigator and open up the Database Objects tree. From there, a list of schemas (users) will appear. Scroll down to your username and open it up. Then open up the Stored Program Units tree. A list of your stored procedure should then appear.

Additional Stored Procedures and Triggers

There are countless ways in which stored procedures and triggers can be used to enforce business rules and to process data in an application. In this section, a few of the most commonly used triggers and procedures are described.

Generating unique or consecutive identifiers using the table

Many of the keys used in tables are based on a number sequence. For example, in our DEPARTMENT table, the DNUMBER is an integer that should increase for each new department. To automatically generate a new DNUMBER, create a query to capture the largest current DNUMBER value and add 1 to it. Then assign this new value to the DNUMBER item in the DEPARTMENT data block. A trigger to do this could be created at the block level and should execute before any new record is inserted into the database. A PRE-INSERT trigger on the DEPARTMENT data block would be used for this example:

```
BEGIN
    SELECT MAX( dnumber ) + 1
    INTO :department.dnumber
    FROM department;
END;
```

A PRE-INSERT trigger executes just before the INSERT statement for a new record is sent to the database.

Generating unique or consecutive identifiers using an Oracle Sequence

One problem with the above method is that many users working on the same form to insert new records will run into concurrency problems. For each new record to be inserted, a full table scan must be done to find the largest identifier.

One solution to this problem is to use an Oracle Sequence. An Oracle Sequence is a schema object that keeps track of a simple integer and automatically increments this counter when it is accessed.

For example, in our DEPARTMENT table, the DNUMBER is an integer that should increase for each new department. To automatically generate a new DNUMBER, create an Oracle Sequence using the SQL*Plus tool:

```
CREATE SEQUENCE department_seq
INCREMENT BY 1
START WITH 1
MAXVALUE 99999
NOCYCLE;
```

The above department_seq sequence will begin counting from 1 and increment by 1 until it reaches 99999. After that, accessing the sequence will produce an error. This is reasonable since it is highly unlikely an organization will ever have more than 99999 departments.

The next step is to assign the next value of the sequence to the DNUMBER item in the DEPARTMENT data block. A trigger to do this would be created at the block level and should execute before any new record is inserted into the database. A PRE-INSERT trigger on the DEPARTMENT data block would be used for this example:

```
BEGIN
-- Get the next value for DNUMBER from the
-- department_seq sequence.
SELECT department_seq.nextval
INTO :department.dnumber
FROM dual;
END;
```

The dual table is a dummy table that contains exactly one record (row). We can use it in a SELECT...INTO statement to consistently return a single value. The nextval accessed in the sequence will return the current sequence value and then automatically increment it to the next value.

A PRE-INSERT trigger executes just before the INSERT statement for a new record is sent to the database.

Oracle Sequences are not applicable for master-detail forms such as purchase orders where an item number needs to be assigned in the detail table. For example, purchase order items are typically numbered: 1, 2, 3.... The next purchase order will also number the items 1, 2, 3, ... An Oracle Sequence is designed to deliver unique identifiers for primary keys and should not be used for such item numbers.

Checking constraints at the client

In any database system, it is always desirable to constrain the values certain columns can take on. It is possible to add constraints to the database tables themselves in order to enforce constraints, however, the enforcement only takes place when a transaction reaches the database. In addition, many constraints on the data that involve values of data from other tables may not be easily implemented as table constraints.

Many types of constraints on data can be checked in the client using triggers. For example, in our EMPLOYEE data entry form, we may want to enforce a constraint that no employee can act as their own supervisor. Thus for any record, SSN may not equal SUPERSSN. To implement such a constraint, add the SUPERSSN field to the EMPLOYEE form and then create a WHEN-VALIDATE-ITEM trigger on the SUPERSSN item in the EMPLOYEE data block:

```
BEGIN
    IF (:SUPERSSN = :SSN) THEN
        MESSAGE('Employees may not supervise themselves!');
        RAISE FORM_TRIGGER_FAILURE;
    END IF;
END;
```

The FORM_TRIGGER_FAILURE will cause the execution of the item validation to be halted and the user will have to change the SUPERSSN before moving on to another item.

ADDING ALERTS (POP-UP MESSAGES)

In the previous example, the MESSAGE procedure is used to display the error along the status bar at the bottom of the Forms window. A better approach may be to force the user's attention to the problem. This can be accomplished by creating a pop-up dialog box that forces the user to read the message and click an OK button (or some other button). In Oracle Forms, this is called an Alert.

To set up an Alert:

- Use the Object Navigator to display the Alerts area. Pull down the Navigator menu and choose Create. Click on the default name that is given for the new alert (something like ALERT4) and rename it: SUPERVISOR_ALERT
- Bring up the Property Palette for this Alert and fill in the following properties: Title: Supervisor Alert Message

  Message: Employees may not supervise themselves!

  Alert Style: STOP

  Button 1 Label: OK

  Leave the Button 2 Label and the Button 3 Label blank

  Default Alert button: Button 1

  Leave all of the other properties with their defaults and close the Property palette.
- Change the above WHEN-VALIDATE-ITEM trigger on the SUPERSSN item in the EMPLOYEE data block to:

```
DECLARE
    return_alert NUMBER;
BEGIN
    IF (:SUPERSSN = :SSN) THEN
```

```
        return_alert := SHOW_ALERT ('SUPERVISOR_ALERT');
        RAISE FORM_TRIGGER_FAILURE;
    END IF;
END;
```

The SHOW_ALERT procedure calls up the specified alert and obtains the return value (based on the button the user clicks on) to assign to a local variable called return_alert.

Below is an example of the Alert in action:

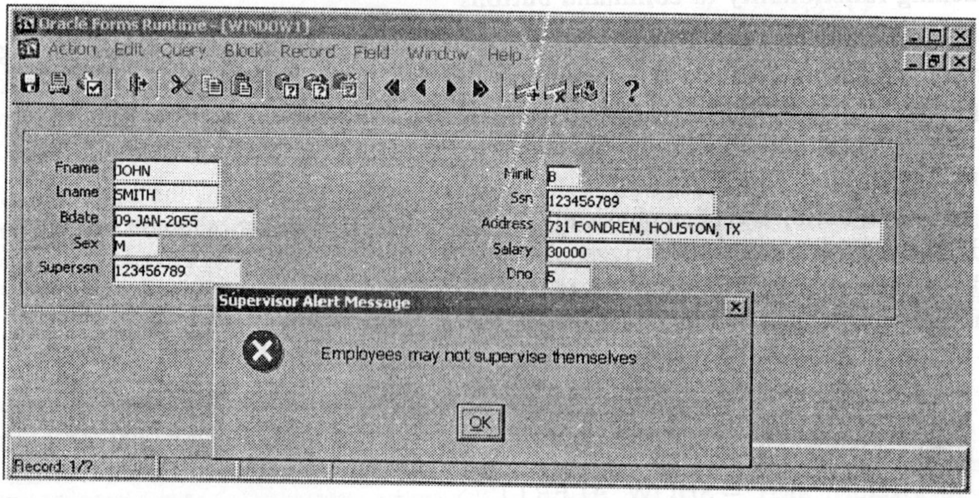

In general, Alerts may provide several different buttons for the user to click on. For example, to confirm exiting a form, a POST-FORM trigger might invoke an "Are you sure you want to Exit" Alert with "Yes" and "No" buttons. Or, to confirm deleting a record, a PRE-COMMIT trigger might invoke an "Are you sure you want ot delete this Employee?" Alert with "Yes" and "No" buttons. Based on the return_alert value, either a commit or rollback might be issued.

Populate items with default values

There are many cases where default values can be suggested for certain data items based upon values already supplied in other data items. The method here is to use a POST-ITEM or WHEN-VALIDATE-ITEM trigger to populate another field, only if the other field is currently blank. For example, to populate the SUPERSSN data item of the EMPLOYEE block based upon the MGRSSN of the employee's department, the following WHEN-VALIDATE-ITEM trigger code might be used on the DNO data item:

```
BEGIN
    IF :SUPERSSN IS NULL THEN
        SELECT department.mgrssn
        INTO :employee.superssn
        FROM department
```

```
        WHERE department.dnumber = :employee.dno;
    END IF;
END;
```

Note that the IF statement uses :SUPERSSN IS NULL to check to see if any value has been supplied for SUPERSSN. If nothing was typed into the SUPERSSN data item, then its value is NULL. If the user types anything at all into the SUPERSSN data item, then the IF statement will evaluate to false and no value will be suggested.

Attaching functionality to command buttons

Command buttons can be added on a form to carry out functions such as exiting a form, committing/saving changed records and so on. The basic command button object contains properties for the button Label (the text provided on the button itself). Additional properties include visual attributes including the ability to display a bitmap image in place of the button's normal appearance.

Once a button has been physically placed on a form, functionality is added but writing a WHEN-BUTTON-PRESSED trigger. As one might expect, this trigger executes when the user clicks on the button. So, for example, to create a button to exit the form when the user clicks on it the WHEN-BUTTON-PRESSED trigger might look like:

```
DECLARE
    return_alert NUMBER;
BEGIN
    return_alert := SHOW_ALERT ('EXIT_ALERT');
    IF (return_alert = alert_button1) THEN
        EXIT_FORM;
    END IF;
END;
```

The above code assumes there is an Alert called EXIT_ALERT with two buttons: "Yes" and "No". If the user clicks on the first button ("Yes") then the EXIT_FORM procedure is called and the form will exit (close). If the user clicks on any other button, then the Alert will close and the form will remain open.

Passing parameters between forms

There are many occasions that require the passing of data from one form to another. One such example is when we query a certain record on one form and then wish to call up another form with the same record automatically retrieved. In general, data values can be passed between forms using GLOBAL variables (treat :GLOBAL as a block available in all forms) or by using Parameter lists. In the example, below, the parameter list features will be used to demonstrate how data can be passed from one form to another.

For this example, we wil make use of two forms: A basic EMPLOYEE form with all fields and the EMPLOYEE/DEPENDENT master/detail form. The idea is to place to button on the EMPLOYEE form that when pressed, will call the EMPLOYEE/DEPENDENT form and automatically query the dependents for the employee being viewed on the EMPLOYEE form. The main steps are:

- On the EMPLOYEE form, create a button and label it "Query Dependents". Create a WHEN-BUTTON-PRESSED trigger with the following code (comments are enclosed in the code):

```
DECLARE
    /* Declare pl_id as the identifier for the parameter list */
    pl_id ParamList;
BEGIN
    /* See if that parameter list already exists. If so, destroy it */
    pl_id := Get_Parameter_List('tmpdata');
    IF NOT Id_Null(pl_id) THEN
        Destroy_Parameter_List( pl_id );
    END IF;
    /* Create a fresh parameter list */
    pl_id := Create_Parameter_List('tmpdata');

    /* Add a new parameter to this list called EMPLOYEESSN */
    /* Assign this parameter the current value of the :SSN field */
    Add_Parameter(pl_id, 'EMPLOYEESSN', TEXT_PARAMETER, :SSN);

    /* Now run a new form called 'empdepn' (must be in the same */
    /* directory) as the employee form we are now editing. */
    /* Pass along the identifier of our parameter list (pl_id) */
    Run_Product(FORMS, 'empdepn', SYNCHRONOUS, RUNTIME,
        FILESYSTEM, pl_id, NULL);
END;
```

- Compile and save this form.
- Now open up the empdepn (EMPLOYEE/DEPENDENT) form.
- Using the Object Navigator, create a new PARAMETER called EMPLOYEESSN. This parameter will automatically be assigned a value based on the parameter list passed to the form by the above RUN_PRODUCT procedure call.
- Create a new trigger called WHEN-NEW-FORM-INSTANCE. This trigger will execute whenever the form is first run.

```
DECLARE
    /* Declare a forms block identifer */
    blk_id Block;
```

```
BEGIN
    /* Obtain the block ID of the EMPLOYEE block. This is the */
    /* Master block in the empdepn master/detail form. */
    blk_id := Find_Block('EMPLOYEE');
    IF NOT Id_Null(blk_id) THEN
        /* Check to make sure our parameter has a value. If this form */
        /* were executed by itself, then the parameter will be null. */
        /* If this form is called from EMPLOYEE then the parameter will */
        /* be passed along and assigned to :PARAMETER.employeessn */
        IF (:PARAMETER.employeessn is not null) THEN
            /* Since we have a parameter, use it to alter the WHERE Clause */
            /* property so that it becomes WHERE ssn=
                                        :PARAMETER.employeessn */
            SET_BLOCK_PROPERTY(blk_id,DEFAULT_WHERE,'ssn='
                                        || :PARAMETER.employeessn);
            /* Navigate to the EMPLOYEE block and execute a query automatically */
            GO_BLOCK('EMPLOYEE');
            EXECUTE_QUERY;
        END IF;
    END IF;
END;
```

- Compile and save the empdepn form.
- Now run the EMPLOYEE form, query an employee record and click on the "Query Dependents" button. The empdepn form should appear with the dependents automaticaly queried.

LAB ASSIGNMENT—19

1. Create an Oracle Sequence (using SQL*Plus) that will generate new Department numbers for the DEPARTMENT table. Add the requisite PRE-INSERT trigger code to insert a unique DNUMBER each time a new department record is created.
2. Create an alert that displays a warning if an employee's salary is larger than their supervisor's. In a WHEN-VALIDATE-ITEM trigger, run a query to check if the employee's salary is greater than their supervisor's and if so, show the alert.
3. Put in some validation code that will check to make sure if a DEPENDENT is a SON or DAUGHTER, then the DEPENDETN's BDATE must be less than the EMPLOYEE's BDATE. If this is not the case, show an alert.
4. After you learn how to create Reports create a simple DEPARTMENT data entry form with a button that, when pressed, will run a report for that department by passing along the DNUMBER as a parameter.

14 Oracle Reports

Objectives :

- Oracle Reports Basics
- Starting Developer Tools Under Windows 95/98/NT/2000
- The Oracle Reports Object Navigator
- Creating Menus in Oracle Forms
- Assigning Commands to Menu Items
- Graphics and the Chart Wizard
- Oracle Schema Builder
- Adding Relationships between Tables

ORACLE REPORTS BASICS

The Oracle Reports Builder allows the developer to create sophisticated reports in a variety of layouts and contains many customization features.

STARTING DEVELOPER TOOLS UNDER WINDOWS 95/98/NT/2000

A typical installation of Developer creates several folders under the Start Programs menu. The main items for the Oracle Reports 6i programs are found under the menu item: Oracle Reports 6i and include the following items:

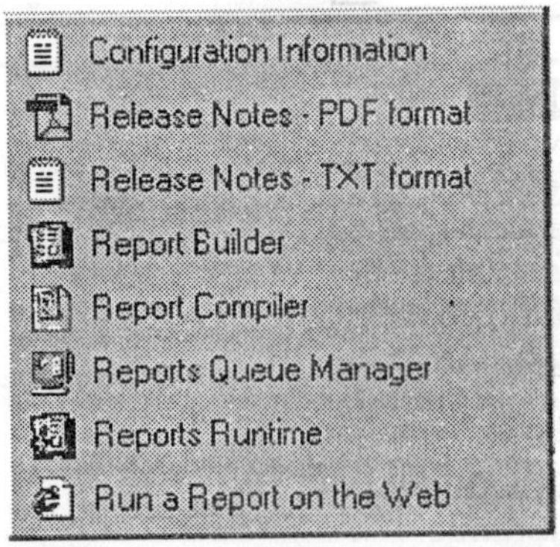

To run Oracle Reports Builder under Windows 95/98/NT/2000, click on the Start -> Programs -> Oracle Reports 6i -> Report Builder menu item.

As with Oracle Forms, an initial screen will appear:

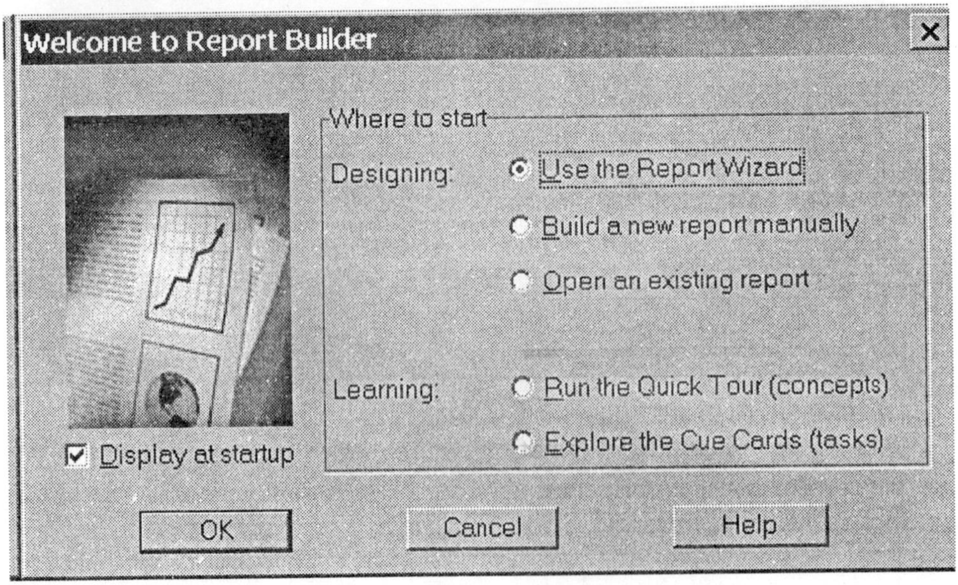

Click on the Cancel button to proceed directly to the Object Navigator.

THE ORACLE REPORTS OBJECT NAVIGATOR

The Oracle Reports main screen is called the Object Navigator (similar to Oracle Forms) and can be seen in the following figure:

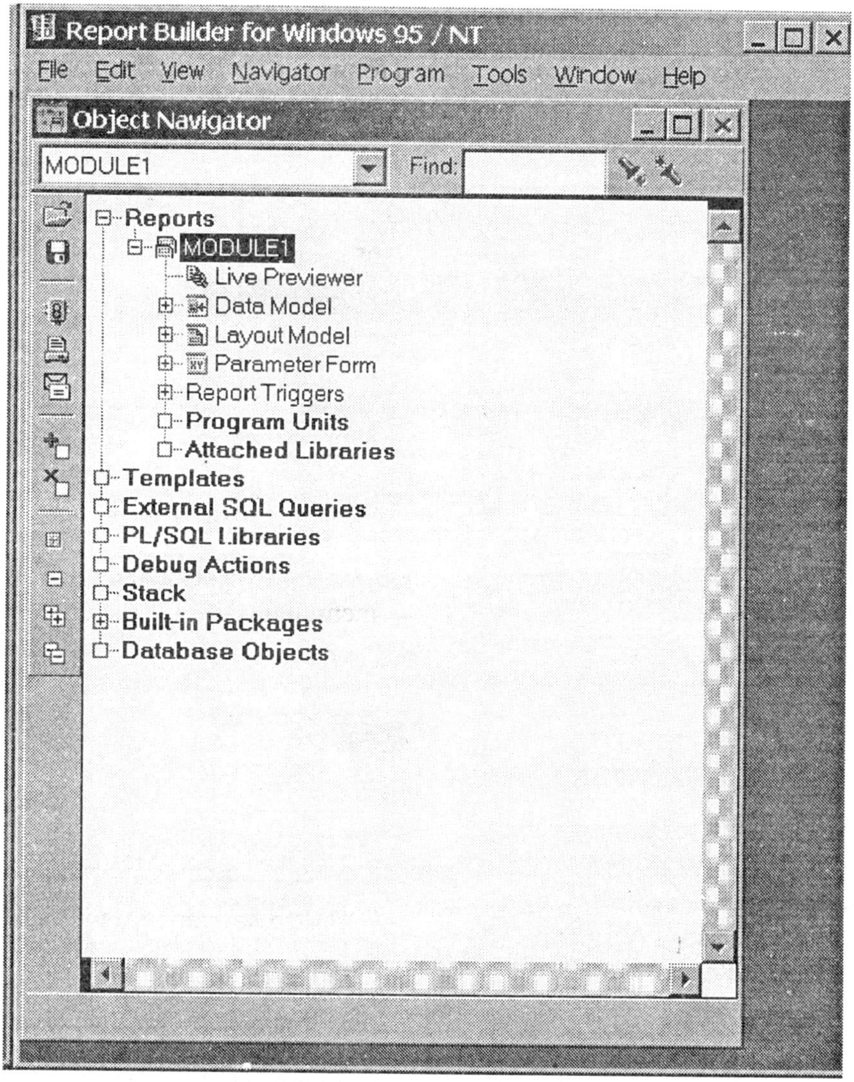

The main sections of the Object Navigator are:

1. Data Model - Contains information about queries used for a report.
2. Layout - Contains information about how a report is formatted including headers, footers, margins, fonts, etc.

3. Parameter Form - Contains information about the initial screen that is displayed when a form first runs.
4. Report Triggers - PL/SQL code that can be executed before, during or after a report has been executed.

As with Oracle Forms, the first step in using Oracle Reports is to Connect to an Oracle server. This is accomplished by pulling down the File menu and selecting the Connect menu item.

Fill in your Oracle Username and Oracle Password (press the tab key to move between the fields).

For the Database field, type in the service name for your Oracle database. For example, if you are using Personal Oracle Lite, the Database: would be ODBC:POLITE. Contact your system administrator to learn the service name for your Oracle database and provide that information in the Database: field.

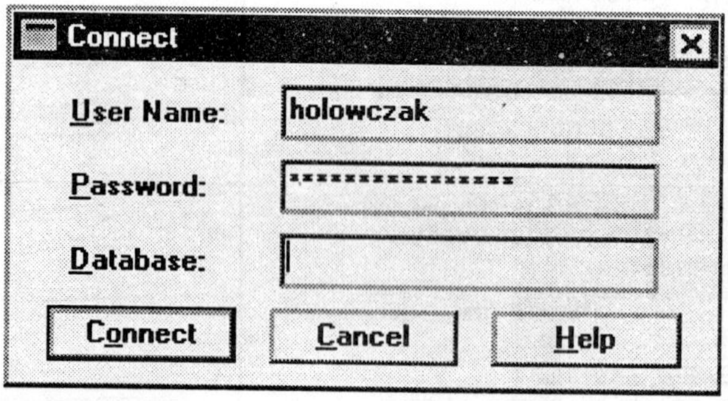

Click on the Connect button to complete the connection (Under some versions of UNIX, the button is labeled OK). If the user name or password is mistyped or incorrect, the dialog box will be re-displayed. Be sure to provide your Oracle username and password (not your UNIX host password).

Creating Reports in Oracle Reports

Creating reports follows a 4 step process:

1. Define the Data Model - This step specifies which queries should be run on the database including how multiple queries are related and how they are grouped. This step must be done by hand. Queries that have been created elsewhere can be imported into Oracle Reports.
2. Define the Layout - This step specifies the layout of the report including the overall orientation of query results and the suppression of repeating groups. There are a number of default report layouts that can automatically be applied to a data model.
3. Create and/or Customize the Parameter Form - If some user input is required in order to run the report, then a parameter form must be customized. All reports have a default parameter form.
4. (optional) Create any triggers or program units that will be executed with the report.

Oracle Reports 3.0 and 6.0 support a wizard that takes the developer through all of these steps. This approach will be demonstrated next.

Creating a Single-Table Report

In this section, we go through the steps for creating a report that views the contents of a single table.

Specify the Data Model and Layout

The first step is to specify the data model and layout of the report. We will use the Report wizard to accomplish this. From the Object Navigator, pull down the Tools menu and choose Report wizard...

The first screen for the reports wizard will appear prompting for the style of the report and for the Report Title.

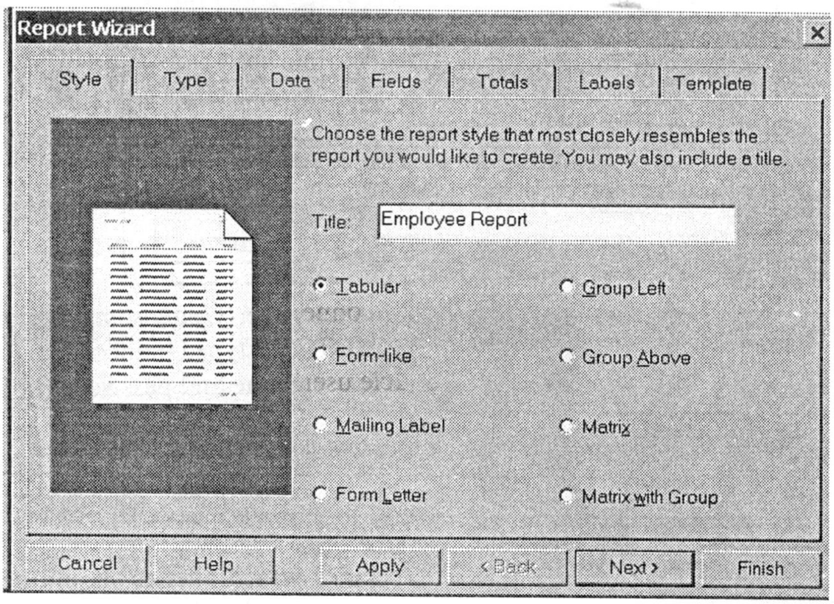

The eight layout choices include:

1. Tabular - Simple table with column headings at the top and data records in consecutive rows below.
2. Form-Like - Column headings on the left hand side with data values next to them on the right.
3. Mailing Label - No column headings and records grouped into repeating sections sized to print directly to a sheet of mailing labels.
4. Form Letter - Arbitrary placement of data items within a text body.
5. Group-Left - A Master/Detail/Detail style where the master records are grouped on the left hand side with details to the right.

6. Group-Above - A Master/Detail/Detail style where the master records appear above the detail records.
7. Matrix - Column labels on both the left and the top with data values in the middle. Similar to a spreadsheet.
8. Matrix with Group - A combination of Master/Detail (Group-Above) and Matrix.

For this report, type in "Employee Report" as the title, choose the Tabular Layout and click on the Next button.

The next step is to specify the Type of query the report will be based on. The two main choices are a SQL query and an Oracle Express (OLAP) query. For this example, choose the "SQL Statement" and click the next button.

The next step is to specify the query that will form the basis of the report. In this case, type the following query in the SQL Query Statement: text box:

```
SELECT FNAME, LNAME, SSN, SALARY, DNO
FROM EMPLOYEE ;
```

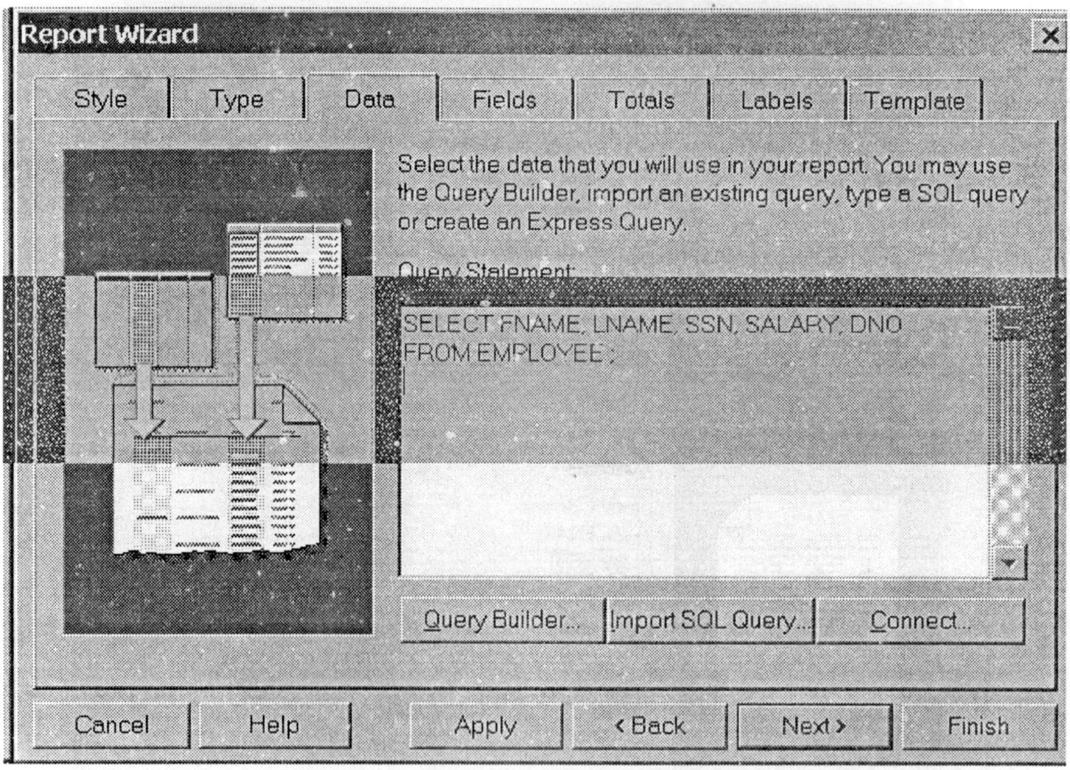

Then click on the Next button to move to the next step.

Note. If you did not Connect to the database, you will be prompted for the Username, Password and Database.

In the next wizard dialog box, specify which columns from the SQL Query will be displayed in the report output. To specify all columns, click on the double right arrow to bring all of the *Available Fields* to the *Displayed Fields* side.

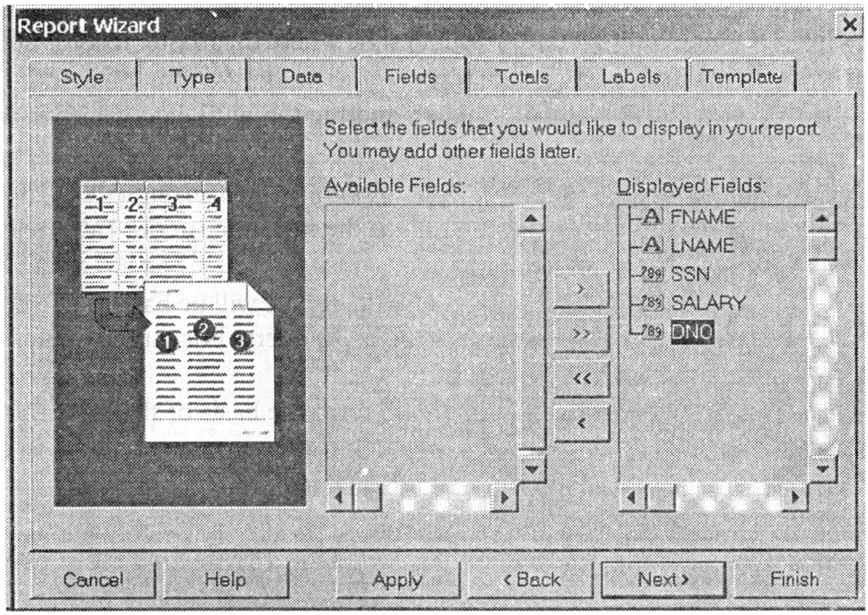

Click on the Next button to move to the next dialog box.

In the next step, aggregate functions can be applied to the fields on the report. For this example, we will display the average salary as well as a count of employees. Highlight the SALARY field and click on the *Average* button. Then highlight the SSN field and click on the *Count* button.

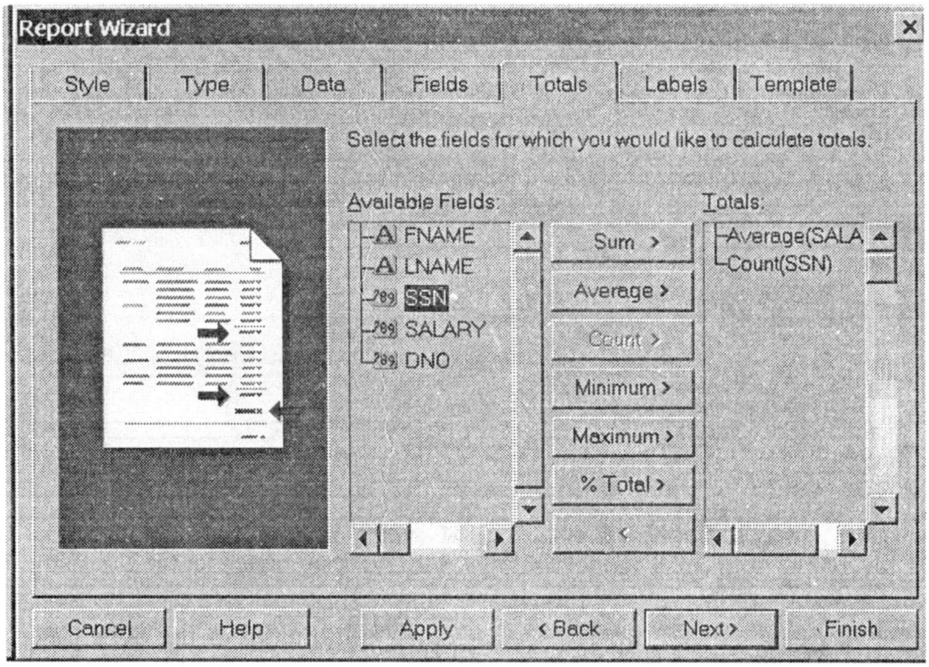

The next dialog box allows you to change the field labels and display widths for various fields in the report.

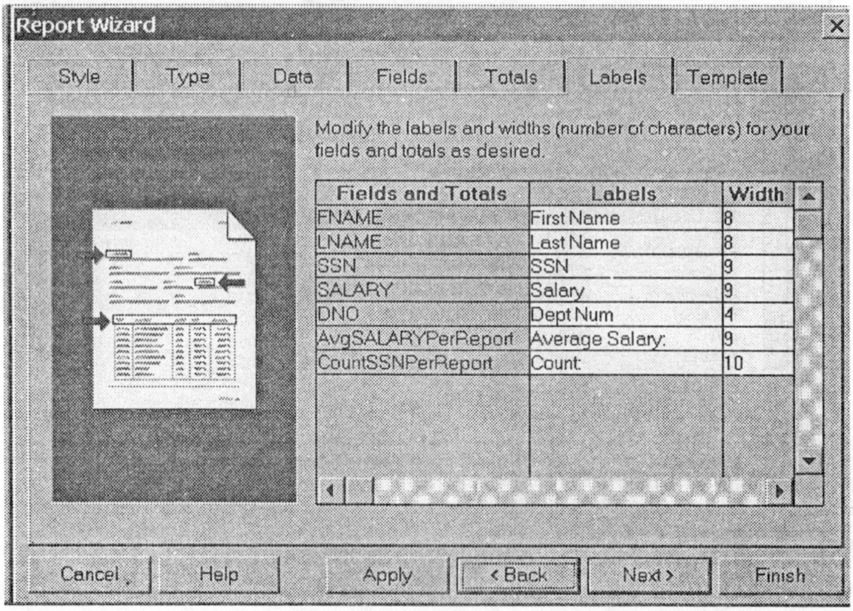

As a final step, a design template can be applied to the report. Design templates include specifications for fonts, colors and layout of the report. For this example, choose the Corporate 2 template and then click on the Finish button.

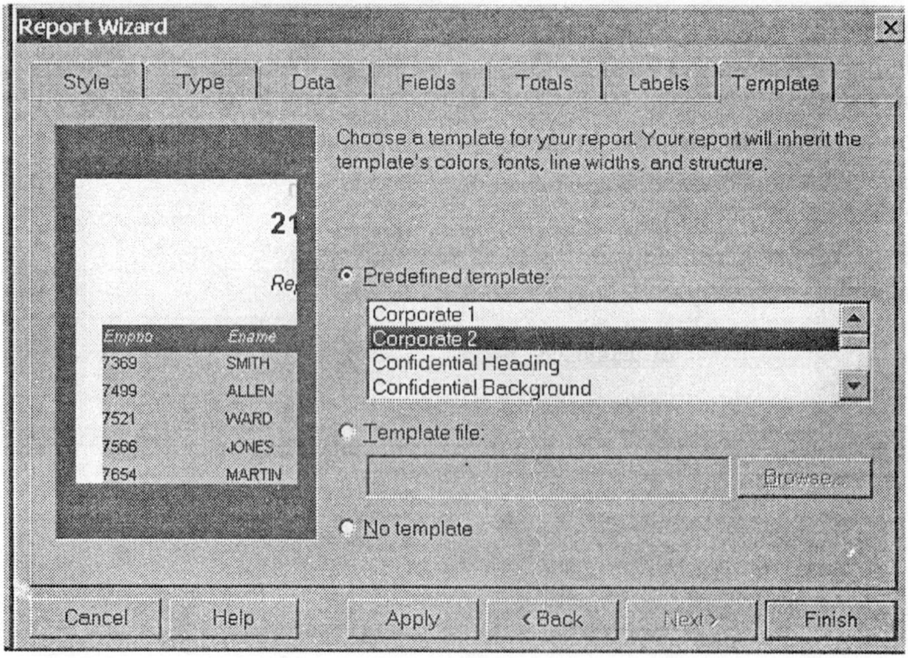

After a short delay, the Reports Live Previewer will appear showing the executing report.

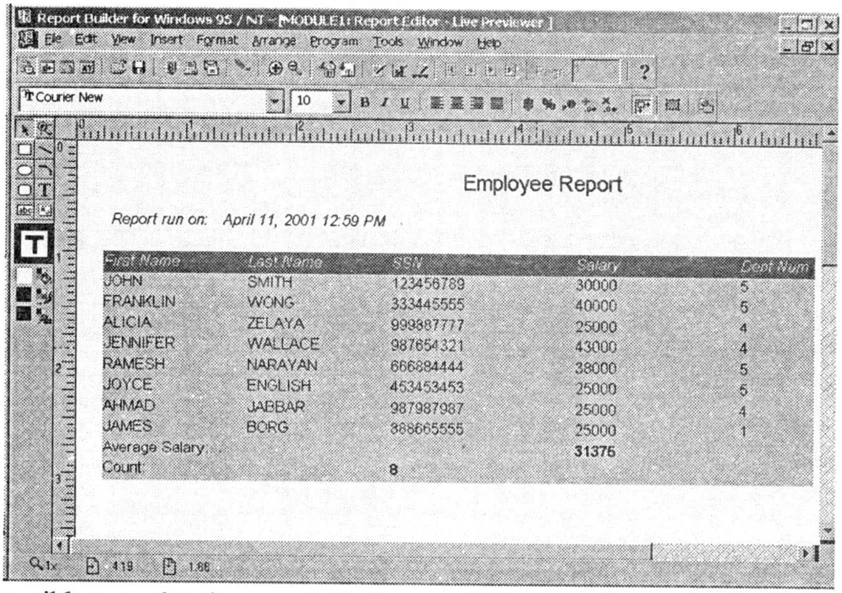

It is possible to make changes to the layout of the report by using the tool palette on the left hand side. When you have finished touching up the report, close the Reports Live Previewer and the Object Navigator will reappear. To view the report again, pull down the Program menu and choose Run Report.

Saving, Generating and Running the Report

To save a report, pull down the File menu and choose the Save option. This is similar to saving an Oracle Form. The source code for Oracle Reports are saved in files with an .rdf file name extension. Compiled and generated reports are saved with a .rep extension.

For this example, save this report as employee.rdf

Once the report is saved, it can be run by pulling down the View menu and choosing the Runtime Preview menu item.

As the report is running, an Activity screen will appear giving an indication of the processing that is currently underway.

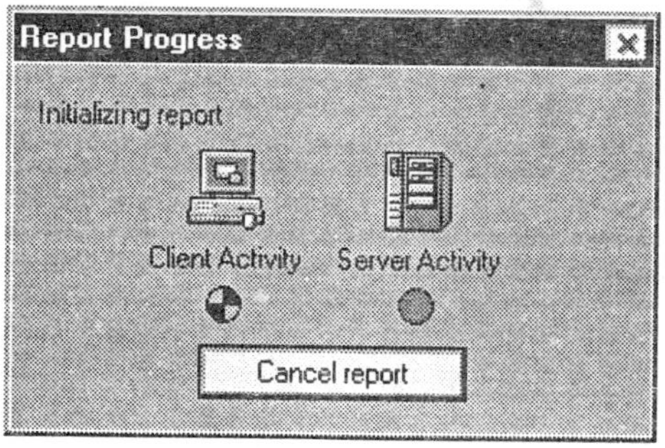

The Activity will go through 3 stages: Client Activity while the queries are prepared, Server Activity when the queries are executed and finally Client Activity as the report is formatted. When this is finished, the report will appear on screen.

Example: Creating a Report

For this exercise, create a report to display all of the records in the DEPARTMENT table including a join with the EMPLOYEE table to display the last name of the department manager.

- Start up the Report wizard. Use "Departments" as the title and enter the following SQL Statement as the query:
- SELECT dnumber, dname, mgrstartdate, mgrssn, lname
  FROM department, employee
  WHERE department.mgrssn = employee.ssn;
- Summarize the report with an average of the Salary column.
- Save the new report as departmg.rdf

The finished report should look something like the following:

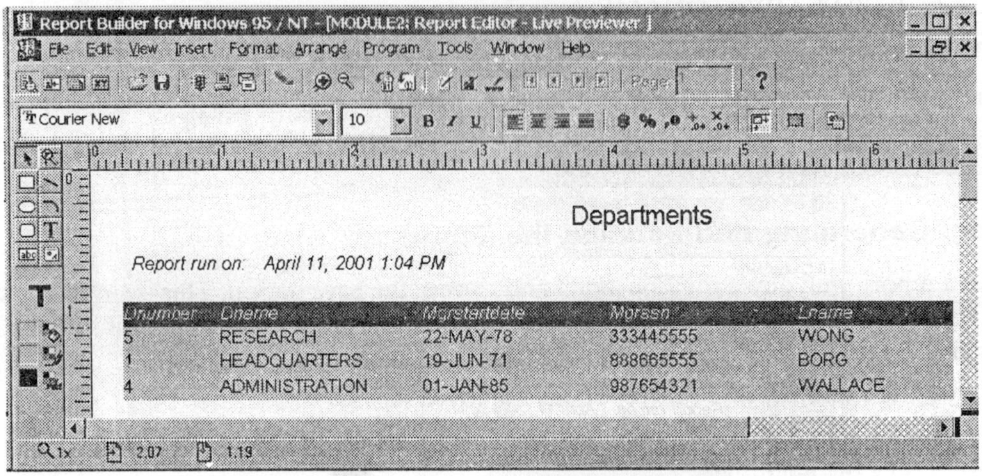

Creating a Master-Detail Report

In this section, the steps for creating a report that views the contents of two tables in a Master-Detail (one to many) relationship are given. To avoid any confusion, Save and Close any existing reports before proceeding.

Specify the Master-Detail Data Model and Layout

As in the single-table report, we begin by specifying the data model and layout for the Master-Detail report by using the Report Wizard.

Invoke the wizard by pulling down the Tools menu and choosing Report wizard. Following these steps to complete the wizard:

1. For the Report Title use: Departments and Employees
2. For the *Report Style*, choose *Group Above.*

3. Choose a SQL Statement and the SQL Query:
4. SELECT DNAME, FNAME, LNAME, SALARY
   FROM DEPARTMENT, EMPLOYEE
   WHERE DEPARTMENT.DNUMBER = EMPLOYEE.DNO;
5. Designate the DNAME field as a *Group field* (Level 1). Click on the DNAME field and then on the right arrow button.
6. Display all fields in the report.
7. Choose Average Salary as a *Totals* field. Click on the SALARY field and then click on the Average button.
8. Touch up the fields and labels as follows:
9. Fields and Totals Labels
10. DNAME Department Name
11. FNAME First Name
12. LNAME Last Name
13. SALARY Salary
14. AvgSALARYperDNAME Average:
15. AvgSALARYperRep Average For all Employees:
16. Use the Corporate 2 template.

From this point, click on Finish to display the Live Report Preview:

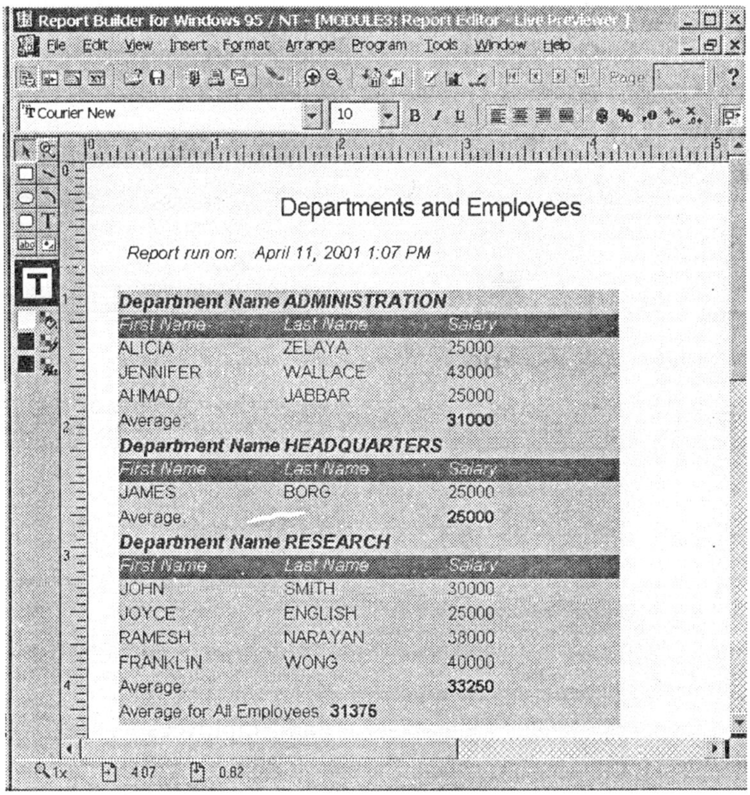

Example: Creating a Master-Detail Report

In this exercise, a master-detail report will be created that displays each EMPLOYEE record, with a group of DEPENDENT below.

Create a new Report using the wizard. Give a title: "Employees and Their Dependents"

Select the Group Above report type and use the following SQL query:

```
SELECT employee.fname, employee.lname,
       employee.bdate AS EmpBdate,
       employee.sex AS EmpSex, dependent.dependent_name,
       dependent.bdate AS DepBdate,
       dependent.sex AS DepSex, dependent.relationship
FROM employee, dependent
WHERE employee.ssn = dependent.essn;
```

Note the use of column aliases (AS) to differentiate the bdate and sex columns.

Select the lname, fname, empsex, empbdate fields as the "Group 1" fields. These should all be from the EMPLOYEE table.

Select all fields to display in the report and do not select any fields for the calculate totals step.

- Touch up the report in the live previewer to fit on one screen.
- Save the report as file: empdepen.rdf

The report should look similar to the following when completed:

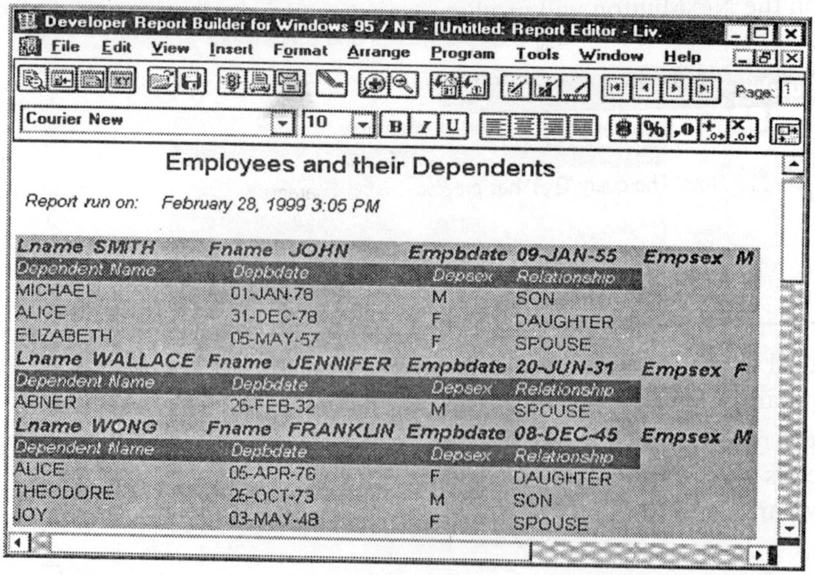

Parameter forms in Oracle Reports

For each of the Oracle Reports examples thus far, all of the records in the respective tables were returned as part of the report. However, there may be situations where only a subset of the database records are required. In these cases, we would like to prompt the user to enter some criteria that can be used to filter the report. In Oracle Reports, a *Parameter Form* fulfills this role.

Parameter forms are simple Oracle forms that prompt the user for some information before a report is executed. This information can become part of the WHERE clause in the report query and is used to filter the records returned in the report. Parameters in Oracle Reports can either be filled in by the user on a parameter form or can be filled in automatically by passing the parameters in from another Oracle Forms form (see the example of parameter passing in the previous section on Oracle Forms).

In the following example, a simple parameter form is automatically created by Oracle Reports to restrict a query on the EMPLOYEE table by showing only employees in a given department number (DNO) supplied by the user.

1. Create a new report using the report wizard. Specify "Employees" as the report title and use a Tabular report layout.
2. Use the following SQL query exactly as written. Note the use of the full colon in the WHERE clause.
3. SELECT *
   FROM employee
   WHERE employee.dno = :DNO_PARAMETER;

In the above query, :DNO_PARAMETER is the name of a run time parameter. When the report is executed, the user will supply a value for this parameter thus completing the WHERE clause for the query.

Clicking on the Next button will produce the following alert:

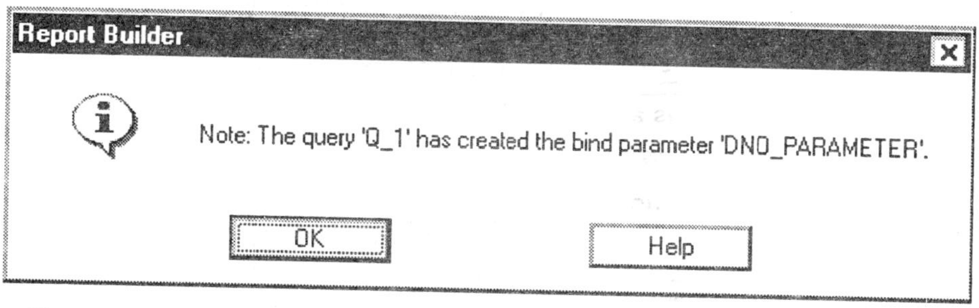

6. Choose all of the columns (fields) for display in the report. Do not choose any fields for summary information.
7. When the report wizard is finished, the report and parameter form (based upon the parameters given in the SQL query) will be created. As the live previewer is running, the new parameter form will be displayed:

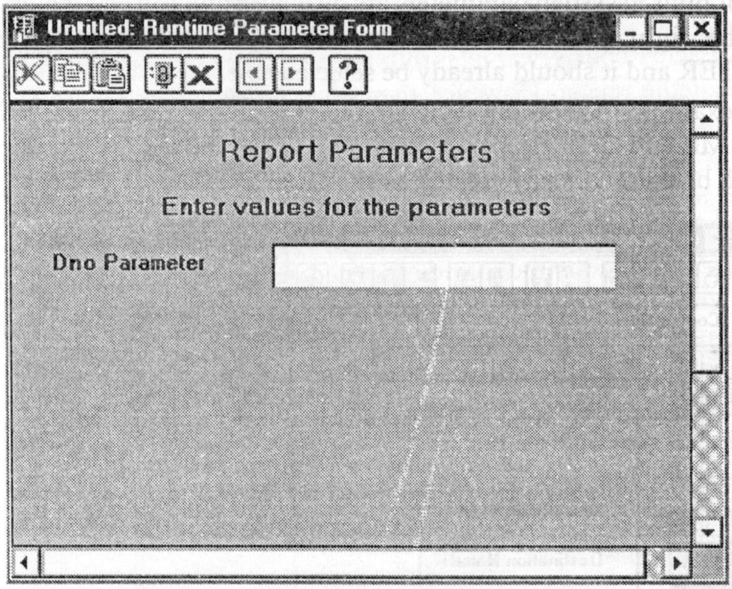

For this example, choose department 5 (type the number 5 in the field) and press the enter key. Notice that only employees in department 5 are displayed in the live previewer.

Building a Custom Parameter Form

At this point, whenever the report is run, a default parameter form showing the DNO_PARAMETER will be displayed. However, it is possible to create a custom parameter form as shown in the following steps.

1. Switch to the Object Navigator, pull down the Tools menu and choose the Parameter Form Builder. This is shown below:

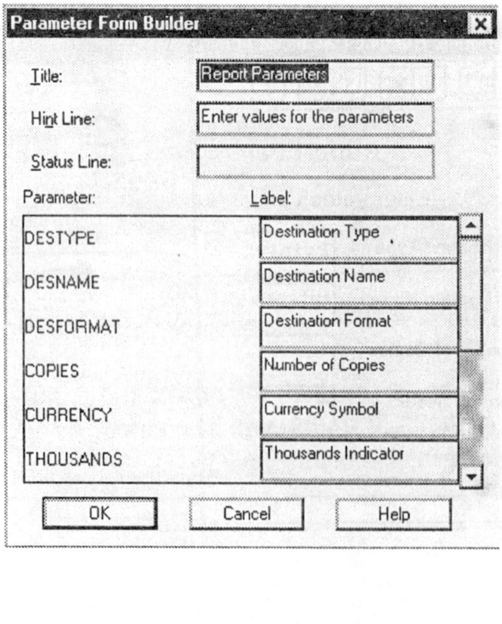

A number of built-in system parameters are displayed and can be highlighted by clicking on them with the right mouse button. Note that at the bottom of this list is the DNO_PARAMETER and it should already be selected.

2. For this example, in addition to the DNO_PARAMETER also select the DESTYPE, DESNAME and COPIES parameters. Then click the OK button. A new parameter form will be automatically created as shown below.

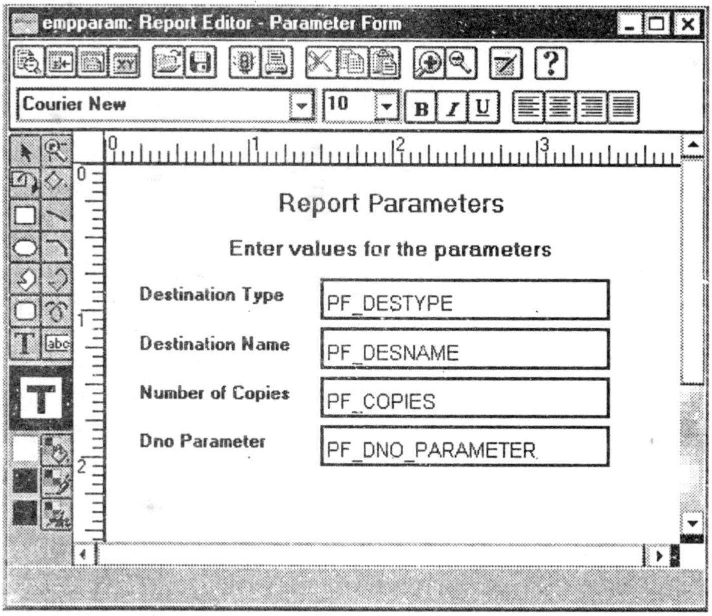

3. Save the report as empparam.rdf. When the form is executed (pull down the Program menu and choose Run Report), the new parameter form will be displayed as shown below:

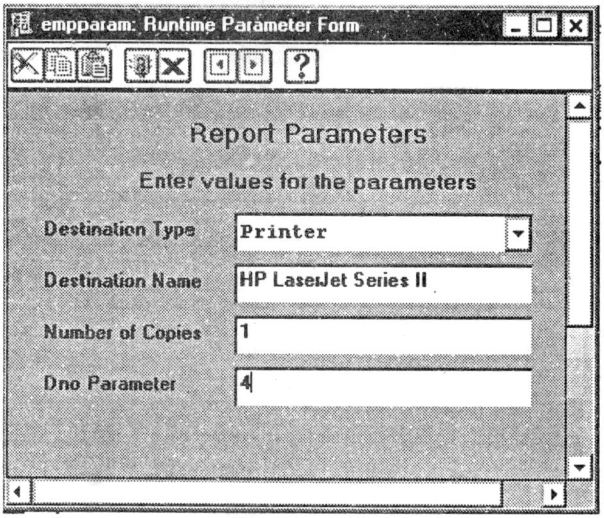

In the above example, 1 copy of the report will be sent to the printer named "HP LaserJet Series II". The report will only show employees in department 4.

Other Destination Type options include Screen, File and E-mail.

Parameter forms can be highly customized to include list of values user prompts and other user-friendly features. The techniques used for Oracle Forms can be easily applied to parameter forms in Oracle Reports.

CREATING MENUS IN ORACLE FORMS

Note. The properties for Menus in different versions of Forms seem to change with every minor revision. Please keep in mind, the version of Forms you are working with may differ slightly from what is shown in this tutorial.

Thus far, we have covered the basics for creating forms and reports using Oracle Developer. Some advanced features such as using stored procedures (Program Units) have also been introduced.

In a complete Database System, the applications consist of many forms and reports that might be used by a number of users. Access to forms and reports is typically accomplished through *menus*. In Oracle Developer, menus can be created to guide users into forms and reports of interest. Menus are designed as part of the Oracle Forms designer.

In Oracle Forms, every form runs with one of the following:

1. The default menu which includes the Action, Edit, Block, Field, Record, Query, Window, Help menus. The structure of the default menu cannot be changed.

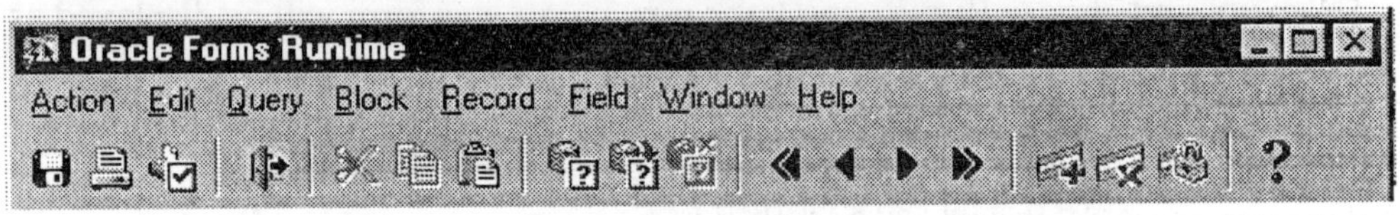

2. A custom menu that you define as a separate module and then attach to the form for runtime execution.
3. No menu at all.

The default menu is part of the form module. However, custom menu modules are separate from form modules. So, when a single-form application runs using a custom menu, there will be two executable files:

- an .FMX form module
- an .MMX menu module

In a multi-form application, Multiple forms can share the same menu, or each form can invoke a different menu.

To explicitly specify the default menu in Forms 6i:

1. Select the name of the form/module in the Object Navigator. Click with the right mouse button and choose Properties from the pop-up menu.
2. In the Menu Module property, type DEFAULT &SMARTBAR to get the default menu and a button bar below it. If you want the form to run without a menu, leave the Menu Module property blank.

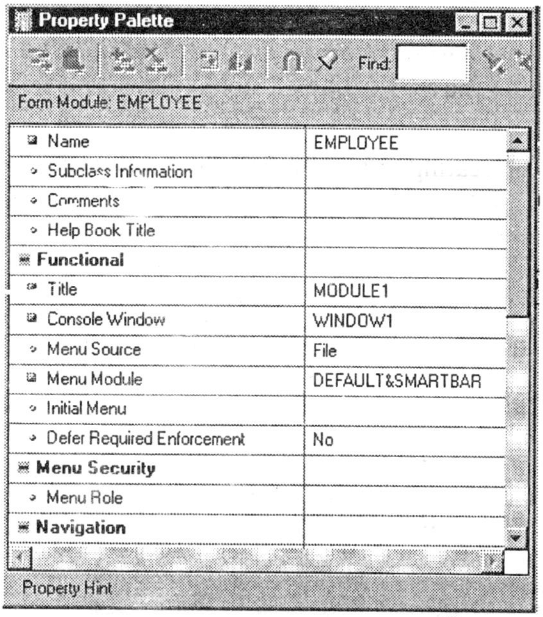

To explicitly specify the default menu in older versions of Developer:

1. Select the name of the form/module in the Object Navigator. Click with the right mouse button and choose Properties from the pop-up menu.
2. In the Menu Module property, type DEFAULT. If you want the form to run without a menu, leave the Menu Module property blank.

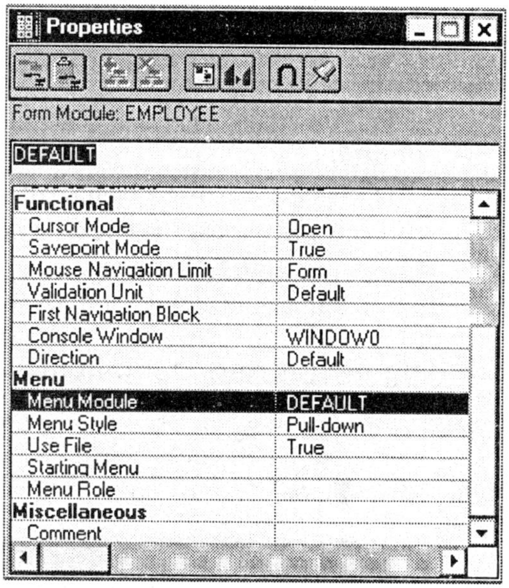

The default menu is suitable for control over the current form being executed, however, it does not contain custom menu items pertaining to a specific application. In the following section, the steps to create a custom menu structure will be introduced.

The Oracle Forms Menu Hierarchy

The Oracle Forms menu hierarchy contains three object categories:

1. Menu modules - Like form modules, a menu module can contain its own items (menus and menu items), program units and other objects.
2. Menus - Including main menus, individual menus, and submenus
3. Menu items

Creating a Custom Menu

Designing a custom menu requires five basic steps:

1. Creating a menu module
2. Creating menus and menu items
3. Assigning commands to menu items
4. Saving and generating the menu module
5. Attaching a menu module to a form

Creating a Menu Module

The first step in designing a custom menu is to create a menu module. There are several ways to create a new menu module:

1. Pull down the File menu, highlight the New menu item and then select the Menu menu item.
2. Navigate down to the Menus subtree in the Object Navigator, pull down the Navigator menu and choose the Create menu item.

A new menu module will be created and a default name will be assigned. Click on this default menu name and assign it a more meaningful name such as mymenu.

Creating menus and menu items

Creating menus and menu items can be accomplished using the Menu Editor. To activate the menu editor, first highlight the name of your menu, then pull down the Tools menu and click on the Menu Editor item.

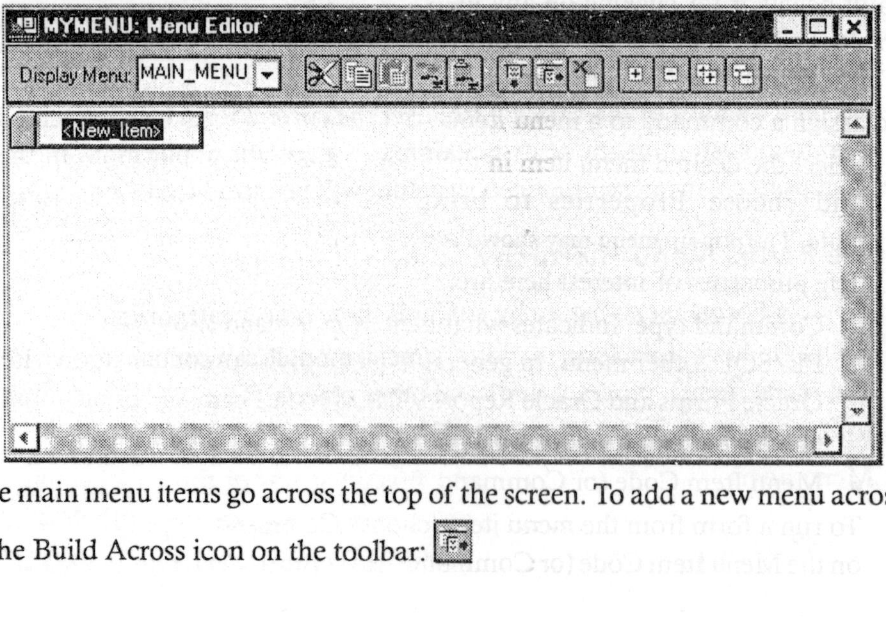

The main menu items go across the top of the screen. To add a new menu across the top, click on the Build Across icon on the toolbar:

Sub-menus and menu items appear below each one. To add a new sub-menu or menu item, click on the Build Down icon on the toolbar: 

To change the name of a menu or menu item, click in the menu object and over-write the name that appears there.

Using the icons, create and re-label several menus and menu items to appear as follows:

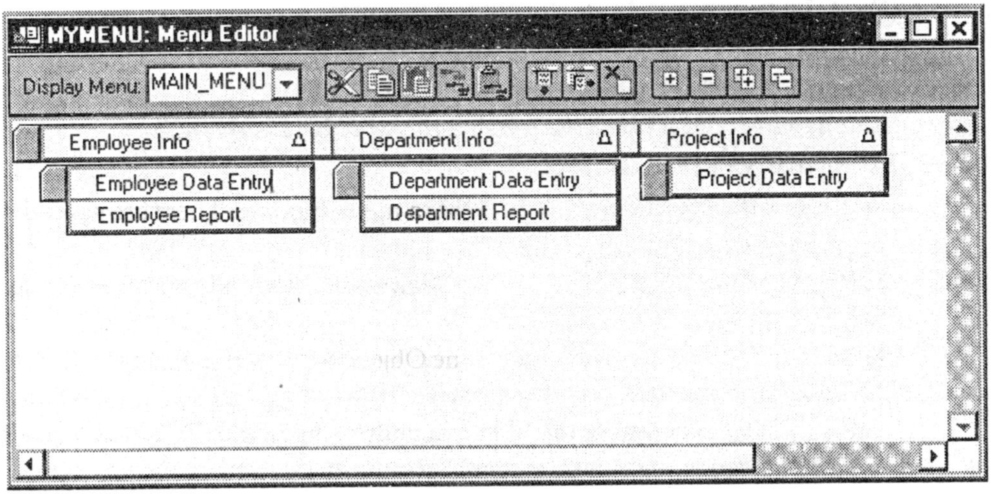

Once this is completed, the basic menu structure will be in place. The next step is to add functionality to each menu item.

ASSIGNING COMMANDS TO MENU ITEMS

The default behavior for clicking on any menu is for that menu's items to be displayed. The next step is to assign commands to each of the menu items so that when a user clicks on a menu item, a form, report or SQL*Plus script is executed.

To assign a command to a menu item:

1. Select the desired menu item in the Menu Editor. Click with the right mouse button and choose Properties to bring up the properties of that menu item. **Note.** The pop-up menu may show Property Palette.
2. The properties of interest here are:
   - Command type: Indicates what kind of command should be run: Form, Report, PL/SQL, other menu. In general, the PL/SQL command type is used to launch Oracle Forms and Oracle Reports. The specific Form and Report command types are maintained for backwards compatibility only.
   - Menu Item Code (or Command Text): The text of the actual command to run.

To run a form from the menu item, choose Command Type PL/SQL. Double click on the Menu Item Code (or Command Text) property and type in the PL/SQL editor:

```
BEGIN
   RUN_PRODUCT(FORMS, 'employee', SYNCHRONOUS, RUNTIME,
         FILESYSTEM, '', '');
END;
```

RUN_PRODUCT is a PL/SQL built-in function that runs another Oracle Developer product. The parameters to RUN_PRODUCT are:

- Product: FORMS or REPORTS
- Document/Module: name of the file in single quotes
- Command Mode: SYNCHRONOUS or ASYNCHRONOUS
- Executable Mode: RUNTIME
- Location: FILESYSTEM or DATABASE
- Parameter List: A list of parameters to pass to the form or NULL
- Display: Type of display to show the product on. Can be NULL to indicate the current display.

Note. Starting with Forms 5.0, (which uses PL/SQL version 2.3) you may not use NULL in the call to RUN_PRODUCT here. You must use two single quotes (indicating a zero length character string).

Compile this code by clicking on the Compile button. Then close the PL/SQL editor.

Repeat the above steps for each menu item.

A final menu item should be created to Exit the application. Call the menu: Exit Application and enter the following PL/SQL code:

```
BEGIN
      EXIT_FORM;
END;
```

EXIT_FORM is a built-in procedure that exits the current form.

A View of the complete mymenu is shown below:

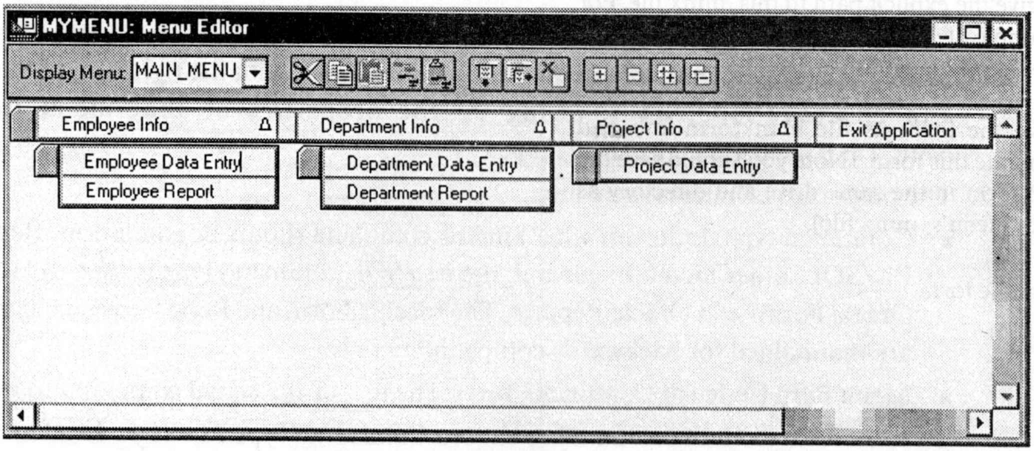

Save and Generate the Menu Module

At this point, all of the menu structure has been created and commands for each menu item have been specified. The menu module must now be saved to a file (with a .mmb extension) and Generated or Compiled.

To save the menu module, make sure the name of the menu is highlighted, pull down the File menu and choose the Save menu item. Specify a file name with a .mmb extension. This is the "source code" for the menu. For this example, use the file name mymenu.mmb.

To generate or compile the menu module, pull down the File menu, click on the Administration menu item and choose Generate from the flyout menu. In some versions of the Forms Builder, the menu item might be called Compile File. Generating or compiling a menu module results in a file with a .mmx extension. In this example, the generated menu module becomes: mymenu.mmx

Attaching a Menu Module to a Form

A custom menu must be attached to a form in order to be displayed. Typically, a form with no data entry on it is used as the main screen to host the custom menu.

The following steps are different depending on the version of Forms being used.

For Oracle Forms version 6i

1. Create a new form with no blocks or items on it. Pull down the File menu, select New and then select Form.

Click on the name of the form in the object navigator and rename it as blankform.

2. Open up the property palette for the form and set the following properties:

   Menu Source: File - The menu information will come from a file.

   Menu Module: mymenu.mmx - The file name of the compiled menu module. You may have to give the explicit path to this .mmx file. For example, if this file is on your A: drive then type a:\mymenu.mmx

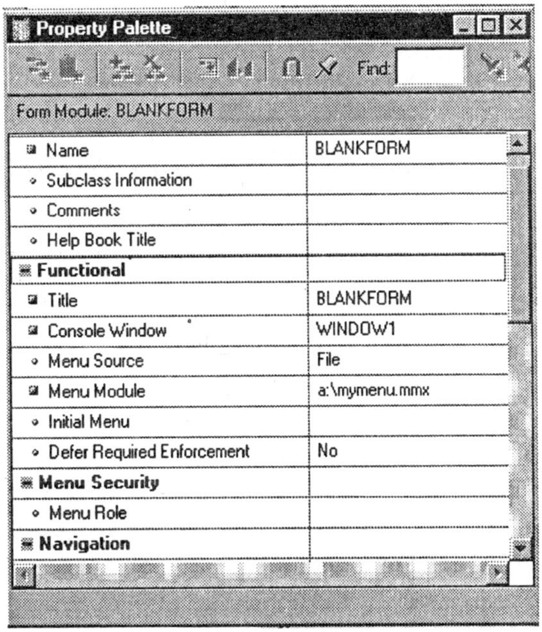

3. Save the form as file blankform.fmb and generate this form. (Note you should save the this form in the same drive and directory as your menu's .mmx file).

4. Run the form.

Notice that when running this blank form, the default menu is replaced by the mymenu Menu Module.

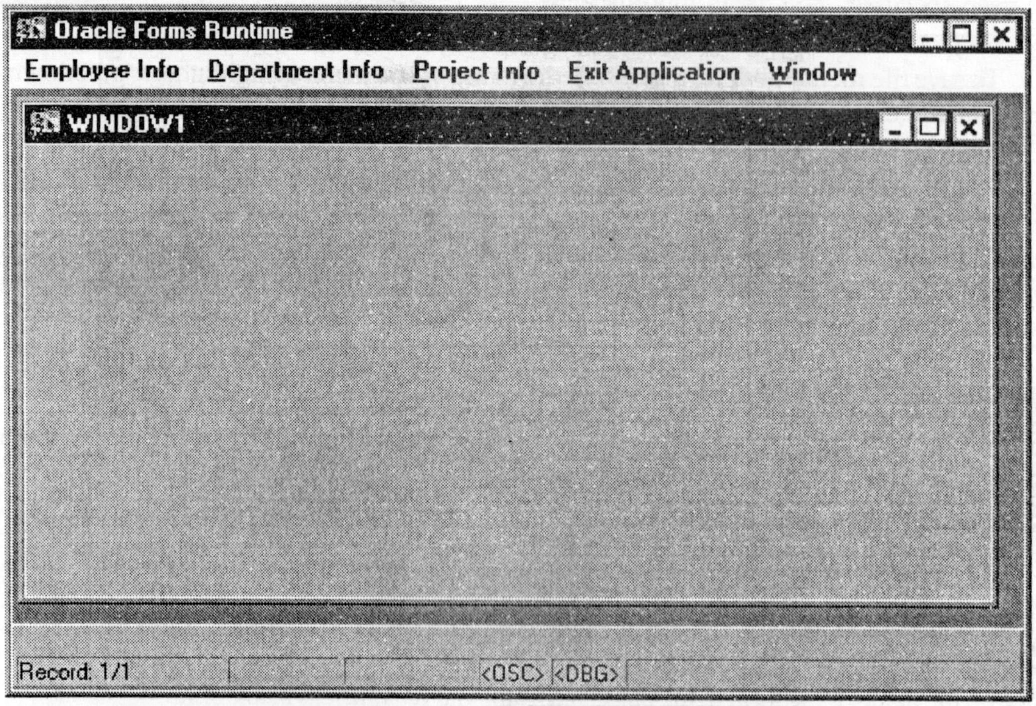

The blank form that is used to host the menu need not be blank. You may wish to use the Layout Editor to place some graphics and a title of the application on the canvas.

Another use for this space would be for some simple instructions the user can read to get started with the database application.

GRAPHICS AND THE CHART WIZARD

The Oracle Graphics Designer can be used to create a variety of graphs and charts including bar charts, line plots and pie graphs. Typically, a graphic object designed with Oracle graphics is included on either a form or a report. The Oracle Forms Designer includes a wizard that will automatically construct an Oracle graphic object using data from an existing data block.

Adding a Chart to a Form

In the following example, an Oracle Graphics object will be added to a basic Master/Detail form. As a first step, create a new Master/Detail form using the DEPARTMENT table (DNUMBER and DNAME columns) as the master block and the EMPLOYEE table (FNAME, LNAME, DNO and SALARY columns) as the detail block. The chart added to this form will compare the SALARY values of the employees in a given department.

An example layout is shown below (note the DNO column in the EMPLOYEE block is not displayed):

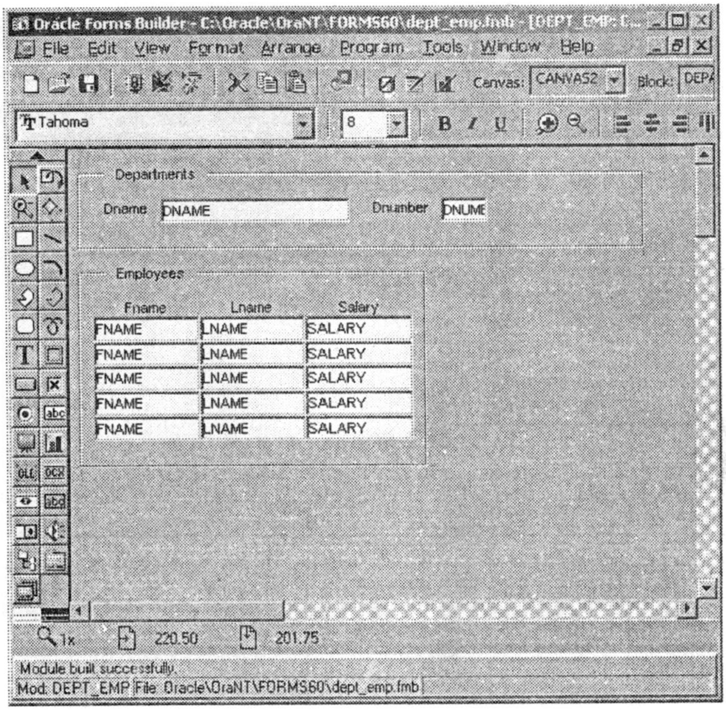

Be sure to save this form on disk before moving on to create the chart.

To start the Chart Wizard, click on any open area of the form while in the layout view. Then pull down the Tools menu and choose the Chart Wizard. The first screen of the Chart Wizard will appear as below:

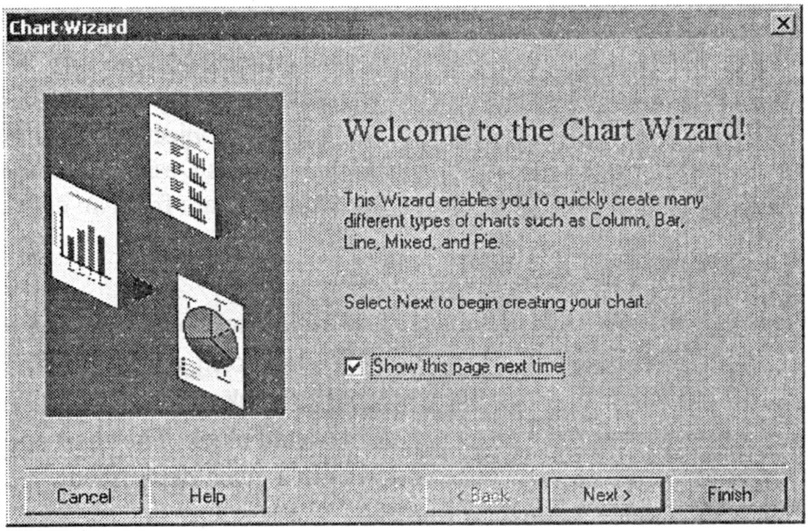

Click the Next button to move to the next step in the wizard. In the next step, choose the type of chart (and subtype if applicable) to be created. For this example, choose Pie and Depth as shown below and click on the Next button:

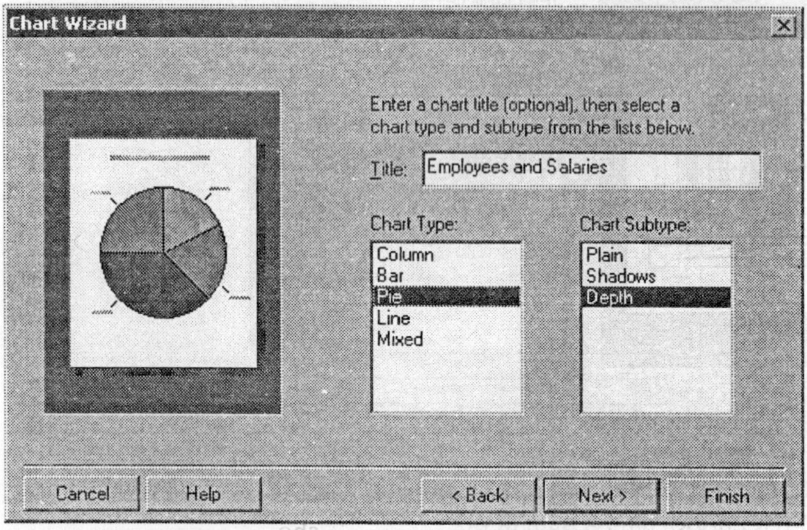

The next step is to choose which data block the chart should be based on. All of the data blocks on the current form should be displayed. For this example, choose the EMPLOYEE block as shown below and click on the Next button:

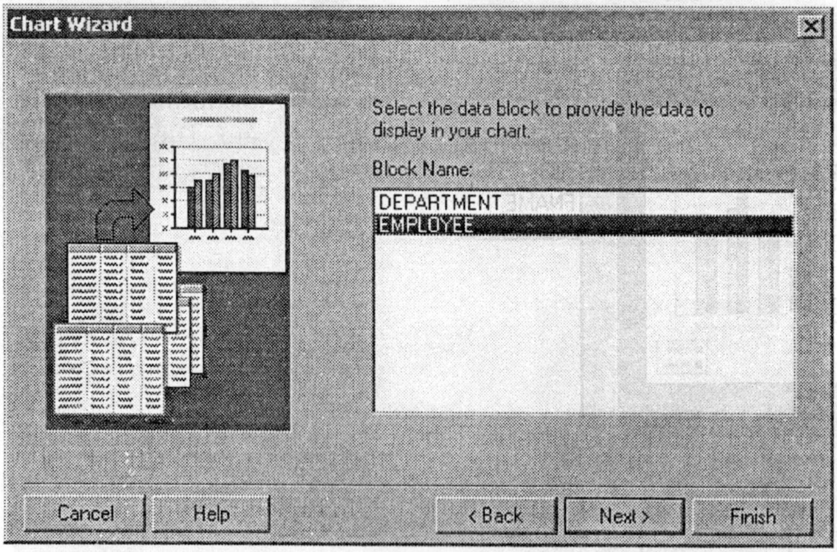

The next step is to choose which field in the data block should be used for the X-Axis (or category labels) for the chart. For this example, choose the LNAME field as shown on next page and click on the Next button:

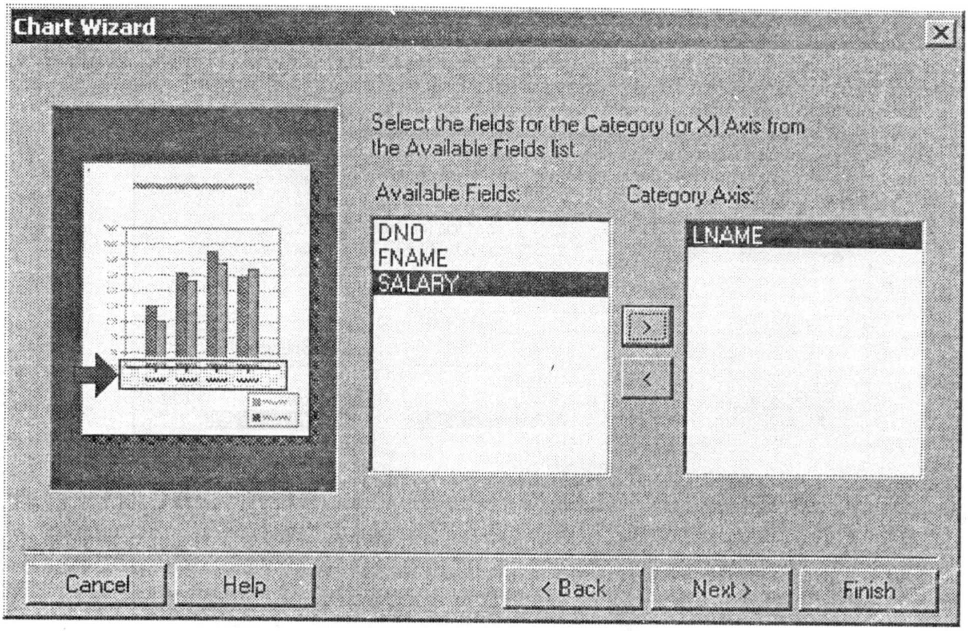

The next step is choose which field in the data block should be used as the Y-Axis values. For this example, choose the SALARY field as shown below and click on the Next button:

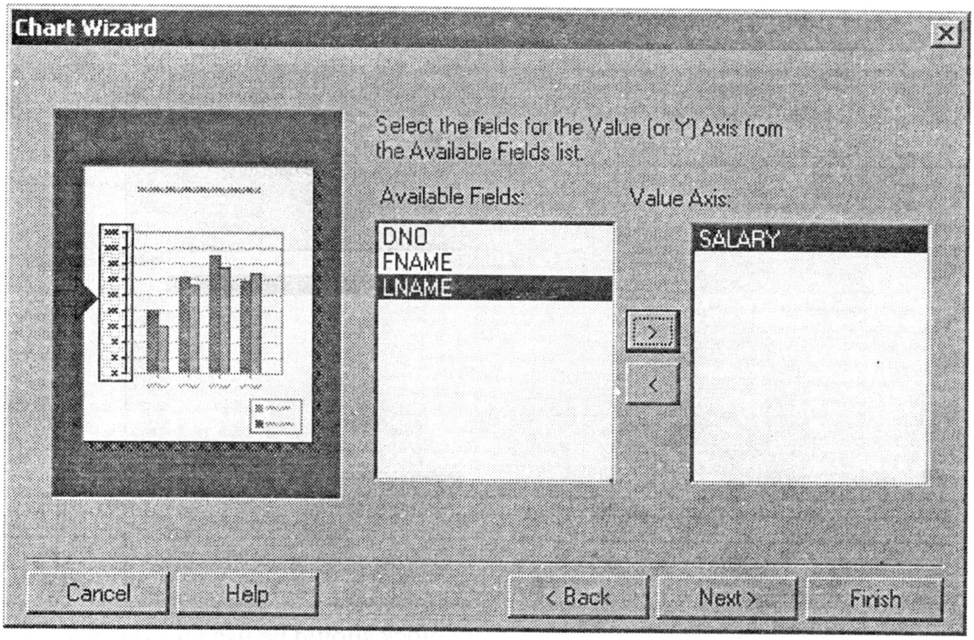

In the last step for the wizard, the new Oracle Graphics object must be saved in a file. Give a new name for the graphics object such as employee.ogd as shown below and click on the Finish button:

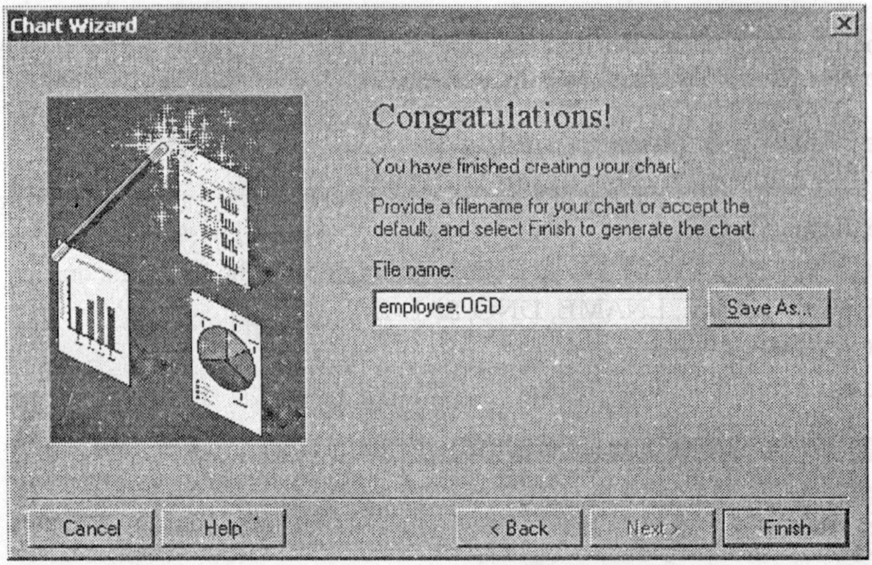

At this point, the graphics object will be created and placed on the form. Use the mouse to move and re-size the object as desired. When finished, save the form again and run it. The following figure shows the form as it is running. Notice that when the form is queried and as new department records are retrieved, the employees and their associated salaries for that department are displayed in the pie chart.

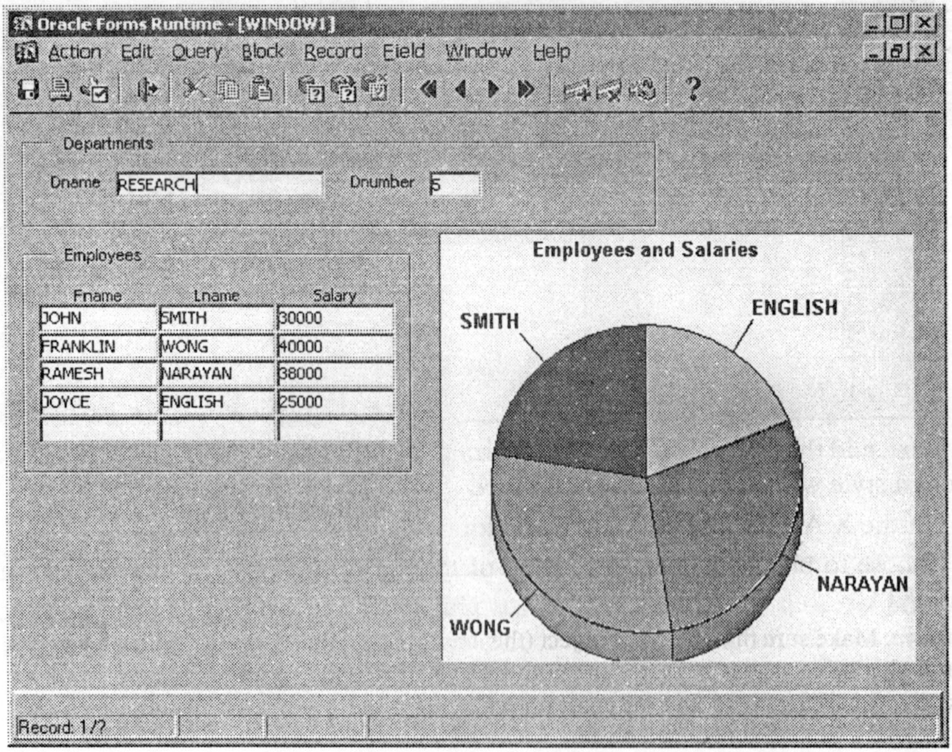

When copying forms files that use Oracle Graphics, be sure to also copy the associated graphics object files. These files typically have an .OGD file extension.

Example: Adding a Chart to a Report

For this exercise, add a bar chart depicting the employees salaries to a report showing additional Employee data.

Start by creating a basic tabular Report making use of the following query:

SELECT FNAME, LNAME, DNO, SALARY

FROM EMPLOYEE

The basic report is shown below:

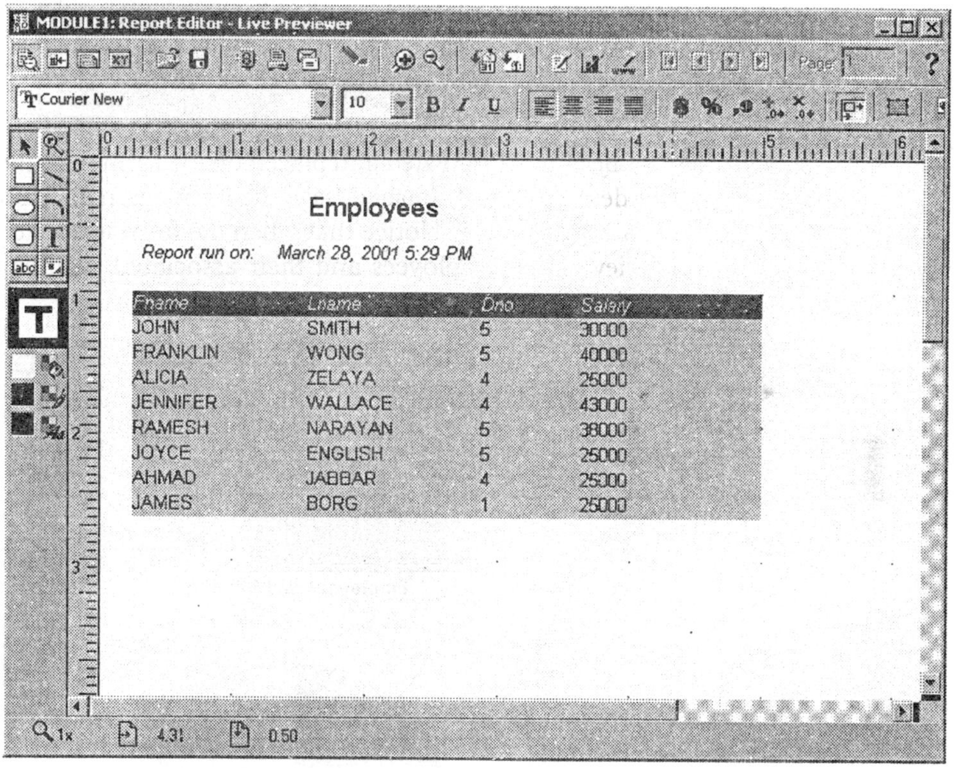

Next, add the Chart using the Chart wizard. Specify "Salaries" as the chart title, and use a Bar chart style with "Depth" as the sub-type.

For the X Axis, choose LNAME and for the Y Axis choose SALARY.

Choose to place the chart at the end of the report and give the chart object the name "repsal.ogd".

Note. Make sure that the chart object (the .ogd file) and the report file are in the same directory. By default chart objects may be stored in another location. If they are not together, you will get an error such as "Reports is unable to find the chart object".

Below is the final output of the report with the embedded Oracle Graphics chart object:

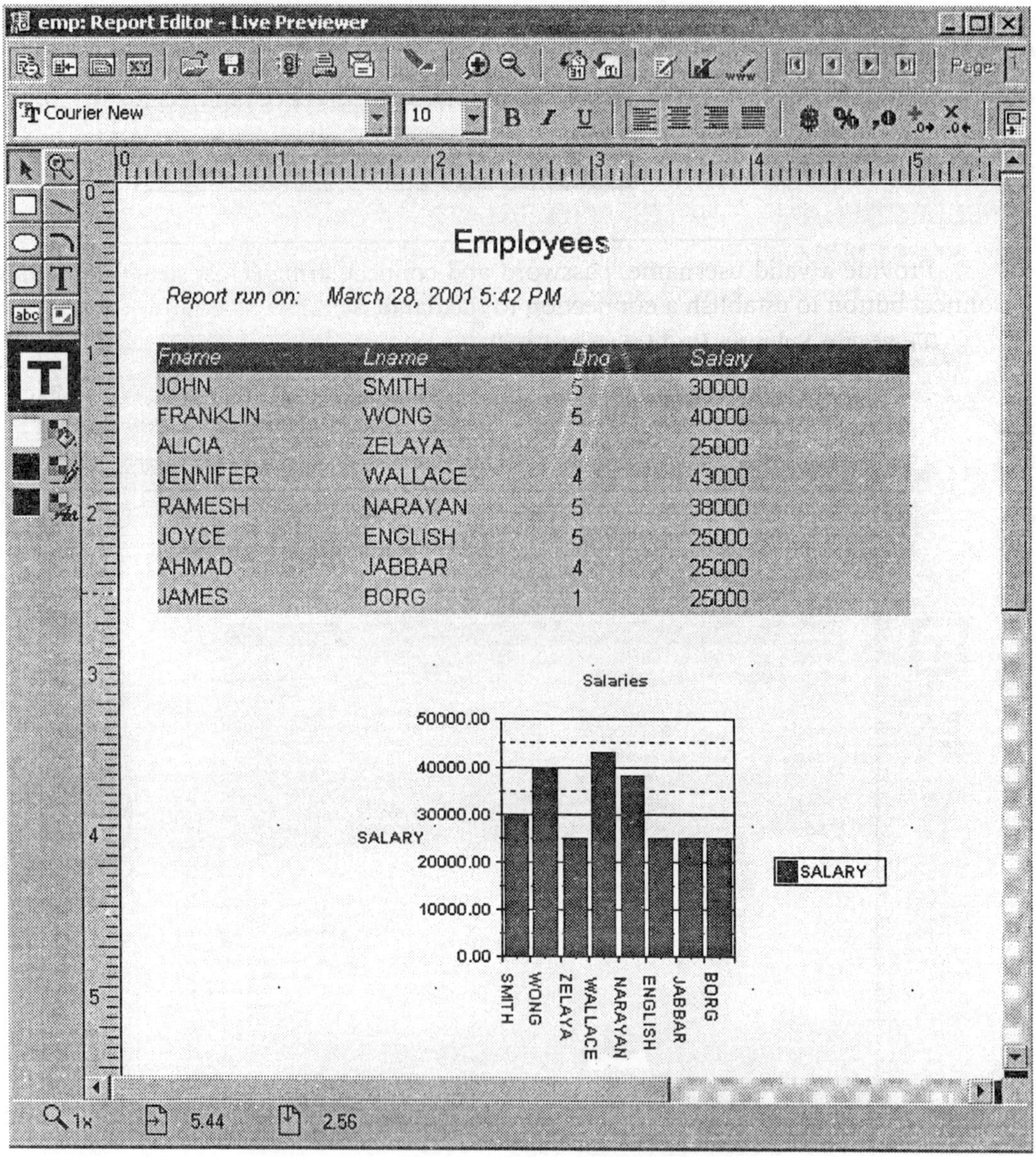

ORACLE SCHEMA BUILDER

The Oracle Schema Builder provides an easy to use graphical user interface for defining and modifying tables, views and other schema objects.

To run the Schema Builder, choose it from the Oracle menu. As with most Oracle development tools, the first step will be to connect to the database. The Connect dialog box will appear as on next page.

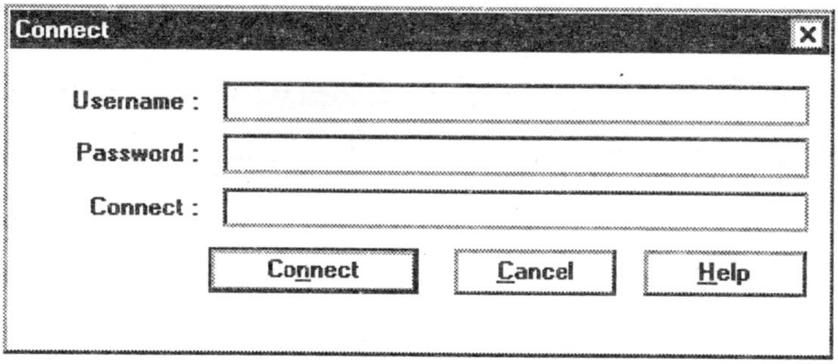

Provide a valid username, password and connect string (Host string) and click on the Connect button to establish a connection to the database.

The main Schema Builder screen will appear:

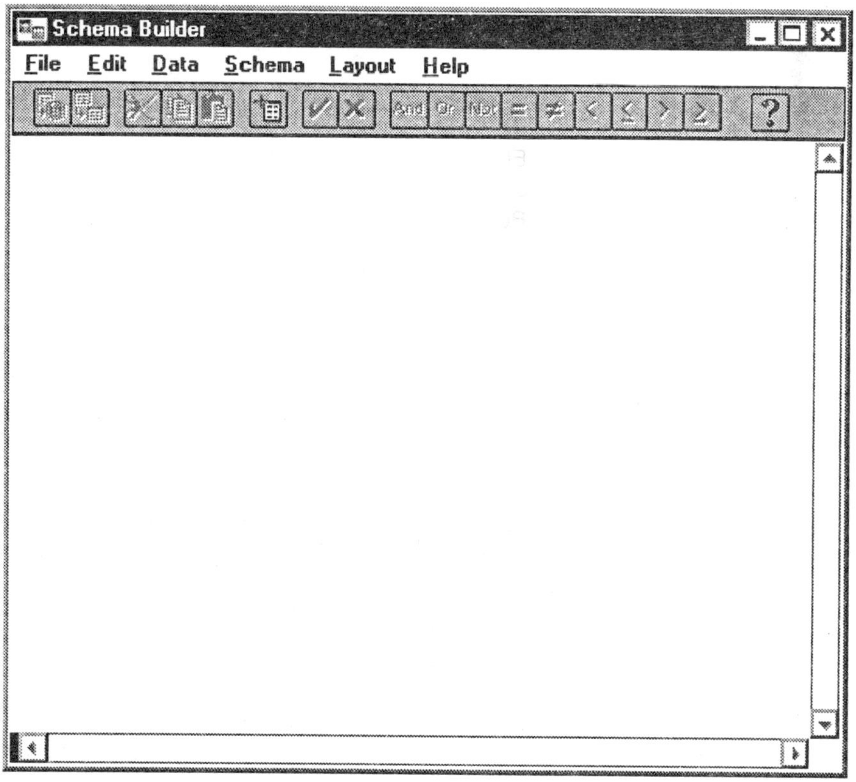

Creating New Schema Objects

Creating a new table is a straight forward process. First, pull down the Schema menu and choose the Create Table menu item. A small menu will appear. Choose Table. The mouse pointer will change to an arrow with a + sign. Click in the open space of the Schema Builder main screen and the new table will be created.

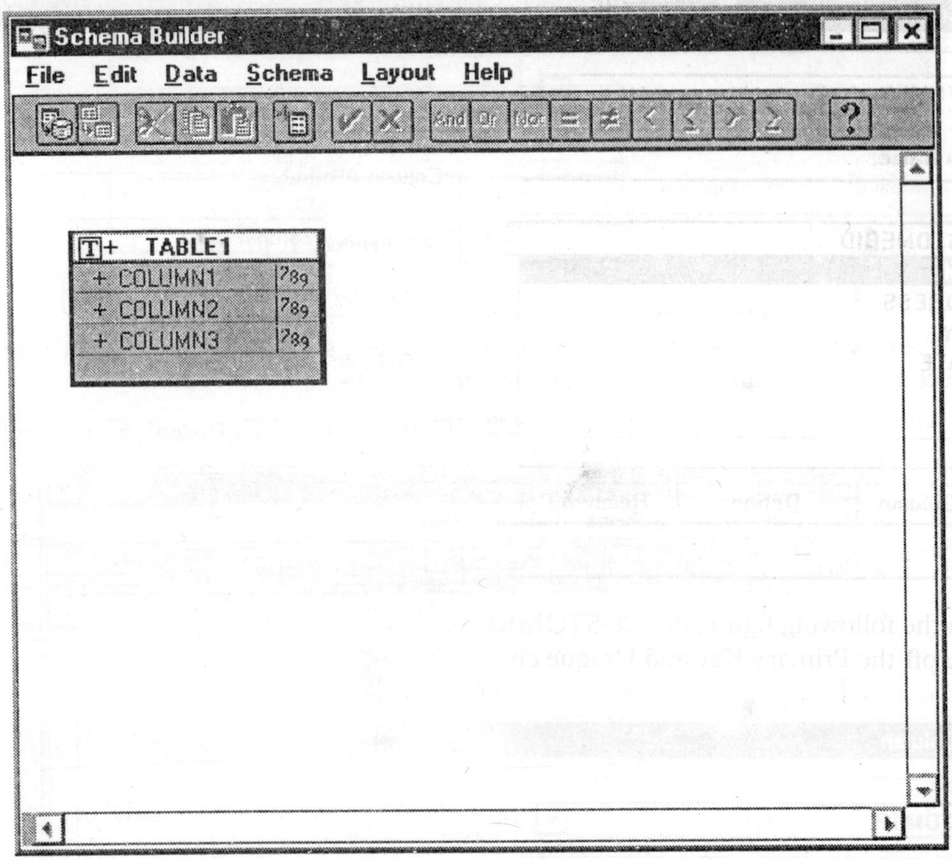

Note that the new table is given a default name (TABLE1) and it contains several examples columns.

To change the name of the table, click on the current name and type over it with a new name. Do not use spaces in the table name. When finished, press Enter or Return to set the new name for the table.

To change the name of a column, click on a column name and type over the existing name.

To add more columns to the table, simply click the lower right hand corner of the table display and drag it downwards. Additional columns will appear with their default names.

To change the data type and other characteristics of columns, double click on the column name. The Define Column dialog box will appear. Highlight the column you wish to modify and change its datatype and other options on the right hand side. In the figure on next page, the NAME column has been changed to VARCHAR(20) and a NOT NULL constraint has been added by checking off the Required checkbox.

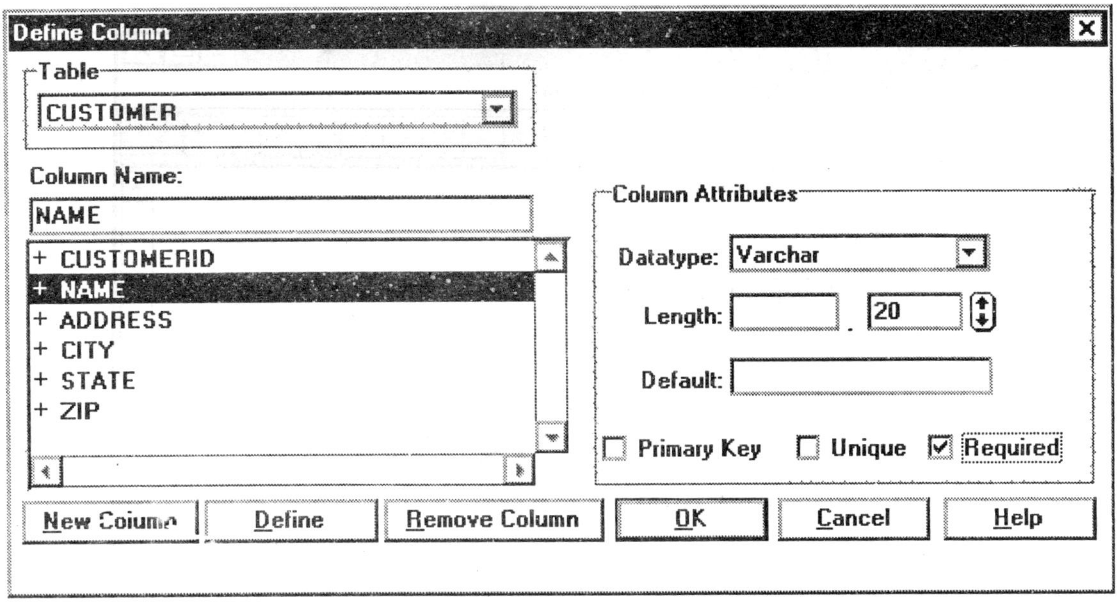

In the following figure, the CUSTOMERID column has been designated as the key by checking off the Primary Key and Unique check boxes.

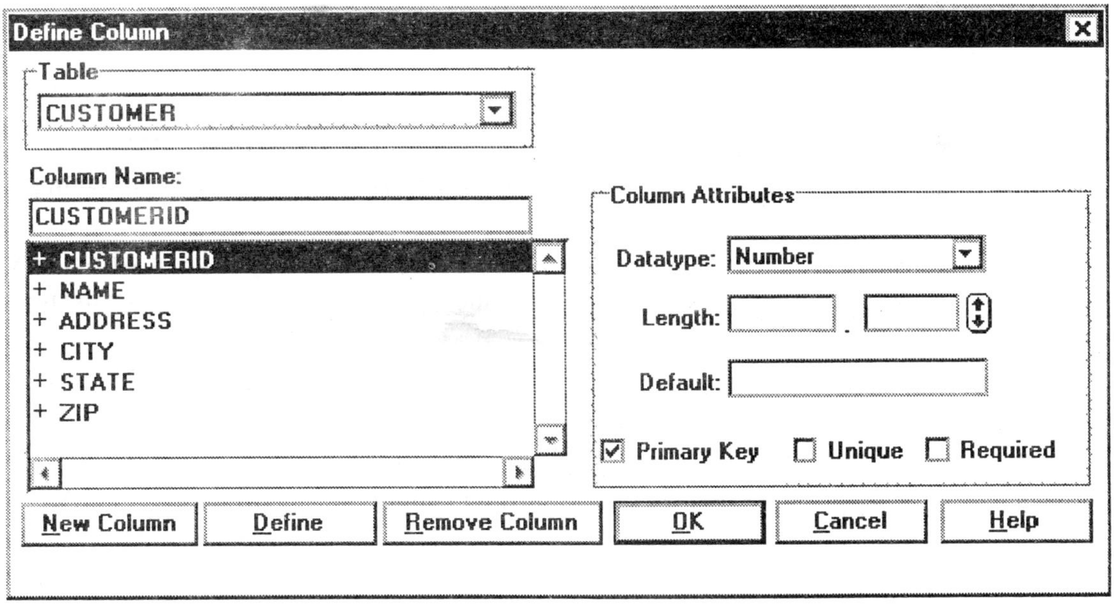

In the following figure, each of the columns in the CUSTOMER table have been defined:

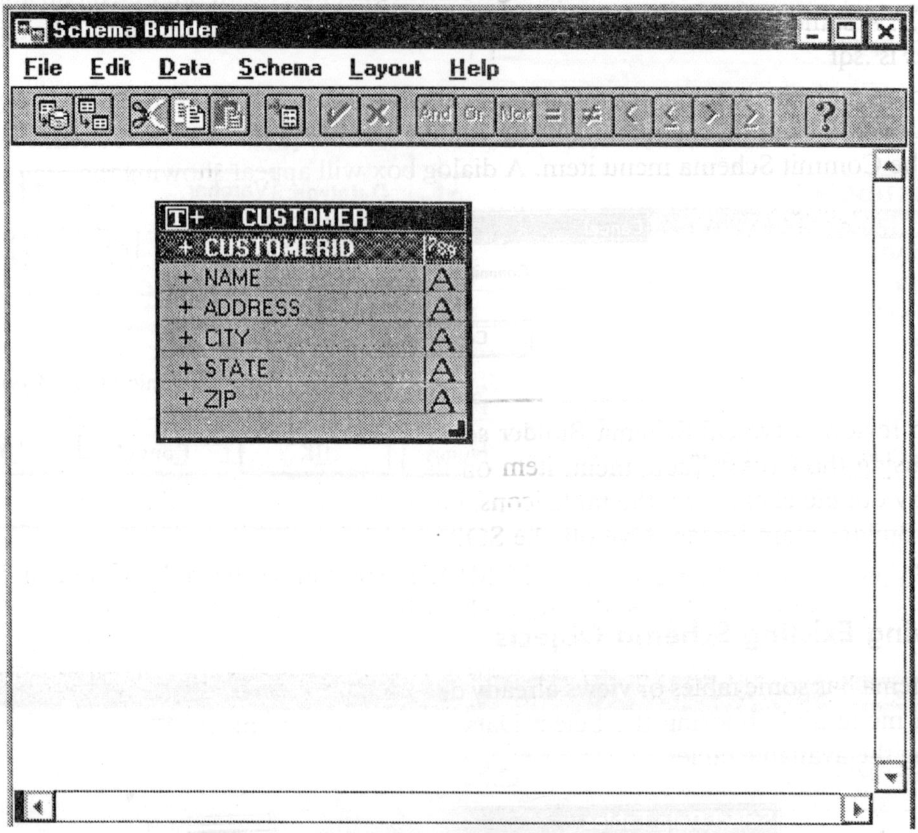

Once each of the columns has been renamed and defined, the table must be saved in the database. To see the SQL statements that will be sent to the database server, pull down the Schema menu and choose the Show SQL menu item.

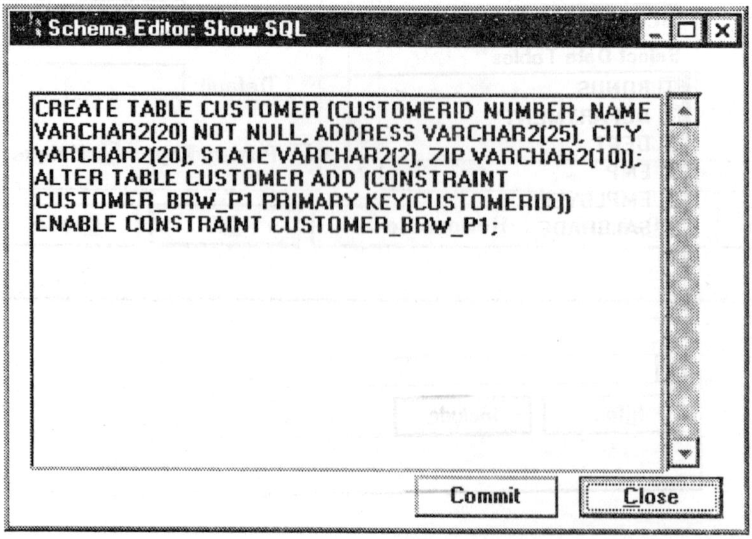

At this point, the SQL statements that will be used to create the schema can be saved into a text file for future use. To save the SQL statements, pull down the File menu and choose Save SQL. A standard windows file save dialog box will appear. The default file extension for SQL files is .sql

To commit the schema in the database, either click on the Commit button in the Show SQL dialog box or, from the main Schema Builder screen, pull down the Schema menu and choose the Commit Schema menu item. A dialog box will appear showing the progress.

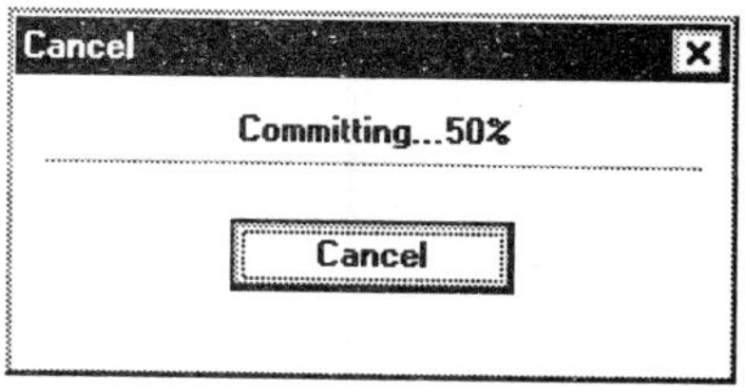

To review, a typical Schema Builder session would consist of adding new tables to a schema using the Create Table menu item on the Schema menu. Columns in tables can be defined by double clicking on the table icons. Once all of the tables have been defined in the Schema Builder main screen, save off the SQL to a file and then commit the schema in the database.

Displaying Existing Schema Objects

If the schema has some tables or views already defined, these can be displayed by pulling down the Data menu and choosing the Select Data Tables menu item. A dialog box will appear displaying the available tables.

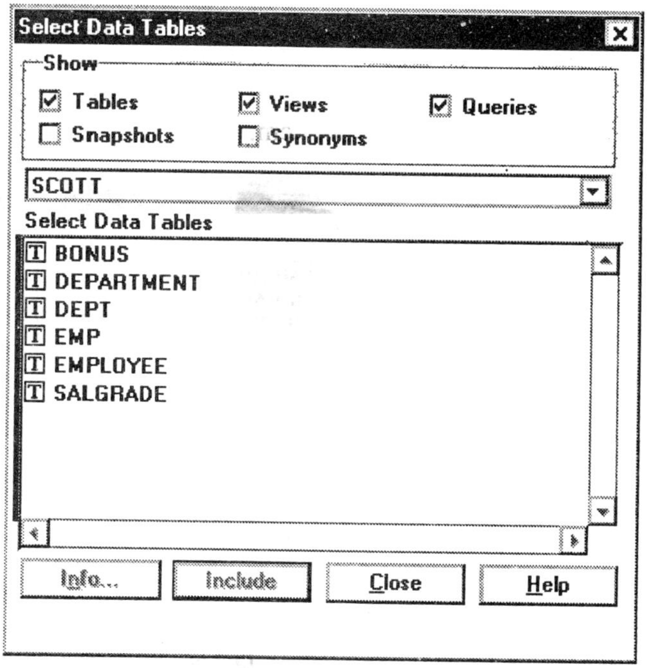

To include a table in the Schema Builder main screen, highlight a table and click on the Include button. The table should appear on the main screen and the name of the table will be grayed out in the dialog box.

In this example, the EMPLOYEE and DEPARTMENT tables were included in the main screen. When all of the desired tables have been displayed, click on the Close button to close the dialog box. Below is the resulting main screen after the EMPLOYEE and DEPARTMENT tables were added:

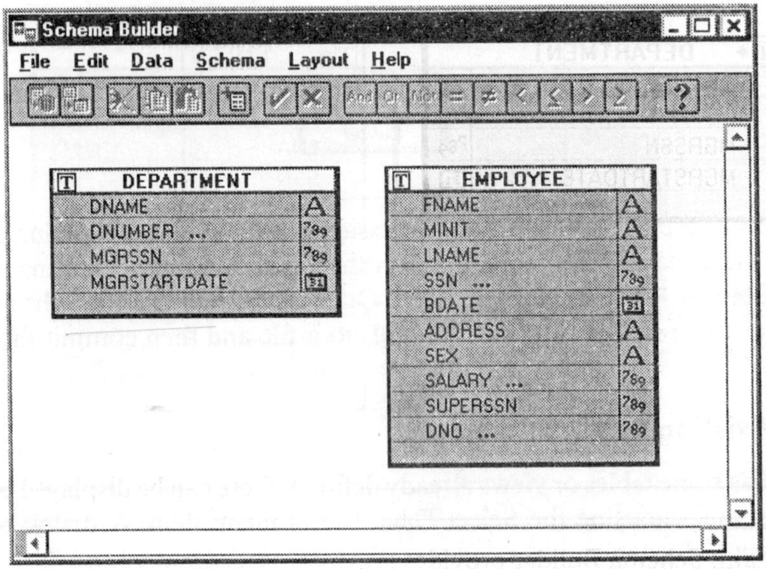

ADDING RELATIONSHIPS BETWEEN TABLES

Once the tables have either been created or displayed in the Schema Builder main screen, relationships between tables can be defined. In this example, the DNUMBER column of the DEPARTMENT table is related to the DNO columns in the EMPLOYEE table. The DNUMBER column in DEPARTMENT must be defined as a Primary Key.

To create the appropriate constraints for this relationship, pull down the Schema menu and choose the Define Relationship menu item.

A dialog box will appear with spaces for the Foreign Key and Primary Key. Fill these in as appropriate for the relationship. In this example, the Foreign Key is EMPLOYEE.DNO and the Primary Key is DEPARTMENT.DNUMBER as shown in the figure below:

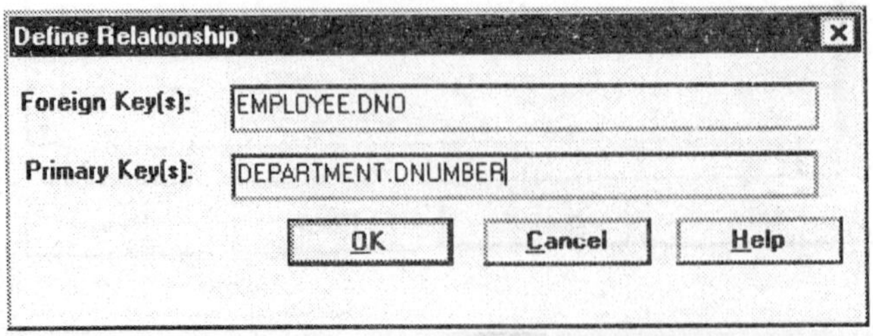

Click the OK button to confirm the relationship. The display will then change. A line will appear linking the Primary Key and Foreign Keys.

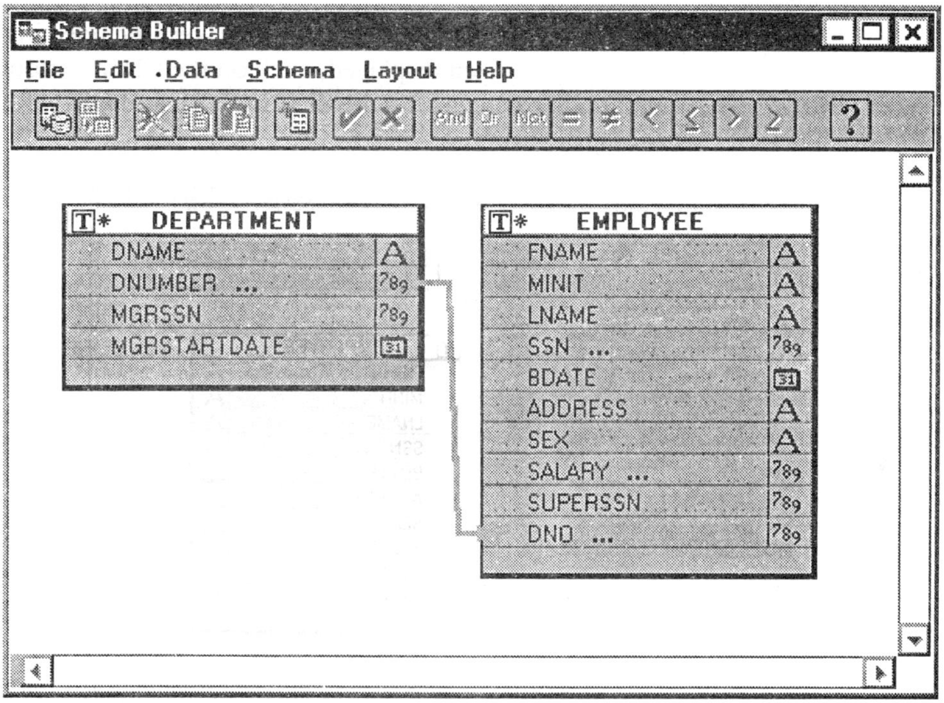

Once again, Schema Builder provides a view of the SQL that will be used to create the Foreign key constraints that will implement the relationship in the database schema. To see the SQL, pull down the Schema menu and choose the Show SQL menu item.

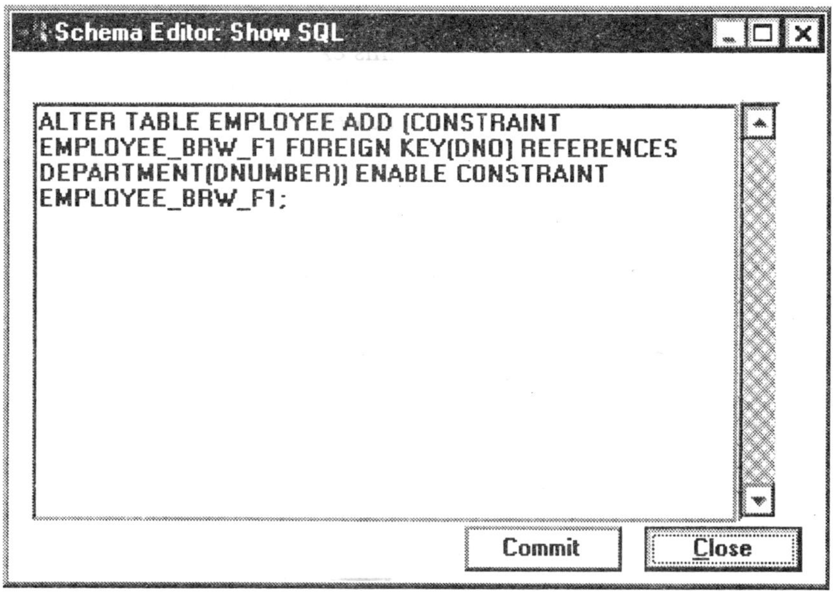

As before, the SQL statements to create the foreign key constraints can be saved to a file using the File menu and Save SQL menu item.

Finally, to commit the changes to the database, pull down the Schema menu and choose the Commit Schema menu item.

The next time both DEPARTMENT and EMPLOYEE are displayed in Schema Builder, the relationship will automatically appear.

15 Objects & Basic Database Administration

Objectives :

- Object Views
- Methods
- Large Objects
- Tablespace
- The Oracle Database Administrator
- Data Dictionary
- Remote Data Access

Lab Assignment-20

OBJECT VIEWS

Oracle provides object views as a means for defining objects used by existing relational tables. For example, there is a previously created relational database application and we want to implement object-relational concepts into our application without rebuilding and recreating the entire application. We need to overlay Object-Oriented (OO) structures such as abstract datatypes on existing relational tables. Object views allow us to create abstract datatypes within tables that already exist.

If the student table is already created as relational table, we could create the student_name_ty datatype, and use object views to relate them to student table.

In the following example, let us assume that the student table has been created as relational table with the following commands:

```
CREATE TABLE STUDENT
(STUDENT_ID NUMBER(4) PRIMARY KEY,
FIRST_NAME VARCHAR2(15),
LAST_NAME  VARCHAR2(15));
```

Although the student table is already created, we can create the abstract datatype, STUDENT_NAME_TY for FIRST_NAME and LAST_NAME as given in the next page:

```
CREATE OR REPLACE TYPE STUDENT_NAME_TY AS OBJECT
(FIRST_NAME VARCHAR2(15),
LAST_NAME  VARCHAR2(15));
/
```

We can optionally create an object that is based on all the columns of the STUDENT table. This object will be named as STUDENT_TY:

```
CREATE OR REPLACE TYPE STUDENT_TY AS OBJECT
(STUDENT_ID NUMBER(4),
NAME  STUDENT_NAME_TY);
/
```

Now the object view can be created, based on the STUDENT table using the datatypes we have defined. An object view starts with the create view command. The following is the command to create STUDENT_OV object view:

```
CREATE VIEW STUDENT_OV (STUDENT_ID,NAME)
AS SELECT
STUDENT_ID, STUDENT_NAME_TY(FIRST_NAMER, LAST_NAME)
FROM STUDENT;
```

For creating object views based on existing relational tables, the order of operation is :

1. Create the student table.
2. Create the STUDENT_NAME_TY datatype.
3. Create the STUDENT_NAME_TY datatype.
4. Create the STUDENT_OV object view, using the datatype.

The two main benefits of using object views are :

1. They allow us to create abstract datatypes within tables that already exist. Since we can use the same abstract datatype in multiple tables within our application, we can improve our application's adherence to standard representation of data and ability to re-use existing objects.
2. Object views allow two different ways to enter data into the base table. We can enter data into student table via the student_ov object view, or we can enter data into the student table directly. The flexibility of data manipulation for object views being able to treat the base table as either a relational table or an object table- is a significant benefit for application developers.

METHODS

A method is a block of PL/SQL code used to encapsulate the data access method for an object. Within ORACLE, methods are specified as part of the abstract datatype specification and their body is specified as part of the CREATE TYPE BODY command. USERS can execute methods on the datatype for which the methods are defined.

In the case of object views, when we define methods that apply to abstract datatype, by applying those datatypes to existing tables, we can apply those methods to the data in those tables.

When we create an abstract datatype, we can use the Create Type command. When we create a method, we can use the Create Type Body command.

Before creating the body for a method, we must name the method within the type declaration. For example, a new datatype MARKS_TY AS OBJECT

```
(M1 NUMBER(3),
M2 NUMBER(3),
M3 NUMBER(3),
MEMBER FUNCTION TOTMARKS(M1 IN NUMBER, M2 IN NUMBER, M3 IN
NUMBER )
RETURN NUMBER);
```

TOTMARKS is a function since it returns a value. It is a member of the MARKS_TY datatype. To define the TOTMARKS function, the CREATE TYPE BODY commands are used. Now, to create TOTMARKS function within the marks_ty datatype.

```
CREATE OR REPLACE TYPE BODY MARKS_TY AS
MEMBER FUNCTION TOTMARKS(M1 NUMBER, M2 NUMBER, M3 NUMBER)
RETURN NUMBER IS
BEGIN
RETURN(M1+M2+M3);
END;
```

After the TOTMARKS function is created, it is associated with the MARKS_TY datatype. If a table uses this datatype, then it can use the TOTMARKS function.

If marks_TY is used as a datatype for a column named MARKS in the students, then the table structure will :

```
CREATE TABLE STDMARKS
(STUDENT_ID NUMBER(4), MARKS MARKS_TY)
```

Now to invoke the TOTMARKS function, which is part of the marks_ty datatype,

```
SELECT MARKS.TOTMARKS (MARKS.M1, MARKS.M2, MARKS.M3 )
FROM STUDENTS;
```

Like the attributes of an abstract datatype, the member methods are referenced via the column names that use the datatypes.

LARGE OBJECTS

The long datatype can be used to store character data up to 2 GB in length per row. The Long Row datatype provides storage for long binary data.

There are four types of Large Objects (LOB's) available.

LOB DATATYPE	DESCRIPTION
BLOB	Binary LOB, Binary data, up to 4 GB in length, stored in the database.
CLOB	Character LOB character data up to 4 GB in length, stored in the database.
BFILE	Binary file; read only binary data stored outside the database, length is limited by the operating system.
NCLOB	A CLOB column that supports a multibyte character set.

Multiple LOBs can be created on a table. For example, let us create a proposal table to store the data of proposals that you submit.

```
CREATE TABLE PROPOSAL
(PROPOSAL_ID NUMBER(10) PRIMARY KEY,
PROPOSAL_TEXT CLOB,
BUDGET BLOB,
COVER_LETTER BFILE);
```

A Proposal_id is assigned because multiple proposals are sent to the same recipient.

Proposal_text	A CLOB containing the text of the proposal
Budget	A BLOB containing a spreadsheet showing calculations of the cost and profit for the proposed work.
Cover_letter	A binary file stored outside the database that contains cover letter that accompanied the proposal.

For each row in the proposal table, there will be up to 3 LOB values stored.

Oracle will use the normal database capabilities to support data integrity and concurrency for the proposal and budget entries but not for the cover_letter values. Since the cover_letter column uses BFILE datatype, data is sorted outside the database. Internally, the database stores only a locator value that allows it to find the external file. Oracle does not guarantee the data integrity of BFILE files is stored outside the database. Oracle does not guarantee that the data integrity of file exists when we insert a record outside the database. Oracle does not even validate that the file exists when we insert a record using a BFILE datatype. Data concurrency and integrity is only maintained for internally stored LOBs. The data for LOB columns whether stored inside or outside the database, is not physically stored within the proposal table. Within the proposal table, ORACLE stores locator values that point to data locations. For BFILE datatypes, the locator points to an external file and for BLOB and CLOB datatypes the locator points to a separate data location that the database creates to hold the LOB data. Thus, the LOB data is not necessarily stored directly with the rest of the data in the proposal table.

Storing the data out-of-line like this allows the database to avoid having to scan LOB data each item it reads multiple rows from the database. The LOB data is read only when required. Otherwise the locator values will be read.

Manipulating and selecting LOB values : LOB data can be selected and manipulated via the DBMS_LOB package. Other methods for manipulating LOB data include using API (Application Programming Interfaces) and OCI (ORACLE Call Interface) programs. LOBs are much more flexible, than long datatypes in terms of data manipulation possibilities.

Initializing Values: The proposal_ID column is the primary key column for the proposal table. There are three LOB columns identified in the proposal table, one BLOB column, one CLOB and one BFILE. For each of the LOB column, Oracle will store a locator value that tells it where to find any out-of-line data stored for the record.

When inserting a record into a table that contains LOBs, use DBMS_LOB package to tell Oracle to create an empty locator value for internally stored LOB columns. An empty locator value is different from a null value. If an internally stored LOB column's value is null, then set to an empty; locator value before updating it to non-NULL value.

```
INSERT INTO PROPOSAL
VALUES (2,'THIS IS THE NEW PROPOSAL TEXT', EMPTY_BLOB(),
BFILENAME ('c:\NOIDA', NOIDA.doc));
```

The inserted record has a proposal_ID of 2. The proposal_text column is set equal to a short character string for now. In order to set the budget column to an empty locator value, the EMPTY_BLOB function is used. The BFILE_name() tells ORACLE exactly where to find the Cover_letter - *i.e.*, in the C:\ NOIDA directory and its name is NOIDA.DOC. Within the BFILENAME function, the first parameter is always the directory name and the second parameter is the name of the file within that directory.

When you select the value from a LOB column, ORACLE will use the locator value to find the data that is associated with the LOB data. The user does not know or specify the locator values.

Updating LOB values

Before modifying a LOB value, the row must be located. Normally row locking occurs in the background when an update command is executed, ORACLE dynamically locks the row, performs the transaction and then unlocks the row. If we are updating a row that contains a LOB value, then we need to explicity lock the row before we execute the update command or the command will fail.

To lock the record, the record is selected using the UPDATE clause.

```
SELECT PROPOSAL_TEXT FROM PROPOSAL
WHERE PROPOSAL_ID = 2 FOR UPDATE;
```

Now the record with Proposal_id 2 has been selected for update and has an exclusive lock on the row.

```
UPDATE PROPOSAL SET PROPOSAL = 'This column is updated today'
WHERE PROPOSAL_ID = 2;
```

To release the lock, commit the change:

```
COMMIT;
```

The Cover_letter column can also be updated. We can use the BFILENAME function to change the file name.

```
UPDATE proposal SET COVER_LETTER =
BFILENAME (('C:\NOIDA','NOIDA.DOC'));
WHERE PROPOSAL_ID = 2;
```

Since the Cover_letter column uses BFILE datatype, the row need not be locked before performing update. Exclusive lock is only needed for update of internally stored LOBs. The BFILE columns can be updated with NULL value without first setting them to empty locator values. If we had inserted a record with a NLL value for Budget (a BLOB column), we cannot update the budget column's value unless it is set to a value of EMPTY_BLOB() via an update command.

After setting the value to EMPTY_BLOB() and establishing an empty locator value, we can update the budget column value by,

Using DBMS_LOB to Manipulate LOB values.

The DBMS_LOB package can be used to change or select LOB values. SQL function SUBSTR and INSTR can be performed on LOB values, and for appending to LOB values, comparing LOB values and reading them. The string comparison and manipulation procedures and functions are available within DBMS_LOG package.

Function	Description
SUBSTR	Function used to perform the SQL SUBSTR function on a LOB value.
INSTR	Function used to perform the SQL INSTR on a LOB value.
GETLENGTH	Function used to perform the SQL LENGTH function on a LOB value.
COMPARE	Function used to compare two LOB values.
READ	Procedure used to read a piece of a LOB value.
WRITE	Procedure used to write data into the LOB value at a specified point within the LOB value.

Procedure	Description
APPEND	Procedure used to append the contents of one LOB value to another LOB value.
ERASE	Procedure used to erase all or part of a LOB value.
TRIM	Procedure used to perform the SQL RTRIM function on a LOB value.
COPY	Procedure used to copy all part of a LOB value from one LOB column to another.

While using BFILEs, the maximum number of files that can be opened is limited by the setting of the SESSION_MAX_OPEN_FILES parameter in the database's Init.Ora file. The default maximum number of concurrently open BFILE files is 10.

BFILE- specific Procedure and Functions within the DBMS_LOB package.

Procedure	Description
FILEOPEN	Procedure used to open files for reading.
FILECLOSE	Procedure used to close specific files. For every FILEOPEN call, there must be a matching FILECLOSE call.
FILECLOSEALL	Procedure used to close all open files.
FILEGETNAME	Procedure used to get the name of the external file referenced by a BFILE locator value.
FILEEXISTS	Procedure used to determine if the external file referenced by a BFILE locator value exists.
FILESOPEN	Function used to determine if the external file is open.

READ

The READ procedure reads a piece of a LOB value. In the proposal table, for example, the PROPOSAL_TEXT which is a CLOB column, can be retrieved using the SELECT statement.

```
SELECT PROPOSAL_TEXT
FROM PROPOSAL
WHERE PROPOSAL_ID = 2;
```

However, since a CLOB column can contain a large amount of data (4GB), the SELECT statement is not normally used. Instead, the READ procedure is used to read any portion of the column.

The same functions and operations can be used against longer CLOB strings.

The read procedure has 4 parameters, which must be specified in this order.

1. The LOB locator.
2. The number of bytes or characters to be read.
3. The offset (starting point of the read) from the beginning of the LOB value.
4. The output data from the READ procedure.

If the end of the LOB value is reached before the specified number of bytes is read, the READ procedure will return an error. As the READ procedure requires the LOB locator as input, the READ procedure is executed within PL/SQL blocks. We will need to select the LOB locator value, provided that as input to the READ procedure and then display the text read via DBMS_OUTPUT package.

A READ example :

To use the READ procedure, we need to know the locator value of the LOB we want to read. The locator value must be selected from the table that contains the LOB. Since the locator value must be supplied as input to the READ procedure, we should use PL/SQL variables to hold the locator value. The READ procedure, in turn, will place its output in a PL/SQL variable. We can use the DBMS_OUTPUT package to display the output value.

From the proposal table, to select first 50 characters from PROPOSAL_TEXT column.

READING INFORMATION FROM CLOB DATA TYPE.

```
SET SERVEROUTPUT ON
DECLARE
LOCATOR_VAR CLOB;
AMOUNT_VAR INTEGER;
OFFSET_VAR INTEGER;
OUTPUT_VAR VARCHAR2(50);
BEGIN
AMOUNT_VAR:= 50;
OFFSET_VAR:= 1;
SELECT PROPOSAL_TEXTINTO LOCATOR_VAR
```

```
FROM PROPOSAL WHERE PROPOSAL_ID =2;
DBMS_LOB.READ(LOCATOR_VAR, AMOUNT_VAR,OFFSET_VAR,OUTPUT_VAR);
DBMS_OUTPUT.PUT_LINE('START OF PROPOSAL TEXT :' || OUTPUT_VAR);
END;
/
SET SERVEROUTPUT OFF
```

The locator value was selected from the proposal table and stored in a variable named locator_var. Then the READ procedure was called, using the values that have been assigned. As a result of the execution of the READ procedure, the output_var variable will be populated with the data that was read.

To select a different portion of the Proposal_Text CLOB, you have to just change the amount and offset variable. If you want to change the size of the output variable too, then, if 20 characters are to be read from the proposal_text, starting from the 10th character onwards, the amount_var:= 20 and offset: = 10 in the PL / SQL block.

If the proposal_text is created as VARCHAR2 column, then SUBSTR function is used. However, for a VARCHAR2 column, the maximum length is limited to 4000 characters. LOB columns can contain Binary data (BLOB datatypes). The READ procedure can be used to select data from BLOBs the same way as selecting CLOBs. For BLOBs, the output buffer is declared to use RAW datatype. In PL/SQL raw and VARCHAR2 datatype (used for output variable for CLOB and BLOB reads) have maximum length of 32,767.

TABLESPACE

A tablespace is an area of disk consisting of one or more disk files. A tablespace can contain many tables, indexes, or clusters. As a tablespace has a fixed size, it can get full as rows are added to its tables. When this happens, the table can be expanded by someone who has DBA authority. The expansion is accomplished by creating a new disk file and adding it to the tablespace or by extending the existing datafiles. New rows can then be added to existing tables, and those tables will therefore have rows in both files. One or more tablespace, together, make up a database.

Each table has a single area of disk space called a segment set aside for it in the tablespace. Each segment, in turn, has an initial area of disk space set aside for it in the tablespace called the initial extent. Once it has used up this space, the next extent, another single area of disk space, is set aside for it. When it has used up as well, yet another next extent is set aside. This process continues with every table until the whole tablespace is full. At that point, someone has to add a new file to the tablespace to extend the tablespace's files before any more growth in the tables can take place.

Every database also contains a system tablespace, where the ownership records and addresses are kept. It contains the data dictionary, and the names and locations of all of the tablespaces, tables, indexes, and clusters for this database.

The database is created and named by the system database administrator, who usually also sets up tablespaces and grants use of them to individual users.

Create tablespace: The create tablespace command allows one or more files to be assigned immediately to the tablespace. It also specifies a default space for any table created without an explicit storage clause mentioned in the create table statement.

```
CREATE TABLESPACE MYSPACE DATAFILE 'HOME.ONE SIZE 1000K
DEFAULT STORAGE (INITIAL 25K NEXT 10K
MINEXTENTS 1 MAXEXTENTS 100
PCTINCREASE 0)
PERMANENT;
```

The initial file assigned to this tablespace is included in the command, as well as its size in bytes. The number bytes is an integer and can be followed by a K (to multiply by 1024 - about a thousand) or a M(to be multiplied by 1048576- about a million). Default storage sets up the storage a table will get if storage is not specified in the create table statement. Here the initial default extent is 25K bytes and the next (incremental) extent is 10K bytes.

Minextents allows us to set aside additional extents beyond the first at the time a table is created. These will not necessarily be contiguous (physically adjacent) with the initial extent, or with each other, but the space will at least be reserved.

Maxextents is the limit of additional extents allowed.

Pctincrease is a growth factor for extents. When set to a non-zero value, each incremental extent will be the specified percentage larger than the one before it. This has the effect of reducing the number of extents, and noncontiguous space, used by a table that grows at a constant rate, you should set pctincrease to 0.

```
CREATE TABLESPACE MYSPACE1 DATAFILE 'HOME.TWO' SIZE
1000K
DEFAULT STORAGE (INITIAL 25K NEXT 10K
MINEXTENTS 1 MAXEXTENTS 100
PCTINCREASE 0)
PERMANENT;
```

Note. The permanent keyword in the create tablespace command tells Oracle that you will be storing permanent objects (such as tables) in the tablespace. If the tablespace is only used for temporary segments, then you can specify the temporary keyword instead. The default value is permanent.

The create table command for the STUDENT table using the tablespace is as follows:

```
CREATE TABLE STUDENT
(
STUDENT_ID NUMBER(4) PRIMARY KEY,
STUDENT_NAME VARCHAR2(20)
}
TABLESPACE MYSPACE
;
```

THE ORACLE DATABASE ADMINISTRATOR

Types of Oracle Users

At your site, the types of users and their responsibilities may vary. For example, at a large site the duties of a database administrator might be divided among several people.

- Database Administrators
- Security Officers
- Application Developers
- Application Administrators
- Database Users
- Network Administrators

Database Administrators

Because an Oracle database system can be quite large and have many users, someone or some group of people must manage this system. The *database administrator* (DBA) is this manager. Every database requires at least one person to perform administrative duties.

A database administrator's responsibilities can include the following tasks:

- installing and upgrading the Oracle Server and application tools
- allocating system storage and planning future storage requirements for the database system
- creating primary database storage structures (tablespaces) after application developers have designed an application
- creating primary objects (tables, views, indexes) once application developers have designed an application
- modifying the database structure, as necessary, from information given by application developers
- enrolling users and maintaining system security
- ensuring compliance with your Oracle license agreement
- controlling and monitoring user access to the database
- monitoring and optimizing the performance of the database
- planning for backup and recovery of database information
- maintaining archived data on tape
- backing up and restoring the database
- contacting Oracle Corporation for technical support

Security Officers

In some cases, a database might also have one or more security officers. A *security officer* is primarily concerned with enrolling users, controlling and monitoring user access to the database, and maintaining system security. You might not be responsible for these duties if your site has a separate security officer.

Application Developers

An *application developer* designs and implements database applications. An application developer's responsibilities include the following tasks:

- designing and developing the database application
- designing the database structure for an application
- estimating storage requirements for an application
- specifying modifications of the database structure for an application
- relaying the above information to a database administrator
- tuning the application during development
- establishing an application's security measures during development

Application Administrators

An Oracle site might also have one or more application administrators. An *application administrator* is responsible for the administration needs of a particular application.

Database Users

Database users interact with the database via applications or utilities. A typical user's responsibilities include the following tasks:

- entering, modifying, and deleting data, where permitted
- generating reports of data

Network Administrators

At some sites there may be one or more network administrators. Network administrators may be responsible for administering Oracle networking products, such as Net9.

Database Administrator Security and Privileges

To accomplish administrative tasks in Oracle, you need extra privileges both within the database and possibly in the operating system of the server on which the database runs. Access to a database administrator's account should be tightly controlled.

- The Database Administrator's Operating System Account
- Database Administrator Usernames
- The DBA Role

The Database Administrator's Operating System Account

To perform many of the administrative duties for a database, you must be able to execute operating system commands. Depending on the operating system that executes Oracle, you might need an operating system account or ID to gain access to the operating system. If so, your operating system account might require more operating system privileges or access rights than many database users require (for example, to perform Oracle software installation). Although you do not need the Oracle files to be stored in your account, you should have access to them.

In addition, Enterprise Manager requires that your operating system account or ID be distinguished in some way to allow you to use *operating system privileged* Enterprise Manager commands.

Database Administrator Usernames

Two user accounts are automatically created with the database and granted the DBA role. These two user accounts are:

- SYS (initial password: CHANGE_ON_INSTALL)
- SYSTEM (initial password: MANAGER)

These two usernames are described in the following sections.

You will probably want to create at least one additional administrator username to use when performing daily administrative tasks.

SYS

When any database is created, the user SYS, identified by the password CHANGE_ON_INSTALL, is automatically created and granted the DBA role.

All of the base tables and views for the database's data dictionary are stored in the schema SYS. These base tables and views are critical for the operation of Oracle. To maintain the integrity of the data dictionary, tables in the SYS schema are manipulated only by Oracle; they should never be modified by any user or database administrator, and no one should create any tables in the schema of the user SYS. (However, you can change the storage parameters of the data dictionary settings if necessary.)

Most database users should never be able to connect using the SYS account. You can connect to the database using this account but should do so only when instructed by Oracle personnel or documentation.

SYSTEM

When a database is created, the user SYSTEM, identified by the password MANAGER, is also automatically created and granted all system privileges for the database.

The SYSTEM username creates additional tables and views that display administrative information, and internal tables and views used by Oracle tools. Never create tables of interest to individual users in the SYSTEM schema.

The DBA Role

A predefined role, named "DBA", is automatically created with every Oracle database. This role contains all database system privileges. Therefore, it is very powerful and should only be granted to fully functional database administrators.

Database Administrator Authentication

Database administrators must often perform special operations such as shutting down or starting up a database. Because these operations should not be performed by normal database users, the database administrator usernames need a more secure authentication scheme.

- Selecting an Authentication Method
- Using Operating System Authentication
- OSOPER and OSDBA
- Using an Authentication Password File

Selecting an Authentication Method

The following methods for authenticating database administrators replace the CONNECT INTERNAL syntax provided with earlier versions of Oracle (CONNECT INTERNAL continues to be supported for backward compatibility only):

- operating system authentication
- password files

Depending on whether you wish to administer your database locally on the same machine where the database resides or to administer many different databases from a single remote client, you can choose between operating system authentication or password files to authenticate database administrators.

On most operating systems, OS authentication for database administrators involves placing the OS username of the database administrator in a special group (on UNIX systems, this is the DBA group) or giving that OS username a special process right.

The database uses password files to keep track of database usernames that have been granted administrator privileges.

Using Operating System Authentication

If you choose, you can have your operating system authenticate users performing database administration operations.

1. Set up the user to be authenticated by the operating system.
2. Make sure that the initialization parameter, REMOTE_LOGIN_PASSWORD, is set to NONE, which is the default value for this parameter.
3. Authenticated users should now be able to connect to a local database, or to connect to a remote database over a secure connection, by typing one of the following commands:

   CONNECT / AS SYSOPER

   CONNECT / AS SYSDBA

If you successfully connect as INTERNAL using an earlier release of Oracle, you should be able to continue to connect successfully using the new syntax.

OSOPER and OSDBA

Two special operating system roles control database administrator logins when using operating system authentication:

OSOPER and OSDBA.

OSOPER	Permits the user to perform STARTUP, SHUTDOWN, ALTER DATABASE OPEN/MOUNT, ALTER DATABASE BACKUP, ARCHIVE LOG, and RECOVER, and includes the RESTRICTED SESSION privilege.
OSDBA	Contains all system privileges with ADMIN OPTION, and the OSOPER role; permits CREATE DATABASE and time-based recovery.

The Grant Command

In most multi-user database management systems you need to be a special user - DBA or owner - or you need to get explicit permission from either the DBA or owner to perform any operation, even to run a simple query. This permission is given using the GRANT command. The syntax of the GRANT command is given below:

GRANT {ALL | privilege}
ON {table-name [(column-comma-list)] | view-name[(column-comma-list)]}
To {PUBLIC | user-list}
[WITH GRANT OPTION]

Another format of the syntax where the column-comma-list is moved up, is given below:

GRANT {ALL | privilege-list [(column-comma-list)]}
ON {table-name | view name}
TO {PUBLIC | user-list}
[WITH GRANT OPTION]

If 'ALL' is specified then all the privileges for the object for which the user issuing the GRANT has grant authority, will be granted. If a 'privilege-list' is specified, then, only the listed privileges will be granted. The 'ON' clause specifies the object on which the privileges are granted. It can be table or view. If the optional column-comma-list is specified the privileges will be restricted to those columns. If the column list is not specified, then the grant will be for the entire table/view. The 'TO' clause is used to identify the users to whom the privileges are granted. The keyword 'PUBLIC' means that the privileges are granted to all known users of the system- all the users who have valid User ID and password. If the 'user-list' is specified, then the privileges will be granted to the user(s) specified in the list. If the 'WITH GRANT OPTION' is specified, it means that the recipient has the authority to grant the privileges that were granted to him to another user.

The following are some examples of the GRANT command :

1. **Grant the SELECT authority on the BOOK table to all users.**
   GRANT SELECT
   ON BOOK
   TO PUBLIC;
2. **Grant the SELECT, DELETE and UPDATE authority on EMP table to user 'ALI'.**
   GRANT SELECT, DELETE, UPDATE ON EMP TO ALI;
3. **Grant the SELECT, DELETE and UPDATE authority with the capability to grant those privileges to other users on EMP table to user 'ALI'.**
   GRANT SELECT, UPDATE ON EMP TO ALI WITH GRANT OPTION;
4. **Grant ALL privileges on BOOK table to user 'DON'.**
   GRANT ALL ON BOOK TO DON;
5. **Give the system privileges for creating tables and views to 'POBBY'.**
   GRANT CREATE TABLE, CREATE VIEW TO POBBY;
6. **Grant the UPDATE authority on the ENAME column of the EMP to user 'PRABIN'.**
   GRANT UPDATE (ENAME) ON EMP TO PRABIN;

THE REVOKE COMMAND

The REVOKE command is used to take away a privilege that was granted. The syntax for REVOKE is given below:

REVOKE {ALL | privilege-list}
ON {table-name [(column-comma-list)] | view-name [(column-comma-list)]}
FROM {PUBLIC | user-list}

Another format of the syntax where the column-comma-list is moved up is given below :

REVOKE {ALL | privilege-list [(column-comma-list)]}
ON {table-name | view-name}
FROM {PUBLIC | user-list}

If 'ALL' is specified then all the privileges for the object specified will be revoked. If a 'privilege-list' is specified then only those privileges will be revoked. The 'ON' clause specifies the object from which the privileges are removed. It can be a table or view. If the optional 'column-comma-list' is specified, the privileges will be restricted to those columns. If the column list is not specifies, then the revoke will be for the entire table/view. The 'FROM' clause is used to identify the users from whom the privileges are taken away. The keyword 'PUBLIC' means that the privileges are revoked from all known users of the system. The user issuing the Revoke command should be the user who granted the privileges in the first place. Dropping a domain, base table or view will cause an automatic REVOKE for all privileges on the dropped object for all users.

The following statements explain how the privileges are revoked :

1. **REVOKE the system privileges for creating tables from 'RUCHIN'.**
   REVOKE CREATE TABLE FROM RUCHIN;
2. **REVOKE the SELECT privileges on EMP table from 'SHARAD'.**
   REVOKE SELECT ON EMP FROM SHARAD;
3. **REVOKE THE UPDATE privileges on EMP table from all users.**
   REVOKE UPDATE ON EMP FROM PUBLIC;
4. **Remove all privileges on EMP table from user 'Lee'.**
   REVOKE ALL ON EMP FROM LEE;
5. **Remove DELETE and UPDATE authority on the ENAME and ADDRESS columns of the EMP table from user 'SAHIL'.**
   REVOKE DELETE, UPDATE (ENAME, ADDRESS) ON EMP FROM SAHIL;

EXAMPLES

Creating Users

Example: **To create a log in name for user, NOIDA.**

SQL> CREATE USER NOIDA IDENTIFIED BY COLLEGE;

Here, log in name is NOIDA and password is COLLEGE.

After creating the users, the DBA has to grant appropriate privileges to the users in order to work on the database.

A collection of privilege is called a Role. There are 3 standard roles,

Connect, Resource and DBA.

Example: **To GRANT roles for users, NOIDA.**

SQL> GRANT CONNECT, RESOURCE TO NOIDA;

Here, two roles have been assigned to the user.

To view the roles that have been assigned

```
SQL> SELECT * FROM SESSION_ROLES;
ROLE
--------------
CONNECT
RESOURSE
```

Each of these roles represents a collection of privileges.

To view the privileges that have been assigned

```
SQL>  SELECT * FROM SESSION_PRIVS;
PRIVILEGE
--------------------
CREATE SESSION
ALTER SESSION
```

UNLIMITED TABLESPACE
CREATE TABLE
CREATE CLUSTER
CREATE SYNONYM
CREATE VIEW
CREATE SEQUENCE
CREATE VIEW
CREATE DATABASE LINK
CREATE PROCEDURE
CREATE TIGGER

The CONNECT role, does not allow the user to create TRIGGERS and procedures. To perform these operations, the RESOURCE role is required.

REVOKING the ROLE: The Roles that are granted to any user can be revoked by the use of the DCL, REVOKE

Example: **SQL > REVOKE RESOURCE FROM NOIDA;**

Even if all the roles are REVOKED from the user, the user is still part of the database and the tables created by the user will exist in the database.

To Remove a USER: To remove a user from the database,

SQL> DROP USER NOIDA;

If any objects created by the user exist in the database, Oracle does NOT remove the user.

SQL> DROP USER NOIDA CASCADE;

The CASCADE option drops the user along with all the objects owned by the user. It invalidates the views, synonyms, stored procedures, functions or packages that refer to objects in the schema of the user, which has been dropped.

Using tables in Another Schema

The user who creates the tables is the owner of the table. The owner can grant privileges on the objects owned to other users. For example, in order to allow another user to use the owner's tables, the owner must GRANT THE PRIVILEGES TO THE OTHER user.

Example: **To allow user GRNOIDA to use the table, SALARY of user NOIDA:**

NOIDA is the owner of the table, SALARY.

SQL> GRANT SELECT ON SALARY TO GRNOIDA;

The USER, GRNOIDA can execute SELECT statements on the table, SALARY. The table name must be prefixed by the owners name or schema name.

SQL> SELECT * FROM NOIDA.SALARY;

Example: **To allow user GRNOIDA to display and update ONLY BASIC of the SALARY of user NOIDA:**

SQL> GRANT SELECT, UPDATE (BASIC) ON SALARY TO GRNOIDA;
SQL> GRANT ALL ON SALARY TO GRNOIDA;

Synonym: The user can create a synonym (a substitute file name) for any table.

Example: **User GRNOIDA can create a synonym for the table, SALARY.**

SQL> CREATE SYNONYM MYSAL FOR NOIDA.SALARY;

SQL> SELECT * FROM MYSAL;

To view the details of the synonym:

SQL> SELECT * FROM USER_SYNONYMS;

Object Privileges: The user can grant the following privileges:

Tables and Views	:INSERT, DELETE, SELECT
	UPDATE
	UPDATE (column_name)
Tables only	:ALTER
	REFERENCES
	INDEX (columns in a table)
	ALL (all of the above)

Procedures, Functions and Packages : EXECUTE

WITH GRANT OPTION: Privileges can be granted to other users with a special option, WITH GRANT OPTION.

This option will allow the granted user to grant the rights that have been received to other users.

Example:

SQL > GRANT SELECT, UPDATE ON SALARY TO GRNOIDA WITH GRANT OPTION;

The user, GRNOIDA can pass on the SELECT and UPDATE privileges to any other user.

Connecting to Another User: Any user can connect to another user's schema provided the password and the connect string is known.

SQL> CONNECT NOIDA /COLLEGE@ORACLE;

Will connect the user to NOIDA.

Here, the password is COLLEGE and the host string is ORACLE.

REVOKING PRIVILEGES: Privileges can be revoked using DCL, REVOKE.

Example:

SQL> REVOKE UPDATE ON SALARY FROM GRNOIDA;

SQL> REVOKE ALL ON SALARY FROM GRNOIDA;

The ALL option can be used to revoke all the privileges granted to the user.

Granting access to the public (all users)

SQL> GRANT SELECT ON CUSTOMER TO PUBLIC;

Now, all the database users can SELECT the Customer table, with the schema name as prefix.

SQL> SELECT * FROM NOIDA.CUSTOMER;

The DBA can create a synonym that is PUBLIC.

SQL> CREATE PUBLIC SYNONYM CTM FOR NOIDA.CUSTOMER;

Any user can now query the file using the name, CTM.

Creating Roles for Applications

Suppose people in the SALES department have to be granted rights to certain files, then instead of granting these privileges individually, a ROLE can be created (ROLE is collection of privileges) and granted to any user of the SALES department.

CREATE ROLE SALESROLE;

GRANT SELECT ON PRICES TO SALESROLE;

GRANT SELECT, INSERT, DELETE, UPDATE ON DAILYSALES TO SALESROLE;

Note. Prices and dailysales are tables.

SALESROLE is now ready and can be granted to any user.

GRANT SALESROLE TO NOIDA:

COPY COMMAND

Note. The copy command can be used to copy a table from one schema to another.

Example:

SQL > COPY FROM NOIDA/COLLEGE@ORACLE CREATE MYSAL USING SELECT * FROM SALARY;

will copy the table named, SALARY from NOIDA schema whose password is COLLEGE in the database named ORACLE. The table created is named, MYSAL.

Syntax

COPY FROM <db> TO <db> <option> <tablename> {(<cols>)} USING <sel>;

<db>: database string, e.g., scott/tiger@xyz

<option> : One of the keyword: APPEND, CREATE, INSERT OR REPLACE

<tablename>: name of the destination table

<cols>: a comma-separated list of destination column aliases

<sel>: any valid SQL SELECT statement

A missing FROM or TO clause uses the current SQL*Plus connection.

SQL> COPY FROM NOIDA/COLLEGE@ORACLE CREATE MYSAL (NO,BASIC) USING SELECT EMP_NO, BASIC FROM SALARY;

will copy only the two columns, EMP_NO and BASIC from SALARY. These columns will be named as NO and BASIC in the table MYSAL which is created.

DATA DICTIONARY

The data dictionary is a set of tables and views owned by the DBA users (login name SYS and SYSTEM). The data dictionary is a central pool of information for the ORACLE RDBMS and for the users. The tables and views of the data dictionary is automatically maintained by Oracle and has information about database objects, users, privileges etc.

Some of the commonly used data dictionary views are listed below.

ALL_USER: To display names of all users of the database.

SELECT * from all_user;

Information about all users of the database is displayed.

USER_CONSTRAINTS: To find out if the table has a primary key.

For example, if the table EMP has a primary key.

SELECT CONSTRAINT_NAME, CONSTRAINT_TYPE FROM USER_CONSTRAINTS WHERE TABLE_NAME = 'EMP';

CONSTRAINT_NAME	C
SYS_C00879	P

The P indicates that a primary key has been defined.

USER_cons_columns: To find out the name of the column which is the primary key.

SELECT * FROM USER_CONS_COLUMNS

WHERE CONSTRAINT_NAME = 'SYS_C00879';

USER_CATALOG: To display all tables, views, synonyms and sequence for which user is the owner.

Select * from user_catalog;

USER_OBJECTS: To display all types of objects *i.e.*, clusters, database links, functions. Indexes, packages, package bodies, procedures, sequences, synonyms, tables, triggers and views.

SELECT * FROM USER_OBJECTS;

USER_OBJECT_SIZE : To display in bytes the size of PL / SQL objects.

SELECT * FROM USER_OBJECT_SIZE;

USER_SOURCE: To display the source of stored objects accessible to the user.

Select * from user_source;

USER_SYNONYMS: To display the synonyms created by the user.

SELECT * FROM USER_SYNONYMS;

USER_COL_GRANTS: To display the grants on columns for which the user is the owner, grantor or grantee.

SELECT * FROM USER_COL_GRANTS;

USER_COL_GRANTS_MADE: To display all grants on columns of objects owned by the user.

SELECT * FROM USER_COL_GRANTS_MADE;

USER_COL_GRANTS_RECD : To display all grants on columns for which the user is the grantee.

SELECT * FROM USER_COL_GRANTS_RECD;

USER_COL_PRIVS: To display the grants on columns for which the user is the owner, grantor or grantee.

SELECT * FROM USER_COL_PRIVS;

USER_COL_PRIVS_MADE: To display all grants on columns of objects owned by the user.

SELECT * FROM USER_COL_PRIVS_MADE;

USER_COL_PRIVS_RECD: To display all grants on columns for which the user is the grantee.

SELECT * FROM USER_COL_PRIVS_RECD;

USER_TAB_GRANTS: To display the grants on objects for which the user is the owner, grantor or grantee.

SELECT * FROM USER_TAB_GRANTS;

USER_TAB_GRANTS_MADE: To display the grants on objects for which the user is the owner.

SELECT * FROM USER_TAB_GRANTS_MADE;

USER_TAB_GRANTS_RECD: To display the grants on objects for which the user is the grantee.

SELECT * FROM USER_TAB_GRANTS_RECD;

USER_VIEWS: To display the text of views owned by the user.

SELECT * FROM USER_VIEWS;

REMOTE DATA ACCESS

Data may be stored in many databases and so there must be a method to locate and access such data. The method is to create DATABASE LINKS.

Database links require SQL * Net to be running on each of the machines involved in the remote data access.

To create the link:

Syntax

CREATE DATABASE LINK <link name>
CONNECT TO <username> IDENTIFIED BY <password>
USING 'connect string';

Example: CREATE DATABASE LINK DELHI
CONNECT TO STUDENT IDENTIFIED BY GOOD
USING 'ORACLE'

Note. The 'CONNECT STRING' will be dependent on network protocol used.

To use the link: SELECT * FROM SALARY@DELHI;

To view the link: SELECT * FROM USER_DB_LINKS;

To remove the link: DROP DATABASE LINK DELHI;

LAB ASSIGNMENT—20

1. Create a new user DON, BON and JOHN with password SITRI.
2. Grant read only privileges to everybody on product_mast table. Allow only the Product_no, Description, Cost_price columns.
3. Create a USER as IT_OFFICER, which has the privileges of querying, updating and deleting all issues transactions only.
4. Grant this role to the users DON, BON and JOHN.
5. Create an index on ITNO column of product_mast table.
6. Give the name of data dictionary views that are used for getting information about the transactions.
7. Change the password of Don by new password China.
8. Delete the indices that are no longer required.
9. Grant write permission to everybody on employee table.
10. Delete the user JOHN.

FAQ
(Frequently Asked Questions)

Q.1 *What are the components of physical database structure of Oracle database?*

Ans. ORACLE database is comprised of three types of files. One or more data files, two or more redo log files, and one or more control files.

Q.2 *What is a tablespace?*

Ans. A database is divided into two logical storage units called tablespaces. A tablespace is used to group related logical structures together.

Q.3 *What is system tablespace and when is it created?*

Ans. Every Oracle database contains a tablespace named system, which is automatically created when the database is created. The system table space always contains the data dictionary tables for the entire database.

Q.4 *Explain the relationship among database, tablespace and data file.*

Ans. Each databases is logically divided into one or more tablespaces, one or more data files are explicitly created FOR EACH TABLE SPACE.

Q.5 *What is schema?*

Ans. A schema is a collection of database objects of a user.

Q.6 *What is Table?*

Ans. A table is the basic unit of data storage in an ORACLE database. The tables of database hold all of the user accessible data. Table data is stored in rows and columns.

Q.7 *What is a view?*

Ans. A view is a virtual table. Every view has a query attached to it.

(The query is a select statement that identifies the columns and rows of the table(s) the views uses.)

Q.8 *Can a view be based on another view?*

Ans. Yes.

Q.9 *What are the advantages of views?*

Ans. Provide an additional level of table security, by restricting access to a predetermined set of rows and columns of a table.

- Hide data complexity.
- Simplify commands for the user.
- Present the data in a different perspective from that of the base table.

Q.10 *What is a Sequence?*

Ans. A sequence generates a serial list of unique numbers for numerical columns of a database's tables.

Q.11 *What is Synonym?*

Ans. A synonym is an alias for a table, view, sequence or program unity.

Q.12 *What are the type of synonyms?*

Ans. There are two types of synonyms , private and public.

Q.13 *What is an Index?*

Ans. An index is an optional structure associated with a table to have direct access to rows, which can be created to increase the performance of data retrieval. Index can be created on one or more columns of a table.

Q.14 *What is data block ?*

Ans. Oracle database's data is stored in data blocks. One data block corresponds to specific number of bytes of physical database space on disk.

Q.15 *What is a rollback segment ?*

Ans. A database contains one or more rollback segments to temporarily store "undo" information.

Q.16 *What are the uses of rollback segment?*

Ans. Rollback segments are used:

To generate read-consistent database information during database recovery to rollback uncommitted transactions for users.

Q.17 *Describe referential integrity?*

Ans. A rule defined on a column (or set of columns) in one table that allows the insert or update of a row only if the value for the column or set of columns (the dependent value) matches a value in a column of related table (the referenced value). It also specifies the related table (the referenced value). It also specifies the type of data manipulation allowed on referenced data and the action to be performed on dependent data as a result of any action on referenced data.

Q.18 *What are the referential actions supported by FOREIGN KEY integrity constraint?*

Ans. UPDATE and DELETE restrict - a referential integrity rule that disallows the update or deletion of referenced data.

DELETE cascade - when a referenced row is deleted all associated dependent rows are deleted.

Q.19 *What do constitute an Oracle instance?*

Ans. SGA and Oracle background processes constitute an Oracle instance (or) Combination of memory structure and background process.

Q.20 *What is SGA?*

Ans. The System Global Area (SGA) is a shared memory region allocated by Oracle that contains data and control information for one Oracle instance.

Q.21 *What are the componenets of SGA ?*

Ans. Database buffers, Redo Log buffer, the shared pool and cursors.

Q.22 *What is cursor ?*

Ans. A cursor is a handle (a name or pointer for the memory) associated with specific statement.

Q.23 *What is user process?*

Ans. A user process is created and maintained to execute the software code of an application program.

It is shadow process created automatically to facilitate communication between the user and the server process.

Q.24 *What is the function of Lock (LCKn) process?*

Ans. Lock (LCKn) are used for inter-instance locking when the oracle parallel server option is used.

Q.25 *What is the maximun number of lock processes used?*

Ans. Though a single LCK process is sufficient for most Parallel Server System

Upto ten locks (LCK0,....,LCK9) are used for inter-instance locking.

Q.26 *Define transaction.*

Ans. A transaction is a logical unit of work that comprises one or more SQL statements executed by a single user.

Q.27 *What is SAVE POINT?*

Ans. For long transactions that contain many SQL statements, intermediate markers or savepoints can be declared which can be used to divide a transaction into smaller parts. This allows the option of later rolling back all work performed from the current point in the transaction to a declared save point within the transaction.

Q.28 *What are the different types of PL/SQL program units that can be defined and stored in oracle database?*

Ans. Procedures and functions, packages and database triggers.

Q.29 *What is procedure?*

Ans. A procedure consists of a set of SQL and PL / SQL statements that are grouped together as unit to solve a specific problem or perform a set of related tasks.

Q.30 *What is the difference between procedures and functions?*

Ans. A function returns a value to the caller whereas a procedure does not.

Q.31 *What is a package?*

Ans. Package is a collection of related procedures, functions, variables and other package constructs together as a unit in the database.

Q.32 *What are the advantages of having a package?*

Ans. Increased functionality (for example, global package variable can be declared and used by any procedure in the package) and performance (for example, all objects of the package are parsed complied, and loaded into memory once)

Q.33 *What is a database trigger?*

Ans. A database trigger procedure is a set of SQL and PL/SQL statements that is automatically executed as a result of an insert in, update to, or delete from a table.

Q.34 *What are the uses of database trigger?*

Ans. Database triggers can be used to automatic data generation, audit data modification, enforce complex integrity constraints, and customize complex security authorizations.

Q.35 *What are the differences between database triggers and integrity constraints?*

Ans. A declarative integrity constraint is a statement about the database that is always true.

A constraint applies to existing data in the table and any statement that manipulates the table.

A trigger does not apply to data loaded before the definition of the trigger, therefore, it does not guarantee all data in a table that conforms to the rules established by an associated trigger. A trigger can be used to enforce transitional constraints whereas a declarative integrity constraint cannot be used

Q.36 *What are roles?*

Ans. Roles are named groups of related privileges that are granted to users or other roles.

Q.37 *What are the uses of roles?*

Ans. **REDUCED GRANTING OF PRIVILEGES**—Rather than explicity granting the same set of privileges to many users a database administrator can grant the privileges for a group of related users granted to a role and then grant only the role to each member of the group.

DYNAMIC PRIVILEGE MANAGEMENT—When the privileges of a group must change, only the privileges of the role to be modified. The security domains of all users granted the group's role automatically reflect the changes made to the role.

SELECTIVE AVAILABILITY OF PRIVILEGES—The roles granted to a user can select, enable (available for use) or disabled (not available for use). This allows specific control of a user's privileges in any given situation.

APPLICATION AWARENESS—A database application can be designed to automatically enable and disable selective roles when a user attempts to use the application.

Q.38 *How to prevent unauthorized use of privileges granted to a Role?*

Ans. By creating a role with a password.

Q.39 *What is the basic difference between a join and a union?*

Ans. A join selects columns from 2 or more tables. A union selects rows.

Q.40 *What is normalization and what are the five normal forms?*

Ans. Normalization is a design procedure for representing data in tabular format. The five normal forms are progressive rules to represent the data with minimal redundancy.

Q.41 *What are foreign keys?*

Ans. These are attributes of one table that have matching values in a primary key in another table, allowing for relationships between tables.

Q.42 *Describe the elements of the SELECT query syntax.*

Ans. SELECT element FROM table WHERE conditional statement.

Q.43 *Explain the use of the WHERE clause.*

Ans. WHERE is used with a relational statement to isolate the object element or row.

Q.44 *What techniques are used to retrieve data from more than one table in a single SQL statement?*

Ans. Joins, unions and nested selects are used to retrieve data.

Q.45 *Explain an outer join.*

Ans. An outer join includes rows from tables when there are no matching values in the tables.

Q.46 *What is a subselect? Is it different from a nested select?*

Ans. A subselect is a select which works in conjunction with another select. A nested select is a kind of subselect where the inner select passes to the where criteria for the outer select.

Q.47 *What is the difference between group by and order by?*

Ans. Group by controls the presentation of the rows, order by controls the presentation of the columns for the results of the SELECT statement.

Q.48 *What keyword does an SQL SELECT statement use for a string search?*

Ans. The LIKE keyword allows for string searches. The % sign is used as a wildcard.

Q.49 *What are some SQL aggregates and other built-in functions?*

Ans. The common aggregate, built-in functions are AVG, SUM, MIN, MAX, COUNT and DISTINCT.

Q.50 *How is the SUBSTR keyword used in SQL?*

Ans. SUBSTR is used for string manipulation with column name, first position and string length is used as arguments. For example, SUBSTR (NAME, 1, 3) refers to the first three characters in the column NAME.

Q.51 *Explain the EXPLAIN statement.*

Ans. The explain statement provides information about the optimizer's choice of access path of the SQL.

Q.52 *What is referential integrity?*

Ans. Referential integrity refers to the consistency that must be maintained between primary and foreign keys, every foreign key value must have a corresponding primary key value.

Q.53 *What is a NULL value? What are the pros and cons of using NULLS?*

Ans. A NULL value takes up one byte of storage and indicates that a value is not present as opposed to a space or zero value. It's the DB2 equivalent to TBD on an organizational chart and often correctly portrays a business situation. Unfortunately, it requires extra coding for an application program to handle this situation.

Q.54 *What is a synonym? How is it used?*

Ans. A synonym is used to reference a table or view by another name. The other name can then be written in the application code pointing to test tables in the development stage and to production entities when the code is migrated. The synonym is linked to the AUTHID that created it.

Q.55 *What is an alias and how does it differ from a synonym?*

Ans. An alias is an alternative to a synonym, designed for a distributed environment to avoid having used the location qualifier of a table or view. The alias is not dropped when the table is dropped.

Q.56 *When can an insert of a new primary key value threaten referential integrity?*

Ans. Never. New primary key values are not a problem. However, the values of foreign key inserts must have corresponding primary key values in their related tables and updates of primary key values may require changes in foreign key values to maintain referential integrity.

Q.57 *What is the difference between static and dynamic SQL?*

Ans. Static SQL is hard-coded in a program when the programmer knows the statements to be executed. For dynamic SQL the program must dynamically allocate memory to receive the query results.

Q.58 *Compare a subselect to a join.*

Ans. Any subselect can be rewritten as a join, but not vice versa. Joins are usually more efficient as join rows can be returned immediately, subselects require a temporary work area for inner select results while processing the outer select.

Q.59 *What is the difference between IN subselects and EXISTS subselect?*

Ans. If there is an index on the attributes tested an IN is more efficient since DB2 uses the index for the IN. (IN for index is the mnemonic).

Q.60 *What is a Cartesian product?*

Ans. A Cartesian product results from a faulty query. It is a row in the results for every combination in the join tables.

Q.61 *What is a tuple?*

Ans. A tuple is an instance of data within a relational database.

Q.62 *Any SQL implementation covers data types in couple of main categories. Which of the following are those data types ? (Check all that apply) A. NUMERIC B. CHARACTER C. DATE AND TIME D. BLOBS E. BIT*

Ans. A,B,C. Not all SQL implementations have a BLOB or a BIT data types.

Q.63 *We have a table with a CHARACTER data type field. We apply a ">" row comparison between this field and another CHARACTER field in another table. What will be the results for records with field value of NULL ? (Check one that applies the best) A. TRUE B. FALSE C. UNKNOWN D. ERROR E. IGNORED.*

Ans. C. NULL in a row when compared will give an UNKNOWN result.

Q.64 *Any database needs to go through a normalization process to make sure that data is represented only once. This will eliminate problems for creating or destroying data in the database. The normalization process is done usually in three steps which results in first, second and third normal forms. Which best describes the process to obtain the third normal form? (Check one that applies the best) A. Each table should have related columns. B. Each separate table should have a primary key. C. We have a table with multi-valued key. All columns that are dependent on only one or on some of the keys should be moved in a different table. D. If a table has columns not dependent on the primary keys, they need to be moved in a separate table. E. Primary key is always UNIQUE and NOT NULL.*

Ans. D. All columns in a table should be dependent on the primary key. This will eliminate transitive dependencies in which A depends on B, and B depends on C, but we're not sure how C depends on A.

Q.65 *What is auditing ?*

Ans. Monitoring of user access to aid in the investigation of database use.

Q.66 *What are the different levels of auditing?*

Ans. Statement auditing, Privilege auditing and Object auditing.

Q.67 *What is Statement auditing?*

Ans. Statement auditing is the auditing of the powerful system privileges without regard to specifically named objects.

Q.68 *What is Privilege auditing?*

Ans. Privilege auditing is the auditing of the uses of powerful system privileges without regard to specifically named objects.

Q.69 *What is distributed database?*

Ans. A distributed database is a network of databases managed by multiple database servers that appears to a user as single logical database. The data of all databases in the distributed database can be simultaneously accessed and modified.

Q.70 *What is a SQL * NET?*

Ans. SQL * NET is Oracle's mechanism for interfacing with the communication protocols used by the networks that facilitate distributed processing and distributed databases. It is used in Client-Server and Server-Server communications.

COMPETITIVE QUESTIONS ASKED BY REPUTED COMPANIES LIKE INFOSYS, SATYAM, HCL, TCS, ORACLE, PEOPLESOFT, BAAN etc.

SET–1

1. Examine the structure of the EMPLOYEES and NEW_EMPLOYEES tables:

   EMPLOYEES
   EMPLOYEE_ID NUMBER Primary Key
   FIRST_NAME VARCHAR2(25)
   LAST_NAME VARCHAR2(25)
   HIRE_DATE DATE

   NEW_EMPLOYEES
   EMPLOYEE_ID NUMBER Primary Key
   NAME VARCHAR2(60)

   Which UPDATE statement is valid?

   A. UPDATE new_employees SET name = (SELECT last_name|| first_name FROM employees WHERE employee_id =180) WHERE employee_id =180;

   B. UPDATE new_employees SET name = (SELECT last_name||first_name FROM employees) WHERE employee_id =180;

   C. UPDATE new_employees SET name = (SELECT last_name || first_name FROM employees WHERE employee_id =180) WHERE employee_id =(SELECT employee_id FROM new_employees);

   D. UPDATE new_employees SET name = (SELECT last_name|| first_name FROM employees WHERE employee_id = (SELECT employee_id FROM new_employees)) WHERE employee_id =180;

2. The EMP table contains these columns:

LAST_NAME	VARCHAR2 (25)
SALARY	NUMBER (6,2)
DEPARTMENT_ID	NUMBER (6)

   You need to display the employees who have not been assigned to any department. You write the SELECT statement:

   SELECT LAST_NAME, SALARY, DEPARTMENT_ID
   FROM EMP
   WHERE DEPARTMENT_ID = NULL;

What is true about this SQL statement?

A. The SQL statement displays the desired results.

B. The column in the WHERE clause should be changed to display the desired results.

C. The operator in the WHERE clause should be changed to display the desired results.

D. The WHERE clause should be changed to use an outer join to display the desired results.

3. Examine the description of the EMPLOYEES table:

EMP_ID	NUMBER(4)	NOT NULL
LAST_NAME	VARCHAR2(30)	NOT NULL
FIRST_NAME	VARCHAR2(30)	
DEPT_ID	NUMBER(2)	
JOB_CAT	VARCHAR2(30)	
SALARY	NUMBER(8,2)	

Which statement shows the department ID, minimum salary, and maximum salary paid in that department, only if the minimum salary is less than 5000 and maximum salary is more than 15000?

A.
```
SELECT dept_id, MIN(salary), MAX(salary)
FROM employees
WHERE MIN(salary) < 5000 AND MAX(salary) > 15000;
```

B.
```
SELECT dept_id, MIN(salary), MAX(salary)
FROM employees
WHERE MIN(salary) < 5000 AND MAX(salary) > 15000
GROUP BY dept_id;
```

C.
```
SELECT dept_id, MIN(salary), MAX(salary)
FROM employees
HAVING MIN(salary) < 5000 AND MAX(salary) > 15000;
```

D.
```
SELECT dept_id, MIN(salary), MAX(salary)
FROM employees
GROUP BY dept_id
HAVING MIN(salary) < 5000 AND MAX(salary) > 15000;
```

E.
```
SELECT dept_id, MIN(salary), MAX(salary)
FROM employees
GROUP BY dept_id, salary
HAVING MIN(salary) < 5000 AND MAX(salary) > 15000;
```

4. You created a view called EMP_DEPT_VU that contains three columns from the EMPLOYEES and DEPARTMENTS tables: EMPLOYEE_ID, EMPLOYEE_NAME AND DEPARTMENT_NAME.

The DEPARTMENT_ID column of the EMPLOYEES table is the foreign key to the primary key DEPARTMENT_ID column of the DEPARTMENTS table.

You want to modify the view by adding a fourth column, MANAGER_ID of NUMBER data type from the EMPLOYEES table.

How can you accomplish this task?

A. ALTER VIEW emp_dept_vu (ADD manager_id NUMBER);

B. MODIFY VIEW emp_dept_vu (ADD manager_id NUMBER);

C. ALTER VIEW emp_dept_vu AS
```
SELECT employee_id, employee_name,
    department_name, manager_id
FROM   employees e, departments d
WHERE  e.department_id = d.department_id;
```

D. MODIFY VIEW emp_dept_vu AS
```
SELECT employee_id, employee_name,
    department_name, manager_id
FROM   employees e, departments d
WHERE  e.department_id = d.department_id;
```

E. CREATE OR REPLACE VIEW emp_dept_vu AS
```
SELECT employee_id, employee_name,
    department_name, manager_id
FROM   employees e, departments d
WHERE  e.department_id = d.department_id;
```

F. You must remove the existing view first, and then run the CREATE VIEW command with a new column list to modify a view.

5. Examine the SQL statement that creates ORDERS table:

```
CREATE TABLE orders
    (SER_NO        NUMBER UNIQUE,
ORDER_ID        NUMBER,
ORDER_DATE      DATE NOT NULL,
STATUS VARCHAR2(10)
    CHECK (status IN ('CREDIT', 'CASH')),
PROD_ID NUMBER
    REFERENCES PRODUCTS(PRODUCT_ID),
ORD_TOTAL       NUMBER,
PRIMARY KEY (order_id, order_date));
```

For which columns would an index be automatically created when you execute the above SQL statement? (Choose two.)

A. SER_NO
B. ORDER_ID
C. STATUS
D. PROD_ID
E. ORD_TOTAL
F. composite index on ORDER_ID and ORDER_DATE

6. You are granted the CREATE VIEW privilege. What does this allow you to do?
A. Create a table view.
B. Create a view in any schema.
C. Create a view in your schema.
D. Create a sequence view in any schema.
E. Create a view that is accessible by everyone.
F. Create a view only if it is based on tables that you created.

7. Which clause would you use in a SELECT statement to limit the display to those employees whose salary is greater than 5000?
A. ORDER BY SALARY > 5000
B. GROUP BY SALARY > 5000
C. HAVING SALARY > 5000
D. WHERE SALARY > 5000

8. Examine the structure of the EMPLOYEES and NEW_EMPLOYEES tables:

EMPLOYEES

EMPLOYEE_ID NUMBER Primary Key
FIRST_NAME VARCHAR2(25)
LAST_NAME VARCHAR2(25)
HIRE_DATE DATE

NEW_EMPLOYEES

EMPLOYEE_ID NUMBER Primary Key
NAME VARCHAR2(60)

Which MERGE statement is valid?

A.
```
MERGE INTO new_employees c
USING employees e
ON (c.employee_id = e.employee_id)
WHEN MATCHED THEN
   UPDATE SET
   c.name = e.first_name ||','|| e.last_name
WHEN NOT MATCHED THEN
   INSERT VALUES(e.employee_id, e.first_name ||', '||e.last_name);
```

B. MERGE new_employees c
USING employees e
ON (c.employee_id = e.employee_id)
WHEN EXISTS THEN
UPDATE SET
c.name = e.first_name ||','|| e.last_name
WHEN NOT MATCHED THEN
INSERT VALUES(e.employee_id, e.first_name ||','||e.last_name);

C. MERGE INTO new_employees c
USING employees e
ON (c.employee_id = e.employee_id)
WHEN EXISTS THEN
UPDATE SET
c.name = e.first_name ||','|| e.last_name
WHEN NOT MATCHED THEN
INSERT VALUES(e.employee_id, e.first_name ||','||e.last_name);

D. MERGE new_employees c
FROM employees e
ON (c.employee_id = e.employee_id)
WHEN MATCHED THEN
UPDATE SET
c.name = e.first_name ||','|| e.last_name
WHEN NOT MATCHED THEN
INSERT INTO new_employees VALUES(e.employee_id, e.first_name ||','||e.last_name);

9. Which two statements are true regarding the ORDER BY clause? (Choose two.)
A. The sort is in ascending order by default.
B. The sort is in descending order by default.
C. The ORDER BY clause must precede the WHERE clause.
D. The ORDER BY clause is executed on the client side.
E. The ORDER BY clause comes last in the SELECT statement.
F. The ORDER BY clause is executed first in the query execution.

10. Which constraint can be defined only at the column level?
A. UNIQUE
B. NOT NULL

C. CHECK

D. PRIMARY KEY

E. FOREIGN KEY

11. Mary has a view called EMP_DEPT_LOC_VU that was created based on the EMPLOYEES, DEPARTMENTS, and LOCATIONS tables. She granted SELECT privilege to Scott on this view.

Which option enables Scott to eliminate the need to qualify the view with the name MARY.EMP_DEPT_LOC_VU each time the view is referenced?

A. Scott can create a synonym for the EMP_DEPT_LOC_VU by using the command CREATE PRIVATE SYNONYM EDL_VU FOR mary.EMP_DEPT_LOC_VU; then he can prefix the columns with this synonym.

B. Scott can create a synonym for the EMP_DEPT_LOC_VU by using the command CREATE SYNONYM EDL_VU FOR mary.EMP_DEPT_LOC_VU;
then he can prefix the columns with this synonym.

C. Scott can create a synonym for the EMP_DEPT_LOC_VU by using the command CREATE LOCAL SYNONYM EDL_VU FOR mary.EMP_DEPT_LOC_VU;
then he can prefix the columns with this synonym.

D. Scott can create a synonym for the EMP_DEPT_LOC_VU by using the command CREATE SYNONYM EDL_VU ON mary(EMP_DEPT_LOC_VU); then he can prefix the columns with this synonym.

E. Scott cannot create a synonym because synonyms can be created only for tables.

F. Scott cannot create any synonym for Mary's view. Mary should create a private synonym for the view and grant SELECT privilege on that synonym to Scott.

12. Examine the description of the MARKS table:

STD_ID NUMBER(4)
STUDENT_NAME VARCHAR2(30)
SUBJ1 NUMBER(3)
SUBJ2 NUMBER(3)

SUBJ1 and SUBJ2 indicate the marks obtained by a student in two subjects.

Examine this SELECT statement based on the MARKS table:

```
SELECT subj1+subj2 total_marks, std_id
FROM marks
WHERE subj1 > AVG(subj1) AND subj2 > AVG(subj2)
ORDER BY total_marks;
```

What is the result of the SELECT statement?

A. The statement executes successfully and returns the student ID and sum of all marks for each student who obtained more than the average mark in each subject.

B. The statement returns an error at the SELECT clause.

C. The statement returns an error at the WHERE clause.

D. The statement returns an error at the ORDER BY clause.

13. From SQL*Plus, you issue this SELECT statement:

SELECT * FROM orders;

You use this statement to retrieve data from a database table for _____. (Choose all that apply.)

A. updating

B. viewing

C. deleting

D. inserting

E. truncating

14. Which three SELECT statements display 2000 in the format "$2,000.00"? (Choose three.)

A. SELECT TO_CHAR(2000, '$#,###.##') FROM dual;

B. SELECT TO_CHAR(2000, '$0,000.00') FROM dual;

C. SELECT TO_CHAR(2000, '$9,999.00') FROM dual;

D. SELECT TO_CHAR(2000, '$9,999.99') FROM dual;

E. SELECT TO_CHAR(2000, '$2,000.00') FROM dual;

F. SELECT TO_CHAR(2000, '$N,NNN.NN') FROM dual;

15. Which three statements about subqueries are true? (Choose three.)

A. A single row subquery can retrieve only one column and one row.

B. A single row subquery can retrieve only one row but many columns.

C. A multiple row subquery can retrieve multiple rows and multiple columns.

D. A multiple row subquery can be compared using the ">" operator.

E. A single row subquery can use the IN operator.

F. A multiple row subquery can use the "=" operator.

16. Which are DML statements? (Choose all that apply.)

A. COMMIT ...

B. MERGE ...

C. UPDATE ...

D. DELETE ...

E. CREATE ...

F. DROP ...

17. The DBA issues this SQL command:

CREATE USER scott
IDENTIFIED by tiger;

What privileges does the user Scott have at this point?

A. no privileges

B. only the SELECT privilege

C. only the CONNECT privilege
D. all the privileges of a default user

18. Examine the description of the STUDENTS table:
STD_ID NUMBER(4)
COURSE_ID VARCHAR2(10)
START_DATE DATE
END_DATE DATE

Which two aggregate functions are valid on the START_DATE column? (Choose two.)
A. SUM(start_date)
B. AVG(start_date)
C. COUNT(start_date)
D. AVG(start_date, end_date)
E. MIN(start_date)
F. MAXIMUM(start_date)

19. Which SELECT statement will get the result 'elloworld' from the string 'HelloWorld'?
A. SELECT SUBSTR('HelloWorld',1) FROM dual;
B. SELECT INITCAP(TRIM ('HelloWorld', 1,1)) FROM dual;
C. SELECT LOWER(SUBSTR('HelloWorld', 1, 1) FROM dual;
D. SELECT LOWER(SUBSTR('HelloWorld', 2, 1) FROM dual;
E. SELECT LOWER(TRIM ('H' FROM 'HelloWorld')) FROM dual;

20. You need to display the last names of those employees who have the letter "A" as the second character in their names.
Which SQL statement displays the required results?
A. SELECT last_name FROM EMP WHERE last_name LIKE '_A%';
B. SELECT last_name FROM EMP WHERE last_name ='*A%'
C. SELECT last_name FROM EMP WHERE last_name ='_A%';
D. SELECT last_name FROM EMP WHERE last_name LIKE '*A%'

21. Which four are correct guidelines for naming database tables? (Choose four.)
A. must begin with either a number or a letter
B. must be 1-30 characters long
C. should not be an Oracle Server reserved word
D. must contain only A-Z, a-z, 0-9, _, *, and #
E. must contain only A-Z, a-z, 0-9, _, $, and #
F. must begin with a letter

22. In which case would you use a FULL OUTER JOIN?
A. Both tables have NULL values.
B. You want all unmatched data from one table.

C. You want all matched data from both tables.

D. You want all unmatched data from both tables.

E. One of the tables has more data than the other.

F. You want all matched and unmatched data from only one table.

23. Examine the structure of the EMPLOYEES table:

Column name	Data type	Remarks
EMPLOYEE_ID	NUMBER	NOT NULL, Primary Key
EMP_NAME	VARCHAR2(30)	
JOB_ID	VARCHAR2(20)	NOT NULL
SAL	NUMBER	
MGR_ID	NUMBER	References EMPLOYEE_ID column
DEPARTMENT_ID	NUMBER	Foreign key to DEPARTMENT_ID column of the DEPARTMENTS table

You need to create a view called EMP_VU that allows the users to insert rows through the view.

Which SQL statement, when used to create the EMP_VU view, allows the users to insert rows?

A. CREATE VIEW emp_vu AS SELECT employee_id, emp_name, department_id FROM employees WHERE mgr_id IN (102, 120);

B. CREATE VIEW emp_vu AS SELECT employee_id, emp_name, job_id, department_id FROM employees WHERE mgr_id IN (102, 120);

C. CREATE VIEW emp_vu AS SELECT department_id, SUM(sal) TOTALSAL FROM employees WHERE mgr_id IN (102, 120) GROUP BY department_id;

D. CREATE VIEW emp_vu AS SELECT employee_id, emp_name, job_id, DISTINCT department_id FROM employees;

24. When should you create a role? (Choose two.)

A. to simplify the process of creating new users using the CREATE USER xxx IDENTIFIED by yyy statement

B. to grant a group of related privileges to a user

C. when the number of people using the database is very high

D. to simplify the process of granting and revoking privileges

E. to simplify profile maintenance for a user who is constantly traveling

25. You need to perform certain data manipulation operations through a view called EMP_DEPT_VU, which you previously created. You want to look at the definition of the view (the SELECT statement on which the view was created.)

How do you obtain the definition of the view?

A. Use the DESCRIBE command on the EMP_DEPT_VU view.

B. Use the DEFINE VIEW command on the EMP_DEPT_VU view.

C. Use the DESCRIBE VIEW command on the EMP_DEPT_VU view.

D. Query the USER_VIEWS data dictionary view to search for the EMP_DEPT_VU view.

E. Query the USER_SOURCE data dictionary view to search for the EMP_DEPT_VU view.

F. Query the USER_OBJECTS data dictionary view to search for the EMP_DEPT_VU view.

26. Which two statements about creating constraints are true? (Choose two.)

A. Constraint names must start with SYS_C.

B. All constraints must be defined at the column level.

C. Constraints can be created after the table is created.

D. Constraints can be created at the same time the table is created.

E. Information about constraints is found in the VIEW_CONSTRAINTS dictionary view.

27. The STUDENT_GRADES table has these columns:

STUDENT_ID NUMBER(12)
SEMESTER_END DATE
GPA NUMBER(4,3)

The registrar has asked for a report on the average grade point average (GPA) for students enrolled during semesters that end in the year 2000. Which statement accomplishes this?

A. SELECT AVERAGE(gpa) FROM student_grades WHERE semester_end > '01-JAN-2000' and semester_end < '31-DEC-2000';

B. SELECT COUNT(gpa) FROM student_grades WHERE semester_end > '01-JAN-2000' and semester_end < '31-DEC-2000';

C. SELECT MID(gpa) FROM student_grades WHERE semester_end > '01-JAN-2000' and semester_end < '31-DEC-2000';

D. SELECT AVG(gpa) FROM student_grades WHERE semester_end BETWEEN '01-JAN-2000' and '31-DEC-2000';

E. SELECT SUM(gpa) FROM student_grades WHERE semester_end > '01-JAN-2000' and semester_end < '31-DEC-2000';

F. SELECT MEDIAN(gpa) FROM student_grades WHERE semester_end > '01-JAN-2000' and semester_end < '31-DEC-2000';

28. The EMPLOYEES table has these columns:

LAST_NAME VARCHAR2(35)
SALARY NUMBER(8,2)
COMMISSION_PCT NUMBER(5,2)

You want to display the name and annual salary multiplied by the commission_pct for all employees. For records that have a NULL commission_pct, a zero must be displayed against the calculated column.

Which SQL statement displays the desired results?

A. SELECT last_name, (salary * 12) * commission_pct FROM EMPLOYEES;

B. SELECT last_name, (salary * 12) * IFNULL(commission_pct, 0) FROM EMPLOYEES;

C. SELECT last_name, (salary * 12) * NVL2(commission_pct, 0) FROM EMPLOYEES;

D. SELECT last_name, (salary * 12) * NVL(commission_pct, 0) FROM EMPLOYEES;

29. Evaluate the SQL statement

DROP TABLE DEPT;

Which four statements are true of the SQL statement? (Choose four.)

A. You cannot roll back this statement.

B. All pending transactions are committed.

C. All views based on the DEPT table are deleted.

D. All indexes based on the DEPT table are dropped.

E. All data in the table is deleted, and the table structure is also deleted.

F. All data in the table is deleted, but the structure of the table is retained.

G. All synonyms based on the DEPT table are deleted.

30. Which statement explicitly names a constraint?

A. ALTER TABLE student_grades ADD FOREIGN KEY (student_id) REFERENCES students(student_id);

B. ALTER TABLE student_grades ADD CONSTRAINT NAME = student_id_fk FOREIGN KEY (student_id) REFERENCES students(student_id);

C. ALTER TABLE student_grades ADD CONSTRAINT student_id_fk FOREIGN KEY (student_id) REFERENCES students(student_id);

D. ALTER TABLE student_grades ADD NAMED CONSTRAINT student_id_fk FOREIGN KEY (student_id) REFERENCES students(student_id);

E. ALTER TABLE student_grades ADD NAME student_id_fk FOREIGN KEY (student_id) REFERENCES students(student_id);

31. Which two tasks can you perform using only the TO_CHAR function? (Choose two.)

A. convert 10 to 'TEN'

B. convert '10' to 10

C. convert 10 to '10'

D. convert 'TEN' to 10

E. convert a date to a character expression

F. convert a character expression to a date

32. Management has asked you to calculate the value 12*salary*commission_pct for all the employees in the EMP table. The EMP table contains these columns:

    LAST_NAME VARCHAR2(35) NOT NULL
    SALARY NUMBER(9,2) NOT NULL
    COMMISSION_PCT NUMBER(4,2)

    Which statement ensures that a value is displayed in the calculated column for all employees?

    A. SELECT last_name, 12*salary*commission_pct FROM emp;
    B. SELECT last_name, 12*salary*(commission_pct,0) FROM emp;
    C. SELECT last_name, 12*salary*(nvl(commission_pct,0)) FROM emp;
    D. SELECT last_name, 12*salary*(decode(commission_pct,0)) FROM emp;

33. In which scenario would Top N analysis be the best solution?

    A. You want to identify the most senior employee in the company.
    B. You want to find the manager supervising the largest number of employees.
    C. You want to identify the person who makes the highest salary of all employees.
    D. You want to rank the top three sales representatives who have sold the maximum number of products.

34. The EMPLOYEES table has these columns:

    LAST_NAME VARCHAR2(35)
    SALARY NUMBER(8,2)
    HIRE_DATE DATE

    Management wants to add a default value to the SALARY column. You plan to alter the table by using this SQL statement:

    ```
    ALTER TABLE EMPLOYEES
    MODIFY (SALARY DEFAULT 5000);
    ```

    Which is true about your ALTER statement?

    A. Column definitions cannot be altered to add DEFAULT values.
    B. A change to the DEFAULT value affects only subsequent insertions to the table.
    C. Column definitions cannot be altered to add DEFAULT values for columns with a NUMBER data type.
    D. All the rows that have a NULL value for the SALARY column will be updated with the value 5000.

35. Which two statements complete a transaction? (Choose two.)

    A. DELETE employees;
    B. DESCRIBE employees;
    C. ROLLBACK TO SAVEPOINT C;

D. GRANT SELECT ON employees TO SCOTT;
E. ALTER TABLE employees SET UNUSED COLUMN sal;
F. SELECT MAX(sal) FROM employees WHERE department_id = 20;

36. Which SQL statement defines a FOREIGN KEY constraint on the DEPTNO column of the EMP table?

A. CREATE TABLE EMP
(empno NUMBER(4),
ename VARCHAR2(35),
deptno NUMBER(7,2) NOT NULL,
CONSTRAINT emp_deptno_fk FOREIGN KEY deptno
REFERENCES dept deptno);

B. CREATE TABLE EMP
(empno NUMBER(4),
ename VARCHAR2(35),
deptno NUMBER(7,2)
CONSTRAINT emp_deptno_fk REFERENCES dept (deptno));

C. CREATE TABLE EMP
(empno NUMBER(4),
ename VARCHAR2(35),
deptno NUMBER(7,2) NOT NULL,
CONSTRAINT emp_deptno_fk REFERENCES dept (deptno) FOREIGN KEY (deptno));

D. CREATE TABLE EMP
(empno NUMBER(4),
ename VARCHAR2(35),
deptno NUMBER(7,2) FOREIGN KEY
CONSTRAINT emp_deptno_fk REFERENCES dept (deptno));

37. You want to display the titles of books that meet these criteria:

1. Purchased before January 21, 2001
2. Price is less than $500 or greater than $900

You want to sort the results by their date of purchase, starting with the most recently bought book.

Which statement should you use?

A. SELECT book_title
FROM books
WHERE price between 500 and 900

```
AND purchase_date < '21-JAN-2001'
ORDER BY purchase_date;
```

B.
```
SELECT book_title
FROM books
WHERE price IN (500,900)
AND purchase_date < '21-JAN-2001'
ORDER BY purchase_date ASC;
```

C.
```
SELECT book_title
FROM books
WHERE price < 500 OR > 900
AND purchase_date < '21-JAN-2001'
ORDER BY purchase_date DESC;
```

D.
```
SELECT book_title
FROM books
WHERE (price < 500 OR price > 900)
AND purchase_date < '21-JAN-2001'
ORDER BY purchase_date DESC;
```

E.
```
SELECT book_title
FROM books
WHERE (price < 500 OR price > 900
AND purchase_date > '21-JAN-2001')
ORDER BY purchase_date ASC;
```

38. Examine the description of the EMPLOYEES table:

EMP_ID	NUMBER(4) NOT NULL
LAST_NAME	VARCHAR2(30) NOT NULL
FIRST_NAME	VARCHAR2(30)
DEPT_ID	NUMBER(2)
JOB_CAT	VARCHAR2(30)
SALARY	NUMBER(8,2)

Which statement shows the maximum salary paid in each job category of each department?

A.
```
SELECT dept_id, job_cat, MAX(salary)
FROM employees
WHERE salary > MAX(salary);
```

B.
```
SELECT dept_id, job_cat, MAX(salary)
FROM employees
GROUP BY dept_id, job_cat;
```

C. SELECT dept_id, job_cat, MAX(salary)
FROM employees;

D. SELECT dept_id, job_cat, MAX(salary)
FROM employees
GROUP BY dept_id;

E. SELECT dept_id, job_cat, MAX(salary)
FROM employees
GROUP BY dept_id, job_cat, salary;

39. Which three are true regarding the use of outer joins? (Choose three.)

A. You cannot use IN operator in a condition that involves an outer join.

B. You use (+) on both sides of the WHERE condition to perform an outer join.

C. You use (*) on both sides of the WHERE condition to perform an outer join.

D. You use an outer join to see only the rows that do not meet the join condition.

E. In the WHERE condition, you use (+) following the name of the column in the table without matching rows, to perform an outer join.

F. You cannot link a condition that is involved in an outer join to another condition by using the OR operator.

40. Which substitution variable would you use if you want to reuse the variable value without prompting the user each time?

A. &

B. ACCEPT

C. PROMPT

D. &&

41. In which scenario would an index be most useful?

A. The indexed column is declared as NOT NULL.

B. The indexed columns are used in the FROM clause.

C. The indexed columns are part of an expression.

D. The indexed column contains a wide range of values.

42. Evaluate the SQL statement:

```
SELECT a.emp_name, a.sal, a.dept_id, b.maxsal
FROM employees a,
   (SELECT dept_id, MAX(sal) maxsal
   FROM employees
   GROUP BY dept_id) b
WHERE a.dept_id = b.dept_id
AND a.sal < b.maxsal;
```

What is the result of the statement?

A. The statement produces an error at line 1.

B. The statement produces an error at line 3.

C. The statement produces an error at line 6.

D. The statement returns the employee name, salary, department ID, and maximum salary earned in the department of the employee for all departments that pay less salary than the maximum salary paid in the company.

E. The statement returns the employee name, salary, department ID, and maximum salary earned in the department of the employee for all employees who earn less than the maximum salary in their department.

43. Which statement describes the ROWID data type?

A. binary data up to 4 gigabytes

B. character data up to 4 gigabytes

C. raw binary data of variable length up to 2 gigabytes

D. binary data stored in an external file, up to 4 gigabytes

E. a hexadecimal string representing the unique address of a row in its table

44. Examine the structure of the EMPLOYEES table:

EMPLOYEE_ID NUMBER Primary Key
FIRST_NAME VARCHAR2(25)
LAST_NAME VARCHAR2(25)

Which three statements insert a row into the table? (Choose three.)

A. INSERT INTO employees VALUES (NULL, 'John', 'Smith');

B. INSERT INTO employees(first_name, last_name) VALUES('John', 'Smith');

C. INSERT INTO employees VALUES ('1000', 'John', NULL);

D. INSERT INTO employees (first_name, last_name, employee_id) VALUES (1000, 'John', 'Smith');

E. INSERT INTO employees (employee_id) VALUES (1000);

F. INSERT INTO employees (employee_id, first_name, last_name) VALUES (1000, 'John', ' ');

45. Which two statements about sequences are true? (Choose two.)

A. You use a NEXTVAL pseudo column to look at the next possible value that would be generated from a sequence, without actually retrieving the value.

B. You use a CURRVAL pseudo column to look at the current value just generated from a sequence, without affecting the further values to be generated from the sequence.

C. You use a NEXTVAL pseudo column to obtain the next possible value from a sequence by actually retrieving the value from the sequence.

D. You use a CURRVAL pseudo column to generate a value from a sequence that would be used for a specified database column.

E. If a sequence starting from a value 100 and incremented by 1 is used by more than one application, then all of these applications could have a value of 105 assigned to their column whose value is being generated by the sequence.

F. You use a REUSE clause when creating a sequence to restart the sequence once it generates the maximum value defined for the sequence.

46. Which operator can be used with a multiple-row subquery?

A. =

B. LIKE

C. BETWEEN

D. NOT IN

E. IS

F. <>

47. You need to produce a report for mailing labels for all customers. The mailing label must have only the customer name and address. The CUSTOMERS table has these columns:

CUST_ID NUMBER(4) NOT NULL

CUST_NAME VARCHAR2(100) NOT NULL

CUST_ADDRESS VARCHAR2(150)

CUST_PHONE VARCHAR2(20)

Which SELECT statement accomplishes this task?

A. SELECT * FROM customers;

B. SELECT name, address FROM customers;

C. SELECT id, name, address, phone FROM customers;

D. SELECT cust_name, cust_address FROM customers;

E. SELECT cust_id, cust_name, cust_address, cust_phone FROM customers;

48. Examine the structure of the EMPLOYEES and DEPARTMENTS tables:

EMPLOYEES

Column name	Data type	Remarks
EMPLOYEE_ID	NUMBER	NOT NULL, Primary Key
EMP_NAME	VARCHAR2(30)	
JOB_ID	VARCHAR2(20)	
SALARY	NUMBER	
MGR_ID	NUMBER	References EMPLOYEE_ID column
DEPARTMENT_ID	NUMBER	Foreign key to DEPARTMENT_ID column of the DEPARTMENTS table

DEPARTMENTS

Column name	Data type	Remarks
DEPARTMENT_ID	NUMBER	NOT NULL, Primary Key
DEPARTMENT_NAME	VARCHAR2(30)	
MGR_ID	NUMBER	References MGR_ID column of the EMPLOYEES table

Evaluate this SQL statement:

```
SELECT employee_id, e.department_id, department_name, salary
FROM employees e, departments d
WHERE e.department_id = d.department_id;
```

Which SQL statement is equivalent to the above SQL statement?

A. SELECT employee_id, department_id, department_name, salary FROM employees WHERE department_id IN (SELECT department_id FROM departments);

B. SELECT employee_id, department_id, department_name, salary FROM employees NATURAL JOIN departments;

C. SELECT employee_id, d.department_id, department_name, salary FROM employees e JOIN departments d ON e.department_id = d.department_id;

D. SELECT employee_id, department_id, department_name, salary FROM employees JOIN departments USING (e.department_id, d.department_id);

49. Which SQL statement generates the alias Annual Salary for the calculated column SALARY*12?

A. SELECT ename, salary*12 'Annual Salary' FROM employees;

B. SELECT ename, salary*12 "Annual Salary" FROM employees;

C. SELECT ename, salary*12 AS Annual Salary FROM employees;

D. SELECT ename, salary*12 AS INITCAP("ANNUAL SALARY") FROM employees

50. Which four statements correctly describe functions that are available in SQL? (Choose four.)

A. INSTR returns the numeric position of a named character.

B. NVL2 returns the first non-null expression in the expression list.

C. TRUNCATE rounds the column, expression, or value to n decimal places.

D. DECODE translates an expression after comparing it to each search value.

E. TRIM trims the heading or trailing characters (or both) from a character string.

F. NVL compares two expressions and returns null if they are equal, or the first expression if they are not equal.

G. NULLIF compares two expressions and returns null if they are equal, or the first expression if they are not equal.

SET–2

1. **Table Name : Combos**

Row_id	A	B	C
1.	Cat	NULL	Dog
2.	Lion	Dog	NULL
3.	NULL	Bird	Ferret
4.	Lynx	Ant	Bat
5.	Fly	Bee	Beetle
6.	fish	Fish	Cricket

SELECT MAX (*a*), MIN (*b*), MAX (*c*), FROM combos

What is returned when the sample code is executed?

1. lynx ant ferret
2. lynx fish ferret
3. lynx NULL ferret
4. lynx bee lion
5. Nothing is returned because an error occurs.

2. Create view employees as select j.id, j.description, p.id, p.last_name, p.first_name from jobs j, people p where j.id = p.job_id and p.active = 'y'

What is the problem with the create view statement above?

1. All view names must begin with of the following prefixes : vw, VW, v, or V.
2. Everything after the AS keyword must be enclosed in parantheses.
3. When two tables are contributing to a view, only join conditions can be included in the WHERE clause. The additional "AND p.active = 'Y' " is not allowed in the create view statement.
4. The proper syntax for the statement is " CREATE VIEW AS employees (SELECT j.id, j.description, p.id, p.last_name, p.first_name)."
5. When two columns contributing to a view have the same name, at least one new column name (alias) must be used in the SELECT list.

3. Which one of the following join types will always create a cartesian product?

1. LEFT OUTER JOIN
2. CROSS JOIN
3. INNER JOIN

4. FULL OUTER JOIN
5. RIGHT OUTER JOIN

4. In SQL, what is the process of comparing the data in specified columns from one or more tables and using the comparison results to form a new set containing information from both tables that qualify?
1. The INSERT
2. The ALTER TABLE
3. The JOIN
4. The UPDATE
5. The DELETE

5. Which one of the following represents a correct SQL query?
1. SELECT S.TITLE, min(start_time) FROM shows s JOIN networks n ON s.net_id WHERE n.name = 'NBC' GROUP BY s.title
2. SELECT g.description, AVG(b.price) FROM books b JOIN ON b.book_id = genre.id where b.author_id = 5 GROUP BY g.description
3. SELECT i.product, i.qty FROM inventory I JOIN RIGHT sales s on i.id = s.prod_id WHERE s.sales amt >10000
4. SELECT s.id, SUM(credit_hrs) FROM students s MIDDLE JOIN classes c WHERE s.id = c.student_id AND c.active = 'Y' GROUP BY s.id
5. SELECT e.last_name, e.first_name FROM employees e LEFT OUTER JOIN payroll p ON e.salary_id = p.id WHERE last_name LIKE 'A%'

6. How are multiple column = value pairs delimited in the SET clause of an UPDATE statement?
1. With square-brackets (SET[price = 0][status = '1'}
2. With double-pipes(SET price = 0 || status = '1')
3. With parentheses(SET (price = 0) (status = '1'))
4. With single or multiple spaces (SET price = 0 status = '1')
5. With commas (SET price = 0, status = '1')

7. UPDATE books SET sales_1999 > (SELECT SUM(qty * price) FROM sales WHERE sales.book_id = books.id AND sales.date BETWEEN '01/01/1999' AND '12/31/1999')
What is the problem with the query above?
1. There is no reference in the subquery to the table from the UPDATE statement.
2. The BETWEEN keyword cannot be used with character or date fields.
3. You cannot use an arithmetic operator within the SUM() function(SUM(qty * price), for example)
4. You cannot use a subquery in the SET clause of an UPDATE statement.
5. There should be an equal sign(=) introducing the subquery.

8. **Table Name :** vtable

Column Name	Null/Not Null	Data Type
A	Null	Char(5)
B	Not Null	Number(5)
C	Not Null	Char(20)

Select distinct A from vtable;

If the ten records in vtable above have two "Blue" four "White" and three NULL for the values of column "a", the SQL statement above outputs how many rows?

1. 3
2. 4
3. 7
4. 8
5. 10

9. What SQL keyword must immediately follow the UNION ALL statement?
   1. ORDER
   2. WHERE
   3. JOIN
   4. SELECT
   5. INTO

10. If you want a column to be part of the result set, after which SQL keyword does it belong?
    1. HAVING
    2. SELECT
    3. FROM
    4. WHERE
    5. GROUP BY

11. SELECT category, type, AVG(price)
    FROM prducts
    Group by category, type
    Order by 1,2

    If there are three distinct categories in the "products" table, and each one has five different types, how many rows are returned by the query above?
    1. 1 row
    2. 3 rows
    3. 5 rows

4. 8 rows
5. 15 rows

12.

ANIMALS	
Family	**Name**
Mammal	Dog
Mammal	Lion
Mammal	Bear
Bird	Eagle
Fish	Guppy
Bird	Pelican
Fish	Bass

TYPES	
Family	**Blood_type**
Mammal	Warm-blooded
Fish	Cold-blooded
Bird	Cold-blooded

SELECT name from animals a, types t where a.family = t.family and a.name > t.blood_type

How many rows are retuned by the query above?

1. One row
2. Two rows
3. Three rows
4. Four rows
5. Five rows

13. Part

Pno	Name	Price
1	Axle	280.00
2	Wheel	190.00
3	Handle	12.00
4	Door	310.00
5	Mirror	NULL

select * from part where price > (select price from part where name = 'Handle') order by 1
Referring to the above, what result does the query deliver?

1.

pno	name	price
2	Wheel	190.00
1	Axle	280.00
4	Door	310.00

2.

pno	name	price
1	Axle	280.00
2	Wheel	190.00
4	Door	310.00

3.

pno	name	price
1	Axle	280.00
4	Door	310.00
2	Wheel	190.00

4.

pno	name	price
1	Axle	280.00
2	Wheel	190.00
4	Door	310.00
5	Mirror	NULL

5.

pno	name	price
5	Mirror	NULL
2	Wheel	190.00
1	Axle	280.00
4	Door	310.00

14. Which one of the following represents a correct order for the keywords in an INSERT statement in which the values are coming from an existing table?

1. INSERT, VALUES, WHERE, ORDER BY
2. INSERT, INTO, SELECT, FROM, WHERE
3. INSERT, INTO, WHERE, AND, VALUES
4. INTO, INSERT, VALUES, FROM, WHERE
5. SELECT, FROM, WHERE, INSERT, INTO

15. Which one of the following is valid SQL statement that does NOT require any other clauses (such as FROM, WHERE, or ORDER BY clauses)?
    1. PUSH
    2. START
    3. DROP
    4. STOP
    5. REMOVE
16. What is the main difference between a UNION statement and a UNION ALL statement?
    1. A UNION statement can be used to combine any number of queries; a UNION ALL statement can be used to combine a maximum of two queries.
    2. A UNION statement eliminates duplicate rows; a UNION ALL statement includes duplicate rows.
    3. A union statement cannot be used with aggregate functions; a UNION ALL statement can be used with aggregate functions.
    4. A UNION statement can only combine queries that have parallel fields in the SELECT list; a UNION ALL statement can combine queries with differing with SELECT list structures.
    5. There is no difference between the two statements; they are interchangeable.
17. **Table Name :** Sites

Description	X_coord	Y_coord
Disney World	9	1
White House	10	7
Space Needle	1	10
Mount Rushmore	5	9
Statue of Liberty	10	8
Grand Canyon	4	5

SELECT description from sites where x_coord >5 AND y_coord <5

How many rows are returned by the SQL statement listed above?

1. Zero rows
2. One rows
3. Two rows
4. Three rows
5. Four rows

18. **Table Name : vtable**

Col a	Col b	Col c	Col d	Col e
5	4	2	3	0

SELECT a-b / (e + c) + d FROM vtable
What is the output of the above SQL statement?
1. 0.2
2. 2
3. 3.5
4. 6
5. The statement causes an error due to an attempt to divide by zero.

19. SELECT a.* from atable a left outer join btable b on a.fk_b = b.ib
Left outer join ctable c on a.fk_c = c.id
Tables atable, btable and ctable each contain 100 rows, and the primary key for each table is "id". How many rows are returned by the query in the sample code above?
1. 0 rows
2. 100 rows
3 1,000 rows
4. 10,000 rows
5. 1,000,000 rows

20. Enteries

Eno	Name	Phone
1	Quick and Dirty	1112223333
2	Starve Bucks	1112224444
3	JeffyGrease	1114443333
4	Stuffed Stuff	1112225555

MenuGuide

Dishcode	Eno	Course	Price
1	1	whatever	3.00
2	1	hash noodles	15.00
3	2	smashed potat	20.00
4	3	small potatoes	4.00
5	3	singing beans	3.00
6	4	fishy stuff	NULL
7	4	square pizza	5.00

Recommended2001

Eno	Name	Phone
1	Quick and Dirty	1112223333
11	Pleasant Regrets	9992223333
12	Try Harder	8882224444
4	Stuffed Stuff	1112225555
23	BBB's Choice	1114443333
2	Starve Bucks	1112224444
1	Quick and Dirty	1112223333

Select distinct e.no, e.name, e.phone
from Enteries e Inner join Menuguide m on e.eno = m.eno
where m.price between 2.0 and 10.0 and
not exists (Select * from Recommended2001 r where e.no = r.eno)
referring to tables Enteries, MenuGuide, Recommended2001 in the scenario above, which records are selected by the statement?

1. 1 Quick and Dirty 1112223333
   3 JeffyGrease 1114443333
   4 Stuffed Stuff 1112225555
2. 3 JeffyGrease 1114443333
   4 Stuffed Stuff 1112225555
3. 12 Try Harder 8882224444
   1 Quick and Dirty 1112223333
   3 JeffyGrease 1114443333
   5 Stuffed Stuff 1112225555
4. 3 JeffyGrease 1114443333
5. 1 Quick and Dirty 1112223333
   4 Stuffed Stuff 1112225555

21. **Table Name :** locations

Row_id	Description	Climate	Cost_rank
1	Northwest	Mild	1
2	West Coast	warm	1
3	Northeast	Mild	2
4	Midwest	Extremes	3
5	Southeast	Hot	3
6	Southwest	Hot	3

SELECT count (*) from locations Group by climate, cost_rank
How many rows are returned by the SQL statement listed above?

1. One row
2. Two rows
3. Three rows
4. Four rows
5. Five rows

22. Which one of the following is a reason that an insert statement might cause an error instead of executing correctly?
    1. The insert statement was attempting to insert a record into a view rather than a table.
    2. The insert statement was attempting to insert a record into a view that was created from more than one table.
    3. The insert statement was attempting to insert to a record using a combination of constants and values from an existing table.
    4. The insert statement was attempting to insert a record with a non-NULL value into a table that has the column defined as NULL.
    5. The insert statement was attempting to insert a record into table by selecting a record from same table.

23.

Tools

Name	Price	Type
Drill	155.00	A
Sawzall	192.00	N
Mitre saw	292.00	M
Router	86.00	I
RAD	145.00	M
Jigsaw	128.00	I
Screwdriver	77.00	P

Tool_type

Type	Usage
A	Always
I	Often
M	Sometimes
N	Rarely
P	Never

SELECT name, price from tools where type IN (SELECT type from tool_type where usage > 'Sometimes')

How many rows are returned by the query above?

1. Zero rows
2. One row
3. Two rows
4. Three rows
5. Four rows

24. Tool_job

Tool_id	**job_id**
1	0
1	1
1	2
2	1
3	1
3	2
3	3
4	4

select distinct tool_id from tool_job tj1 where job_id IN (select tj2.job_id from tool_job tj2 group by tj2.job_id having count (*) = 1)

Referring to the table above, to what command does the query respond?

1. Display all tools that can do at least some of the listed jobs.
2. Display all generic tools for listed jobs.
3. Display all tools that can do unique listed jobs.
4. Display all tools that can do all of the listed jobs.
5. Display all tools that can do none of the listed jobs.

25. **Table Name :** Old_cust

Cust	**Name**	**Tenure**
10	Tom	2
20	Mike	4
30	Betti	6
40	Barb	2
50	Greg	5

Table Name : Customer

cust	name	owes_us
10	Tom	20.00
20	Mike	30.00
30	Betti	NULL
40	Barb	0.00
50	Greg	40.00

update customer set owes_us = owes_us * 0.9 where cust in (Select cust from old_cust where tenure >2)

Referring to the tables customer and old_cust above, what rows are updated by the statement?

1. 10 Tom 18.00
   20 Mike 27.00
   50 Greg 36.00
2. 20 Mike 20.00
   50 Greg 30.00
3. 20 Mike 27.00
   50 Greg 36.00
4. 10 Tom 18.00
   20 Mike 27.00
   30 Betti 0.00
   40 Barb 0.00
   50 Greg 36.00
5. 20 Mike 27.00
   30 Betti NULL
   50 Greg 36.00

26.

Products		
Name	**Price**	**Type**
Soap	2.00	C
Aspirin	2.00	B
Floss	2.00	D
Brush	3.00	A

SELECT price, Sum(price), count(price)
From products group by price
How many rows are returned by the query above?

1. Zero rows
2. One row
3. Two rows
4. Three rows
5. No rows are returned because the query causes an error to occur.

27. Select AVG(price) from products where 1 = 1
If the "products" table contains eight records with different values in the "price" column (NULL, NULL, 2, 3, 3, 4, 5, 7), what is the result of the sample code above?

1. Error (You cannot retrieve the average of a column that contains nulls.)
2. 2.4
3. 3.5
4. 4
5. 4.2

28. What SQL structure allows you to specify the columns/values for an INSERT statement in a different order than that is which they appear in the table?

1. The column list, as in "INSERT INTO employees(emp_id, last_name, first_name)"
2. The ORDER BY clause
3. The values list, as in "INSERT into employees values(24,'Simth','Barney')"
4. The SET statement
5. The ALTER table statement.

29.

Animals	
Family	**Name**
Mammal	Dog
Mammal	Lion
Fish	Guppy
Bird	Eagle
Fish	Guppy
Bird	Pelican
Fish	Bass

Types	
Family	Blood_type
Mammal	Warm-blooded
Fish	Cold-blooded
Bird	Cold-blooded

SELECT name from animals a. where exists (select * from types t where t.family = a.family and a.family LIKE 'b%')

How many rows are returned by the query above?

1. One row
2. Two rows
3. Four rows
4. Five rows
5. Seven rows

30. Expenses

Dept	Type	Dollar
A	P	100
A	D	0
A	S	50
A	P	100
B	P	NULL
B	P	10
B	D	100
B	S	400
C	D	320
C	S	100

Select type from expenses group by type order by type desc.

Referring to the Expenses table in the scenario above, what is the result of the query?

1. **type**
   P
   D
   S
2. **type**
   D
   P
   S

3. **type**
S
P
D

4. **type**
S
P

5. **type**
S
P
D

31.

Table Name	A	B
Column1	Fname	Idnumber*
Column 2	Lname	Salary
Column 3	Idnumber*	Startdate

* Indicates unique columns

Referring to the table above, what SQL keyword or keywords do you use to return all of the rows from table "a" and any corresponding rows from table "b"?

1. WHERE NOT
2. CROSSREF
3. LEFT JOIN
4. IF EXISTS
5. SELECT INTO

32. Supplier

Sno	Name
1	Smith
2	Blake
3	Stone
4	Gale
5	Fox

Part

Pno	Name
1	Axles
2	Wheels
3	Handles
4	Doors

Sales

Sno	Pno
1	2
1	3
2	1
3	3
3	4

Referring to the Supplier, Part and adjoining Sales tables above, which supplier sold which parts?

1. Smith: Wheels, Handles
   Blake : Axles
   Stone : Handles, Doors
   Fox :
2. Smith : Wheels, Axles
   Blake : Handles
   Stone : Doors
   Fox: Handles
3. Smith: Wheels, Handles
   Blake : Axles
   Stone : Doors
   Fox: Handles
4. Smith: Wheels, Handles
   Blake : Axles
   Stone : Doors
   Fox:
5. Smith: Wheels, Handles
   Blake : Axles
   Stone : Handles, Doors
   Fox: Wheels

33. What separates multiple criteria in an SQL WHERE clause?
1. Commas
2. The Keyword FROM
3. Spaces
4. Periods
5. The keywords AND or OR

34. UPDATE products
SET products.qty_sold = products.qty_sold +1,
Products.qty_left = products.qty_left -1,
Products.qty_to_order = 1000 - SUM(products.qty_left),

Products.price = products.price * 1.05
Where products.category = 90 AND products.status = 'A'
What is the problem with query above?

1. The use of an alias for products is required when the table name is used. This frequently is an UPDATE statement.
2. The multiple conditions of an UPDATE statement's WHERE clause must be either separated by commas or differentiated with parentheses.
3. You cannot SET a column's value by using the same column on the right side of the equation.
4. Aggregate functions cannot be used in the SET clause of an UPDATE statement.
5. You cannot use an asterisk ("*") as an arithmetic operator within the SET CLAUSE of an UPDATE statement.

35. SELECT id, last_name, first_name, salary FROM employees e, payroll p
WHERE e.id = p.id
AND salary > ALL
(SELECT AVG(pa.salary) FROM payroll pa
GROUP BY pa.type)
ORDER BY 2,3
What is the problem with the query above?

1. The GROUP BY statement in the subquery is invalid because the column to which it refers is not in the SELECT list of the subquery.
2. You cannot refer to a table in the subquery that is also a joined table in the main query.
3. The ">" operator cannot be used in conjuction with the ALL keywork to introduce a subquery.
4. The "id" column in the SELECT list is ambiguous and needs to be qualified with a table name or alias.
5. The ORDER BY clause must refer to column names rather than their positions in the SELECT list.

36. CREATE table report
(empno INT, salary decimal(8,2), AVGsalary decimal (8,2), EMPcount INT, DMAX decimal(8,2))
EMP

Empno	Dept	Job	Salary	Comm
10	AAA	analyst	80000.00	.00
20	AAA	salesrep	60000.00	10000.00
30	BAA	dba	50000.00	1000.00
40	BAA	webmaster	40000.00	50000.00

Insert INTO report select empno, salary, DINFOAVGsalary, dinfo.empcount, dinfomax.dmax from emp, (SELECT dept, avg(salary), as avgsalary, count(*) as empcount from emp group by dept) as DINFo, (SELECT dept, max(salary) as DMAX from EMP group by Dept) AS DINDFOMAX where emp.job = 'salesrep'

AND EMP.DEPT = DINFO.DEPT AND EMP.DEPT = DINFOMAX.DEPT

Refering to the Emp table and the insert statement above, what are the contents of the report table?

1. | EMPNO | SALARY | AVGSALARY | EMPCOUNT | DMAX |
|---|---|---|---|---|
| 10 | 80000.00 | 70000.00 | 2 | 80000.00 |

2. | EMPNO | SALARY | AVGSALARY | EMPCOUNT | DMAX |
|---|---|---|---|---|
| 40 | 60000.00 | 70000.00 | 2 | 80000.00 |

3. | EMPNO | SALARY | AVGSALARY | EMPCOUNT | DMAX |
|---|---|---|---|---|
| 20 | 60000.00 | 70000.00 | 2 | 80000.00 |

4. | EMPNO | SALARY | AVGSALARY | EMPCOUNT | DMAX |
|---|---|---|---|---|
| 30 | 50000.00 | 45000.00 | 2 | 50000.00 |

5. | EMPNO | SALARY | AVGSALARY | EMPCOUNT | DMAX |
|---|---|---|---|---|
| 40 | 40000.00 | 45000.00 | 2 | 50000.00 |

37. What SQL statement do you use to create new rows in an existing table using data from individual rows in another table?

1. update with a correlated subquery.
2. insert with a select statement subquery.
3. insert with a correlated subquery.
4. select into.
5. update with a subquery.

38. Select e.name, max(t.logindate) lastlogin

From loginAuditTrial t

Join employee e

ON e.netid = t.netid

Where e.type = 'salary'

Considering the query shown above, which one of the following statement completes the query and sorts the results by "LastLogin"?

1. Group by e.name, max(t.logindate)
2. Group by e.name
3. Group by e.name order by e.name max(t.logindate)
4. Group by e.name order by max(t.logindate)
5. Group by MAX(t.logindate)

39. **Table Name :** Customer

cust	name	owes_us
10	Tom	20.00
20	Mike	30.00
30	Betti	.00
40	Barb	NULL

update customer set owes_us = owes_us * 1.1

Referring to the table above, what is the result of running the update statement ?

1.

cust	name	owes_us
10	Tom	22.00
20	Mike	30.00
30	Betti	.00
40	Barb	NULL

2.

cust	name	owes_us
10	Tom	22.00
20	Mike	33.00
30	Betti	.00

3.

cust	name	owes_us
10	Tom	22.0
20	Mike	33.0
30	Betti	.0
40	Barb	.0

4.

cust	name	owes_us
10	Tom	22.00
20	Mike	33.00
30	Betti	.00
40	Barb	NULL

5.

cust	name	owes_us
10	Tom	22.00
20	Mike	33.00

40. Which one of the following is possible using update statement?

1. Inserting new rows into a table if they do not already exist
2. Changing the datatype of a particular field
3. Updating a column in one table with data from another table
4. Deleting a column from a table (changing the number of columns in a table from four to three for example)
5. Setting the new value of a column to the average for the table without using a subquery.

SET–3

1. SELECT c.page, c.line from chapters c JOIN books b on c.book_id = b.id where b.genre = 'Mystery'

   Which one of the following produces the same result as the sample code above?

   1. select page, line from chapters c where book_id = (SELECT * from books b where genre = 'Mystery')
   2. select c.page, c.line from chapters c where exists (SELECT * from books b where b.genre = c.genre AND b.genre = 'Mystery')
   3. SELECT c.page, c.line from chapters c where EXISTS (SELECT b.id from books b where b.genre = 'Mystery')
   4. Select page, line FROM CHAPTERS C WHERE C.* IN (SELECT * from books b where b.genre = 'Mystery')
   5. Select page, line FROM CHAPTERS C WHERE book_id IN (SELECT id from books b where genre = 'Mystery')

2. Eateries

Eno	name	phone
1	Quick and Dirty	1112223333
2	Starve Bucks	1112224444
3	Jeffy Grease	1114443333
4	Stuffed Stuff	1112225555

MenuGuide

Dishcode	eno	course	price
1	1	whatever	3.00
2	1	hash noodles	15.00
3	2	smashed potato	20.00
4	3	small potato	4.00
5	3	singing beans	3.00
6	4	fishy stuff	NULL
7	4	square pizza	5.00

SELECT name as Eateries, phone from Eateries where exists (SELECT * from MenuGuide m1 where price < (SELECT AVG(price) from MenuGuide) AND m1.eno = Eateries.eno)

Reffering to tables Eateries and MenuGuide in the scenario above, what is the result set produced by the query?

1. | | |
   |---|---|
   | JeffyGrease | 1114443333 |
   | Stuffed Stuff | 1112225555 |

2. Quick and Dirty 1112223333
JeffyGrease 1114443333
Starve Bucks 1112224444

3. Quick and Dirty 1112223333
Starve Bucks 1112224444
Stuffed Stuff 1112225555

4. Quick and Dirty 1112223333
JeffyGrease 1114443333
Starve Bucks 1112224444
Stuffed Stuff 1112225555

5. Quick and Dirty 1112223333
JeffyGrease 1114443333
Stuffed Stuff 1112225555

3. Select s.first_name, s.last_name FROM students s where s.id not in (SELECT a.id from add_info a where a.status = 'Expelled')

Which one of the following produces the same results as the sample code above (assume each students exists in the "add_info" table only once, and NO fields contain NULL values)?

1. SELECT first_name, last_name from students s, add_info a where s.id = a.id AND a.status = 'Expelled'
2. SELECT first_name, last_name from students s where exists (SELECT * from add_info a where a.status = 'Expelled')
3. SELECT s.first_name, s.last_name from students s where s.id IN (SELECT a.id from add_info a where a.status <>'Expelled')
4. SELECT s.first_name, s.last_name from students s JOIN add_info a ON s.id = a.id where a.status <> 'Expelled' ORDER COLUMNS BY s.first_name, s.last_name
5. SELECT s.first_name, s.last_name from students s JOIN add_info a ON s.id = a.id where a.status = 'Expelled'

4. **Table Name :** Products

Category	Type	Price
Indoor	Kitchen	1.50
Outdoor	Garden	6.00
Indoor	Bathroom	4.75
Outdoor	Garden	20.20
Indoor	Bathroom	4.25
Office	Desktop	9.80

SELECT category, COUNT (DISTINCT type) from products GROUP BY category
How many rows are returned by the SQL statement listed above?

1. One row
2. Two rows
3. Three rows
4. Four rows
5. Five rows

5. CREATE TABLE clients AS (client_id INTEGER NOT NULL,client_name VARCHAR(30) NOT NULL, industry_code INTEGER NULL, contact_name VARCHAR(30) DEFAULT 'Unknown Contact' NOT NULL, sign_year INTEGER NOT NULL)
What is the problem with create Table statement above?
   1. The AS keyword is used in CREATE TABLE statement.
   2. The keywords NOT NULL and DEFALUT must be separated by a comma.
   3. The closing parenthesis (")") must be on the same line of code as the last column listed.
   4. Columns that are declared as character cannot also be specified as NOT NULL.
   5. You cannot have a column specified as NULL appear in a table before a column specified as NOT NULL. All NULL columns must be grouped together at the end of the table.

6. Supplier

Sno	Name
1	Smith
2	Blake
3	Stone
4	Gale
5	Fox

Part

Pno	Name
1	Axles
2	Wheels
3	Handles
4	Doors

Sales

Sno	Pno
1	2
1	3
2	1
3	3
3	4

Referring to the Supplier, Part and adjoining Sales Tables above, which supplier sold which parts?

1. Smith : Wheels, Handles
   Blake: Axles
   Stone: Doors
   Fox:
2. Smith : Wheels, Axles
   Blake: Handles
   Stone: Doors
   Fox: Handles
3. Smith : Wheels, Handles
   Blake: Axles
   Stone: Doors
   Fox: Handles
4. Smith : Wheels , Handles
   Blake: Axles
   Stone: Handles, Doors
   Fox: Wheels
5. Smith :Wheels, Handles
   Blake: Axles
   Stone: Handles, Doors
   Fox:

7. **UPDATE** products SET products.qty_sold = productds.qty_sold +1,
products.qty_left = products.qty_left -1,
products.qty_to_order = 1000 - SUM(products.qty_left),
products.price = products.price * 1.05
WHERE products.category = 90 AND products.status = 'A'

What is the problem with the query above?

1. You cannot use an asterisk ("*") as an arithmetic operator within the SET clause of an UPDATE statement.
2. You cannot SET a column's value by using the same column on the right side of the equation.
3. The use of an alias for products is required when the table name is used this frequently in an UPDATE statement.
4. Aggregate functions cannot be used in the SET clause of an UPDATE statement.
5. The multiple conditions of an UPDATE statement's WHERE clause must be either separated by commas or differentiated with parentheses.

8. Customer

cust	name	owes_us
10	Tom	20.00
20	Mike	30.00
30	Betti	.00
40	Barb	NULL

update customer set owes_us = owes_us *1.1

Referring to the above table, what is the result of running the update statement?

1.

cust	name	owes_us
10	Tom	22.00
20	Mike	33.00

2.

cust	name	owes_us
10	Tom	22.00
20	Mike	33.00
30	Betti	.00
40	Barb	NULL

3.

cust	name	owes_us
10	Tom	22.00
20	Mike	33.00
30	Betti	.0
40	Barb	.0

4.

cust	name	owes_us
10	Tom	22.00
20	Mike	33.00
30	Betti	.00

5.

cust	name	owes_us
10	Tom	22.00
20	Mike	30.00
30	Betti	.00
40	Barb	NULL

9. SELECT AVG(price) from products where 1=1

If the "products" table contains eight records with different values in the "price" column (NULL,NULL, 2,3,3,4,5,7) what is the result of the sample code above?

1. Error (You cannot retrieve the average of a coluumn that contains nulls.)
2. 2.4
3. 4
4. 4
5. 4.2

10. If you want a column to be part of the result set, after which SQL keyword does it belong?
    1. Group by
    2. Having
    3. FROM
    4. SELECT
    5. WHERE

11.

Scores	
Name	**Score**
Jim	74
Sam	37
Betty	100
Ken	91
Val	55
Lee	79
Sue	88

Grades		
Grade	**From_score**	**To_score**
A	92	100
B	83	91
C	74	82
D	65	73
F	0	64

SELECT grade FROM grades g
WHERE g.from_score > SELECT MIN(score)* 2 FROM scores)
AND g.to_score < (SELECT MAX(score) FROM scores)\
What is the output of the query above ?
1. A
2. B
3. A
   B
4. B
   C

5. A
   B
   C

12. **Table Name : vtable**

Column a	Column b	Column c	Column d	Column e
5	4	2	3	0

SELECT a-b /(e+c) + d FROM vtable

What is the output of the above SQL statement?

1. 0.2
2. 2
3. 3.5
4. 6
5. The statement causes an error due to an attempt to divide by zero.

13. Tools

Name	Price	Type
drill	155.00	A
sawzall	192.00	N
mite saw	292.00	M
router	86.00	I
RAD1	45.00	M
jigsaw	128.00	I
screwdriver	77.00	P

TOOL_TYPE

Type	Usage
A	Always
I	Often
M	Sometimes
N	Rarely
P	Never

SELECT name, price FROM tools WHERE type in (SELECT type FROM tool_type WHERE usage > 'Sometimes')

How many rows are returned by the query above?

1. Zero rows
2. One row

3. Two rows
4. Three rows
5. Four rows

14. **Table Name:** employees

first_name	last_name	age
James	Catillo	32
Diane	Kelly	28
Arthur	Peebles	47
Sandra	Arnold	25
Ronald	Sanders	31

SELECT last_name, age of employees WHERE age>=30
How many rows are returned by the SQL statement listed above?

1. Zero rows
2. One row
3. Two rows
4. Three rows
5. Four rows

15. What SQL statement do you use to create new rows in an existing table using data from individual rows in another table?

1. Update with a correlated subquery
2. Insert with a correlated subquery
3. Insert with a select statement subquery
4. SELECT INTO
5. Update with a subquery

16.

Table Name	a	b
Column 1	fname	idnumber*
Column 2	lname	salary
Column 3	idnumber*	startdate

Referring to the table above, what SQL keyword or keywords do you use to return all of the rows from table "a" and any corresponding rows from table "b"?

1. CROSSREF
2. IF EXISTS

*indicates unique columns

3. SELECT INTO
4. WHERE NOT
5. LEFT JOIN

17. SELECT CASE WHEN COUNT (*) = 0 THEN 'Do not coincide' ELSE 'Coincide' END FROM t1 WHERE (SELECT COUNT (DISTINCT T1.C1) FROM t1) = (SELECT COUNT (DISTINCT T1.C1) FROM t1 INNER JOIN t2 ON t1.cl = t2.cl) AND (SELECT COUNT (DISTINCT T2.C1) FROM t2) = (SELECT COUNT (DISTINCT T2.C1) FROM t2 INNER JOIN t1 ON t1.cl= t2.cl)

T1

c1
1
2
3
4

T2

c1
1
2
3
4

Referring to the query and tables T1 and T2 in the scenario above, which actions produce the output "Do not coincide"?

1. INSERT INTO T1 VALUES(1) run the query
2. INSERT INTO T2 VALUES(1) run the query
3. INSERT INTO T1 VALUES(1)INSERT INTO T1 VALUES(1) run the query
4. INSERT INTO T2 VALUES(NULL) run the query
5. All choices yield "Coincide".

18. **Table Name :** animals

row_id	family	animal	color
1	mammal	dog	brown
2	mammal	zebra	black, white
3	fish	shark	gray
4	bird	gull	white
5	bird	pelican	white
6	fish	trout	gray

```
SELECT a1.animals, a2.animal, a1.color
FROM animals a1
JOIN animals a2
ON a1.color = a2.color
WHERE a1.animals <> a2.animal
AND a1.row_id > a2.row_id
```

How many rows are returned by the query above

1. Zero rows
2. One row
3. Two rows
4. Three rows
5. Four rows

19.
```
UPDATE books SET sales_1999 >
(SELECT SUM(qty * price)
FROM sales
WHERE sales.book_id = book.id
AND sales.date BETWEEN '01/01/1999 AND 12/31/1999')
```

What is the problem with the query above ?

1. You cannot use a subquery in the set clause of an UPDATE statement.
2. You cannot use an arithmetic operator within the SUM() function (SUM(qty*price), for eample).
3. There is no reference in the subquery to the table from the UPDATE statement.
4. There should be an equal sign (=) introducing the subquery.
5. The BETWEEN keyword cannot be used with character or

20. Account

acc_no	acc_type	amount
10	c	356.12
31	m	1387.64
25	c	12500.00
22	m	40356.15
61	c	12500.00
12	m	6000.76

SELECT acc_no, acc_type, amount, 'tiny' AS category from account WHERE amount < 100 UNION SELECT acc_no, acc_type, amount, 'small' as category1 from account WHERE amount <5000 UNION SELECT acc_no, acc_type, amount, 'big' as category2 from account WHERE amount >= 5000 AND amount <10000 UNION SELECT acc_no, acc_type, amount, 'big' as category3 from account WHERE amount >= 10000 ORDER BY amount, acc_type.

Referring to the table above, how many rows does the query return?

1. Zero
2. Three
3. Four
4. Five
5. Six

21. **Table Name :** creatures

row_id	name	rank	legs
1	mouse	3	4
2	ant	1	6
3	bat	2	2
4	cat	4	4
5	fish	5	0
6	bird	6	2

SELECT * FROM creatures, which one of the following order by statements causes the rows from the query above to be returned in the following order by "row_id": 5,6,3,4,1,2?

1. ORDER BY legs DESC, name DESC
2. ORDER BY name, rank, row_id DESC
3. ORDER BY rank, legs
4. ORDER BY rank DESC,name
5. ORDER BY legs, rank DESC

22. SELECT id, last_name, first_name, salary FROM employees e, payroll p WHERE e.id = p.id AND SALARY > all (select avg(PA.SALARY) from payroll pa GROUP BY pa.type) Order BY 2,3

What is the problem with the query above?

1. The ">" operator cannot be used in conjunction with the ALL keyword to introduce a subquery.
2. The ORDER BY clause must refer to column names rather than their positions in the SELECT list.
3. The "id" column in the SELECT list is ambiguous and needs to be qualified with a table name or alias.
4. The GROUP BY statement in the subquery is invalid because the column to which it refers is not in the SELECT list of the subquery.
5. You cannot refer to a table in the subquery that is also a joined table in the main query.

23. Account

acc_no	acc_type	amount
10	c	356.12
31	m	1387.64
25	c	12500.00
22	m	40356.15
61	c	12500.00

SELECT acc_type, amount, 'small' as category1 FROM account WHERE amount <= 10000 UNION ALL SELECT acc_type, amount, 'BIG' as category2 FROM account WHERE amount > = 10000 ORDER BY amount, acc_type

Referring to the table above, how many rows does the query return?

1. Zero
2. Two
3. Three
4. Four
5. Five

24. Emp

empno	dept	day_sal	ed_level
10	100	50.00	15
12	100	60.00	16
20	100	40.00	14
30	200	40.00	15
40	200	30.00	15
42	200	45.00	14
50	300	70.00	NULL
60	300	30.00	17
70	300	70.00	16

1. select * from emp where day_sal BETWEEN 40.0 and 60.0
2. select * from emp where day_sal >= 40.0 and day_sal < 60.0
3. select * from emp where day_sal >= 40.0 and day_sal <= 60.0
4. select * from emp where day_sal > 40.0 and day_sal <= 60.0
5. select * from emp where day_sal > 40.0 and day_sal < 60.0

Referring to the Emp table and the queries in the scenario above, which queries always retrieve the same rows?

1. 1, 2
2. 1, 3

3. 1, 4
4. 1, 5
5. 3, 4

25.

Table name : t1

c1
1
2
4

Table name : t2

c1
1
3
2

SELECT * FROM t1 RIGHT OUTER JOIN T2 ON t1.c1 = t2.c1

Referring to the tables above, what is the result of the query?

1.

c1	c1
1	1
2	2
NULL	3

2.

c1	c1
1	1
2	2

3.

c1	c1
NULL	1
1	3
2	3
1	2

4.

c1	c1
2	1
4	1
4	3
4	2

5.

c1	c1
1	3
2	3
1	2

26. Which one of the following is a valid SQL statement that does NOT require any other clauses (such as FROM, WHERE, or ORDER BY clauses) ?

1. START
2. REMOVE
3. DROP
4. PUSH
5. STOP

27. DELETE FROM employees line change if you want to delete all records from employees for whom the emp_id either does NOT contain a value, or the value does not match the hire_id from the same table, what needs to be added to the query above?

1. WHERE NOVAL (emp_id) OR emp_id <> hire_id
2. WHERE emp_id IS BLANK OR emp_id != hire_id
3. WHERE emp_id IS BLANK AND (emp_id MOD hire_id >0)
4. WHERE emp_id IS NULL OR emp_id <> hire_id
5. WHERE emp_id =0 OR emp_id NOT = hire_id

28. Tool_job

Tool_id	Job_id
1	0
1	1
1	2
2	1
3	1
3	2
3	3
4	4

Jobs

Job_id
1
2
3

SELECT tool_id, COUNT(*) FROM tool_job tj1 GROUP BY tj1.tool_id HAVING COUNT(*) = 1

Referring to the sample code above, to what command does the query respond?

1. Display all tools that can do none of the listed jobs.
2. Display all tools that can do some of the listed jobs.
3. Display all specialized tools.
4. Display ali tools that can do all the listed jobs.
5. Display all generic tools.

29.

Products		
Name	**Price**	**Type**
Soap	2.00	C
Brush	3.00	A
Comb	1.00	A
Floss	3.00	A
Aspirin	5.00	B
Vitamins	4.00	C
Aspirin	3.00	B

DELETE FROM products WHERE price = (SELECT AVG(price) FROM products WHERE type = 'B')

How many rows are deleted in the above query above?

1. Zero rows
2. One row
3. Two rows
4. Three rows
5. Four rows

30. SELECT category, type, AVG(price)
FROM products
GROUP BY category, type
ORDER BY 1,2

If there are three distinct categories in the "products" table and each one has five different types, how many rows are returned by the query above?

1. 1 row
2. 3 rows
3. 5 rows
4. 8 rows
5. 15 rows

31. **Table Name : Bus**

Vid	Seats	Age
1	10	10
2	20	4
3	10	6
4	40	6
5	10	NULL

Table Name : Car

Vid	seats	age
10	4	6
20	10	4
30	10	4
40	8	10

1. DELETE FROM bus b, car c WHERE c.seats >= b.seats AND c.age <= b.age
2. DELETE FROM car c WHERE exists (SELECT * FROM bus b WHERE b.seats > = c.seats AND b.age<= c.age)
3. DELETE FROM bus b WHERE EXISTS (SELECT * FROM car c WHERE c.seats >= b.seats AND c.age <=b.age)
4. DELETE FROM bus WHERE vid IN (SELECT DISTINCT b.vid FROM bus b, car c WHERE c.seats >= b.seats AND c.age <= b.age)

Referring to tables bus and car in the scenario above, which two statements delete the same rows?

1. 1, 2
2. 1, 3
3. 1, 4
4. 2, 3
5. 3, 4

32. **Table Name :** HR

Emp_id	dept	sex	sal
1	A	M	80000.00
3	A	F	20000.00
4	A	F	25000.00
5	B	M	50000.00
6	B	F	60000.00
8	C	F	90000.00
9	D	M	70000.00
10	E	M	90000.00

SELECT DISTINCT dept FROM hr AS hr1 WHERE sex = 'M' AND dept = ANY (SELECT sex from hr AS hr2 WHERE hr1.dept = hr2.dept AND sal <(SELECT AVG(sal) FROM hr AS hr3 WHERE hr3.dept = hr2.dept)) ORDER BY dept

Referring to the table above, which department does the query return?

1. A
2. B
3. C
4. D
5. E

33. Which one of the following represents a correct SQL query?

1. SELECT i.product, i.qty FROM inventory I
   JOIN RIGHT sales s ON i.id = s.prod_id
   WHERE s.sales_amt > 10000
2. SELECT g.description, AVG(b.price) FROM books b JOIN ON b.book_id = genre.id WHERE b.author_id = 5
   GROUP BY g.description
3. SELECT s.title, MIN(start_time) FROM shows s JOIN
   JOIN networks n ON s.net_id = n.id WHERE n.name = 'NBC'
   GROUP BY s.title
4. SELECT s.id, SUM(credit_hrs) FROM students s
   MIDDLE JOIN classes c where s.id = c.student_id AND c.active = 'Y' GROUP BY s.id
5. SELECT e.last_name, e.first_name FROM employees e
   LEFT OUTER JOIN payroll p ON e.salary_id = p.id
   WHERE last_name LIKE 'A%'

34.

T1

C1
1
2
4

T2

C1
1
3
2

SELECT * FROM T1 FULL JOIN T2 ON T1.C1 = T2.C2

Referring to the tables above, what is the result of the query?

1.

cl	**cl**
1	1

	NULL	3
	2	2
	4	NULL
2.	**c1**	**c1**
	1	1
	2	1
	2	2
	4	1
	4	3
	4	2
3.	**c1**	**c1**
	1	1
	2	2
	4	NULL
4.	**c1**	**c1**
	1	1
	NULL	3
	2	2
5.	**c1**	**c1**
	1	1
	1	3
	1	2
	2	3
	2	2
	3	NULL

35. **Table Name :** Expenses

Dept	**Type**	**Dollar**
A	P	100
A	D	0
A	S	50
A	P	100
B	P	NULL
B	P	10
B	D	100
B	S	400
C	D	320
C	S	100

SELECT e1.dept, SUM(e1.dollar)
FROM expenses e1 GROUP BY e1.dept
HAVING SUM(e1.dollar) > 250
ORDER BY 1

Referring to the Expenses table in the scenario above, what is the result of the query?

1. A 250
   B 600
   C 500
2. A 250
   B 510
3. A 1000
   B 510
   C 420
4. B 510
   C 420
5. A 250
   B 510
   C 420

36. Which one of the following is a valid INSERT statement in ANSI SQL?

1. INSERT INTO students
   SELECT VALUES (95,'Bill', 'Gates')
2. INSERT INTO students (id, first_name, last_name)
   SELECT id, first_name FROM new_students
   WHERE last_name IS NULL
3. INSERT INTO students (id, first_name, last_name)
   values (118,'Kim','Rugger')
4. INSERT INTO students (id, first_name, last_name)
   (118,'Kim','Rugger')
5. INSERT INTO students (id, first_name, last_name)

37. Which one of the following represents a correct order for the keywords in an insert statement in which the values are coming from an existing table?

1. INSERT, VALUES, WHERE, ORDER BY
2. SELECT, FROM, WHERE, INSERT, INTO
3. INTO, INSERT, VALUES, FROM, WHERE
4. INSERT, INTO, SELECT, FROM, WHERE
5. INSERT, INTO, WHERE, AND, VALUES

38.

Scores	
Name	**Score**
Jim	74
Sam	38
Betty	100
Ken	91
Val	55
Lee	79
Sue	88

Grades		
Grade	**From_score**	**To_score**
A	92	100
B	83	91
C	74	82
D	65	73
F	0	64

SELECT grade FROM grades WHERE (to_score - from_score) >8 and from_score <= (SELECT Max (score) FROM SCORES)

How many rows are returned by the query above?

1. Zero rows
2. One row
3. Two rows
4. Three rows
5. Four rows

39. Which clause of an UPDATE statement allows you to affect only certain rows of a table?
    1. The WHERE clause
    2. The ORDER BY clause
    3. The ROWS AFFECTED clause
    4. The SET clause
    5. The UPDATE clause

40. Which one of the following pairs of aggregate functions do you use with character fields?
    1. MIN(field) and SUM(field)
    2. COUNT(field) and SUM(field)
    3. AVG(field) and Max(field)
    4. COUNT(field) and MAX(field)
    5. AVG(field) and COUNT(field)

SET–4

1. **Table Name :** Eateries

Eno	name	phone
1	Quick and dirty	1112223333
2	Starve Bucks	1112224444
3	JeffyGrease	1114443333
4	Stuffed Stuff	1112225555

Table Name : Recommendedlist

Eno	eateryname	phone
4	Stuffed Stuff	7772225555
11	Pleasant Regrets	9992223333
12	Try Harder	8882224444
23	BBB's Choice	1114443333
1	Quick and Dirty	8882223333

UPDATE Eateries SET Eateries.phone = (Select r.phone from RecommendedList r where r.eno = Eateries.eno) where Eateries.eno IN (Select eno from RecommendedList)

Referring to tables Eateries and RecommendedList in the scenario above, how many Eateries records are updated by the statement?

1. Zero
2. One
3. Two
4. Three
5. Four

2. **Table Name :** Pets

Row_id	Name	Domestic	Care_factor
1	Cat	Y	2
2	Lion	N	10
3	Dog	Y	4
4	Bird	N	2
5	Fly	N	1
6	Fish	N	8

Select row_id, name, domestic from pets where name Like '%i%' AND care_factor >=5
How many rows are returned by the SQL statement listed above?

1. One row
2. Two rows
3. Three rows
4. Four rows
5. Five rows

3. Create table t1(c1 INT unique NULL, c2 INT PRIMARY KEY)
Create table t2(c1 INT PRIMARY KEY,c2 INT REFERENCE t1(c2))
    1. insert into t1 values(1,1)
    2. insert into t1 values(2,3)
    3. insert into t1 values(NULL,4)
    4. insert into t1 values(2,5)
    5. insert into t1 values(3,0)
    6. insert into t2 values(1,1)
    7. insert into t2 values(2,3)
    8. insert into t2 values(1,3)
    9. insert into t2 values(1,4)

Referring to the definitions of the tables t1 and t2 in the scenario above, which one of the sequentially executed insert statement fails?

1. 4
2. 3, 4
3. 4, 8
4. 4, 8, 9
5. 3, 4, 8, 9

4.

Animals	
Family	**Name**
Mammal	Dog
Mammal	Lion
Fish	Guppy
Bird	Eagle
Fish	Guppy
Bird	Pelican
Fish	Bass

Types	
Family	**Blood_type**
Mammal	Warm-blooded
Fish	Cold-blooded
Bird	Cold-blooded

Select name from animals where family IN (Select famliy FROM types where SUBSTRING(blood_type,4,3) = 'd-b')

How many rows are returned by the query above?

1. Zero rows
2. One row
3. Three rows
4. Five rows
5. Seven rows

5. Create table clients as (client_id INTEGER NOT NULL,
Client_name VARCHAR(30) NOT NULL,
Industry_code INTEGER NULL,
Contact_name VARCHAR(30) DEFAULT 'Unknown Contact' NOT NULL,
Sign_year INTEGER NOT NULL)

What is the problem with the CREATE TABLE statement above?

1. The AS keyword is not used in a CREATE TABLE statement.
2. The keywords NOT NULL and DEFAULT must be separated by a comma
3. Columns that are declared as character cannot also be specified as NOT NULL

4. You cannot have a column specified as NULL appear in a table before a column specified as NOT NULL. ALL NULL columns must be grouped together at the end of the table.
5. The closing parenthesis (")") must be on the same line of code as the last column listed.

6. SELECT COUNT(title)
FROM books b
WHERE b.genre = 'Horror'
AND b.title IS NULL

Why is the query above a poor attempt at finding a count from the books table in which the title is missing for a specific genre?

1. This query never returns a value higher than "1" because the "COUNT(title)" functions counts the unique values.
2. The proper syntax for the last line of the query is "HAVING b.title AS NULL"
3. The conditions in the WHERE clause need to be reversed. Otherwise, all Horror titles(NULL or non_NULL) will be included in the count.
4. The "COUNT(title)" function does not identify NULL values in that field.
5. The proper syntax for the last line of the query is "HAVING NULL b.title"

7. SELECT firstname, lastname, ssn, yearsofservice FROM employees which ORDER BY clause is added to the code above to sort the above rows by years of service, with those who have been with company longest coming first?

1. ORDER BY 'yearsofservice'
2. ORDER BY yearsofservice asc
3. ORDER BY 'yearsofservice' desc
4. ORDER 'yearsofservice' desc
5. ORDER BY yearsofservice desc

8. **Table Name :** Expenses

Dept	Type	Dollar
A	P	100
A	D	0
A	S	50
A	P	100
B	P	NULL
B	P	10
B	D	100
B	S	400
C	D	320
C	S	100

Select 'High Expenses' count(*) from expenses where dollar > 100
UNION
Select 'Low Expenses', count(*) from expenses where dollar <=100
UNION
Select 'Unknown Expenses', count(*) from expenses where dollar IS NULL order by 1

Referring to the Expenses table in the scenario above, what is the result of the query?

1. Unknown Expenses 1
   Low Expenses 7
   High Expenses 2
2. Unknown Expenses 2
   Low Expenses 7
   High Expenses 1
3. Unknown Expenses 1
   Low Expenses 7
   High Expenses 2
4. Unknown Expenses 2
   Low Expenses 7
   High Expenses 1
5. Unknown Expenses 7
   Low Expenses 2
   High Expenses 1

9. SELECT a.type, a.description, b.type, b.description FROM a ????? b ON a.type = b.type

To return all types and descriptions from both tables, regardless of whether or NOT they have a corresponding value in the other table, which type of JOIN is used in place of the "????" above?

1. JOIN ALL
2. MID OUTER JOIN
3. LEFT OUTER JOIN
4. FULL OUTER JOIN
5. RIGHT OUTER JOIN

10. Create view ActiveCustomers
AS SELECT c.name, c.phone, SUM(i.total) YTDSales
FROM customer c
JOIN invoice i ON c.custno = i.custno
WHERE i.year = 2000
Group BY c.name, c.phone
DELETE FROM ActiveCustomers
WHERE c.creditstatus = 'over120'

If the DELETE statement shown above is run against the ActiveCustomers' view, also shown above, what data is deleted?

1. All customers that have bad credit status one or more in voices for the year 2000 along with all invoices for those customers dated in the year 2000.
2. No customers or invoices are deleted since the DELETE statement produce an error when used with the view as defined.
3. All customers that have bad credit status and one or more invoices for the year 2000 along with ALL invoices for those customers.
4. All customers that have a bad credit status, whether they have an invoice dated in the year 2000 or not.
5. All customers that have one or more invoices for the year 2000 and have a bad credit status.

11. SELECT mth, SUM(amount) sls96, 0 sls97
FROM sales
WHERE mth = 12 AND yr = '1996'
GROUP BY mth
UNION
SELECT mth, 0 sls96, SUM(amount) sls97
FROM sales
WHERE mth = 12 AND yr = '1997'
GROUP BY mth

The table "sales" has positive "amount" values for every month of the year for 1995 through 1998. How many rows are returned by the query above?

1. 1
2. 2
3. 12
4. 24
5. No rows are returned because the query causes an error to occur.

12.

Animals	
Family	**Name**
Mammal	Dog
Mammal	Lion
Fish	Guppy
Bird	Eagle
Fish	Guppy
Bird	Pelican
Fish	Bass

Blood_types	
Family	**Blood_type**
Mammal	Warm-blooded
Fish	Cold-blooded
Bird	Cold-blooded

Other_info	
Blood_type	**Life_exp_code**
Warm-blooded	1
Cold-blooded	2

SELECT MAX(a.name) FROM animals a where a.family IN (SELECT t.family FROM blood_types t WHERE t.blood_type IN (SELECT o.blood_type FROM other_info o WHERE life_exp_code = 2))

What is the value returned when the query above is executed?

1. Robin
2. Five
3. No rows are returned because the statement causes an error to occur.
4. Six
5. minrow

13. SELECT a, AVG(b), c FROM vtable
WHERE a > c
GROUP BY a, c
ORDER BY 2 DESC, 4

What is the problem with the query above?

1. A SELECT statement cannot list regular columns ("c") after aggregate functions ("AVG(b)").
2. Once the ORDER BY clause uses the keyword DESC, all columns in the ORDER BY clause must use either ASC or DESC(such as ORDER BY 2 DESC, 4 ASC).
3. The GROUP BY clause must contain all elements of the SELECT list (regular columns as well as aggregate functions).
4. The ORDER BY clause contains a select list number that is out of range.
5. An ORDER BY clause cannot refer to an aggregate function in the SELECT list.

14. CREATE TABLE VTABLE (a INTEGER NOT NULL, b VARCHAR(10) NULL, c VARCHAR(10) NOT NULL, d DATE NOT NULL DEFAULT '01/01/2000') referring to the sample code above, which one of the following INSERT statements successfully inserts a row into table "vtable"?

1. INSERT INTO vtable (a.b.d) VALUES (70,'Archie', '12/31/1999')
2. INSERT INTO vtable (a,b,c,d) VALUES (27,'Reggie',NULL, '09/17/1999')
3. INSERT INTO vtable SELECT * from vtable WHERE d IS NULL
4. INSERT INTO vtable (a,c) VALUES (5, 'Jughead')
5. INSERT INTO vtable VALUES(20,'Veronica')

15. What SQL structure allows you to specify the columns/values for an INSERT statement in a different order than that in which they appear in the table?
    1. The SET statement
    2. The column list, as in "INSERT INTO employees (emp_id, last_name, first_name)"
    3. The ALTER TABLE statement
    4. The values list, as in "INSERT INTO employees VALUES (24, 'Smith','Barney')"
    5. The ORDER BY clause

16.

Products		
Name	**Price**	**Type**
Soap	2.00	C
Brush	3.00	A
Brush	2.00	A
Soap	5.00	B
Aspirin	4.00	C
Comp	3.00	B

Old_products	
Name	**Price**
Toothbrush	2.00
Deodorant	6.00
Mouthwash	2.00
Shampoo	4.00
Conditioner	3.00

INSERT INTO old_products
SELECT name,MIN(price) FROM products GROUP BY name

How many rows are inserted in the query above?
1. Zero rows
2. Two rows
3. Four rows
4. Six rows
5. Eight rows

17. 1. SELECT city, state, count(*)
2. FROM customers
3. GROUP BY city, state
4. UNION ALL
5. SELECT city, state, count(*)
6. FROM employee
7. GROUP BY city,state

If you wanted to sort the result returned by the UNION ALL statement above, where do you place the ORDER BY clause?
1. Between lines 1 and 2, and between lines 5 and 6
2. Between lines 3 and 4, and after line 7
3. After line 7
4. After the UNION ALL
5. An ORDER BY cannot be used in a query along with a UNION ALL

18. **Table Name : Ranges**

Range	From_num	To_num
1	0	2
2	3	5
3	6	8
4	9	11
5	12	14
6	15	17

SELECT range FROM ranges WHERE from_num > ANY (SELECT to_num FROM ranges)

How many rows are returned by the SQL statement listed above?
1. Zero rows
2. Two rows
3. Three rows

4. Four rows
5. Five rows

19. **Table Name :** Athletes

Column Name	Null/Not Null	Data Type
Row_id	NOT NULL	Integer
Name	NOT NULL	Varchar(30)
Sport	NULL	Varchar(30)
Rank	NULL	INTEGER

Which one of the following statements, when executed against the table above, causes an error to occur?

1. SELECT * FROM athletes
   WHERE rank = 1
   AND sport = 'Basketball'
2. UPDATE athletes
   SET rank = NULL
   WHERE rank > 20
3. INSERT INTO athletes (row_id, sport, rank)
   VALUES (100,'Football',1)
4. DELETE FROM athletes
   WHERE name = 'Donald Duck'
5. SELECT MIN(rank)
   FROM athletes
   WHERE sport = 'Golf'

20. **Table Name :** Customers

Row_id	Gender	Department	Purchase
1	Female	Housewares	27.75
2	Male	Garden	42.20
3	Female	Home improvement	97.50
4	Female	Kitchen/bathroom	28.60
5	Male	Furniture	225.75
6	Female	Garden	34.40
7	Male	Hardware	16.50

SELECT department, count(*) FROM customers
WHERE gender LIKE '%male'
AND purchases > 30.00
GROUP BY department ORDER BY 1
How many rows are returned by the query above?
1. Zero rows
2. Two rows
3. Three rows
4. Four rows
5. Six rows

21. **Table Name : students**

First_name	Last_name	Year_in_school
Albert	Edwards	1
Rita	Benter	3
Stan	Mustak	1
Karen	Glanville	2
Bulah	Simms	3

SELECT s.* FROM students s WHERE first_name LIKE 'B%' OR last_name LIKE 'B%'
How many columns are returned by the SQL statement listed above?
1. Zero columns
2. One column
3. Two columns
4. Three columns
5. Four columns

22. **Table Name : old_cust**

Cust	Name	Tenure
10	Tom	2
20	Mike	4
30	Betti	6
40	Bard	2
50	Greg	5

Table Name : customer

Cust	name	owes_us
10	Tom	20.00
20	Mike	30.00
30	Betti	NULL
40	Bard	.00
50	Greg	40.00

UPDATE customer SET owes_us = owes_us * 0.9 WHERE cust IN (SELECT cust FROM old_cust WHERE tenure > 2)

Referring to the table customer and old_cust above, what rows are updated by the statement?

1. 20 Mike 27.00
   50 Greg 36.00
2. 10 Tom 18.00
   20 Mike 27.00
   30 Betti .00
   40 Bard .00
   50 Greg 36.00
3. 10 Tom 18.00
   20 Mike 27.00
   50 Greg 36.00
4. 20 Mike 20.00
   50 Greg 30.00
5. 20 Mike 27.00
   30 Betti NULL
   50 Greg 36.00

23. UPDATE players
SET number = 0,
First_name = 'Player',
Last_name = e.last_name
WHERE p.sign_date IS NULL
OR p.sign_date <
(SELECT MIN(e.hire_date) FROM employee e)

What is the problem with the query above?

1. Only one column can be updated at a time when there is a WHERE clause present.
2. Subqueries are not allowed in the WHERE clause of UPDATE statement.
3. The WHERE clause must identify only one row to be updated.

4. The field "sign_date" cannot be used with the IS NULL argument because it is date or datetime field.
5. There is an error in the SET statement.

24. **Table Name : T1**

C1
1
2
7
NULL

1. Select count (*) from t1
2. Select count(*), SUM(*) from t1
3. Delete * from t1
4. INSERT INTO t1(4)
5. SELECT * FROM t1 WHERE Not c1 IS NULL.

Referring to table t12 in the scenario above, which SQL statements are syntactically correct?

1. 1, 2
2. 2, 3, 5
3. 3, 4, 5
4. 4, 5, 2
5. 5, 2, 1

25. SELECT month, monthname
FROM vtable
WHERE month > 6
OR month < 12

If vtable consists of month(which hold the numbers 1 through 12) and monthname (which holds the month names January through December), How many rows are returned by the above sample code?

1. 5
2. 6
3. 7
4. 11
5. 12

26. To which one of the following do you need to add only the words "TABLE employees" in order for the statement to execute correctly on the employees table?

1. SELECT
2. ALTER

3. DROP
4. UPDATE
5. INSERT INTO

27. **Table Name :** emp

Empno	dept	day_sal	ed_level
10	100	50.00	15
12	100	60.00	16
20	100	40.00	14
30	200	40.00	15
40	200	30.00	15
42	200	45.00	14
50	300	70.00	NULL
60	300	30.00	17
70	300	70.00	16

1. DELETE FROM emp WHERE day_sal BETWEEN 40.0 AND 60.0
2. DELETE FROM emp WHERE day_sal >= 40.0 And day_sal < 60.0
3. DELETE FROM emp WHERE day_sal > 40.0 And day_sal <=60.0
4. DELETE FROM emp WHERE day_sal >= 40.0 AND day_sal < = 60.0
5. DELETE FROM emp WHERE day_sal > 40.0 AND day_sal < 60.0
6. DELETE FROM emp WHERE day_sal IN (40.0, 45.0, 50.0, 60.0)

Referring to emp table and the queries in the scenario above, which queries always delete the same rows?

1. 1, 2, 3
2. 1, 4, 2
3. 1, 4, 3
4. 1, 4, 5
5. 1, 4, 6

28. **Table Name :** T1

Ident	irand
10	532
11	41
12	127
...	....
452	833

SELECT * from t1 WHERE MOD(ident,9) = 0

The table T1 has column ident whose values are 10,11,12,........,452 referring to the query used to generate the result set in the scenario above, How many rows does the result set have?

1. 49
2. 50
3. 51
4. 52
5. 442

29.

Roster	
Student_id	**Class_id**
1	80101
2	80102
3	80104
4	80102
5	80104
6	80203
7	80201
8	80201

Classes		
Class_id	**Class_name**	**Level**
80101	History I	easy
80102	History II	Easy
80104	History IV	mid-range
80201	Calculus I	mid-range
80203	Calculus III	Hard

SELECT class_id, COUNT(*)
FROM roster r WHERE EXISTS (SELECT class_name FROM classes c WHERE c.class_id = r.class_id AND level = hard) GROUP BY class_id

What is the error in the SQL statement above that prevents it from executing correctly?

1. The GROUP BY clause should be contained within the parentheses.
2. When the keyword EXISTS is used, the subquery must begin with "SELECT*."
3. The column "class_id" in the select lsit of the main query is ambiguous and must be qualified with a table name or alias
4. If the GROUP BY clause is present, the ORDER BY clause must also be used.
5. The column "level" is a character field, so the value "hard" should be single-quoted.

30. 1. SELECT * from table1 WHERE id NOT IN (SELECT id from table2)
2. SELECT table1.* FROM table1, table2 WHERE table1.id = table2.id
3. SELECT table1.* FROM table1 RIGHT JOIN table2 ON table1.id = table2.id WHERE table2.id IS NULL
4. SELECT table1.* FROM table1 LEFT JOIN table2 ON table1.id = table2.id WHERE table2.id IS NULL
5. SELECT table1.* FROM table FULL JOIN table2 ON table1.id = table2.id WHERE table2.id IS NULL

Which two queries in the scenario above have the same results?

1. 1, 2
2. 1, 3
3. 1, 4
4. 1, 5
5. 2, 5

31.

Roster	
Student_id	**Class_id**
1	80101
2	80102
3	80104
4	80102
5	80104
6	80203
7	80201
8	80201

Classes		
Class_id	**Class_name**	**Level**
80101	History I	Easy
80102	History II	Easy
80104	History IV	mid-range
80201	Calculus I	mid-range
80203	Calculus III	Hard

SELECT COUNT(DISTINCT class_id)
FROM roster r WHERE class_id IN (SELECT class_id from classes where level LIKE '%a%')

What is the value returned when the query above is executed?

1. One
2. Two
3. Three
4. Four
5. Five

32. **Table Name :** Expenses

Dept	Type	Dollar
A	P	100
A	D	0
A	S	50
A	P	100
B	P	NULL
B	P	10
B	D	100
B	S	500
C	D	400
C	S	100

Create View exp AS SELECT * FROM expenses.

Referring to the table and view above, which rows are deleted from the table when the statement "DELETE FROM exp WHERE dollar > 100 " runs.

1. B S 500 C D 400
2. B P NULL B S 500 CD 400
3. The statement does not run

4. B P NULL B D 100 B S 00 C D 400
5. B S 500 C D 400 C S 100

33.

Products		
Name	**Price**	**Type**
Soap	2.00	C
Brush	3.00	A
Comb	1.00	A
Floss	3.00	A
Vitamins	5.00	B
Aspirin	4.00	C
Toothpaste	3.00	B

DELETE FROM products WHERE price = (SELECT AVG(price) FROM products) AND type <> 'B'

How many rows are deleted in the query above?

1. Zero
2. One
3. Two
4. Three
5. Four

Appendix

Glossary of Database Terms

(Useful for Interview/Viva-Voce Purpose)

A

Abstract data types. The ability to define more complex data domains that support inheritance for storing objects, in SQL3.

Accessibility. A design goal to make the application usable by as many users as possible, including those with physical challenges. One solution is to support multiple input and output methods.

Access. Refers to the process of obtaining data from, or placing data into a disk storage device, register, or RAM. (*i.e.*, accessing a memory location).

Access control. The management of permissions for logging onto a computer or network.

Access strategy. The method by which a database management system locates physical data.

Access time. Time required to perform an access. Usages, e.g., 1) seek to location on a disk, 2) amount of time to read or write to a memory location, 3) the time to position to the correct location in a disk drive and carry out a read or write operation.

ActiveX. A model developed by Microsoft for writing programs so that other programs and the operating system can call them.

Ad hoc query. A temporary query for which neither the specification nor the output are saved.

Address. A specific location in memory where a unit record, or sector, of data is stored.

Aggregate function. A function that produces a single result based on the contents of an entire set of table rows. Also called a set function. Often used with the GROUP BY and HAVING clauses, aggregate functions generate one summary value from a group of values in specified column. Aggregate functions include AVG, COUNT, COUNT (*) MIN, and MAX.

Aggregation. The generic name for several SQL functions that operate across the selected rows. Common examples include SUM, COUNT, and AVERAGE.

Alias. A temporary name for a table or a column. Often used when you need to refer to the same table more than once, as in a self-join.

ALL. An SQL SELECT clause often used with subqueries. Used in a WHERE clause to match all the items in a list. For example, Price > ALL (...) means that the row matches only if Price is greater than the largest value in the list.

ALTER TABLE. An SQL data definition command that changes the structure of a table. To improve performance, some systems limit the changes to adding new columns. In these situations to make major changes, you have to create a new table and copy the old data.

ANSI. American National Standards Institute

ANY. An SQL SELECT clause often used with subqueries. Used in a WHERE clause to match at least one of the items in a list. For example, Price > ANY (...) means that the row matches as long as Price is greater than at least one item in the list.

Application. A complete system that performs a specific collection of tasks. It typically consists of integrated forms and reports and generally contains menus and a Help system.

Application Program. A sequence of programmed instructions that tell the computer how to perform an end use task (*i.e.*, accounting, word processing or other work for the computer system user).

Argument. A value (also called "parameter") supplied to a function.

Arithmetic operators. Addition (+), subtraction (–), multiplication (*), and division (/) are arithmetic operators. They can be used with all numeric columns. Some systems also supply modulo (%), for finding the integer remainder after a division operation on two integers.

ASCII. American Standard Code for Information Interchange. An eight-bit code for character representation; includes seven bits plus parity.

ASP. Active Server Pages. Server-side scripting technology to make interactive web pages. Based on VBScript.

Association. A many-to-many relationship between entities.

Asynchronous Data. Data sent usually in parallel mode without a clock pulse. Time intervals between transmitted bits may be of unequal lengths.

Atomic value. A value that contains only a single component. A field is the intersection of a single column with a single row, and contains an atomic value.

Attribute. A data value that describes one characteristic of an entity. It is also called a "field" or a "column". A field is represented by a column within an object (entity). An object may be a table, view or report. An attribute is also associated with an SGML (HTML) tag used to further define the usage.

Authentication. Providing a verification system to determine who actually wrote a message. Common systems use a dual-key encryption system.

Automatic Back-up of Files. This gives a user the security to make changes to a file without worrying about accidentally destroying it; there is always another copy. One weakness of this method is that files take up twice the room on a disk.

Auxiliary Memory. Memory other than main memory; generally a mass storage subsystem, it can include disk drives, backup tape drives, controllers and buffer memory. Typically, auxiliary memory is non-volatile.

Auxiliary Storage Device. Devices, generally magnetic tapes and magnetic disks, on which data can be stored for use by computer programs. Also known as secondary storage.

B

B$^+$-tree. An indexed data storage method that is efficient for a wide range of data access tasks. Tree searches provide a consistent level of performance that is not affected by the size of the database.

Back End. A back end is that part of a programming system that the user never sees. It is most commonly used to refer to the "data" part of a database system when it is separated from the user interface.

Backup. Copying computer files from one location to another. The second location is usually a tape drive or some other media. The medium is then physically moved to a safe location away from the original computer. A backup strategy is a key part of Fault Tolerance.

Backup Device. Disk or tape drive used with a fixed Winchester disk drive to make copies of files or other data for off line storage, distribution or protection against accidental data deletion from the Winchester drive, or against drive failure.

Backup File. File copies made on another removable media device (disk, tape or sometimes a remote hard disk system) and kept to ensure recovery of data lost due to equipment failure, human errors, updates, disasters and the like.

Backup and recovery. The combination of manual and machine procedures that can restore lost data in the event of hardware or software failure. Routine backup of databases and logs of computer activity are part of a backup and recovery program.

Bandwidth. Measures the data-carrying capacity of a communications channel. Usually measured in bits per second (bps).

Base query. Same as ground query.

Base station. The central radio transmitter/receiver that maintains communications with a mobile telephone. Most countries require several hundred base stations, in order to give approximated full coverage for mobile subscribers.

Base table. A table that contains data about a single basic entity. It generally contains no foreign keys, so data can be entered into this table without reference to other tables. For example. Customer would be a base table; Order would not.

Baud Rate. A variable unit of data transmission speed equal to one bit per second.

BCNF. Boyce-Codd Normal Form Relations are in third normal form and there are no Boyce-codd dependencies.

Benchmarking. The process of testing a piece of hardware or software to determine its general or specific performance characteristics.

Between . An SQL comparison operator that determines whether an item falls between two values.

Binary. A number system like the decimal numbers, but using 2 as its base and having only the two digits 0 (zero) and 1 (one). It is used in computers because digital logic can only determine one of two states—"OFF" and "ON". Digital data is equivalent to a binary number.

Binary data type. A data type provided by some systems for storing bit patterns.

Binary search. A search technique for sorted data. Start at the middle of the data. If the search value is greater than the middle value, split the following data in half. Keep reducing by half until the value is found.

Bit. The smallest unit of data. Consists of a single binary digit that can take the value of 0 or 1.

Bit data type. A data type provided by some systems for storing true/false data.

Bitmap index. A compact, high-speed indexing method where the key values are compressed to a small size that can be stored and searched rapidly.

BLOB. Binary Large Object. A data domain for undefined, large chunks of data. A BLOB (or simple object) type can hold any type of data, but the programmer is often responsible for displaying, manipulating, and searching the data.

Block. A group of BYTES handled, stored and accessed as a logical data unit, such as an individual file record. Typically, one block of data is stored as one physical sector of data on a disk drive.

Bluetooth. A radio technology built around a new chip that makes it possible to transmit signals over short distances between computers and handheld devices without the use of wires. (www.bluetooth.com). Named after the Danish king Harald I Bluethooth who reigned form 940-985 A.D.

Boolean algebra. Creating and manipulating logic queries connected with AND, OR, and NOT conditions.

Boolean expressions. Expressions that evaluate as "true" or "false" rather than return a specific value.

Boolean operators. The logical operators AND, OR and NOT.

Boyce-Codd dependency. A (part of the) key being dependent on a non-key attribute.

Browser. A software application that is used to allow users to read an HTML document in a user-friendly readable format. Two well-known browsers are Microsoft Internet Explorer and Netscape Navigator.

Buffer. A temporary data storage area that compensates for a difference in data transfer rates and/or data processing rates between sender and receiver.

Buffer cache. Memory allocated for data storage.

Buffered Seek. In buffered mode, head motion is postponed until a string of step pulses can be sent to the drive. These pulses represent the number of tracks that the head is to be stepped over, and are sent much faster than the heads can move. The pulses are saved or buffered and then the optimum head movement to the correct track is performed.

Byte. A sequence of adjacent BINARY digits or BITS considered as a unit, 9 bits in length. One byte is sufficient to define all the alphanumeric characters. There are 8 BITS in 1 BYTE. The storage capacity of disk drive is commonly measured in MEGABYTES, which is the total number of bits storable, divided by eight million.

C

Cache Memory. Cache Memory allows the system to load bytes of data from the hard disk to memory. The system may then refer to memory for information instead of going back to the hard disk, thereby increasing the processing speed.

Candidate key. One or more attributes that will uniquely identify one tuple in a relation. A candidate key is a potential primary key.

Cardinality. The number of rows in a table.

Cartesian product. All the possible combinations of rows from the tables. Such a result is generally caused by not including all the necessary joins.

Cascade. Propagation of an update or delete through related tables in a database.

Cascading delete. When tables are linked by data, if you delete a row in a higher-level table, matching rows in other tables are deleted automatically. For example, if you delete Customer 1173, all orders placed by that customer are also deleted.

CASE. Computer-Aided Software Engineering. Computer programs that are designed to support the analysis and development of computer systems. They make it easier to create, store, and share diagrams and data definitions. Some versions can analyze existing code and generate new code.

CDMA. Code Division Multiple Access. A technology for digital transmission of radio signals between, for example a mobile telephone and a base station. The system uses the same frequency to allow multiple conversations. Each conversation is cut into snippets and then remodulated and reassembled in the other end.

CGI. Common Gateway Interface. With Web servers, CGI is a predefined system for transferring data across the Internet. Current scripting languages hide the details, so you can simply retrieve data, as it is needed.

Character. An information symbol used to denote a number, letter, symbol or punctuation mark stored by a computer. In a computer a character can be represented in one (1) byte or eight (8) bits of data. There are 256 different one-byte binary numbers, sufficient for 26 lower case alphas, 26 upper case alphas. 10 decimal digits, control codes and error checks.

Character data type. A data type used to store character data such as letters, numbers, and special characters.

Character set. A list of letters and special characters (repertoire) and its internal mapping to computer codes.

Class. A descriptor for a set of objects with similar structure, behavior, relationships. That is, a class is the model description of the business entity. A business model might have an Employee class, where one specific employee is an object in that class.

Class diagram. A graph of classes connected through relationships. It is designed to show the static structure of the model and is similar to the entity-relationship diagram.

Class hierarchy. A graph that highlights the inheritance relationships between classes.

Clause. A functional subunit of an SQL statement. A portion of the SQL statement that is complete enough for its effects on the statement to be understood.

Client. A software application on your computer, which is used to extract or download some application, data or service from a host system.

Client/Server. A technique for organizing systems where a few computers hold most of the data, which is retrieved by individuals using personal computer clients.

Client/Server architecture. A 'networked' environment where a smaller system such as a PC interacts with a larger, faster system. This allows the processing to be performed on the larger system, which frees the user's PC. The larger system is able to connect and disconnect from the clients in order to process the data more efficiently.

Client-server system. A multi-user system in which a central processor (the server) is connected to multiple intelligent user workstations (the clients).

Closure. The property that is the fundamental structure in which the data is stored in the same structure that it retains in its final state and the structure in which it can be described. For example, the queries operate on a table and produce a table.

Clustered index. An index in which the bottom, or leaf level is the data itself. A table can have only one clustered index.

Code. A set of unambiguous rules specifying the way in which digital data is represented physically, as magnetized bits, on a disk drive. One of the objectives of coding is to add timing data for use in data reading.

Collating sequence. See sort order.

Column. A component of a table that holds a single attribute of the table; also called a "field".

Command. 1) An instruction sent by the central processing unit (CPU) to a controller for execution. 2) English-like commands entered by users to select computer programs or functions. 3) A CPU command, which is a single instruction such as "add two binary numbers" or "output a byte to the display screen." 4) Any SQL statement, such as INSERT of CREATE DATABASE.

Commit. Decision to proceed with the actual posting of a change to the database.

Comparison operators. Operators used for comparing one expression to another in a WHERE or HAVING clause. Comparison operators include equal to (=), greater than (>), less that (<), greater than or equal to (>=), less than or equal to (<=), and not equal to (! = or <>).

Composite indexes. Indexes based on more than one column in a table.

Composite key. A key—whether primary, unique or foreign— consisting of more than one column. Sometimes known as concatenated key.

Comprehensive data sub-language. A single language that handles all communications with the database.

Computed attribute. An attribute for which the value is calculated from other attributes. While computed attributes may be stored in relations, they are not usually done so. Most often they are produced as needed in the resolution of a query.

Conceptual View. The schema of a database.

Concurrency control. Strategies such as locking that prevent two or more users from changing the same piece of data concurrently.

Concurrent access. Performing two (or more) operations on the same data at the same time. The DBMS must sequence the operations so that some the changes are not lost.

Connection column. A column that participates in a join, allowing one table to link with another or with itself. Connecting columns are columns from one or more tables that contain similar values.

Consistency. The goal of making an application easier to use by using the same features, colors, and commands throughout. Modern applications also strive for consistency with a common design guide.

Constraint. A restriction placed on a form, table, field or other objects to either force an action to happen in a certain way, or to prevent an action from happening all together. Constraints enforce referential integrity, and promote fault tolerance.

Constraints. A restriction you specify on the data in a database. Clauses in the CREATE TABLE statement (CHECK, PRIMARY KEY, UNIQUE, REFERENCES, FOREIGN KEY) that help enforce referential integrity and business rules.

Control. A programming term that refers to just about any windows object that a user can see and manipulate. Examples of controls are pushbuttons, drop-down boxes, menus, and scroll bars.

Correlated subquery. A subquery that must be re-evaluated for each row of the main query. Can be extremely slow. Can often be avoided by creating a temporary table and using that in the subquery instead.

Crash. A malfunction in the computer hardware or software, usually causing loss of data.

Create table. An SQL data definition command to create a new table. The command is often generated with a program.

Create view. An SQL command to create a new view or saved query.

Criteria. A set of characteristics or limitations applied to the values of an attribute to select some of the tuples of a relation during a query.

Cross-join. Arises when you do not specify a join condition for two tables. It matches every row in the first table with every row in the second table. Also known as the Cartesian product. It should be avoided.

Cursor. An object used to store the output of a query for row-by-row processing by the application programs.

Cyclic-Redundancy-Check (CRC). Used to verify data block integrity. In a typical scheme, 2 CRC bytes are added to each user data block. The 2 bytes are computed from the user data, by digital logical chips. The mathematical model is polynomials with binary coefficients. When reading back data, the CRC bytes are read and compared to new CRC bytes computed from the read back block to detect a read error. The read back error-check process is mathematically equivalent to dividing the read block, including its CRC, by a binomial polynomial. If the division remainder is zero, data is error free.

Cylinder. The cylindrical surface formed by identical track numbers on vertically stacked disks. At any location of the head-positioning arm. all tracks under all heads are the cylinder. Cylinder number is one of the three address components required to find a specific address, the other two being head number and sector number.

D

DAO. Data Access Objects. Microsoft's cursor-level programming for tracking through a table one row at a time. You retrieve and alter data using predefined methods and properties of the objects.

Data. Information processed by a computer, stored in memory, or fed into a computer.

Data Access. When the controller has specified all three components of the sector address to the drive, the ID field of the sector brought under the head by the drive is read and compared with the address of the target sector. A match enables access to the data field of the sector.

Data administration. One of the three general categories for which SQL is used. The other two are data definition and data manipulation. Data administration includes activities such as granting and revoking permissions to users.

Data cache. The area of memory allocated for data storage.

Data control. Another term for data administration.

Data definition. The process of creating (or removing) a database and its objects.

Data dictionary. The system tables that contain descriptions of the database objects and how they are structured.

Data Directory. A collection of definitions, rules and advisories of data, designed to be used as a guide or reference with the data warehouse. The directory includes definitions, examples, relations, functions and equivalents in other environments, such as ISIS, IFIS, PPS and DSE.

Data independence. Separates the data from the programs, which often enables the data definition to be changed without altering the program.

Data integrity. Keeping accurate data, which means few errors and means that the data reflect the true state of the business. A DBMS enables you to specify constraints or rules that help maintain integrity, such as prices must always be greater than 0.

Data manipulation. Retrieving and modifying data, through SQL statements SELECT, INSERT, DELETE, and UPDATE.

Data Manipulation Language (DML). The part of SQL that operates on the data.

Data mining. Searching databases for unknown patterns and information. Tools include statistical analysis, pattern-matching techniques, and data segmentation analysis.

Data modification. Changing data, through SQL statements INSERT, DELETE, and UPDATE

Data Processing. The process of computer handling, manipulating, and modifying data such as arithmetic calculation, file lookup and updating, or word processing.

Data redundancy. Having the same data stored in more than one place in a database.

Data replication. In a distributed system, placing duplicate copies of data on several servers to reduce overall transmission time and costs.

Data retrieval. Finding and displaying data in the database via queries (SELECT statements).

Data structure diagram. A diagram that shows how the objects in a database fit together. It is also called an "entity relationship (E-R) diagram."

Data type. A type of data that can be held by a column. Each DBMS has predefined system domains (integer, float, string, etc.). Some systems support user-defined domains that are named combinations of other data types.

Data volume. The estimated size of the database. Computed for each table by multiplying the estimated number of rows and the average data length of each row.

Data warehouse. A specialized database that is optimized for management queries. Data is extracted from online transaction processing systems. The data is cleaned and optimized for searching and analysis.

Database. A collection of related tables containing data and definitions of database objects.

Database. A collection of all the data needed by a person or organization to perform needed functions.

Database Administrator (DBA). The person ultimately responsible for the functionality, integrity and safety of a database.

Database design. The process of setting up the objects in the database (principally, but not exclusively, tables and their columns).

Database device. The physical or logical device on which a database is stored.

Database manager. The person with primary responsibility for the design, construction, and maintenance of a database.

Database owner. The creator or owner of a database, a concept most useful in systems that allow more than one database.

Date data type. A data type used for storing date information.

DBA. Database Administrator. Person in charge of the technical and operational support for a database or all databases for an organization.

DBMS. Database Management System. Special software to create and maintain a database and enable individual business applications to extract the data they need without having to create separate files or data definitions in their computer programs must generally be supported by a data administrator.

DDL. Data Definition Language. Component of a database management system that defines each data element as it appears in the database.

Deadlock. A pathological state of a computer system reached when none of a group of competing processes can proceed because each is waiting for resources locked by the other (s).

Deadlock. A situation that exists when two (or more) processes each have a lock on a piece of data that the other one needs.

Decimal data type. A data type used for storing decimal data.

DECT. Digital Enhanced Cordless Telecommunications. A standard for cordless telephony.

Default. A value entered by the system for specified columns when the user supplies no explicit value.

Default values. Values that are displayed and entered automatically. Used to save time at data entry.

Degree. The number of columns in a table.

DELETE. An SQL data manipulation command that deletes rows of data. It is always used with a WHERE clause to specify which rows should be deleted.

Denormalization. The opposite of normalization.

Derived tables . A name sometimes applied to views, which are also known as "virtual tables".

DES. Data Encryption Standard. A standard method for encrypting data. It is a single-key technique.

DHTML. Dynamic HTML, a way of describing web pages that can change according to user input without having to send requests back to the server.

Digital. Any system that processes digital binary signals having only the values of a 1 or 0. An example of a non-digital signal is an analog signal that continuously varies, e.g., TV or audio.

Direct Access. Generally refers to an auxiliary memory device, having all data online. A tape drive without a tape mounted is not direct access, but a Winchester Drive is direct access.

DirectX DirectX is a Microsoft standard that provides programmers a way to gain access to hardware under Windows. DirectX is used mostly for games, computer based training, and multimedia programs.

Disk Pack. A number of metal disks packaged in a canister for removal form the disk drive. Winchester Drives do not have disk packs.

Disk storage. Auxiliary memory system containing disk drives.

Disk/Platter. For rigid disks, a flat, circular aluminum disk substrate, coated on both sides with a magnetic substance (iron oxide or thin film metal media) for non-volatile data storage. The substrate may consist of metal, plastic, or even glass. Surfaces of disks are usually lubricated to minimize wear during drive start-up or power down.

DISTINCT. An SQL keyword used in the SELECT statement to remove duplicate rows from the output.

Distinguished nulls. Unknown pieces of information whose values are not precisely known.

Distributed data processing. A system in which data is distributed across multiple servers.

Distributed database. Multiple independent databases that operate on two or more computers that are connected and share data over a network. The databases are usually in different physical locations. Each database is controlled by an independent DBMS.

DML. Data Manipulation Language. Language associated with a database management system, which is used by endusers and programmers to retrieve modify and/or store data in the database.

Domain. The collection of all possible values of an attribute. The domain of an attribute may be finite or infinite.

DROP TABLE. An SQL data definition command that completely removes a table from the database—including the definition. Use it sparingly.

DSS. Decision Support System. A system that collects data, analyzes models, and presents the results in a manner to help mangers make decisions. From a database perspective, the demands that analysis and presentation place on the system are different from those of a transaction processing system.

DTD. Document Type Definition. A DTD defines the names and contents of all elements that are permissible in a certain document. A DTD is used to specify XML document structure.

Dual-key encryption. An encryption technique that uses two different keys: one private and one public. The public key is published so anyone can retrieve it. To send an encrypted message to someone, you use the person's public key. At that point, only the person's private key will decrypt the message. Encrypting a message first with your private key can also be used to verify that you wrote the message.

Dummy values. False values you enter as placeholders or tests.

Dynamic SQL. SQL as used in applications that must be able to generate SQL code at runtime.

E

Embedded SQL. SQL code embedded into the source code of the host language.

Entity. A person, place or thing about which you want to store data; this can include people, places, events in time, and concepts.

Entity integrity. An integrity rule requiring that each row has a primary key and that no primary key allows nulls.

Entity-relationship (ER) diagram. Design tool used primarily for relational databases in which entities are modeled as geometric shapes. Identifies the data / information required by the business by displaying the relevant entities and the relationships between them.

Entity-relationship modeling. Identifying the important subjects about which information will be stored; identifying their attributes; and identifying the relationships among these entities. Also known as "entity modeling".

Equi-join. An SQL equality join condition. Rows from two tables are joined if the columns match exactly. Equi-join is the most common join condition. Rows that have no match in the other table are not displayed.

Escape character. A character used in a LIKE clause with the ESCAPE keyword to strip a wildcard of its magic meaning and force SQL to interpret it as a literal.

Exclusive lock. Sometimes called a "write" lock, it gives one user exclusive use of a row, page, or table during data modification activities.

Execute. To perform a data processing operation described by an instruction or a program in a computer.

Expert system. A system with a knowledge base consisting of data and rules that enable a novice to make decisions as effectively as an expert.

Expression. A constant, column name, function, or any combination thereof connected by arithmetic (and sometimes bitwise) operators.

F

FAQ. Frequently Asked Questions. An acronym that refers to a text file on the Internet that contains answers to frequently asked questions. FAQ's are a valuable resource for gaining knowledge on particular subjects of interest. FAQ's are compiled by subject matter.

Fault Tolerance. The ability of a system to respond gracefully to an unexpected hardware or software failure. There are many levels of fault tolerance, the lowest being the ability to continue operation in the event of a power failure. In database design, fault tolerance also means anticipating user mistakes and including ways to prevent or control them.

Feasibility study. A quick examination of the problems, goals, and expected costs of a proposed system. The objective is to determine whether the problem can reasonably be solved with a computer system.

Field. Same as attribute. A grouping of characters into a word, group of words, or number; e.g., a person's name or age; fields can be specified as different types, e.g., text, numeric, integer, etc.

Fifth normal form. A relation is in fifth normal form if it is in fourth normal form and it cannot be decomposed into smaller relations without loss of information.

File. The separately named unit of storage for all data and programs on most computers. For example, a relation or a whole database may be stored in one file.

File Name. Each file has a name, just like the name on the tab of a file folder.

File server. The server component of a recourse sharing system. It does not contain any database management software.

Fillfactor. An indexing option provided by transact SQL that allows you to control how full to make each page of a new index. This number affects performance because of the time it takes for the system to split index pages when they become 100 percent full.

Firewall. A piece of software, or a combination of hardware and software that isolates an intranet from the Internet, allowing only trusted traffic to travel between them.

Firmware. A computer program written into a storage medium that cannot be accidentally erased, e.g., ROM. It can also refer to devices containing such programs.

First normal form. First of the five normal forms. It requires that tables have a fixed number of columns and that there be no repeating groups.

Fixed Disk. A disk drive with disks that cannot be removed from the drive by the user, e.g., Winchester Disk Drive.

Fixed length. Some data types can have either fixed or variable length. Choosing the correct one may have storage and performance implications.

Flat file . A collection of data records having minimal structure.

Floppy Disk. A flexible plastic disk coated with magnetic media and packaged in a stiff envelope.

Foreign key. A column (or combination of columns) in one table whose value(s) matches the primary key(s) in another table.

Fourth normal form. A relation is in fourth normal form if it is Boyce-Codd normal form and it has at the most only one independent multi-valued dependency.

Free-form language. A computer language with no requirements for line length or line breaks.

Front End. The client part of a program that contains the user interface.

FTP. File Transfer Protocol is the most common way to transfer files from one computer to another over the Internet.

Functional dependency. A particular relationship between two attributes. This relationship is such that by knowing the value of one of the attributes (A), the value of the other (B) can be uniquely determined. In this case B is said to be dependent on A.

G

GIF. Graphics Interchange Format. A file compression format used for transferring graphics files over the internet.

GIS. Geographic Information System. Designed to identify and display relationships among business data and locations.

GPRS. General Packet Radio Service. A packet-linked technology that may enable high-speed (up to 115 kilobit per second) access to wireless Internet a GSM network. GPRS is IP-based, and may allow users to be online 24 hours.

GPS. Global Position System. Based on US defense satellite system, enables tracking of individuals. This technology may prove helpful when navigating a car in the city, or help emergency rescue-team to locate the person in need of help.

GQL. Graphical Query Language is a graphical query tool used to access information stored in an SQL database.

GRANT. The SQL command to give someone access to specific tables or queries.

Granularity. The size of the smallest unit, which can be independently locked. A database may apply locks at the database level, the relation level, the tuple level, or on the value of a single attribute within a tuple.

Ground query. Queries in which all the attributes are taken directly from relations; none are taken from the output of other queries.

Group view. A view with GROUP BY clause in its definition.

GSM. Global System for Mobile Communications. The world's most widely used mobile system. Used on the 900 MHz and 1800 MHz frequencies in Europe, Asia and Australia, and the MHz 1900 frequency in America.

GUI. Graphical User Interface.

H

Hard Disk Drive. Commonly called rigid disk drives, or Winchester disk drives. An electromechanical device that can read rigid disks. Though similar to floppy disk drives, the hard disks have higher bit density and multiple read/write surfaces.

Hardware. Computer equipment (as opposed to the computer programs and software).

Hashed key. Direct access storage of a row of data, where the key value is converted to a physical storage location.

Head. An electromagnetic device that can write (record), read (playback), or erase data on magnetic media.

Head Crash. A head landing occurs when the disk drive is turned on or off. This function normally does not damage the disk as the disk has a very thin lubricant on it. A head crash occurs when the head and disk damage each other during landing, handling or because a contaminant particle gets between them. Head crash is a catastrophic failure condition and causes permanent damage and loss of data.

Hexadecimal (HEX). A number system based on sixteen, using digits 0 through 9 and letters A through F to represent each digit of the number. (A = 10, B = 11, C = 12, D = 13, E = 14, F =15).

Host language. A programming language used to develop an application that uses embeddec SQL or that calls stored procedures.

Host variable. Variable(s) in the host language used to store values retrieved by the SQL statements.

HTML. Hyper Text Markup Language, a subset of SGML, provides a tag set used to create ar HTML document. The tags or elements tell the browser how to display the information. The tags are used to 'mark,' in a hierarchical format, the different components of the document.

Hyperlink. A hyperlink is a logical link between two related pieces of information in the same document or between different documents. It will allow you to quickly jump from one document or location ιo another transparently.

Hypertext. A hypertext document is a combination of text, links to other documents, sound, graphic images, and film clips.

I

Identifer. The name of a database or database object.

Inclusive range. A range, specified with the keyword BETWEEN, in which you search for the lower value and upper value of the range as well as the values included in the range.

Index. A method used to reorder tuples or to display them in a specific order. Also a data structure used to give rapid, random access to relations. Indexes are most often used with large relations.

Input. 1. Data entered into the computer to be processed. 2. User commands or queries.

Input/Output. The process of entering data into or removing data from a computer system.

INSERT. SQL command that inserts data into a table. One version inserts a single row at a time. The other variation copies selected data from one query and appends it as new rows in a different table.

Instance. Each row in a table represents an occurrence, or instance, of the entity.

Integrity. The assurance that the database data is accurate and correct. One type of integrity is Entity integrity, where the table in question has to be entirely consistent with the entity that it models. In this case, the table must have a primary key.

Intersection. A set operation that displays rows that two or more tables have in common.

Inversion. An index from which the tuples in a main relation with a particular value for an attribute can be determined.

IP address. Every device on the Internet is assigned an address that is used for communicating from device to device.

ISAM. Indexed Sequential Access Method. A data storage method that relies on an index to search and retrieve data faster than a pure sequential search.

ISO. International Standards Organization.

Isolation level. The extent to which a transaction is affected by the actions of other transactions on the same data.

J

Java. A programming language developed by Sun Microsystems that is supposed to be able to run unchanged on diverse computers.

Join. A query, which uses data from more than one relation. The relations must have at least one attribute (called the join or linking attribute) in common.

Join column. A column used to set conditions for a join.

K

Key. A field in a record that uniquely identifies a particular instance of that record so that it can be retrieved, updated, deleted or sorted.

Key values. Primary keys uniquely identify a row, while foreign keys provide a way to refer to those unique values from another table.

Keyword. A word used as part of SQL syntax, also called a "reserved word."

L

LAN. Local Area Network. A grouping of devices, such as PC's, fax machines and printers, physically connected together by Ethernet wiring, within a fairly limited location.

Literal value. A kind of constant value; the representation itself is the value.

Load Balancing. Distributing processing and communications activity evenly across a computer network so that no single device is overwhelmed.

Locking. A concurrency-control mechanism to protect data both from being modified by more than one user at a time and from being read while a transaction is in progress.

Logical connectives. Used to connect or change the truth value of predicates to produce more complex predicates.

Logical independence. The concept that relationships among tables, columns, and rows can change without impairing the function of application programs and ad hoc queries.

Logical operators. AND (joins two or more conditions and returns results when all the conditions are true), OR (connects two or more conditions and returns results when any of the conditions is true), and NOT (negates a condition).

Logical security. Determining which users should have access to which data. It deals with preventing three data problems: (1) unauthorized disclosure, (2) unauthorized modification, and (3) unauthorized withholding.

Lookup table. A table used primarily for reference purposes, rather than for data entry or modification.

Lost-update problem. Multi-user updates can overwrite each other if a database has no concurrency control.

LRU-MRU. Least Recently Used, Most Recently Used: an algorithm often used in data caching. Most recently used items are put in the cache, displacing least recently used ones.

M

Main Memory. Random-access memory used by the CPU for storing program instructions and data currently being processed by those instructions.

Many-to-many relationship. One or more tuples in one relation may be related to one or more tuples in a second relation by a common value of a join attribute. This implies that each value of the join attribute may appear any number of times in either relation or in both.

Memory. Any device or storage system capable of storing and retrieving information.

Metadata. Data about data, typically stored in a data dictionary. For example, table definitions and column domains are metadata.

Multiprocessor. A computer containing two or more processors.

Multitasking. The ability of a computer system to execute more than one program or program task at a time.

Multi-User. The ability of a computer system to execute programs for more than one user at a time.

N

Natural join. A display of only one from each pair of columns whose matching values created the join on the basis of equality. See also equijoin.

Negation. Specifying that a query is to select all tuples except those, which have a particular value for a given attribute. Such queries are often unsafe, and many databases do not support negation.

Nested query. A statement that contains one or more subqueries.

Nested sort. A sort within another sort.

Network database. An older DBMS type that expanded the hierarchical database by supporting multiple connections between entities. A network database is characterized by the requirement that all connections had to be supported by an index.

Non-loss decomposition. The process of splitting a table into smaller tables without losing any information.

Nonprocedural language. A language that allows you to specify the results you want without describing the method for getting them.

Nonrelated subquery. A subquery that can be evaluated independently of the outer SQL statement.

Normal form. A condition of relations and databases intended to reduce data redundancy and improve performance or rules and processes for putting relation and databases into normal form.

Normal forms. See normalization.

Normalization. Process of creating small stable data structures form complex groups of data when designing relational databases.

Null. A null represents a missing or inapplicable value in a column of a database table.

O

ODBC. Abbreviation of Open Database Connectivity, a standard database access method developed by microsoft Corporation. The goal of ODBC is to make it possible to access any data from any application regardless of which database management system (DBMS) is handling the data. ODBC manages this by inserting a middle layer, called a database driver, between an application and the DBMS.

OLAP. On-Line Application Processing. The use of a database for data analysis. The focus is on retrieval of the data. The primary goals are to provide acceptable response times, maintain security, and make it easy for users to find the data they need.

OLTP. On-Line Transaction Processing. The use of a database for transaction processing. It consists of many insert and update operations and supports hundreds of concurrent accesses. High-speed storage of data, reliability, and data integrity are primary goals, Examples include airline reservations, online banking, and retail sales.

One-to-many. A master-detail relationship in which one row in the first table may relate to many in the second, but a row in the second table can relate to only one row in the first.

One-to-one relationship. Exactly one tuple in one relation is related by a common join attribute to exactly one tuple in another relation. This implies that each value of the join attribute appears no more than once in each of the relations.

Operating System. An operating system is a program, which acts as an interface between the user of a computer and the computer hardware. The purpose of the operating system is to provide an environment in which a user may run programs. The goal of the operating system is to enable the user to conveniently use the computer's resources such as the CPU, memory, storage devices and printers.

Outer join. A join that displays nonjoining rows from either one or the other of a pair of joined tables.

Output. Processing data being transferred out of the computer system to peripherals (*i.e.*, disk, printer, etc.). This includes responses to user commands or queries.

Owner. The creator of a database object is the owner of that object and usually has full privileges on that object.

P

Parameter. A variable within an application written in SQL module language.

Partial dependency. The value of a non-key attribute is dependent on only part of the key (usually on one attribute of a multiattribute key).

PDA. Personal Digital Assistant. Usually a hand-held device, such as the Palm Pilot or Psion.

Permissions. Authority to run certain actions on certain database objects or to run certain commands.

Persistent query. A query that is stored for reuse.

PHS. Personal Handyphone System. Digital mobile telephone system according to Japanese standard (1900 MHz).

Physical data independence. The independence of the physical storage of data from a database's logical design.

Plug-in. A software component that is downloaded from a Web server to a Web client, where it is integrated with the client's browser, providing additional functions.

Precompiled queries. Named collections of SQL statements for which execution plans have already been figured out, in Transact SQL.

Predicate. A statement that may be either true or false.

Primary key. A column or combination of columns in a database table that uniquely identifies each row in the table.

Primary memory. The internal memory of a computer, usually consisting of RAM chips, on which the data and programs currently being used must reside.

Privileges. See permissions.

Procedural language. A traditional programming language that is based on following procedures and is typically executed one statement at a time. Can be compared to SQL, which operates on sets of data with one command.

Procedure. A subroutine or function that is designed to perform one specific task. It is generally wise to keep procedures small.

Program. A sequence of instructions stored in memory and executed by a processor or microprocessor.

Project. A query in which only some of the attributes in the source relation appear in the output.

Projection. Listing the columns that will be included in the results of a selection from the database.

Protocol. A set of conventions governing the format of messages to be exchanged within a communications system.

Q

QBE. Query-By-Example, a tabular language for expressing queries, in which a query is specified by sketching an abbreviated 'schema' of the output desired, along with any criteria which should be applied to the attributes desired.

Qualification. Conditions on the rows to be retrieved, described in the WHERE or HAVING clause.

Queries. Requests for retrieval of data from the database; sometimes also used to refer to SQL statements in general.

Query. A command, written in a query language, for the database to present a specified subset of the data in the database.

Query language. A high-level computer language used to retrieve specific information from database. SQL (Structured Query Language) is the most common of the query languages. SQL is a data manipulation language for relational databases.

Query optimizer. The part of the DBMS that calculates the most efficient way to perform a given query.

Query resolution. The process of collecting the data needed to answer a query.

R

RAID. Redundant Array of Independent Drives. A disk drive system that consists of multiple drives with independent controllers. There are several levels of RAID offering different features. The goal is to split the data to provide faster access and automatic duplication for error recovery.

Random Access Memory (RAM). Memory where any location can be read from or written to in a random order. Random access memory usually refers to volatile memory where the contents are lost when power is removed. The user addressable memory of a computer is random access memory.

Read. To access a storage location and obtain previously recorded data.

Read lock. A lock, which allows the user receiving the lock to read all or part of a database but not to modify it. Some database management systems will allow many users to have simultaneous read locks on a unit of data.

Read Only Memory (ROM). A chip that can be programmed once with bits of information. This chip retains this information even if the power is turned off. When this information is programmed into the ROM, it is called burning the ROM.

Record. A set of related fields that describes a specific entity. Also called "tuple" or "row".

Recovery. Restoring the database to a consistent state after a software or hardware failure.

Recursive query. A query in which the output of the query is then used as input for the same query.

Referential integrity. The rules governing data consistency, specifically the requirement that a foreign key must either match its primary key exactly or else be completely null.

Referential Integrity. A feature provided by relational database management systems (RDBMSs) that prevents users or applications from entering inconsistent data. Most RDBMSs have various referential integrity rules that you can apply when you create a relationship between two tables.

Relation. A named two-dimensional table of data. Each relation consists of a set of named columns and an arbitrary number of rows. The columns correspond to the fields describing each tuple in the table or relation. The rows correspond to each instance of the entity described by the table or relation.

Relational data model. Logical database model that treats data as if it were stored in two-dimensional tables. It can relate data stored in one table to data in another as long as the two tables share a common data element.

Relational Database. A type of database management system (DBMS) that stores data in the form of related tables. Relational databases are powerful because they require few assumptions about how data is related or how it will be extracted from the database. As a result, the same database can be viewed in many different ways. An important feature of relational system is that a single database can be spread across several tables. This differs from flat-file databases, in which each database is self-contained in a single table.

Relationship. Relationships in a relational database are represented by common data values stored in the two tables. This type of relationship allows you to retrieve related data from the database by manipulating the relationships in a simple, easy way.

Repeating subquery. See correlated subquery.

Reserved words. Words that have a special significance in SQL and cannot be used as variable names or in any other way that differs from their intended use.

Restriction. One of the basic query operations in a relational system, also called selection. A restriction determines which rows will be selected from a table.

REVOKE. The SQL command used to remove permissions that were granted to certain users.

Roll forward. If an error occurs in processing transactions, the database can be restarted and loaded from a known checkpoint. Then partially completed transactions can be rolled forward to record the interrupted changes.

Rollback. A database system transaction feature. If an error occurs in a sequence of changes, the preceding changes can be rolled back to restore the database to a safe state with correct data.

Row Value. The most visible values in a database; the row values are the values that each row of a database contains. A row value is typically made up of multiple components because each column in a row contains a value.

Rows. The set of data values associated with one instance of the entity that the table describes: one set of columns.

Rule. A specification that controls what data may be entered in a particular column.

S

Safe query. A query in which the output is guaranteed to be finite.

Schema. A description of a database. It specifies (among other things) the relations, their attributes, and the domains of the attributes. In some database systems, the join attributes are also specified as part of the schema.

SCSI. Small Computer Systems Interface.

Second normal form. A relation is in second normal form (2NF) if it is in first normal form (1NF) and every non-key attribute is fully functionally dependent on the primary key. In other words, every non-key attribute must be determined by the whole key, not some subject of the key.

Secondary memory. The external storage of a computer , usually consisting of magnetic or optical disks, on which data and programs are stored in the intervals between the times when they are actually in use.

Sector. A sector is a section of a track whose size is determined by formatting. When used as an address component, sector and location refer to the sequence number of the sector around the track. Typically, one sector stores one user record of data. Drives typically are formatted from 17 to 26 sectors per track. Determining how many sectors per track to use depends on the system type, the controller capabilities and the drive encoding method and interface.

SELECT. The primary data retrieval command for SQL. The main components are SELECT ... FROM ... INNER JOIN ... WHERE.

Select list. The asterisk (for all columns) or a list of columns and expressions to be included in the query results.

Selection. Specifying conditions for retrieving rows from a table. See also restriction.

Self-join. Select from a table by comparing values in one or more columns of the same table.

Sequel. A query language.

Sequential Access. Writing or reading data in a sequential order, such as reading data blocks stored one after the other on magnetic tape (the opposite of random access).

Serial data type or property. A facility to maintain a sequentially increasing number.

Server. A computer where the server software resides. Such services as filing, mail, communications and authentication are a few of the services that are available.

Servlet. A small program that runs on a server. Unlike embedded programs, such as those found in ActiveX web pages or Java applets, these programs do no have to be downloaded to the user via the wab page. This allows much faster loading of web pages, and much faster execution of scripts.

SET. SET or Secure Electronic Transaction is a system for ensuring the security of financial transactions over the Internet. SET may authenticate both user and merchant in order to approve the transaction.

Set function. A function that produces a single result based on the contents of an entire set of table rows. Also called an aggregate function.

Sets. Groups of rows to which aggregates apply.

SGML. Standardized Generalized Markup Language. The mother of all markup languages. XML is 'SGML light'. HTML is a loose application of SGML.

Shared lock. A lock created by non-update ("read") operations. Other users many read the data concurrently, but no transaction can acquire an exclusive lock on the data until all the shared locks have released.

SMS. Short Messaging Service. A service for sending messages of up to 160 characters to mobile phones that use Global System for Mobile (GSM) communication.

Software. Application programs, disk operating system and other programs (as opposed to Hardware). The instructions or programs, usually stored on floppy or hard disks, which are used to direct the operations of a computer, or other hardware.

Sort order. A collating sequence (or collation) for a character set, determining which characters come before and after other characters.

SQL. A unified language for defining, querying, modifying, and controlling the data in a relational database (originally an acronym for Structure Query Language).

SSL. Secure Sockets Layer. A protocol for managing the security of message transmissions in a network. The idea is that the programming for keeping your messages confidential ought to be contained in a program layer between an application (such as your Web browser) and the Internet's TCP/IP layers. The current rate of SSL encryption is 128.

Statement. An SQL data definition, data manipulation, or data administration command.

Storage Capacity. Amount of data that can be stored in a memory, usually specified in kilobytes (KB) for main memory and floppy disk drives and megabytes (MB) for hard disk and tape drives.

Stored Procedure. In Database Management Systems (DBMSs), an operation that is stored with the database server. Typically, stored procedures are written in SQL. Stored procedures execute faster than ordinary SQL requests because they have been compiled and optimized by the server. By keeping the requests on the SQL server, they do not have to be coded into the user's front end, thereby allowing the program to load and execute faster.

Strings. Groups of one or more letters, numbers, or special characters (such as the question mark or asterisk).

Subquery. A SELECT statement that nests inside the WHERE clause of another SELECT statement.

Synchronous Data. Data sent, usually in serial mode, with a clock pulse.

System administrator. The person who has overall responsibility for the data in the database, and for its consistency and integrity.

System catalog. The system tables containing descriptions of the database objects and how they are structured.

System tables. See system catalog.

T

Table. A representation of data values as rows and columns.

Table list. The list of tables, views, or both following the FROM keyword in a SELECT statement.

Table scan. Reading each row in a table rather than using an index to locate a particular data element. (For small tables, a table scan can be the most efficient access method.)

Tape Drive. A sequential access memory device whose magnetic media is tape in a cassette, reel or continuous loop.

TCP/IP. Transmission Control Protocol/Internet Protocol. The network protocol used by the Internet and by intranets.

Terminator. A character, word, or menu option marking the end of an SQL statement.

Theta join. A join based on any valid comparison operator, such as equal (=), greater than (>), or not less than (!<).

Third normal form. Third normal form requires that each non-key column gives information about the key column. A non-key column may not describe another non-key column.

Three-valued Logic. A variation of Boolean logic used in SQL where the expression may be TRUE, FALSE or UNKNOWN. Unknown occurs when Nulls are compared with other values or with each other.

TIFF. Tagged Image File Format is a graphic file format used to transfer graphic images across the Internet.

Time data type. A data type that stores time information.

Transaction. The fundamental unit of change in many (transaction-oriented) databases. A single transaction may involve changes in several relations, all of which must be made simultaneously in order for the database to be internally consistent and correct.

Transaction log. A log in which changes to the database are recorded (usually for recovery purposes). The method is implementation dependent.

Transaction management. Ensuring that transactions are either completed or conceled so that the database is never left in an inconsistent state.

Transaction Processing. A programming technique where a number of related commands are placed in a group called a transaction. When the transaction runs, each command is executed in turn. A log is kept detailing exactly what every command is going to do to the database. No changes are committed to the database, however, until the last command executes successfully. At that point, all the transactions are committed at once. If any command fails before the transaction completes, the entire transaction is "rolled back," and no change are committed. Transaction processing is an important technique for both preserving referential integrity and for promoting fault tolerance.

Transaction table. Tool for converting character strings from one character set to another.

Transitive dependency. A functional dependency between two or more non-key attributes in a relation.

Trigger. A detectable event that causes another action to happen.

Trigger actions. The actions for which a trigger is specified.

Trigger conditions. The conditions that cause a trigger to take effect.

Tuple. A set of related attributes that describes a specific entity. Also called "row" or "record".

Two-phase commit. A strategy in which changes to a database are made temporarily to a buffered version of the database. Once it has been determined that all parts of an update can be made successfully, the changes are posted to the actual database.

U

Unique indexes. An index with no duplicate primary keys.

Unmodified comparison operator. A comparison operator not followed by ANY or ALL.

Unsafe query. A query in which the output is possibly infinite. This most often occurs in queries which are recursive or which contain negation. Such queries are disallowed by many database management systems to prevent unsafe queries.

UPDATE. An SQL data manipulation command that changes the values in specified columns. A WHERE clause specifies which rows will be affected.

URL. Uniform Resource Locator. The URL is the path information in an HTML coded source file used to locate another document or image.

User-defined data types. Data types created by the user, defined in terms of the system data types, with characteristics such as null status and length (where appropriate). Users can apply rules and defaults to these data types.

User-defined transaction. Transactions you define with transaction commands such as BEGIN TRANSACTION and COMMIT TRANSACTION.

V

Validation rule. A rule specifies what data may be entered in a particular column: it is a way of defining the domain of the column. Rules are sometimes referred to as "validation rules," since they allow the system to check whether a value being entered in a column falls within the column's domain.

Value. A single data element, such as the contents of one column-row intersection. May represent either a variable or a constant.

Value expression. An expression that combines two or more values.

Value function. A function that performs an operation on a single character string, number or date-time.

Vector aggregate. An aggregate that returns an array of values, one per set.

View. A database component that behaves exactly like a table but has no independent existence of its own. Multi-table views draw from 2 or more tables.

Viewed table. Another term for "view" (as opposed to "base" table).

Virtual Table. A view.

VOIP. Voice Over Internet Protocol. Describes the process of transmitting voice via data IP packages.

VSAM. Virtual Sequential Access Method. A data storage method that uses virtual addresses instead of physical locations in the index. A true VSAM technique also provides multilevel indexes and other storage features. It has largely been replaced by B^+- tree indexes.

W

W3C. World Wide Web Consortium.

WAP. Wireless Application Protocol, which is a family of protocols allowing mobile devices to access wireless services.

WAP Gateway. A WAP gateway is a twoway software. Its main function is to offload the WAP mobile device from a lot of computational layers.

WAP Server. A WAP server is a web server. The computer programmers use WML instead of HTML.

WAN. Wide Area Network. A network that is spread across a larger geographic area. Parts of the network are outside the control of a single firm. Long-distance connections often use public carries.

WCDMA. Wideband Code Division Multiple Access. A technology for wideband digital radio communications of Internet, multimedia, video and others. Also known as 3G.

Web Server. A computer that delivers (serves up) web pages.

Wildcards. Characters used with the SQL LIKE keyword that can represent one character (underscore) or any number of characters (percent sign, %)

WMLScript. Scripting language for WAP devices. Based on JavaScript, but less powerful.

Word. Number of bits processed in parallel (in a single operation) by a CPU. Standard word lengths are 8, 16, 32, and 64 (1, 2, 4, or 8 bytes).

Write. To access a storage location and store data on the magnetic surface.

Write lock. A lock, which allows the user receiving the lock to read and to modify the database. Write locks almost always imply exclusive control of the database; no other users will be allowed to have either read or write locks as long as one write lock is active.

WWW. World Wide Web. A hypermedia application used for access of data over the Internet. The WWW is based on the HTML standard of marking up 'documents.'

WYSIWYG. What You See Is What You Get.

X

XML. Extensible Markup Language. W3C's standard for Internet Markup Languages. WML is one of these languages.

Bibliography

1. The Power of Oracle 9i by Rajiv Parida, Vinod Sharma, *Firewall Media.*
2. Keeping Ahead—SQL Server 7.0, *Firewall Media.*
3. MCSE—Administering SQL Server 7.0, *Firewall Media.*
4. Oracle PL/SQL: Programming, 2nd Edition *by Steven Feuerstein & Bill Pribyl.*
5. Oracle PL/SQL: Guide to Oracle8i Features *by Steven Feuerstein.*
6. Oracle Built-in Packages *by Steven Feuerstein, Charles Dye & John Beresniewicz.*
7. Advanced Oracle PL/SQL: Programming with Packages *by Steven Feuerstein.*
8. Oracle Web Applications: PL/SQL Developer's Introduction *by Andrew Odewahn.*
9. Oracle PL/SQL: Language Pocket Reference *by Steven Feuerstein, Bill Pribyl & ChipDawes.*
10. Oracle PL/SQL: Built-ins Pocket Reference *by Steven Feuerstein, John Beresniewicz & Chip Dawes.*
11. Oracle 8 PL/SQL: Programming by *Scott Urman.*
12. Oracle 8: Architecture by *Steven Bobrowski.*
13. Understanding SQL by *Gruber.*
14. SQL Unleashed by *Ladanyi.*
15. Teach Yourself SQL in 21 Days by *Stephen.*
16. SQL and Relational Databases by *Soren Vang.*

Index

T

U

V

W

Index

SYMBOLS

A

B

C

J

L

M

N

O

P

T

U

V

W